CHILDREN,
NOT WIDGETS

CHILDREN, NOT WIDGETS

How to Fight and Fix the Willful Miseducation of Students and the Dismantling of Public Education

JODY LONGO-SCHMID, PhD

Emerald Calabria, LLC

Learning shapes the future

Published by Emerald Calabria, LLC
http://www.emeraldcalabria.com/

Copyright 2022 by Jody Schmid

Printed in the United States of America on acid-free paper

ISBN-13: 978-1-7377385-0-3 (hbk)
ISBN-13: 978-1-7377385-1-0 (pbk)
ISBN-13: 978-1-7377385-2-7 (ebk)

Library of Congress Control Number: 2021945600

Cover design by Tim Barber

This book is dedicated to those who choose public service, especially those who work on the front lines. Current and former educators—like my late father—serve our nation's interests by developing the strengths of all students, fighting for more equitable schooling, and demanding more and better-targeted resources for children, families, communities, and public schools.

Contents

Acknowledgments

This book would not have been possible without the 83 teachers and administrators who willingly and openly shared their thoughts, time, and expertise with me. I would also like to thank my family for their care and support over the many years that I spent working on the book.

Abbreviations

ACA	Affordable Care Act
AFDC	Aid to Families with Dependent Children
ACT	American College Testing
AFT	American Federation of Teachers
AIS	academic intervention services
AP	Advanced Placement
APPR	annual professional performance reviews
AYP	adequate yearly progress
BLM	Black Lives Matter
BLOB	big learning organization bureaucracy
CACFP	Child and Adult Care Food Program
CCSS	Common Core State Standards
CSP	Charter Schools Program
DOE	Department of Education
EAHCA	Education for All Handicapped Children Act
EBT	Electronic Benefit Transfer for Children
ELA	English language arts
ELL	English language learner
ESEA	Elementary and Secondary Education Act
ESSA	Every Student Succeeds Act
EVLN	exit, voice, loyalty, and neglect
GED	General Educational Development test (high school equivalency diploma)
GI Bill	Servicemen's Readjustment Act
GSS	General Social Survey
HBCUs	historically Black colleges and universities
HCV	housing choice vouchers
HEDI	highly effective, effective, developing, and ineffective
HELP	Senate Health, Education, Labor, and Pensions Committee

HP	humanistic paradigm of teaching
HQT	highly qualified teacher
HUD	Housing and Urban Development
IASA	Improving America's Schools Act
IDEA	Individuals with Disabilities Education Act
IRS	Internal Revenue Service
MMP	market-managerial paradigm
NAACP	National Association for the Advancement of Colored People
NAEP	National Assessment of Educational Progress
NAFTA	North American Free Trade Agreement
NCG	networked community governance
NCLB	No Child Left Behind
NEA	National Education Association
NGA	National Governors Association
NIMBY	not in my backyard
NPM	new public management
NPR	National Partnership for Reinventing government
NPS	National Park Service
NSLP	National School Lunch Program
OECD	Organisation for Economic Co-operation and Development
OTL	opportunities to learn
PAR	peer assistance and review
PERB	Public Employee Relations Board
PIC	public information campaign
PISA	Program for International Student Assessment
PRO	Protecting the Right to Organize Act
PSM	public service motivation
PTA	Parent Teacher Association
RttT	Race to the Top
RTW	right to work
SAT	Scholastic Aptitude Test
SES	socioeconomic status
SFSP	Summer Food Service Program
SGM	student growth measures
SIG	School Improvement Grant
SINI	school in need of improvement
SLO	student learning objective
SNAP	Supplemental Nutritional Assistance Program

SOP	standard operating procedures
STEM	science, technology, engineering, and math
TFA	Teach for America
TPA	traditional public administration
UFT	United Federation of Teachers
VAM	value-added models
WIC	Women, Infants, and Children
WPEA	Whistleblower Protection Enhancement Act
YIMBY	yes in my backyard

Policy Feedback and Education Reform

Concepts and Perspectives

Most of our hopes and dreams for public education rely on how well teachers teach, and federal education policies (typically) need educators to serve as their primary implementers. Yet we know very little about how public discourse and policies influence educators' political and social experiences, identities, and behaviors. This book identifies the images and rationales that policy makers used to advance four national education reforms: No Child Left Behind (NCLB), NCLB waivers, Race to the Top (RttT), and the Every Student Succeeds Act (ESSA). It then uses 83 interviews with teachers and administrators to explore the effects of those changes. The primary purpose is to understand how public discourse and policies influence teaching, learning, and policy implementation; however, by interviewing educators from a wide variety of backgrounds and schools, the book provides insights into how public policies interact with educators' backgrounds, and the racial and socioeconomic backgrounds of their students, to affect children's educational outcomes and the democratic social purposes of schools. The latter includes the ability of public schools to create a level playing field in society by shaping students' knowledge and abilities, as well as their civic skills and engagement. I conclude by using educators' voices to construct a broad-based policy agenda that advances equity while still improving opportunities for all.

My interest in this topic stems from teaching American history, government, and economics to high school students. During that time, I began exploring research on *policy feedback* and on *social capital*. The former examines how experiences with government shape citizens' political identities and behaviors. The latter considers how relationships contribute to the well-being of individuals, groups, and communities and the efficiency and effectiveness of governments (Bourdieu, 1986; Portes, 1998; R. Putnam, 2000). These fields have developed in isolation from one another, but I began to create a dialogue between them to understand how political, social, and economic institutions interact with the social contexts of schools to inequitably influence educational outcomes. More directly, though, a large body of research documents the importance of teachers for student achievement; research also shows that public policies do not work when policy makers are misinformed about the values and beliefs of citizens and policy implementers. The government may even create the very problems that it is trying to resolve. In consequence, this study's findings are important for scholars, policy makers, and educators, especially as the nation continues to negotiate the current pandemic and economic crisis.

Policy makers, for instance, hoped to close the achievement gap between underprivileged children and their more advantaged peers and between American students and their international peers by (a) using student test scores to rate and rank schools and educators; (b) penalizing public schools and educators through poor performance reviews and decisions to restructure or close schools; and (c) fostering competition for public resources through merit pay, charter schools, and other forms of school choice. These policies are based on the belief that the two most important variables for teaching and learning are individual teachers and individual students. If mapped, that process would look as follows:

Teacher + Individual Student = Learning

No one would deny that teachers and students are critical for educational outcomes, but informants argued that this equation ignores the social and relational aspects of teaching and learning.

Learning in the classroom is co-constructed through the interactions between students, as well as between teachers and students. It is further influenced by variables *outside of the classroom,* such as family backgrounds, the socioeconomic composition of the school and community, and the organizational environment of the school. Learning is also *cumulative, contingent,* and often *nonlinear.* Prior experiences, skills, and knowledge influence the acquisition of new knowledge and skills; children may not catch what is being thrown out owing to different learning styles or other issues; and students sometimes take a step back before moving forward or make no gains and then suddenly take a giant leap as everything "clicks." These complexities require teachers to use multiple methods, adjust lessons across classrooms, and "adjust as they go" within specific units or lessons. They also make it difficult to standardize education and create issues with using student test scores to evaluate schools and teachers. Yet these are the very methods advocated by policy makers to improve public education under recent reforms.

Educators were not opposed to using test scores as a *gauge* of student performance; however, high stakes testing under recent reforms resulted in dysfunctional behaviors more than real improvements in instruction and public education. For example, rewarding or penalizing schools (NCLB) and teachers (RttT and NCLB waivers) based on student test scores created the incentive to "drill and grill" tested material, but the time spent preparing and administering those exams also reduced teachers' ability to develop untested knowledge, skills, and competencies. These issues challenged the profession's ability to meet its core moral purpose—to develop children as caring, well-adjusted, competent, and educated human beings—by marginalizing the development of critical thinking, problem solving, and "noncognitive" skills and behaviors, such as socioemotional skills (e.g., empathy, trust, tolerance of diverse opinions) and other so-called soft skills (e.g., perseverance, conscientiousness, self-control). Veronica, a suburban elementary teacher, explained,

> [There] are a lot of teachers who are teaching to the test because they feel like they have to, and I think it makes learning less enjoyable for students. . . . No Child Left Behind did that, but RttT is going to make it worse because now teachers' jobs are on the line. I think we're creating this world of test takers. Kids know how to take a test, but we're not creating students that can actually think outside the box and offer creative or innovative solutions to problems. . . . The social aspect of the classroom is huge . . . but that's going away. . . . I think it's the students who are being harmed, but it hurts us as a society too.

Like Veronica, most interviewees conveyed that these skills and behaviors should play a role in public education because they improve individual success and broader societal outcomes. Research supports their perspective.[1]

Another issue was that schools spent less time teaching nontested subjects, such as social studies and science in elementary school. Meagan, a suburban elementary teacher, told me,

> We are told [by administrators] that if we get to science and social studies that is all right but we don't need to . . . which is appalling. . . . [The state has] eliminated the social studies test in fifth grade, which I'm not opposed to . . . but they can get away with [it]. . . . It is really sad because some kids love school because of science and social studies. They want us to . . . [infuse both into] reading, but that is just read science and social studies . . . [not] doing experiments for example. . . . The whole philosophy is that if they can read well everything else will come. But . . . you need to really understand the concepts . . . discuss and debate them . . . manipulate them. . . . So, it is *very frustrating* [said with great emphasis].

This change obviously harms students, but it also harms us as a democratic society. Without social studies students are unlikely to develop civic skills and knowledge; science affects our ability to understand and transform our natural and physical worlds.

When combined, these developments created social justice issues. Test results are highly correlated with socioeconomic background and minority children are disproportionately likely to be poor. Persistent poor performance harms children's feelings of self-efficacy, self-worth, and self-confidence; impedes their ability to persevere; and causes some to engage in neglect (i.e., opting out and acting up through absenteeism, dropping out, or refusing to participate, study, or do homework). These claims are evident in the words of a suburban elementary (Carley) and a secondary art (Tom) teacher:

CARLEY: I'm finding that kids are giving up . . . we are not allowed to do things that kids need developmentally . . . because we are spending so much time on these tests and those skills that are needed for the tests . . . we are losing all kinds of other forms of learning, and therefore children who primarily learn in these other ways, like . . . kids who are more tactile . . . need to manipulate things to learn. And that's just one other form of learning.

TOM: By middle school, you . . . see alienation because they either can't perform at the expectation level of those tests, or they don't have the support at home. . . . That has always been an issue, but we're now starting . . . tests younger. . . . Art, gym, technology, music, and so forth used to be a place where kids could be safe from that testing . . . environment . . . form relationships with teachers, and work on things where a test didn't rank them and where they could draw on other abilities. Now, that is not the case because there's testing there too. We're doing as much as we can . . . [to limit the impact, but] children learn differently and . . . [some] struggle with testing. There are cumulative effects . . . [to] being told year after year . . . their peers are so-called better because of a test. . . . [Many struggle because of] things that go on outside . . . [but are] ranked with their peers who have that support at home, and . . . opportunities outside of school. It's not a level playing field.

Those who fell on the wrong side of the bell curve—low-income and minority children, English Language Learners (ELLs), and children with academic, behavioral, and emotional issues—were also less likely to be exposed to more complex skills and knowledge, as some states, school districts, and educators tried to "fix" low achievement by standardizing individual behaviors through organizational practices or "drill and grill" teaching.

Just as problematically, by penalizing those who care and rewarding those who teach high achievers or teach to the test, recent reforms encouraged high-quality teachers to leave the students and schools that need them the most, such as children with academic, behavioral, and emotional issues and/or the underresourced schools that disproportionately serve low-income and minority children. Participants claimed that only a small portion of those who exited teaching were less effective. Many more were *ethical leavers*. To them, recent reforms violated the moral imperatives of teaching, as a profession, and the ethical imperative of any policy intervention to "first do no harm."

A recent study supports that education reforms contributed to a growing teacher shortage, defined as the inability to staff vacancies at current wages with individuals qualified in the needed fields. Shortages are most severe in the underresourced schools that disproportionately serve low-income and minority children and in math, science, bilingual, and special education (Sutcher et al., 2016). This situation is unlikely to improve without changes in policy and discourse. Three-quarters of those I interviewed would not recommend teaching to others. Don, a suburban high school social studies teacher, described why:

Everyone talks about how China is doing so well. Their respect for teachers is so much higher. . . . [Teachers are] proportionally paid to those of the higher end . . . [But] the disheartening part . . . [is the] lack of respect for what we do. When your leaders don't respect . . . teachers . . . people below them will have the same attitude and that perpetuates to the children who might want to teach . . . It has gotten worse . . . [After]

25 years . . . [I do] not want my kids to be teachers . . . I love teaching . . . it is the greatest job ever . . . It's not the money. I don't think I am underpaid . . . [or] overpaid . . . No one goes into this . . . to be rich . . . there is a complete lack of respect . . . then they . . . [say] education is so important . . . Politicians don't walk the walk . . . we are reluctant to tell people we are teachers . . . you have to justify your position . . . people love to bash educators . . . [I say] "why do you think you should be paid so much" . . . they say, "Well, I am highly educated!" Who . . . educated you? Shouldn't the person who educated you get to share in those rewards?

Informants agreed that low pay discourages some from entering the profession, but opinion polls support their claim that low status (lack of respect), too little autonomy, and poor working conditions are key contributors.

Americans express high trust and confidence in teachers (61%), yet 54 percent do not want their children to become one—the highest rating since the question was asked in 1969—primarily due to low pay and poor benefits, student behaviors, low status, and a belief that teachers are overworked (PDK, 2018).[2] Research further supports their claim that applications to teacher education programs have gone way down over the past decade (Ayers, 2016; Will, 2019) and a recent poll of teachers confirms that 55 percent do not want their children to become one (Will, 2019). Anecdotal evidence and my informal conversations with teachers suggest that the pandemic has exacerbated these issues (Lieberman, 2021).

The educators in this study perceived that policy makers often portray their concerns as "self-interested" because it helps to suppress the voice of those who advocate redressing the broader socioeconomic issues that influence educational outcomes. Instead, the focus is on "failing" public schools and teachers. This negative discourse initially suppressed political and economic voice (policy feedback) through reduced union participation among younger teachers and increased political cynicism among educators of all ages. That changed in 2018 when teachers began engaging in strikes, walkouts, and walk-ins at capitols in states like West Virginia, Kentucky, Oklahoma, Arizona, North Carolina, Colorado, Washington, and California. Such widespread protest drew attention to the fact that school funding never fully recovered from the Great Recession of 2008. An unprecedented number of teachers from both political parties also successfully ran for national, state, and local office in 2018—many of them in deep red and purple states, where tax cuts had resulted in education funding decreases.[3]

Across the country, teachers gained strength from parents, students, and other stakeholders, who joined them in large numbers to protest rising class sizes, overtesting, poor teacher compensation, deteriorating working conditions, and increasingly impoverished public schools (Balingit, 2018a; CBPP, 2018; D. Goldstein, 2018d). Parents also began opting their children out of standardized tests in large numbers due to concerns about the ill effects of overtesting and the narrowing of the curriculum as a result of recent accountability reforms and the Common Core State Standards (CCSS; Bakeman, 2018; Zernike, 2015).

Broad support for teachers' views is further evident in the successful pursuit of school funding adequacy lawsuits in many states; a strike at a charter school network (D. Goldstein, 2018a, 2018b); and opinion polls where Americans said that teachers are underpaid, there is too much standardized testing, and test scores are not the best way to judge schools, teachers, or students (PDK, 2015, 2018).[4] Close to two-thirds also declared that they would support teachers in their community if they went on strike for higher salaries, including 6 in 10 Republicans (PDK, 2018).[5] By mobilizing a broader community of stakeholders through their unions, personal networks, and social media, teachers created political and social capital and successfully pushed for raises and more education spending in many states. This *policy feedback* is critical because the most recent federal reform—the ESSA of 2015—provides state governments with more discretion to regulate and evaluate schools, teachers, and students.[6]

Will the ESSA live up to its name and ensure equal educational opportunity for America's 50 million schoolchildren? This research suggests that, like previous federal and state reforms, the answer to that question will largely depend on how educators respond to that policy in practice and through collective voice. Those responses, in turn, will be influenced by their social contexts (e.g., local communities, schools as organizations, teaching as an occupation, teachers' unions), as well as their experiences with previous policies.

The chapters that follow explore how recent education reforms interacted with social contexts to construct educators experiences and behaviors and examine the consequences—both intended and unintended—for teaching, learning, and future policies. My hope is that the juxtaposition of policy makers' views (Chapter 2) with those of educators (Chapters 3 through 11) will create a way forward that improves public education for all children while also fostering the broader democratic and transformative ends of public schools. The next section specifies the general perspective of this book and the empirical gaps that it addresses.

Perspectives on the Policy Process

Traditional models of the policy process are "linear," or move from citizen participation up to government action in the form of political debate and public policies. In contrast, research on *policy feedback* explores how experiences with elected officials, public servants, and public policies alter citizens' demands for future policies (Figures 1.1 and 1.2).[7] The empirical literature shows that the government influences citizens' willingness and capacity to mobilize and become politically engaged through resource and interpretive effects (Mettler & Soss, 2004).

Resource effects occur when political institutions confer needed civic skills and knowledge or provide the economic means, capacity, or incentive to participate.[8] *Interpretive effects* influence citizen engagement by conveying meanings and information about civic obligations, inclusiveness of membership in the polity, and policy makers' responsiveness to individual and collective needs or concerns. This information is gathered from policy designs (e.g., the visibility of benefits and burdens), the construction of policy targets, and the behaviors of public servants. It influences group consciousness, civic predispositions, and citizens' sense of political efficacy (Pierson, 1993; A. Schneider & Ingram, 1993, 2005b).

Phrased another way, public policies allocate more than benefits and burdens; they are sites of political and social learning. Some policies, such as Social Security and the GI Bill (the Servicemen's Readjustment Act of 1944), construct a "deserving" target population.

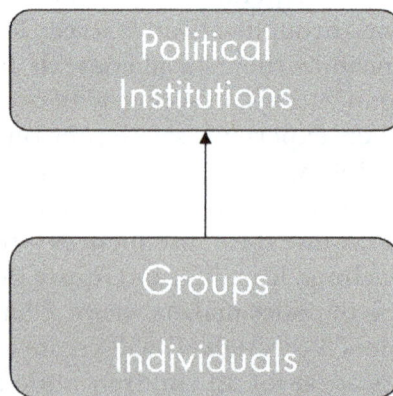

Figure 1.1. Traditional policy approaches

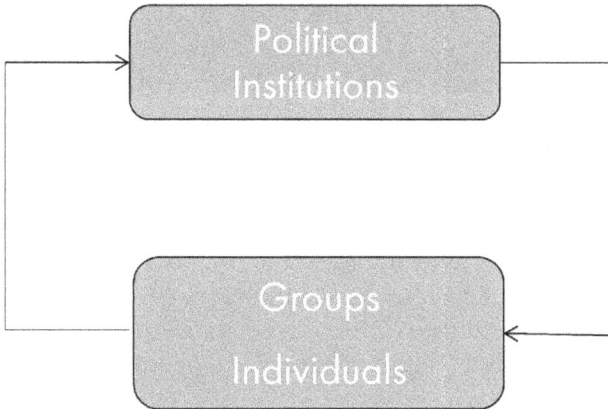

Figure 1.2. Policy feedback approaches.

Other policies construct an "undeserving" population. Means-tested and/or paternalistic policies, such as Aid to Families with Dependent Children (AFDC), are especially likely to convey that negative message when compared to entitlements like Social Security Disability Insurance. Research shows that the former policies increased political engagement and encouraged demand-making by providing resources, fostering feelings of civic belonging, and instilling a sense of affect and obligation toward the government and/or other members of society (Campbell, 2003; Mettler, 2002); the latter discouraged political participation and demand-making by differentiating between citizens in ways that fostered isolation, apathy, and alienation among recipients.[9]

Public policies are not the only ways that citizens encounter their government, yet the empirical literature clearly shows that public policies do not simply address societal problems. The government inequitably affects how citizens perceive their rights and responsibilities as citizens and their willingness to organize, exercise political voice, and influence future policies. It does so by conveying messages about policy targets; informing individuals about their status as citizens; ordering social, political, and economic relations; and shaping individuals' beliefs about themselves and their group (H. Ingram & Schneider, 1993; Mettler & Soss, 2004).

Gaps in the Empirical Literature on Policy Feedback

The empirical literature has provided many important insights into how experiences with the government influence political participation. Most studies, however, focus on policies that confer individual benefits, such as welfare, Social Security, and veterans' assistance (but see Flavin & Griffin, 2009; Patashnik, 2008). There is a need for studies that explore policies—like NCLB and RttT—that create "winners" (e.g., charter schools and highly performing public schools and teachers) and "losers" (e.g., schools and teachers in need of improvement), as well as policies that impose burdens through taxes and restrictions on social, political, and economic behaviors.

Another area in need of exploration is how the government interacts with social contexts to construct citizen engagement and participation. As shown in Figure 1.3, citizens experience public discourse and policies as individuals, yet also as members of networks, social groups, and communities—like unions, occupations, professions, and school districts. In fact, the government often uses social groups to delimit service entitlement and achieve other objectives. This was the case with Title I of the Elementary and Secondary Education Act (ESEA), which labeled low-income children "culturally deprived" to justify and delimit participation in the program (Stein, 2004), and with the citizen participation requirements included in many Great Society programs, like Head Start, which were designed to increase voice (participation and civic engagement) in previously marginalized low-income and minority communities. Policy makers also create groups through policy that had not previously existed (e.g., drunk drivers).

Studies further focus on how politicians (deliberately or unintentionally) design policies to *increase feedback* from political allies; however, it is possible to design policies or frame citizens in ways that defang, weaken, or demobilize political opponents.[10] Unions are the perfect example of both. Historically, government at all levels restricted labor mobilization by imposing risks on workers. This included actual violence (beating up strikers), legal penalties (jailing and fining strikers), and symbolic violence (discouraging workers from joining by stigmatizing members through narratives that linked unions to communism). By reducing membership density and dues, these actions hindered the ability of unions to mobilize on behalf of change. With the adoption of the National Labor Relations Act (1935), though, the federal government guaranteed private-sector employees the right to organize and bargain collectively. In return, labor unions

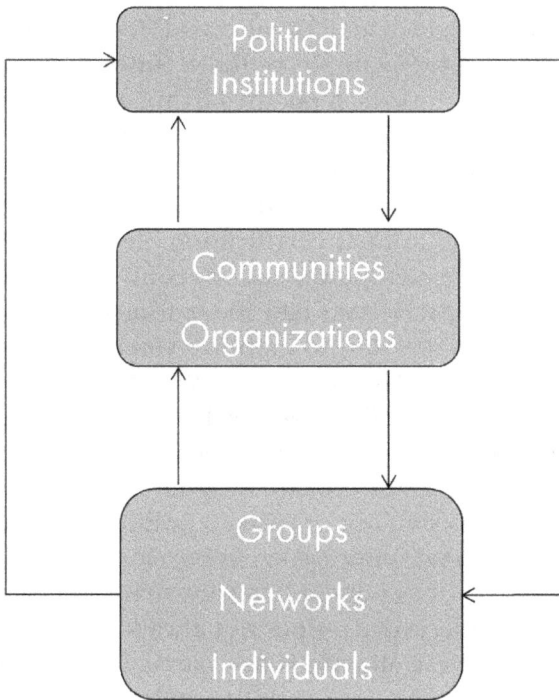

Figure 1.3. Policy feedback loops.

generated positive feedback for pro-labor policies (e.g., minimum wage laws and workplace protections). They also expanded the size of the government by lobbying for programs that helped middle- and working-class citizens and mobilizing grassroots support for Democratic and Republican candidates who supported an expanded welfare state (see Dark, 1999; Greenstone, 1969). Beginning with Wisconsin in 1959 (Umhoefer, 2016), many states—like the one that is the subject of this analysis—also adopted laws that permitted public employees to bargain collectively as a way of reducing strikes and public service disruptions. The federal government began doing so in 1962.[11] Together, these policies expanded economic and political voice through resource effects (e.g., higher wages and increased union membership and dues) and interpretive effects (e.g., feelings of political efficacy).

More recently, conservatives created cross-state networks that successfully lobbied for policies that reduced the organizational resources of public-sector unions (membership size and revenues) and suppressed the political participation of unions and individual employees in ways that harmed Democrats (Hertel-Fernandez, 2018). Act 10 in Wisconsin, for example, reduced union membership from 14.2 to 8.3 percent of workers. It put the birthplace of public-employee unions near the bottom third of state union membership by stripping public employees of any meaningful collective bargaining power; making it harder to collect dues; and forcing union leaders to engage in resource-draining annual certification elections. With 132,000 fewer members, public-employee unions contributed less money to political campaigns; they also had fewer foot soldiers to lobby on behalf of public services and to mobilize voters against anti-union candidates, like former Governor Scott Walker.[12]

Beyond showing that political actors deliberately use legislation as a means of disadvantaging their opponents, recent research (Hertel-Fernandez, 2018) does not provide insights into the strategies that policy makers use to shut out or weaken political opponents within particular institutional venues, such as bureaucracies, the judiciary, or Congress. It also does not explain why such *weaponized policy feedback*—even when successful—does not always reduce political and economic voice. These shortfalls are particularly critical in light of two recent developments: a rash of teacher strikes and political protests—mostly in states that do not allow public employees to engage in collective bargaining (see Chapter 7)—and the Supreme Court's 5–4 decision in *Janus v. AFSCME Council 31* (2018).

Janus reversed the Court's prior distinction between "mandatory agency fees" and "voluntary union dues." Only the latter could be used for lobbying or other political activities. The former were designed to prevent nonmembers from freeriding off their dues paying coworkers by requiring them to pay partial fees that would cover the union's costs of handling grievances and negotiating new contracts for members and nonmembers alike (*Abood v. Detroit Board of Education*, 1977). Instead, the conservative majority held that "fair share" agency fees violated free speech because it is impossible to define what is political with a union that negotiates with the government. The case, the third to come before the Supreme Court in five years, was financed by a small group of foundations with ties to the same business-economic interest groups that had successfully lobbied for state-level laws that reduced the power of unions, including right to work (RTW) laws.[13]

They vary from state to state, but—like *Janus*—RTW laws allow workers to benefit from union contracts and representation in a grievance against their employer without paying dues, partial or otherwise. Research shows that they contributed to a 70-year decline in private-sector unionization.[14] *Janus* has now made RTW the law of the land for public employees.[15] Based on the experiences of states that adopted RTW laws, most have predicted that *Janus* will result in large decreases in public-employee union membership and thereby negatively affect political contributions to the Democratic Party and policy feedback for its preferred policies.[16] Yet, inexplicably and contrary to expectations, labor union approval is growing in America. The current approval rate, 68 percent, is at its highest level since 1965; approval rates have risen among Democrats, Republicans, and Independents (Brenan, 2021); and, 52 percent see unions as mostly helping the economy, up from 39 percent in 2009 (J. Jones, 2016).[17] The public also views unions' diminished ranks more negatively than positively (51% mostly bad vs. 35% mostly good; Fingerhut, 2018). Perhaps more critically, total union membership grew by 262,000 in 2017—especially among workers aged 24 years and younger, who account for 76 percent of increased membership but less than 40 percent of total employment (Schmitt, 2018)—and, since then, self-reported membership in a labor union has remained steady (Brenan, 2021). This study contributes to the existing literature by showing how social contexts—not just political and economic ones (e.g., political parties or the economic effects of the novel coronavirus)—explain these developments.

Finally, most policy feedback studies focus on how self-interest compels individuals to protect public programs (e.g., Campbell, 2003). Yet one recent study (L. Jacobs & Mettler, 2018) found that assessments of how the Affordable Care Act (ACA) had helped fellow citizens actually tempered individual concerns about increased tax burdens—even amid growing partisan divisiveness and declining trust in government—and research outside the policy feedback field shows that individuals are motivated by altruism, social justice, and other communal or public-regarding considerations.[18] While making an important contribution, the ACA policy feedback study (L. Jacobs & Mettler, 2018) is limited to public opinion; focuses on taxes; and, again, does not explore the influence of micro- and meso-social contexts. There is a need for more research on how burdens beyond taxes (e.g., restrictions on political, social, and economic behaviors) and values beyond self-interest affect policy feedback, and whether both are influenced by social contexts.

Gaps in the Empirical Literature on Policy Implementation

The literature on policy implementation suffers from many of the same gaps as empirical studies on policy feedback. Defined as "the process of carrying out . . . policy directives" (Nakamura & Smallwood, 1980, p. 1), most research focuses on the motives and behaviors of policy implementers (Honig, 2006; Odden, 1991).[19] Some studies attribute implementation failures to conflicts between political goals and the interests and preferences of policy implementers. Others conclude that policies are poorly implemented because frontline workers do not understand what they are supposed to do or lack the necessary skills, knowledge, capacity, or time.[20] Either way, the research (largely) assumes that policy implementers are the most important determinants of successful implementation (Honig, 2006; Odden, 1991).[21] There is a need for studies that explore how citizens and social contexts contribute to policy implementation.[22]

The literature also largely separates the democratic process of making laws from the bureaucratic process of carrying them out. In contrast, Schattschneider (1960, p. 288) argued that "policies produce politics," meaning public policies construct the experiences of citizens and policy implementers in ways that influence their behaviors and, as a result, future political action. This might occur because policies generate new problems; redistribute power and influence in ways that create new political alliances; or reconstruct the values, beliefs, and preferences of citizens and policy implementers. In these cases, as illustrated in Figure 1.4, the government creates "feedback loops" that influence subsequent policies.

The Problem

The literatures on policy feedback and implementation both largely silence how social contexts influence the political behaviors of public servants as citizens and policy implementers; yet research from a wide array of disciplines suggests that interests, preferences, and behaviors are constructed through social interaction.[23] In terms of education, these interactions take place within schools as communities but are also structured by schools as organizations, teaching as an occupation, teachers' unions, and education as a public institution. This empirical gap is especially critical for those professions and occupations that involve "coproduction." That term conveys the importance of citizens for the quality of public goods and services

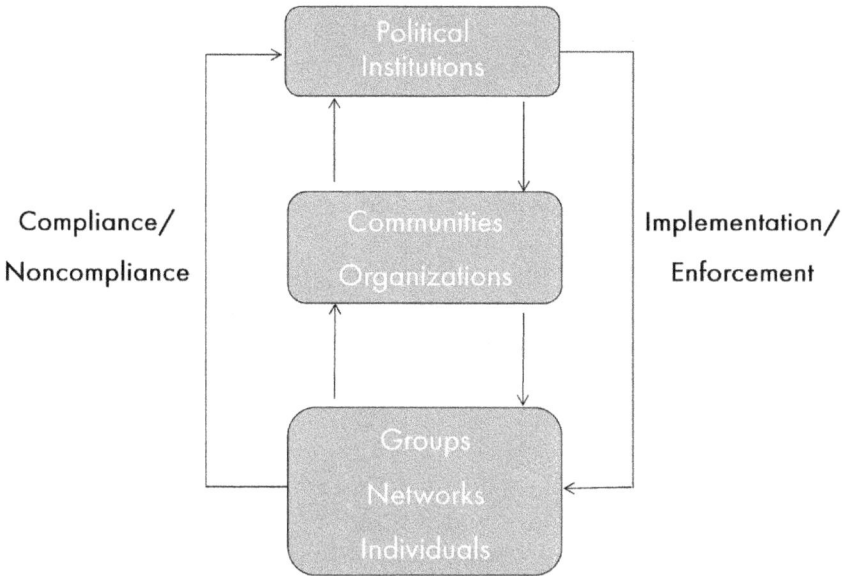

Figure 1.4. Implementation feedback loops.

(Ostrom, 1996) and acknowledges that many public servants—such as police officers, park rangers, emergency responders, public health workers, administrators, and teachers—are not the sole producers of collective and individual outcomes (e.g., an educated workforce, academic achievement and attainment, a student's report card). In consequence, their behaviors are likely to be influenced by their social contexts, not just structured by public policies and discourse.

Study Purpose

This research addresses gaps in the public policy literature by exploring how recent education reforms and discourse interacted with schools and communities to influence the behaviors of educators as citizens and policy implementers. It examines the contingencies and *microfoundations* of policy feedback—meaning the behaviors of individual educators, parents, students, and taxpayers—as a result of these interactions across four national education reforms, beginning with NCLB.

Enacted during the George W. Bush administration, NCLB was the most significant expansion and alteration of the federal role in education since the original ESEA of 1965 (McGuinn, 2006) and commentators dubbed the reforms of the Obama administration (NCLB waivers and RttT) "NCLB on steroids" (Mathis, 2011). Such large-scale change offers a natural experiment for understanding how public policies interact with the social contexts of schools to inform the perceptions and behaviors of educators. Natural experiments approximate those controlled by scientists in laboratories but occur *spontaneously* in nature and are therefore not controlled by the researcher. In this study, recent education reforms served as "events," and I examined educators' reactions to these "natural experiments" to learn how public policies and discourse inform individual and group behaviors. The central questions that guided this research follow:

RQ1: How did policy makers justify different forms of regulation? How did they use language and institutions (e.g., congressional hearings or the rules of debate) to achieve their preferred ends? How did current policies and discourse influence policy feedback and subsequent policies?

RQ2: What are the similarities and differences between (a) the kinds of reasoning and assumptions public policy makers used to justify different forms of regulation in schools and (b) the lived realities of teachers and administrators?

RQ3: Do relationships in schools and teaching interact with public policies and policy designs to structure educators' political and social experiences, identities, and behaviors?

RQ4: What are the implications for teaching, learning, policy implementation, public education, and policy feedback?

The next section discusses the methods and data that I used to link public policies and discourse to educators and their school communities.

Methods, Data, and Data Analysis

Traditional policy analysis focuses on the relationship between discrete policy problems, policy configurations, and program outcomes in an effort to find the "proper" combinations of incentives to motivate, encourage, or deter specific behaviors. In education, traditional approaches would examine which "inputs" (e.g., teacher certification, resource allocation) have the desired effects on "outputs" (e.g., standardized test scores, graduation rates).[24] In contrast, this research mostly relied on narrative policy analysis (NPA)—an interpretive method that uses narrative inquiry to examine policy effects. It compares stories across a single or multiple informants to understand how people communicate ideas and make sense of their worlds as related to policy.[25]

The usefulness of this method emerged early in the research process. I noticed educators often told stories rather than providing more direct responses to my questions. Many of these stories were actually "narratives." They had a plot; a cast of characters; and a beginning, middle, and end. Although there were many reasons for this, there were patterns across informants. For instance, when and why respondents told stories was important. Stories were also frequently a way for participants to make sense of their experiences, especially when they were conveying tacit knowledge that was difficult to get across in other ways, expressing emotions, and discussing things that made them uncomfortable. In essence, narratives helped educators communicate across a practitioner–nonpractitioner divide and open up their worlds while affording themselves distance when needed. Just as importantly, national policy makers frequently told stories to convey ideas and justify political choices. By analyzing stories at both levels, I could construct shared meanings and points of contestation to generate an overarching narrative about how public discourse and policies interact with social contexts to construct the political and social experiences, identities, and behaviors of educators.

Data

I used several sources of data, some of which are public and some of which were collected specifically for this study.

National data. Similar to other inductive forms of content analysis, this research focuses on the communication of meanings. Thus words or discourse are my data (Merriam, 1998). The primary sources of national data were congressional hearings and debates between January and December 2001 (NCLB); the rhetoric of President George W. Bush (NCLB), President Barack Obama (NCLB, NCLB waivers, RttT, and the ESSA), and secretaries of education Rod Paige (NCLB), Margaret Spellings (NCLB), and Arne Duncan (NCLB Waivers, RttT, and the ESSA); and the rhetoric of members of both houses of Congress and the leaders of the House and Senate education committees (NCLB, NCLB waivers, RttT, and the ESSA).

Debates, hearings, and speeches compose the public aspect of policy making. Policy makers frame issues, events, and people in ways that create alliances and generate support for their preferred policies. In the process, they provide power, authority, and resources to those designated to fix perceived problems. Rather than trying to establish the "authenticity" of the messages, I examined the images and rationales key policy makers used to advance and continue a radically new approach to public education. I supplemented this analysis with a content analysis of each policy's mandates, instruments, and regulatory requirements, public opinion polls, media accounts, and other empirical studies. All of these influence the experiences, identities, and behaviors of citizens, interest groups, elected officials, public servants, and policy implementers.

I first developed a set of focusing questions that were grounded in the relevant theoretical and empirical literatures on policy change (see Appendix A). I used these focusing questions to open-code the data (debates, speeches, hearings, policies, and regulatory language) and develop themes and analytic categories. The actual data sets varied depending on the theme or construct, such as comparing ideological positions for a particular policy target, causal stories, use of symbolic devices, or preferred policy tools.

Over the course of the debates on NCLB, my analysis showed that there was *policy learning*, as policy makers adopted one another's language to justify new forms of regulation and accountability. Such learning influenced how legislators politically and culturally reconstructed public schools and public schoolteachers in comparison with other affected groups (e.g., administrators, parents, charter schools, and the private and religious providers of supplemental services). In consequence, I used the themes and constructs from my qualitative analysis to construct a quantitative analysis of the debates on the Conference Report that eventually became NCLB (see Tables 2.3–2.7 in Chapter 2). That analysis was especially important for constructing similarities and differences across two administrations (George W. Bush and Barack Obama) and between national policy makers and educators.

State and local data. The practitioner data were collected using an interview protocol that I developed and field-tested on 11 informants during fall 2005 and spring 2006. That protocol used Spradley's (1979) guide to ethnographic interviewing to develop a series of open-ended questions that were designed to elicit general and specific information about teachers' and administrators' jobs (see Appendix B for the protocol).[26] It also drew from other sources, such as Lortie's (1975) ethnography on teaching. Many of his descriptions and data are out of date—having been collected in the 1960s and early 1970s—but using some of his questions allowed me to further exploit recent education reforms as natural experiments by constructing a "before" and "after" analysis of teachers and teaching. The field test showed that early questions created rapport, drew informants in, and made more difficult questions easier to handle later on. As such, I mostly kept the same protocol but formalized many of the questions that I had informally asked during the pilot interviews.

The first section of the protocol gathered data about how educators' backgrounds, teaching assignments, and school contexts influence their experiences, identities, and behaviors. The second examined how recent reforms affected administrators, teachers, parents, students, teaching as an occupation, and schools as organizations and communities. The third explored how forces within society at large influence public schools and teaching. For example, I asked educators to comment on recent headlines on public education, public schools, teachers, teachers' unions, and teaching. I then used those comments to flesh out their reactions to how each of these groups was being politically and socially constructed.

Participant selection. Since federal education reforms were serving as natural experiments, I recruited teachers and administrators who had only worked under the policy interventions, never worked under the policy interventions, and worked before and after the policy interventions. Informants were also selected for maximum variation in terms of age, years of experience, grades or subjects taught, tested versus nontested subjects and grades, and different occupations (e.g., administrators, teachers, speech pathologists, psychologists). I further sampled educators at various stages of their careers, including teachers who had retired, left teaching, or become administrators. For purposes of this analysis, the word *educator* refers to administrators and teachers, and *teacher* is broadly construed to represent anyone who works *directly* with students in the learning process, such as subject area teachers, special education teachers, speech pathologists, psychologists, librarians, and aides. Where differences emerged between teachers—as broadly construed in this study—I bifurcated the label to alert the reader.

Finally, I purposively interviewed educators from districts and schools that differed along several key factors: district size; level of need/level of resources; racial and socioeconomic composition; policy label (schools in good standing, in need of improvement, or being restructured, taken over, or closed); geographic location (urban, rural, or suburban); and public, private, and charter schools.[27] Research indicates that all of these influence educators' experiences at work; however, this *sampling for difference* also ensured that the interview population in general resembled the teaching workforce in the state, as well as the variations in educators' work situations. This helped me disentangle the multiple meanings ascribed to a federal policy by different communities while also distilling those meanings held in common. It was further useful for elaborating on how accountability policies—like NCLB, NCLB waivers, RttT, and the ESSA—interact with educators' backgrounds, and the racial and socioeconomic backgrounds of their students, to affect children's educational outcomes and the democratic social purposes of schools.

Data sample. In total, I conducted 83 interviews with teachers and administrators in 39 school districts across the state.[28] Participants included 21 males and 62 females. Of those, 14 percent never worked under NCLB and RttT (i.e., they retired or left teaching or administration prior to 2001), 22 percent only worked under NCLB and RttT (i.e., entered the field of education after 2001), and 64 percent worked before and after NCLB and RttT. The average age was 43 years and the average years teaching was 17, but participants' experience ranged from 1 to 40 years (see Figures C.1–C.14 in Appendix C).

While 11 of the teacher interviews were conducted as part of a pilot study and took place prior to the subject state receiving its RttT grant, I reinterviewed 4 of the 11 after the adoption of RttT to see how that policy had changed their political and social experiences, identities, and behaviors. Most of the remaining 72 interviews were conducted between spring 2011 and spring 2013; however, I sporadically returned to the field through spring 2014—to both reinterview and conduct new interviews—in order to understand whether educators' perceptions of RttT had changed as they developed more experience with its implementation. In addition, 16 respondents—including some who had participated in the original pilot project—continued to informally reach out to me through October 2020. These informal discussions allowed me to update my findings to reflect recent developments and changes in education policy, such as recent teacher strikes, the adoption and implementation of the ESSA, and the novel coronavirus. Along with the interview protocol, this interview strategy allowed me to identify and separate changes in educators' experiences and attribute them to NCLB, RttT, or more recent developments. Nevertheless, about two-thirds of the interviews involved a single encounter that lasted approximately two hours.

Data Analysis

The process of analyzing the data was largely the same for both the national and practitioner data. I printed hard copies of the full-length transcriptions and stored them and any field notes in binders. Drawing on the work of Corbin and Strauss (2008), I then used a process of open and selective coding to analyze them. I first read the entire "interview" transcript (i.e., interview, debate, speech, testimony, law) to make sense of the overall themes and compare what was going on in one "interview" to the others. I then annotated each by making comments in the margins, highlighting quotes or stories, and making notes of themes and analytic categories. Finally, I recoded, re-sorted, and reanalyzed the data to capture the overarching themes and subthemes that were common across individuals or "data sets" and highlight comments or themes that were unique to particular individuals, situations, or circumstances (Corbin & Strauss, 2008).

I kept running notes on emerging themes and constructs, including those that were shared across informants and those that were unique to individual participants or situations. Early notes, along with my thoughts and interpretations, were used to create a "start list" of important themes and constructs (M. Miles & Huberman, 1984). That list guided the kinds of probing questions I asked and the initial codes for organizing my national and educator data, but I continued to update both to account for newly emerging themes and constructs. The outcome of this process was that I created groups of related concepts and then constructed categories that represented particular social or political phenomena (Corbin & Strauss, 2008).[29]

Trustworthiness

Some of my interviews were with retirees who had been away from teaching for a while. As such, they may have been more likely to remember their most positive and negative experiences rather than their "everyday worlds." It is also possible that current educators skewed the research by only offering their most positive portrayals of themselves, their colleagues, and their teaching. Recognizing these issues, I built safeguards into this study. First, I fleshed out the experiences of teachers and administrators through the use of open-ended interviews, which allowed educators to divert from the questions and interview protocol. Second, I structured the interviews as conversations to establish rapport and build trust and openness. In doing so, I found that teachers and administrators were quite open in terms of discussing negative experiences and behaviors. This may have resulted from the fact that participants knew I was not identifying their schools or state, but the interview protocol was also designed to draw educators in slowly. Third, by eliciting "stories," my questions allowed informants to open up their emotions without "naming them," meaning participants could put themselves in the middle of their narratives while also affording themselves emotional distance if needed. Fourth, I interviewed educators from a wide variety of settings and backgrounds. I used this diversity to compare and contrast educators' stories, develop overarching narratives and identify differences among them. These areas of agreement and divergence helped me make sense of how participants viewed education reforms, as seen through their descriptions and stories.

Audiences and Contributions

I have more than one purpose for writing this book, and those purposes are likely to interest different audiences. The book is organized so that chapters and sections of interest may be read independently.

The primary purpose is to inform policy makers about how public policies and political discourse interact with schools and communities to affect teaching, learning, public education, and the implementation of education policies. These findings are therefore useful as state policy makers reform their evaluative regimes under the ESSA and national policy makers consider changes to the ESSA when it comes up for renewal. My efforts to inform policy, however, have theoretical and empirical implications for scholars who are interested in politics, public administration, public management, and education policies. Scholars typically partition these fields; this book explores the linkages between them. Theoretically, it shows how recent education reforms were part of a broader shift in public service paradigms. Empirically, it explores how these paradigms and their corresponding education policies influenced the political and social experiences, identities, and behaviors of educators, parents, students, taxpayers, and community members. I use these findings to develop a model of policy feedback that has applications in fields outside of education and to map a broad-based policy agenda that will promote equity, foster the broader social democratic and transformative ends of public schools, and provide choice while still improving public education for all children.

Last, but not least, this book is intended for educators and the scholarly audience of historians, sociologists, economists, and political scientists who study and theorize about unions, occupations, and professions. Outside of education, research explores how the free market (i.e., competition and choice) and hierarchies (i.e., the organization of private firms and public agencies) affect consumer choice and worker motivation; however, professionalism, according to Freidson (2001), is often treated "as an aberration" rather than something that has "a logic and an integrity of its own" (pp. 11–12). In this book, educators discuss the reforms and rhetoric that marketized public education while also expanding the bureaucratic power of the government. Their words are important for understanding how unions, occupations, and professions influence policy feedback, policy implementation, and the efficiency, effectiveness, and fairness of government programs.

Unions, for instance, do not solely engage in collective bargaining; they are well-positioned to lobby for policies that more broadly distribute wealth and opportunity for two reasons. Unions are one of the few political and economic interest groups that directly represent the interests of working-class Americans; and, like professions and occupations, they have a federated membership structure that enables them to mobilize local social ties on behalf of policy feedback at the state and national level. When policy makers deliberately and persistently make it harder for some groups—such as young people, minorities, unions, farmers' associations, occupations, or professions—to exercise voice through voting, lobbying, organizing, and protesting, they do not solely create barriers for collective action. Such weaponized policies reduce individual civic engagement. If primarily targeted against those who demand programs that benefit middle-class, working-class, and low-income citizens, these policies have the potential to exacerbate socioeconomic inequality and foster political, social, and economic unrest.

The Plan of This Book

In this chapter, I provided an overview of the theoretical arguments that inform this research. The remainder of the book is divided into four parts, each of which may be read independently from other sections of the book.

Part I compares the rhetoric of policy makers and educators. Chapter 2 examines the images and rationales that key policy makers used to justify replacing an equity regime with an accountability regime; it also explores the role of policy feedback in that development. Chapter 3 provides educators' responses to this political and social reconstruction of education, including, but not limited to, their perceptions of how policy makers framed policy targets, such as public schools, administrators, teachers, parents, children, taxpayers, unions, charter schools, and the private and religious providers of supplemental services.

Part II examines the pre–education reform environment. I argue that you cannot make educators more accountable without first knowing what accountability already looks like, how it is achieved, and at what costs and benefits to society. Chapter 4 focuses on how and why different forms of accountability evolved in teaching; it also examines how public discourse and policies influenced the economic and political mobilization of teachers—meaning voting, lobbying, organizing, or protesting through unions and teachers' associations—in ways that resulted in more professional authority (policy feedback). Chapter 5 explores educators' understandings of how professional accountability differs from other forms of accountability and the costs and benefits for society.

Part III examines how recent education reforms influenced the political (Chapter 6) and social (Chapter 7) experiences, identities, and behaviors of educators in a northeastern state. These chapters focus on how educators, as part of a shared professional culture, individually and collectively interpreted and responded to recent reforms and the effect on teaching and learning.

Part IV provides insight into how the government influences the efficiency, effectiveness, and fairness of public services by affecting voice and everyday acts of participation. It builds theory on policy feedback by developing a model for how the government interacts with social contexts to influence the political, economic, and social behaviors of citizens, public servants, and policy implementers. Chapter 8 shows that recent education reforms are part of a broader shift in public service paradigms. Chapter 9 explores educators' perceptions of how these paradigms and their corresponding education policies influenced the behaviors of important coproducers of education (e.g., parents, students, taxpayers). Chapter 10 draws from all of the preceding chapters to explore the links between policy feedback, policy implementation, democratic participation, and democratic performance. It largely focuses on the field of education but provides examples from other policy areas to build a model that is testable through future research.

When combined, these sections show that policy makers willfully dismantled public services by framing the government as the problem, rather than the solution, and citizens as consumers, rather than community members. The unproven claim that markets would better achieve important social democratic goals—such as increased civic engagement and socioeconomic integration—as economic growth trickled down in ways that would "lift all boats," justified allotting public resources to an unregulated private sector. This created what some have referred to as a "*consumerocracy,*" where public services are evaluated based on how well they serve individual wants versus collective ends. The book elaborates on why the construction of education as a good that is produced by teachers and consumed by individuals—versus a good that is produced collectively for the benefit of society—jeopardizes the broader benefits provided through a strong system of public education. It further shows how market-based education reforms resulted in unequal, unproductive, and undemocratic outcomes rather than real improvements to public schools.

I conclude, in Chapter 11, by using these "lessons from the field" to develop a new education policy agenda. The novel coronavirus, the renewed Black Lives Matter (BLM) movement, and teacher protests and strikes in many states have increased support for reimagining and reinvesting in public education. As mapped in Chapter 11, the book develops a broad-based policy agenda that focuses on the social, economic, and political contexts of schools—not just the behaviors of individual educators, parents, and students—to promote equity, achieve the broader social democratic and transformative ends of public schools, and provide choice while still improving public education for *all* children.

At the onset of this book, it is important to note that informants agreed more than they disagreed; however, research supports this study's conclusion that these views are not partisan. Educators share similar understandings with respect to educational issues and policies even though their political affiliations (political parties and political ideologies) generally match those of citizens at large and the communities where they live (Editorial Projects in Education, 2017). Instead, these observations provide a counter discourse to the supposedly commonsense logics that have been used to justify tax cuts for the most well-off, deregulating the private sector, disinvesting in the public sector, and expanding policies that focus on "individual" accountability. In education, this included using competition, choice, and high stakes testing to hold schools, educators, parents, and students accountable. According to their words, policy makers have continued to rely on these policy instruments—despite their failure to improve public education—because of a belief that there are no better alternatives. This book provides those alternatives.

Conclusion

Summing up, public policies convey messages that have consequences for beliefs and behaviors, but social contexts influence how these messages are received and implemented. This book explores what that looks like for administrators and teachers. The findings are important for those that seek to understand how the government directly influences children's educational outcomes through its policies, as well as how it indirectly does so by affecting demands for future policies.

PART I

Social Constructions, Policy Feedback, and Education Reform

As mentioned, empirical research shows that public policies and political rhetoric generate socially constructed identities for policy "targets," who are defined as the victims or perpetrators of policy problems and the objects of policy solutions.[1] Sometimes, changes in how a group is constructed result from shifting mores, such as portraying alcoholism as a disease (dependency) rather than the result of deviant behavior. Other times, these changes are designed to achieve political ends.[2] The goal is to win the allegiance of the largest number of people and generate positive feedback for specific policies; however, these social constructions develop categories of deservedness and undeservedness that raise or lower the standing of groups; create "groups" that would not have existed or borne a negative stigma without the force of law (e.g., drunk drivers); and influence all subsequent understandings of a group's potential and the merits or pitfalls of providing for their needs.[3] They also shape citizens' beliefs about the nature of government and teach them different lessons about their role in the polity and the efficacy of exercising political voice, which is a form of policy feedback.[4] Chapter 2 uses a qualitative and quantitative analysis of education policies and discourse to examine how policy makers reconstructed the policy problem, solution, and targets in ways that justified political change in the form of NCLB. It then explores how NCLB, public discourse, and the actions of policy makers constructed policy feedback in ways that resulted in subsequent education reforms (RttT, NCLB waivers, and the ESSA). Chapter 3 uses 83 interviews with

27

educators to compare and contrast their views with those of policy makers and set up the chapters that follow—where educators discuss how education reforms and discourse influenced their political and social experiences, identities, and behaviors.

2

The Political and Social Construction
of Education Reform

Sociologists and political scientists recognize that formal and informal political institutions generate "positive feedback," meaning they
create constituencies that have a vested interest in either maintaining
the status quo, expanding existing programs, or blocking those who
oppose existing political arrangements (see, e.g., Pierson, 1996). Such
was the case with demands to index Social Security to inflation and
thereby increase payments to recipients. Yet research also shows that
political institutions generate negative feedback (K. Weaver, 2010)
by mobilizing groups that perceive the government has penalized
or ignored them and/or those who believe that "the state"—defined
as public institutions (e.g., Congress, public schools, public policies)
and public servants—is inefficient, ineffective, or not working as
intended. Less discussed is how public discourse fosters or suppresses
policy feedback by, for example, legitimizing the claims of some and
delegitimizing those of others. There is also a need for research
that examines institutional strategies for demobilizing, weakening,
or shutting out political opponents within specific venues, such as
Congress, bureaucracies, or the judiciary. This chapter rectifies
those shortfalls by showing how policy makers used *both* discourse
and institutions to "mobilize bias" (Schattschneider, 1960) in favor
of an accountability regime across two presidential administrations
(George W. Bush and Barack Obama). That status quo was then
maintained under the administration of President Donald Trump.

Constructing the Mediocre Status Quo: Institutions, Narratives, and Policy Feedback

The great promise of public education is that it will enable all children—regardless of their backgrounds—to share equally in the American dream, even as it prepares them for the responsibilities of democratic citizenship. Throughout most of our nation's history, state and local governments have borne responsibility for fulfilling that promise. This shifted with the adoption of the ESEA of 1965. Passed during the height of the civil rights movement, the ESEA recognized that the promise of equal opportunity was a mirage for many low-income children owing to the inverse relationship between poverty and educational achievement. It was part of an "equity regime" that sought to equalize opportunity by expediting desegregation and providing federal resources to schools with high concentrations of economically disadvantaged children (D. Cohen & Moffit, 2009; McGuinn, 2006).

The ESEA has been revisited numerous times. Early amendments retained the federal government's focus on affording equal educational opportunity while expanding it to children with disabilities and English language learners (ELLs). Recent education reforms—NCLB, NCLB waivers, and RttT—also maintained the goal of improving educational outcomes for these groups but did so by mandating higher standards for *all* students, backed by testing and other forms of accountability. These policies framed resources as incentives that should be withheld if schools did not produce specified outcomes. This chapter shows how policy makers facilitated these developments through the *mobilization of bias*—a phrase that describes how vested interests and policy makers maintain their positions of privilege by organizing issues in or out of politics (Schattschneider, 1960, p. 71).

Sometimes policy makers use formal and informal institutions to exclude opposing viewpoints and policy solutions, but those in power also frame issues and policy targets in ways that discredit the opposition and its favored policies. I am using Bourdieu's (as cited in Lamont & Lareau, 1988) concept of *symbolic violence* to convey the latter. He deployed that phrase to describe the capacity of a class or dominant group to advance their interests by controlling normative ideas about what is superior or inferior. In terms of recent education reforms, the evolution of the ESEA resulted in growing negative feedback from liberals and conservatives yet neither side could generate enough support to overcome the resulting stalemate.

During the administration of George W. Bush, policy makers altered the playing field by using discourse (symbolic violence) and formal and informal institutions to delegitimize the concerns and preferred policies of some and magnify those of others.

It is important to note that the transformation from a federal "equity regime" to an "accountability regime" did not start with NCLB (McGuinn, 2006). It began under President Ronald Reagan with the publication of *A Nation at Risk* by a federal U.S. Department of Education (DOE) task force. That report acknowledged that the average citizen was more educated and knowledgeable than a generation ago, yet then described an educational system that was rudderless and sinking fast (National Commission on Educational Excellence, 1983). It is an example of how policy makers—in this case federal bureaucrats—may intentionally generate negative feedback to stimulate demands for reform.[1] President Reagan initially stymied the report's call for national reforms; he used the bully pulpit to urge state and local governments to improve public schools while questioning an expanded federal role. However, he and the report opened a "policy window" (Kingdon, 1984) for states to adopt accountability reforms. Those efforts eventually generated positive feedback for national reform by mobilizing groups that had a stake in standards, testing, and school choice.[2] They argued that standards, backed by testing and competition, would improve teaching and learning by holding public schools accountable for student outcomes (Hanushek, 2002).[3]

This "excellence movement" was first institutionalized during the administration of President Bill Clinton, a New Democrat, with Goals 2000 and the Improving America's Schools Act (IASA) of 1994. As evidenced by only 16 states complying with the law and the failure of Congress to reauthorize it during Clinton's second term in office, ideological and institutional barriers remained (McGuinn, 2006).[4] That changed after the election of George W. Bush when conservative interests joined a new breed of civil rights groups to support accountability and school choice as a way to foster equity (DeBray-Pelot, 2007; Rhodes, 2014). These groups had diverse agendas. What united them in their support for NCLB was the claim that excellence for all would achieve equity by "raising all boats." Many predicted that President Obama would diverge from the policies of George W. Bush. Instead, he expanded the accountability regime through executive policy making (RttT and NCLB waivers). This section elaborates on these claims.

Political Institutions, the Evolution of the Equity Regime and Negative Policy Feedback

Education's rise to prominence as a social policy began in the 1960s, when it became a substitute for—versus a complement to—the more direct forms of New Deal public assistance. Under the Great Society, liberals argued that education and job training would mitigate socio-economic inequality by helping low-income Americans participate in the labor market.[5] This claim is perhaps best evidenced by Title I of the ESEA. As part of an "equity regime," it provided federal funds to schools that served low-income children to redress the "cultural deprivations" of poverty, improve their educational outcomes, and expand their employment opportunities (Kantor & Lowe, 2006). Like other policies at the time, it was backed by an even broader vision of state–society relations, which L. Cohen (2003) calls the "Consumer's Republic." She used that phrase to convey that policy makers, business and labor leaders, and civic groups agreed to primarily use private markets—supported by public resources—to deliver economic prosperity and reconstruct the nation's economy after World War II. They argued that the free market was better suited for delivering important social democratic goals, such as political freedom, democratic participation, social integration, and socioeconomic equality.

Early expansions of the equity regime benefited *all* Americans—not just low-income and minority students—through the provision of low-cost student loans and increased funding for public schools, colleges, and universities. Private businesses and the defense industry also profited from government-funded research and the production of trained human capital. These benefits generated strong positive feedback for the equity regime—despite it sharply increasing the costs of education at all levels of government. That began to change during the 1970s as the contentious politics of desegregation and public school finance reform increased skepticism about the efficacy of federal involvement in education (D. Cohen & Moffit, 2009; Pincus, 1985).

Liberals and negative feedback. On the left, critics complained that the equity regime had not fulfilled its promise. While the federal government had a positive record of expanding educational opportunities through desegregation, the ESEA did not resolve inequities between districts, either in terms of their overall level of resources or the average amount spent per pupil.[6] The policy was never fully funded; it did not penalize states with large disparities in per pupil spending between districts; and, its funding formula was designed to ensure that most schools received federal support. Because of this policy design, it was not uncommon for impoverished districts with large numbers of low-income children to be short-changed, while schools in relatively wealthy districts—with few low-income children—received benefits.[7]

Conservatives and negative feedback. Support for the equity regime also began to wane among conservatives. President Ronald Reagan, for example, reduced funding for the ESEA as part of his New Federalism, which returned responsibility for some programs to state and local governments, so that fewer underprivileged children were served under Title I in the 1980s than during the 1970s. This occurred despite strong bipartisan support for the program in Congress (Cross, 2004; Davies, 2007). A more conservative Supreme Court also began delimiting remedies to reduce de facto segregation in public schools.[8] De facto segregation (occurring primarily in the North and West at that time) is harder to redress than de jure segregation (separation by law in the South) because it appears to result from "natural" conditions, such as where people choose to live; yet research shows that all three levels of government had played a role.

The GI Bill and the Federal Housing Administration (FHA), for instance, subsidized business loans and homeownership for millions of former soldiers and families, who left rural and urban areas to move to sprawling suburbs; however, both linked policy instruments with local discretion in ways that enabled communities to overtly and covertly discriminate against African American soldiers and families when they applied for business loans or mortgages. Federal infrastructure policies, such as the Interstate Highway Act, further accelerated the movement of corporations, jobs, workers, and tax revenues to the suburbs and the metropolitan fringe. When combined with urban renewal programs and "redlining"—an FHA policy instrument that labeled racially and ethnically mixed neighborhoods "too risky" for federal loans—the practice of gutting and isolating low-income and minority neighborhoods to construct highways that moved suburban commuters to work in urban areas increased the property values of white neighborhoods and decreased the property values of low-income and minority communities.[9]

Together, these developments contributed to the segregation of low-income and minority students in underfunded public schools. Local public services are largely funded through property taxes and public schools are organized around geographic catchment areas. By contributing to disparities in property values and property taxes, the government therefore played a key role in ensuring that low-income and minority communities differed substantially in the kinds of services that they could provide their residents, including public schools, fire, police, parks, roads, and bridges. Unredressed private behaviors—such as allowing builders, neighborhood associations, and real estate companies to keep African Americans out of white neighborhoods and therefore local schools—also played a role (K. Jackson, 1987). The federal Fair Housing Act was not adopted until 1968.[10]

Despite these developments, in *San Antonio Independent School District v. Rodriguez* (1973), the Supreme Court held that the use of local property taxes to finance public schools did not violate the 14th Amendment's equal protection clause because education was not a fundamental right protected by the U.S. Constitution. That decision disproportionately harmed low-income and minority students, but it also restricted policy feedback at the national level. It forced those who wanted to challenge the inequitable financing of public education to expend more resources litigating these inequalities on a state-by-state basis, assuming that there are any relevant provisions within a state's constitution. At the same time, the federal DOE began to weaken the ties between Title I and school desegregation efforts to ensure the political survival of the ESEA. In consequence, Title I of the ESEA was increasingly viewed as a substitute for—versus a complement to—desegregation policies (Kantor & Lowe, 2006), even though research shows that segregation is a large contributor to racial disparities in educational achievement and attainment (G. Orfield & Lee, 2005) and increases the likelihood that students will drop out of high school (Balfanz & Legters, 2004).

These actions (and inactions) resulted in the 1980s being both the high-water mark for integration and the period when the "achievement gap" between white and Black students was the narrowest (Grissmer et al., 1998). This book is not making arguments about the merits or pitfalls of busing as a remedy to desegregate schools. There are better ways to improve integration, reduce the achievement gap between low-income and minority children and their peers, and improve public school performance for all children (see Chapter 11). The point is that policy makers—for all intents and purposes—served notice that the federal government would no longer be an active partner in the fight for equity and desegregation. It is therefore not surprising that growing numbers of African Americans would start to view accountability through school choice, standards, and testing as the only way to improve their children's educational outcomes (for how this influenced the adoption of NCLB, see Rhodes, 2014).

Of equal importance, these federal actions created space for negative feedback from the right—where critics used the achievement gap between low-income and minority children and their more advantaged counterparts and between American students and their international peers to argue that America was spending more on education and getting fewer returns on its investments.[11] As mentioned, this negative feedback resulted in state reforms that were designed to increase the academic achievement and attainment of *all* students through standards backed by testing and school choice. Eventually, those reforms generated positive feedback for similar national ones. Presidents George H. W. Bush (R) and Bill Clinton (D) both agreed with these demands, but ideological and ideational differences remained in Congress. The remainder of this chapter shows how policy makers mobilized bias to overcome the resulting stalemate and adopt and expand accountability reforms during the administrations of George W. Bush and Barack Obama.

Policy Narratives, the Mobilization of Bias, and Interest Group Behaviors

Schattschneider (1960) argues that political entrepreneurs draw attention to the negative consequences of existing political arrangements to expand the conflict and mobilize new interests. Issue expansion is a form of policy feedback that transforms cohesive policy subsystems into conflicting interest group networks; it fosters change through a process of divide and conquer. By the time George W. Bush was elected, issue expansion had resulted in three disconnected and increasingly divided policy networks: conservatives, liberals, and "New" (centrist conservative) Democrats (DeBray-Pelot, 2007). Each told a different narrative about the problem in education, its victims, and its perpetrators. Policy narratives are causal stories that portray events, problems, and policy targets in ways that favor particular solutions. They protect or challenge existing political arrangements; justify beneficiaries and costs; create alliances; and provide power, authority, and resources to those designated to "fix" the problem. The public policy literature suggests that these causal stories are strategic (Stone, 1997).

"Winners" (those who benefit from existing arrangements) maintain their policy monopoly by containing the scope of the conflict through, for instance, structuring alternatives out of politics and restricting participation to those who support the status quo. "Losers" seek to destabilize the status quo by expanding the conflict. This includes defining an issue in ways that mobilize previously apathetic individuals or groups, changing the policy venue to a decision-making authority that supports the losing group's favored solutions (e.g., the courts), or portraying an event as purposefully caused to rally the troops. Those seeking to avoid blame, on the other hand, will try to persuade people that an event or action resulted from an accident, a mechanical problem, an unforeseen side effect, or a risk that did not pay off (Stone, 1997).

Policy narratives are strategic for another reason: Political actors use them to mobilize support or opposition by manipulating *perceived* costs and benefits. One tactic involves portraying the state as an important source of "outside help" for weaker individuals or groups against more powerful ones (e.g., David vs. Goliath). A second makes it appear as if the benefits or costs are widespread or diffuse by either aggregating potential winners and losers into a much broader class of people or by converting economic interests into social interests, and vice versa. An example of this is the debate about dismantling the federal school lunch program in 1995. Defenders of the program expanded the crisis beyond the children no longer eligible for a free or reduced-price lunch (social group) by identifying the economic groups that would suffer as a result of reduced demand, such as small businesses (i.e., bakers, dairies, and farmers) and their employees (Stone, 1997). A third tactic makes it appear as if a small (unworthy) few are benefiting while the "many" are (inappropriately) paying the costs. A fourth constructs the policy prescription in ways that concentrate costs on those who are perceived to be part of an undeserving or "deviant" group. These individuals are typically unable to attract public sympathy; they are also less likely to protest because mobilization requires admitting that they are part of a poorly regarded group.[12]

As shown in Table 2.1, this section uses J. Wilson's (1980) typology of interest group politics to show how and why these tactics mobilized bias behind a "meta-narrative" about the mediocre status quo.[13] Meta-narratives convert competing primary narratives into a new dominant story to overcome political gridlock (Roe, 1994), like the stalemate between conservatives, liberals, and New Democrats.

Conservatives and the narrative of failed government. Conservatives in Congress and their interest group allies blamed an intrusive federal equity regime for the achievement gap between low-income and minority children and their more advantaged peers and between American students and their international peers. They

Table 2.1. Causal stories and interest group politics

Narrative	Conservatives' narrative of failed government	(Liberal) Democrats' narrative of failed promises	New Democrats' narrative of good intentions gone bad	George W. Bush's narrative of failed expectations
Problem	Intentional cause	Intentional cause	Inadvertent cause	Intentional to inadvertent cause
Villains	Contenders (the system: Democrats and their interest group allies, such as the DOE, teachers' unions)	Contenders (policy makers failed to redress the effects of socioeconomic inequality and the inequitable financing of public schools)	Inadvertent (national policy makers)	Contenders and implied contenders (the system/soft bigotry)
Victims	Diffuse (society, taxpayers, parents, children, and state and local governments)	Concentrated (low-income and minority children and the schools that serve them)	Diffuse (society, taxpayers, parents, children, and state and local governments)	Diffuse (society, taxpayers, parents, children, and state and local governments)
Solution	Block grants; eliminate DOE; competition/choice	More resources; target Title I (Robin Hood)	Accountability through resources, reform, results (the 3 Rs)	Flexibility (block grants); accountability through standards, testing, and competition/choice
Benefits	Concentrated	Concentrated	Rhetorically diffuse	Rhetorically diffuse with some concentrated
Costs	Concentrated	Diffuse and concentrated	Diffuse	Rhetorically concentrated, but actually diffuse
Type of politics (J. Wilson, 1980)	Interest group	Client/interest group	Majoritarian	Interest group/entrepreneurial

argued that America was spending more on public education, but getting fewer returns on its investments because Democrats, federal and state bureaucrats, and special interests—especially teachers' unions—extracted resources from government through an inefficient and ineffective maze of bureaucratic rules, regulations, and red tape.[14] Congressman Thomas (R-CA), for instance, complained,

[As] a result of 40 years of Democratic control of this body, the federal education system takes more than 30 cents of every education dollar to support its own administrative bureaucracy, rather than the needs of our children. (*Congressional Record*, December 13, 2001, H10108)

Some also implicated teachers and public schools by portraying them as part of what President Reagan's secretary of education, William Bennett, called "the BLOB" (big learning organization bureaucracy).[15] This moral tale praised private and charter schools as "unsung heroes" in need of government help. They prevented poor and minority children from being "trapped in failing public schools," but were victims of the BLOB's ability to use its "public school monopoly" (exclusive right to provide public education) and political resources (e.g., campaign contributions and lobbying) to prevent school choice. The policy prescription created hostile *interest group politics* between the education establishment (e.g., the DOE, teachers' unions, school board associations) and the new insiders (charter and private schools) by advocating school choice, the abolishment of the DOE, the elimination of some federal categorical grants, and the conversion of other federal programs into a block grant. Winning in these cases is a function of group strength (J. Wilson, 1980) and neither side had a clear majority.

(Liberal) Democrats and the narrative of failed promises. Many Democrats, especially liberals, also took an offensive position against the status quo; however, their *narrative of failed promises* blamed unequal resources for the achievement gap between low-income and minority children and their peers and attributed the problem to partisanship, a failure of political will, and the ability of policy makers to underfund public education because it is a discretionary program at the national level. Congresswoman Jackson-Lee (D-TX) stated,

> [Children] are our country's greatest asset. . . . The lack of will to make critical and sometimes difficult decisions on children and education issues has damaged the ability of the United States to guarantee . . . the next generation will achieve a higher standard of living than their parents. (*Congressional Record,* May 17, 2001, H2306)

The policy prescription created a combination of *client* and *interest group politics* by advocating tinkering—providing more and better targeted federal aid—and/or large-scale policy change to create more opportunities to learn (OTL) for low-income and minority children. Policies to improve OTL included revising the federal aid formula so that it was solely targeted to high-need, low-resource schools and expanding social programs outside of K–12 education (e.g., increased funding for preschool, day care, health care, better nutrition, public housing, and other programs that serve low-income children).

Normally, policies that concentrate benefits on one group while diffusing costs onto a larger population (*client politics*) are more likely to be adopted. Those slated for benefits (low-income and minority children and the schools that serve them) are highly incentivized to lobby in their favor; those slated for burdens (taxpayers) lack the incentive to mobilize in opposition because individual costs are small (dispersed across all taxpayers) and "members" typically do not perceive that they are part of a larger group. This is especially true when policy makers are able to hide benefits and costs—a strategy that is difficult for programs, like education, that have a specific line item in the federal budget.[16] Instead, the *Robin Hood* approach left Democrats vulnerable to being labeled "tax and spend liberals," especially since opponents could use test score data to suggest that federal funding had not reduced the achievement gap between low-income and minority students and their peers. The policy solution also created *interest group politics* by penalizing (mostly) suburban schools and then directing more resources to schools that serve high percentages of low-income and minority children—primarily those in urban and rural areas. [17]

New Democrats and the narrative of good intentions gone bad. Centrist Democrats tried to break the stalemate through the *narrative of good intentions gone bad*. Their claim that the ESEA had (inadvertently) failed to redress gaps in achievement by (misguidedly) focusing on "inputs" (what was spent on education) without a concomitant focus on "outputs" (academic achievement and attainment) was attractive to both parties. It enabled Congress to escape blame while also justifying an expanded federal role—so long as resources were accompanied by accountability for results. Consider the words of Republican congressman Isakson (R-GA),

> I am a subscriber to a great quote: "Our children are a message we send to a time we will never see." The last generation of American politicians, though unintended, sent a mixed message. Our richest and most affluent children have prospered and succeeded and grown, but our poorest and our most disadvantaged have not. . . . The gap between them and our best and most affluent has widened. (*Congressional Record,* December 13, 2001, H10094)

Just as importantly, this narrative implied that the policy prescription would diffuse benefits across society as a whole by more efficiently and effectively providing a quality education to *all* children. Thus it symbolically altered the playing field from *interest group* to *majoritarian politics*—where adoption depends on the popularity of the policy. This was an important development because public opinion polls showed that Americans supported a federal role in education and believed their own schools were doing a good job, but were concerned about the performance of public schools in general (PDK, 2000). It is therefore not surprising that this narrative diffused across parties, especially once it gained support from President G. W. Bush. The rallying cry was "resources, reform, results."[18] In return for more funding and flexibility (opportunity and freedom), the federal government would demand accountability for results (personal responsibility).

George W. Bush and the narrative of failed expectations. Education reform was part of Republican George W. Bush's electoral platform. He took office with unified party control over both houses of Congress but his mandate for reform was tenuous due to a contested presidential election and the polarized environment in Congress with respect to education policy. The narrow Republican majority in the House (221–213) created issues because many conservatives supported proposals to abolish the DOE, block grant federal aid, and privatize education through charter schools and school vouchers—all of which Democrats opposed. The Senate, on the other hand, was split 50–50, with Vice President Dick Cheney breaking the tie. However, on June 5, Senator Jim Jeffords (R-VT) became an independent who voted with the Democrats. This resulted in a Democratic majority and (liberal) Ted Kennedy (D-MA) becoming the chair of the Senate Health, Education, Labor, and Pensions (HELP) Committee.

One way President G. W. Bush gained support across the aisle was by (largely) adopting the New Democrats' approach. He expanded the crisis by claiming that mediocre public schools had affected *all* students and impeded America's ability to compete globally; Bush also framed society, taxpayers, and *all* children as the beneficiaries of higher performing public schools. He opined that "nearly one third of college freshmen . . . must take a remedial course before they are able to even begin regular college level courses" and stated that "we will reclaim America's schools, before ignorance and apathy claim more young lives" (Bush, 2001; U.S. House of Representatives, 2001c, p. 6).[19] Like conservatives, though, Bush alleged that "the system" had served its own interests at the expense of society, parents, and children; he also portrayed poor and minority children as the primary beneficiaries of school choice (Bush, 2001; U.S. House of Representatives, 2001c). The proposed solution would normally invoke *interest group politics,* but Bush instead created *entrepreneurial politics* by symbolically altering the playing field. His narrative of *failed expectations* made it appear as if the costs would be concentrated on the unworthy few while the benefits would be diffused across the larger population.[20] In this case, it appeared as if only those schools and educators that had failed children—through the soft bigotry of low expectations—would be penalized by Bush's policy prescription.

The spread of the narrative of failed expectations shows why framing is so important in politics. By portraying those who opposed his reforms as bigots, President Bush effectively silenced educators' concerns about testing and school choice. As powerful interest groups, teachers' unions posed a threat to his agenda through their Democratic allies in Congress. Just as importantly, his narrative downplayed the costs borne by states, local public schools, and taxpayers as a result of testing and accountability; it also hid the benefits received by a few concentrated interests (e.g., publishing and testing companies, charter schools, and the private and religious providers of supplemental services).

As passed by large bipartisan majorities in both houses of Congress, NCLB required states test students in English/language arts (ELA) and mathematics in Grades 3–8 to measure annual progress and publish annual report cards that disaggregated those test scores by school and district, for special education, for low-income children, and for racial and ethnic subgroups. Those report cards were designed to provide the means to name and shame "failing schools"—defined as schools and districts where students did not make adequate yearly progress (AYP)—thereby furnishing an incentive to remove or avoid the stigma of failure. Students in failing schools were allowed to transfer to better performing public and public charter schools within their district and to obtain supplemental services—like tutoring—from private, nonprofit, and public providers at the expense of their home districts (U.S. Department of Education [DOE], 2002). The theory of action (Stone, 1989) was that public information (school report cards) and the competition for public resources would stimulate positive changes in public schools and teaching, especially in schools in need of improvement (F. Hess & Petrilli, 2009).

Stone (1997) argues that the success or failure of a narrative is indicated by whether it becomes the dominant story. Another way to study the success of a narrative is whether it gets co-opted by the other side in a conflict. My analysis suggests that the narratives of low expectations (Bush) and unintended consequences (New

Democrats) meet only the second criteria. The narrative of low expectations diffused across parties because it enabled Democrats to impose costs on public schools and teachers—an important part of their political base—without overtly naming and shaming them. The narrative of unintended consequences allowed Republicans and some conservatives—like George W. Bush—to advocate federal interventions, even while they claimed that "the system" had failed children. They argued, "We should not throw the baby out with the bathwater." Despite widespread diffusion, though, neither narrative became the dominant story. Instead, policy makers "mobilized bias" behind a meta-narrative about the mediocre status quo to justify support for NCLB.

Constructing the mediocre status quo. The *narrative of the mediocre status quo* drew on *A Nation at Risk* and the narratives of low expectations and unintended consequences to blame student apathy on poor-quality schools and teachers versus a lack of resources or the inequitable distribution of resources. Senator Bayh (D-IN), a New Democrat, contended,

> [Our journey began] with the common school movement. . . . [We then] realized that the dream of a good education for too many poor children was . . . a cruel illusion . . . [so the ESEA] was born. Today we . . . recognize that the status quo is no longer good enough. Too many children, particularly poor children, are still at risk of falling behind . . . [failures of] the system which for too long we have been unwilling to fundamentally change. . . . No longer will we tolerate the two-track system which embodied . . . what the President [G. W. Bush] referred to as the "soft bigotry of low expectations," trapping too many poor children in ghettos of ignorance and, therefore, ghettos of poverty. . . . Every child can learn and . . . should be given that opportunity. (*Congressional Record*, December 17, 2001, S13331)

Some stressed that America could not compete globally due to the achievement gap between American students and their international peers.[21] Others focused on the failure of the ESEA to fulfill the promise of equal opportunity, as evidenced by the achievement gap between low-income and minority students and their academic peers.[22] The common solution for these *two achievement gaps* was more resources and flexibility combined with accountability for results.[23]

One large concern, however, was that NCLB would disproportionately punish schools that served large numbers of low-income and minority children owing to the link between socioeconomic status (SES) and educational performance (e.g., scores on standardized tests, grades, academic attainment). Democrats were concerned about the defection of liberals, public schools, public school teachers, and teachers' unions; Republicans risked losing those who valued compassionate conservativism. Over the course of the debates, members of Congress began using clinical reasoning to mask the more punitive nature of NCLB.

Clinical reason looks for problems within individuals versus social structures. It uses "imaging techniques," both literally and figuratively, to render "hidden" individual characteristics visible, such as police tests of blood alcohol levels or school exams to test student competencies. Problem areas are then identified through comparisons with statistical norms. Stone (1993) argues that clinical reasoning has become an attractive form of social control and political "gatekeeping" because it defuses "intense political conflict" by appearing to provide an independent source of knowledge—defined as information that is nonpolitical and insulated from overt, covert, or unintentional manipulation. In this case, clinical reasoning resulted in two narratives that hid the punitive nature of NCLB by linking the policy to three broader American values: individual freedom, equal opportunity, and personal responsibility.

The *narrative of tough love* advocated providing more resources (equal opportunity) and freedom (choice and flexibility through block grants), but using standardized tests to "keep score" and hold schools accountable for results (personal responsibility). Senator Carper (D-DE) said,

> Sometimes on our side of the aisle we are viewed as just wanting to throw money at every problem. We are all love. Sometimes those on the other side . . . are viewed as just being tough . . . not willing to provide the resources that are needed. . . . The beauty of this legislation . . . is that it takes the toughness and it mixes it with a measure of love . . . greater funding and greater flexibility in exchange for greater accountability for results. . . . One of our sports heroes . . . Vince Lombardi . . . used to say about football: Unless you are keeping score, you are just practicing. (*Congressional Record*, December 17, 2001, S13337)

The *narrative of diagnostic testing*, on the other hand, framed test scores as a "neutral" (objective and scientific) way to rate and rank schools and students—so that states and school districts could ascertain problem areas, develop prescriptive remedies, and provide resources to treat these issues. It emerged during the House hearings on NCLB (U.S. House of Representatives, 2001b) when Congressman Ted Strickland (D-OH), a psychologist by training, claimed that the purpose of testing was "diagnostic" and "prescriptive." It should be used "to determine what learning impediments might exist" and then prescribe "what methods might be best to help a particular student learn better."

Strickland actually used these ideas to convey *why testing should not be used* as "a measure of accountability or a factor in decisions about how much money a school district wins as a bonus or loses as a sanction." However, his arguments were co-opted by both parties to portray testing as a nonpunitive accountability tool.[24] As shown in Table 2.2, clinical metaphors dominated the debates on the Conference Report and enabled many to justify voting for NCLB, despite public opinion polls that showed mixed support for testing (PDK, 2001).[25]

Rhetoric aside, testing—diagnostic or otherwise—was mostly portrayed as an *information regime*; it would provide data to evaluate and take action against schools and educators, which is a more punitive use of test scores.[26] My analysis suggests that, like the narrative of the mediocre status quo, the conversion of testing into a nonpunitive accountability tool was not organic. Policy makers used formal and informal institutions to shut out opposing viewpoints. For brevity and to show the difference between the use of formal and informal institutions, I will focus on one example from President G. W. Bush and two from Congress.

Informal Political Institutions and the Mobilization of Bias

President G. W. Bush mobilized bias by inviting a bipartisan group of legislators to his ranch in Texas to discuss education reform shortly before taking office. He hoped this *informal working group* would give him the sixty votes needed to break a Senate filibuster and bring Senator Ted Kennedy into the fold. His strategy worked. Realizing some form of legislation was going to be adopted, Senators Kennedy (D-MA) and Dodd (D-CT) later joined the group that would translate Bush's blueprint into NCLB (DeBray, 2006).[27] Unlike previous efforts to reauthorize the ESEA, that informal working group relegated the DOE (formal institution), and therefore the traditional education lobby, to a minor role.

By the time the National Conference of State Legislatures, the National Governors Association (NGA), teachers' unions (the National Education Association [NEA] and the American Federation

Table 2.2. NCLB metaphors

Narrative	Total statements (%)	Percent of statements that were from Democrats	Percent of Democrats' statements	Percent of statements that were from Republicans	Percent of Republican's statements
Medical/clinical[a]	(27)	65	36	35	19
Business[b]	(21)	51	21	49	20
Safety valve[c]	(14)	31	8	69	19
War[d]	(12)	50	11	50	12
Technical/rationalist[e]	(9)	47	9	53	10
Ecological[f]	(9)	50	9	50	10
Punitive[g]	(5)	33	3	67	6
Art/craft[h]	(3)	43	3	57	4
Total statements[i]	190 (100)	51	100	49	100

[a]Testing helps diagnose and treat educational problems. [b]Education is an investment (vs. a journey). Market incentives (competition, choice, and focusing on the "bottom line") will improve public education. [c]Children (and parents) are trapped in failing schools and need a safety valve (school choice). [d]The education reform battle must be won to fight the balkanization of America into two hostile groups, the events of September 11, and the War on Terror. [e]Discussions of metrics or the need to measure, the use of machine metaphors (e.g., "the engine of the American dream" and "the whole is better than the moving parts"), and education and education reform as providing tools and building blocks. [f]Fragile, complex systems need vigilance and care. [g]The need for "tough love" to face cold, hard truths; keep score; and foster personal responsibility. [h]Education as a journey to develop human beings. [i]There were 140 speeches during the debates on the Conference Report that had "content" (discussed the legislation in some way rather than simply thanking those responsible for NCLTB). There were fewer speakers than speeches because some members of Congress made more than one speech. The total statements in Tables 2.2–2.7 do not add up to the number of speeches because some speakers did not use metaphors or made no statements about a specific policy target (a nonevent), whereas others offered more than one. In some charts, I showed these nonevents to provide further illumination with respect to the data.

of Teachers [AFT]), and lobbyists for public schools, school boards, and administrators had fully mobilized, the legislation had already reached the Conference Committee in Congress (formal institution). Conference committees reconcile differences in legislation that has passed both houses of Congress before reporting a unified bill back for consideration by the House and Senate. Because the leaders of both parties agreed to keep those discussions private until the reconciled bill was reported out of that committee, traditional education interests were relegated to the role of "veto player." They could block some of the most controversial provisions, yet could not influence the general course of the bill.[28] This strategy suppressed negative feedback from those groups that opposed NCLB.

Formal Institutions and the Mobilization of Bias

The leaders from both parties in Congress also weaponized the rules of the game. For instance, early on in the process there were four national hearings on what would eventually become NCLB, one in the Senate and three in the House. Congress mobilized bias through who was called to testify and how members framed the witnesses and their testimonies. The only witness in the Senate was G. W. Bush's secretary of education, Rod Paige (U.S. Senate, 2001). He was also the sole witness in the first House hearing. Members of Congress testified in the second hearing, which also had the most diverse testimony, suggesting strong disagreement—at least in the early stages of debate. The final hearing called only six witnesses. Four were from outside the "education establishment" (U.S. House of Representatives, 2001a, 2001b, 2001c, 2001d). The overall impression from these hearings (tone, rhetoric, who was called to testify, how their testimony was framed, and who spoke the most) is that public schools, public school educators, and teachers' unions promote the status quo because it serves their interests. Charter schools and the private sector, on the other hand, are deserving of public funds; they ensure that low-income and minority children have opportunities but have been blocked from receiving help because the "education establishment" is afraid of competition from school choice.

This claim is evident in the way some lauded Dr. Gail Foster, who was representing the Black Alliance for Educational Options, and denigrated the president of the AFT (Randi Weingarten). Congressmen Schaffer and Hoekstra (U.S. House of Representatives, 2001a) stated:

MR. SCHAFFER (R-CO): Dr. Foster . . . your testimony, of all those who have come here today . . . [speaks to] looking at children first, and institutions . . . later.

MR. HOEKSTRA (R-MI): Dr. Foster . . . thank you . . . [for] standing up for America's families . . . our parents . . . our kids. . . . Your organization is awesome. . . . Your statement . . . was awesome. . . . Listening to Ms. Weingarten talk about . . . [taking over] 40 schools . . . congratulations. And you are ready to take over 40 more. What happened to the kids . . . this year. . . . Those kids were locked into that school . . . with no opportunity . . . [and so I] applaud the voice . . . speaking eloquently not as a Democrat or a Republican . . . but speaking up for . . . parents.

David versus Goliath was also a common narrative during congressional debates on NCLB. It was used to both support school choice and oppose providing more resources to schools that were labeled in need of improvement (SINI). As with clinical narratives about testing, it masked the punitive nature of an accountability regime by alluding to the need for safeguards to ensure SINI schools would "do right by the kids."[29]

Another way Congress mobilized bias was through the rules of debate. Education chair and majority leader John Boehner (R-OH), for example, facilitated agreement by asking members of the education committee to withhold submitting amendments until the House floor. He then used the rules to favor initiatives G. W. Bush supported while silencing those he opposed. Some amendments not debated—but supported by Democrats and teachers' unions—included funding for reduced class sizes and school construction and a proposal to better target Title I funds to schools that disproportionately serve economically disadvantaged students. In contrast, the House debated Republican amendments for school vouchers and Straight A's, which was a proposal to block grant federal monies. In addition, the debate on accountability was restricted to a single amendment that would have eliminated the proposed new tests altogether. This forced members to vote for or against accountability by voting for or against testing and, as evident in the words of Congressman Tierney (D-MA), silenced legitimate debates about the merits and pitfalls of testing. He complained that Republicans had prevented debate on "the validity or concept of testing[,] . . . whether we provide sufficient resources to schools to administer" fair and comprehensive tests, and "whether or not this type of testing" is good for students or the best way to hold state and local governments accountable (*Congressional Record,* May 17, 2001, H2303-05).

Boehner's tactic paid off. Many Democrats admitted that NCLB included measures that they opposed—such as funding for charter schools and private tutoring—yet stated that they were voting for it because it included things that they supported, such as more funding for high-need, low-resources schools, and excluded things that they strongly opposed—like Straight A's (block grants), private school choice, and a proposal to abolish the federal DOE.[30] Members from both parties also used this *language of pragmatism* to urge their colleagues to support the bill.[31] While not everyone agreed with this logic, gaining some of what they wanted allowed many to put up with the things they previously had opposed.[32]

Two final points deserve mention. Political actors are embedded in institutions where they develop relationships that facilitate collective action. Policy makers used this *social capital* to influence interest group behaviors. DeBray-Pelot (2007, 83), for instance, tells a story about how Senator Kennedy (D-MA) tried to quell early protests by the NEA by saying "you may not have noticed but we don't control the White House, the Senate, or the House. I'm doing my best but I'm not going to let you stop this." She writes, "Having decided . . . to compromise with the Republicans and the White House, Kennedy could not meet the group's demands, so he minimized contact with them" but personally called and demanded that the NEA not oppose the bill. The NEA took no position on NCLB.

Policy makers also used their social capital, as well as events at that time, to persuade one another to vote for or against NCLB.[33] In terms of the latter, the claim that mediocre public schools were causing the nation to fall behind in a global economic race had gained traction after *A Nation at Risk* yet was especially evocative during the debates on the Conference Report because they occurred shortly after the terrorist attacks of September 11, 2001. This "focusing event" (Kingdon, 1984) helped legislators demobilize the opposition by shaming those who opposed the policy or tried to propose more extreme reforms; it also enabled many to justify their policy choices and/or avoid criticism for supporting NCLB.[34] They argued that bipartisan unity was critical to addressing domestic issues and maintaining American's confidence in the government during a difficult time.[35] This claim is apparent in the debate on the Conference Report but also in the common usage of war metaphors (see Table 2.1).

Mobilizing Bias by Constructing Villains and Victims

A final way policy makers mobilized bias was through the framing of policy targets. Empirical research shows that public discourse generates socially constructed identities for policy targets. These social constructions influence how citizens are treated through public policies, how they are served by policy implementers, and their willingness to mobilize and exercise political voice (policy feedback). Advantaged groups (e.g., small businesses, scientists, the military, the middle class, homeowners) are highly regarded socially. Owing to this social capital, they are (typically) portrayed as entitled to government assistance and rarely assigned policy burdens—even when unorganized. Contenders (e.g., Wall Street bankers, wealthy individuals, labor unions, the gun lobby) are politically powerful yet often ill regarded socially due to perceptions that they have gotten more than their fair share; gained their positions of power through unfair, underhanded, or self-interested actions; and/or abused their power. These groups have political capital because they maintain strong group loyalty (social cohesion) and are typically well organized and easily mobilized. The combination of political power and public perceptions ensures that they are more likely to suffer symbolically—rather than substantively—but also less likely to be the overt targets of government assistance. For instance, policy makers may provide "hidden" benefits through tax incentives and lucrative government contracts or reward them by privatizing public programs and reducing former policy burdens through deregulation (A. Schneider & Ingram, 1993).

When compared with these groups, those society portrays as dependents and deviants lack political *and* social resources. Deviants (e.g., criminals and drug addicts) are viewed as dangerous or of no value to society, owing to their illegal, immoral, or irresponsible behaviors, and so policies designed to control their activities are (typically) backed by sanctions. Dependents (e.g., children and the mentally ill) are framed as deserving of government largesse so long as they are not viewed as the cause of their problems. Even then, they are frequently framed in paternalistic and uncomplimentary ways (e.g., incompetent or incapable of resolving their own problems because of a lack of capacity, character, or discipline). An example is Title I of the ESEA, where policy makers justified federal intervention by arguing that poor children were "culturally deprived." Despite these differences, government assistance for both is typically justified through moral reasoning, rather than portrayed as an entitlement of citizenship (advantaged groups); both also face barriers to inclusion owing to limited material resources and restrictions on political participation and representation (A. Schneider & Ingram, 1993).

Tables 2.3–2.7 provide a quantitative analysis of how Congress framed policy targets during the debates on the Conference Report. Table 2.3 shows how Congress characterized the federal government, the education bureaucracy, and state and local governments. Table 2.4 displays how Congress portrayed public schools; *at-risk public schools* (low-resource public schools, public schools that primarily serve low-income and minority children, and schools that are labeled in need of improvement [SINI]); and *non–public school others* (charter schools and the private and religious providers of supplemental educational services). In comparison, Table 2.5 presents how legislators framed public education. The remaining two tables reveal how members of Congress framed actors within schools. Table 2.6

compares the framing of administrators and teachers; Table 2.7 does the same for parents, children in general, and low-income and minority children. When combined with my qualitative analysis, these tables show that Congress blamed federal rules and regulations and poor-quality public schools and teachers—rather than a lack of resources—for the mediocre status quo; framed children as a resource for the nation rather than as entitled citizens; portrayed low-income and minority children as deserving an opportunity to succeed rather than being entitled to more equal funding; and, characterized parents and non–public school others as a moral force that would ensure public schools and public schoolteachers "do right by the kids."

In more detail, Table 2.3 shows that both parties constructed bureaucrats at all levels of government as contenders and deviants. They serve "the system" (i.e., their own interests) at the expense of society; have created an inefficient and ineffective maze of rules, regulations, and red tape; and, "do not know their local communities." Most (77 percent) also framed the federal government as part of the problem. In contrast, 69 percent characterized state and local governments as allies of society (an entitled group).[36] To counter concerns that NCLB would create a "slippery slope" that encouraged more federal involvement over time, speakers from both parties used the language of cooperative federalism. They acknowledged that education was primarily a state and local function, yet said that the federal government had an important role to play and applauded NCLB for providing state and local governments with more resources and flexibility (block grants) but (responsibly) stressing accountability for results.

While *local governments* were positively constructed, that was not the case with local public schools. Table 2.4 shows that, across political parties, public schools and at-risk public schools were only framed as allies of society in 2 and 3 percent of the statements, respectively. Only a few discussed non–public school others (a nonevent); of those who did, none framed this group as mediocre and 44 percent characterized it as a societal resource. The fact that members talked about public schools (192 statements) more than at-risk public schools (119 statements)—the supposed target of the legislation—and that both were portrayed in similar, largely negative ways is consistent with my qualitative analysis that policy makers expanded the crisis by implying that public schools *in general* were mediocre.[37]

There were some partisan differences. Republicans were far more likely to frame non–public school others as entitled to public funds because they provided poor and minority children with a needed

Table 2.3. NCLB target groups: federal government, education bureaucracy, and state and local governments

Narrative	Federal			Bureaucracy			State and local		
	Total (%)	Dem % of total (as a % of Dem. state.)	Rep % of total (as a % of Rep. state.)	Total (%)	Dem % of total (as a % of Dem. state.)	Rep % of total (as a % of Rep. state.)	Total (%)	Dem % of total (as a % of Dem. state.)	Rep % of total (as a % of Rep. state.)
Allies of society[a]	(23)	68 (40)	32 (12)	(0)	0	0	(69)	31 (48)	69 (86)
Pathologies of localism									
Unequal finance							(16)	80 (28)	20 (6)
Ignore/mask failure							(15)	71 (24)	29 (8)
Hijack test[b]									
Pathologies of federalism									
Mandates/lack of flexibility	(47)	34 (39)	66 (52)						
Limit choice	(30)	29 (21)	71 (36)						
Don't know parents or local communities									
Pathologies of bureaucracy									
Bureaucratic maze/red tape				(53)	19 (45)	81 (55)			
Serve the system				(37)	33 (55)	67 (32)			
Don't know local communities				(10)	0	100 (13)			
Total statements	94 (100)	40 (100)	60 (100)	49 (100)	22 (100)	78 (100)	94 (100)	45 (100)	55 (100)

[a]For state and local governments, these narratives portrayed them as entitled or in need of flexibility and discretion. Conversely, the national government was characterized as having an important role to play. [b]Mostly, this narrative argues that public schools ignore disadvantaged students or "mask failure." It was typically used to justify reporting test scores for educational "subgroups," but some argued that state governments need to be regulated to ensure they set high standards and that state tests were "diagnostic" (used to treat problem areas).

"safety valve" and forced public schools to perform by providing competition. Democrats were far more likely to portray public schools as (entitled) allies of society. Still, these positive constructions made up only 3 percent of Democratic statements about public schools.

Of interest, the Bush administration's proposal included a private school voucher component, which G. W. Bush asserted would help children escape "failing public schools." It was removed before the House and Senate education committees reported their bills to the floor and replaced with the "supplemental services" component of NCLB. Under this compromise, students in persistently "failing schools" would be able to obtain tutoring from private and religious providers; they were also allowed to transfer to better performing public and public charter schools within their districts. However, because Congress debated both public *and* private school choice, members' statements may be used to qualitatively compare the construction of public schools, public charter schools, private schools, and the private and religious providers of supplemental services.

Metaphorically, public schools were often described in ways that brought to mind the prison system. Students were "quarantined in," "sentenced to" or "trapped in government-owned schools" that were mediocre, unsafe, or full of drugs. Descriptively, they were beleaguered, in need of "reinvigoration" from outside the system, did not care about parents or children, or used their public monopoly to mask failure and pursue their own interests at the expense of taxpayers, children, and society. Their nonpublic counterparts were framed as providing opportunities for parents and children, especially low-income and minority students; they were robust, competitive, and successful.[38] My qualitative analysis suggests that the language of "entrapment," "imprisonment," and "enslavement" was not accidental. It was typically used to link school choice with the civil rights movement to communicate that the freedom to choose would provide poor and minority children with the opportunity to participate in the American dream. If Democrats used this language, they were typically discussing public charter schools. Republicans used these ideas to justify public and private school choice.

Senator Gregg (R-NH), for example, avowed that the "portability amendment" would fund a school choice demonstration project that was needed to help

> [people] left behind . . . [not] the wealthy . . . [but] low-income people, most . . . in urban schools . . . [that are] failing. . . . You cannot . . . compete

Table 2.4. NCLB target groups: public schools, at-risk public schools (e.g., low-resource, primarily serve low-income and minority children, SINI), and private providers/charter schools

Narrative	Public			At-risk public			Private providers/charter schools		
	Total (%)	Dem % of total (as a % of Dem. state.)	Rep % of total (as a % of Rep. state.)	Total (%)	Dem % of total (as a % Dem. state.)	Rep % of total (as a % of Rep. state.)	Total (%)	Dem % of total (as a % of Dem. state.)	Rep % of total (as a % of Rep. state.)
Heroes, allies of society: valence positive[a]	(2)	75 (3)	25 (1)	(3)	100 (5)	0	(44)	24 (28)	76 (54)
Moral but beleaguered dependents: valence mixed[b]	(30)	74 (39)	26 (18)	(26)	87 (36)	13 (10)	(29)	7 (5)	93 (43)
Beleaguered (mediocre) dependents: valence negative[c]	(33)	54 (33)	46 (35)	(27)	56 (23)	44 (34)	(0)	0	0
Contenders: valence negative[d]	(25)	36 (16)	64 (35)	(26)	45 (18)	55 (42)	(23)	100 (61)	0
Deviants: valence negative[e]	(10)	53 (9)	47 (11)	(18)	71 (18)	29 (14)	(4)	50 (6)	50 (3)
Total statements	192 (100)	56 (100)	44 (100)	119 (100)	66 (100)	34 (100)	48 (100)	37 (100)	63 (100)
Nonevent[f]	33	33	18	46	46	62	80	80	67

[a]Public schools help society meet individual and collective ends. Non–public school others provide low-income and minority children with a needed "safety valve" and force public schools to "do right by the kids" by providing needed competition. By the time Congress debated the Conference Report, most speakers were discussing public charter schools and the private and religious providers of supplemental services, but in a few cases, this was expanded to include private school choice. [b]For public schools, this narrative conveyed that they were serving more needy populations (e.g., economically disadvantaged children, children with academic or behavioral issues, children with mental health issues) with too few resources. For non–public school others, this involved discussing them as "victims" of the public school monopoly to show that they needed government assistance and sponsorship. [c]This narrative asserted that poor teaching or administrative practices were the unintended result of too few resources or the need for training and development. [d]Public schools were portrayed as monopolistic and self-interested. Non–public school others were described as a drain on public resources or equally in need of regulation and accountability as public schools. [e]For public schools, this story included ignoring the needs of disadvantaged students, masking failure (allowing poor and minority children to slip through the cracks by hiding their achievement gaps within overall successes) or engaging in social promotion (moving children on to the next grade despite poor performance). When linked to discussions about civil rights or unequal opportunities, this narrative was part of a story about the "two-track" system for low-income and minority children and their more advantaged peers. Both parties used this narrative to advocate the need to disaggregate student test scores by racial and other subgroups. Democrats also used it to demand resources and provide SINI schools with training; Republicans also used it to justify school choice. This narrative further includes stories about public schools being unsafe, violent, or full of drugs. Republicans were more likely to use the latter characterization; however, it was not a dominant story and was mostly used to discuss the need to address declining values. Private/charter schools were typically not the focus of these negative narratives. The focus was on "other" privates, such as the need to ensure student privacy as a result of telemarketers. Those narratives are included here because they were part of a public versus private narrative. [f]A nonevent is a nonstatement. This category shows the percentage of speakers who did not tell a narrative about a particular target group.

and participate in our society . . . when you go through a school which does not teach . . . is filled with violence . . . drugs. . . . Every day a child . . . is falling further . . . behind . . . that school is . . . denying that child the opportunity to participate in the American dream. . . . [Those with] a fairly decent income . . . can leave the public school system and go to a private school. . . . Single, mostly low-income, mothers . . . [do not have that option, so] poor . . . mostly minority children . . . [are sentenced to] schools affluent families would never tolerate. (*Congressional Record,* June 12, 2001, S2062–S2063)

Senator Gregg does not mention how middle-class and wealthier Americans have access to better performing *public* schools. He says they exit public schools for private schools. That is because his narrative is largely about inferior public services as compared to superior private ones.

This claim is especially evident when he compares educating children with making a Big Mac or a Whopper:

It is fairly obvious . . . that if you create competition you usually improve a product. . . . Somebody chooses McDonald's over Burger King . . . because they think the product is better. . . . Our public school systems have not ever had the competition necessary to improve the product. The purpose of choice . . . is not to undermine the public school system; it is . . . to create an incentive for reform . . . [and give] kids who have been locked in a failing school . . . an opportunity. (*Congressional Record,* June 12, 2001, S2063–S2064)

Like Senator Gregg, Republicans were far more likely to focus on the benefits of market competition but some Democrats used this language as well.[39]

Also of interest, as shown in Table 2.5, *public education* was framed in more positive ways than *public schools*. Public education was deemed an ally of society because it promotes democracy and enables the United States to compete economically. Despite these differences, the benefits associated with each were largely framed in similar ways. Both were primarily important for meeting individual and collective *economic* ends—a framing that is consistent with *A Nation at Risk* but did not match public opinion polls at the time. Americans rated "preparing people to become responsible citizens" first and "helping people become economically self-sufficient" second; however, "promoting cultural unity," "improving social conditions," "enhancing people's happiness and enriching their lives," and "dispelling

Table 2.5. NCLB debates: tales about goals/ends of public education, public schools, and federal education policy

Narrative	Total statements (%)	Percent of statements that were from Democrats	Percent of Democrats' statements	Percent of statements that were from Republicans	Percent of Republicans' statements
Future nation: democracy[a]	(17)	62	17	38	19
Making progress: civil rights[b]	(14)	77	16	23	9
Great society: socioeconomic equality[c]	(12)	82	15	18	6
Opportunity society[d]	(31)	59	28	41	38
International: global economic competitiveness[e]	(22)	55	18	45	28
International: "city on a hill"[f]	(2)	100	3	0	0
International: national security[g]	(2)	100	3	0	0
Total statements	93 (100)	66	100	34	100
Nonevent			66		60

[a]Education is important for democracy and for transcending divisions in a democratic society. [b]Education is the means to achieve civil rights. [c]Education is a means to achieve socioeconomic equality or provide equal opportunities. [d]Education is a means of providing a better quality of life for individuals (higher SES) and/or enabling individuals to reach their potential or achieve the American Dream. [e]An educated society is important for competing in a globalized economy. [f]Other nations are watching. America needs to be a "beacon of democracy" by demonstrating fairness, economic opportunity, and so forth. [g]An educated society is important for our national security.

inequities" were all almost tied for second place with economic self-sufficiency (PDK, 2000).

Moving onto educators, early in the debates, some Republicans overtly framed teachers' unions as contenders and deviants for supporting a status quo that harmed low-income and minority children, as well as taxpayers and society. Some also described charter and private schools as a deserving group that was being victimized by teachers' unions. These David versus Goliath narratives often implicated Democrats because teachers' unions are an important part of their political base and a large source of political contributions.[40] Some even characterized teachers and administrators as victims of teachers' unions. In discussing his support for the portability (school choice) amendment, for instance, Senator Ensign (R-NV) pronounced,

School choice, be it private or public, has been proven to drive reform. . . .
A lack of competition breeds mediocrity. . . . I will bet . . . everyone here
has sought out the best schools for our children. . . . Parents strongly
support public school choice . . . even vouchers. . . . I have had conversations with public school superintendents, principals, and teachers . . .
they are afraid of stating their support publicly because of the teacher
unions. In fact, public school teachers send their own children to private
schools at a higher rate than the general population. (*Congressional
Record,* June 12, 2001, S6077)

By the time Congress debated the Conference Report, however,
teachers' unions were a "nonevent." They were indirectly implicated
in the mediocre status quo through the narrative of low expectations
but were not overtly discussed.

This silence supports A. Schneider and Ingram's (1993) claim that
contenders (unions) are poorly regarded yet politically powerful.
In consequence, elected officials typically exercise caution when
framing and regulating these groups. It is also why unions are not
included in Table 2.6, which displays the framing of educators during
the debates on the Conference Report. As exhibited in that table,
administrators were also portrayed as a nonevent in public school
performance. Teachers, in contrast, were largely framed as needing
training and development.

Another trend was that legislators often framed educators as allies
of society if they supported NCLB and as part of the problem if they
did not. Liberal congressman George Miller (D-CA) stated,

I am optimistic that we can set high standards. . . . There already is . . .
pressure from those who resist change . . . want to maintain the status
quo. . . . Those are the same people that have given us the results that
Americans find so repugnant. We need to change the system. . . . Those
that say they cannot get students proficient in 12 years . . . thank God
they were not in the room with President Jefferson when he launched
Lewis and Clark . . . [or] John Kennedy when he launched the program
to put a man on the moon. . . . Their response . . . they are going to
dumb down tests . . . teach to the tests. That is the response of the
American education system in this country? (*Congressional Record,* July
18, 2001, H4122)

He then claimed to be "shocked to hear" from so many educators that
the 10-year requirement for 100 percent proficiency was impossible
and exclaimed "Maybe they are in the wrong field" (*Congressional*

Table 2.6. NCLB target groups: public school teachers and administrators

Narrative and valence	Teachers			Administrators		
	Total statements (%)	Dem % of Total (as a % of Dem. state.)	Rep % of total (as a % of Rep. state.)	Total statements (%)	Dem % of total (as a % of Dem. state.)	Rep % of total (as a % of Rep. state.)
Heroes, allies of society: valence positive[a]	(14)	40 (10)	60 (19)	(38)	40 (25)	60 (60)
Moral but beleaguered dependents: valence mixed[b]	(9)	40 (6)	60 (13)	(0)	0	0
Beleaguered (mediocre) dependents: valence negative[c]	(59)	66 (68)	34 (47)	(62)	75 (75)	25 (40)
Contenders/deviants: valence negative[d]	(18)	50 (16)	50 (21)	0	0	0
Total statements	110 (100)	57 (100)	43 (100)	13 (100)	62 (100)	38 (100)
Nonevent	45		40		91	91

[a]These narratives almost exclusively described teachers as an important resource rather than deserving discretion as a result of their professional training or as heroes due to their commitment to working with children. Administrators were more commonly described than teachers as professionals in need of discretion. Republicans were more likely to stress the need for discretion, but this was primarily used to discuss the need for less federal involvement in education. As such, the expressed support for professional autonomy was symbolic. [b]This category portrayed educators as being "stifled by the system" or beleaguered as a result of societal problems or a lack of resources. These statements framed educators as needing government's help rather than as autonomous agents. These stories stressed educators were in need of professional training, development, and assistance. Republicans were more likely than Democrats to discuss the need to recruit from outside the "educational establishment" (nontraditional routes into teaching) to redress the mediocre status quo. For the most part, however, the emphasis on teacher training was a way for Democrats and Republicans to show that Congress had delivered resources to a highly mobilized group. The legislation did not do much for teachers because, as part of a political compromise, funding for salary increases and smaller class sizes—both of which teachers support—had been combined into a block grant with other programs that allowed states to choose where to invest the money. Nonetheless, the consistent portrayal of teachers as being in need of professional training, development, and assistance implied "those who can't teach." [d]These narratives portrayed teachers as part of the problem (contenders bordering on deviants), because they are part of the education establishment; have low expectations; or need regulation, accountability, or competition to ensure that they "do right by the kids."

Record, December 13, 2001, H10103). This is an example of symbolic violence and the weaponization of public discourse. It silenced educators' concerns by framing them as protecting the mediocre status quo if they objected to NCLB.

Finally, Table 2.7 shows that Congress largely framed parents as a nonevent in public school performance. When discussed at all, most characterized them as entitled to government support in the form of information, choice, and supplemental services—either because they are victims of failing schools or because parental voice and choice created an incentive for schools to "get their house in order" (see, e.g., *Congressional Record,* December 17, 2001, S13328). Those narratives that implicated parents in the mediocre status quo were typically describing economically disadvantaged parents. This language, which was somewhat sympathetic yet often paternalistic, is consistent with a broader societal narrative that portrays parents as an entitled group but low-income parents and citizens—especially welfare recipients—as dependents or deviants (Bensonsmith, 2005; A. Schneider & Ingram, 2005b). Senator Gregg (D-NH), for instance, continued with his earlier narrative,

> [NCLB empowers parents that] have a child who is in a failing school and who is being left behind and is from a low-income background. . . . In most instances . . . it is not parents but parent. They usually come from single-parent families. That is unfortunate, but that single parent is usually struggling to make ends meet and really does need to have some options available to her—usually it is a "her"—when she is trying to address the education failures of the school her child attends. (*Congressional Record,* December 17, 2001, S13327)

Far fewer portrayed children as a nonevent and even less did so for underprivileged children. The bipartisan focus on the poor performance of low-income and minority children implied that both were either deviant (did not work hard) or incapable dependents. This was true even when they were portrayed as victims of low expectations or poorly performing schools.[41]

Again, there were some partisan differences. Democrats typically framed parental voice (speaking up and participating) as a means of ensuring that public schools "do right by the kids" in a similar way to how neighborhood watch groups or citizen militias serve society by keeping their "eyes on the street." Republicans also deployed this moral framing but mostly portrayed parents as changing the system through their role as consumers of education and used that language

Table 2.7. NCLB target groups: parents, children, and low-income and minority children

Narrative	Parents				Children			Low-income and minority children	
	Total (%)	Dem % of total (as a % of Dem. state.)	Rep % of total (as a % of Rep. state.)	Total (%)	Dem % of total (as a % of Dem. state.)	Rep % of total (as a % of Rep. state.)	Total (%)	Dem % of total (as a % of Dem. state.)	Rep % of total (as a % of Rep. state.)
Heroes, allies of society: valence positive[a]	(71)	41 (76)	59 (67)	(34)	52 (34)	48 (34)	(13)	59 (12)	41 (15)
Beleaguered dependents (victims of society): valence mixed[b]	(23)	23 (14)	77 (29)	(26)	44 (22)	56 (30)	(33)	67 (34)	33 (31)
Beleaguered dependents (victims of background): valence negative[c]	(0)	0	0	(6)	55 (6)	45 (6)	(35)	65 (35)	35 (34)
Contenders/deviants: valence negative[d]	(6)	57 (10)	43 (4)	(34)	58 (38)	42 (30)	(19)	63 (19)	37 (20)
Total statements	112 (100)	38 (100)	62 (100)	193 (100)	52 (100)	48 (100)	295 (100)	64 (100)	36 (100)
Nonevent		**69**	**45**		**46**	**25**		**29**	**47**

[a]Parents were heroes and "allies of society" because they served as "system changers." Their freedom to choose or participate puts pressure on public schools to perform. Children were typically framed as the "future of our democracy" or the "engines of our economy." [b]Parents and children were typically characterized as needing help because they were "trapped in failing schools" or the victims of "low expectations." Children were also characterized as needing help due to growing issues with mental health, violence, and drugs. This framing portrayed children as being "at risk" in some way as a result of their families or backgrounds. It was mostly used for economically disadvantaged children. [d]This category typically conveyed that the targets were contenders or deviants through the language of "personal responsibility." For example, speakers discussed the need for parents to participate and for children to work hard. The general message was "we will give you the tools and opportunities, but you need to use them." This framing was far more common for children, and low-income and minority children, and was often conveyed through discussions about poor performance compared to international peers (all children) or domestic peers (low-income and minority children). It also included narratives about growing mental health issues as well as increases in violence and drug abuse.

to justify school choice.[42] Another difference is that Democrats were more likely to characterize children in sympathetic yet uncomplimentary ways. Partially, this was to justify more resources (tinkering); however, their narratives also support F. Hess and McGuinn's (2002) claim that Democrats tried to shake the label of "tax and spend liberals" by linking federal funding (opportunity) with accountability for results (personal responsibility) rather than portraying federal resources as an entitlement.[43] Conversely, Republicans were more likely to portray children as deviant, but their narratives about drug abuse, school violence, and mental health issues were often used to justify more spending (tinkering).

More broadly, this research finds that Republicans were far more likely to deploy "divide and conquer strategies." This finding makes sense given that Democratic constituencies benefitted from maintaining the ESEA but providing more resources to schools that served large numbers of low-income and therefore minority students (tinkering). One example is that Republicans often characterized low-income and minority children as being "enslaved by ignorance." This narrative helped them link NCLB to the next phase of the civil rights movement, portray themselves as compassionate conservatives, and connect Democrats and the education establishment to the mediocre status quo.[44] It is a classic case of weaponizing discourse to "divide and conquer" since teachers and their unions largely opposed NCLB, the mediocre status quo without tinkering disproportionately harmed low-income and minority children, and all of these groups are part of the Democratic Party's base.

A second divide-and-conquer strategy involved (implicitly or explicitly) associating teachers and public schools with segregation through G. W. Bush's narrative of low expectations. A third co-opted the language of liberalism to contrast compassionate conservatism with failed liberal spending. In the words of Senator DeWine (R-OH),

> [our] society is becoming more . . . divided . . . along economic and educational lines. . . . Scholars and sociologists have been warning us for many years that this was where our Nation was headed . . . if we didn't properly educate our children. . . . We have not heeded these warnings . . . [and] our Nation today is . . . split into two Americas: One where children get educated and one where they do not. This gap in educational knowledge and . . . economic standing is entrenching thousands upon thousands of children into an underclass and into futures filled with little hope and little opportunity. . . . So how do we bring society . . . together . . . bring about equality and opportunity so that all children . . . have the

chance to lead full, meaningful, and productive lives . . . in the same way that we have always done it. . . . Education should provide all children, regardless of their economic circumstances or family backgrounds . . . the tools . . . to make it as adults . . . to rise above individual situations of poverty and instability . . . hopelessness and despair. It truly has been, for generation after generation . . . their ticket out of poverty . . . away from despair . . . to opportunity. (*Congressional Record,* December 17, 2001, S13339–S13340)

Senator DeWine links (mediocre) public schools and public school teachers to the problem of the "two Americas"—a phrase liberals use to discuss socioeconomic inequality. He later recommended adopting NCLB to restore opportunity through accountability, teacher training, and recruiting from other professions, especially the military.

In sum, traditional policy analysis examines how citizens' demands lead to political change. This research, on the other hand, shows that NCLB actually contradicted public opinion (policy feedback). NCLB focused on the behaviors of "failed" schools and teachers and portrayed that failure as affecting *all* students, yet Americans gave the public schools in their *own communities* the highest ratings in the 30-year history of the PDK poll; they also said that parents (53%) had a greater effect on student achievement than teachers (26%) and students (17%) and that parents had a greater influence on student learning (60%) than schools (30%; PDK, 2000). In addition, Americans listed a lack of fiscal support as one of the top three issues facing public schools; that issue had actually risen to first and tied for first in 2000 and 2001, respectively. Moreover, they favored strengthening public schools over using school choice as a way of improving educational performance (PDK, 2000, 2001).

The Mobilization of Bias and Policy Feedback in the Obama Administration

Politics sometimes makes strange bedfellows, but widespread congressional support for NCLB fell apart almost immediately due to growing concerns about federal overreach (conservatives) and the ill effects of NCLB on schools that served large numbers of low-income and minority children (liberals)—especially once the G. W. Bush administration's promise of significant new funding did not materialize (Welner & Weitzman, 2005). Bush and his first secretary of education, Rod Paige, responded to a reenergized left by framing educators and their allies in increasingly negative ways.

Paige (2003a, 2003b), for example, claimed that research demonstrates that teachers underestimate the intelligence of low-income children and opined that "some of the biggest skeptics [of NCLB] are those whose job it is to believe in children." He then stated that NCLB should be applauded because

> any system and any person that gives up on any child because of what he looks like or who his parents are is no less discriminatory than a jeering mob blocking the schoolhouse door. It is every inch the bigotry that once exiled some people to the back of the bus.

Similarly, G. W. Bush noted, at the annual National Association for the Advancement of Colored People (NAACP) convention, that NCLB had been adopted to

> challenge the soft bigotry of low expectations . . . a system that gives up on people. . . . When . . . schools . . . are not teaching and will not change, our parents should have a different option. . . . Wealthier white families . . . defeat mediocrity by moving. That is not the case for lower-income families. . . . I strongly believe in charter schools, and public school choice . . . to move their child out of a school that's not teaching. (Bush, 2006)

Blaming educators' bigotry for past and prospective injustices if they oppose accountability is a classic case of symbolic violence; they may only escape this stigma if they support NCLB.

Bush and Paige also attacked teachers' unions. Paige called the NEA a "terrorist organization." He later apologized but then accused the NEA of using "obstructionist scare tactics" to stymie the implementation of NCLB; compared the NEA to the "real soldiers of democracy"—the nation's teachers; and framed the union as racist because its "high-priced Washington lobbyists . . . made no secret that they will fight against bringing real, rock-solid improvements in the way we educate all our children regardless of skin color, accent or where they live" (Paige, 2004; Pear, 2004). His speech weaponized discourse (divide and conquer) by framing teachers as part of the "immoral them" if they stand with their unions (see also Paige, 2007).

Bush and Paige further silenced opposing viewpoints by having the DOE reject state requests for more flexibility with respect to implementing NCLB, like the waivers issued during the Clinton administration (McGuinn, 2006). These waivers acknowledged that states have developed vastly different educational systems and that there are large differences in state DOE and school district capacities (D. Cohen & Moffit, 2009). Because waivers are also an institutional strategy to stem negative policy feedback, it is not surprising that more than half of state governments considered, and five passed, laws or resolutions challenging NCLB by 2004—once they realized that they would not get waivers—or that the nation's largest teachers' union, the NEA, filed a lawsuit.[45] This negative feedback sought to change policy by seeking out more favorable institutional venues (state governments and the courts).

Partially to quell these negative responses, Bush's second secretary of education—Margaret Spellings—provided states with increased flexibility, so long as they adopted standards and annual testing; improved teacher training; disaggregated test scores by student subgroups; and distributed test information to parents. While more palatable to many, this flexibility resulted in considerable variation between states in terms of academic rigor and policy implementation; yet it still did not appease conservatives, as evidenced by the introduction of legislation in the House and Senate by more than 50 Republicans to allow states to opt out of NCLB's testing mandates (Rhodes, 2014; Weisman & Paley, 2007).

Many of these Republicans had gone along with new federal mandates because they hoped that NCLB's charter school and supplemental services provisions would demonstrate the efficacy of choice and open the door for broader market-based policies. Instead, a lot of the private providers of supplemental services had gone out of business and only a small portion of parents who were eligible for choice had exercised that option (Mesecar, 2015; U.S. DOE, 2006). Once Democrats retook control of Congress in 2006, the stage was set for the failed reauthorization of NCLB as scheduled in 2007, despite months of hearings, negotiations, and public debate (Rhodes, 2014). More states then began informing the U.S. DOE that they planned to disregard key pieces of NCLB if Congress failed to make changes (McNeil, 2011). There was also growing negative feedback from Americans as a result of NCLB's policy design.[46]

The goal was for 100 percent of U.S. students to be proficient in ELA and mathematics by the year 2014, but the accountability model actually resulted in growing numbers of schools being labeled SINI. First, states used student proficiency (status) scores versus improvement scores to rate and rank schools. This meant that a student could grow two grade levels during a single school year and still count against a school's AYP rating if the student was below the established proficiency bar for that year. Second, test scores were reported in *normative* terms (above and below average based on a statistical mean) and so, by statistical design, some students had to "fail" simply because they fell on the wrong side of the bell curve. Third, entire schools were labeled "failing" as a result of a single subject or subgroup, such as special education. Fourth, the mandated targets continued to increase after Congress failed to revamp NCLB in 2007. In fact, President Obama's secretary of education, Arne Duncan, projected that 82 percent of schools would be labeled by 2012 and face escalating consequences, including being restructured, taken over, or closed, if no action were taken (Resmovits, 2011b). All of these concerns had been expressed during the early debates on NCLB but were marginalized through the weaponization of political discourse (symbolic violence) and political institutions.

Given these issues and his electoral platform, many expected President Obama would move away from market-based accountability policies. Instead, he gave Congress a 2011 deadline to revise NCLB. When that did not happen, he invited states to apply for waivers from some of NCLB's toughest requirements, including the afore-mentioned AYP measurement system, in return for adopting his preferred (and incentivized) reforms, such as developing, adopting, piloting, and implementing teacher and principal evaluation systems that support student achievement (U.S. DOE, 2012). In addition, the $4.35 billion RttT grant competition incentivized states to develop performance measurement systems that linked teacher and princi-pal evaluations to student test scores; use student growth measures (SGMs) for teacher accountability; adopt college- and career-ready standards, such as the Common Core; implement targeted inter-ventions for low-performing schools; and expand charter schools (U.S. DOE, 2009).

As policy interventions, NCLB waivers and RttT more clearly focused on growth over set targets, individual educators over school districts, and motivating through "carrots" (grants and waivers) more than "sticks" (sanctions); yet, like NCLB, the theory of action (Stone, 1989) was that principals and teachers would improve their work effort to obtain respectable test scores and this would result in higher performing schools. Both also continued NCLB's focus on "fixing" low-performing schools through reconstitution, closure, and increased competition from charter schools (U.S. DOE, 2011). The latter reforms are based on a belief that competition and either threatening or actually firing, replacing, or putting large percentages of adminis-trators, teachers, and support staff on probation would improve a school's human capital by motivating educators to work harder. The largest reconstitution effort was the federal School Improvement Grant (SIG). SIG was created as part of NCLB, but not funded until 2007 (Government Accountability Office [GAO], 2011); it was greatly expanded by the Obama administration (U.S. DOE, 2011).[47]

By 2015, 42 states and the District of Columbia were operating under a waiver. Thus the Obama administration had leveraged federal education funding and waivers in ways previously unseen in education politics; in effect, it had used executive policy to replace NCLB for most of the nation's 50 million students (Camera, 2015). Earlier, I argued that policy makers co-opt one another's narratives. As evident in the discourse of the Obama administration, this enables them to tap into taken-for-granted meanings, build coalitions, and generate support for their preferred policies.

In defense of his reforms, President Obama exclaimed, "The status quo is morally inexcusable, it's economically indefensible, and all of us are going to have to roll up our sleeves to change it." He then advocated "tough love" as a way to spur "bottom-up" transformation (Obama, 2010). The narrative of David versus Goliath is less prominent but still evident in his administration's rhetoric:

PRESIDENT OBAMA: There are going to be elements within the teachers union . . . [that are] resistant to change. . . . People inherently are resistant to change. . . . Teachers aren't any different from any politicians or corporate CEOs. . . . Certain habits . . . have been built up that they don't want to change. . . . [RttT is] not based on politics . . . who's got more clout . . . what . . . groups are looking for. . . . It's based on what works. (Shear & Anderson, 2009)

ARNE DUNCAN: Too much is at stake . . . to restrict choice and innovation. . . . States that do not have public charter laws or put artificial caps on the growth of charter schools will jeopardize their (RttT) applications. . . . We cannot continue to do that same thing and expect different results. We cannot let another generation of children be deprived of their civil right to a quality education. (A. Duncan, 2009)

My analysis suggests that these narratives diffused across parties and administrations because they helped policy makers negotiate intense political conflict by suppressing dissenting voices at a time of partisan gridlock in Congress, but negative feedback continued to grow.

Like Clinton and G. W. Bush, President Obama had tried to suppress this negative feedback and promote bipartisanship through waivers; instead, his strategy sowed division within the Democratic Party, where opposition from the left had already been mounting, much like the implementation of NCLB had sowed division between G. W. Bush and conservatives. The expanded federal role also inflamed opposition on the right—as evident in conservatives dubbing his reforms "Obamacore" to link them with executive "overreach" through the Affordable Care Act (Carey, 2016; Whitman, 2015).

These issues created common ground between teachers and Republicans—like Lamar Alexander (R-TN), the chair of the Senate HELP Committee—especially once underresourced (mostly urban and rural) schools were joined by suburban communities that were concerned about the narrowing of the curriculum due to testing and the CCSS. These groups fostered an "opt out" movement that revitalized teachers' unions by providing grassroots support for their concerns.

Arne Duncan tried to silence this negative feedback by shaming parents, stating that "white suburban moms" were just upset "their child isn't as brilliant as they thought they were and their school isn't quite as good as they thought." He later apologized (S. Simon, 2013) and President Obama began to call for limits on testing (Zernike, 2015).[48] These actions are not surprising—middle- and upper-income Americans are more likely to vote (Piven & Cloward, 1989). Still, by expanding the conflict, these individuals and groups were able to successfully lobby for reform and the ESSA passed by large bipartisan majorities in the House and the Senate (Layton, 2015b).[49]

Similar to previous reforms, interest groups and policy makers—such as Senators Lamar Alexander (R-TN) and Patty Murray (D-WA), ranking HELP Committee chairs and key architects of the rewrite—admitted that there were issues with the ESSA. However, they stressed the need for pragmatism to correct the mediocre status quo; claimed the policy would "unleash a flood of excellence" from the "bottom up" by restoring power to local communities (resources and flexibility);[50] linked education reform to an improved economy—rather than advocating a reduction in poverty and socioeconomic inequality to improve educational performance, as had been the case under the original ESEA;[51] and, often continued to advocate disciplining poorly performing schools to encourage educators to work harder. Tales about the need for personal responsibility were further implicit in the portrayal of federal interventions as providing a chance for students to succeed—rather than ensuring equal OTL.[52]

The latter two claims are apparent in the words of President Obama and Education Secretary Arne Duncan:

ARNE DUNCAN: [The ESSA] enshrines . . . the expectation that where schools serve students poorly or have low graduation rates . . . where groups of students aren't making progress, there will be accountability and action for change. (Kerr, 2015)

PRESIDENT OBAMA: [The goals of NCLB] were the right ones. . . . But in practice, it often fell short . . . forced schools . . . into cookie-cutter reforms. . . . [The ESSA reaffirms the] American ideal that every child, regardless of race, income, background, the ZIP Code where they live, deserves the chance to make out of their lives what they will. (Resmovits, 2015)

The ESSA's policy design further supports these claims.

Some of the ESSA's provisions are genuine improvements. For example, it included preschool development grants and an arts education fund; it also substituted "a well-rounded education" for "core academic subjects," making it less likely that schools would downgrade the teaching of social studies and the arts to a focus on ELA, math, and science. In addition, the ESSA scaled back some sanctions, such as the AYP requirements, and the ability of the federal DOE to influence or incentivize states to adopt national standards or policies that use student test scores to evaluate, reward, and punish educators. States must still adopt "challenging" standards; however, they have greater latitude in the number and types of measures used to evaluate performance and are encouraged to reduce testing by eliminating unnecessary state tests (Camera, 2015; Kerr, 2015; A. Klein, 2015).

At its core, though, the ESSA primarily promotes a punitive, test-based accountability regime that uses market-based economic models (competition, choice, incentives, and sanctions) to improve public education. States are still required to test students in ELA and math in Grades 3–8, at least once in high school, and at benchmarks for science; they must publish those results by district and school and for different student "subgroups" (e.g., ELL, special education, racial minorities, students living in poverty). States and districts are also required to use evidence-based interventions in schools that perform in the bottom 5 percent and where fewer than two-thirds graduate. Moreover, the ESSA continues to divert resources away from public schools through charter school expansion and is likely to reduce teacher training by requiring states to open more pathways for teachers to become certified (Camera, 2015; Kerr, 2015; A. Klein, 2015).

It is unlikely that schools, educators, parents, and students will experience much on-the-ground change for another reason. As mentioned, most states had waivers that allowed them to develop their own strategies for measuring student progress, raising achievement, and turning around struggling schools; states had also already invested millions of dollars in their accountability systems, as well as the CCSS and associated tests. By requiring states demonstrate that they have challenging academic standards, the law incentivized states to continue their already approved systems. Meanwhile, the need to draft and submit ESSA plans created burdens and technical challenges at a time when gubernatorial elections resulted in many new faces at the head of state DOEs. Both of these removed some attention from the testing flexibility options and resulted in state plans that mostly reinforced existing regimes (Gewertz, 2018; A. Klein, 2018b).[53]

There is also evidence that the ESSA is suppressing the negative feedback that often promotes change. For instance, by permitting state laws that allowed students to opt out of exams but requiring states to mark those students as "not proficient" (Lahm, 2017), the ESSA has weakened the opt-out movement. Test participation rates rose slightly even in states where the opt-out movement had been particularly strong (A. Klein, 2018a). In addition, the ESSA's institutional strategy of restoring state control requires interest groups to lobby 50 governments to achieve political change versus focusing their efforts at the national level. Sometimes this strategy (intentionally or unintentionally) builds feedback from below and results in national political change. This was the case with the excellence movement beginning with President Reagan, but not opt out. While strong in a handful of states—like New York, New Jersey, Connecticut, and Colorado—the new political terrain appears to have made it more difficult to recruit new members, construct coalitions, and mobilize the other forms of social and political capital that enable individuals and groups to build momentum for reform from the ground up (Gewertz, 2018; Ujifsa, 2016). Teachers' unions have also expressed support for the ESSA, admitting that it did not resolve many issues yet advocating pragmatism in light of its improvements over previous federal reforms (AFT, 2015; NEA, 2015). This book sits within that political environment.

Discussion: Narratives, Institutions, and the Construction of Political Change

Pierson (1996) shows how postwar social programs created an "army of beneficiaries" with vested interests in maintaining the status quo, expanding existing programs, and/or blocking those who oppose existing political arrangements. This chapter, in contrast, confirms that policy makers are able to "weaponize" discourse (symbolic violence) and institutions (the formal and informal rules of the game) to overturn existing political arrangements. The meta-narrative about the mediocre status quo expanded the crisis, and therefore those who had an interest in resolving it, by linking poor educational performance to declining economic competitiveness. It also converted socioeconomic inequality into a nonstory by blaming educational failure on individual schools, teachers, and students. When combined with the narratives of low expectations and diagnostic testing, this language portrayed the benefits of NCLB as diffuse and the costs as being borne by the (unworthy or immoral) mediocre few. The stigma associated with the mediocre status quo symbolically and materially altered the playing field.

Symbolic resources are embodied in public perceptions about a group and its ability to mobilize. For instance, a group's attractiveness may decline if it is perceived to have unfairly or disproportionately benefited from government rewards (A. Schneider & Ingram, 2005a). *Material resources* include a group's organizational capacity, meaning its size, monetary resources, and other factors that affect mobilization and collective action. Both of these resources help groups construct political and social capital. By blaming public schools, teachers, and teachers' unions for the mediocre status quo, and framing them as self-interested if they opposed testing and school choice as the best way to improve public education, policy makers impeded their ability to contest the accountability regime. They also conferred actual resources on a new group of beneficiaries (e.g., testing and publishing companies, charter schools, private consulting firms for school turnarounds, and private and religious providers of supplemental services); these groups then had a vested interest in continuing and expanding the accountability regime.

Conclusion

In the 1970s, Marion Wright Edelman established the Children's Defense Fund (CDF) as a research and advocacy group for children. Its intent was to counter the effects of growing poverty. The CDF's slogan was "Leave No Child Behind." Thirty years later, policy makers co-opted that slogan to justify moving from an equity regime to an accountability regime. They argued that excellence (for all) would close the achievement gap by "raising all boats." By that time, education had risen to the top of the policy agenda, yet both parties struggled to construct a majoritarian narrative. The Republican Party embraced individualism but struggled to extend the "mantle of opportunity" owing to its support for localism and its opposition to an activist government. Democrats supported an activist social agenda; however, they struggled to appease growing middle-class opposition to redistributive social programs (F. Hess & McGuinn, 2002). By stressing equal opportunity (increased funding for schools that served underprivileged children), freedom from the federal government (block grants and choice), and personal responsibility (accountability for public schools, educators, and students), recent education reforms enabled Democrats to shake the "tax and spend" label and Republicans to advance compassionate conservatism as the best way to achieve an opportunity society.

The claim that accountability would advance America's economic interests by improving the performance of *all* students obscured questions about whether academic achievement is linked to economic productivity and whether our system of education could or should be run like a business—with its focus on efficiency and effectiveness—as opposed to a human service, with its focus on autonomy, participation, and broader social values. The remainder of this book uses 83 interviews with teachers and administrators to explore how the accountability regime and its associated rhetoric affected their political and social experiences, behaviors, and identities, as well as teaching, learning, and public education.

3

Public Discourse and Policy Feedback

Chapter 2 discussed how one tactic for achieving political ends is to impede opponents' ability to mobilize by influencing their symbolic and material resources, such as public perceptions and organizational capacity. Marginalized groups (e.g., the homeless, the unemployed, the poor, the incarcerated) are more likely to be scapegoated for public problems and less likely to benefit from public resources because negative stereotypes (typically) cause them to remain silent rather than draw attention to themselves through protest (A. Schneider & Ingram, 2005b). I referred to this as *symbolic violence* and showed how policy makers promoted the transition from an equity regime to an accountability regime by blaming public schools and public school educators for the two achievement gaps and the nation's declining economic competitiveness. This chapter uses 83 interviews with administrators and teachers to explore their views on how and why public discourse changed with respect to education and the subsequent effects on policy feedback and public policies.

The State, Symbolic Violence, and Policy Feedback

During the 1960s and 1970s, previously marginalized groups—such as women, minorities, and the economically disadvantaged—mobilized to demand political, social, and economic change. Such protest included economically marginalized occupations, like teaching, where the number of strikes increased from 25 (between 1960 and

71

1965) to more than 1,000 (between 1975 and 1980), involving more than 1 million teachers (Toch, 1991). Economic protest eventually spilled over into the political arena, as teachers' unions fought to expand education funding at all levels of government. Their demands (voice) resulted in the inclusion of ELLs, women, and the disabled in the equity regime. This claim is evident in the adoption of Title IX in 1972, which required, among other things, that schools receiving federal funds provide girls with equal opportunities to compete in sports, and the Education for All Handicapped Children Act (EAHCA) in 1975, which required public schools to provide special needs children with a free and appropriate education in the least restrictive environment. The equity regime was also expanded beyond K–12 education through grants and low-cost student loans, as well as increased federal funding for public colleges and universities. Teachers' unions further mobilized for the first time on behalf of a presidential contender. In return for their support, President Jimmy Carter (D) created the federal DOE, which elevated education to a cabinet-level position and provided teachers with more voice at the national level.

While all of these changes are examples of policy feedback, mobilization is rarely a one-way street. Informants said that the expansion of the equity regime sparked the countermobilization of business-economic interests, conservatives, and religious groups. Some viewed the DOE, educators, and schools of education as a threat to their values because they promoted a more progressive curriculum. Johanna, a retired suburban elementary schoolteacher, exclaimed,

> I don't know why they are picking on teachers. . . . [I hear] they consider the colleges to be too liberal . . . liberal people . . . instructing our young. . . . They feel threatened by this . . . want to promote a certain way of viewing our history, a certain lens, and . . . [ensure that] those views are the ones that are continued . . . especially the religious right, to promote their beliefs.

Others mobilized out of a concern that federal and state court decisions and state and school district organizational and curricular reforms had broadened educational opportunities at the expense of school district efficiency and effectiveness and the teaching of traditional academic subjects.[1] The remainder of this section explores and provides context for educators' narratives about how this countermobilization normalized a new discourse that reinvented education policy.

The Business–Economic–Political Complex and Education Reform

According to informants, the movement to change education policy began in the late 1970s with economic distress and concerns about declining productivity and economic competitiveness.[2] From 1969 to 1979, America lost 32 million to 38 million jobs to global competition and it became a debtor nation for the first time in nearly four generations. Economists do not agree on what caused slowed productivity but do agree that it curtailed a long period of upward mobility. Americans were still well-off when compared to historical and international standards; however, real median family income actually fell between 1973 and 1979, and many Americans felt fearful about their economic futures. They were also experiencing economic insecurity as deindustrialization, meaning the shift from manufacturing to a service economy, negatively affected wages and benefits. Service sector jobs are typically nonunionized, offer lower wages, and provide few, if any, benefits. In addition, many firms began experimenting with flexible labor practices, such as contracting out different aspects of the production process and hiring part-time or temporary employees. These changes reduced workers' access to health insurance and pensions through their employers while unstable wages and the need to "follow the jobs" increased the risks associated with homeownership.[3] One consequence was that problems that had once been (largely) confined to the working poor—such as restricted access to affordable health and pension plans, job insecurity, bankruptcy, and foreclosure—spread to the middle class (Hacker, 2006).

Economic uncertainty reshaped Americans' relationships with the government at a time when reduced union membership and dues (organizational resources) were negatively affecting labor's ability to lobby for public policies that helped low-income, working-class, and middle-class Americans.[4] Fears about the viability of American democracy and capitalism were further exacerbated by a series of high-profile fiscal crises in both the public and private sectors. For example, New York City and Chrysler verged on bankruptcy in 1975 and 1979, respectively (Troy, 2005).[5] While the federal government bailed out Chrysler, Republican president Gerald Ford adopted a "tough love" approach for New York City. The crisis was averted at the last minute when Albert Shanker, then president of the United Federation of Teachers (UFT), agreed to use $150 million from the union's pension fund to buy Municipal Assistance Corporation bonds. Ford eventually relented and persuaded Congress to approve federal loans—which New York City paid back with interest—but he had angered many voters when the *New York Daily News* headlined "Ford to City: Drop Dead."[6] He later acknowledged that his handling of the New York City fiscal crisis cost him the presidency when his opponent, Jimmy Carter, narrowly carried New York State.

Although these fiscal crises were especially affecting manufacturing and the nation's older urban centers, the economic downturn harmed state and local governments across the country as rising unemployment reduced tax revenues and simultaneously grew the costs of social programs. Many localities had to increase taxes just to provide the same level of services due to inflation and escalating energy costs. Informants who were teaching at the time said that these economic trends contributed to social and political unrest in the form of antibusing crusades, taxpayer revolts—like those that led to Proposition 13 in California and 2 ½ in Massachusetts—and the election of anti-tax-and-spend school boards. This political feedback reduced the flow of revenues to public schools and resulted in teacher layoffs, salary freezes, program cuts, school bankruptcies, and school closings in some extreme cases. It is therefore not surprising that the 1970s were also a time of rising teacher activism (McGirr, 2002; Toch, 1991).

Americans have often looked to their schools in times of crisis. The 1970s were no different. The media began reporting a 12-year decline in scores on Scholastic Aptitude Tests (SATs), which are used for college admissions, as early as 1975. Educators at the time argued that declining scores resulted from a positive trend—rising college attendance and therefore increased numbers of students taking those exams—but the National Assessment of Educational Progress (NAEP) in 1981 reported a decline in students' abilities to think and write; the National Science Foundation complained that a decrease in graduation requirements had negatively affected the proportion of students who pursued math, science, and foreign languages; and, business groups claimed that the nation's graduates did not have the necessary skills to compete in a technology society.[7] They blamed this job-skill mismatch for the nation's lost advantage in manufacturing and other industries, asserting that the nation's top competitors—the former Soviet Union, Japan, and Germany—provided more rigorous academic programs that focused on science, technology, engineering, and math (STEM; Hayes, 2004). Within this environment, the New York Stock Exchange commissioned a report by a group of economists to study Japan's growing dominance in industry. Although the report was supposed to focus on business techniques, it cited

Japan's educational system as the primary driver for its superior economic performance and concluded that America would need to raise the achievement levels of *all* students to compete economically (Jennings, 1990).

Per respondents, this narrative gained traction through the publication of *A Nation at Risk* by a federal DOE task force. Paul, a retired suburban middle school English teacher, pronounced,

> This large outcry . . . started as far back as the 1950s Sputnik. . . . It has grown and education has consistently been in the top three things that Americans think we need to improve . . . [because it] has been . . . politicized by both parties. . . . [Partly due] to global economic competition . . . jobs leaving and being outsourced . . . fear that we are falling behind and the schools are expected to do more to help us compete . . . the debate, though, is really caused by . . . [politicians claiming] our schools are failing . . . [then a] growth in think tanks . . . books and reports . . . *A Nation at Risk*. . . . [Politicians have] middle-class America and above thinking that the next generation is not going to be better off . . . worried about their kids.

By portraying *all* of the nation's educational institutions as "mediocre" (i.e., kindergarten through colleges and universities) and linking that mediocrity to declining economic productivity, policy makers (bureaucrats within the DOE and then elected officials) legitimized the inclusion of business-economic interests in education reform. The latter groups threw their support behind the burgeoning "excellence in education" movement at the state level and then built up the conservative parapolitical sphere (e.g., think tanks and interest groups) on behalf of national reform.[8]

Educators did not agree on what business-economic and conservative political interests hoped to achieve through education advocacy. Across age groups, four claims topped the list. While different, each narrative asserted that *political elites*—policy makers, interest groups, and others who hold a disproportionate amount of political power and influence owing to wealth, privilege, skill, or connections (hierarchy)—worked with the private sector (the market) to pursue a business-economic agenda in general and for public education specifically.

Publicly fund the development of trained human capital. Some participants maintained that business-economic interests hoped to promote the production of trained human capital as the most important goal of public education and the use of business-economic models as the best way to achieve that goal. The words of Jack, an elementary school principal, exemplify this narrative:

> [Business leaders] have historically gotten involved in education because they want trained labor. . . . Other countries track their students at an early age . . . decide who's going . . . to college or . . . [will] be laborers. . . . The latter get basic skills . . . vocational training. . . . State standards were a way to attract and retain businesses . . . compete with [other] states and globally . . . by offering trained labor. . . . The Common Core [CCSS] is also an example . . . to compete economically by providing skills that are viewed as necessary in the workplace.

Historical research supports this claim and recent research documents the role of conservative and business-economic interests and leaders, such as Bill Gates, in the adoption of the Common Core Standards.[9]

Transfer blame for the economic crisis. A second common narrative was that business-economic interests tried to squash demands for government programs and regulations by blaming the economic crisis on unions and the public sector. By spreading the belief that these policies had forced businesses to close or move overseas to a less hostile tax and regulatory climate, this symbolic violence helped them lobby against laws that create the right to bargain collectively, increase the minimum wage, and protect workers, consumers, and the environment. Molly, a suburban high school social studies teacher, declared,

> [This] whole thing about running schools like a business is part of an overall cultural shift that began in the '80s. . . . Business was washing its public face . . . scrubbing it clean, and they threw their dirty water all over the public sector. . . . Things were tough economically and people were scared. . . . It gave business an opportunity to set the tone . . . demand things . . . "we need concessions or else we have to move plants and jobs down south where they don't regulate as much," and . . . [then] overseas. They kept blaming government regulation for everything. . . . Now people just take it for granted that private is good and public is bad . . . state employees are lazy . . . [the] state kills jobs through taxes and regulation. . . . Business always talks about . . . how the profit motive and competition promotes . . . efficiency and effectiveness . . . you never hear them talk about . . . [things] like pollution . . . who cleans up the mess? Government . . . our tax dollars . . . they would not be successful without . . . things government has provided, like roads and bridges and public education.

The argument that taxes and regulations had "killed jobs" and necessitated more spending for unemployment and social welfare programs also helped business-economic interests increase support for privatizing the public sector, deregulating the private sector, and reducing corporate taxes.

According to my interviews, public schools and teachers were not initially blamed for economic decline; they became a target because the public sector is more highly unionized than the private sector, teachers are one of the most powerful public-sector unions, public sector unions are a large source of political contributions for Democrats, and public and private sector unions (typically) support welfare state expansion. Don, a suburban high school social studies teacher and district union president, explained,

[The] last presidential election—the 10 largest PACs (political action committees) . . . 7 were Republican and 3 were Democrat. Of those three, they were all public service unions. . . . If you crush . . . [those] you take care of the problem. And teachers are one of the strongest. . . . So, I think the argument that there are too many bad teachers and that we need to be able to fire bad teachers to compete is political. It is scapegoating, but so much of this is political to get back at the unions. . . . [I'm a] Republican . . . and I'm telling you a lot of it is about Republicans.

Don's narrative is a classic tale about symbolic violence. It was much more commonly expressed by educators in their forties and older, but, as mentioned in Chapter 1, research supports their claim that conservatives weaponized public discourse and policies to discredit unions, reduce their organizational resources (membership and dues), suppress union voice, and reduce political contributions to Democrats (Hertel-Fernandez, 2018). In contrast, educators *of all ages* stated that public employees in general make an especially attractive scapegoat during tough economic times because they have more job security and better benefits than the average American; their salaries and benefits are also funded through taxes.[10]

Privatize public education for profit. Chloe, an urban middle school English teacher, offered a third common narrative, which discussed how the private sector first exploited our natural resources and now wanted to privatize public programs—like education, Medicare, and Social Security—for profit:

[Government] is allowing big business to control everything. . . . Education is the last frontier. It had been untouchable. But . . . No Child

> Left Behind is a boom for big business. The book vendors are making a fortune on test prep. The testing companies . . . on all of the exams. The private tutoring companies . . . it is a multimillion-dollar industry.

Research supports these educators' claim that business-economic interests funded think tanks to produce *advocacy research*—research done for the express purpose of justifying policies versus scientifically advancing knowledge—with the goal of promoting a business-economic agenda, including, but not limited to, recent policies that hold schools and educators accountable through testing and school choice.[11] These accountability reforms provided the means to privatize public education and/or gain access to public resources.

Avoid redressing the "real" issues in education. A fourth common narrative asserted that accountability reforms were adopted to avoid politically unpopular solutions. In the words of Liam, a retired suburban high school English teacher and former district union president,

> [there are data that] say a good teacher is critical. . . . Everyone can agree with that, but that is another way of saying . . . anxiety, mental health . . . medical issues, and many other things do not interfere with a child's ability to learn. We as a society are failing to take responsibility for our own. . . . [There has been] a gross misreading of the data by Gates and other business and political elites. . . . Good teachers are critical . . . [but] other factors . . . have a strong influence. . . . [They] say . . . "The public is angry. Let's direct that anger away from banking and Wall Street . . . towards public employees . . . unions . . . public programs." . . . [And] politicians . . . said that this is a good way to go.

As a group, educators framed the "real" problems—both in terms of the economy and public education—as a loss of jobs that pay livable wages, socioeconomic inequality, poverty, hunger, segregation, homelessness, family decay, inadequate health care, and a lack of affordable day care, housing, and preschool. These solutions are less popular because they require raising taxes, whereas accountability implies that schools can do more with less—a fifth common narrative.

Reduce taxes and spending. As mentioned, the ESEA never fully redressed the inequitable financing of public schools and large gaps remain in per pupil spending across districts (B. Baker et al., 2018; Epstein, 2011). Some participants alleged that accountability policies—like NCLB and RttT—were a response to state lawsuits challenging these inequalities at a time when public opinion polls showed that Americans believed that there were large differences in per pupil spending, the amount spent affected the quality of education a great deal, the lack of financial support was the largest problem facing public schools, and finances were the main obstacle to improving schools in their communities (PDK, 1998, 2000, 2001).[12] Business-economic elites reportedly used think tanks and the media to counteract and change these views by reframing the issue as the inability of "failing" public schools to use resources effectively. That narrative helped justify accountability reforms instead of raising (federal, state, and local) taxes to provide public schools with more resources.

Other informants focused specifically on property taxes. They argued that business-economic interests fight to keep the property tax system as the primary vehicle for financing public schools—despite the resulting inequalities—because it creates a "natural alliance" with homeowners in favor of capping public school expenditures. Unlike federal and state income taxes, which are withdrawn from citizens' paychecks and used to support many different public programs, property taxes are *regressive and highly visible*—they disproportionately affect low-income property owners and those with fixed incomes, such as the elderly, and people know the exact amount that they are paying. Meanwhile, as a human service, educators' salaries and benefits are the largest component of school budgets These realities enable business-economic interests to frame teachers and their unions as being both self-interested *and* disinterested in the needs of lower- and fixed-income homeowners if they support budget increases. Returning to Liam's narrative,

> [property] taxes . . . created a natural antagonism between the community and their schools and teachers. . . . Corporations want to avoid higher corporate . . . and income taxes. . . . [and] politicians have . . . gone along . . . keeping that burden on homeowners, many of whom do not have a stake in the school. . . . [They] created an antagonistic climate . . . [especially] during economic difficulties. . . . Any real effort to change the system has been stymied. . . . [At] state hearings . . . one businessman . . . said . . . "keep . . . the property tax . . . it creates tension between the schools and the community . . . kept pressure on the unions and the teachers to keep costs down and salaries low." . . . I remember thinking, "Of course, as long as it is on the property tax, it unites citizens behind the business agenda of keeping school costs low."

Property taxes also create a "natural alliance" between homeowners, business-economic interests, and state policy makers. Middle- and upper-income citizens are more likely to own homes; these groups are also more likely to vote (Hall & Yoder, 2019; McElwee, 2014; Piven & Cloward, 1989; U.S. Census, 2021). These realities encourage state governments—like the one that is the subject of this analysis—to cap property taxes to "curry favor" with these groups.[13]

On a broader scale, a majority of informants declared that politicians have made *taxes in general* an issue, with about half of these respondents claiming that the purpose was not solely to gain votes.[14] Those who favor smaller government want to "starve" public programs by reducing available revenues. Either way, these participants expressed a belief that business-economic interests and their political allies are engaged in a zero-sum game with those that support a more expansive role for the public sector. Because the "winner" depends on public opinion, business-economic interests stir up anger against the latter groups—especially unions and public servants—to reduce their power (symbolic and material resources) and therefore their ability to fight proposals that starve the public sector through tax cuts. Molly, from whom we heard earlier, disclosed,

> I think this all started with Reagan. . . . [He] was a really amazing performer because he believed in what he was saying and he made other people believe it too. And, he put a compassionate face on things that were not compassionate . . . legitimized things, like breaking the airline traffic controller's strike . . . that had previously been off-limits. And conservatives realized . . . they could do these things. . . . [But] they are linking into something in the larger political culture . . . the whole personal responsibility thing . . . "you can give a man a fish or teach him to fish." . . . No one is entitled to anything, they have to work for it, and so welfare is now workfare and teachers should not have tenure because it is like a job entitlement. It is not. . . . It says that if you want to fire a teacher, you have to give due process. That is the American way . . . but teachers are being presented as . . . shady . . . getting special treatment . . . [since many private workers] no longer . . . [have these benefits. It's like how they provide] tax breaks to the wealthiest few under the lingo that "they've earned it" while those "others," whoever they are [*laughing*], have not.

Some—like Molly—specifically linked anti-union sentiments to American political culture, but most of those who told this narrative said that anti-union discourse was a way for conservatives and business-economic interests to take power back after a period of quiescence in the 1960s.

Educators did not use this language, but their claims are consistent with A. Schneider and Ingram's (1993) theory of target groups. As discussed in Chapter 2, taxpayers and homeowners are constructed as an "advantaged" or entitled group in American political culture. Because of this, they are more likely to be overtly rewarded through public policies. Unions and business-economic interests are viewed as "contenders." They are therefore more likely to be rewarded through less visible means. Capping property taxes overtly appeals to homeowners, but hiding economic benefits in the tax code reduces negative feedback from nonbeneficiaries. The focus is on what the government overtly spends (e.g., public school expenditures) rather than on what it gives back to individuals and business-economic interests through tax breaks (tax expenditures). The negative framing of unions reduces the symbolic resources (public perceptions) and the material resources (membership size and dues) of a group that would normally be able to counter the demands of business-economic interests and ensure that these benefits are more equitably distributed.

Most respondents made similar claims with respect to the negative framing of public servants and public programs. According to this narrative, business-economic and conservative interests portray the public sector as inferior to justify lower taxes, privatization, and deregulation while reducing the power of those with the resources to fight back. This symbolic violence allegedly started with public sector unions and bureaucrats; it then spread to teachers and other public servants.[15] The diffusion of symbolic violence may be one reason why younger teachers were less likely to discuss their unions in a political context, focusing instead on the portrayal of teachers. Owing to the historical time period in which they teach, they have been directly affected by negative discourse about teachers rather than indirectly harmed through anti-union rhetoric.

Michael, an urban high school librarian, provided perhaps the best description from any age group of how this type of symbolic violence works,

> [In] New Jersey . . . the governor . . . is calling teachers greedy. . . . [He and] others are labeling teachers as the new welfare cheats . . . the new welfare queens because if you can slap a negative label or . . . image on someone, then you can go after them . . . convince people that teachers are making too much money and that they are taking taxpayers for a ride because then they can justify paying them less. . . . No one goes into teaching for the money, but people need to realize that teaching is end-loaded. You don't make a good salary considering your level of education when you start teaching but you do pretty well at the end of

your career . . . [after working] for a long time. . . . [My friend] started teaching in the '70s . . . at $2,000 a year. The state pension was good but that was the trade-off. . . . Now they want to take that pension away because times are tough. But they're reneging on the deal.

Like A. Schneider and Ingram (1993), Michael is conveying how policy makers label groups in ways that help achieve political ends. In this case, such symbolic violence involves linking teachers to "welfare queens," a pejorative term that is used to convey that poor women—especially unwedded Black women—exploit taxpayers by having more children to avoid work and increase their welfare payments (Bensonsmith, 2005).

Research suggests that conservatives used concerns about "welfare queens" to stoke public anger and win elections by portraying Democrats as the party of handouts and wasteful liberal spending (spending on minorities and the economically disadvantaged). This language resulted in bipartisan support for workfare as adopted by Democratic president Bill Clinton and a Republican controlled Congress (Bensonsmith, 2005; Katznelson, 2005). Similarly, informants described how the claim that teachers—especially older, more expensive teachers—do not need to work hard because they have been given a "job entitlement" eroded Democrats' support for tenure and seniority and created bipartisan support for using student test scores to hold educators accountable.

Over the long term, the ability of business-economic and conservative interests to move some ideas and claims to the foreground, while pushing others to the background, helped generate broad support for market-based reforms across both political parties.[16] Education policy debates "normalized" these new assumptions and priorities, by making them appear like common sense (Fairclough, 1989), and institutionalized them through accountability reforms. I am referring to these "common sense" logics as a *market managerial paradigm* (MMP).

The Market Managerial Paradigm and Education Reform

The MMP prioritizes the efficiency, effectiveness, and academic goals of public schools—especially as they pertain to economic ends like the development of human capital or marketable job skills—over other goals, such as civic engagement and the development of socioemotional skills. To achieve these *instrumental ends*, the MMP advocates corporate models of governance, including "the carrot and the stick" (e.g., incentives, sanctions, competition, choice) and top-down hierarchical controls. It is evident in recent reforms that advocated using student test scores to rate and rank schools (NCLB) and educators (RttT and NCLB waivers) and then reward or penalize them through merit pay, poor performance reviews, and decisions to restructure, close or convert public schools to charter schools. Within this framework, according to informants, principals are "mid-level managers" who transmit data to central office staff and carry out central office directives once those data have been used to make decisions. These data-driven monitoring systems are a form of *social control*—a way to manage principals, teachers, and the public—rather than a means of engaging citizens, fostering site-based decision-making, or enabling parents to make decisions about their children, as was the intent of public information under recent reforms. This is because parents and taxpayers are viewed as "consumers" of education rather than as citizen coproducers. Many of these ideas are not new. There is a long history of applying business-economic models to public education, including the organization and management of teachers and students, the physical design of school buildings, and the curriculum (Cuban, 2004; Tyack, 1974).

In comparison, the educators in this study focused on the transformative and humanistic ends of public education. This *humanistic paradigm* (HP) includes the academic goals of public education (academic achievement and attainment) yet also focuses on other ends, such as developing children as caring, well-adjusted human beings; fostering inclusion; reducing socioeconomic inequality; and increasing civic engagement. One goal is to develop individuals who voluntarily follow the rules and contribute to society, versus doing so solely when compelled or controlled by authority figures, but educators also mentioned fostering feelings of self-efficacy and equal worth and developing children as lifelong learners. District administrators under this framework largely focus on budgetary and other business functions while schools are viewed as learning communities. Administrators support—rather than control—teaching and learning, and principals create *communities of practice* that engage educators in site-based decision-making about the curriculum, pedagogy, and day-to-day school operations.

There are two other key differences between the MMP and the HP. The latter recognizes the importance of parents and the broader community for educational outcomes; it advocates the creation of *associational ties* between and among public schools, citizens, private institutions (e.g., local businesses, developers, hospitals), elected officials, and other public institutions (e.g., public libraries, local police, housing authorities, social service agencies) to develop trust and encourage these groups to work together. The HP further acknowledges that public education is (often) a site of political, social, economic, and cultural conflict owing to its transformative nature and the lack of consensus about what teachers should accomplish—beyond raising student achievement and attainment—and the best means of achieving those ends. For learning to occur, educators must minimize conflict through the development of shared beliefs, values, and attitudes within schools and classrooms. The resulting *social cohesion* reduces the need for more coercive forms of social control (detention, suspensions, expulsions) by creating feelings of belonging, security, and identification with place. It also fosters a commitment to the common good by developing *social trust*—a belief in the honesty, integrity, and reliability of others. Sometimes those involved must advocate putting individual needs over organizational ends, but that is not the same as pushing individual rights in ways that are harmful to others or the collective. Instead, it involves nurturing individuals while recognizing that members have a responsibility to something larger than themselves (see Chapters 5 and 9).

Table 3.1 compares and contrasts the HP and MMP. The remainder of this section *summarizes* educators' views on how the MMP transformed education by promoting myths, misunderstandings, and distortions about public schools and public school educators while making them appear like commonsense. Where applicable, I point out those chapters that provide more detail.

Myths about educational performance. Research supports informants' claim that accountability, as a rationale for reform, was highly influenced by a number of myths about educational performance that stemmed from misunderstandings in some cases and the misuse of state, national, and international test data in others.[17] Not every educator mentioned all four myths described here or discussed them in equal detail, but these claims were pervasive across "groups" (i.e., different occupations; educators in urban, rural, and suburban schools; public, private, and charter school educators; older versus younger educators).

Public school quality has declined. Per these respondents, the primary way public discourse distorts performance is by failing to acknowledge that test scores are reported in *normative* terms, meaning above average and below average based on a statistical

Table 3.1. Market-managerial and humanistic paradigms

	Market-managerial paradigm	Humanistic paradigm
Purpose of education	Instrumental ends (e.g., raise academic achievement, attainment, and test scores, increase global competitiveness, improve marketable job skills)	Instrumental, transformative, and humanistic ends (e.g., reduce socioeconomic inequality, increase democratic participation, develop critical thinking and socioemotional skills, improve feelings of self-worth, create lifelong learners, develop a caring society)
Framing of teaching and learning	Teaching as a technology (standardized and mechanized); teachers matter; learning is teacher directed and measurable over a period of time (it has a start and an end)	Teaching as a moral practice (holistic, developmental, and relational); communities matter; learning is inclusive and relational (many actors over a lifetime) but takes place within prescribed standards
How to best manage public schools	Schools as businesses; top-down: hierarchical controls and data-driven monitoring systems to standardize education; bottom-up: market controls (e.g., explicit rewards and incentives), such as merit pay for teachers and competition from charter schools; democracy as public opinion	Schools as learning communities; site based: shared/communal responsibilities; data informed, but also experiential; democracy as participation: trust and associational ties are critical
Theory of motivation/control	Externally driven; bureaucratic and competitive; explicit rewards; examples: scripting/merit pay	Internally/externally driven; normative: shared beliefs and values; implicit rewards but also relational; example: norms of teaching
Educator evaluation	Clinical/performative; visible work and measurable activities; efficiency and effectiveness: targets and testing	Experiential/performative; visible and invisible work; effectiveness: professional competence (e.g., professional development plans and portfolios)
Culture/ethos	Individualistic; performative and competitive; performance as serving institutional interests; ethos of self-interest: do right by the organizational regime	Constrained competition: humanistic and performative; performance as professional judgment, commitment, and service; ethos of care: do right by the kids/community/ occupation

mean. As mentioned, this means that, by statistical design, there will *always* be some students who "fail" simply because they fall on the wrong side of the bell curve. It does not (necessarily) mean that those students are uneducated. The latter depends on what the test is designed to measure and how high the bar is set for passing and failing. The federal DOE sets these *cutoff points* for the NAEP and state DOEs for the exams that were used to evaluate students, and thus schools and teachers, under NCLB, NCLB waivers, and RttT. These processes allegedly became *politicized* and distorted as policy makers and interest groups realized that lowering the bar could help avoid federal penalties and raising it could help justify closing public schools and replacing them with charter schools. I support these claims in Chapters 6 and 7.

Inadequate resources and the inequitable distribution of resources are not the problem. During the 1990s, the perception that public school quality had declined led researchers and policy makers to explore the relationship between expenditures and student performance to determine if additional resources had improved average achievement. The evidence from these studies was mixed. However, research supports respondents' claims that it was (mis)used to promote the idea that resources do not matter in education and provided the justification for holding schools and teachers accountable—rather than redressing the large gaps in funding that disproportionately affect the highest poverty schools and students of color.[18]

American schools cannot compete with schools in other nations. Given policy makers' use of student test scores to blame public schools for the nation's lost economic advantage, it is not surprising that many educators mentioned the role of the Organisation for Economic Co-operation and Development's (OECD) Program for International Student Assessment (PISA) in the adoption of recent education reforms. The PISA compares "educational performance" across more than 60 countries by assessing the ability of a sample of 15-year-olds to apply the skills and knowledge they might need in the future (PISA, 2001). Educators acknowledged that American students did not compare well to their international peers (see National Center for Education Statistics [NCES], 2010b) but claimed that the PISA is not an accurate or fair assessment of students, educators, or schools.

One common narrative was that the PISA does not measure what schools teach—only students' ability to demonstrate the skills that a select group of individuals (political and economic elites) believe are important for success in a knowledge economy (the OECD supports this claim; see PISA, 2001). The focus on producing trained human capital is not surprising, given that the PISA is part of the OECD; however, unlike American educators, many countries are less committed to the humanistic and transformative ends of public education. They track their students at an early age into elite (college-bound) and vocational schools, and only offer the PISA at elite schools. In consequence, American students are being compared to other nations' elite students on material their teachers may or may not be prioritizing or may teach in later grades because they are also focusing on other knowledge and skills.

These apples-and-oranges comparisons are magnified by a second complaint. White middle-class and upper-income parents are disproportionately likely to boycott the "testing culture" by opting their children out of state, NAEP, and PISA exams (for support of this claim, see Campanile, 2015; Pizmony-Levy & Saraisky, 2016). Because testing is highly correlated with socioeconomic status (Reardon, 2011), the PISA is now even more likely to over-assess students who struggle in the United States. Sam, a suburban high school science teacher, explained,

> [People] play with numbers. . . . It instills the crazy fear that our country is falling behind. . . . PISA . . . was supposed to be a random selection of ninth-grade students. . . . [They are pulled] out of class. . . . My daughter . . . was randomly chosen. . . . You could sign a letter saying you did not want your child to take the test. . . . I know . . . a lot of other parents . . . who are involved . . . have *very good* students . . . [said] their children are tested enough and did not want them missing more school to take a test so that some bureaucrat could rate and rank. . . . This is going to be used by the *New York Times* to say "American students do not do as well as the kids in Sweden" [*laughing*]. . . . [The test] is comparing apples and oranges because many of those nations track their students at an early age and only the students who are tracked for college are taking these tests . . . their top 10 percent with our whole and many of our top 10 percent are opting out . . . [because] we think of the individual first. If it's better for the individual to opt out, then . . . we do. It's a totally different culture.

Sam's statement that "we think of the individual first" is the third common apples-and-oranges argument. International comparisons do not take into account the influence of important cultural and socioeconomic factors. Studies show, for instance, that the high rate of socioeconomic inequality and childhood poverty in the United States when compared to other economically developed countries negatively affects student achievement. Research further supports informants' claim that American students are highly competitive with their international peers when poverty and socioeconomic inequality are taken into account.[19] Educators complained that policy makers and the media ignore these realities when reporting on American public schools.

Private, parochial, and charter schools outperform public schools. Albert Shanker, who was president of the AFT from 1974 to 1997, developed the idea to create publicly funded, yet privately managed, charter schools as a way for *teachers* to create and run small schools that were relatively free from bureaucratic rules and regulations. He viewed this public–private hybrid as a way for teaching as a profession to experiment and innovate on how to *better serve needy students,* especially those who had dropped out or were at risk of dropping out due to disengagement and other behavioral issues.[20] Shanker eventually turned against charter schools because the movement was co-opted by conservatives and business-economic interests to privatize public education.

Similarly, almost all of the educators in this study linked charter schools to a movement to privatize education and more than half alleged that charter schools were being used to silence their voices by restricting unionization and removing due process protections, such as tenure and seniority. As evidence, they cited the fact that most charter schools are not unionized. Liam, from whom we heard earlier, had this to say,

> Obama and Duncan . . . [Bill] Gates . . . very bright guy . . . has good ideas and intentions . . . bought into this idea . . . the teacher alone . . . matters. . . . They know . . . children in these urban environments are not getting the benefits of those in suburban schools . . . use that to justify giving up on public schools. . . . There is also an insidious argument that . . . public school teachers are self-interested while charter schools are idealistic. Some . . . are, but others are very astute hedge fund managers [*laughs*]. . . . So, *no tenure* has become a really big rallying cry. . . . There was . . . white flight and now . . . Black flight. . . . If . . . middle-class minorities leave the public school system in droves . . . you lose your political voice in the public schools and the only voice left on behalf of disadvantaged children . . . [and] immigrants are the unions. . . . And, in this environment where the charters take the money out of the public school . . . [they've] imposed a penalty. . . . One local urban district, they have taken away millions to set up . . . [charters. It has eliminated their ability] to redress the issue[s]. . . . You have to do what is right for your

child. . . . I am not attacking charter schools. I don't like this ideology that they are idealistic and public school teachers are self-interested.

Like Liam, most educators in this study were not resistant to the idea of charter schools. For them, the real issue was the misappropriation of data to claim that private, parochial, and charter schools outperform their public school counterparts as a way to justify the transfer of public resources and force public schools to do more with less—or go out of business.

Chapters 9 and 10 support educators' claims that charter schools perform no better, and often worse, than public schools; that school vouchers have not improved overall performance; and that the playing field is not even. Public schools must take everyone. Public charter schools do not discriminate against who is allowed entrance, but they "counsel out" students with learning, behavioral, and emotional issues. Chapter 11 offers possible reforms to preserve choice while leveling the playing field and resolving other issues discussed in this study.

Myths about teaching and learning. The myths about performance in the last section are closely tied to a number of myths about teaching and learning.

Only teachers matter. Studies support that teachers are the single most important *school-related variable* in terms of student achievement and attainment and find that some teachers consistently outperform others, even within the same school. My informants did not contest these findings. Instead, they argued against the recent claim that public schools could vastly improve educational outcomes simply by replacing ineffective teachers and discussed how that myth resulted in ineffective and unjust policies.

First, the myth that only teachers matter downplays other important factors that influence children's educational outcomes, such as *school-related variables* (e.g., administrative support, school facilities, per pupil spending), *outside-of-school variables* (e.g., levels of poverty, hunger, segregation, socioeconomic inequality, and resources within a community), *student-related variables* (e.g., motivation and effort), and *family-related variables* (e.g., food insecurity, language spoken in the home, frequent moves, and parental employment, income, education, and marital status). Research supports these claims.[21] Katy, a retired suburban elementary teacher and high school substitute, declared,

We have a huge distribution of wealth and . . . a lot of needs at the bottom . . . going unmet. Schools cannot do it all. . . . Children are coming in hungry . . . exhausted because their parents were fighting or . . . they had nowhere to stay the night before, and you're going to use the test scores to judge a teacher or a school? There are a lot of things going on at home. . . . We need to focus on the whole child. . . . Education is more than . . . just academics . . . more than what goes on in the class-room. . . . "It takes a village." . . . Deal with the village. . . . [But] those issues are complicated and expensive. So, they focus on . . . schools . . . [and] teachers. . . . Government and society need to . . . step up to the plate . . . think more broadly.

In this study, every informant in some way conveyed the impor-tance of these external variables for educational outcomes and most expressed that they are being ignored because they are more difficult and expensive to redress—it is easier to blame schools and teachers.

Second, this myth presumes that schools will replace ineffective teachers with more effective ones. For that to occur, there must be a steady supply of effective teachers *and* an equal distribution of highly qualified teachers (HQTs) across schools. Yet research finds that approximately one-third of America's teachers leave during their first three years and almost half during the first five (National Commission on Teaching and America's Future [NCTAF], 2010). This high turnover has contributed to a growing teacher shortage, especially in schools that disproportionately serve low-income and minority children.[22] Chapter 7 shows how recent reforms have exac-erbated these issues.

Third, teacher effectiveness—like student test scores—is quanti-fied in normative terms (i.e., above average and below average when compared to a mean). Again, this means that there will always be some teachers who appear to be less effective simply because—by statistical design—they fall on the wrong side of the bell curve. Respondents argued that most ineffective teachers voluntarily exit early in their careers; those who fall on the wrong side of the bell curve may therefore be relatively less effective but still good teachers who may eventually become great ones. They are also more likely to be new or more innovative because it takes anywhere from three to five years to become consistently effective; the most innovative teachers are often given the most difficult students; and effective innovations require the willingness to take risks that may not pay off in the short-term. Kathy, a suburban elementary teacher, stated,

I would say that it took me the first three years to become really profi-cient in terms of classroom control. . . . You are always learning . . . but you definitely need that base in terms of classroom control and then . . . [you continue] tinkering with it. In terms of methods, content, and presentation, I'm still learning, and that is the way it should be. . . . You need to constantly grow and take risks . . . or you will get stale, which is bad for . . . a professional but incredibly bad for the children. You need to bring that excitement that comes with learning new things into the classroom all the time or else it is stifling for the kids.

The myth that only teachers matter reportedly resulted in policies that discouraged risk taking and penalized new teachers who were learning the ropes. Chapter 7 addresses this claim.

Standardized testing is a neutral way to assess performance. Informants contested policy makers' portrayal of testing as a "neutral" way to evaluate schools, educators, and students. They argued, and research supports, that *all* assessment regimes overtly and implicitly codify knowledge, skills, and behaviors that are unevenly distributed across social classes and groups. They do so to rate and rank.[23] Research shows, for instance that boys tend to do better on standardized math tests while girls do better in reading. A recent study suggests that the test format is partly to blame. Boys outperform girls on state tests that rely more heavily on multiple-choice questions—a common way to assess math knowledge—while girls outperform boys on tests where a larger proportion of the total score is determined by constructed response questions, where students write their own answers in a sentence or an essay. These differences explained about 25 percent of the variation in gender achievement gaps between states (Reardon et al., 2018). Parts III and IV elaborate on other ways that testing, and therefore recent reforms, institutionalizes the effects of class, race, ethnicity, and gender on school, educator, and student performance.

Learning is a rational process. Educators further questioned the portrayal of learning as an individualized and linear process that occurs mostly through memorization and imitation. Valerie, a retired suburban special education teacher and supervisor, conveyed these ideas in her discussion of why public schools cannot be run like a business:

[We could never treat] educating human beings the same as the business of producing a Ford on an assembly line. . . . You want . . . every Ford . . . to be exactly alike . . . [so] the raw materials . . . have to be the same . . . [and put] together in exactly the same way. . . . Children . . . come to school from very different places and with very different abilities. The range of normal is *huge*: socially, physically, cognitively, developmentally, and so forth. And that is . . . without even looking at their environments . . . [which] are *drastically* different, and so kids come to school with *totally* different experiences. . . . The end result is that . . . you have 30 *very* different raw materials . . . one way . . . is not going to meet all of those children's needs. . . . There are research-based practices that, when used, will meet most children's needs. . . . We should be using those . . . while always recognizing . . . some children, even . . . without special education needs, are going to need accommodations. . . . Children rarely learn on an inclined plane. There are drops, plateaus, huge spikes . . . their interests change too . . . [so] even with one . . . child, you may need to change how you teach.

Chapters 5, 6, 7, and 9 show how the relational, contingent, and nonlinear aspects of learning make it difficult to standardize teaching and create issues with high stakes testing (vs. the previous use of testing to gauge student performance).

Teaching is a technical enterprise. The aforementioned myths about learning are important for another reason; they reportedly resulted in policy makers (inappropriately) characterizing teaching as a technical enterprise where knowledge is taught in specified ways and demonstrated at prescribed moments in time. Certainly teaching involves technical skills, but educators portrayed it as an art and a profession more than a science or a technology (see Chapter 5). Returning to Katy's narrative,

[it's an] art. You have to find a way to get to each child . . . be entertaining to get their attention and get your point across . . . a profession. . . . You have to keep up with your training . . . keep improving your skills . . . act like a professional . . . [not] punch in and out like a job . . . do whatever it takes to get the work done . . . policing yourself . . . because intrinsically it is what you believe needs to be done. . . . Every day . . . and every child . . . [is] different, and so you are constantly engaging your brain and your skills to do the job.

Per respondents, the characterization of teaching as a technical occupation has had four negative repercussions: It treats children like a "product" that can be shaped and molded by standardizing content and pedagogy in the same way that the assembly line standardizes the production of automobiles; it fosters a belief among policy makers and citizens that teachers should be able to accomplish more than they already do; it opens up education reform to those who have no training; and, it results in waves of reform that are based on current events or emotion more than research, data, or factual analysis.

Educators described such reforms as "fads and fetishes." They are based on a belief that it is possible to quickly and easily accomplish meaningful reform. When that does not occur, it leads to disillusionment (see also Cuban, 2010; Payne, 2010; Ravitch, 2010). A retired suburban elementary teacher, Sophia, decried,

> There are a lot of fads. . . . [There was a] huge movement . . . open classrooms . . . tearing down walls. . . . My school sent me and some other teachers to observe . . . "Look around, everyone is learning!" . . . that was *so* not the case [*laughing*]. . . . A lot of these ideas come from people who . . . did really well . . . were self-motivated but that is not the case with the majority. . . . They need to be engaged by the teacher . . . will try to get away with something or do the least amount of work [*laughing*]. It is a human thing. . . . Children do want to learn but they need . . . that back and forth that produces learning. . . . The open classroom model came and went. . . . [Now, we have inclusion, which I support]. . . . "Don't worry, you will have aides." . . . [But] children . . . want the attention of the teacher. . . . Class size . . . don't worry . . . you have an aide. . . . You cannot tell a seven- or eight-year-old "wait, wait!" when they have a question. . . . [It squashes] their natural exuberance for learning. It is a horrible thing to do to a child.

Almost every educator conveyed that most people, because they went to school, believe that "teaching is easy" and that "anyone can do it." In reality, the production of educational outcomes is complex. As mentioned, education is coproduced; schools, as organizations and public institutions, have multiple goals; and principals and teachers perform a variety of tasks, many of which cannot be measured (Koretz, 2002). Educators are further affected by a variety of district, state, and federal mandates. They need to balance these mandates with the needs of individual students and the common good. These realities mean real reform takes time and must address the external factors that affect student performance.

Myths about teachers' unions, tenure, seniority, and teacher evaluations. In Chapters 4 and 5, teachers describe how they were forced by historical circumstances to adopt business unionism as a way to influence their organizational environments; discuss how collective bargaining improved teachers' working conditions, salaries, and benefits; and elaborate on the resulting societal benefits. Their words show how collective bargaining (economic voice) increases both political voice (lobbying and campaigning) *and* professional voice (formal and informal protests on behalf of children, parents, and colleagues or in defense of occupational norms, knowledge, and practices). A majority—but especially those in their forties or older—expressed a belief that conservative political and business-economic interests have perpetuated myths and distortions about unions as a way to silence voice and regain control over education.

Business unionism harms society. One myth is that unions protect teachers at the expense of society and the power of union leaders at the expense of members and non-members alike. A handful of teachers acknowledged that union leaders have sometimes been resistant to change and/or too focused on salaries, benefits, and other aspects of teachers' contracts.[24] Like their colleagues, however, most of these participants said that this is not a concern because school districts and elected school boards retain most of the power in collective bargaining. This and other research supports that claim (see Chapters 4 and 5). It further shows that union presidents have moved away from industrial-style bargaining to find win-win solutions with school districts (Moore et al., 2007); unions are roughly in line with members' views on issues such as teacher evaluations, salaries, and benefits (Bill & Melinda Gates Foundation, 2010); and unions help teachers improve public education—not just salaries and benefits (see Chapter 4). They do so by fighting for education reforms and other policies that help children and families, as well as by voicing against racism, segregation, an exploitative economy, and socioeconomic inequality (L. Weiner, 2012).

Participants in this study framed the "real issue" as too much business power—not excessive union demands. The United States today has one of the lowest rates of unionization in the industrialized world, socioeconomic inequality has grown as union membership has declined, and nations that outperform American students on international tests (e.g., PISA) have strong teachers' unions. Liam continued,

> [The] demand for unions and public employees to take concessions is . . . a means of taxing public employees. . . . Then they want to take away the right to collective bargain . . . that is taxation without representation [*laughs*]. . . . Teachers, firemen, policemen have pensions and union protection and many others do not . . . 7 percent of the private sector is organized . . . 20 percent of the public sector. . . . There is a ready-made base of resentment . . . a clever politician can use . . . [say] aggressive unions . . . are responsible for the economic crisis . . . to avoid

raising the revenues necessary to support public services. . . . But this is . . . hidden taxes on the earned income of public employees . . . to fund existing public programs. . . . [I am] disappointed with the failure of the Democratic mainstream to . . . aid . . . unions. . . . I thought we would have had a commonsense discussion like "Only 7 percent of the private sector is unionized. How can unions be responsible for economic insecurity? Why are you so threatened by unions? . . . How can they be breaking your bank?"

Research supports that there is a correlation between unionization and socioeconomic equality and between unionization and improved educational performance. Union density benefits working- and middle-class Americans even when they are not members of a union (see Chapters 4 and 11).

RTW laws also provide a natural experiment for examining participants' claims that unions do not harm the economy or kill jobs. As discussed in Chapter 1, these laws allow employees to benefit from union contracts—including the right to union representation in a grievance against their employer—without paying dues; they have contributed to a steep decline in private sector union membership and are now the law of the land for public employees as a result of the Supreme Court's decision in *Janus*. Policy makers claimed RTW laws would increase job growth and income. Unions argued that the ability of some employees to benefit from collective bargaining without paying their fair share of the costs of negotiating and enforcing those agreements (free riding) would reduce union membership; make it harder for unions to sustain themselves financially; undermine union bargaining strength; and reduce wages and benefits for *all* workers, as growing numbers of nonunionized employers put pressure on unionized employers to compete by reducing labor costs. Research supports the claims of unions (see Chapters 1 and 11).

More specifically, many states—especially in the South—have already adopted RTW laws. Others recently considered and either adopted (Indiana) or failed to adopt (New Hampshire) these laws. This uneven adoption is a natural experiment for how unions affect workers and society. Research supports that wages for union *and* nonunion members are 3.2 percent lower, on average, in RTW states; RTW laws reduced access to health insurance and pensions; and the recent adoption of an RTW law (Indiana) did not create jobs or decrease unemployment. Just as interesting, every state has lost manufacturing jobs due to cheaper labor overseas since the adoption of the North American Free Trade Agreement (NAFTA) in 1994, but

RTW states all lost a higher share of their manufacturing sector than New Hampshire, which did not adopt RTW.[25]

Teachers' unions protect incompetent teachers. Chapter 4 shows that tenure and seniority for the most part do not protect incompetent teachers. These policies were actually adopted to increase the efficiency and effectiveness of public schools but resulted in the unintended side effect of improving teacher retention and professionalism. They did so by encouraging voice on behalf of parents, students, colleagues, and the norms of teaching. An elementary teacher, Meagan, explained,

> In part, it was to protect people who may have had the "wrong" political views or . . . [gave] a grade that a parent with influence did not like. In these cases, teachers were dismissed without cause. . . . [Tenure allows] a teacher to do the job . . . in a manner that is consistent with their professional norms. . . . Sometimes you need to single out a child . . . treat them differently to best serve that child, but mostly teachers need to . . . treat all children the same as much as possible. . . . You are dealing with other people's children . . . *in loco parentis*. . . . Tenure protects you against things that could be . . . misconstrued . . . blown out of proportion. . . . Sometimes parents . . . [cannot] be neutral observers . . . administrators may ask teachers to go against . . . the best interests of a child . . . think about the bottom line. . . . [Teachers could be] forced to do things because emotions and money are involved.[26]

Prior to the adoption of these policies, teachers were dismissed because of their political views, the capricious decisions of administrators, their racial background or sexual orientation, and to avoid paying higher salaries as they gained more years of experience. Many were forced to go against the norms of teaching to retain their jobs (see Chapters 4 and 5).

Respondents said that school districts have always been able to fire teachers, but more than half acknowledged that some administrators may not be doing the work to build a case against ineffective ones. Don, a suburban high school social studies teacher, admitted,

> [We've] had bad teachers . . . told administrators not to give them tenure and they [do]. . . . It hurts the reputation of the department . . . the school . . . reflects poorly on all teachers. . . . One bad situation can really turn a student off . . . become anti-education. . . . Some . . . teach bigger classes because this teacher can't handle behavioral problems. Nobody wants

to be in Johnny's class. . . . Then people get mad at tenure. . . . No one is against reform . . . [or] getting rid of crappy teachers. . . . Due process is there for a reason. . . . Make sure . . . someone who gets tenure is a damn good teacher because . . . they'll continue to be a good teacher.

Some claimed that principals hoped these ineffective teachers would leave or that fellow teachers would encourage them to do so. Others said that some principals want to avoid the "paperwork."

Despite these claims, my interviews suggest that these are minor issues. Ineffective teachers typically exit early in their careers because the occupation is so stressful, especially for those who are less successful. In addition, studies support participants' claims that those who choose teaching possess a service ethic and are called to work with children.[27] Administrators typically share these values because most are former teachers. The calling to serve ensures that most administrators want to remove ineffective teachers and that most teachers will monitor their colleagues to ensure that they do not reflect negatively on the profession and their schools.[28] Sometimes this involves using their social ties to encourage ineffective colleagues to leave, but teachers are involved in hiring decisions in many schools and in evaluating their peers in some schools. Interestingly, administrators told me that teachers in these cases are actually stricter in terms of hiring, firing, and tenure decisions, and one administrator and one union president professed that more teachers were dismissed or required to seek professional development under these arrangements. These claims are fleshed out in Chapters 5 and 11.

On a less positive note, educators acknowledged that the teaching workforce is not distributed evenly. High-need, low-resource schools have historically struggled with turnover and a shortage of applicants. Principals in these schools also have less time to oversee teachers because of a lack of resources and an abundance of socioeconomic issues. According to some, these realities can result in ineffective teachers being transferred within the district rather than being fired. Still, as articulated by an urban eighth-grade English teacher (Stephanie), this is not a major issue:

Tenure is a system of due process. . . . The principal has to . . . go in and document. . . . In an urban district . . . some things are not confronted because all of the crises . . . like a lockdown in your building because somebody was shooting outside. . . . The "dances of the lemons" [*Waiting for Superman,* dir. Davis Guggenheim, 2010] is easier. . . . This is not making excuses . . . but there's a different reality. . . . Do I think urban schools have bad teachers? No, I think there are some bad teachers in all types of districts. But it's not a major problem like they're claiming. I also think that there are some bad professionals in every profession.[29]

Principals and teachers both said that the best way to protect against ineffective teachers is to ensure a steady supply of effective ones and to appoint administrators—especially principals—from a pool of knowledgeable and experienced teachers. As discussed in Chapter 7, however, recent discourse and policies have discouraged young people from entering the profession, encouraged effective teachers to leave, and resulted in some districts—especially urban ones—hiring administrators with little or no teaching experience.

Traditional teacher evaluation systems are inadequate. Educators did not dispute that there are issues with traditional methods of evaluating teachers—such as principal observations, portfolios, and professional development plans. They took issue with the claim that observations are subjective but "numbers" (test scores) objectively distinguish strong from weak teachers. Chapter 6 explains why standardized tests—including student growth models (VAMs)—are not an objective, accurate, or fair way to evaluate school and educator performance. The point here is that most respondents expressed a belief that this misperception was perpetuated by "outside groups" (e.g., think tanks, private foundations, corporate-funded research at universities and colleges) as a way to support recent reforms, including closing "failed" public schools and eliminating tenure and seniority by forcing school districts to use student test scores for decisions about dismissal and promotion. States like Florida, where teacher contracts are now renewed annually based on performance, support their claim (NCTAF, 2011).

Until now, I have described the role of policy makers and business-economic interests in the construction of recent education reforms, but (mostly) not elaborated on the involvement of the media and entertainment industry. That role is described separately in the next section because some respondents included that group in their definition of political elites and others either framed them as business-economic elites or as part of a business–economic–political complex.

The Media and Entertainment Industry: Moral Entrepreneurs and Education Reform

As mentioned, research shows that public policies and discourse create socially constructed identities for citizens and policy implementers; however, historical custom, popular culture, advertising, and the media and entertainment industry (written and spoken news, movies, magazines, television shows, video games, and so forth) also play a role. These moral entrepreneurs craft, perpetuate, and change social constructions by stereotyping and typifying the behaviors of individuals or groups. Once institutionalized through public policies, these narratives take on the power of the state and shape individual beliefs and actions (H. Ingram & Schneider, 2005; Stone, 2005). Respondents discussed two ways that the media and entertainment industry motivated and shaped the adoption of recent education reforms: influencing public opinion and influencing popular culture.

Influencing public opinion. According to the vast majority of informants, the media and entertainment industry helped policy makers and business-economic interests create positive feedback for an accountability regime by blaming educators and public schools for declining economic competitiveness, portraying educators as incompetent, claiming that teachers and their unions care more about salaries and benefits than the welfare of children, and alleging that competition would ensure public schools and public school educators "do right by the kids." The complaint that public school teachers are mostly portrayed as incompetent and self-interested was widespread but more prevalent among urban teachers.

Urban educators were also more likely to argue that the media and entertainment industry "mythologizes" them in ways that suggest "only teachers matter." This lets the rest of society off the hook. Stephanie, from whom we heard earlier, pronounced,

> [*Waiting for Superman* is] very misguided. . . . I used to love movies like *Dangerous Minds* [dir. John N. Smith, 1995] and *Freedom Writers* [dir. Richard LaGravenese, 2007]. . . . These movies inspired me to teach in urban schools. . . . Jonathan Kozol . . . pointed it out. . . . Society's art, like these movies, is a *reflection of* the way that society sees us but also *influences* the way . . . society sees us . . . presenting us like we can solve the world's ills just by being good teachers. . . . [This] does my students a disservice because . . . it's a myth . . . people buy and even teachers get sucked into it. But then it lets everyone else off the hook. . . . If you are not doing what Erin Gruwell [from *Freedom Writers*]

did, then there is something wrong with you. But the truth is, that is a Hollywood version.

Over time, these negative portrayals influenced public opinion and helped policy makers justify the MMP as the best way to resolve the crisis.

The majority of informants also claimed that the media and entertainment industry inappropriately characterizes research in ways that appear to support providing more public funding for school choice, such as downgrading negative findings about charter schools and expanding positive findings beyond what the research suggests. They compared this reporting to what they perceive to be the mostly negative portrayals of public schools and public school teachers. Studies support this view.[30] Many also pointed to articles like the one in the *Los Angeles Times* that published student test scores to "out" supposedly "bad teachers," which led to one teacher committing suicide (Lovett, 2010). By failing to discuss widespread, research-based academic concerns about using value-added models (VAMs) to evaluate teachers (see Chapters 6 and 7), these stories imply that unions oppose test-based accountability for "self-interested" reasons, or outright accuse them of doing so.

Stephanie's narrative demonstrates the third common example. These participants said recent movies and documentaries normalized a business-economic agenda by hiding how it benefits the private sector while radically reinventing public education. They cited many movies and documentaries, such as *The Lottery* (dir. Madeleine Sackler, 2010) and *The Cartel* (dir. Bob Bowdon, 2009), yet most frequently used the 2010 documentary *Waiting for Superman* (dir. David Guggenheim, 2010) to support these claims.

Directed by David Guggenheim, *Waiting for Superman* follows five American children as they seek entry to a charter school through the lottery system.[31] Respondents said its broader message was that we need to privatize public education to promote equity and America's ability to compete economically. Privatization in the movie does not solely engender school choice and competition from charter schools; it also involves eliminating tenure and seniority to force teachers to compete for good evaluations. The movie suggests that these market reforms will help children in general and minority children in particular by forcing teachers and public schools to "do right by the kids."

As compared to this supposedly commonsense logic, informants claimed the "real" beneficiaries of these reforms are the charter school movement and its corporate backers. The clearest losers are public education and the vast majority of students whose schools will lose funding and effective teachers as a result of public tax dollars being diverted to charter schools and growing teacher shortages. Returning to Carley's narrative,

> [Why] should anyone have to wait for Superman? Why not adequately fund the public school system? Why do we need to privatize it to improve it? We are asking the wrong questions to get the answers that we want to hear, and they are self-serving answers. They help those who are asking the question in a way to get the answer they want. Instead of asking the hard questions, they want to burn and churn teachers.

In Chapter 2, I showed how policy makers mobilized bias in favor of an accountability regime. Here, respondents were conveying that the film distorts data and presents information in ways that mobilize bias in favor of its preferred (market) reforms.

One way the movie bolsters market reforms is by largely relying on interviews with charter school founders, their corporate backers, and public figures who are well known for advocating merit pay, restricting collective bargaining, and privatizing education through vouchers and charter schools.[32] Throughout the film, these actors and charter school teachers are portrayed as unsung heroes: They set high expectations and use their time and resources to push failing public schools and recalcitrant teachers' unions to "do right by the kids." In comparison, union leaders and public school teachers are largely ignored, given abbreviated interviews, or shown protesting reform.[33]

The film also mobilizes bias through what information is left out. Some informants mentioned how charter schools often have smaller classes, a longer school year, and Saturday classes—all of which provide teachers with more instructional time. They also typically siphon off the most motivated students (see Chapters 9 and 10). For instance, the Harlem Children's Zone—mentioned in the film—includes agencies that provide a wide variety of social services to students and families as a way to bolster academic achievement. Even so, Jeffrey Canada kicked out his entire first class of middle school students because their test scores were too low (Tough, 2009). Per respondents, public schools would also improve if they had more resources and "counseled out" students with academic, behavioral, and emotional issues. A suburban elementary teacher, Veronica, said,

> [Students] put their names into the lottery. Those parents are active. . . .
> And, they have rules in those schools that, if the child is not doing well,
> they can kick the child out because there is always somebody on the list
> that can take that child's place. We can't do that. . . . So, of course they
> would have good test scores . . . public schools serve everyone.[34]

Guggenheim also fails to discuss how market actors hope to profit
from the money that investors have poured into charter schools and
how a network of charter schools, venture capitalists, and (neoliberal
and neoconservative) thinks tanks have influenced political leaders at
all levels—through campaign contributions and by funding advocacy
research—to adopt policies that close public schools while expanding
charter schools (see also Burch, 2008; Scott, 2009).

Just as problematically, Guggenheim provides no examples of
successful public schools or dedicated public school teachers. Instead,
he shows "the dances of the lemons," where principals trade ineffective teachers; they supposedly cannot fire them because tenure,
unions, and the evaluation system protect "bad teachers." Some
participants further complained that he does not interview any charter school teachers who support unions. The impression is that charter schools outperform public schools because they are not weighed
down with bureaucratic rules and red tape as a result of unions.
Meanwhile, teachers in one of the charter school networks that he
praises, Green Dot Schools, and in Finland, which he eulogizes, are
unionized, granted tenure, and play a strong role in collective decision making and school leadership. Just as importantly, schools in
Finland are much more homogeneous; there is less socioeconomic
inequality; school financing is not highly unequal—like it is in the
United States—and citizens are provided with universal access to
social supports, such as day care, preschool, and health care. All of
these affect student performance.[35]

Some also noticed the lack of information about the "failed public
schools" that are supposedly the focus of the film. In consequence,
there is no counternarrative to the proposed solutions: closing "failing schools," firing ineffective teachers, and creating more charter
schools. Molly, from whom we heard earlier, exclaimed,

> I think the movie had a certain idea of what policies it wanted adopted
> and then it structured everything to fit those policies. The so-called
> educational experts were all people who supported those policies, like
> charter schools and eliminating tenure. Many . . . are also the people who
> will benefit from expanding charter schools, which is very self-serving. . . .

> You don't really hear from public school teachers . . . what they think the problems are and how . . . we should resolve them. They don't address societal issues at all . . . like socioeconomic inequality, poverty, hunger, and so forth. It really places all the blame on unions for protecting bad teachers. . . . If they could just get rid of bad teachers and expand the number of charter schools, then everything would be great. They ignore the fact that some charter schools have unions and many of the countries they say we can't compete with have strong teachers' unions too. It was just very biased.

In addition, Guggenheim does not discuss how many families lack the ability to enter the lottery or send their children to a charter school, whether that is because they are working two jobs—and therefore lack the time to do so—or lack transportation. A handful of teachers also said we do not hear from the vast majority of Americans who believe that their children's schools are doing a good job.

According to those I interviewed, these biases resulted in a one-sided presentation of the problem *and* the appropriate political solutions. Money is not the problem; Americans spend more per student yet lag behind their international counterparts. The weak economy, globalization, deindustrialization, popular culture, growing socioeconomic inequality, and rising poverty in general and among children specifically are also not the issue. The "real" problem is that American students are unmotivated because there are too many ineffective teachers. The "appropriate" response is therefore to fire bad teachers and penalize failing public schools by closing them and funding charter school transfers. Participants said that these solutions are contrary to what many other highly performing nations have done, such as redressing poverty, hunger, homelessness, and socioeconomic inequality and attracting and retaining HQTs by raising salaries, improving working conditions, funding college, and providing mentoring. Most also noted that America must redress the inequitable financing of public schools and recruit administrators from a pool of highly experienced teachers—rather than retired businessmen, as promoted in debates on NCLB—if it hopes to compete with these nations (see Chapters 2 and 11).

Influencing popular culture and shaping the behaviors of citizen coproducers. The second way the media and entertainment industry generated positive feedback for an accountability regime was by shaping popular culture in ways that reduced public school performance, thereby stimulating demands for education reform. The negative portrayal of authority figures and the glamorization of

violence, drugs, and gangs reduces academic performance by fostering social and behavioral issues (e.g., skipping school and reducing
work effort). Movies, television, music, and video games also impede
learning by glorifying the consumer culture and reducing children's
willingness and ability to focus, work hard, and persevere.

Video games, for instance, reportedly alter children's brains in
ways that have increased diagnoses that affect learning (e.g., learning
disabilities). This is especially true for boys, who spend more time
playing these games, and may be one contributor to the growing
male gender gap across a wide array of educational behaviors and
outcomes, such as grades, disciplinary infractions, college attendance, and high school and college graduation rates. Respondents
pointed to the fact that American colleges and universities now
enroll roughly six women for every four men (see Chapter 11). Like
the consumer culture at large, these games hinder the development
of needed socioemotional and other so-called soft skills that help
students do well in school and life. They do so by creating an artificial world that is fast paced, revolves around children, and is full
of visual and auditory stimulation—one where individual wants are
immediately satisfied but new wants are constantly developed.

The combination of these issues has fostered a decline in empathy
and leadership skills; it has also reduced students' willingness and
capacity to individually persevere and collectively work together to
achieve common ends. Carley, from whom we heard earlier, stated,

> [We] were outside playing and organizing our own activities. . . . [It]
> taught us a lot of lessons and life skills . . . how to problem solve . . .
> leadership skills . . . get along with others . . . work together as a group.
> They don't do that anymore, so kids can't problem solve in a group. . . .
> [They] look to adults to do it for them. . . . With the consumer culture,
> kids get everything the moment they want it. . . . Parents are using tech-
> nology and TV to babysit . . . not talking to their kids and being available
> emotionally. . . . Everything on TV and video games happens so quickly
> . . . a lot of visual and auditory stimulation. So, kids get bored easily . . .
> [are] more aggressive because they don't play and are not learning those
> socioemotional skills . . . don't know how to work together collectively. . . .
> It does affect our public life.

Informants expressed a belief that two long-term effects on society
are a decline in communal values and a reduced tolerance of diverse
opinions and needs.[36]

It is important to note that respondents did not blame children or privilege the media and entertainment industry in their discussion of the decline in communal values. Like Liam below, they argued that policy makers encouraged and exacerbated this development through public discourse and policies:

[There has been] an erosion of community values. . . . Part of it began with Reagan. . . . He did an awful lot to destroy the idea of community, which was never his intention, because he overemphasized the individual . . . government is not the solution. It is the problem. He provided . . . the jargon and the ideology . . . to attack all forms of government . . . suddenly, it is not our government and our community. . . . We were funding them and they were taking my money . . . like you got no benefits from it. . . . He opened the door . . . to draw on the simmering public anger with the economy . . . to get rid of the burden of government . . . unions . . . welfare. . . . Even an intelligent guy like [Paul] Ryan . . . is a big follower of Ayn Rand . . . the individual's right to be . . . totally independent of any form of society . . . if you get rid of government . . . we will have this blossoming of wealth because the individual will be free of any constraints. But, if you study history, this is just not true. . . . The Industrial Revolution, where gradually the community had to reassert itself to prevent Social Darwinism from taking over . . . the law of the jungle . . . [individuals claw] their way to the top . . . everything from poverty to mental illness is your own fault. . . . They are great fans of Rand but they don't understand Emerson's . . . more noble American version of individualism . . . [that] says "I don't care where he comes from or what his first language is, he is going to rise because . . . a public school system that guarantees a quality education and a ladder up." . . . The fundamental concept behind public education is that a person is not free if they have no choices . . . are hemmed in by poverty or . . . a lack of education. . . . [Now] every hand up is a hand out . . . to people who are too lazy to get a job.

As mentioned, that rhetoric created what some have referred to as a "*consumerocracy*"—where public services are evaluated based on how well they serve individual wants versus collective ends; it "trickled down" in ways that negatively affected the quality of public services by reducing the willingness of citizens to work together to promote the common good.

Parts three and four of the book show how declining cooperation negatively affects the efficiency, effectiveness, and fairness of public goods and services, like education. The point informants were making is that the resulting declines in public school performance—as well as the perceived effects of those declines on the economy—were then blamed on educators and used to justify accountability reforms.

Discussion: Symbolic Violence and Political Behaviors

Stone (1997) argues that policy makers need to construct a new narrative to sell political, social, and/or economic reform. This chapter discussed informants' perception that policy makers, business-economic interests, and the media and entertainment industry advanced the MMP by blaming public schools and educators for declining economic competitiveness. The goal was to improve public school efficiency and effectiveness, but educators described how the resulting policies actually impeded educational performance. In part, this was due to how the *market forms of social control* (e.g., competition and choice) interacted with schools as communities to alter the behaviors of educators (Chapters 6 and 7); however, recent discourse and reforms also reportedly polarized public schools and encouraged citizens to blame educators, vote down school budgets, and exit public schools rather than work together to solve collective problems (Chapter 9).

The vast majority of respondents conveyed that negative rhetoric about the government, public servants, and public programs has reduced the quality of *public services in general* by reducing citizens' willingness to contribute to the common good. Jess, a suburban elementary teacher, declared,

> [They're] always telling us that government is the bogeyman. . . . After decades . . . people believe it . . . are more cynical . . . less inclined to participate. . . . I largely mean conservatives but it has spread across parties . . . [it] gets votes. . . . Public servants . . . make a nice target. . . . The reason you can't get a job . . . [The reason] taxes are too high . . . teachers, firemen, policemen. . . . No one goes into these . . . to get rich. . . . You would *never* hear elected officials denigrate our men and women in the service, and they shouldn't. God bless them for the service. . . . But we serve our country too. The military protects us from external threats . . . policemen from internal threats, but teachers, firemen, nurses . . . bureaucrats, also serve. . . . They may be the force but we're the hearts and hands . . . we go beyond the call of duty . . . [like] the military. . . . It's easiest to see . . . during . . . crises . . . teachers . . . throwing their bodies in front of shooters or during 9/11 carrying children on their backs to . . . safety. . . . [But we] do the extraordinary . . .

through the ordinary. . . . [We develop] human beings. . . . We deserve respect . . . not to be called "thugs" [citing Sarah Palin] because we voice.

Three claims, though, topped the list for how the MMP and the resulting "consumerocracy" impeded *public school performance* by focusing on individual rights (freedom from the government) at the expense of collective responsibilities.

First, the MMP degraded our inclination—as a society—to tax ourselves to provide public goods and services, like education. Returning to Paul's narrative,

> [It] was not normal for people to complain about . . . school taxes. People generally believed . . . education was how we as a society advanced. . . . This was true of . . . elderly people . . . people who never had kids . . . [taxes] were an investment in their community . . . [You] wouldn't see someone going to a board meeting and questioning why their taxes were paying for special needs students . . . [to] have more money for the gifted and talented . . . voting down the budget for school sports because their child was not an athlete. You see things like this all the time. . . . It is much more individualistic . . . "what's in it for me." . . . It has harmed us collectively, which harms us individually. My parents were poor . . . [never complained] about paying taxes . . . felt they had duties that went along with the privilege of being Americans . . . thought in terms that were larger than their individual selves.

Paul is discussing school taxes and budgets, but informants mentioned how decades of anti-government rhetoric increased support for politicians who promise to reduce taxes at all levels of government. This has forced public schools in general to do more with less, yet is especially harmful for the performance of schools in high-need, low-resource communities that rely on national and state funding (see Part IV).

Second, public discourse justified reforms that fostered an abandonment of the public sphere in favor of private alternatives. As evident in Paul's narrative, it also encouraged parents to use their social and cultural capital to demand special programs for their own children but, in doing so, unknowingly or consciously reduced revenues for "other people's children." Such behaviors tend to privilege those with economic capital because they are more vocal and less dependent on public services. Diane, a suburban elementary teacher, explained,

> They're taking away music and art . . . [and after-school programs]. People don't care as long as "my kid" is okay. . . . I can afford to have my kid play on a private team. . . . What about that really talented kid whose parents don't have the money . . . maybe their kid is talented but the poor kids are going to lose every time once they hit high school and beyond because their parents couldn't afford to give them those opportunities.

These developments reportedly reduced the performance of public schools by decreasing social cohesion, social trust, and the willingness to tolerate differences and help one another (see Part IV).

Third, recent reforms and discourse fostered growing teacher shortages through a combination of increased turnover and reduced entry into the profession. Some were *ethical* leavers—they left to protest the violation of the moral imperative that any reform intervention must "first do no harm." Others left as Americans' declining trust in fellow citizens, educators, and public schools made their jobs more difficult by, for example, reducing cooperation from parents and encouraging cuts in school budgets (see Part III).[37]

Research and public opinion polls mostly support these claims. Support for public education has actually remained generally stable for the past 20 years, with most Americans expressing high trust and confidence in educators (61%) and continuing to rank too little funding as the biggest issue facing public schools (PDK, 2000–2018). Yet research and public opinion polls confirm that trust in government and fellow citizens has been declining since the 1980s, when the gap between the rich and the poor began to expand, as growing numbers of citizens felt shut out of the American dream and lost their sense of a shared fate. Americans, like educators, also mostly blame these developments on public discourse and policies and worry that declining trust is negatively affecting our public life (Cass, 2013; Rainie et al., 2019; Uslaner, 2010, 2012).

According to a recent poll (Rainie et al., 2019), two-thirds of Americans believe that interpersonal trust has worsened in the last 20 years (71%) and that low interpersonal trust makes it harder to solve the country's problems (70%). In an open-ended question, those who believe that there has been a decline in interpersonal trust were asked to name some major reasons for this development. By far, the most commonly cited explanation was unredressed social ills and policy problems (43%), but some other reasons include political polarization and gridlock (16%); the performance of the news media (biased reporting, one-sided coverage, disinformation, and misinformation; 11%); technology, the internet, and social media

(12%); the performance of Trump and Republicans (4%); the performance of Democrats (2%); and the rise of extremism and hate (1%). Research further documents growing teaching shortages, due to high turnover and low entry into the profession, and opinion polls show that most Americans (54%) do not want their children to become teachers—the highest rating since 1969—because of low pay, negative student behaviors, low status (lack of respect and autonomy), and a belief that teachers are overworked.[38]

Studies also support that policy makers and the media and entertainment industry eroded American's willingness to invest in public schools and created demands for accountability reforms by blaming schools and educators for declining economic performance (e.g., Berliner & Biddle, 1996; Morgan & Poppe, 2012). Research finds that a civic-oriented public discourse leverages more community support for public schools than one that focuses on children and parents as consumers. The resulting civic engagement helps communities resolve a range of collective action problems, including the willingness to tax ourselves to provide public education. The framing of education as a public good was especially critical for America's historical commitment to a broader vision of public education, including the common school movement and the construction of high schools and community colleges—even though, at the time, very few expected to benefit from the latter (Glaser et al., 2002; Goldin & Katz, 1999).

Finally, studies verify educators' claim that recent reforms failed to close the achievement gap. Race-based gaps have (somewhat) narrowed over the past several decades, but those gains resulted from federal antipoverty and desegregation policies rather than from accountability reforms. In the meantime, income-based gaps have increased as a result of growing numbers of children living in poverty.[39]

My interviews suggest that the discrepancy between some opinion polls and educators' perceptions relates to generic public opinion versus their experiences with how public discourse and policies influence beliefs and behaviors in their districts. Diane continued

> [These] think tanks . . . doing all of the research, and the publishing
> . . . [and] test making companies are making money off of all of this. . . .
> We are being blamed and scapegoated, like we're wasting public money.
> Politicians . . . talking about how it is the taxpayer's money and how we
> use it unnecessarily. They rile up the taxpayer . . . to get elected . . . it
> has real consequences in terms of how people *feel* about public schools

and teachers . . . and these feelings they create have real implications [for public schools].

Like public opinion polls, educators expressed that most parents are supportive of teachers and public schools; however, a small increase in aggressive voice at the national level may appear quite large or threatening at the local level, depending on where educators work. It also has a tendency to spread more quickly at the local level (see Chapter 9)—especially if it is being fostered and magnified by national- and state-level political and/or economic actors to win elections, influence policy, or earn ratings and advertising dollars.

As a whole, this book shows that words matter. There is a powerful connection between talk and action, words and deeds. In education, rhetoric about the need for more personal responsibility to fix inefficient and ineffective public schools resulted in a movement away from the federal equity regime, which was characterized by the commitment to level the playing field through the infusion of federal resources to schools that served large numbers of low-income children (Title I). Under the accountability regime, the primary role of the federal government is to ensure local schools teach basic skills by holding schools, educators, and students accountable for test scores.

Conclusion

Chapter 2 showed how policy makers supported market-based accountability policies by magnifying policy feedback from some and suppressing it from others. In this chapter, educators discussed the theory of action (Stone, 1989) behind these reforms. Both public *and* charter school educators expressed bafflement at the portrayal of public schools and public school teachers as a "Goliath" that steals society's tax dollars while characterizing the private sector as a "David" that serves the public realm by protecting citizens and disadvantaged children.[40] Both groups instead portrayed public schools and public school educators as allies of society; they level the socioeconomic playing field and promote democracy by shaping children's knowledge, skills, and behaviors, as well as their civic capacities and engagement.

Unlike their private, religious, and charter school counterparts, public schools must accept everyone—no matter the child's race, language, economic status, or disability. Indeed, public schools are one of the primary places where citizens experience people who are not like them and so they are also the primary vehicle for social integration. The next two sections examine the pre- and post-reform environments to explore educators' perceptions of how the MMP and its preferred reforms affected children's educational outcomes and the benefits that are achieved through a strong system of public education.

PART II

Policy Feedback in the Pre–Education Reform Environment

In the last part of the book, I showed how stories, especially the narrative of the mediocre status quo, politically and culturally reconstructed teachers and public schools in ways that justified new forms of regulation and accountability. This section argues that you cannot make educators more accountable without first knowing what accountability (already) looks like, how it is achieved, and at what costs and benefits to society. It explores these questions through interviews with educators *who taught before* and *before and after* the adoption of NCLB and RttT (Appendix C provides a breakdown of participants' backgrounds). Per these respondents, the major form of accountability prior to recent education reforms was a moral or ethical commitment to caring. This *ethos of care* involved going beyond what is formally required at work (i.e., the academic ends of public schools) to develop children as well-rounded and well-adjusted human beings. It also encompassed professional and political voice on behalf of colleagues, students, and parents. Chapter 4 documents the role of policy feedback in the development of this form of professional accountability and then explores how teachers used their professional solidarity to influence subsequent policies. Chapter 5 examines how professional accountability interacts with social contexts to influence teaching, learning, schools as organizations, and public education.

4

Unions, Professional Voice, and Policy Feedback

Research shows that public policies do not simply redress socie-tal issues; they influence citizens' perceptions of their "rights and responsibilities as members of a political community" (Mettler & Soss, 2004, p. 61). Public discourse also plays a role. Civic engagement is not solely a function of individual dispositions, characteristics, or preferences. The state—again, defined as public servants and public institutions (e.g., Congress, public schools, public policies)—shapes the political, social, and economic behaviors of citizens, including, but not limited to, demands for future policies. In this chapter, teachers explain why they began to mobilize politically and econom-ically, the role of the government in that development, and how they used their newly gained political, social, and economic resources to influence subsequent policies (policy feedback).

The State, Collective Action, and Professional Voice

Federal policies after World War II were designed to encourage mass consumption as the primary route to a prosperous and democratic America. For instance, expanded social welfare programs and federal support for collective bargaining raised wages, increased demand for consumptive goods, boosted business growth, and expanded public and private sector employment. By sparking a long period of economic growth and mobility, postwar social programs created an "army of beneficiaries" that had a vested interest in maintaining the status quo, expanding existing programs, and/or blocking those who opposed existing political arrangements, especially those who had been left out of the resulting economic gains (L. Cohen, 2003; Pierson, 1996). Teachers were among the latter (Lortie, 1975). To rectify the situation, they began mobilizing in the 1960s and their organizational resources continued to grow so that, by the 1980s, their unions had become powerful political and economic interest groups. The NEA endorsed a presidential candidate for the first time in 1976, throwing its support behind Democratic hopeful Jimmy Carter. That same year, 291 of the 349 congressional candidates endorsed by the NEA were elected (Merry, 1980; Methvin & Herndon, 1979).

Today, the NEA and AFT send the largest share of delegates to Democratic National Conventions; surveys rank teachers' unions as the most effective interest groups at the state level; and teachers outrank parents, civil rights groups, and religious groups in terms of their perceived influence over local school board elections. Teachers' unions have also been highly successful at influencing state and local policies, including—but not limited to—those that affect the teacher workforce.[1] This chapter shows how the state played an active—albeit mostly unintended—role in these developments. It *contextualizes* policy feedback by describing how historical barriers to collective political, social, and economic action negatively influenced the ability of teachers to exercise voice, how they overcame those barriers, and the role of the state in these developments. I conclude by discussing how teachers used their newly gained political and economic resources to benefit the group and then describing the effects of those actions on teaching as a profession and the performance of public schools. The next chapter explores the broader benefits for society.

Contextualizing Teacher Mobilization

By the 1990s, teachers were considered to be part of the middle class, but retired teachers told me that their working conditions and wages were abysmal during the 1960s and 1970s—both in relation to their level of education and when compared to unionized workers in other fields (see also Lortie, 1975). Paul, a retired suburban elementary and middle school English teacher, and former district union president, illustrates this pervasive claim:

When I started teaching, I had three days a week where I had no time away from students. . . . Zero minutes. . . . I had to take the children to lunch and eat lunch with them, and then . . . the playground . . . [as] part of their physical education. On the other two days, I had one free period because they went to either art or music . . . that was the only time all week. . . . [I had to] do anything that was not teaching, like grading or lesson planning. . . . [If I had to go] to the bathroom . . . I had to send a student . . . to get the principal or the secretary to . . . watch my room. . . . You really didn't go to the bathroom. . . . Our first three children . . . were not covered . . . [by] health insurance. We had . . . to take out a loan to get them out of the hospital. . . . I had a better job . . . in high school. . . . I worked for a baker and we were unionized. If you . . . made it a yearly salary, I would have been paid $5,400 a year [as a baker]. I made $4,200 [as a teacher]. . . . I got a 15 minute break in the morning, a 15 minute break in the afternoon and an hour lunch as a baker, none of which I got as a teacher. . . . We also had no personal days. My retired father had to drive my wife to her doctor's appointments when she was pregnant . . . to the hospital when she was having the baby. . . . It was really an unsustainable system.

Because teachers made so little, most supplemented their salaries with part-time jobs at night and on weekends and with full-time jobs during the summer. Paul, for instance, worked in construction and as a bank teller. The need to supplement their salaries through outside employment ensured teachers had little time for professional development.

Low pay and poor working conditions *feminized* teaching by making it less attractive to male workers. As evident in the statements of a retired physical education (Maria), retired high school English (Rose), and current elementary (Lisa) teacher, it became one of the few occupations open to women, and the proportion of female applicants rose:

MARIA: In the 1950s and 1960s there was not really too much of a choice for women. It was teaching or nursing [*laughs*]. . . . I had worked for the Red Cross . . . teaching swimming and I really liked . . . working with young people. . . . It made sense to teach phys ed. . . . I identified with the children and I liked sports. . . . I had something to offer.

ROSE: [When] I chose teaching there were . . . fewer doors open for females. . . . I didn't want to be a nurse . . . a secretary . . . a hairdresser, and teaching . . . was going to be challenging . . . something I would enjoy. . . . I'm a people person . . . loved English . . . reading . . . language . . . [and] young adults as you can converse with them.

LISA: From the time that I was little, I always adored my teachers . . . was always playing school . . . with my friends. . . . And when you went to your guidance counselor to determine if you were college entrance, it was, "Well, are you going to be a nurse or a teacher?"

Historical research supports that the construction of teaching as "women's work" that would be abandoned upon getting married and having children reduced the status of the occupation and resulted in low pay and high turnover. Like nursing and social work, teaching remained a feminized, semiprofession well into the 1970s. It was considered a low-status occupation in general but also when compared to those requiring a similar level of education, such as clerical work (Etzioni, 1969; Lortie, 1975).

Informants acknowledged that low pay and poor working conditions were not the only reasons for the low entry of male teachers and high turnover (exit) for all teachers. The hierarchical nature of schools as organizations resulted in limited autonomy. This system of administration had emerged during the Progressive Era, when muckraking journalists, urban political and economic elites, good government reformers, "outside" professionals (i.e., doctors, lawyers, etc.), and schools of education installed a Taylorist bureaucratic-management model to rationalize and standardize teaching and learning. This "factory model" diverted power away from school boards—often controlled by local ward bosses—and concentrated it in the office of the superintendent. The latter transformed one-room schoolhouses into bureaucratically administered school districts, standardized the curriculum, and *cellurized* teaching—so that elementary teachers taught a single grade and secondary teachers taught a single subject, rather than multiple grades and subjects within a one-room schoolhouse. School districts also standardized instruction through other organizational practices, such as using exams and grades to place students by ability. Known as *tracking,* the practice of homogenously grouping students was designed to allow teachers to better target instruction. The goal was to increase the efficiency and effectiveness of teachers by having them repeatedly teach a much narrower curriculum (i.e., single grade, single subject, similar ability levels). Reformers alleged that this "one best system" would enable schools to more cheaply produce a better "product," largely defined as future workers (Tyack, 1974).

While social progressives hoped to remove the politics from education, Tyack (1974) shows how this hierarchical-bureaucratic model actually maintained political control of schools yet shifted power from teachers and other local constituencies to business-economic elites and professional men. The latter seized control of local school boards and maintained this model well into the 1970s. Liam, a retired suburban high school English teacher and former district union president, described how it worked in his district:

> The community was expanding . . . [and] developers and builders had a lot of power. . . . The superintendent told me . . . [they] would meet . . . and tell him that he had to keep . . . property taxes low. . . . This was like 1975 . . . but this had been going on since the . . . 1960s. . . . These builders and developers worked closely with Town Hall, with the party in power . . . sold the community based on low taxes and the ability to afford homes . . . constantly harping on . . . the need to curb the power of unions to ensure that teachers' salaries do not increase taxes. There was also the Chamber of Commerce starting out and one of the board members was very open about the agenda. . . . It was a competitive environment with other suburban communities. That was the philosophy that dominated the management side.

Again, as a human service, educators' salaries are the largest component of school budgets. Political-market accountability—the ability of residents to vote down school budgets, vote out school board members, or exit to another locality with lower property taxes—favors business-economic interests in two ways: it puts pressure on elected school boards to extract more labor from teachers in the form of lower salaries and larger class sizes and it encourages state and local governments to keep property taxes low. Both groups are competing for votes and residents; however, state and local governments are also worried about increased spending on unemployment and social programs if businesses leave and take jobs with them.

When combined, these developments created a *high turnover model of teaching*, meaning they discouraged entry and encouraged exit, which suppressed teacher professionalism by removing the incentive to (a) invest in ongoing training and (b) mobilize on behalf of better working conditions and wages. Such collective action might benefit "the group," but it was less likely to benefit individual teachers unless they planned to remain in the occupation—and few did. The feminization of teaching at a time when collective bargaining and political voice were controversial for women further discouraged collective action (e.g., strikes and protests). Ted, a retired rural high school English teacher and district union president, explained,

[In] the 1950s and early 1960s . . . teaching was viewed as a second income . . . mostly made up of women, who left teaching when they got married or continued to teach but their husbands were the primary income earners. . . . There was no health insurance and salaries were simply too low. . . . Male teachers . . . worked nights at a second job and during the summer picked up a third . . . to feed their families. . . . Women were not politically active . . . appalled about walking the picket line . . . had no concept, until . . . Gloria Steinem . . . the women's movement, that they had rights . . . didn't want them [*laughing*]. Their place was in the classroom and then they would go home . . . get dinner ready for their own families.

The women's movement eventually normalized political and economic voice. Until then, though, the struggle to recruit members diluted the organizational resources of teachers' unions and reduced their ability to foster change.

Despite these narratives, teachers were not an unorganized group. They joined administrators to form teachers' associations that, while largely social forums, did provide some minimal economic benefits. Still, as described by a retired rural high school teacher (Joe), the composition of the teacher workforce combined with the historical era to work against collective economic and political demand-making:

The teachers asked me to be their representative for the teachers' association. . . . We had two or three faculty meetings a year . . . to bring a couple of things up to the supervising principal. . . . [I requested] medical benefits. . . . He said that he could probably get the school to pay for half if the teachers would cover the other half. . . . [But they] did not want the townspeople to be able to say that they were paying a teacher's doctor's bill. It was a pride thing. . . . And they said . . . it wouldn't be fair . . . because the school would be covering benefits for . . . teachers who had families, and single people . . . would get much less. . . . It was not because the Board of Education would not give it to us. It was because we were professionals. . . . Unions are for Teamsters and Longshoremen . . . not for professionals. Do doctors have a union? Do attorneys have a union? Noooooooooo [*he is telling this story like he is an old school marm lecturing an errant student on ethics*].

Respondents agreed that this organizational environment began to change in the 1960s when a combination of demographic, sociopolitical, institutional (local and state reforms), and economic forces altered the *willingness* and *capacity* of teachers to engage in collective action.

Demographic and sociopolitical forces and teacher mobilization. The school-age population expanded rapidly from the 1950s to the mid-1960s as soldiers returning home from World War II and Korea married and started families. This "baby boom" (demographic changes) resulted in the mass hiring of teachers. Many had different life experiences and were more inclined to challenge the previous hegemony of administrators, elected officials, and business-economic interests. Ted continues,

> [They hired] an enormous amount of . . . teachers and they had a much more militant attitude. . . . The Vietnam War . . . [sparked] protest on college campuses. . . . Those young people were teaching . . . long-term faculty . . . for lack of a better description . . . the schoolmarms [*laughs*] . . . saying "We believe in what you are doing but we don't want to be seen out on the picket line. It isn't professional." . . . [The] "Young Turks" . . . saying "We do have the right. They are taking advantage . . . not treating us like professionals." It was almost as difficult in the early years . . . to bargain with our own members as . . . with administrators . . . [and] the Board of Education . . . such a divergent age group . . . such different life experiences and . . . [views of] acceptable behaviors and what rights they had as professionals.

Like Ted, others described how positive experiences with political protests during college encouraged a new generation of teachers to voice individually and collectively. This is an example of sociopolitical changes but also interpretive effects (feelings of political efficacy).

Respondents agreed that these newly hired teachers were also more inclined to favor the collective resolution of political, social, and economic problems because of their own or their families' positive experiences with unions and/or government programs. Johanna, a retired suburban elementary teacher, elaborated on this type of interpretive effect:

> [Once we got a union] I remember . . . trying to decide if I should join. . . . I wasn't making a lot of money and "Why should my money go to dues" and "I am a professional" . . . those were my thoughts. . . . [Many] did not want to be associated with the union. . . . My mother said, "You should absolutely join it. We are a union family. The union . . . provided us with our middle-class lifestyle. . . . Everything we have, we owe to the union. You might consider yourself a professional, but . . . why should you benefit from everything it is going to provide you and for everything unions have already provided you without having to pay

your dues? Why should you get all the privileges and advantages and not have to contribute?" . . . My father worked on the railroad, and he was union president.

Earlier, Paul mentioned having positive encounters with unionization while working as a baker in high school. He said those experiences played a prominent role in his efforts to unionize teachers. Johanna describes how she decided to join the union because her family had benefited from her father doing so.

My interviews suggest that New Deal and postwar social and economic policies, including federal support for collective bargaining, increased support for unions and a more activist government by demonstrating to growing numbers of citizens that collective bargaining and public programs could expand the middle class and improve their lives. Parents then transferred those views to their children. Many further mentioned that they had only been able to attend college because of federal and state policies that had expanded the middle class, provided low-interest student loans, and/or funded the development of public colleges and universities. Once there, they had personal experiences that altered their sociopolitical identities in ways that made them more willing to engage in collective political, social, and economic action. This is an example of how resource and interpretive effects often work together.

The mass hiring of teachers (demographic changes) worked in tandem with these sociopolitical developments to foster teacher mobilization in other ways. For instance, it brought more men into the occupation at a time when the burgeoning women's movement made it acceptable to remain in the workforce after having children. The potential for career longevity provided women with the incentive to mobilize on behalf of equal rights, including equal pay for equal work, but their demands for better, more standardized wages drew support from male teachers too by calling attention to the practice of principals routinely making hiring, firing, tenure, and wage compensation decisions based on personal preferences. Returning to Johanna's narrative:

[In] my first job, I replaced someone on leave. She was the principal's girlfriend . . . then wanted to come back to that job. . . . He had no reason *not* to give me tenure, but he said . . . "Are you going to go off and get pregnant? I don't know if I can recommend you . . . I'm tired of these young women getting tenure and then going on maternity leave. Are you pregnant or are you planning on getting pregnant?" . . . It was before Title IX in 1972. Legally, I could not have sued him. . . . [Luckily] I had two principals and the . . . other principal recommended me. . . . [It shows] the games that were played.

Johanna does not specifically mention being offered less pay due to her gender; however, she and others said that this was often the case. More broadly though, the need to negotiate individually with principals worked against those who demanded higher wages or equal pay for equal work because principals could refuse to hire or find reasons to fire them. A number of institutional developments (eventually) altered the playing field. Johanna mentioned Title IX—a national reform—but teachers more commonly described state and local reforms.

Local reforms and teacher mobilization. As teacher shortages spread with the baby boom, many districts began using the benefits associated with tenure and seniority to encourage teachers to remain in the field. These reforms were first adopted during the Progressive Era to deal with the unintended side effects of school district consolidation. It became more difficult and costly to evaluate and rehire teachers on an annual basis as the size of school districts grew. School boards and administrators realized that they could reduce personnel costs by granting tenure to effective teachers after three years. Tenured teachers still must be evaluated, just not on an annual basis. Tenure and seniority further reduce personnel costs by decreasing turnover (exit) and therefore the costs of hiring and training new teachers. Tenure encourages teachers to remain in a district (loyalty) by providing them with more professional voice. Seniority does so by "end loading" salaries. Teachers do not make a lot at the beginning of their careers, especially considering their level of education, but they receive more the longer they remain in a district. Many districts also began building other benefits into teacher contracts to encourage loyalty, such as allowing experienced teachers their first choice of schools, classes, and "nonacademic" duties (e.g., monitoring a hallway during classes vs. the more onerous duties of monitoring the cafeteria or parking lot during lunch and the arrival and dismissal of students).

Tenure and seniority have been controversial since first adopted over a century ago. Critics argue that school districts rarely fire ineffective teachers because these policies make the costs of removal too high and claim that this disincentivizes hard work and suppresses performance.[2] Informants, on the other hand, said that tenure is not a "job guarantee"; it provides due process. School districts must show cause for dismissal and teachers must receive representation at a hearing before a neutral third party; however, they may be dismissed for unfitness, incompetence, insubordination, seditious utterances, and unprofessional or immoral conduct. Liam told this story to explain why due process is important:

> [When] I was in the service . . . there was a private . . . accused of insubordination. . . . Before the officers could take away the one stripe or his pay, they had to have a hearing. . . . He was entitled to representation . . . to cross-examine the officer's testimony . . . and a neutral party had to render an opinion. . . . After listening, I did not think he was guilty . . . he was being punished because he was . . . a pain in the butt . . . no evidence he disobeyed a direct order. . . . He ended up winning. . . . I bring this up because the army did not fall apart because the officer lost the case . . . [and this] was during the Cold War. . . . Teachers spend a lot of time going to college and getting a master's degree . . . borrow up to the hock. . . . [Many] are raising families. . . . Yet, people are advocating removing their license to teach or dismissing them without . . . due process. . . . People say they can't fire teachers. . . . We had teachers fired . . . [if] incompetent . . . even if they have tenure. No one is arguing that they should be kept. . . . But, I have had many firing issues that were about personality conflicts.

Almost every retiree said that teachers had been inappropriately dismissed for non-performance-related issues, such as gender, racial background, sexual orientation, taking an unpopular position on a public issue outside of school, or the capricious decisions of administrators. They also agreed that tenure and seniority were adopted first to redress organizational issues and then to alleviate a hiring crisis—not to protect teachers.

When asked about other associated benefits, teachers of all ages discussed how tenure and seniority increase *professional* and *economic voice*. Johanna provided perhaps the best story about this second unintended side effect:

> My husband . . . [was] a second year teacher. . . . He would not allow a student to graduate . . . [because he] had not done any of the work . . . but his mom was on the school board. . . . [The principal] told him that he should pass the student . . . or else he would . . . not get tenure. . . . If you set a policy, you do not back down because someone has power. What kind of message does that send to the other kids? My husband refused. . . . Thirty years later, that young man came back . . . through

Facebook and . . . [said] he had done the very best thing for him . . . caused him to get his act together [*getting emotional*]. . . . He got his GED [high school equivalency diploma] . . . went in the service. . . . Sometimes it is the ones who give you the hardest time that are the most grateful. . . . You have to care enough to do the right thing by kids even when it's hard to do. My husband cared enough to hold his ground even under threat of something bad. . . . [The student] got that later on . . . there ended up being no bad consequences for my husband but he didn't know that going in.

Tenure *directly* encourages professional and economic voice by reducing the ability of administrators and school boards to dismiss teachers for non-performance-related purposes. Tenure and seniority *indirectly* do so by preventing the firing of more experienced teachers to achieve savings. The latter are reportedly more willing to challenge the capricious decisions of administrators, school boards, and powerful parents because on-the-job experience provides lessons about the importance of individual and collective voice. It also fosters a belief that their professional knowledge should be respected. This *social learning* differs from economic incentives. Tenure and seniority provide the latter by reducing turnover and therefore providing teachers with a fiscal stake in collective economic and political action.

State reforms and teacher mobilization. In the late 1960s, the state that is the subject of this analysis, like many others, also unintendedly contributed to teacher mobilization. It did so by granting public employees, like teachers, the right to bargain collectively. Participants framed this law as a *symbolic* victory. It did not level the playing field; however, teachers' experiences under the law contrasted sharply with earlier periods when all levels of government discouraged unionism through actual violence (police brutality), legal barriers (arresting and fining those on strike), and symbolic violence (portraying union members as communist to impose social costs on workers). Now, the state required that public employers—like school districts—bargain in good faith. It also established the Public Employee Relations Board (PERB) to mediate, arbitrate, and resolve work disputes for union- *and* non-union-affiliated employees alike.

Although an improvement over past practices, teachers said the law still favors public employers. It imposes monetary remunerations on workers who go on strike and potential jail time for their union leaders but imposes no economic penalties on public employers (e.g., school districts) that refuse to negotiate in good faith. PERB also allegedly hires people who do not share the "professional mind-set" of teachers (e.g., lawyers and business leaders); it is therefore more likely to favor hierarchical controls over the profession's need to exercise independent voice.[3]

These power asymmetries make sense. The law was actually designed to decrease strikes during a time of growing militancy among state and local employees, including a teachers' strike in a large city in 1962. The outcome of that strike encouraged teachers in other districts to demand collective bargaining and, when combined with the mobilization of other public employees, increased demands for state lawmakers to "do something." Paul remarked,

> [We] had NEA upstate . . . unionization began in the city, with AFT . . . [But the] law was changed because of pressure from teachers' associations . . . lobbying . . . saying, "I have to make more. I can't raise a family on those low salaries" . . . The state had no intention of empowering . . . . public employees . . . [thought the law was] unusable because they put all the teeth . . . on the side of the [school] board . . . [and] didn't give teachers any positive power. Strikes continued to be illegal . . . [and are] hurtful to their students . . . the community . . . relationships with administrators . . . [other] teachers . . . [The] negative financial penalties . . . harm teachers and their families. Strikes are an action of last resort, but . . . the only action available if the board is behaving unreasonably . . . the law did *not* give teachers any power . . . but the first rule of negotiations is . . ."get your foot in the door . . . come back and get more . . . open the door a little wider."

The AFT's adoption of business unionism had quickly increased the salaries and benefits of its affiliated teachers; nonetheless, the NEA continued to define itself as a teachers' association, rather than a union. These differences diluted union bargaining strength at the state level.[4] By allowing collective bargaining statewide, the law opened up space for the creation of a single, state-level teachers' union.

It is difficult to understand the importance of this development without explaining the nature of schools as organizations. Prior to unionization, male and female teachers alike described their work environments as paternalistic—but they were not using that word to denote gender differences. While most principals were male, participants were describing how the hierarchical authority structure of schools restricted teachers' control over what and how they taught. Ted explained,

[It] was not really a male/female thing because male . . . and female administrators treated teachers of both genders that way. . . . The role itself lent administrators a certain moral authority that was unquestionable. . . . They made the policy decisions . . . [and] decisions about how the classroom should be run. . . . If you had a question . . . about discipline or pedagogy, you went to your administrator . . . [not] another teacher . . . you referred to administrators by their titles . . . doctor, or sir and madam, or Mr. Smith and Ms. Smith. You never referred to them by their first name or on a collegial basis, like "Hey John" [*laughs*]. There was that gap between the practitioners . . . and the administrators.

In other words, *the role itself* provided principals and administrators with tremendous *moral authority* both within and outside of the classroom. Informants referred to male and female principals as "father figures" and claimed that they brought their personal and professional concerns to them. Principals resolved disputes between teachers, dealt with student discipline issues, and socialized and trained new teachers.

Teachers were not necessarily arguing that this paternalism was problematic, nor did they portray the hierarchical authority structure as "fixed." The principalship evolved from the position of "head teacher," which was often rotated between teachers until it morphed into an administrative position that involved teachers permanently leaving the classroom. Even then, most principals and district-level administrators were former teachers and school districts typically promoted from within rather than hiring from outside the district. These organizational realities meant that most administrators had previously been socialized into teaching and therefore shared the occupation's values and training. A retired teacher said, "You have to remember that administrators were ex-teachers. They *were* us. It wasn't really us versus them." Teachers were also quite close with their administrators and frequently socialized outside of work—first at functions that were organized by teachers' associations, which were typically run by principals, and then later through teachers' unions, before state law prohibited administrators from joining. When combined, this socialization improved social cohesion and reduced social conflict. The hierarchical, paternalistic nature of schools was only problematic if there were personal issues between a principal and a teacher. Then teachers had no recourse.

It was that early amendment to the state's collective bargaining law that enabled school boards to "divide and conquer." By prohibiting management (administrators) from joining employee unions (teachers), this institutional strategy ensured that union leaders would have to convince fellow teachers that they were equal to administrators, had the right to make demands of administrators, and were not unprofessional for joining a union. Teachers told me that their social ties were critical for all three. In Paul's words,

> [Our state union talked about] getting small groups of teachers together and then making bigger groups of friends. I don't like to say "cadres" because it sounds communist. . . . [It was influencing teachers] through their social ties. . . . We used that networking to discuss everything . . . [and] convince people to join. . . . If we did not have the social group, we were nothing. That's how information was passed along. . . . [Teachers had been] isolated in their classrooms . . . that is what we fought against. . . . That's good for the other side.

The development of a single, state-level union was also quite critical because it created more social cohesion and consolidated organizational resources (e.g., dues and membership) under a single umbrella. Teachers today are still affiliated with two different unions at the local and national levels, but state level resources may be channeled up (national government) or down (local level) for coordinated political and economic action.

Just as importantly, teacher networks combined with this *federated structure* to pass along information at a time when there was no social media. Those social ties were critical for allowing teachers to engage in social learning at a faster rate than "isolated" school boards. Paul elaborated on the importance of this form of *social capital*:

> That social learning was critical. It wasn't just going on within the district and it wasn't directed by the state union. It was . . . teachers' social ties across schools. We had *never* met as a group before. . . . [After the collective bargaining law, we] started meeting to discuss how we were doing with negotiations, what was working, what wasn't. . . . It was our own union self-ties. We were all leaders of unions. From those local ties, it got aggregated up. . . . [These ties were important because] there are no negative repercussions for school boards and administrators . . . [but they] did not get that initially. So, teachers . . . made a lot of gains very quickly . . . by making the other side think . . . [we] had more power. . . . [Our state union was also] better than any union I know . . . at educating their people very quickly on how to negotiate. They got us way ahead of the school boards. . . . There are all kinds of things . . . that don't require power. They require . . . the psychology of negotiations. . . . The

boards . . . had no idea how to negotiate. The tables started turning once school boards started bringing in lawyers and . . . people who had studied the negotiations process. Then, they stopped the fast-forward mode . . . and now they've reversed it.

Together, these narratives show how the unintended consequences of state laws are sometimes more important than the intended ones. **Economic forces, local political forces, and teacher mobilization.** By the mid-1970s, teachers' working conditions had deteriorated even further owing to a combination of social, economic, and political forces. With the end of the baby boom, public school enrollment declined from 46 million to 39 million between 1971 and 1982. Inflation, an economic downturn, taxpayer revolts, and the election of "anti-tax-and-spend" school boards in many communities also negatively affected school district revenues and budgets. The combination of the two resulted in layoffs, salary freezes, program cuts, school closures, and, in some extreme cases, bankruptcies (Toch, 1991). Educators told me that the crisis was especially acute in urban areas.

Lorna, an elementary teacher and district union president, described what it was like to be hired and work in an urban district at that time:

> I went to apply for a job . . . with my mother because I was scared to death to be in the neighborhood. . . . [The] school was supposed to have 120 teachers . . . they were hiring 20. . . . The secretary . . . went in to talk with the principal . . . [then said,] "Here is the list of openings. . . . Just erase the name of anyone who is currently assigned to the class you want. . . . Anyone who brings their mother to a job interview here is a good person." . . . The principal . . . this dapper man in the heart of the "ghetto" [*using finger quotes*] . . . no guards in front of the schools . . . crime . . . gangs . . . in the streets . . . said to me, "You have experience. We don't usually get teachers with any experience." I had one year teaching . . . in a Catholic school . . . 64 children in my class . . . three reading groups. . . . He said, "You know about grouping . . . [could you] lead the seminar." . . . I'm 22 years old. . . . Then he said, "Here are the rules . . . don't call the office *ever*. . . [*pauses for effect*] and don't let them out of your room [*laughs*]. If that means you have to take your desk and move it to the door to block it, that's . . . not considered a fire hazard. . . . Just don't call us and we won't call you, and you will get an S [satisfactory] rating." . . . We used to get $600 more a year to teach . . . a bonus . . . [because we] were the . . . bottom of the bottom. . . . We had to *beg* to get textbooks . . . our school was so poor . . . never enough of anything. You bought your own chalk . . . erasers.

As the economic crisis spread, teachers across the state became more militant.

My interviews indicate that economic crises alone, however, are not sufficient for fostering more militant forms of collective action, such as strikes. Teachers' political and organizational environments are also critical due to the organization of public schools around geographic catchment areas and the ways that political-market accountability inequitably affects salaries, working conditions, and the provision of services across school districts. Teachers care about their students and their ability to do a good job; they also care about how they are treated by their district and how that compares to teachers in other districts. Liam, for instance, mentioned how business-economic elites had used their control over the school board to keep taxes low by suppressing salaries and increasing class sizes. These actions kept housing affordable and helped grow the community, yet teachers could not afford to live there due to low wages. He discussed how that influenced the decision to go on strike:

[We] were the lowest paid in . . . [our local area and] had the highest class size. . . . [We also had] a teacher in her second year . . . [fired due to] a personality conflict with the principal . . . had tenure in another district . . . [and] was highly regarded. . . . Her husband was transferred . . . to this district. . . . The teachers signed a petition and then 29 of her 30 students' parents signed a letter. . . . [Some on the board] felt the teacher was unfairly fired, but . . . [said] it was a union effort at gaining power and control . . . if they did not back their managers, then it set a precedent. . . . [The faculty] felt it was an injustice. . . . We wanted . . . a fair dismissal clause . . . [for teachers to get] a hearing. . . . There were also other issues . . . pay, class size and their *attitude* [*said emphatically*] toward us at the bargaining table. . . . "We are the authority and you obey us." . . . [We got] a lot of sympathy because many parents felt . . . 30 students in an elementary classroom is high. The high school was worse. . . . I had 33 students in all five of my classes . . . that was the contractual maximum. . . . [The] board made a really insulting offer. . . . Most . . . elementary teachers were female, and it was a different time. . . . Elementary principals . . . [told] the superintendent . . . "*My* teachers will not go on strike. If the union is lucky, maybe 10 percent of *my* teachers will go on strike." It was paternalistic. But . . . the elementary schools . . . turned out to be the backbone of the strike because of their anger

The right to bargain collectively under state law facilitated collective action in two ways: It spread the belief that teachers' professional voice should be respected and it made teachers less inclined to accept the paternalistic attitudes of administrators, school boards, and business-economic elites.

The very high strike participation rates—over 80 percent in Liam's district and exceeding 95 percent in other districts—are evidence of these changing attitudes toward collective action. Despite these stories, teachers agreed that the state's collective bargaining law actually minimizes strikes. It does so by imposing high social and economic costs on public servants and union leaders that go on strike.

The Costs of Collective Action

Greene (Greene & Kahlenberg, 2012) argues that collective bargaining is undemocratic because teachers use their economic solidarity and physical concentration in school buildings to advance their own interests at the expense of geographically disbursed parents, students, and taxpayers (see also Moe, 2011). I have referred to this as *social cohesion*. Contrary to this view, teachers described how all of the power rests with administrators and democratically elected school boards. The latter receive no penalties for failing to negotiate in good faith while teachers bear high *economic costs* if they go on strike in protest. One suburban teacher said his first paycheck was $1.12 because, per state law, the district took two days' pay for every day the teachers were on strike. Another usually worked a full-time job in the summer and a part-time job during the school year to supplement his income. That year, he worked two full-time jobs during the summer. Others discussed how they were married and their spouses worked in the same district, which meant that they had to support their family with no income during the strike—a common narrative among male teachers whose wives did not work at a time when that was the norm.

These economic costs reduce social cohesion partly because they are not distributed equally. Union leaders are more severely affected, but Paul provided a range of examples to illustrate this point:

> [The state union] told us that, if we [the union leaders] were caught, we would probably be immediately imprisoned. . . . We stayed away from our homes, only going there at odd hours . . . [had] our members check for process servers. . . . Our treasurer . . . was arrested. . . . [The other] officers . . . unanimously decided . . . we should turn ourselves in . . . [but the state union] reps were adamant that this was not an option. . . . [It]

would effectively kill the strike . . . [because it] would be leaderless. . . . They argued the good of the many should take precedence. . . . I thought it was wrong. . . . It is my biggest regret . . . other than . . . [my] family. . . . Seeing their father on TV apparently in trouble . . . was unsettling to the children. The phone was ringing at all hours . . . with calls from media . . . and by harassers. . . . [There were no answering machines at the time and my] wife did not want to disconnect because that was our only means of communication. . . . We settled on a ring code [a series of rings and hang-ups] I would use. . . . [The strike] lasted a little more than 19 days. . . . [So we lost] over a month's salary . . . financially all were hurt but some . . . just purchased new homes . . . were about to retire and this would affect their final average salary [used to calculate retirement]. . . . [The union said] to go in . . . but they wouldn't. . . . [A few] had political aspirations and were being pressured by a political party. . . . There were marital problems.

Paul is actually describing a combination of economic and *social costs*. He mentions rising divorce rates due to income insecurity or because the spouse was opposed to unions in general and strikes in particular. This is an example of personal social costs but my interviews show that strikes impose high collective social costs as well.

The most common example of collective social costs was the creation of long-term issues in the workplace. Some—like Brian, a retired urban elementary teacher—mentioned tensions between teachers who crossed the picket lines and their colleagues:

I was not a rah-rah union guy . . . I did it because my fellow teachers . . . [Some] broke the strike. . . . It caused some *incredibly* hard feelings . . . *awful.* . . . It lasted 30–40 years. . . . People still ask, "Why do you think he went in?" [*laughs*] . . . The union leaders went to jail. . . . People thought . . . it would be over quickly . . . 30 days later we were still reeling . . . lost two days' pay for every day we were out on strike. . . . It was tough. . . . I always had good relationships with my administrators. . . . There are schools where the administrators . . . bully the teachers. I have a former student who . . . contacted me on Facebook . . . told me she became a teacher because of me [getting emotional]. It really touched me. . . . Her principal is bullying the teachers. It happens. . . . And so, I do think unions are important.[5]

Other informants described how strikes create long-term issues with administrators. One suburban teacher said, "It changes the way you feel about a person when they hand you an injunction letter as you are standing on the picket line." Teachers also care about students and their relationships with the community. Strikes impede learning because districts typically hire unprepared teachers and use "nonacademic" means of keeping students engaged, such as assemblies where large groups of students are watched over by a handful of adults; they also make teachers' jobs more difficult by reducing cooperation from parents and the community.

As a group, teachers conveyed how these high social costs provide the motivation to avoid a strike; in fact, the majority suggested that social costs are more important than economic ones for discouraging strikes. Thus, the concentration of teachers in school districts—where they form strong personal relationships—works in favor of parents, students, and taxpayers rather than promoting the interests of teachers, as Greene (Greene & Kahlenberg, 2012) argues. School boards and administrators are able to use these social penalties, not just economic ones, to encourage some teachers to defect. This divide-and-conquer strategy reduces social cohesion and enables school districts to stack the deck in their favor during negotiations.

Even so, loyalty is a complex emotion that should never be taken for granted. Earlier, Liam said that elementary principals had misguidedly believed that "their" teachers would not go on strike. Brian and others discussed how even the course of time, for many, did not diffuse feelings of anger, bitterness, and betrayal against colleagues and substitute teachers who had crossed the picket lines or against administrators who had bused teachers in from other states. Informants also mentioned how some residents supported the teachers, by refusing to send their children to school during the strike, while others supported the school board. In addition, some, like Lorna, verbalized how they could not count on solidarity from other public servants—even when they were experiencing similar things:

> [Our] almost strikes in the 2000s, the cops and the firefighters united with us. And we had a *wonderful* rally . . . all the city workers joined us. . . . It was a different feeling than the 1970s. There was total disapproval by the whole city . . . the city was bankrupt. They just thought we should work for no money. . . . [More recently] we were able to convince people that it . . . really was about children. . . . [The mayor also] wants to use the money that we have been contributing . . . as part of the health . . . [and] pension fund . . . to stave off . . . [layoffs and] divide the older teachers from the younger. . . . [Make them think] they will not lose their jobs if the older teachers . . . [give in, but] we know how hard we fought.

Loyalty inspires action, but it often pales in the face of other concerns, such as economic consequences, personal and collective social costs, and concerns about students, parents, and the community. Participants said they must have tremendous social cohesion to successfully negotiate with school boards and administrators.[6] Reduced social cohesion—whether due to a lack of support from fellow teachers, the public, other public servants or, in Lorna's case, because the mayor is using younger teachers' fears about losing their jobs to encourage older teachers to give concessions—makes it much harder to sustain collective action.

The Benefits of Collective Action

Although teachers' reasons for engaging in collective economic action were complex, one reported side effect was that teachers began to view themselves as the appropriate source of professional knowledge. That attitudinal change altered their behaviors in ways that increased economic, professional, and political voice (policy feedback) at all levels of government. This section focuses on the link between collective bargaining (economic voice) and professional and political voice. That connection explains how teachers were able to use their newly gained economic resources to benefit the group and then society (Chapter 5).

Collective bargaining and professional voice. Respondents said unionization did not change the hierarchical authority structure of schools as organizations; however, it increased professional voice by spreading out formal and informal sources of authority. Paul explained:

> [We] became stakeholders. . . . [It took] maybe five years, but you could . . . see a loss of that paternal grant. . . . [Faculty were] less and less likely to ask that principal for a personal favor, or to step into a dispute . . . would go to a union rep . . . and principals became more like administrators than "father figures." . . . This did not just spread power to unions. It spread the authority around. . . . They've done studies on . . . formal and informal leaders. . . . That is what happened. . . . So X, Y, and Z were union reps, but A, B, and C were known for being good at developing curriculum, an expert on a specific topic . . . good at mentoring . . . [had] good techniques for . . . discipline. And people would go to . . . [them] for help and advice. . . . Mostly, teachers did not have problems with the principal, but . . . it was *really* a problem . . . [when] there was nowhere else to go. Leadership got spread out *a lot.*

As collective bargaining fostered the development of other sources of help, teachers were less inclined to rely on administrators. The creation of informal sources of help appears to be especially critical for the development of effective teachers.

Teachers of *all ages* told me that teacher preparation programs provide important content-based knowledge and pedagogical skills (how to teach), but teachers need on-the-job experience to learn different ways to present content and manage large numbers of students. Formal mentorship and informal socialization enable teachers to discuss classroom experiences and learn through those social interactions. This *social learning* directly reduces turnover and indirectly does so by creating the social cohesion that improves teachers' willingness to share their knowledge and skills. This is what society gains from collective bargaining. In contrast, "trial by fire" reduces the efficiency and effectiveness of public schools by fueling a high turnover model of teaching and increasing feelings of inefficacy, isolation, and burnout (see Chapter 5).

Just as importantly, teachers began using collective bargaining to formalize these informal sources of professional authority. Liam stated:

> [Initially] there was some division. . . . Those who wanted the union to just deal with bread-and-butter issues and those who said, "No, we should make sure we have a decent curriculum . . . class sizes and humane work schedules." . . . The union chose to focus on both. So, the union got *professional voice* as well as the *union voice* [my italics]. . . . This seems extraordinary now. . . . There used to be a committee . . . [that] made sure the curriculum was appropriate for each grade level, but *there were no teachers on it* [my italics]. . . . They were local elites . . . we demanded . . . the right to representation . . . on any committee that dealt with curriculum . . . that created teachers as experts on different things. . . . Teachers became more and more involved in decisions about what . . . and how to teach . . . voluntarily doing . . . [this] because they cared about having autonomy . . . [and it] spread to other things.

This narrative shows how economic voice (using collective bargaining to improve salaries and working conditions) and professional voice (the formal or informal defense of occupational norms, knowledge, and practices) often go hand in hand.

For the most part, though, teachers' narratives suggest that professional autonomy was an unplanned by-product of union demands for smaller class sizes, a reduction in outside-of-the-classroom contractual duties (e.g., parking lot, lunchroom, and hall duty), and a free period every day to grade papers, plan lessons, confer with colleagues, meet with students, talk to parents, and so forth. Some of these concessions directly provided teachers with more free time, but smaller classes indirectly do so by reducing the workload associated with grading and discipline issues. Teachers voluntarily used this time to become more involved in their organizational environments (e.g., serve on committees); develop curriculum and mentor fellow teachers; and discuss pedagogy, the curriculum, student discipline, and other classroom issues with colleagues.

All of these developments improved the efficiency and effectiveness of schools (see Chapter 5); however, the bonds that were built as a result of having more time to socialize and mentor colleagues also increased *social cohesion* and what I earlier referred to as *social trust*—a belief in the honesty, integrity, and reliability of others. Liam continues,

> [There] were real problems in terms of no time off from the classroom.... Elementary teachers ... could not even go to the bathroom.... We also began a general attack on teachers doing noninstructional duties. That was primarily a secondary [schoolteacher] issue . . . lunchroom duty, parking lot duty, bathroom duty, and so forth. . . . [We] created this rhetoric of "GE does not hire engineers to patrol the parking lot" [*laughs*].... The elementary teachers . . . did not have those noninstructional duties . . . [but had] bus duty . . . and they had to eat lunch with their students. We demanded they hire aides.... It turned out to be one of the best things we ever did because it gave teachers at all levels more time to prepare, to tutor students, to make copies, or whatever.... It built a bond between teachers. We saw what we could do when we were united, but teachers also had some time during the day where they could talk to one another and help one another. Before, they were really isolated in their classrooms. So, it definitely built up solidarity.

As forms of social capital, social cohesion and social trust improve the ability of groups to engage in political action (see Chapter 10), but Liam's claim that "we saw what we could do when we were united" shows how *social learning* removed the stigma that had caused many to opt out of the union; it created a link in teachers' minds between unionization and professionalism, not just unionization and improved salaries and benefits.

Once union membership became more concentrated, collective bargaining enabled teachers to enforce that they, versus administrators or business-economic and political elites, were the appropriate source of knowledge with respect to pedagogy and the curriculum. Increased autonomy then combined with better salaries and benefits to reduce turnover, improve the status of the occupation, and encourage college-bound students—especially men—to become teachers at a time when federal laws, such as affirmative action, increased the number of minorities entering the profession through expanded access to college. Rose and Lisa conveyed these ideas:

ROSE: [Over] the course of my teaching career . . . [administrators] respected your professionalism more and allowed you to use that expertise. . . . [Before the union] it was more a paternalistic kind of situation. . . . "We have to tell them what to do." Whereas, later on, they allowed you to use . . . your professional expertise . . . [and it] was more enjoyable for me. . . . I had more autonomy . . . [and could really engage my] creativity.

LISA: In the '70s, it was the type of administration that . . . [was more like] "paternalistic dictatorships." . . . Your principal told you what to do [*clapping*], and that's what you did. . . . Then it swung over. . . . [In the] late '70s, early '80s . . . teachers were asked to give input. . . . We were stakeholders. . . . We gained a lot more professional autonomy . . . a lot more control over pedagogy and content. . . . [With collective bargaining, we] became partners in the whole educational process . . . that translated into more teachers staying in the classroom. . . . Salaries and benefits helped, but . . . professionalization . . . [reduced] turnover because teachers felt like they had more autonomy and . . . could be more creative in the classroom.

The teaching workforce is still predominantly female, but it is no longer uncommon today to see male and minority teachers. Teachers *of all ages* told me that this diversity is important because children need role models (see Chapter 11).

Collective bargaining and political voice. Again, research recognizes that politicians *intentionally* design policies to increase positive feedback from allies and thereby advance their favored policies; my interviews suggest that the state's collective bargaining law *unintendedly* increased political participation through interpretive and resource effects.

In terms of *interpretive effects*, positive experiences with collective bargaining fostered a link in teachers' minds between school board elections and their organizational environments. After seeing how this engagement advanced their economic *and* professional interests,

teachers individually and collectively began to recognize the impor-
tance of becoming more active in state and national politics (see also
Briney, 1958; Rosenthal, 1966; Zeigler, 1967). Consider the words of
Liam and Ted:

LIAM: [The] union worked really hard to get someone elected as the head of
the board who was . . . not pro-union necessarily, but pro-education . . .
a moderate Republican . . . understood . . . that class size was important
and that we could recruit better teachers if we paid decent salaries. . . .
We also worked really hard to get parents elected . . . brought class sizes
down from 30 in the elementary to 20 to 23. . . . [A teacher stopped
me in the grocery store and] was enthusing about what a difference it
made . . . what she could do for the kids . . . not about what it did for her.

TED: [The collective bargaining law] informed teachers of the importance
of . . . reaching beyond the confines of our school district . . . to influence
politics at the state and national level . . . where decisions were being
made in terms of public policy . . . that affect the classroom. . . . [In
1972, we] threw our support behind Jimmy Carter. . . . He created the
Department of Education, and teachers got their foot in the door. . . .
That was proof of the pudding. . . . We supported a political candidate
. . . who made and fulfilled a promise.

Together, these narratives show how the successful mobilization of
teachers at all levels of government demonstrated the efficacy of
political voice.

With respect to *resource effects,* the state's collective bargaining law
helped teachers' unions resolve "collective action problems"—issues
that occur when individuals are unable to work together to achieve
common ends (Olson, 1965/1971). Typically, small groups are better
able to mobilize and dominate larger ones because the latter face
higher *organizational costs*: They are more likely to have varied and
conflicting interests and individual members find it easier to free ride
off the labor of others without getting caught. To counteract these
issues, Olson advocated providing "select incentives" to those who take
part in collective action while withholding them from those who do
not. This is what occurred once the state amended the law to (a) make
the local union—once organized and recognized under state law—the
sole legal representative for all teachers in the district, even those who did
not elect to join, and (b) allow the union to collect "fair share agency
fees" (partial dues) from those who did not join yet still benefited from
collective bargaining and union representation.[7] As Olson predicted,
the need to pay partial dues (about 80%) incentivized teachers to join.

Increased membership size and dues provided teachers' unions with the tangible organizational resources to engage in economic and political voice, but these *resource effects* were not the intent of policy makers. The state wanted the union to provide legal services to *all* teachers in the district. The union argued that it would create a "fairness issue." Rather than take nonmembers out of the union's legal and contractual responsibilities, the state chose to make nonmembers contribute a portion of the fees that were paid by members and prohibited the union from using those dues for political purposes.[8] Over time, the union used collective bargaining and political voice to obtain other organizational resources that reduced the costs of collective economic and political action.

One amendment required that school districts provide space and time for unions to discuss wages, hours, and working conditions. Teachers used this contractually mandated union time to discuss public policies that affect teachers, public schools, children, and families. The union also gained the right to post announcements about district, state, and national policies in teachers' mailboxes and teachers' lounges in addition to information about their contracts and negotiations with the district. The state further required that school districts give union presidents time off for union business, including travel to political conventions or meetings at the union's central office. Moreover, it began allowing members to "check off" if they want to contribute part of their paycheck to the union's political action fund. These examples show how teachers translated what had mostly been symbolic benefits into a resource for mobilizing rank-and-file members for coordinated economic and political action. Paul best summarized these benefits:

> Our contract said . . . the first meeting [of the month] was . . . our time to meet as a union. . . . There were discussions . . . [about contributions to the union's political action arm and] state . . . and school policies. I suppose that is political, but we weren't discussing political candidates. . . . The political arm was another law change that happened much later on. . . . [It] is a separate entity . . . none of the money is from dues. It is all voluntary . . . has a separate board. . . . The money goes to fund political candidates and political ads. . . . [Some] is given back to the local union to use for political purposes, such as school board elections [and] for mailing activities at the state or local level. . . . [The political action fund] also pays for the polling center. . . . By the way, the state union gets a lot of demographic information about members and nonmembers . . . and can use it for political purposes. That's not under

. . . [the political action arm of the union]. . . . The membership form that you fill out has a lot of different information that the state union can use. They're getting that information as an economic organization, but it's useful for political activities too.

Paul, like a handful of others, also mentioned a fifth resource gained through public policy. As the exclusive representative of teachers, the state union is provided with a complete list of *all* teachers. That list includes important demographic information that the union may use to identify, contact, and mobilize teachers for political action as well as employment-related issues. Obviously, this is an important organizational resource for mobilizing teachers.

Summing up, my interviews suggest that the state's collective bargaining law materially and symbolically altered the *relative position* of the players on the field. While it never fully redressed the power imbalance between public employers and public servants, none of those I interviewed complained about the law. On the contrary, most said that they felt lucky to work in a state that does not discourage unionization like many other states do. In Liam's words,

[The] strike was a tremendous strain on the faculty. . . . Parents were with us overall, but . . . they were getting abuse on the picket lines. . . . The board called in the sheriff's department, and they were busing in scabs from different places to teach. We were disappointed . . . that unemployed . . . [recently graduated] and teachers from other states would cross the lines, but . . . [we] were lucky because the board did not ask for the leaders to go to prison. That happened in another . . . district. . . . The union just had to pay the fines, and we lost two days' pay for every day on strike, but that was hefty. . . . We definitely recognized that . . . the law that guaranteed the right to bargain . . . was an extraordinary thing and that many of our fellow teachers did not have that in other states.

Like Liam, teachers (typically) only mentioned state-imposed economic costs for two reasons. First, they were conveying why going on strike is never a "win" for teachers; it is an action of last resort. Second, they were falsifying the claim that collective bargaining is undemocratic.

Teachers cannot use their economic solidarity and physical concentration in school buildings (social cohesion) to advance their own interests at the expense of parents, students, and society; the teeth in the law work in favor of administrators and elected school boards.

What teachers gain through collective bargaining depends on the school district's willingness to negotiate in good faith, the level of support from the community, and teachers' willingness to incur high social and economic costs if they go on strike as an action of last resort. For these reasons, social contexts are quite important. The fact that teachers across the state were similarly suffering from economic stagnation during the mid-1970s but not every local union went on strike supports this claim. Teachers in schools with a history of refusing to negotiate in good faith were more likely to go on strike than those who had been treated with dignity and respect.

Discussion: The State, Collective Voice, and Public Service Quality

A 1957 survey by the NEA showed that two-thirds believed teachers should not participate in political activity beyond voting and only one in three felt it was appropriate to informally discuss electoral candidates with other teachers. Such political activities included influencing school board elections, even though this study and other research show that the composition of school boards directly affects educators' working environments (Briney, 1958; Methvin & Herndon, 1979). This chapter explored how and why teachers' unions emerged as powerful political and economic interest groups despite these views. As shown, teachers initially pursued economic gains through their unions but then used their professional solidarity to influence public policies through lobbying, campaign contributions, and other forms of political voice.

Economic voice improved public school performance by making it easier to recruit and retain effective teachers through higher salaries, improved working conditions, and increased autonomy. Informants provided many examples of how political voice benefited citizens, but two topped the list: teachers' unions lobbied for policies that benefitted children, families, public schools, and communities; they also successfully demanded teaching and curricular reforms. The latter improved teaching and learning by strengthening teacher credentialing; enriching the quality of mentoring and professional development programs; helping to recruit and retain teachers in hard-to-staff schools and subjects; introducing standards by subject and grade; implementing course requirements for high school graduation; and using testing to assess student progress. While the overall goal was to help *all* students meet higher standards, such policy feedback also emphasized a more equitable distribution of HQTs across schools. All of these changes were adopted before similar national policies (NCLB, NCLB waivers, and RttT).

Some—like Chris, a former suburban elementary teacher and current elementary school principal—clarified that, unlike their national counterparts, these state policy reforms improved practice by establishing *schools as learning communities*:

> [Afterward, we] collaborated . . . graded each other's [state] tests . . . [to] get exemplars . . . [ask] questions. . . . If you shut your door and it becomes a competition for test scores, that knowledge and growth will get lost. . . . [We lose] the great things each of us has to offer . . . learn from one another and . . . help people who might be struggling. . . . If you trust one another, you are willing to share your successes but also what did not work. . . . Trust is important. . . . Competition will weaken that trust. . . . Teachers come with different skill sets and different passions about what interests them. Students are inspired by what teachers feel passionate about. . . . We don't want them all to look exactly alike, but we do want them to learn from one another. . . . These kinds of differences add to the fabric of the building.

State standards and testing encouraged grade-, school-, and district-level collaboration, but schools as organizations remained "loosely coupled" (Meyer & Rowan, 1977). Teachers could still "shut their doors" and exert some control over how they taught, even as the state increasingly directed what they taught. It was one factor in informants' expressed support for these policies. They further applauded the inclusion of teachers and their unions in the development and implementation of state standards and tests and using state exams as a *gauge* of performance. Tests provided a general idea of how a child, teacher, and school were doing; they were not used to make high-stakes decisions, except with the "exit" exams in some subjects that students needed to pass to graduate from high school. Even then, there were alternative means for students to graduate.

Others—like Liam in the following quotation—applauded the increased willingness of political and economic elites *at all levels of government* to seek out their advice with respect to the curriculum, pedagogy, and education policies:

> It is definitely a profession . . . like medicine . . . in the 1980s. . . . This was where we were going. Teachers were more organized and gaining control over our profession and more autonomy in the classroom. There was a lot of excitement, and we were also working with the business

community, like IBM, but they were not coming in to micromanage . . . [or tell] us the cheapest way of mass-producing our product like what is going on in many respects now . . . how to do it faster, better, cheaper, and in the same way . . . a cookie-cutter approach. That was not the case . . . it was more about supporting schools and teachers.

Respondents contrasted this development with earlier periods, when teachers were left out of policy decisions and policymakers tried to limit union voice to bread-and-butter issues (salaries and benefits). Both suppressed professional voice and policy feedback, but the latter created tensions between teachers and their communities by leaving the impression that unions only cared about salaries and benefits. Unions worked to overcome these negative stereotypes (symbolic violence) by improving the teacher workforce and fighting for policies that benefit children, families, public schools, and communities.

As evidence that unions improved the quality of the teacher workforce and therefore public education, they cited that, by the 1990s, teaching was a "competitive market" in the northeastern state that is the subject of this analysis. The profession drew applicants from highly ranked colleges and universities, the supply of teachers exceeded demand, and school districts had more choice in terms of whom they hired. Informants acknowledged that the weak economy increased competition for all jobs but cited southern states as their "counterfactual." There, RTW laws suppressed unionism, states were slower to adopt teaching reforms, and low wages and poor working conditions resulted in teacher shortages. Kristen, an urban elementary teacher, elaborated on these claims. She had worked in the South before returning to teach in this northeastern state:

> I went to teach down south because the job market in the North was horrible . . . like 100 . . . or 200 applicants for every job. . . . There are no unions down there. . . . They couldn't even get substitutes. . . . They were *desperate* for teachers. . . . The principal interviewed me. . . . He wanted to know if I had any more friends that wanted to come down and teach. . . . His exact quote was, "We just love you Yankee teachers!" . . . And, when he introduced me at the first faculty meeting, he said how well prepared the teachers always were when they came from our colleges. He said any time he sees a certification from this state that he knows they will be a good teacher. . . . So, it wasn't just a "Yankee thing" [*laughs*]. It was our state. He said that teachers from this state were very well prepared.

Participants discussed charter schools as a second counterfactual: only 7 percent of charter schools are unionized; they pay less, on average, than public schools; and they have significantly higher rates of turnover (Burian-Fitzgerald, 2005; Rebarger & Zgainer, 2014).

Surprisingly few studies examine how unions affect school, teacher, and student performance. The main issue is the lack of available student achievement data from the time when most schoolteachers were unionizing (the 1960s and 1970s). To get around this issue, recent studies have taken advantage of three natural experiments. The first group of studies used the uneven rates of unionization across states to examine the issue. Unionism is positively linked to standardized test scores (e.g., NAEP and college aptitude testing [ACT and SAT]) and graduation rates; student performance is also significantly better in states with *high union density* (those where over 90% of teachers are unionized) when compared to those where less than 50 percent are covered by collective bargaining or meet-and-confer agreements.[9] Although not a causal analysis, B. Baker (2014) supports another claim made by informants: Unionization increases funding fairness, as well as teacher and public school performance.[10]

Han (2016) benefited from a second natural experiment. In 2010–2011, four states—Indiana, Idaho, Tennessee, and Wisconsin—began severely restricting collective bargaining. These actions reduced teachers' salaries (by approximately 9%) and decreased teacher quality through high turnover and teacher shortages. The latter disincentivized the dismissal of ineffective teachers owing to a lack of higher quality replacements. By comparison, the states that allowed collective bargaining had higher dismissal rates for low-quality teachers, and union density reduced the dropout rate—an important finding since studies show that areas with lower dropout rates have more upward socioeconomic mobility.

The third natural experiment compared unionized and nonunionized charter schools in California. Matsudaira and Patterson (2017) found that unions increased student performance on math exams and had a positive, but statistically insignificant, effect on reading scores, especially for lower performing students. This finding refutes an earlier synthesis of studies that suggests unionism leads to modest gains in test scores and possibly graduation rates but may be harmful to the very lowest- and highest-achieving students (Carini, 2002). That synthesis may have been inappropriately affected by the inclusion of lower quality studies.

One further point deserves mention. Loyalty, as both an emotion and a work commitment, was evident in discussions about early state reforms. For example, many said they felt "proud" to work in a "progressive state" that allowed collective bargaining, respected professional voice, and treated teachers with dignity and respect. My interviews suggest this pride of place increased both individual and collective political participation (*interpretive effects*). Even so, unionization was facilitated through teachers' social ties and their desire to socialize with fellow teachers—more than a desire to engage in political activities—and *teachers of all ages* said that unions are still (largely) a source of social engagement, versus political or even economic action. In the words of Molly, a current suburban high school social studies teacher,

> I don't really think of my union as a political entity. . . . We can check off to have some of our paycheck go to . . . the political action arm of the union. . . . They use that money to fund political candidates and political ads, and the state union has a polling center and . . . teachers volunteer . . . to run the phones. . . . In our contract, we have one faculty meeting a month . . . set aside for the union. . . . [We mostly discuss] the social and economic things the union does . . . picnics or a Friday happy hour . . . getting people to serve on committees . . . [collecting] money for scholarships . . . [or to] adopt families for Christmas. . . . They do ask people to run for the union . . . discuss our contracts but . . . [not] political candidates. It's political only in the sense we discuss state . . . federal [education and budgetary] policies. . . . They may ask people to go to rallies at the state capital . . . [or discuss the need to get] candidates to run for the school board who are not anti-tax-and-spend . . . [the union doesn't say] vote for so-and-so.

Molly is describing *resource effects*—when political institutions provide the economic means, capacity, or incentive to participate in politics or when they confer needed civic skills and knowledge—but she prioritizes the union's social functions. She values how these social actions benefit the students, the faculty, the school, and the community (social capital).

I discuss teachers' social behaviors more fully in the next chapter. For now, it is important to note that this study suggests that *active* union participation has never been high among teachers. In my sample, 23 percent had in some way served the union. Among those who had not, about 9 out of 10 expressed that their interactions with the union were largely through social events. Just as interesting, most of those who actively participated in the union also declared socialization *was* the end goal. Others said they served because they were complaining and a fellow teacher said they should "do something about it" or "guilted" them into service. Either way, union participation stemmed from teachers' social ties more than a commitment to collective bargaining or political participation. Returning to Lorna's narrative,

> [My] friend was chapter leader, and my mother had passed away. . . . My mother had been president of the Catholic Women's Association. . . . [My Jewish] friend knew what she was doing with the Italian guilt. . . . I said to her, "If she didn't die, what were you going to do?" And she said [*laughing*], "If she didn't die, we were going to tell you it would help you get over having to take care of your sick mother. It would get you out of the house."

Clearly, teachers' social ties are important in terms of union service, but, as shown, they are also important for individual and collective (political, economic, and professional) voice.

Conclusion

In the 1950s, educators believed that it was unprofessional to join unions and engage in political voice beyond the individual act of voting. This chapter showed how collective political and economic action spread partly—albeit unintentionally—as a result of a state law that allowed public employees to bargain collectively. While it provided mostly symbolic resources, that law activated a link in teachers' minds between collective political and economic voice and the group's economic and professional interests (interpretive effects). Over time, teachers used collective voice to expand the law in ways that provided organizational advantages (resource effects). The latter altered the content and character of future policies by helping the union redress collective action problems (Olson, 1965/1971).[11] These findings suggest that scholars should pay more attention to how the state facilitates or hinders the ability of organized interests—like farmers' organizations, renter and consumer associations, and unions, occupations, and professions—to mobilize members and engage in collective voice. Government policies do not simply alter individual perceptions about the efficacy of economic and/or political action (interpretive effects); they also alter the economic and political playing field by subsidizing groups (resource effects).

This chapter further indicates that recent political efforts to reduce union membership, and thereby defund and defang political opponents, are misguided. Teachers' unions do not engage solely in collective bargaining and political mobilization. They improve funding fairness and increase the efficiency and effectiveness of public schools by fostering professional voice and providing the social cohesion to address the broader political, social, and economic issues that influence children's educational outcomes. These societal benefits contradict the arguments of scholars—like Moe (2011) and Greene (Greene & Kahlenberg, 2012)—that teachers' unions are the same as other special interests, such as the sugar lobby and the Tobacco Institute, because they use their social cohesion to benefit themselves at the expense of society. The next chapter explores these broader societal benefits in more detail.

5

Professionalism, Social Accountability, and Policy Feedback

Durkheim argued that each occupation has its own "morality"—ideas, sentiments, and "ways of seeing" and "feeling" (cited in Bosk, 2003, p. 5)—and Bosk (2003) found that surgeons share a "collective conscience." If policy makers hope to make professions and occupations more accountable, they must first understand how that collective conscience is formed and how it benefits society. Chapter 4 showed how unionization contributed to the development of a collective identity among teachers. They used the resulting solidarity to improve salaries, benefits, and working conditions and to gain more voice in the development of policies that affect teaching, learning, and public schools. Over time, political and economic voice (policy feedback) expanded professional authority by providing teachers with more autonomy at work and occupational control over the labor market (e.g., licensing and training requirements). This chapter compares professionalism—as a means of controlling teachers' work—with its counterparts (managerialism and consumerism); it explores the effects of professional accountability on teaching, learning, and public schools before the expansion of hierarchical accountability (managerialism) and market accountability (consumerism) under recent reforms.

Exploring Professional Accountability

According to Freidson (2001, p. 11), professional authority will not expand unless the professions are able to "neutralize or at least effectively counter" the arguments of those who favor control by managers (managerialism) on one end and the market (consumerism) on the other. Advocates of *consumerism* believe that individuals and firms should be free to purchase or offer goods and services under a "buyer beware" philosophy. Because the average person has enough knowledge and capacity to make rational choices, government regulation is unnecessary; a firm that engages in abusive and unethical practices will not be able to recruit enough workers and customers to remain in business. Those who favor *managerialism*, on the other hand, contend that an advanced, formal education (e.g., management degree) is superior to consumer purchasing power and the knowledge of "trained specialists" (e.g., laborers, professionals, tradesmen) for the efficient and effective production of goods and services. Despite these differences, both ideologies view work as an instrument to other ends (e.g., consumption, moving up the corporate ladder, being part of the middle class); assume that it is human nature to "shirk," or avoid hard work; and contend that rewards are not intrinsic, or inherent, in the work itself. Owing to these beliefs, both advocate external forms of control and tying extrinsic rewards, like salaries and benefits, to performance (Freidson, 2001).

By comparison, Freidson (2001) sees "monopoly"—occupational control over the work—as the essential characteristic of the ideal typical profession. By definition, *professionalism* involves the official recognition that an occupation requires the use of complex, formal knowledge and skills and the exercise of discretion. *Official recognition* is conferred when the government enforces the professional monopoly through, for example, licensing and certification requirements. You cannot practice medicine without a license. *Formal knowledge* is that which is gained through university training and a residency requirement. These experiences provide members with the concrete, abstract, and theoretical foundations to *create and expand knowledge*, but they also create the commitment, solidarity, and community to *monitor and enforce compliance with a professional code of ethics*; they socialize members into the norms of the occupation and instill an occupational code and lifestyle. This is what gets created above and beyond learning. Why might the government give professions this kind of control?

Professionalism is based on the belief that those who have been trained and socialized are better able to judge the performance of their colleagues. The work is complex, lacks uniformity, and cannot be routinized; workers also need to remain relatively free from "outside" control to be true to their professional norms and practices. Managerialism threatens the ethical commitment to clients because managers tend to put quantity and cost (efficiency) over quality; they may routinize work and restrict innovation to achieve efficiency gains. Consumers, in contrast, may sanction qualified professionals while supporting unqualified ones—either because they lack the prerequisite knowledge to judge service quality or because, like managers, they are focusing on costs. Whether stemming from above (hierarchy or managerialism) or below (the market or consumerism), such external controls have the potential to create a race to the bottom that typically results in social justice issues because upper-income and highly educated individuals are better able to access superior services (Freidson, 2001).

More broadly, professions are given autonomy because society recognizes that they serve some higher value. Physicians save lives; lawyers ensure justice; and the clergy protects society's moral foundations. Although this list varies across societies—chefs, for instance, are included in France because its people value the culinary ideal of eating well—professional discretion is based on a *widespread belief* that members are "morally involved" with the client and the work. In consequence, members will use their knowledge and skills to advance the interests of their clients versus their personal or occupational concerns. Phrased another way, there is a widespread belief that members have internally embraced a code of ethics, errors—by and large—are not the result of deliberate neglect, the profession has adopted procedures for reviewing the behaviors of its members, and the profession will prosecute ethical violations and protect against professional malfeasance (Freidson, 2001). Table 5.1 compares professionalism with consumerism and managerialism in terms of worker commitment and productivity.

The last chapter showed how unionization contributed to the development of a professional identity among teachers but (largely) left three questions unanswered. First, if you give teachers more professional autonomy, do they self-regulate beyond their initial training? Second, do members police against deviance and mistakes? And third, does professionalism benefit society? My interviews suggest that an *ethos of care* is the key to answering all three questions. As such, the remainder of this section explores teaching as a caring occupation, particularly how and why teachers' affective ties are important for teaching and learning, how they serve as a source of professional accountability, and how they improve the efficiency and effectiveness of schools by facilitating *individual* and *collective social controls*.

Table 5.1. Theory of action about worker commitment and productivity

	Professionalism	Markets (consumerism) and hierarchy (managerialism)
Why do people work?	Intrinsic rewards: There is something in the work itself that motivates over and above the extrinsic rewards, such as a calling to do good in society (i.e., God put us on this earth for a reason. This work is where I realize who I am).	Instrumental ends: Rewards are not inherent in the work itself. Work is an instrument to other ends, such as making a living or moving up the corporate ladder (i.e., extrinsic rewards).
How do you maximize worker performance? Control worker deviance?	Instill a work ethic, protect voice, and provide interesting, challenging, and worthwhile work.	It is human nature to shirk. The way to motivate workers is to tie extrinsic rewards (i.e., salary, benefits, or hierarchical position) to effort. Workers also need surveillance. This may include incentives (the market) or a formal system of control (i.e., observation or supervision).
Who should control or regulate the work?	Professionals have answered the calling and have spent years training for the job. Professions police their own through formal controls but also through social controls.	Consumers control the work through voice and exit under consumerism. Public and private managers (i.e., hierarchy) control the work under managerialism.

Teaching as a "Caring Occupation"

Most research on organizations, occupations, and professions neglects the study of emotions because they are perceived to be private and unregulated (Fineman, 2000). Two strands of research challenge those assumptions. The first documents the vital role emotions play in organizational life; the second shows how some jobs require or prescribe the use of emotions. Such is the case in the service sector when workers are provided with scripts that standardize and sell a particular experience along with a work product.[1] This *emotional labor* differs from *emotion work,* where employees manage their emotions for their own noncompensated benefit. It also differs from *caring* occupations—like teaching—where members manage their emotions in accordance with professional norms, client expectations, and the demands of the job; they are not closely supervised and retain some autonomy over their emotion management (Hochschild, 1983).[2]

Like other research, this study finds that the act of teaching requires more than technical skills and content knowledge. It contains an affective domain, including—but not limited to—the ability to genuinely understand and empathize with students, parents, and colleagues.[3] Teaching involves a great deal of human interaction, "often in crowded conditions, with large numbers of pupils who are frequently energetic, spontaneous, immature and preoccupied with their own interests" (Nias, 1996, p. 296). Genuine and feigned emotions—what Hochschild (1983) calls "deep acting" (summoning actual emotions) and "surface acting" (displaying outward signs of emotions that are not internally felt)—improve teaching and learning by building excitement in the classroom, engaging students in learning, and minimizing behavioral issues. Consider the words of a suburban elementary teacher (Terry) and an urban middle school science teacher (Peter):

TERRY: I stand on my desk and march and sing . . . [in] a tiara. . . . I am the "Learning Fairy." I bestow magic learning dust on them. . . . First graders just go "Yee-yah. Yeah. This . . . is . . . it!"[shaking her fists high up in the air to emphasize each word]. My own kids are grown . . . but every day I get to . . . be a kid again with my kids in school. . . . I am six years old, but trapped in a 53-year-old body. . . . In my heart, I am six years old . . . in my soul.

PETER: Ever since I can remember I have lived and breathed science . . . always running tests. . . . My mom . . . getting mad at me because I would have jars of things in the refrigerator . . . lose a tooth . . . keep my teeth in different liquids and see how they would dissolve. . . . [It] drew me to the profession . . . that creative side. . . . I could craft lessons . . . and I liked that I could be goofy . . . the whole mad scientist thing. . . . I can be myself when I am working . . . become that character . . . use humor . . . to engage children in learning.

Teachers typically draw on many different emotions, depending on the lesson and the "mood" of the class.[4] This makes it difficult to standardize teaching and exert control through bureaucracy (managerialism) and/or markets (consumerism).

Teachers are not—and cannot be—uniform in terms of the emotions on which they draw to improve teaching and learning. Too much acting also negatively affects educational outcomes. Students know if their teachers are dispassionate about teaching or fabricating genuine caring for students. They are less likely to work hard and more likely to engage in disruptive behaviors in these classrooms. Ron, a high school physics teacher, explained,

[We all] want people to care about us. Students . . . make that judgment within 30 seconds. If they think you are indifferent . . . it is a real struggle. But if . . . you are concerned . . . they will really pull for you. Then, you . . . build that rapport over time . . . every day . . . constantly communicating back and forth. . . . Each month you forge a deeper relationship and rapport. . . . You can lose it too. . . . It's more fragile at first, but becomes more durable over time.

Such disruptive behaviors harm individual students but also negatively affect the performance of the class because teaching and learning are collectively constructed.

Teaching as a "Collective Performance"

As discussed, a common misperception is that teaching and learning are constructed through the interaction between individual teachers and individual students. This belief downplays how teachers need to manage large numbers of students—with diverse abilities, backgrounds, and dispositions—in crowded (and compulsory) situations, often with limited resources. Paul, a retired suburban elementary and middle school English teacher, discussed how these realities require teachers to channel individual and collective dispositions, experiences, abilities, and behaviors so that students are able *and* willing to learn:

[It] took . . . the first month . . . to get on the same page. There was learning . . . [but also] a great deal of testing and negotiating. . . . Mostly it is going to end up my way. . . . [You cannot teach] the same lesson . . . exactly the same way . . . [because each class has] different dynamics . . . depending on who you congregate together. . . . The IQs of the students are almost exactly the same . . . same ratio of girls to boys . . . socioeconomic status, and no two classes would be exactly the same. . . . [Owing to] the way that those students react to each other . . . it is like . . . slicing through butter with a hot knife to teach one . . . pulling teeth to teach the other. . . . It is not the sum of the individuals, it is how they mix together to form a collective. . . . [The teacher has] to find what . . . will work. . . . [Try] different things. . . . The teacher is responsible . . . [but it] is not me as an individual teacher producing an outcome, it is me with a group of students . . . it is a collective good.

In other words, like all collective bodies, teachers need to create social order and social cohesion to meet their core functions and tasks. Their ability to do so is complicated by the frequent conflict between individual and collective ends. If teachers narrowly focus on improving individual achievement (core task)—through explicit rewards or by putting overt pressure on unmotivated students—they may actually reduce learning by creating adversarial relationships. The resulting us-versus-them environment (e.g., teachers vs. students, low-performing vs. high-performing students, favored vs. disfavored students) reduces social cohesion and necessitates more overt forms of social control (e.g., calling home, detention, suspension).

Research supports informants' claim that peers matter; students perform better when pooled with higher achieving students owing to positive behavioral effects more than academic ones.[5] Paul described such *peer* effects—the ability of students to influence one another academically and behaviorally—in the previous narrative; however, respondents discussed how one student may influence an entire class, how students model their behaviors according to the norms of their peer groups, and how both may create "balloon effects" (a small incident blows up into something big), "snowball effects" (once a class starts going downhill, it is difficult to stop its descent), and "tipping points" (it gets disproportionately harder for teachers to manage students and ensure learning once the number of academically or behaviorally challenged students becomes large enough).

Teachers use their emotions and their relationships to mitigate or stop disruptive and unhelpful behaviors *before they occur.* The ability to do so is one reason why experience is critical for teacher performance. Novice teachers are hyperfocused on what one teacher called "the whats" and "the hows" of teaching (content and pedagogy) while "learning the ropes." They spend more time "putting out fires" (managing students) and less time teaching content until they develop the ability to predict and prevent negative behaviors. In the words of a brand-new suburban art teacher (Gloria),

> it's hard . . . to look beyond the day-to-day because you have to focus on so many new things at once . . . content, developing projects and lesson plans . . . the rules of the school. . . . Little things . . . can snowball. Kids . . . take advantage . . . if you let the little things slide. Then you have to deal with something bigger down the road.

With time, teachers learn how to create an environment that encourages students to rise individually and collectively in ways that improve performance.

Terry's and Peter's narratives showed how teachers create this environment by using their emotions to build excitement in the classroom and engage students in learning. Others, like Paul and Don, a suburban high school social studies teacher, discussed using peer relationships to challenge individual students and make them feel individually and collectively safe to try new things. More than one teacher described this as creating a "caring community":

DON: [When] you have a bad day, they know and they really pull for you. . . . It's a community. . . . Sometimes, someone will walk by . . . and peak in, and the kids and I will look at each other like, "Why is he looking in here?" We're all in it together [*laughing*]. We need to do better than "the other guys" [other classes]. . . . I even do it for homeroom. I didn't like the word. . . . [It] was too warm and fuzzy [*laughing*] . . . so we [voted and] renamed it the "Morning Meeting Room" [*laughing*]. . . . It is all part of the whole idea of "Come on board, we're all in this together." You try to rope them in [*laughing*].

PAUL: [Eighth]-grade students hate to be up in front of the class . . . love attention, but . . . not . . . people . . . staring at them. . . . So, you draw them in and then you pull them out over the precipice. . . . [For example, as] part of a poetry unit, . . . they had to write a poem. They were guaranteed an "A" if they sang it in front of the class. . . . The performance . . . was not part of the assignment, but . . . every year, 99 percent . . . would sing their poem. . . . After the second, third, fourth student did it, they would realize that they could do it. . . . When they got finished . . . they would just be happy with the whole thing . . . laugh while doing it and the other students would laugh with them. . . . There was a lot of direct teaching . . . [also] coworking . . . and students teaching and learning by doing. . . . [Many did] duets . . . they would have to do their own, so . . . they would have to do two.

In these classrooms, social order is present, but the mechanisms through which it is achieved are not "visible." Yet Don and Paul are clearly using their relationships to encourage students to pull their behaviors in line in ways that improve individual and collective outcomes. Don even professed that this *social accountability* is important in homeroom. Social accountability is an informal source of control that occurs as a result of individuals being embedded in a group. They fulfill their obligations owing to feelings of loyalty, trust, and respect for fellow members and/or because they are closely aligned with the group's norms and values.

The collective nature of teaching and learning is one of reasons why the occupation stresses *humanistic ends,* not just instrumental ones (e.g., student achievement and attainment). When asked to elaborate, participants discussed three such ends. The first involves developing children as caring, well-adjusted human beings who voluntarily follow the rules—rather than behaving, learning, or contributing only when being compelled to do so by authority figures. The second is to foster the intrinsic love of learning that creates life-long learners. Lisa, a suburban elementary teacher, offered a story about this humanistic end:

> You don't teach them, you help them to learn . . . facilitate . . . put it out there . . . in such a way that they're going to want to grab onto it and hook into it, and love it, and love to learn the rest of their lives. . . . The academic part is . . . [important, but there is] so much else. . . . My husband had an angioplasty. . . . I showed them how the balloon worked. . . . [One student later became] a doctor . . . said, "Remember . . . the balloon?" . . . [We] can effect change. It's scary sometimes. But it's so rewarding to know that we really make a difference.

The third involves developing *noncognitive skills and behaviors.* I referred to these as socioemotional and other so-called soft skills (e.g., empathy, trust, perseverance, self-control). The next section uses a discussion of feeling and expression rules to elaborate on how the humanistic ends of teaching improve academic outcomes (core task) but also *transform* society, meaning they change students' life outcomes and create a more egalitarian, democratic, and caring society.

Teaching as a Humanistic Occupation

According to Hochschild (1983), societies develop "feeling and expression rules" that regulate internal feelings as well as facial or bodily displays. These social norms create zones of acceptable and unacceptable behaviors, communicate what is owed to others emotionally, and provide information that serves as a source of action. Guilt and shame, for example, are internal and external signals, respectively, that the rules were not followed or that something owed was not paid. Fear, on the other hand, warns us of danger and encourages flight away from precarious situations.

Feeling and expression rules vary across social contexts. Some societies, for instance, expect displays of grief at a funeral, while others discourage them or encourage individuals to celebrate life instead of death. Human beings are also unequal in their capacity to engage in *emotion management*—the ability to modify one's emotions and facial and bodily displays to bring them in line with social expectations—and their willingness to comply with feeling and expression rules. Some differences relate to personal dispositions and upbringing; however, institutions—like schools and churches—play a role in socializing our young (Hochschild, 1983). Many informants referred to this role by using the phrase *in loco parentis,* which is Latin for "in the place of a parent."

Participants argued that schools should foster the development of socioemotional and other so-called soft skills and behaviors because they help students meet social norms and expectations and thereby improve their academic, employment, and life outcomes; they also help create a caring society. These claims are apparent in a story Fred, a suburban elementary teacher, told about how he conveyed to his students that it was important to fulfill one's obligations, even while grieving, after his father passed; his grief also helped them learn how to express sympathy:

> I lost my dad in 2004. . . . It was something real . . . how you deal with pain, with life. Nobody talks about this stuff . . . but they need to hear it and see . . . role modeling. That is how we learn. . . . I remember hanging up my wall phone . . . the kids . . . said, "What's the matter?" and I said, "My father just died." . . . This was two days before the moving-up ceremony. I came back . . . to read their names as they go by. So cool, so hard, but I spent a year with these guys. I couldn't just go and leave them. I had to be there.[6]

Research supports informants' claims that socioemotional skills and behaviors improve academic, life, and work outcomes by encouraging individuals to work hard, persevere, and "think outside the box."[7] The phrase *in loco parentis,* however, is also part of a cautionary tale about the dark side of feeling and expression rules and the socialization function of public schools.

As a legal doctrine, *in loco parentis* provides schools and teachers with broad authority over children. For much of our nation's history, it was used to discipline human behaviors in ways that were harmful to the least well-off—minorities, the poor, immigrants, and children with learning, emotional, or behavioral issues. Efforts to standardize educational experiences and behaviors perpetuated inequalities by favoring "the norm," which tended to advantage middle- and upper-income students and those with power or status in society. These issues are far less prominent today because federal laws and civil rights and liberties lawsuits since the 1960s haven given parents and students more legal authority and rights; the professionalization of teaching also resulted in changing mores and practices. Nonetheless, as evident in the words of a suburban counselor (Sue), the unequal capacity to comply with societal norms still sometimes disciplines differences in human behavior in ways that harm the least well-off:

> [Many of those I counsel] suffer from mental illness . . . drug . . . and behavioral issues. . . . You have to really think outside of the box. Every child . . . family is different. . . . They all want to be understood . . . [not] judged. . . . [Many] have not had positive relationships . . . [at school and] struggled to get help. . . . Many . . . parents . . . struggled with school . . . did not graduate or got a GED . . . lack . . . academic skills but . . . also struggle when they interact . . . [don't] know what to ask . . . have limited social skills . . . act inappropriately . . . say inappropriate things. . . . Then they are not taken seriously. . . . [So] I work with the families to help them interact with schools. You have to be careful . . . [when telling them] how to act appropriately . . . not to swear . . . and so forth . . . walk a fine line because you do not want them to feel judged but you have to help them . . . so that they and the child get the help they need.

Informants' words and nonverbal cues indicate that teachers are aware of these issues. This claim was especially prominent in their discussions of why society should not standardize teaching and learning and in their displays of discomfort when elaborating on the need for social order to meet their core tasks.[8] Unlike widgets, the "product" that they are manipulating to meet their work outcomes are autonomous human beings who deserve to be treated with respect.

Certainly children need to be taught "the rules"—including, but not limited to, formal and informal norms—so that they internalize and follow them within and outside of school buildings. However, if they are to become autonomous and caring adults, they must also have the capacity to negotiate, debate, and challenge ways of seeing and constructing the world. When parents and students feel like they are being marginalized, treated unfairly, "put down," or compelled to behave in ways that make them uncomfortable, they *withdraw*. The lack of cooperation and participation reduces both individual *and* collective academic outcomes; it also has negative consequences for democratic societies (see Chapters 9 and 10). My interviews indicate that educators use their relationships with parents and students to maximize the democratic aspects of teaching, learning, and public education while minimizing the compulsory ones.

The relational aspects of teaching, learning, and classroom management are one of the primary reasons why educators emphasize a normative commitment to addressing children's emotional and social needs. It is also this normative commitment that makes teaching a profession, not a technical occupation. Policy makers may view these humanistic ends as moral or ethical imperatives, but they enable educators to perform their core tasks while also advancing societal interests by developing caring, well-adjusted, and educated human beings.

Teaching as a Profession: The Ethos of Care and Invisible Work

As mentioned, professions must remain relatively free from hierarchical controls (managerialism) and market pressures (consumerism) to meet core tasks while remaining true to professional norms, ethics, and practices (Freidson, 2001).[9] In education, the latter includes the *ethos of* care—an occupational norm to "do right by the kids" through *voice* (formal and informal protests on behalf of children, parents, and colleagues or in defense of occupational norms, knowledge, and practices) and a service ethic. In the words of Carley, a suburban elementary teacher,

> [a] little boy had no school clothes and I bought them. . . . It sets a precedent but . . . [you] have to go with your heart. . . . They wanted . . . our report cards online. . . . A lot of parents don't have computers . . . cars . . . flexible work schedules. . . . It is not great for the environment, but I kept thinking about one . . . single father . . . working so hard . . . to juggle his work schedule . . . [to come] to the parent–teacher conference. . . . [He said,] "I don't have a computer." . . . I fought tooth and nail to keep the paper report cards. You couldn't do that if you didn't have tenure because it was not a popular thing to do but it was the right thing to do. . . . What my heart knows is the right thing to do. . . . And they did change it back.

Carley exemplifies a *service ethic* in her commitment to going beyond what is required at work (buying clothes for a student); she *voiced* against a policy that harmed students and parents.

Most expanded voice to include any development that affects

teaching, children, families, public schools, and public education. Others extended the service ethic to parents, communities, and fellow Americans.[10] Janet, a suburban elementary teacher, told this story about a colleague offering care to her student outside of school:

> [Teachers] do a lot of things that are outside of their contracts to help students. Relationships are very important in teaching. I had a friend who was teaching ninth grade, and one of the boys in her class invited her to his wedding. . . . And she was thinking, "You're in ninth grade" [*laughing*]. . . . She shows up and was seated in the place where they put the mother of the groom because he had no family and she was the one adult in his life that was connected with him. . . . Teaching is an amazing profession. It really is, but it can be very sad too. This was a positive thing and yet it was also sad.

The situation Janet described is the very definition of *in loco parentis*. Her story sounds extraordinary, but my interviews suggest that these kinds of altruistic behaviors are quite common.[11]

The educators in this study demonstrated very high levels of work commitment. Qualitatively, they described teaching as "all encompassing." It was a calling, a mission, a vocation, and/or a lifestyle rather than a job. Returning to Carley's narrative:

> It's not a 9 to 5. . . . You bring it home with you. . . . They really become a family to you. You care about each and every child . . . have to be willing to put 500 percent into [it]. . . . The best part of teaching is the kids. That's the biggest reward. I absolutely love the children. . . . I'm a people person and they are just little people. . . . I think everybody has something good they can give to this world and if you can find it and tap into it, that's the way to go. . . . I love to learn myself. . . . People say you get summers off. . . . It was not about the hours . . . I want to make sure those kids are getting everything . . . out of that year with me. *Everything.*[12]

Quantitatively, they averaged an additional 10 hours at school every week and 9 hours at home. They also reported spending, on average, $800 of their own money every year on their students. Some examples of this unpaid, *invisible work* include serving on school committees; cleaning up the school and the school grounds; chaperoning student functions; attending school cultural, academic, or sporting events; raising money for or donating time to causes that support children and families in need; mentoring and training new teachers and student teachers; and using union dues to fund public libraries, crisis counseling centers for teens, recreational activities for inner-city children, breast cancer research, Red Cross disaster relief programs, and the Special Olympics. In all of these cases, the ethos of care recognizes that *it takes a village to educate children.*

Although I have described voice and the service ethic as if they are separate, my interviews suggest that the two work hand in hand to promote the humanistic and transformative ends of teaching as a profession. These behaviors also appear to be enforced through professional norms; they are not solely a function of individual dispositions. For example, because many principals are former teachers and other occupations (e.g., speech pathologists and school psychologists) are socialized in the same schools, these participants told narratives that were similar to those of classroom teachers. In addition, teachers' unions do not consign themselves solely to negotiating bread-and-butter issues—meaning salaries, benefits, and working conditions—and advocating policies that provide teachers with more control over the occupation (e.g., certification and licensing requirements) and/or the classroom; they also support the norms of teaching through voice and the service ethic.

With respect to economic and political voice (i.e., strikes, protests, lobbying, and political contributions), informants most commonly cited union demands for more and better targeted resources for public schools, low-income communities, and underprivileged children. The benefits of having a union that will "fight City Hall" (voice) on behalf of the least well-off are apparent in a story an urban elementary school teacher and union president (Lorna) told about her primarily low-income, minority-majority, underresourced school:

> [Kindergarten to second grade] was separated from the . . . [building and the principals] did *nothing* . . . didn't even come out of the office. One principal . . . was a real estate mogul . . . [never took] off his trench coat . . . quickly walked around the halls . . . then would . . . be gone [*laughs*]. . . . All these little babies in the middle of winter had to walk between buildings. It was supposed to be two years, but it turned into a decade. . . . [As the union leader], I spent an incredible amount of time going to the mayor's office and . . . [other places] to fight for a new building. . . . [We finally got a new school] after 15 years of fighting.

Lorna's narrative is an example of how union voice helps teachers remain true to their professional norms. It is a cautionary tale about hiring principals that have not been socialized into teaching but shows how professional accountability may be used to enforce bureaucratic accountability (e.g., administrators and the DOE) and political accountability (e.g., urban mayors). The union forced the latter groups to help those who are often marginalized (low-income and minority parents and students) because they are less likely to speak up, participate, or donate money to political campaigns (voice).

In terms of the service ethic, teachers' unions donate time and money to organizations or causes that improve the health and well-being of children, families, and communities. Two former district union presidents—Liam, a retired suburban high school English teacher, and Ted, a retired rural high school English teacher—had this to say:

LIAM: [Our] union is very involved in a local organization . . . that collects clothes and books for families in need . . . [and provides] crisis counseling for teens, and . . . tutoring to help disadvantaged students. Teachers recognize that what goes on outside school affects their classroom . . . [and] when they were building the library, the union contributed money to that. The schools are the heart of the community, but they need support from outside . . . and they need to provide support to those organizations. It's all connected.

TED: [Healthy], well-fed children, who live in healthy environments, are going to learn better . . . and our society is better off. Otherwise, teachers are spending far too much time being *in loco parentis*. . . . [The union] has made a concerted effort to focus on social justice . . . healthy living . . . hot meals . . . providing opportunities for inner-city kids to get recreational activities . . . disaster relief. It is altruistic, but it is also . . . self-serving. The more stability we can provide, the better we can be at our craft. . . . [Our state-level union alone] spends over a million dollars every year for breast cancer research . . . just over a half million . . . to support the Special Olympics . . . a huge amount . . . to the American Red Cross.

Altruistic behaviors appear to form a *continuum of care* that moves from children and colleagues on one end to schools as organizations, the profession, the community, and society on the other (Figure 5.1).

The way educators described the ethos of care to me suggests that caring behaviors begin close to home and then extend outward in ways that benefit society. For instance, providing care to a student with leukemia extends to providing support to the family and then to donating time and money to organizations that conduct research or provide assistance to others with leukemia. Certainly these behaviors benefit society, but this study indicates that they also increase the

Continuum of Care

Caring for students   Caring for teachers   Caring for the organization   Caring for the profession   Caring for the community   Caring for society

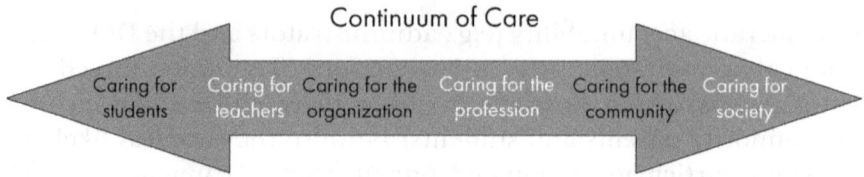

Figure 5.1. Teachers' caring behaviors.

efficiency and effectiveness of teachers and schools. When parents, children, administrators, and teachers perceive that they are part of a caring community, they are more willing to pull their behaviors in line in ways that promote collective outcomes over individual self-interests. As discussed in the next section, this *social accountability* maximizes the democratic aspects of learning (and public education) while minimizing the compulsory ones. It is also the primary way the profession regulates its own.

The Ethos of Care as a Form of Social Accountability

Freidson (2001) claims that the professions have both the right and a collective and individual duty to voice against any development that interferes with the "professional soul"—the set of underlying values that benefit clients and society. They are also obliged to ensure members receive the appropriate training and adhere to a code of ethics. He expressed concern, however, that the professions would only weakly "police their own" (e.g., refusing to refer a client to a colleague) because the complexity of the work makes it difficult to judge colleagues. Bosk (2003), on the other hand, shows that the lack of strong *formal controls* does not (necessarily) equate with weak or nonexistent ones. In his study of physicians at teaching hospitals, he found that *most controls were informal*. They included instilling the appropriate skills and values through training and residencies, where members are socialized into and regulated by the "collective conscience"—the profession's moral framework and expectations. For surgeons, such socialization was especially critical for training them on how to appropriately handle and learn from error, but the use of informal controls was pervasive and, he argues, better at protecting society from professional error and malfeasance than bureaucratic controls.

Like Bosk, my interviews suggest that a moral or ethical commitment to caring—the primary source of accountability in teaching—is instilled and maintained through training, student teaching, and on-the-job socialization. It is largely self-policed, yet also maintained through teachers' relationships with administrators, colleagues, parents, and students. As such, it combines professional accountability with social accountability. It is relational rather than hierarchical, as is the case with bureaucratic accountability, and broader than the relationship that teachers have with their occupation. Consider the words of a suburban high school math teacher (Brenda):

> [Prior to recent education reforms] you were internally motivated to do better. . . . There is professional accountability. Teachers care about their students and want to do right by them. But there is also social accountability. Teachers want people to think well of them. . . . Because we care about those relationships and how we are perceived, we want to do well. It is not like an external thing. It is internal. . . . [I had an 11th-grade student who] would study, study, study . . . [but failed the state exam. To graduate,] she has to take it next June . . . [wait] a whole year . . . for weeks, I was sick . . . to my stomach. . . . I told her I would help prepare her . . . [but it] hits you hard. . . . There are kids that don't try. . . . That hits you hard in different ways. . . . The relationships you form . . . trying to motivate them, show them how to study, how to do well in life. It is not just about your grade in math. It is about seeing your future and how to get there . . . your work ethic, your personality . . . trying to help mold them. . . . This is math, but really, it is about who they are and what they would like to be and what they need to do to get there. It is really exciting but it is also *a lot* of responsibility. So, it's emotional. . . . You take it home with you . . . you can't help it.

Brenda links professional accountability with social accountability but is clearly trying to distinguish between them. According to her, educators want to "do right by the kids" because they have internalized the norms of teaching and care about their students (professional value introjection); however, they also care about what others think of them and know that they are being informally "observed" (e.g., word of mouth) by other members of the community, such as colleagues, parents, students, and taxpayers (social accountability).

As mentioned, *social accountability* occurs as a result of individuals being embedded in a group. This social cohesion provides an informal source of social control. Marilyn, an urban elementary teacher, exemplifies this claim in her story about discouraging a colleague from cheating:

[I caught] my friend . . . cheating on the test. . . . He was walking around the classroom . . . putting his fingers on the desk like this [*she is putting three fingers on the desk to indicate the answer is number 3*]. . . . I said to him, "If I can see that, then everybody else can see that. Are you kidding me? You are putting your career on the line for a test?"

This situation occurred before teachers no longer proctored their own exams to prevent these kinds of behaviors, but it is an example of one teacher shaming another into ceasing an inappropriate behavior. It also shows how social accountability reinforces other forms of accountability. In this case, the teacher had violated the norms of teaching (i.e., professional accountability) *and* a state policy (i.e., political and bureaucratic accountability).

More expansively, relationships appear to create the social cohesion that encourages *all members* of the community (e.g., administrators, teachers, parents, students, residents) to pull their behaviors in line in ways that promote collective outcomes over individual self-interests. Molly, a high school social studies teacher, provided one of the best descriptions of how this informal source of social control works with students:

You have these students for a year . . . know which ones will go AWOL on the test . . . because they struggle in school . . . are . . . poor test takers . . . panic . . . shut down . . . [or are] lazy [*laughs*]. . . . Kids are human beings . . . run the gamut of behaviors. It used to be we were in the room . . . [for testing with our students,] other teachers . . . [and their] students. It was not like you were doing anything that other people did not know about. . . . You could say, "You finished fast. Did you check all your answers . . . [answer] all the questions . . . [write] enough on the essay?" . . . Trying to calm them down in some cases and shame them into doing more in others [*laughs*]. It was not considered cheating. You were looking them in the eye and that connection with a human being, who they knew, caused them to think about their actions or calm down. . . . You weren't even doing it to help your own performance. We did it for each other's students. Students know you even if they're not your student. There was also the possibility they might have you next year so that put some pressure on them too [*laughs*]. We also used to bring food to the students who had . . . failed the year before and . . . [were] taking the state exam for the current . . . and retaking the one from the prior year. You weren't in the room for that, but . . . [dropping food off helped by] in effect saying "I care about you. You can do it." They may be 15, 16, 17, 18 years old, but they need to know adults care about them. They won't ever admit to it [*laughs*], but it's true.

Some of the students did not "know" Molly, but they knew who she was as a result of being embedded within the same community.

With respect to social accountability, Molly used eye contact, dialogue, her presence, the provision of food, and the fact that they had or may have her as a teacher to encourage students to take the exams seriously or keep going when they were struggling. Like others', her story suggests that social accountability improves student performance and increases the efficiency and effectiveness of schools and teachers. It does so by minimizing the need for more overt and costly forms of social control. For instance, she is not berating or reporting a student for detention; instead, she uses her social ties to discourage students from opting out. This is important because studies show that repeated disciplinary actions for lower level issues or threats increase the likelihood of harsher punishments over time (suspensions and expulsions). These actions harm students, schools, and society by contributing to absenteeism, dropping out, and a school-to-prison pipeline; they also create economic and social justice issues by disproportionately harming students of color, students with disabilities, and male students (see Chapter 11).

While respondents acknowledged that teachers have different capacities to care and accepted different ways of demonstrating care, they collectively valued and enforced an ethos of care. Empirically, this claim is supported by the fact that *every* teacher in this study expressed a humanistic commitment to going beyond what was formally required at work to develop children as well-rounded human beings. These findings did not vary by age, gender, or occupational position. They also did not vary across schools or grades, although the form of teachers' emotion work sometimes changed as students aged.[13] It is backed by another theme that ran across interviews: *Good* teachers master their academic content and possess strong pedagogical skills (i.e., the head and the hand of teaching); *great* teachers are passionate about teaching, are enthusiastic about their content areas, and care about their students as human beings (i.e., the heart of teaching). Prior to recent reforms, the normative commitment to a more expansive, humanistic conceptualization of teaching was mostly self-policed, but informants did describe cases where teachers demonstrated a command of content and pedagogy yet lacked "heart" (i.e., a passion for teaching or caring about students). They also provided examples of highly committed teachers who lacked pedagogical skills and content knowledge. My interviews suggest that teachers individually and collectively "policed" the norms of teaching in these cases.

Most typically, collective policing involved using their relationships with one another. In its positive form, this form of social control included mentoring and sharing ideas, but teachers described more coercive forms, such as imposing social costs (e.g., gossip, social exclusion, or withholding social or professional approval) and work-related costs (e.g., voicing their concerns to administrators to encourage them either to remediate the issue or to forgo offering tenure). Patricia, a suburban high school math teacher, disclosed a story about her colleague to convey these complex social processes:

> [There was a teacher] from a very prestigious university but the students just could not stand him. . . . [We] tried helping . . . shared materials . . . [discussed how to] convey content . . . [develop] lesson plans . . . [relate] to the students. . . . [You must find] out what is going on . . . in school and at home . . . go to some of their activities. . . . [Kids will] try to live up to your expectations and accept different kinds of personalities . . . [if] they know you are pulling for them . . . [but] rebel against teachers that . . . don't like kids, or don't like them. . . . [By] the middle of the second year, we realized he was not taking our advice . . . because he didn't like the kids . . . was arrogant . . . shouldn't have to . . . dummy himself down to reach them. . . . The comments were always negative. . . . It was never about "him." . . . *They* were the problem. Teachers . . . make snarky remarks in the faculty lounge . . . use humor [to release tension]. . . . If it's all the time, you're in the wrong field. . . . [We told administrators] "we don't think he should have tenure. He doesn't like the kids. You can't work with that." . . . He was very savvy. . . . They felt . . . he was just young . . . by his third year, the teachers sort of . . . exiled him . . . didn't help . . . [or] sit with him at lunch. . . . I wouldn't say we shunned him. . . . The reception was much colder.

The reasons for policing the norms of teaching are complex; most informants described how ineffective teachers harm students, schools, and teaching as a profession. When parents and students lose trust in a teacher and the school that hired him or her, it makes the job of *all* teachers and administrators more difficult because it reduces voluntary compliance.

Unsurprisingly, many of the narratives that involved the strongest emotions related to a colleague who had violated professional norms. This and the fact that teachers so consistently expressed a commitment to the humanistic norms of teaching suggests that the ethos of care is an occupational norm more than a personal characteristic.[14]

Nevertheless, this study does indicate that professionalism *alone* is insufficient for redressing the unequal ways that external factors influence children's educational outcomes. All levels of government must adopt policies that reduce the unequal costs of caring by more equitably distributing OTL, especially to underprivileged students in high-need, low-resource schools.

Teaching and the Inequitable Costs of Caring

Although education research widely recognizes the unequal distribution of educational resources and academic need across schools and classrooms, many studies portray teachers as if they are uniform in their views and undifferentiated in their work. In contrast, those I interviewed conveyed that educators' experiences vary widely across social contexts, meaning communities, schools, and classrooms. Parents—as educational consumers—have an unequal financial capacity to choose where they live; poverty and academic achievement are highly correlated; children of color are more likely to grow up poor; and the free market and government policies historically relegated low-income and minority students to schools with fewer resources. Those spatial patterns have persisted and still affect teachers and students today (see Chapters 2 and 11). In addition, schools track students based on academic needs.

Tracking is the formal process of grouping students in separate classrooms according to ability or prior achievement to allow differentiated instruction. By comparison, *inclusion* involves providing aides and other resources to allow individual teachers to differentiate instruction within the same classroom. An in-depth discussion of such organizational practices are outside the realm of this book; however, they combine with the aforementioned historical developments to unequally distribute students by race, ethnicity, income, and academic need across schools and classrooms so that those who serve low-income and minority children are also disproportionately likely to teach academically at-risk students in underfunded schools and/or high need classrooms (for more on how tracking does so, see Lucas & Berands, 2002; Oakes, 1985).

Elaine, who retired from an impoverished inner-city school district, imparted some of the best stories about how these issues unequally affect educators and students because she served as a substitute teacher in a variety of better funded suburban schools during her retirement:

[It brought home] how little my kids got . . . a teacher was complaining . . . [because the] air conditioning . . . was not working . . . I taught in a 110-year-old building on the third floor . . . no air conditioning, with windows you could not open because the birds fly in . . . no screens . . . [or] kids had cut them . . . I bought fans . . . it was bearable . . . I never had an aide for a whole day . . . taught 32 kids . . . all very needy . . . [Suburban schools] have beautiful playgrounds while my students had . . . the concrete slab . . . and some swing sets . . . mostly destroyed . . . [I] didn't want to have small children using that playground . . . you didn't know what you are going to find . . . [left over] from kids hanging out there . . . after school . . . [As a substitute teacher] I see the students doing cross-country skiing and all kinds of other sports . . . I don't know why the state cannot spread the wealth. There is no tax base in my old district . . . It is *so* unfair.

Federal and state resources, while helpful, have failed to close the gaps in spending that primarily (a) result from relying on the property tax system to fund public schools and (b) disproportionately harm low-income children and students of color (see Chapters 3 and 11).

It is important to note that educators who serve large numbers of academically at-risk students bear an unequal cost of caring *regardless of where they work*; they are far more likely to deal with a wide array of "wicked problems" in their classrooms. Harmon and Mayer (1986) used that phrase to describe issues where there is widespread disagreement with respect to the definition, the cause, the appropriate solution, and the best way to measure the effectiveness of that solution. Some examples include poverty, homelessness, and family decay. Kristen, who worked in a high-need, low-resource rural elementary school in the South before teaching in a high-need, low-resource urban elementary school in the North, provided a moving description of how "wicked problems" wear on teachers' emotions:

[A] mother came in. . . . She had just been beaten up . . . [had] a baby on her hip . . . said, "You need to help me. I have all my stuff parked outside . . . in a taxi and I don't know what to do." . . . I had . . . desk throwers . . . a little girl whose mother was a cocaine addict and her boyfriend . . . [burned down the home] with her in it, and just poverty. . . . I took the baby . . . grabbed the social worker . . . got her tickets on a bus to go see her mother in another state. . . . Within one week, the boy . . . showed back up in my class. . . . She had gone back . . . [*pause and sigh*] to the guy who had beaten her up . . . [*getting emotional*]. That first year . . . was my toughest . . . [but] will always have that little piece of my heart. . . . I cannot believe how much . . . I cried. I stayed tough. . . . [As] corny as it sounds, I really believe I was supposed to do this . . . [working] in an inner city or a very poor rural district . . . is my calling. . . . I have never, *ever* faltered. . . . I can make the most difference here.

Like others who worked in high-need, low-resource schools, Kristen displayed a very high level of work commitment and *public service motivation,* meaning a desire to serve society; neither totally alleviates the effects of "wicked problems" on educators' performance, emotions, and, for many, their physical and mental health.

These job-related strains are both mitigated and complicated by working with children. In general, educators are more accepting of children's foibles because mistakes are part of learning; however, as human beings, educators want to be treated with respect. Like Emily, an urban teacher, they experience negative emotions—like frustration, anxiety, and anger—when students misbehave:

It's emotional because it involves . . . human beings that you care about . . . not in the early grades, but with fifth and sixth grade. . . . I needed to counsel myself . . . [to exercise] patience with behavioral issues. I was in a very difficult school, and for the first time in my life I had someone swear at me . . . [and call me] a whore [*laughing*]. . . . The reality is . . . you can't teach anything unless you have their behaviors under control. . . . If you are a good teacher, you really labor over whether your students get something . . . care about whether they are happy. . . . If you see students with problems . . . there are all kinds of emotions that come into play. . . . Sometimes it is great because, what is a better feeling than realizing that you have really reached children? But other times it's *terrible.* Your emotions run the gamut.

Many educators admitted that they sometimes struggled to depersonalize negative student behaviors.[15] This is a second area where experience is crucial. Over time, teachers learn strategies that enable them to move beyond negative emotions at work.

As suggested by Emily's narrative, participants reported experiencing frustration or anger over controllable behaviors, such as laziness or swearing at teachers; the strongest emotions, though, typically related to things that were out of their students' control. Health and mental health issues, poverty, homelessness, parental alcohol or drug abuse, family decay, and crime in the community impede academic performance and students' long-term health and well-being. As apparent in the statements of a retired urban elementary teacher (Brian) and an urban middle school English teacher (Ronnie), these issues wear on educators' emotions because they care about their students:

BRIAN: You spend seven hours a day . . . five days a week, 180 days a year, sure you develop feelings for them. . . . It's an emotional job. . . . You see a kid . . . [in] January and he doesn't have a coat, or he is dirty and hungry. . . . [It] was a very, very, very high needs, impoverished district. . . . [Children] didn't have a lot and it was heartbreaking . . . [for instance, reading a] father was killed in a drug-related shooting . . . and then you have to go into school on Monday.

RONNIE: We know some kids don't have enough to eat over the summer. . . . [We] have students . . . in shelters that . . . don't have dinner. We feed them breakfast and lunch. . . . [A student described in her journal] how difficult it was to get to sleep . . . [when] hungry. . . . It's just heartbreaking. . . . It's not just teaching. . . . If they're hungry, how are they going to do it?

Educators said they "never forget" those they were unable to help or who they helped but could not make up for their experiences outside of school. They "worry about" and remember students long after having them.

The importance of "wicked problems" for teaching and learning is evident in the fact that almost every educator explicitly discussed them; most also explicitly advocated the adoption of policies to redress them (see Chapter 11). Some of these policies would directly improve student performance; others would indirectly do so by improving teacher retention, especially in high-need, low-resource schools—like Mark's—where "wicked problems" negatively affect the physical, mental, and emotional well-being of students and educators and influence decisions about whether to remain in teaching in general and the school or district in particular:

[Your relationships are] a positive and negative. . . . Some of my students didn't want to leave [during break]. . . . At school they had stability . . . their day was planned . . . always knew what was going to happen. . . . When they got home, they had no clue what was going to happen, who was going to be there . . . if they were going to get lunch and dinner. . . . [Kids would] go home for a week and lose 10 pounds because they may eat once a day [*heavy sigh*]. . . . As much as they complain and say they hate you [*laughing*] . . . they miss you. . . . You felt . . . needed, and that was . . . rewarding . . . but . . . tough because you knew why.

Mark worked in an urban private and public school before getting tenure in a rural high school. Beyond being high-need, low-resource schools, each was quite different from one another, yet he told similar stories about how economic distress and social issues negatively affected his emotions by harming his students. He also expressed guilt for leaving the urban school he describes in this narrative—as if he had violated a moral code by leaving "his kids"—even though he was laid off due to fiscal cutbacks.

Guilt was a very common emotion across interviews. This study suggests that educators commonly struggle to uphold two widely held moral codes: They believe they *ought* to care about children and *ought* to control negative emotions at work. When teachers say they "feel guilty" after reacting negatively to a difficult student or losing their temper in the classroom, they are supporting Hochschild's claim that negative emotions are often a signal that the rules were not followed.[16] Individually held emotions may or may not indicate a need to reconnect with the norms of teaching, but widely held emotions are a sign that something is going on. For example, organizational factors, working conditions, or the nature of the occupation itself may be heightening negative emotions by making it difficult for teachers to live up to the profession's ideals. These narratives were far more prevalent among those who disproportionately teach large numbers of underprivileged students with inadequate resources, but as shown in the next section of the book, they spread as a result of recent education reforms.

Regardless of the source, educators who worked in impoverished communities and chronically underfunded schools remained disproportionately likely to describe negative work experiences owing to large class sizes, inadequate space, poorly vented or heated buildings, poor technology, outdated textbooks, not enough supplies or textbooks, and a lack of other teaching materials. Some also mentioned difficulties getting to work because the roads were loaded with potholes or had not been plowed as a result of fiscal cutbacks and/or rural isolation. Another complaint involved concerns about their physical safety and the costs associated with having their property vandalized. Loretta, who worked as an urban elementary teacher before becoming a suburban principal, offered this story:

[We] used to rent a parking lot . . . down the block. . . . It was fenced in with a gate. . . . [I worked in the] after-school program . . . in the winter. . . . At six o'clock it was dark. . . . I did not know . . . there were homeless people living . . . in an abandoned car. . . . [I] see movement. . . . My heart was beating so fast . . . thought my life was going to end. . . . I had switched to that parking lot because I had my car broken into [at school]. . . . This happened all the time. They would steal your tires. . . . I had my radio pulled out. . . . The precincts . . . had the highest crime rate in the city. . . . [It] puts a lot of stress on you . . . to worry about . . . personal safety . . . was someone going to . . . mug you . . . [was] your car going to be there . . . intact.

Given how these issues affect the physical, mental, and emotional well-being of educators and students, it is not surprising that informants from these schools reported higher levels of principal and teacher turnover. However, even those in adequately funded schools admitted that the *job itself* sometimes makes it difficult to meet professional ideals. The costs of caring for every student are quite high and often unsustainable given the demands of the job.

Informants said they walk a tight rope between going "the extra mile for individual students" (the ethos of care), serving all students, and maintaining the professional distance they sometimes need to do their jobs (the clinical side of teaching). Teachers' affective ties to students, colleagues, and the occupation appear to help them sustain the very high levels of work commitment that are required for effective teaching, even if relationships are sometimes a source of strain. Participants most frequently reported helping one another deal with organizational and occupational stress through humor and by "lending an ear," but many reported providing outright assistance, such as covering classes or duties during times of crisis.[17] In these cases, teachers are helping their colleagues because they care about them; their colleagues also influence their ability to do their jobs. Teachers are able to close their doors and teach, yet social isolation affects their ability to perform core tasks. This is true when relationships in general are strained—even if their own are not (see Chapter 7).[18]

As a whole, my interviews suggest that teachers manage their relationships because they affect the quality of their work. They care about the quality of their work because they care about the subjects of their work. This often necessitates going beyond the formal requirements of the job to attend to the emotional and social well-being of students, parents, and colleagues, as well as the needs of their schools and communities. In all of these cases, the humanistic values of individual teachers—backed by the humanistic values of teaching as an occupation—are a resource for students, colleagues, schools, and communities (social capital). More broadly, these values are a gift to society in the form of better educated *and* socially adjusted adults.

One final point deserves mention. Despite their strong service ethic, teachers by and large did not view themselves as altruistic or as people who consistently volunteer. In fact, they often downplayed these behaviors. When asked if they volunteered outside of school, for instance, teachers frequently replied "not much" and then indicated that they had little time to do so because of the need to engage in school-related tasks at home (e.g., grading, lesson planning, speaking with parents). Yet, when asked about specific activities, such as ever having participated in a walk-a-thon or donated money to a charity, teachers responded "all the time." Then they would discuss the specific causes to which they contributed time and money. These altruistic behaviors might be invisible to society, but—more interesting—they appear to be invisible to teachers themselves. Why?

My interviews strongly indicate that teachers take these behaviors for granted because the personal and intrinsic value of caring drew many of them into the occupation. Owing to those predispositions *and* the importance of external factors for academic outcomes, they tend to view donations of time and money as something they "do" because they "are" teachers—versus something they do in their role as citizens. Many also derive benefits from performing this invisible work at school and in their communities, including—but not limited to—job satisfaction, enjoyment, love, affection, and validation. This last claim is evident in a story told by Peter, an urban middle school science teacher:

> I had this one student . . . who was really into astronomy. . . . [Before his] birthday, I got in touch with . . . [a famous astronomer] and . . . gave him something my student had written. . . . He sent a book of his and he had written a note addressed to my student on the first page. . . . I presented the book to the student and he was really excited when I told him that someone had signed it inside. He said, "Did you sign it, Mr. So-and-So?" . . . which was really nice, but I said, "No, no, it's even better!" You can imagine how excited he was when he saw the note. I'll never forget his face. He was dumbfounded. He carried that book around with him for the rest of the year. It never left his side [*getting emotional*].

Certainly Peter is going beyond the scope of the job when he has an author sign a book for his student, but he also benefited from doing so. The satisfaction drawn from these noncompensated behaviors makes it less likely that he and other educators will classify them as altruistic.

Summing up, other research supports this study's finding that the personal and intrinsic value of caring draws individuals into teaching and, once there, helps them remain committed to the occupation.[19] It further supports that teachers' work experiences influence their emotions and well-being.[20] Because of this, teachers individually and collectively work to construct an environment that is conducive for meeting the prevailing social and professional definitions of "good teaching." When the prerequisite organizational, material, and relational conditions are not present, they experience reduced feelings of self-efficacy and job satisfaction. This results in burnout, resistance to change, and increased turnover (Nias, 1996). It is therefore not surprising that this and other research show that the emotional health of teachers is important for effective teaching (e.g., Day & Leitch, 2001).

Discussion: Professional Values as Social Capital

Durkheim (1996) maintained that social cohesion becomes more difficult to achieve in modern societies owing to the atrophy of social ties. To counteract these developments, he advocated developing socially integrating institutions—like public education—to pull together the "social fabric." According to him, professions and occupations—like teaching—are also uniquely "marked" to perform this function.[21] Chapter 2 showed that most policy makers recognized the importance of public education for integrating society, but they (largely) did not portray teaching in this way. They also favored the instrumental ends of public education (e.g., providing job skills and improving economic outcomes) over its humanistic, integrative, and transformative ends. Like other educators, a former urban psychologist and current suburban administrator (Sally) conveyed why the atrophy of social ties in an increasingly complex and diverse global society makes these latter three roles especially critical:

> [My former urban community] changed a lot in the past 30 years. You have people there who are lifers. . . . They still largely remain cohesive . . . [and] are very supportive of their school. . . . [But] they now also have a large transient population of drug dealers and prostitutes . . . pockets of . . . [children who are] not part of the original and cohesive group, and the school has to work harder to integrate them because that transient population does not have the ability to become part of that community.

Educators' relationships and humanistic values help create the social cohesion and social trust (social capital) that integrate and transform communities through, for example, the production of better educated *and* socially adjusted adults, the development of a more just and egalitarian society, and increased civic engagement.[22]

It could be argued, though, that teachers' relationships and humanistic values are only important if they influence teaching and learning. This and other research strongly suggests that they do. Some of the causal mechanisms are direct; others are more mediated. Research shows, for instance, that teachers suffer from high levels of stress and burnout; this results in high turnover.[23] Approximately one-third of America's new teachers leave during their first three years, and almost half exit within the first five (NCTAF, 2010). Turnover is especially high in schools that disproportionately serve low-income students and students of color.[24] Some leave the profession altogether; others transfer to schools that have more resources and fewer underprivileged students. In consequence, low-income and minority children are disproportionately likely to be taught by novice or uncertified teachers, those who are working outside of their subject areas, those who graduated from less competitive colleges, and those who scored lower on standardized tests and teacher certification exams.[25] While low pay plays a role in teacher attrition and dissatisfaction at work, research suggests that it is less important than things that help teachers succeed in the classroom. The absence of a "sense of success" is actually the largest contributor to teachers' decisions to leave, but rigid curriculum mandates, ineffective and unsupportive school leadership, the inability to engage in ongoing learning, poor-quality facilities, inadequate resources, and limited opportunities for collaboration all contribute to high turnover.[26]

Some attrition is desirable, especially if it weeds out less effective teachers; yet the need to recruit, hire, and train teachers is a drain on school finances. It harms the occupation, schools as organizations, and society by draining collective knowledge, reducing the number of mentors for new colleagues, and wasting funding that was invested in professional development (see Allensworth et al., 2009; NCTAF, 2007). Although the relationship is not necessarily linear, teacher turnover also negatively affects student achievement because new teachers are less effective than more experienced ones.[27] These instructional costs reduce equity, not just the efficiency and effectiveness of public schools; they are disproportionately borne by low-income students, students of color, ELLs, and students with academic, behavioral, and emotional issues.[28]

On a positive note, research indicates that teachers prefer work environments that are collaborative and inclusive, characterized by trust and reciprocity, and supportive of innovation and personal growth.[29] Teachers who work in collaborative environments continue to improve, and improve more than their colleagues in less supportive environments.[30] Relationships at school also appear to improve teacher retention by reducing isolation, increasing feelings of efficacy and control, and providing implicit rewards that help teachers avoid burnout and sustain their giving.[31] Just as importantly, teachers' emotional investments have been shown to positively influence children's educational behaviors and development, as well as their social and emotional growth and well-being.[32] Studies further show that students are aware of teachers' emotions—even when they try to mask them; children say they value teachers who care about them, while being less motivated by the ones who do not (Sutton & Wheatley, 2003). When combined with educators' narratives in this study, these findings *strongly indicate* that teachers' affective ties improve learning and increase the efficiency and effectiveness of public schools. They do so largely by serving as an informal source of social control in schools and classrooms and by improving teacher retention.

Conclusion

Education reforms frequently overlook the personal and intrinsic nature of teaching and the importance of relationships for teacher effectiveness. These aspects of the job are difficult to measure, but teachers' emotions are also frequently viewed as something to be "managed" to "offset . . . resistance to change" (Hargreaves, 1998, p. 837). In contrast, this chapter showed that educators' emotions and relationships, while individually experienced, are a matter of collective concern. The personal and intrinsic value of caring draws individuals into the profession and influences the quality of those who remain. Teachers' emotions affect their ability and willingness to engage in reform and their affective ties positively influence children's academic and life outcomes.

This research further shows, however, that it is not accurate to portray these caring behaviors as stemming *solely* from educators' personal characteristics or the nature of teaching as an occupation. The social, economic, and political contexts of schools play a role. Socioeconomic inequality, for instance, creates inequitable costs of caring and encourages higher turnover among those who serve underprivileged children. Tracy, an urban special education teacher, elaborated on this issue:

> There's kids at risk everywhere. . . . But . . . inner-city . . . rural schools . . . there's so many children . . . [and] less resources to serve those needs. . . . So the chances of them getting . . . [what] they need is less likely. . . . Sometimes, it can become overwhelming. . . . They're coming to school without breakfast . . . not clothed right . . . [issues] at home. . . . You really have to take care of their basic needs first in order to go forward. . . . It's an emotional job . . . you have to be *very* strong. . . . That's where some people break . . . dealing with a population that has high needs. The stress . . . from that becomes too much . . . not physically, but mentally. . . . That's why a lot of teachers leave the inner city. . . . It does wear you out.

For better or for worse, policy makers and scholars must account for the "feeling" nature of public service. Making public services more humane and caring may be one way to make them more efficient and effective, but, as shown in the next section, public policies may result in the opposite if they fail to account for political, social, and economic contexts.

PART III

Policy Feedback in the Post–Education Reform Environment

As mentioned, NCLB was supposed to close the achievement gap between underprivileged children and their more advantaged peers and between American students and their international peers by using student test scores to rate and rank schools and then penalize poorly performing schools and educators. The goal was for 100 percent of U.S. students to be proficient in ELA and mathematics by the year 2014, but NCLB's accountability model resulted in growing numbers of schools being labeled (SINI). An estimated 82 percent of schools would have faced escalating consequences without subsequent reform. When Congress failed to do so, President Obama allowed states to apply for waivers from some of its toughest requirements (NCLB waivers; U.S. DOE, 2012) and used a $4.35 billion grant competition (RttT) to incentivize the administration's reform priorities (U.S. DOE, 2009).[1] As policy interventions, NCLB waivers and RttT more clearly focused on growth over set targets, individual educators over school districts, and motivating through "carrots" (grants and waivers) more than "sticks" (sanctions); yet, like NCLB, the theory of action (Stone, 1989) was that principals and teachers would improve their work effort to obtain respectable test scores and this would result in higher performing schools. Both also continued NCLB's focus on "fixing" low-performing schools through reconstitution, closure, and increased competition from charter schools (U.S. DOE, 2011). In 2010, the northeastern state that is the subject of this analysis adopted a new teacher and principal evaluation system as part of its RttT initiative. School districts throughout the state were required to conduct annual professional performance reviews (APPRs) that differentiated teacher and principal effectiveness according to four categories: highly effective, effective, developing, and ineffective (HEDI). Student growth and achievement were to make up 40 percent of these ratings, with the remaining 60 percent culled from multiple measures of teacher and principal effectiveness.[2] The state promised to release teacher and principal ratings to parents and required that districts make these evaluations a significant factor in employment decisions (e.g., hiring, tenure, dismissal, supplemental compensation like merit pay). School districts also had to develop and implement teacher and principal improvement plans for those rated ineffective and terminate those with a pattern of ineffective performance, defined as two consecutive ineffective ratings. This section uses open-ended interviews with 83 administrators and teachers to examine how NCLB and RttT influenced educators' political and social experiences, identities, and behaviors, as well as teaching and learning.

6

Education Reform, Policy Tools, and Policy Feedback

The public policy literature recognizes that the government employs a wide variety of tools to move society in its desired direction; the choice of policy instruments is linked to a nation's political culture, including ascendant ideas about the legitimate role of government in society.[1] NCLB, NCLB waivers, and RttT used what policy scholars refer to as "the sermon" (Vedung & van der Doelen, 2007) or a "public information campaign" (PIC; Weiss, 1993). They were designed to encourage educators to adopt policy makers' desired changes through the public reporting of student test scores. The latter provided parents with the information to name and shame "failing" schools (NCLB) and educators (NCLB waivers and RttT); parents could demand supplemental services from public, private, or religious providers or choose better performing public or public charter schools within the district. In addition, federal and state DOEs and school districts could use test scores to fix "failing schools" through personnel decisions, reconstitution, closure, and the expansion of charter schools. These bottom-up (market) and top-down (managerial) controls are consistent with the MMP, which, as shown, now dominates education discourse and policies. This chapter uses 83 interviews with educators to examine how recent reforms affected policy feedback and democratic performance.

Public Policies, Policy Feedback, and Democratic Performance

Studies suggest that policy tools have different effects on democracy, but scholars acknowledge that there is a need for more research on how policy targets react to them within social contexts.[2] For administrators and teachers, these include the physical sites and communities where they work, their organizational and occupational norms, and their political and socioeconomic environments.[3] These social contexts similarly affect parents and students. In addition, scholars disagree about the coerciveness of PICs as a policy tool. Some claim that they are the least coercive tool because the state provides information while allowing individuals to choose how to respond. Yet studies show that PICs often distort democratic processes, disempower citizens, and induce passivity; they alter individual behaviors long beyond other forms of regulation and have cumulative effects that are especially alienating for low-income and low-status groups.[4] My interviews support these latter findings. The interaction between education reforms and social contexts (i.e., local zip codes, individual schools, teaching as an occupation) altered the behaviors of citizens and policy implementers in ways that resulted in what Stone (1997) calls "degenerative politics"—a term that conveys how government policies fall into patterns of allocating benefits and burdens in increasingly ineffective, inefficient, and unfair ways. Part of this resulted from the weaponization of discourse and institutions (see Chapter 2), but testing itself is an undemocratic and degenerative accountability tool.

Testing: An Undemocratic and Degenerative Accountability Tool

As shown in Part I, policy makers increased the legitimacy of recent reforms by constructing testing as a "neutral" (scientific) way to diagnose and treat poor performance. The dominance of this narrative was achieved through symbolic violence; they weaponized discourse in ways that silenced educators' claims that *all* assessment regimes rate and rank knowledge, skills, and behaviors that are unevenly distributed across social classes and groups. In consequence, testing institutionalizes the effects of class, race, ethnicity, and gender on the performance of children. Paul, a retired suburban middle school English teacher, disclosed,

> [It's] a bell curve. . . . Some have to fail. . . . [It is] well documented, that tests will have a cultural bias. . . . Test makers are of a particular culture

... so, people who are subcultures within the culture are penalized. ... If the test is flawed in that way . . . culturally, then they are flawed in every way. . . . If the reason for having a test is to see if the students have had a good education . . . [they] are of no service. . . . [I] don't have faith in anything that tries to measure on paper what you have spent a year accomplishing. . . . Groups of people . . . will defy whatever method . . . not everybody learns the same way, but also because of a lot of very complicated things. . . . [There are cases where] heads of Fortune 500 companies . . . could not read . . . were they uneducated? I don't think so. . . . They must have different kinds of skills . . . you can't test most skills well . . . [We mostly test] knowledge with some skills, but . . . [only] a small range of both. . . . [Mostly tests rate] knowledge as regurgitation. . . . [Some] are better "regurgitators" [*laughs*] . . . that has nothing to do with education. . . . Tests preference some kinds of learning over others and therefore some kinds of individuals over others. . . . [There are] all kinds of learning . . . multiple kinds of intelligence.

Research supports the narratives of Paul and others. The example provided in Chapter 3 was that boys tend to do better on standardized math tests while girls do better in reading. A recent study suggests that the test format is partly to blame. Tests are also "normed" to eliminate questions that nondominant groups answer correctly in higher numbers when compared to the dominant "group" (e.g., middle-class and upper-income students, a racial or ethnic majority, students without academic needs). The assumption is that these questions must be flawed since the majority answered them incorrectly. There are other issues, but these biases make testing an unfair and undemocratic way to reward children.[5]

VAMs—instituted under RttT and NCLB waivers—are better than raw test scores under NCLB because they measure individual growth through a pre- and posttest. Educators, however, expressed extreme skepticism that *any testing model* could account for the complexity of teaching and learning owing to different interests, learning styles, and rates of growth and development. Janet, a suburban elementary teacher, explained,

[Young children] are learning how to learn . . . as much if not more than what to learn. They often don't retain the content over the course of the year. It is hard to evaluate that "how to learn" component in a quantitative fashion. . . . [It] is supposed to be value added. . . . I have all the identified kids . . . that should not matter. . . . But, kids that struggle . . . may not grow as much. . . . And, we are not just being evaluated based on growth . . . [it's also] based on proficiency. In math . . . to be proficient, they must get a 75 percent . . . on that test. It doesn't matter if they have an IEP. . . . I also worry about students that are not identified . . . their growth rates may be lower and they are not identified so the teacher is penalized.

Informants were especially concerned that VAMs, like raw test scores, do not account for the effects of external variables on student performance. They described two types: individual and contextual.

Individual-level *variables* include students' personal characteristics (e.g., motivation and perseverance), as well as their backgrounds and experiences (e.g., level of resources in the home, access to health and dental care, poverty, food insecurity, divorce, domestic violence, frequency of moving).[6] VAMs imperfectly control for some of these variables and do not control for others. For example, they do not account for random events that influence learning during the course of the year or performance on a particular test (e.g., the death of a parent and not eating breakfast or being sick on the day of the test). They also do not account for *interpretive effects,* situations where a student knows the material but did not understand the intent of the question. In the words of a suburban elementary teacher (Kathy),

[performance] on the tests is highly unstable . . . a child . . . [who is] perfectly capable of passing might not do well because they are having a bad day . . . but some children are just terrible test takers. There is also a lot of interpretation that goes into doing well. . . . Many children . . . know the information but they do not understand what the test maker is asking or looking for. . . . My bright children can struggle . . . because tests are written by adults, but when you have children with special needs it becomes even more shaky in this area.

With smaller sample sizes—such as when tests are used to evaluate individual teachers (NCLB waivers and RttT) versus schools (NCLB)—these issues are statistically more likely to cause ineffective ratings because one student is a larger percentage of the overall sample.

Just as problematically, testing creates fairness issues for schools and teachers that disproportionately serve students who struggle (e.g., low-income students, minorities, because they are disproportionately more likely to be poor, ELLs, students with test anxiety, and children with academic, behavioral, and emotional issues). While evident in Janet's earlier narrative, an urban middle school English teacher (Ronnie) and a suburban special education teacher (Nina) told me,

RONNIE: [My] principal said, "We're one bad breakfast away from a 2." . . . We have a lot of kids that have . . . moved around quite a bit . . . [and are] socioeconomically disadvantaged . . . [compared to] a suburban district . . . [where] kids have a lot of advantages.

NINA: They're talking about value added . . . [but my special education] students are all over the map. They don't learn in a straight line. . . . [One student] three years ago had a standard math score of 64. This year . . . he had a 66. . . . Both are far below average but he went up by two points. Do I look at that as . . . fabulous? No, they are both low. . . . Value added doesn't tell you much. . . . It is harder for my students to make large gains.

Again, VAMs are better than raw test scores but still assume that students grow at the same rate, regardless of their experiences, abilities, aptitudes, and motivation.

Educators defined the second variable, *social contexts*, as the organizational and outside-of-school variables that affect teaching and learning. *Organizational variables* include school leadership and climate, the physical plant, books in the library, per pupil expenditures, teacher turnover, and the availability of professional development and after-school programs. Most of these variables are strongly influenced by school finances, which are highly unequal in the United States, with the highest poverty school districts and students of color receiving less funding (Epstein, 2011; Ushomirsky & Williams, 2015). *Outside-of-school variables* include the level of socioeconomic inequality and segregation within a nation or a community and rates of poverty, food insecurity, single-parent families, domestic violence, imprisonment, homeownership, and so forth. Chapter 5 shows how the composition of a classroom affects the performance of students through peer effects. Here, educators are conveying that the composition of the community and the school may tip the balance against positive academic outcomes owing to the prevalence of "wicked problems."

It is important to note that educators were not blaming parents, students, or the community for poor performance. They were making three broader points. First, segregation and the inequitable financing of public schools unequally influence student performance. Research supports this claim.[7] Second, the state that is the subject of this analysis is consistently among the top in the nation in terms of racially and economically segregated schools; its overreliance on property taxes has also resulted in fiscal equity issues that disproportionately harm schools with large numbers of low-income and minority children.

Third, VAMs imperfectly control for these kinds of social contexts and do not (and cannot) account for peer effects. In consequence, like many individual-level variables, these contextual variables are outside of—or unexplained by—the statistical model. Economists call these exogenous variables.

Respondents did not use the words "exogenous variables"; however, their claim that these unaccounted-for variables increase the likelihood that schools (NCLB) and educators (RttT) will be falsely rewarded or penalized based on the students and communities that they serve is consistent with the concept. Sophia, a retired suburban elementary teacher, discussed this type of *attribution error* as it applies to individual teachers:

> I believe in assessment . . . but test scores are affected by so many different things, like . . . his gerbil died or he is sick . . . [can't concentrate] and his score is not going to be a valid assessment of where he is, much less what the teacher taught him. . . . [On the flip side,] a huge improvement . . . may not be the teacher. . . . [My student had] six siblings . . . [no] environmental stimulation . . . could not write . . . [had no] learning disability. . . . [I asked the reading and] speech teacher to take her as an "extra" child. . . . I gave her extra help . . . [too and] never saw a child grow . . . [so fast]. She would be the "abnormal" one who scored practically nil in the beginning . . . [then] did really well. . . . Once she started to read, she took off. . . . I would look very good . . . [VAMs are] better . . . [but] unless you have something like . . . [what I just described] the scores would be stable, or . . . slightly change. . . . It is a bell curve. . . . Typically they are distributed in similar places. They've grown, but the dispersion . . . [shows] some are still struggling and some are doing extremely well . . . the dispersion is similar.

Participants also linked attribution errors to the collective nature of teaching and learning. As shown, learning is co-constructed through the interactions between students and between teachers and students, but it is also constructed over time. Prior experiences, skills, and knowledge influence performance *and* growth by affecting individual dispositions, the motivation to learn, and the ability to acquire new knowledge and skills—whether that is within the same subject or across subjects. Reading levels, for example, influence a student's performance on tests in general; they also affect the ability to pick up new knowledge. Because of this, student performance cannot be attributed to a single teacher at a set point in time. Students are influenced by their first teachers (parents), prior teachers, those concurrently contributing to their knowledge and skills (e.g., administrators, specialists, aides), other students, and members of their communities. Heidi, a suburban high school math teacher, exclaimed, "Learning is a collective effort . . . people teaching a student over a large number of years . . . [other] students and parents. . . . It's hard to link learning to one teacher."

Even if VAMs could account for all of the described individual and collective variables, respondents alleged that there would still be issues with test score validity and reliability; there are *interactive effects* between all of these variables that *no statistical model* is able to capture. Jack, a suburban elementary principal and former elementary teacher, disclosed,

> [Even] with value added . . . [there are] all kinds of biases built into these tests . . . studies showing that value-added scores are all over the place, even for the same teacher depending on the test and class. . . . It's not just who you teach but how kids interact . . . identical classes . . . socioeconomic backgrounds and abilities . . . those classes wouldn't be identical. So the tests themselves are biased . . . can't account for all of the variables that influence individual students . . . having a bad day or not eating breakfast . . . also can't account for all of the random noise that affects teaching because you have human beings interacting with one another. . . . Observations are supposedly subjective but that's really the only way to get at that, but then they want us to attach numbers to that too [*laughs*].

These interactive effects may explain why VAMs do not produce stable ratings for teachers; scores vary between different statistical models, across classes and years, and from test to test.[8]

For all of these reasons, educators portrayed testing as an *unfair, invalid, and unreliable accountability tool.* The definitions of test score reliability and validity have varied historically, as well as across fields, but in terms of teacher and student assessments, *validity* generally refers to whether the scores capture the underlying trait(s) the instrument intends to measure (e.g., teacher quality, student growth, student ability), whereas *reliability* refers to whether the assessment tool produces consistent scores (see American Educational Research Association, 1999; Kane, 2002, 2006; Koretz, 2008). The portrayal of testing in this fashion did not vary across "social groups," meaning by profession (e.g., administrators, teachers, speech pathologists, psychologists, librarians); tested or untested subjects; grade or subject taught; teaching status (i.e., currently practicing, retired, or left teaching); or location in an urban, rural, suburban, private, or charter school. As such, it cannot be attributed to "self-interested" concerns about being held accountable.

Educators further characterized testing as an *undemocratic and degenerative policy tool*. Available data create demands for more data and to expand the applications for the data. These requests then degenerate into demands for punishment, which results in policies that disproportionately harm the least well-off. The most prominent example respondents offered was that early state tests were used as a *gauge* of student performance; policy makers then adopted state "exit exams," which students must pass to graduate. Eventually, these state reforms created positive feedback for national reform, like NCLB, which used student test scores to rate, rank, and punish schools and educators (e.g., closing schools, firing principals and teachers). RttT and NCLB waivers continued these punitive practices, but expanded the "testing culture" by extending it to all subjects and most grades; employing a pre- and posttest model; and using student test scores for teacher evaluations.

The next chapter elaborates on how the expanded testing culture influenced educators' behaviors in ways that degenerated into social justice issues. For now, it is important to note that testing creates social justice issues *even without altering educators' behaviors*. It disproportionately harms low-income students, students of color, ELLs, and children with academic, behavioral, and emotional issues. These groups rank at the bottom of the bell curve owing to test-related biases, academic issues, and the link between academic performance and poverty. Over time, persistent poor performance causes many of these students to become disaffected with school and to alter their behaviors in ways that impede their life outcomes, including dropping out and/or refusing to participate, study, or do homework (*neglect*).

The words of an elementary teacher (Mary) illustrate the widespread concern that persistent poor performance on exams negatively affects children's feelings of self-efficacy, self-worth, and self-confidence over time, causing some to engage in *neglect* rather than to persevere:

> [How] many times can you keep taking a test . . . to show that they are still struggling without them feeling like they are failures. . . . It is just very harsh in terms of their self-concept and self-confidence . . . that has become their idea of school and learning . . . they take tests and fail them. . . . It is a struggle . . . it sets them apart from their peers . . . affects the way they feel about school and whether they want to continue on in school.[9]

More broadly, these individual behaviors spill over to other students and negatively affect the performance of schools and classrooms through peer effects. This, too, creates social justice issues. SES, segregation, and unequal school financing correlate with educational achievement (e.g., grades and test scores) and educational attainment (e.g., high school and college completion); minorities are more likely to grow up in poverty; and low-income and minority children are disproportionately likely to be segregated in high-need, low-resource schools (see chapters 9 and 11). Test scores institutionalize these inequalities across schools and classrooms. The next three sections elaborate on these findings as they relate to the policy tools that were used under NCLB, NCLB waivers, and RttT.

Labeling Schools: An Undemocratic and Degenerative Policy Tool

Research shows that people try to distance themselves from poorly regarded others by, for instance, exaggerating their own positive traits or stressing that they possess "normal" or "mainstream" values. The creation of social distance helps individuals avoid social stigmas but creates social divisions that make it difficult to mobilize the least well-off on behalf of political, social, or economic change.[10] My interviews support these findings. Labeling schools (SINI) reduced reform capacity by encouraging the most well-off families to leave (exit) and reducing trust and social cohesion. In the words of Ronnie, an urban middle school English teacher:

> [Students felt like they were] labeled inferior. The whole school was inferior. I don't think . . . [that they would be] forthcoming that they went to that school, if they met someone new. It was embarrassing. . . . In the paper . . . talked about. And students that did well . . . were highly insulted that they were lumped together with other kids. . . . It was . . . a morale killer for the teachers. . . . We have . . . some poverty . . . some fairly affluent students. . . . If the parents moved . . . two or three blocks . . . [there are] a couple of wealthy districts. . . . [Some] considered just moving . . . [to a district that is] not on any lists.

Some children did not want to tell their neighbors—who lived only a few blocks away but attended a "better" school or district—that they attended the "failed" school or district (cognitive exit); other children felt "insulted" that they were being "lumped together" with students who struggle.

These types of social divisions made it difficult to unite the community behind reform, but exit also tends to exacerbate gaps in performance. Higher performing schools and districts attract higher performing students; being part of a poorly regarded group, on the other hand, adversely affects the aspirations and behaviors of those who are left behind. These claims are discussed in Chapter 9 yet are important for why *every educator* in some way conveyed that labeling is a powerful yet often undemocratic and degenerative policy tool.

Labeling is a powerful policy tool. Negative labels are harmful because most people care about what others think of them and teachers identify so strongly with the profession and their role in society. Stephanie, an urban middle school English teacher, declared,

> [Teachers] say, "I *am* a teacher." It is who they are . . . [When] people attack teachers or teaching . . . [they] are not just attacking their job, you are attacking their identities. . . . [Saying] you are part of a societal problem or that you *are* the problem . . . is really hurtful . . . [for] teachers or fire-fighters or police officers . . . [because they identify so strongly] with their jobs. . . . [I've never seen my friend without his] firefighter shirt . . . my friends constantly wear their school shirts, or carry the umbrella with the school brand. . . . If people told my firefighter friend that he was *the* reason society was going downhill, it would be hurtful because he is so proud of it . . . [and my colleagues] are so proud . . . to tell people they *are* teachers.

Just as importantly, these policy labels are backed by the power of the government and send out moral messages about the school and community. As evident in Ronnie's narrative, the resulting social stigmas directly affect the behaviors of those who live and work in these communities and indirectly do so by affecting how community members are treated by those who do not live there.

Educators also want to "do right by the kids" and the community. Labeling preys on these attachments. This claim is apparent in the guilt and stress educators like Vanessa, an urban middle school math teacher, conveyed after being labeled "subpar" by the state:

> I work in a very [*emotional pause*] needy school district and this is part of the rewards of my job but it also is something that creates some stress. . . . A lot of low-income families . . . free and reduced-price lunch. . . . [It's] a SINI school. . . . We had three years to turn the school around and then last year the cut points were raised . . . we would've made it under the lower cut points but . . . were put in corrective action. . . . It was very upsetting . . . has affected how I feel about . . . teaching. . . . [The kids]

need a lot of structure and discipline, but also a lot of caring. They're very needy . . . not getting as much at home. . . . I have to kick them out of my classroom [*laughs*] at the end of the period . . . end of the day [*laughing*]. They just want a relationship . . . to connect with adults, and I really enjoy that part of my job, but it makes me feel very sad too [*getting emotional*]. . . . Sometimes I feel like it's more than I can physically and emotionally give. . . . It's also a time issue . . . [and] whether it's my place to do this . . . they share things with me about their lives. . . . It's hard to shake it off. . . . I try to counsel them and provide them with encouragement . . . get them help. . . . [I am] a mom to my own son but . . . also . . . the mom to my students. . . . It's hard . . . I pray about it. I pray a lot.

The next chapter shows how increased stress alters educators behaviors in ways that are not welfare enhancing for public schools, students, and teaching as a profession. For now, it is important to note that the perception that they are being labeled greedy and self-interested has reportedly contributed to growing stress among teachers *in general,* not only among those who worked in labeled schools.[11]

Of interest, *every urban educator* conveyed in some way that they were not highly regarded by society—even when their schools were not labeled—and many said that other educators did not respect them. Urban educators were also more likely to frame recent reforms as a way to punish public schools, rather than improve public education, and justify privatization through charter schools and vouchers. These claims are not surprising. Urban districts disproportionately serve low-income and minority children and were disproportionately identified "in need of improvement" under NCLB (Center on Education Policy, 2006); states where minority populations had grown were also more likely to adopt punitive education policies (Nichols et al., 2006).

My interviews suggest that urban educators try to avoid internalizing this social stigma by turning the (inferior) urban label into a *red badge of courage.* Stephanie continued:

[People think suburban] teachers are better because the test scores. . . . That creates animosity. . . . Teachers at my school are very *proud* to be urban teachers . . . sort of look down on suburban teachers. . . . That is not real teaching. . . . [There's] a lot of solidarity among urban teachers. . . . [We're] in the trenches together . . . a struggling school, but . . . stick it out. . . . If anyone has earned the label of hero, it is urban teachers.[12]

These *urban warriors* often appeared militant in their expressions of solidarity and pride, as well as in their claim that suburban educators could not handle working in urban schools. Despite this social solidarity, Stephanie's narrative shows how labeling creates social divisions between "groups" (i.e., teachers from urban vs. rural and suburban schools) that would otherwise have things in common; this makes it more difficult for them to work together to advance collective goals, such as implementing federal policies in ways that help *all* children regardless of the schools they attend.

Many SINI and urban educators also described how public discourse about "failing" schools "infected" their relationships outside of work and forced them to engage in *fight or flight,* meaning defend themselves and/or their schools, hide where they work to avoid a fight, or avoid people who think negatively about urban teachers, urban schools in general, and/or their school in particular, whether that is because it was labeled or an urban school. In Kristen's words,

> [the pressure is] . . . intense. . . . You don't want that label . . . even my in-laws . . . "Oh, it is good your school was not on the list" [*laughs*]. . . . [It is not] just the school community or the parents . . . looking at these tests. . . . I work really hard and I'm good at what I do. . . . There is definitely pride of place. I'm going to stick up for my school no matter what. . . . [But] it does something to your morale. . . . We get judged for being in an urban school . . . our evaluations don't reflect all . . . [we do and we feel] a little defensive . . . discussions, even with family members. . . . They teach in suburban schools and . . . I really have to bite my tongue. . . . [They] have no idea what we're up against on a daily basis. . . . Our children are in no way comparable . . . [yet] testing is on a bell curve. . . . Somebody has to fail for someone to do better. . . . I am okay with testing . . . I don't think teachers are opposed to tests. But . . . you cannot help . . . constantly calculating . . . whether you're going to meet those scores . . . because you *work so hard* . . . [and what] you did the whole year becomes reduced to that [test]. . . . The hardships my students face. . . . It is really precarious . . . [yet they are being] compared to children in the suburban schools where their parents are . . . giving them every advantage. . . . It is just unfair . . . I do everything I can . . . but how can you compete?

Kristen clearly takes pride in her school; this pride of place (loyalty) extends to other urban schools and educators. Labeling is powerful *because* people are embedded in social contexts where they form attachments.

Labeling is an undemocratic and degenerative policy tool. The fact that labeling is a powerful tool is not necessarily a negative finding.

It becomes undemocratic and degenerative when it creates social divisions that make it difficult to achieve common ends. Academic achievement and attainment are highly correlated with poverty, socio-economic inequality, and inequitable school financing (see Chapter 11). In consequence, the state may be shaming schools, students, and educators regardless of whether they have done anything wrong or have the means and capacity to redress educational issues through hard work or effort. Again, educators expressed concern that many of these students then become disaffected with school and engage in *neglect* rather than persevering (see also Chapter 9).

Labeling is undemocratic and degenerative for another reason: It lets other social actors off the hook. Some discussed how NCLB took parents and students off the hook, but educators more commonly complained that it enabled citizens, business-economic elites, and policy makers to blame children, parents, and educators rather than redressing the political and socioeconomic issues that negatively affect academic performance. Stephanie continued:

> [We're not holding society accountable] . . . ignoring poverty . . . violence and hunger . . . children not having lights and electricity. . . . These are not isolated instances. . . . The problems are systemic . . . they affect children's ability to be successful in school. . . . A lot of . . . parents are working two jobs. . . . It is very hard for them to study when they are taking care of and feeding and putting to bed their younger brothers and sisters. . . . They live in a different world . . . children have problems in every socioeconomic class, but there are a specific set of problems that are endemic with children who are underachieving and at the lower end of the bell curve. These problems are not talked about. It is assumed . . . [the] teachers must be bad. . . . All you have to do is stand there in front of my school for an hour and write down what you see and [hear about] what is happening outside of the school . . . no matter how hard teachers try, you cannot sweep all of that under the rug. . . . [We have] to deal with . . . systemic societal problems. And the government doesn't want to do that.

Informants complained that these broader issues have been silenced because they are difficult to resolve and require politically unpopular solutions, like raising taxes. It is easier to blame and penalize schools, educators, and students. The end result is a lack of *distributive justice,* as society increasingly donates more to the most well-off while every-one else fights over a shrinking pie (see Chapter 11).

A further reason why labeling is undemocratic and degenerative is that, as mentioned, it preys on educators' social ties to put pressure on them to do as policy makers wish—even when they believe a policy is socially unjust. This claim is evident in Vanessa's and Kristen's narratives about their students being unfairly compared with their more advantaged counterparts; yet both felt compelled to behave in ways that achieved state aims since failing to do so would harm their students, schools, and teaching as an occupation. My interviews suggest that many educators leave positions where they disproportionately serve underprivileged children and children with academic, behavioral, and emotional issues to avoid feelings of inefficacy, social stigmas, or behaviors that they feel are harmful to these groups (see Chapter 7). Many also leave urban schools because popular culture simultaneously portrays urban educators as Superman (thwarting "the system" through the sheer force of their positive expectations) and as kryptonite (imprisoning children behind a wall of ignorance). This takes society off the hook, but these educators cannot escape negative social regard by retreating into "secondary identities"—such as saying that they work in a suburban, rural, or nonlabeled school.

School Reconstitution and Closures: Undemocratic and Degenerative Policy Tools

As discussed, poorly performing schools were labeled (SINI) and then faced escalating consequences under NCLB, including, but not limited to, being restructured, taken over, or closed. The Obama administration continued and expanded this model by offering temporary RttT grants to turn around 5,000 of the nation's lowest performing schools through four models: *transformation* (replacing the principal, restructuring the school, and evaluating teachers and principals using student test scores); *turnaround* (firing the school's principal and teachers and allowing the new principal to rehire no more than 50 percent of the faculty); *restart* (converting the school into a charter school); and *closure* (transferring all of the students to another school in the district). Transformation was the most common intervention (74%), followed by turnarounds (20%) and restarts (5%), but school closures (1%) also became commonplace, especially in cities across the nation.[13] This section focuses on reconstitution—the practice of laying off and firing staff in low-scoring schools (transformation and turnaround)—and school closures. Chapter 9 examines the use of charter schools to improve the public school system (restart).

School reconstitution. As a human service, educators' salaries and benefits are the largest component of school budgets and their skills are a source of human capital. Recent reforms assumed that it was possible to transform and turnaround low-scoring (SINI) schools by putting a large percentage of administrators, teachers, and support staff on probation or actually replacing them with more capable, collaborative, and committed individuals.

Contrary to the rhetoric of policy makers, this and other research supports informants' claim that the *threat of reconstitution* does not improve performance. In the absence of systemic reform, schools and educators lack the capacity to produce large-scale change and are more likely to engage in dysfunctional organizational behaviors and teaching practices, such as teaching to the test or focusing instruction on students who are at the margins because they are more likely to pass and raise school or teacher performance.[14]

Although the evidence on schools that were *actually reconstituted* is more mixed, it suggests that the provision of a sufficient level of resources is critical for improved performance, but gains may only be short term.[15] Over the long-term, reconstitution often reduces the reform capacity of schools by limiting their stock of social and cultural capital. More seasoned and effective personnel are often the first to exit (retire, leave the profession, or leave for less stressful, punitive, and stigmatized work environments); new hires are typically less effective than those they replace; and HQTs are less likely to seek work in what is perceived to be a stigmatized school.[16] In addition, reconstitution often reduces union voice, professional voice, and site-based decision-making as the focus on incentives, sanctions, and test-based performance reviews shifts the locus of control to district, state, and federal administrators.[17]

I explore these findings in more detail in the next chapter; however, they support respondents' claim that school reconstitutions are an undemocratic and degenerative policy tool. They reduce voice and capacity in the schools that primarily serve low-income and minority students.

School closures. The second tool in the turnaround arsenal, large-scale public school closures, became a fact of life in many American cities—like Chicago, Detroit, New Orleans, New York, and Philadelphia—during both the Bush and Obama administrations, especially after the Great Recession of 2008. Nationwide, the number of closed schools jumped from 242 in 2005–2006 to 1,929 in 2010–2011 (Rich & Hurdle, 2013). New Orleans, the most extreme case, closed all but five of its public schools and vastly expanded charter schools (Journey for Justice Alliance, 2014). School closures differ from reconstitution because all of the staff and students leave.

The school is then sometimes reopened as a new public or charter school.

Decisions to close public schools are complex and cannot be attributed solely to federal education policies. As discussed, housing policies reduced enrollment and tax revenues in many urban and rural districts by encouraging the flight of white homeowners and businesses to the suburbs and metropolitan fringe.[18] Gentrification also played a role. Some urban districts built "boutique" magnet schools to attract middle- and upper-income students. When done correctly, magnet schools integrate public schools and improve performance for underprivileged students (see Chapter 11), but they may also draw the most well-off students away from neighborhood schools.[19] Recent education reforms added to these fiscal and enrollment issues by requiring persistently "failing schools" to fund (a) supplemental services—like tutoring—from public, private, and religious providers and (b) student transfers to other public and public charter schools within the district.

Within this environment, urban mayors—like Democrat Rahm Emanuel in Chicago—argued that it made sense to close schools, especially those that were half empty or housed in old buildings. Although he said that Chicago would save $560 million over a decade by closing schools and laying off more than 850 teachers, the school district later admitted that it had vastly overstated the projected savings and lowered its estimate by $122 million. Even that figure did not factor in the loss of tax revenues from newly unemployed teachers, increased layoffs in the private sector due to reduced consumption, rising costs for unemployment and other social welfare programs, the outlays associated with the depreciation and maintenance of vacant buildings, and the blighting effects that empty buildings have on surrounding neighborhoods.[20] The city also later acknowledged that it needed to spend $7 million to hire 600 adults to provide "safe passage" for children, who now walked farther owing to the closing of their neighborhood schools, and police superintendent Garry McCarthy announced that the city would need to "beef up" police patrols, clean up vacant lots, and secure vacant buildings that might attract gangs. Even with these safety measures, parents complained about their children walking through gang territories, thus exposing them to drugs, gun violence, and other dangers.[21]

While I did not interview any educators who worked in a *school* that was closed as a result of NCLB or RttT, I did speak with administrators and teachers in *districts* where schools had been closed, either due to being labeled "persistently failing," fiscal imperatives, and/or declining enrollment, and one teacher who had worked in a *school* that was closed as a result of declining enrollment. Like the case of Chicago, these interviews indicate that the rhetoric about school closings differs from reality. For instance, policy makers claimed that closing "failed" schools would improve student achievement. My informants agreed with existing research, and a series of articles on the decision to close schools in New York City, that (a) the learning outcomes of displaced students are highly dependent on the characteristics of the receiving schools and (b) most students do not get placed in higher performing schools owing to a lack of available seats.

Because of these realities, schools that already serve a high proportion of academically at-risk students (low-income children and those with academic, emotional, and behavioral issues) receive an even greater percentage of these students. Just as problematically, overburdened educators lose academic time with existing and newly arriving students as they figure out how to best serve a large group of unknown students and families. The need to constantly reorganize teaching and learning drains school resources and further erodes the efficiency and effectiveness of the receiving schools by increasing turnover. Lorna, an urban elementary teacher, had this to say:

> [The] students are *not* being transferred to a better school. They're often transferred to a school that is either the same, meaning it's struggling, or somewhat worse because of all the upheaval and because they are now getting a lot of students who struggle. They also don't know the kids and the families. They're constantly having to recreate the school community because of moving all of these teachers and students around.

The combination of these issues results in declining test scores and often triggers more school closures.[22]

Informants told me that school closures negatively affect student performance *even when* students are transferred to schools that are not struggling. Research supports their claim that moving *itself* disrupts children's social ties in ways that often impede academic achievement and attainment.[23] The ensuing social disruptions often cause negative behavioral changes, including, but not limited to, acting out, nonparticipation, and lateness or absenteeism related to stress, issues with transportation, and concerns about safety if children are leaving their neighborhood schools.

These concerns are evident in the narratives of Stephanie and Trudy about how closing an urban middle and suburban elementary school negatively affected students and the community:

STEPHANIE: [The children] know the school is labeled . . . [and a lot of them] came from the middle school that was shut down. . . . [Some] feel like the school was shut down because . . . [it] was bad in some way . . . [and] they were part of that school being bad. That label affects them. . . . [The] kids who had to . . . travel . . . to another school. . . . It didn't end up being a major issue but . . . [they] had to go to a community where they were not welcome because there had been a long history of gang warfare between these two communities.

TRUDY: [It] was devastating. . . . That school was a community and it was broken up. . . . People were buying homes in my district because they like the fact that we have community schools. We're a walking district. . . . [They are] now disenfranchised from that school and there were some streets where, if you were on the north side of the street you went to one building and . . . the south side . . . went to another. . . . We made it a celebration . . . [so the kids] didn't feel like their school was closed because . . . they did something bad.

In both the labeled (Stephanie) and nonlabeled (Trudy) schools, educators had to deal with how closings and restructurings affected individual dispositions and behaviors. They also had to recreate social cohesion in the receiving schools. Informants said that both of these are harder to do in districts that undergo rapid transformation, like Lorna's. In these cases, school closures threaten individual and collective performance so that the receiving schools often become SINI schools or, if already labeled, become slated for restructuring or closure.

Unsurprisingly, studies—while limited—find that school closures do not improve student achievement; they also show that the effects on high school students are mostly negative, with dropout rates increasing and graduation rates and test scores declining.[24] Studies further support that school closures create social justice issues; they disproportionately harm minority, low-income, ELL, and special education students.[25] For these and other reasons, almost every urban educator—and more than half of the suburban and rural educators—in this study portrayed school closings and restructurings as a "smoke and mirror" game, meaning part of a larger plan to privatize education by increasing demand for charter schools and subsidizing charter schools through public school transfers and, in some cases, the provision of cheap public buildings (for support of this claim, see Vivea, 2013).

Urban educators were also more likely to portray school closings and restructurings as a way to break the power of teachers' unions.

The example they offered was that school districts in many states and cities—like Rhode Island and Washington, D.C.—fired all of their teachers and then selectively rehired some to get around teacher tenure. Many further portrayed school restructurings and closings as a new form of gentrification, where districts create "boutique" magnet schools to appease wealthier residents while closing the then depleted community schools and forcing (mostly low-income and minority) children to attend schools farther away from home (see also E. Simon, 2013). I provide examples of these narratives in Chapter 9, but a recent Pew study supports that 42 percent of vacated school buildings are sold to charter schools. Another 12 percent are used for other educational purposes, such as private schools or universities (Dowdall, 2011).

The views expressed in a series of articles on the decision to close schools in New York City are consistent with informants' claims; they also show a sharp divide between citizens and educators on one hand and policy makers on the other (Chivas, 2010).[26] Parents and students preferred to remain in their community schools, educators expressed strong loyalties to their schools, and both portrayed public schools as the hearts of their communities. An urban elementary teacher (Emily) told me,

> You rarely hear people talk about . . . [how closing schools] is stressful on the community. . . . [They focus on the goal] to the exclusion of the side effects. . . . Schools do a lot . . . [more] than just educate students. They are the hub of their community . . . [funnel services to] needy families. . . . I live next to a community that does not have its own school district . . . the kids are bused . . . [elsewhere]. There is no sense of community there. . . . I think it has a much bigger effect than that community realizes. It also has affected the property values. Who wants to voluntarily move into a town that does not have their own school district?

This narrative about ignoring the negative side effects of school closures because of the focus on punishing rotten apples was common, even among those who did not work in districts that had experienced school closures. So, too, was Emily's claim that public schools are critical for the community in general and needy families in particular; they provide many other services and create the social, political, and economic capital that helps individuals, groups, and communities thrive. Educators argued that policy makers must consider more than fiscal and performative imperatives when making choices about whether to close a school; there are human and intangible costs associated with these decisions.

Interestingly, school closings were one area in which rural educators emerged as "warriors." Every rural educator in this study said that their district was struggling as a result of fiscal distress. Some have contracted out for gym, art, music, and so forth; a couple said that their district had consolidated with a neighboring one, yet still struggled. These educators were also especially likely to discuss how their schools are the hearts of their communities and critical for the provision of many social services, not just academic ones. A high school math teacher (Jim) explained,

> [We] don't have . . . community-type centers. The school is where everything takes place. . . . Our new high school building is really a YMCA. . . . They do everything under the sun. . . . There are districts . . . that are going to be bankrupt . . . if the budget problems continue. Our community lost our major employer. Our tax base is greatly depleted. We have a close friend who is a superintendent at a neighboring district who said they have maybe another four years before . . . [going] bankrupt. We think of schools as a physical entity. . . . [They're] not just a physical plant. . . . There are emotions and memories attached . . . and they are the hub of their communities . . . bring people together for better or for worse [*laughs*]. . . . People look at what will be gained fiscally if they do certain things like . . . merging school districts . . . don't think of what will be lost . . . [or] the human cost. . . . Our school is where everything in our community happens. . . . There is no other physical space to do it.

Jim's claim that public schools cannot be reduced to "a number" or "a physical plant" was quite common; it is very different from the portrayal of public schools as a business that should be run using market logics (the MMP), which, as shown, now dominates education discourse.

As a whole, educators' narratives show that emotions are a powerful motivator in public life. While I did not observe any major differences between administrators and teachers with respect to their rhetoric, some teachers alleged that the business-economic discourse is trickling down to administrators due to fiscal distress. A rural elementary teacher (Sherry), for example, disclosed that her new superintendent exclaimed: "education is a business and I have to take personalities out of the equation when I make my cuts . . . to balance my budget." It remains to be seen how this and other developments will influence future policies. The most recent federal reform—the ESSA—provides greater latitude in terms of the types of measures that states and local districts may use to evaluate performance. Nonetheless, it still requires that states and districts intervene in schools that perform in the bottom 5 percent, as well as in schools from which fewer than two-thirds of the students graduate. Because states had already invested millions into their accountability systems, it is not surprising that state plans submitted under the ESSA mostly reinforced the status quo (see A. Klein, 2018b).

The effects of school reconstitution and closures on democratic participation and policy feedback. Educators' narratives suggest that state plans submitted under the ESSA mostly reinforced the status quo for another reason. School reconstitutions and closures are degenerative. They disproportionately harm our most vulnerable communities; they also reduce democratic participation. In doing so, these policy tools inequitably influence policy feedback in ways that appear to support their continued and expanded use.

There are no systemic analyses of community engagement in the turnaround process, but anecdotal evidence and related studies both support and refute this last claim. School closures have actually triggered strong negative feedback from community members, including complaints to the U.S. DOE's Office of Civil Rights, sit-ins, marches, and other more militant actions, such as a hunger strike by parents of students in Chicago's Walter H. Dyett High School. These actions seem to refute informants' complaint that school closures have become the policy of choice because the generally lower levels of political participation in our most vulnerable communities gives the appearance of support in the form of quiescence. Those involved in these protests, however, agreed with informants' claim that policy makers intentionally suppressed voice from the least well-off to push school closings in these communities.[27] Related studies support these claims.

Research shows that urban mayors, school boards, and administrators weaponize policy feedback by soliciting community participation in ways that will legitimize their preferred solutions. One reason this occurs is that those with higher incomes are more likely to participate in formal feedback processes than those with lower incomes, whose schools are more likely to be affected by the resulting political and administrative decisions (see, e.g., Finnigan & Lavner, 2012). Similarly, as shown in Part I, policy makers from both political parties used institutions and discourse to silence the voice of those who had the most capacity to defeat recent reforms and school district plans to reconstitute or close schools. Such strategies included using formal institutions and public discourse to structure out dissent by portraying teachers' unions as special interests that seek to benefit their own members at the expense of citizens, low income and minority children, and society (symbolic violence).

All of these strategies became less salient as growing numbers of schools were negatively affected by recent education reforms and teachers' unions were able to both draw from *and* offer their strength to parent and community groups that were concerned about the long-term negative effects of accountability reforms. Their efforts included organizing protests and issuing joint reports that showed how government disinvestment and market-based reforms had reduced the performance of schools in low-income communities by creating family and neighborhood instability.[28] Certainly this negative policy feedback has helped draw attention to parents' concerns that too many schools have been closed or converted to charters in historically neglected low-income neighborhoods. Nonetheless, by suppressing opposing voices, this study shows that policy makers at all levels of government structured policy feedback in ways that reproduced the same ineffective policies over a long period of time.

Contrary to popular rhetoric, the threat of school reconstitution or closure and the provision of temporary financial assistance to turnaround low-performing schools does not improve performance. For that to occur, policy makers must redress the long-term social and economic constraints faced by these schools and communities, including how the inequitable and undemocratic distribution of resources have historically harmed those schools most in need of fundamental change (see Chapters 9 and 10).[29]

Test-Based Educator Accountability: An Undemocratic and Degenerative Policy Tool

The Obama administration envisioned a new generation of rigorous evaluation systems as the core of its efforts to build a more effective teaching workforce and improve public education. As mentioned, school districts under the study state's RttT initiative were required to conduct APPRs that differentiated teacher and principal effectiveness based on a combination of SGMs and other measures, including teacher observations. The rationale for using multiple measures is to reduce bias and increase validity (Darling-Hammond et al., 2012). Ideally, as state leaders adopted multimeasure educator evaluation systems, they would have included all of the various stakeholders in their development, piloted the evaluation system before implementing it on a large-scale basis, and then adjusted it based on feedback from the field (Darling-Hammond, 2013). According to respondents, the implementation of APPR was not ideal. It resulted in an evaluative instrument that was inaccurate (not valid and reliable) *and* unfair (not objective, transparent, comprehensible, or democratic). For these reasons, almost every respondent questioned the credibility of APPR. This section focuses on five claims.

Ceding authority to private vendors. Respondents suggested that many of the major issues with APPR arose because the state—in a race to get RttT funds during a recession—gave publishing and testing vendors too much authority to develop and implement the new system. This raised ethical issues for practitioners because the state required school districts to invest in curricular packages and test preparation materials published by those vendors. Jack, an elementary school principal and former elementary teacher, stated,

> [The state] ceded way too much authority to Pearson. . . . [The] focus was on getting Race to the Top money. . . . State Ed even admitted that . . . I saw an article . . . [the chancellor] was using private money to hire fellows . . . [to advise and implement it]. A lot of it was her own money . . . but it also came from Bill Gates and . . . private foundations that were going to benefit from charter school expansion . . . unethical given that the state is now pushing charter schools. . . . [She said that] she was hiring these fellows because . . . people in State Ed being burnt out . . . [said these fellows were] amazing . . . because some had PhDs and Ivy League degrees, but almost all of them had never worked in schools . . . had like 10 years' experience . . . between all of them . . . [yet telling] administrators with decades of experience how to evaluate teachers . . . [and now] having to take hours of training on how to evaluate teachers. . . . [And she] has ties to the data collection company the state is using . . . [but] dismissed concerns that it was a conflict of interest, claiming the state was under pressure to meet the Race to the Top deadlines. So, that makes it okay?

Administrators and teachers provided other examples of ethical issues. For instance, the vendor that developed and implemented the state's assessments was being investigated for improper lobbying practices, and the state's expansion of charter schools followed their heavy lobbying for RttT and large contributions to many political campaigns.

Many educators further complained that the uncensored contributions of publishing and testing vendors had resulted in exams that were laden with errors, were developmentally inappropriate in length, and used developmentally inappropriate and/or "gotcha" questions. Jack and Carley, a suburban elementary teacher, verbalized these widespread concerns:

JACK: [The Commissioner of State Ed] actually used the word "typos" to describe really serious errors . . . developmentally inappropriate . . . and questions that had two right answers . . . [or] where even teachers weren't sure of the answer. He was claiming that there have always been typos. . . . It has *never* been this bad. When you realize how much they are paying Pearson . . . [and] these tests are used to hold students back . . . fire teachers and close schools. . . . [State Ed has] thrown some questions out, but they're saying the tests are still valid . . . listening to . . . private vendors who have a financial stake . . . ignoring the people who have experience, including people in State Ed . . . not just principals and teachers.

CARLEY: A lot of these tests are about . . . testing stamina . . . [and on] the third-grade test, they were using passages that were really more for fifth graders. . . . You feel blindsided. At least make it fair. . . . It feels like a big game. Like a fixed game. . . . It was mean-spirited.

As a result of these errors and issues, educators questioned SGM validity and fairness, and thus the validity and fairness of APPR.

Arbitrary, nontransparent, and unclear state actions. Educators also expressed concerns about the state's arbitrary, nontransparent, and unclear actions. These included, but were not limited to, raising the "cutoff points" for what constituted a 4, 3, 2, or 1 on the exams. Owing to this administrative decision, some students who improved actually regressed or failed. Meagan, a suburban elementary teacher, elaborated on this issue:

[Accountability] has basically become that no child should get below a 3 on the state exams. . . . There is no science . . . [the cutoff scores change] every year and we have no idea why. Two years ago, we were doing so well that they decided to change the cutoff points . . . after the state got the test and graded it . . . to reduce the numbers of 4s. . . . Then you had students who had passed or who would've passed . . . suddenly not passing and needing academic intervention services [AIS]. . . . We felt like the state had set us up for failure. . . . It is all a numbers game . . . just them rereferencing the norm . . . [by] creating a new cutoff point. . . . Some have to fail and some have to achieve above norm. That is how norm-referenced tests work. . . . Then, they assume we are not meeting the needs of a child . . . but they have no basis for that either. You need to look at where that student started and where they were at the end of the year. . . . Even then, children do not learn at the same pace . . . the analogy of the Olympics . . . the 50 meter dash, but this one is an athlete, and you are blind . . . lame . . . have asthma. Nonetheless, you all need to get to the finish line at the same time . . . [or else] the state is going to . . . take money away from the school. . . . That doesn't make any sense. Why . . . take money away from the people that need it the most?

Across policies, these arbitrary actions had negative consequences for students, but also for schools (NCLB) and educators (RttT).

Added to these issues, the state developed an evaluative tool that ascribed numbers to the *observation component* of teachers' evaluations, ignoring educators' expressed concerns that this practice would create issues. Consider the statements of Chris (principal) and Patricia (teacher):

CHRIS: Charlotte Danielson . . . is a great tool [for teacher observations] but . . . [you can't] quantify good teaching. . . . [It's] a profession but also an art. . . . The best teachers have a great mixture of heart, compassion and empathy . . . intelligence . . . content knowledge . . . the pedagogy and personal connections to get that knowledge across effectively . . . [You can't] quantify compassion and empathy . . . but you can feel it . . . when you observe . . . a lot of evidence . . . is very factual . . . [but] you have to give them a 4, 3, 2, 1 based on . . . different domains. . . . [Parents aren't] walking into the school and saying, "This building is filled with exemplary teachers who were rated a 99." . . . They can say, "This building has heart. The teachers care about our children . . . do a lot for the kids."

PATRICIA: Most of teaching is not control by authority. You are managing human beings . . . encouraging them to do the right thing . . . motivating them individually and collectively. . . . It really involves your personality more than people would realize. There are certainly technical aspects . . . [but it] is an art. . . . Testing evaluates the technical aspects and even there . . . [is very] limited. . . . [It] does not get at the intangibles. . . . Teaching is more than a job. I work well beyond 40 hours a week. . . . Saying "your students did not all improve by x percent and therefore you are not a good teacher" . . . misses the point. What if you are doing everything right and working well beyond what is required . . . and two students have a bad day? That test is just a very limited picture of what teachers do. . . . Charlotte Danielson . . . does a good job. . . . But attaching points to it is scary . . . and then the governor arbitrarily raised the percentage of our evaluations that come from student test scores.[30]

Educators did not claim that observations are an "objective" way to evaluate teachers. They were making two broader points: Teacher evaluations had been improving as a result of better assessment tools

(e.g., Danielson) and, although no evaluation system is perfect, observations and professional development plans allow administrators to
account for social contexts and the art of teaching, as described in
Chapter 7. Standardized tests cannot (fully) account for either.

Patricia's narrative is important for another reason. The new point
system was troubling for many because the state reneged on its deal
with the union; it raised the proportion of teacher evaluations that
were linked to student test scores (vs. observation) after outside
groups (e.g., think tanks, private foundations, business-economic
interests) stressed the importance of "numbers" for "objective" evaluations. As evidence to the contrary, educators cited the arbitrarily
raised cutoff points. To them, the willingness of the state DOE to
"raise the bar" after elected officials and business-economic elites
complained that the exams were too easy and students were not
gaining needed job skills showed that numbers are also subjective
(unscientific) and may be manipulated for political reasons.

The words of a high school math teacher (Patricia) and suburban elementary teacher (Veronica) demonstrate how concerns that
the evaluation system had become politicized reduced buy-in from
educators:

PATRICIA: [What's] the science behind this if the state can arbitrarily
change the cutoff points? And, this is assuming the test is even showing
if a student is educated or not, and I don't think there is evidence the
tests show that either.

VERONICA: [The] cutoff point is political. . . . They always had the same. . . .
Then, they changed it . . . didn't announce it [beforehand]. . . . The
ELA scores haven't come back yet, but we're hearing they're going to
change the cutoff point again. . . . [We're] trying to schedule students
for reading next year, but we won't get the scores until some point in
August. . . . [It] makes it very tough for us. It's just handed down. . . . It
feels arbitrary.[31]

For many, the willingness to "renege on the deal" signaled that the
state did not consider teachers to be equal stakeholders in the development and implementation of APPR. Veronica is making another
point. The new cutoff points resulted in more children qualifying
for AIS, yet schools did not get the information until right before
the school year started. This made it difficult for districts to make
personnel decisions and schedule needed services for children.

Respondents also perceived that the state would rather spend
resources hiring "outsiders" to correct the exams than trust educators

to do so. Under previous practice, teachers did not correct their own exams, but they were corrected in-house by other teachers within the same grade or subject area. Allegedly, the state changed this practice because of concerns about cheating, despite no evidence that this was a problem; the arbitrary change in behavior raised ethical issues for educators. Sam, a suburban high school science teacher, explained,

> [We] don't grade the multiple choice and . . . [now we have] to bubble [short answer and send it to the state]. We didn't get anything back until a day . . . *after* graduation. . . . [The information was not enough to] figure out what kids did . . . [or if there was] a grading . . . bubbling . . . compilation error. . . . We used to go back and verify . . . not trying to give kids something . . . [but these] are high-stakes tests. Graduation is on the line . . . they must have had to hire a lot of people. . . . [Yet I'm] teaching one section of biology . . . normally teach chemistry, because two biology teachers retired and the school is not replacing them . . . [There is] no money and state aid is being cut . . . diverted . . . from the classroom . . . to private companies . . . you feel like government is that nebulous . . . "they" . . . don't have a name . . . a face . . . titles. They exist and dictate what we do, but we don't know who they are [*laughing*].

Like Sam, educators questioned the legitimacy and fairness of APPR because schools and teachers could not verify the scores and students got their results *after* graduation.

Lack of state accountability and resources. Sam's point about the state diverting funding away from classrooms to hire outside staff and pay private vendors was part of another complaint. Educators said their school districts were struggling during and after the Great Recession because of a weak economy and cuts in state aid. The state had also adopted a 2 percent limitation on property tax increases—the major source of funding for public schools. RttT was supposed to provide an infusion of federal resources to ameliorate some of these fiscal issues, but many districts had to further cut expenditures to fund principal training and purchase (per state requirements) testing and curricular packages.[32] Mostly, this involved freezing salaries, laying off teachers, and reducing support staff because, as a human service, personnel costs are the largest component of a district's budget. These layoffs, however, increased class sizes; more teachers, such as Sam, also appeared to be teaching outside of their primary areas. Some further reported administrative cuts, which created issues with student discipline, and cuts in extracurricular activities and "nonacademic" courses, such as sports, clubs, art, music, and technology; many mentioned that their districts were considering reducing kindergarten from a full-day to a half-day program.

A suburban aide (Karina) and urban middle school English (Ronnie) and high school art (Sharon) teacher had this to say about the effects of these fiscal issues:

KARINA: I have noticed a huge increase in the class sizes. We went down from four sections to three sections in a grade. My teacher next year is going to have 28 children.

RONNIE: [Because of state budget cuts] there are 19 layoffs . . . class size is . . . bigger . . . we're losing a lot of support people. . . . We'll have a part-time librarian . . . [the budget has] become very contentious. . . . [The] community doesn't want their property taxes to go up. . . . [Many states are taking] collective bargaining rights away. . . . We're under fire . . . the budget is definitely driving this . . . many people are in difficult times . . . you can understand it, but . . . [teachers] are targeted because their salaries are the biggest part of school budgets.

SHARON: Usually we would have an assistant principal who was the head of discipline. Now, because of budget cuts, we have only one principal . . . [for] Grades 7–12. . . . [Class] sizes have gotten bigger . . . they are not filling positions . . . when people retire or leave.

As evident in Ronnie's narrative, these fiscal issues and program cuts often created tensions between school districts and their local communities, which made it difficult to implement the new evaluation system and Common Core Standards as required under the state's RttT grant.

Many of these cuts privilege those with economic capital because they are less likely to rely on public services. For instance, cutting kindergarten disproportionately harms economically disadvantaged children because they are less likely to have been exposed to preschool (R. Strauss, 2013), but extracurricular and so-called nonacademic classes are also critical for students who struggle. Gloria, an art teacher, described why:

[Art, music, gym, and other so-called nonacademic classes help] a lot of kids who . . . don't succeed academically . . . find a place where they can be successful . . . technology and business, as well . . . with all of this testing, subject area teachers have less and less time to build relationships with students because they are so focused on finishing the content. . . . [These other classes] are a place for kids, who maybe would slip through the cracks, to build relationships with adults. . . . Those relationships have to be there . . . for students to feel safe and willing to learn. . . . There is a lot more than just teaching your subject area. You are teaching these kids to be decent human beings.

For the aforementioned reasons, participants argued that the state was failing to fully meet its obligations under a lawsuit settlement that successfully challenged unequal OTL as a result of inequitable school financing. Again, this failure disproportionately harms under-privileged children. In educators' words, the state is not holding *itself* accountable.

Lack of federal accountability and resources. Educators also complained that the federal government has never fully funded its political priorities, including funding all of the children who are eligible for services under Title I of the ESEA, federally mandated services for special education students, and the testing, reporting, and evaluative requirements of NCLB and RttT. By abdicating those fiscal responsibilities, the federal government placed significant new burdens on state and local property taxes, which are already an inequitable and regressive way to fund public schools.[33] According to informants, the federal government should hold itself accountable by playing a key role in funding public education. It has access to a larger and less regressive tax base and is better able to minimize the effects of socioeconomic inequality and segregation on public school performance (see Chapter 11).

Lack of parental, student, and societal accountability. As mentioned, public opinion polls at the time of NCLB's adoption showed that most Americans believed that parents have more influ-ence on academic performance than schools, teachers, and students (PDK, 2000). Yet every informant in some way conveyed that recent reforms take parents, students, and society off the hook, except in the case of high school exit exams.[34] They were not blaming parents or advocating exit exams as a way to hold students accountable; their point was that the failure to account for these important coproducers resulted in unintended negative consequences. These claims are explored in Chapters 7 and 9, but returning to Kathy's narrative,

teachers only have children six-plus hours a day. . . . The responsibility and accountability should be more evenly dispersed. . . . Children are exposed to so much more today. . . . We did a lot of . . . "playing" but it develops your imagination and social skills, and it is good for children to learn from other children too. They are sitting in front of the TV and what they are learning is questionable. . . . Society should be held accountable. . . . Many children are deprived economically . . . do not get enough to eat, which of course affects learning.

Educators of all ages and backgrounds were consistent in their expressed belief that it takes a village to educate children. Society is refusing to deal with the village by redressing socioeconomic inequality, segregation, the inequitable financing of public schools, poverty, food insecurity, family deterioration, and all the other issues that affect public school performance.

Reluctant acceptance. Not every educator expressed overt dissatisfaction with the state's new evaluation system. *Reluctant acceptance* was a minor narrative (i.e., expressed by fewer than a handful of participants). It was primarily a suburban—not an urban or rural—story; more commonly expressed in districts that worked closely with teachers to develop their evaluations; and focused on two points. The first was "Measurement is important. At least tests are only part of the equation." By increasing the percentage of educators' evaluations that stem from their students' test scores, the state lost credibility with these reluctant acceptors, not just with those who were unhappy with APPR. The second was "It's done. We need to work together to minimize the damage." Trudy, a suburban elementary teacher, captured this view:

> [In my district] 80 percent of your students have to meet that goal. . . . That is doable . . . some districts were not as thoughtful when they implemented it. . . . Most of us walk away when we hear people talking negatively. . . . The feeling is "it's here, it's now—deal with it."

Trudy's narrative, though, serves to demonstrate another complaint that teachers and administrators made about the validity of APPR. The evaluative data are not comparable within districts, much less between them. APPR had to be bargained locally. This included classroom observation procedures, the appeals process, local selection of measures of student achievement, and teacher improvement plans. Teachers also set their own student learning objectives (SLOs). In consequence, the "results could be all over the place" and "teachers could game the system." I address these claims in the next chapter.

Summing up, the public policy literature disagrees about the intrusiveness of public information as a policy tool. Certainly public information enhances democracy in many cases. The Freedom of Information Act (1966) provided the public with access to government data, records, and other information; sunshine laws require the government to provide the public with sufficient advance notice of government meetings and to hold those meetings in places that are accessible to the public; and laws requiring the posting of danger-ous chemicals in the workplace and ingredients on food labels have helped workers and consumers. Public information, however, may also be an undemocratic policy tool. Policy labels are powerful because people care about what others think of them and labeling sends out strong moral signals. It may also indiscriminately shame individuals and groups regardless of whether they have engaged in bad behaviors. This was the case with recent education reforms that blamed students, teachers, and schools for problems that were largely outside of their capacity to redress. Consider the statement of a suburban elementary teacher (Meagan):

> [Teachers] are held accountable . . . regardless of what they do . . . what administrators . . . the state and the federal government do or don't do. . . . We do not have a choice in terms of who walks through our doors . . . what effort they expend. . . . It is not like . . . private businesses or even the government where you can fire . . . hire who you want. You are comparing apples and oranges, [yet] trying to use the same means of evaluating them. It is not like a hierarchy. It is . . . a community. . . . You have to think about them differently.[35]

Because of these issues, recent reforms became increasingly degen-erative and undemocratic. They disproportionately shamed and alienated underprivileged children and other marginalized groups, as well as the schools and educators that served them; they also altered the behaviors of educators and students beyond the time period and outside of the environments that were supposedly being regulated by the government.

In terms of educators, for example, recent reforms "infected" their relationships outside of work and increased turnover—especially for educators who primarily served children with academic, behavioral, and emotional issues or worked in schools that disproportionately serve low-income and minority children. For students, testing and labeling negatively influenced their relationships with their peers and reduced educational persistence within a single year and over time. Educators said that both of these outcomes negatively affected educa-tional performance, but also harmed children's future well-being as workers, citizens, and human beings. Phrased another way, recent reforms created a system in which it made sense for students who struggled and those who served them to opt out. Chapters 7 and 9 explore these claims.

Discussion: The State and Political Behavior

Landy (1993, p. 19) argues that public policies cannot be evaluated on efficiency alone because they are sites of political and social learning. They "instruct the public about the aims of government" and their "rights and responsibilities" as citizens. Informants conveyed how policy makers encouraged low-income and middle-class citizens to vote against their interests by convincing them that we could resolve political, social, and economic issues by getting the "government off our backs" (reducing the size and scope of government) and, in education, by holding public schools and educators accountable.[36] A current (Jess) and retired (Johanna) suburban elementary teacher explained,

JESS: I get . . . they've got budgets to balance . . . [but they've convinced the middle class and below that] the wealthy need tax cuts . . . [and citizens] need protections because . . . greedy teachers are asking for *your* money. . . . [Politicians have] been masterful at . . . getting the middle class . . . to protect the rich and bash fellow middle-class people . . . turned the middle class on themselves.

JOHANNA: The public sector is why businesses were able to thrive. . . . Taxpayers leveraged ourselves to provide . . . [roads, bridges, and other] services. . . . [Businesses] don't want taxes . . . hide their money overseas . . . want to benefit from . . . the wealth of our nation . . . [but not] contribute. . . . [With] the 1 percent controlling everything . . . the discrepancy between their income and the rest of us has exploded. . . . [Politicians] are convincing those in the middle and at the low end that they have to bring us down to raise them up . . . knock teachers . . . firemen . . . policemen down or else everyone else is going to suffer . . . playing to the lowest common denominator . . . people's fear . . . divisive thinking . . . [rather than lifting] expectations . . . [Some are] challenging this. . . . Elizabeth Warren . . . said, "Keep your money, but your goods got to the market on public roads. Public police protected you . . . teachers taught your children . . . firemen make sure your buildings are safe. . . . You didn't do it alone."

In doing so, policy makers generated positive feedback for deregulating the private sector, privatizing the public sector, and offering tax breaks to businesses and upper-income citizens.

The theory of action was that a dynamic private market would foster economic growth; the resulting prosperity would then trickle down in ways that obviated the need for public programs and redistributive policies. Instead, the defunding of public goods and services—like roads, bridges, public transportation, public education, and parks—reduced previous gains in income and the quality of life for 98 percent of Americans (see Chapter 11). This is important because those with lower incomes are less likely to vote (Piven & Cloward, 1988; U.S. Census, 2021). Thus, policy makers reduced feedback from those with the most incentive to demand reform.

The majority of informants who were in their forties or older—like Jenny, a suburban elementary teacher—conveyed how these developments were facilitated by rhetoric and court decisions that reduced the power of public and private-sector unions. These organizations have the ability to demand a countervailing agenda to policies that increase inequality owing to their ability to foster widespread collective political and economic action. In her words,

> [policy makers] talk about the need to bring back the middle class of small business owners . . . That is the only part of the middle class that they care about . . . Both parties have distanced themselves from the unions and it is the unions that made this country strong . . . why we had a thriving middle class . . . minimum wage, shorter workweeks, pension plans, health care . . . [no] child labor . . . They are constantly blaming unions . . . but never . . . discuss their contributions to the economy. The unions are not what is responsible . . . The economy is not doing well because of corporate greed . . . [But unions] stand in the way of corporate America . . . They make more than enough money, but they want even more . . . [want] workers to lose collective bargaining so they have to work overtime without . . . pay . . . [and] extend these kinds of behaviors to the public sector. It is about control and money. If they have control, they can make more money.[37]

Research supports their claim that policy makers increased socioeconomic inequality by weakening the ability of unions to fight for benefits, better wages, and policies that help middle-class, working-class, and low-income Americans (see Chapter 11).

Participants of all ages expressed a belief that these developments have contributed to growing political cynicism among Americans. People do not care solely about the efficiency and effectiveness of government programs; they also value distributive and procedural justice. *Distributive justice* denotes the perceived fairness of the allotment of privileges, goods and services, and burdens (e.g., taxes) across social groups in a society. *Procedural justice* conveys the fairness of the processes that allocate resources, resolve disputes, and dispense punishments. For instance, are they open and transparent? Do they consistently treat "like" cases alike (e.g., impartial and neutral)? Do they offer voice and representation to those affected, and do they typically translate into fair outcomes? The broader claim that these informants were making is that the inequitable treatment of citizens and the partial treatment of the private sector in relation to the public sector has increased political cynicism among Americans, but it also appears to have contributed to growing cynicism among educators.

Political cynicism is an attitude that may or may not alter political identities and behaviors. In this study, it appears to have mostly resulted in increased political apathy and nonvoting—with about 10 percent declaring that they had not or would not vote because of recent developments; however, some said that they had changed their political affiliations. These educators (now) consider themselves independents.[38] These claims are apparent in the comments of a suburban high school math (Patricia) and elementary (Janet) teacher:

PATRICIA: I don't consider myself a political person. I do vote but I don't talk about politics. . . . I didn't vote in the last election . . . maybe this makes me a conscientious objector [*laughs*] because I . . . didn't feel like there was a good choice. I didn't think Romney would be good for education, but I also . . . remember reading . . . he'd hidden his money offshore. . . . [It] sends a bad message . . . a politician who is supported by tax dollars but doesn't think he should have to pay taxes. . . . [I read or heard more] Americans are becoming ex-patriots . . . giving up their citizenship. . . . [Many] were doing it to evade being taxed. Why not, when their leaders are evading taxes and telling them that taxes are evil [*laughs*]? Obama . . . I don't think is an immoral person . . . [but] his policies are horrible for public education. . . . More importantly . . . they're really harmful for children.

JANET: I won't vote in the next election. . . . I don't feel like there is really any difference between both parties. . . . The bottom line is that big business is buying elections and . . . funding the research, so their agenda is being adopted. . . . It is also politically unpopular . . . to raise taxes and so there is no political will. . . . It's much easier to point your finger at teachers than to address the problems that actually plague public education. . . . It has changed the way I feel about, not so much government, but politicians.

The two most common reasons offered for changes in political identities and behaviors included politicians "passing the buck"—rather than redressing the "real issues" in education, such as poverty, hunger, homelessness, segregation, inequitable school financing, and growing socioeconomic inequality—and the lack of real choices between political candidates because the two main political parties tend to offer the same policies in general and for education specifically.

Regardless of why educators—as a group—appear to be experiencing increased political cynicism, political disengagement was *far higher among those who were still working* at the time of these interviews; they were therefore directly affected by recent education reforms and discourse. Within this group, younger educators were more likely to express that they were "apolitical" because "politics is a dirty game." Their older colleagues were more likely to discuss actual changes in their political affiliations or behaviors. The "dirty game" narrative included, but was broader than, those that linked disengagement to recent education reforms and discourse. Veronica, a suburban elementary teacher, disclosed,

> I don't feel like politicians are being held accountable. . . . The economy is in a crisis. . . . Many people are unemployed. . . . Politicians try to play up testing and accountability . . . to show that they're not wasting people's tax dollars . . . use the fact . . . [that we] don't perform as high on tests when compared to other nations to justify [those policies]. . . . Teachers make a nice scapegoat . . . the hard work that goes into teaching students . . . is never seen in the headlines. They pick only the bad things because it sells papers and . . . [gets] votes . . . In some countries, teachers are looked up to like doctors . . . [and they] invest in universal health care and preschool and other programs that help children, but no one talks about that. It's made me, at times, question why I'm a teacher. I put in so many extra hours and I'm not compensated . . . not respected. . . . This is why I really don't get involved in politics . . . it's a dirty game . . . Republicans and Democrats . . . they pander to whatever will get them votes. They don't care about the people at the bottom.

It could be argued that higher rates of political apathy among younger educators align with others in their cohorts—Generation X (1965–1980) and Millennials (1981–1997); however, as evident in Veronica's narrative, recent reforms and discourse further increased political disengagement among these informants. In addition, most of those who discussed changes in their political identities and behaviors were in their fifties at the time of these interviews and therefore part of the Baby Boomer generation (born between 1946 and 1964). That generation has a lower rate of political participation than older Americans (the Silent and Greatest generations), yet higher than younger ones (Generation X and Millennials). As such, these findings cannot be attributed to a generational change.

As a whole, my interviews suggest that political cynicism often spreads through social behaviors. Again, *social trust* is a belief in the honesty, integrity, and reliability of others. It helps foster a commitment to the common good. In contrast, political cynicism creates and is created by social distrust; both are influenced by the words and actions of public officials (elected officials and/or other public servants) and both hinder the willingness and ability of individuals and groups to work together to achieve collective political, economic, and social ends. In this case, educators were conveying that recent discourse and policies reduced citizens' trust in public schools and educators. That alone made it more difficult for public officials, educators, and other groups (e.g., businesses, taxpayers, parents, and students) to work together to improve public education, but it also increased political cynicism and reduced support for public schools and other government programs. When combined with the belief that politicians had worked with business-economic elites to adopt policies that advantaged private interests at the expense of society, these developments appear to have increased educators' mistrust of business-economic elites and elected officials at all levels of government.

Many, like Sam from whom we heard earlier, extended that narrative of distrust to bureaucrats within the national and state DOEs, owing to issues surrounding the implementation of RttT and APPR:

> I don't get too involved in politics. . . . I'm going to get a group of kids in front of me and I have to develop positive relationships with them. I'm going to have a good time with them . . . teach no matter what. . . . Do you get a little jaded? Sometimes. . . . Our state used to be the gold standard. . . . I felt *proud* to be a teacher in this state . . . other states wanted to *be* like us. Now . . . they are running around scared, like chickens with their heads cut off . . . so concerned about achievement, which means numbers. . . . [No one] cares about learning because it's not easily measured. And, we need to measure so we can rank . . . I watched my own children take more tests than . . . [they] should ever . . . take . . . had colleagues . . . say "We're going to stop doing social studies and science and prep for the math and reading tests." . . . . They get rid of exams when they have no money . . . the social studies' eighth-grade exam. . . . It's political . . . [It's not] coming from a best practices point of view.

Sam is an example of "reluctant acceptance" yet he is also express-ing increased political cynicism and reduced trust in the state DOE because of recent reforms. His words are powerful when contrasted with Kristen's narrative in Chapter 4 about how she was loyal to her state because its collective bargaining law had empowered teachers to push for reforms that made it the "gold standard" for other states. Both express "pride of place.," but Sam's loyalty has been severely diminished. This is important because the federal and state DOEs need educators to implement education policies.

Others extended the narrative of distrust to teachers' unions. They told me that the union felt pressured to go along with the state's RttT application to get more federal funding during tough economic times. The state then reneged on the deal with respect to the actual policy (APPR) it adopted. The failure to fight the "flawed" Common Core Standards and the new evaluation system reportedly caused many teachers to become disaffected with the union.[39] Liam, a recently retired high school English teacher and former union president, explained,

> [You] cannot have a culture where . . . elected leaders . . . government in general is ridiculed and then . . . say . . . "contribute money so that we can participate in this process" [*laughs*]. . . . Unions . . . have been bashed for decades . . . [undermining them] . . . the recession created the kind of economic insecurity where teachers . . . especially unten-ured . . . are afraid to be more militant. Then . . . APPR, Common Core . . . private-sector vendors . . . selling scripted programs . . . to develop a "teacher proof curriculum" . . . a mechanized system . . . if you say these scripts and use these techniques every child will go to Harvard . . . regardless of poverty or family dysfunction . . . We've taken away the autonomy of the person who they want to save the system. It is totally paradoxical. . . . They want a certain type of individualistic, very bright person . . . to go into teaching. That is not realistic when you . . . [expect them] to work for less, under poor working conditions, with no autonomy.

Liam's claim that many younger teachers do not want to participate in the union *because* it participates in the "dirty game" of politics by lobbying, funding electoral candidates, and so forth shows how political cynicism may reduce collective political and economic voice. His narrative was common, but many felt that declining union support among those in their twenties and thirties also stemmed from different generational experiences.

Unlike Baby Boomers, Generation X and Millennials were not

involved in the movement to unionize teachers and, owing to a decline in union membership in general, are less likely to have grown up in unionized families; they are therefore less likely to have experienced the benefits of collective economic action (e.g., higher familial income) during their formative years. Although this causal narrative is about policy feedback, it is focused more broadly on how weaponized discourse and policies reduced union membership and created downstream effects by influencing the formative experiences of subsequent generations. This is also true of teachers in their forties; however, different formative experiences do not appear to have negatively affected their union participation. My interviews suggest that this relates to what I earlier referred to as "value introjection." They were hired and socialized at a time when the teaching workforce was dominated by the Baby Boomers, who were socialized by older generations and had participated in the drive to unionize teachers. Teachers in their twenties and thirties are less likely to have been socialized by older generations because they were hired during a period of rapid Baby Boomer turnover due to retirements.

Despite these differences, educators typically had more similarities across "social groups" (e.g., occupation, age, employment status, and urban, rural, or suburban public schools and charter schools) than dissimilarities. As shown in Chapter 5, this social cohesion stems from people with similar values being drawn to teaching; it is then strengthened through university programs and on-the-job socialization. Because most administrators are former teachers, this finding also appears to hold true for that group as well. My interviews indicate that this social cohesion has been somewhat eroded owing to the ways that recent reforms and discourse interacted with economic distress.

Like many other citizens, educators are concerned about job security during difficult economic times. Some worry that union demands will anger taxpayers and cause them to reject or reduce school budgets, which would increase layoffs and intensify inhumane working conditions. These fears reportedly diminished union support among younger teachers because they are more likely to lose their jobs as the last hired (tenure and seniority). A suburban elementary teacher (Jess) and an urban elementary teacher and union president (Lorna) stated,

LORNA: [Our local union] is a shell of their former self . . . the new teachers . . . do not understand what we are fighting for . . . [did not] stand in protest . . . on a picket line . . . march . . . in solidarity. . . . Class sizes are going up and so we are losing positions.

JESS: [It takes time for younger teachers to get that] you have to stand up for yourself . . . can't arbitrarily decide . . . [to give up] planning time . . . it's not just you. . . . You're affecting all of us and the contract . . . we collectively fought for. . . . [Someday you'll] want that planning time, and it won't be available. . . . There are fewer [students] . . . from families with union members . . . so they don't have an understanding of why unions came about . . . other than to . . . protect jobs or . . . income . . . feeling the pressures of the testing . . . worried about layoffs.

Both respondents are discussing generational changes, but, similar to other informants, their narratives largely blame fiscal distress and negative public discourse about unions for eroded social cohesion and union support. That rhetoric appears to have convinced younger teachers that Americans do not support salary increases and collective bargaining, despite public opinion polls showing support for both (see Chapter 1).

Many teachers further alleged that school districts, policy makers, and business-economic interests were using economic uncertainty to "divide and conquer"—weaken the union's ability to voice against harmful policy reforms and fight political and administrative demands for "givebacks" in the form of lower wages, larger class sizes, and so forth—by stirring distrust among teachers and between teachers and their unions. Returning to Lorna's narrative,

[the mayor wants everyone to think we'll raise achievement if we have] merit pay . . . get rid of tenure . . . excellent teachers will have jobs . . . "dead wood" will be gone . . . wants the new teachers to . . . turn on the older teachers . . . parents to believe . . . problems are being caused by tenure and the seniority system. . . . Young teachers . . . are becoming anti-union. . . . My former principal . . . did not want me to tell the new teachers . . . why the union was important. . . . She would say . . . "You do not want that old . . . average, mediocre teacher, to keep their job just because they've been here forever when you deserve the position more" . . . then, I would have to say . . . "One day you are going to be that person . . . considered ancient at 45 because . . . [we are getting rid of older teachers] to save money."

Given these developments, it is not surprising that teachers reported increased fears to voice, especially among younger and untenured teachers where administrative retaliation in the form of more difficult classes may reduce test scores and provide justification for firing them. I discuss this latter claim in the next chapter, but recent informal discussions with educators suggest that these concerns have been somewhat ameliorated as a result of teachers observing public support for strikes across the nation and parental protests against testing as a way to evaluate teachers and students. These developments appear to be restoring some informants' faith in citizens for treating teachers with respect, rather than buying into anti-teacher and anti-union rhetoric.

Conclusion

Policies that use information as a political tool assume that people are rational and respond to information in similar ways (Weiss, 1993, 2007). In contrast, this chapter shows that people respond to information emotionally as well as cognitively (through conscious intellectual activity). Educators experienced strong negative emotions as a result of recent reforms and discourse because they perceived both to be undemocratic, harmful, and socially unjust. The consistency of these reactions across those affected by recent reforms (e.g., principals and teachers) and those not affected (e.g., retirees, librarians, speech pathologists, and psychologists) suggests that increased political anger and cynicism were not self-interested responses. Educators believe that testing and accountability are about blaming and shaming, and measuring and punishing, more than resolving educational issues.

7

Education Reform, Social Behaviors, and Policy Feedback

Policy makers portrayed recent education reforms as a less coercive way of regulating schools and educators. Test scores would help diagnose and treat problem areas through the provision of funding, training, and services but schools and educators were relatively free from hierarchical (bureaucratic and political) controls so long as they improved student outcomes. Those I interviewed, in contrast, framed testing as a "disciplinary technology," meaning a form of social regulation—not just political accountability—that disproportionately harms the most vulnerable students and those educators who serve them. This chapter uses 83 interviews with educators to understand how testing, as a form of social regulation, affected teaching and learning.

Post–Education Reform Narratives of Accountability

Foucault (1995) used Jeremy Bentham's concept of the Panopticon—a prototype prison that enabled guards to view every aspect of prisoners' daily lives—to convey how political, economic, and social institutions coerce individuals to behave in certain ways. He argued that institutions use norms, social labels (e.g., groups, ranks, classifications), and the partitioning of time and space (e.g., offices, prison cells, classrooms) to observe and inspect. According to him, perpetual observation is not the end goal of the Panopticon or other institutions; instead, it helps construct norms and abnormalities that may be used to encourage deviants to "discipline themselves" and thereby foster docile and productive behaviors. My interviews suggest that testing—as a form of accountability—works in a similar way.

Testing helps states and local school districts compare schools, principals, teachers, and students; make statements about their potential worth, value, and contribution to society; and allot rewards and punishments in ways that cause them to alter their behaviors. Sandy, a suburban high school math teacher, disclosed,

> They use it [testing] to put a failing grade on the kids . . . the school . . . the teacher. It's meant to find out what the kids need to learn, but there is none of that "Let's get the kid this extra service" . . . they do, but it's a Band-Aid. . . . The kid scored a 2 . . . put them in front of a computer to do 500 problems of adding and subtracting. . . . There is no money . . . to get at the source of the problem. . . . [APPR] is to help the teacher improve, which would be a win-win . . . [but that substructure is not] in place. . . . [A struggling school] just close it down . . . fire all the teachers. . . . [If] students fail my state exam I personally feel accountable, but usually there is some reason . . . they were absent 50 times or whatever. . . . [Administrators are not] making teachers better. They're about politics and testing and discipline.

Compliance, though, tends to result in unintended and dysfunctional behaviors, more than improved performance, largely due to the ways that testing interacts with social contexts.

As a whole, my interviews support Foucault's claim that social control is largely exercised from within (self-regulation), rather than achieved through violence or force, as individuals strive to meet social expectations Consider the words of a suburban elementary teacher (Robin):

> [Teachers] are being held accountable to the public. . . . [Our salaries and school and district] test scores get posted in the newspaper . . . [a Los Angeles teacher committed] suicide because his grades were published. . . . It's stressful. You put a lot of pressure on yourself. You want your students to do well certainly, but it is also a pride thing. I work really hard and . . . what you do becomes reduced to that number. . . . [It is] not just based on my performance, but I'm the one . . . held accountable . . . that's going to be even more true under Race to the Top . . . using test scores to say "this person is a bad teacher." . . . Once you have the data, it snowballs because they can rank teachers and students and schools.

Certainly recent reforms put pressure on educators and students to meet state objectives through the provision of sanctions, rewards, and incentives, but the resulting behavioral changes also stemmed from a human desire to avoid being stigmatized. Then, testing becomes more coercive over time as it provides policy makers with the information to control schools and classrooms.

Testing as a "Disciplinary Technology"

As mentioned, early uses of state standards and testing encouraged grade-, school-, and district-level collaboration, but schools as organizations remained "loosely coupled" (Meyer & Rowan, 1977). Teachers could still "shut their doors" and exert some control over how they taught, even as the state increasingly directed what they taught. It was one factor in informants' expressed support for these policies. They further applauded the inclusion of teachers and their unions in the development and implementation of these reforms and the use of state exams as a gauge of performance rather than to make high stakes decisions. Recent education reforms, however, appear to have opened up classrooms to new and more coercive forms of hierarchical control by expanding the testing culture. Renée, a suburban elementary teacher, best illustrated this claim:

> [The] first principal . . . micromanaged everything . . . press a button . . . the PA system and listen in to people's classrooms from her office . . . walk in and out of classrooms. . . . You had to have all your aims on the board . . . file every piece of paperwork. . . . [She] had an 8 ½ × 14 . . . front and back, like four pages . . . bulletin every week in small print [*laughing*]. . . . You were tested on it. . . . Somewhere in it, she would advise you to do something, which would let her know that you read the whole thing. . . . We have a new superintendent . . . nicknames herself the "Data Diva." . . . We . . . print out our own data . . . four times a year . . . [so they can] assess how you . . . [and] your children are doing. . . . [The tests are] done on the computer . . . everyone in the district is doing it right around the same time. . . . They are individualized . . . by child, teacher and then overall, you against a grade level . . . that's the local assessment. . . . [Then we have] the state tests. . . . [We look at] which school fared the best . . . what our teachers need to work on at that grade level. . . . Sometimes that's all put up at our superintendent's meeting prior to school to both inspire and humiliate you [*laughing*].

Renée describes how administrators "observe" teachers through student test scores. The cellular structure of teaching fosters perpetual observation too; it enables administrators to listen and "pop" into classrooms. This principal further "tested" (controlled) teachers through her weekly newsletter.

Policy makers, administrators, and market actors (e.g., testing and publishing companies) also gained expanded access to classrooms through *consumable learning packages*. Purchased from private vendors, these resources theoretically improve teaching and learning through "scripting" and benchmark exams that may be used to gauge performance. Teachers described scripting as the formally designed curriculum packages that mandate what (specific content) and how (the methods, materials, and language) to teach. Meagan, a suburban elementary teacher, remarked,

> They give us things that we have to follow. . . . "Now you say . . . da da da da da" . . . binders, books, units that we have to do and do it in a certain way. . . . We don't have freedom to implement it in a way that is comfortable . . . [and] best fits the needs of our students . . . based on our professional knowledge. . . . We are also given scripts for test prep.

Per respondents, these packages are attractive to administrators because they facilitate hierarchical control by creating a "teacher-proof" curriculum; they are also easy to disseminate and assess through benchmark exams.

Under NCLB, the use of consumable learning packages appears to have expanded as schools competed with one another for test scores; however, the reporting model also resulted in growing numbers of schools being labeled. These districts had to file a plan with the state DOE that demonstrated how they would use "proven research-based methodologies" to fix poor performance. Because most districts had neither the time nor the resources to demonstrate research-based compliance, they purchased these products from state-approved vendors. Participants said this created a "boon" for testing and publishing companies. Some districts (about 18% of my sample), though, also adopted organizational and procedural controls to ensure that teachers followed the exact "scripts" (the actual language provided in the package). For instance, they required teachers to hand in their schedules and lesson plans at the beginning of the year and then conducted "walk-throughs" to ensure that they followed those schedules, as well as the scripted curriculum. Others adopted a very strong "performative" discourse, which was backed by material rewards (e.g., merit pay), sanctions (e.g., poor performance reviews and more difficult classes and duties), and even public shaming at faculty meetings.

Outside of these districts, my interviews suggest that the loss of professional discretion and autonomy more prominently related to the ways testing encouraged teachers to voluntarily change *what* (content) and *how* (pedagogy) they taught. However, it is not wholly accurate to characterize these behavioral changes as "self-regulation." Testing encouraged teachers to alter their behaviors in ways that pursued—if not achieved—state aims and organizational goals by constructing and disseminating labels that could be used to shame, reward, and punish schools, educators, and students. In doing so, NCLB increasingly replaced professionalism, as a way of organizing knowledge and social relations, with market and hierarchal controls. Later reforms (RttT and NCLB waivers) expanded this trend by linking educators' evaluations to their students' test scores and requiring states to adopt college- and career-ready standards—such as the Common Core.

One way the decline of professionalism occurred across recent reforms was by silencing those aspects of teaching that are essential but difficult to measure. The need to prepare students for state exams, the time spent actually taking those exams, and the focus on testable skills, competencies, and content reduced the amount of time teachers had to develop untested knowledge, skills, and competencies. These claims are apparent in a suburban elementary teacher's (Kathy) explanation of how tests ought to help teachers and how the testing culture actually affects teaching:

> [Testing should help] understand if students are mastering material and, if not . . . [why, but they are not] testing mastery. They are testing exposure. For example, we do not care if students are good writers . . . about grammar, spelling, comprehension . . . so long as they give "four facts." . . . [The] testing culture . . . the response to problems . . . is more testing . . . practice exams . . . less time to teach because we spend so much time taking tests. . . . [It doesn't] make sense . . . fix problems with learning by spending less time on the learning.

The end result was that teachers increasingly lost the capacity to develop children's interests and abilities beyond the tested curriculum.

Teachers provided many examples of lessons and activities that became less salient yet are critical for developing nontested material and engaging multiple ability levels and forms of intelligence.

Most involved building higher order thinking, interpersonal, and/ or civic skills.[1] They also mentioned *teachable* moments—something that is not in your plan book but comes up spontaneously through student questions. A retired (Sophia) suburban elementary teacher had this to say:

> We used to do whole thematic units that incorporated . . . say, dinosaurs into every aspect of learning . . . read books together as a class . . . do research in the library . . . creative writing. . . . My friends . . . tell me they cannot do things like this anymore. . . . That is a shame because . . . along with the fun the children are learning. . . . That is what the children remember . . . those projects, or plays . . . rather than the day they opened up a book and turned to page 25.

Phrased another way, the testing culture reduces "knowledge" to something that is "taught" and then "demonstrated" at prescribed moments in time; teaching is standardized, teacher directed, and then tested. It increasingly alienates teachers *and* students from the learning process, especially the most creative teachers and those students who learn in ways other than direct teaching.[2]

The finding that social control through testing and consumable learning packages increases feelings of powerlessness, alienation, and dissatisfaction is not surprising. Political scientists and sociologists concur that there are consequences to the over- and under-regulation of social life. Educators' words especially reminded me of 19th- and early 20th-century concerns about the ill effects of the market replacing other means of organizing society—such as extended families, guilds, occupations, and communities—as capitalists searched for new ways to expand profits. Some expressed concern that the excessive pursuit of self-interest and individual rights would result in a loss of social ties, which are needed to help individuals and communities thrive. Others worried that workers would become dehumanized and alienated from their natural and social worlds, as they increasingly directed their labor toward the goals of those who owned the means of production.[3]

In this case, teachers are describing how the "commodification" of teaching and learning—meaning control through purchasable tests and learning packages—leads to alienation and the loss of our humanity. Meagan, from whom we heard earlier, elaborated on these ideas:

> I have a hard time . . . [just following] a script. There is a lot that comes up . . . [learning] spontaneously through the interaction between teachers and students, and . . . students' questions. The whole lesson can be taken

in a whole other direction and be just as valuable, if not more valuable because you are engaging students' curiosity. . . . You cannot think of teaching as a business. We are . . . producing good human beings. . . . They want . . . a one-size-fits-all business model of teaching. . . . Kids cannot perform in exactly the same way at exactly the same time. They have different intellects . . . abilities . . . needs . . . [and] interests . . . [and so] we are setting children up for failure . . . to feel like failures.

None of those I interviewed objected to state standards, and most were not opposed to using testing as a *gauge* of student performance. Their main concern revolved around policy-induced pressures to "teach certain things, in certain ways, at certain times" regardless of how it negatively affected students' academic, social, and emotional growth and well-being.

Informants further complained that recent policies created social justice issues by disproportionately harming those groups that are more likely to struggle academically—underprivileged (and there-fore minority) children, ELLs, and students with learning, behav-ioral, or emotional issues. These students were especially likely to be exposed to "drill and grill" teaching as the state, school districts, principals, and teachers tried to "fix" low achievement by stan-dardizing (nonrandomizing) individual behaviors. Certainly this improved test performance for some, but it decreased exposure to more complex forms of knowledge and skills. It also caused many to "opt out" (drop out or refuse to participate, do homework, or study). Returning to Robin's narrative,

the kids that struggle . . . constantly feel like failures. . . . You can see it in their faces and their demeanor as they are taking . . . know we're going to take . . . or after we've taken a test. . . . [There is] less time to teach . . . supposedly what we care about, because we are spending more and more time testing them. . . . [It's] discouraging for them . . . discouraging for us. . . . When you're constantly told you're not good at something . . . it is really human nature to feel less willing to do it. . . . [We're supposed] to lower the dropout rate . . . but they're not changing the way we deal with special needs kids. They're just testing them.

In this way, testing challenged teachers' ability to meet the occupa-tion's core moral purpose—to develop caring, well-adjusted, compe-tent, *and* educated human beings. The remainder of this section explores these claims as reported for school (NCLB) and educator (NCLB waivers and RttT) accountability.

Social Control Under School Accountability (NCLB)

Although most teachers associated their loss of professional discretion under NCLB with time-related factors, some teachers reported experiencing significant new administrative controls. These "Tier 1" and "Tier 2" schools differed from school districts at large. Public managers in Tier 1 schools—10 percent of my sample (four districts)—standardized and routinized teaching through a combination of top-down hierarchical controls and explicit rewards and sanctions. Administrators in Tier 2 schools—8 percent of my sample (three districts)—adopted a very strong "performative" discourse, often backed by explicit rewards (see Figure C.3 in Appendix C). In both cases, though, administrators adopted these controls to meet policy expectations. Two of the five public schools were labeled and trying to improve performance through standardization. The remaining three public and two charter schools were using test scores to keep their customers happy, which was actually the intent of providing public information under NCLB.

Charter school participants declared that these managerial controls were largely profit oriented, meaning they were adopted to attract customers by outperforming the surrounding public schools. Some alleged, however, that administrators viewed their positions as "stepping-stones" to other jobs within the public or private sectors and needed high test scores for positive evaluations.[4] Teachers in the three competitive public schools agreed that administrators wanted to satisfy the local community through improved performance data, but two other themes emerged. Under the first scenario, teachers described the relationship between the school and the community as adversarial or contentious in a budgetary sense. Administrators appeared to view good test scores as a way to encourage the community to pass the budget. Under the second, teachers claimed that the district's "clientele" was competitive. Most were describing parents; some discussed the community or taxpayers, but "relative" test scores were important because they helped the community compete with neighboring ones and children compete with their peers.

Despite some differences, teachers in both Tier 1 and Tier 2 schools told me that their administrators believed that the "norm of competition" would improve performance. This theory of action had very similar effects across public and charter schools.

Externally oriented, performative culture. Teachers described the culture of these schools as *performative* and *hierarchical* because district administrators used top-down controls to focus effort on "the numbers" (e.g., high school graduation and college attendance rates, numbers of students in special education and advanced placement classes, test scores). Consider the words of a suburban elementary teacher (Donna):

> [They] had percentages . . . you have to reduce special ed . . . by 10 percent . . . so many teachers have to be on improvement plans . . . can't have too many . . . exceeding standards . . . if it doesn't look like a bell shape, it can't be accurate. . . . [And] they don't care what it takes for us to have to do our job. They're taking away support . . . and adding to the administration at the top. So it's a top/down, instead of the bottom/up. . . . They redid . . . all the buildings . . . the schools look great . . . the money . . . wasted in landscaping . . . could've been used for the kids. . . . Everything has to look good . . . the façade to the community.[5]

The focus on the "public face"—how the school looked to the community—altered the "private face" of teaching and learning in ways that were (largely) not welfare enhancing (e.g., teaching to the test), as district demands for improved performance indicators diminished the time spent on nonperformative goals. It also reduced the involvement of principals and teachers in the management of their schools (site-based decision-making) and restricted professional discretion and autonomy.

Motivating with the carrot and the stick. Again, teachers described their *work commitment* in terms of intrinsic rewards, such as being good at one's job, a calling to help children, or a desire to do good by improving social justice. Administrators in Tier 1 and 2 schools were able to co-opt some teachers' "backstage" and "offstage" regions (Goffman, 1959), meaning their emotions, emotional displays, and personal and professional relationships, through the use of extrinsic incentives. These inducements included the carrot and the stick, such as material rewards, recognition, or status; they altered teachers' relationships to one another and to the profession. A suburban speech pathologist (Annie) described these market forms of social control:

> [We] do a lot of standing up and clapping for people . . . praising successes . . . celebrations of our test scores if they are up . . . being really sad . . . test scores went down. . . . The principal will say . . . "80 percent of the first graders are reading at grade level . . . 99 percent of the kindergarteners. . . . Stand up everyone and clap. You're a kindergarten teacher—stand up! [*clap, clap*]. This is wonderful! [*clap, clap*]. . . . We

need to . . . get those first-grade test scores up." . . . First-grade teachers feel horrible . . . [and] it starts from there. . . . Teachers who have problems with the principal . . . [get] classes that are loaded with behavioral problems. We've seen that *a lot*. . . . Teachers who are friendly with the principal . . . have *wonderful* classes. Then . . . praised because "aren't they wonderful, their scores are wonderful" when another teacher had children that were much more challenging.

Annie's principal coerced the faculty into recognizing some teachers (clapping) and shaming others (silence with "sad" facial expressions) by giving poor performance reviews to those who did not display the appropriate signals. She then used those reviews to justify withholding material rewards, denying tenure, putting teachers on probation and improvement plans, or, in some cases, firing them.

The material rewards varied depending on the district. Some mentioned merit pay, but a more common example was the use of student placements to reward or punish teachers. Union contracts in some districts put upper limits on the number of students in an elementary classroom and the total number of students taught by secondary teachers. Some teachers were consistently given larger classes, higher overall student numbers, or a disproportionately large number of students who struggle academically. Administrators also influenced teachers' behaviors by rewarding or punishing them with outside duties, denying them personal days, or refusing funds for conferences and supplies. One high school teacher, for example, said that some were consistently given duties where they could correct their work (e.g., monitoring an unused hallway), while others required more stressful interactions with students (e.g., cafeteria duty, parking lot duty, monitoring a study hall). All of these affect work intensity and therefore relative performance. Annie told me that the goal was to reduce the effectiveness of those "targeted for elimination," but some teachers said that these behaviors were also used to *improve district performance* by maximizing the workload of *highly effective* teachers. Another performative strategy involved reducing the workload of less effective teachers or of those who taught grading-intensive classes, like English.

Increased mechanization. Tier 1 districts further combined these incentives with scripting and other routinizing mechanisms to create a "teacher-proof" curriculum. Administrators then gave poor performance reviews to those who did not follow the exact scripts. A suburban elementary school teacher (Kelly) commented,

[We] hand in a schedule in the beginning of the school year that indicates what we are doing every five minutes of our day.... [The principal] has to approve it ... [and checks you're following it. Teachers don't plan their] lessons. They "teach to the book." ... [You] do what ... you're told. ... If you don't ... you might not be meeting standards ... they can ... fire you ... that has happened. ... I use some of ... the little mini lessons ... but improvise ... except during my formal observation. I go verbatim from the book ... memorize the words.[6]

As a whole, participants were not opposed to curricular packages and some expressed that they are helpful, especially for new teachers. They voiced concerns only in those cases where teachers were required to follow the scripts regardless of their own professional judgments and the needs, abilities, and interests of their students, which was the case in all of the Tier 1 schools. My interviews suggest that these practices spread as more districts were labeled.

Exacerbated inequitable costs of caring. As mentioned, prior to recent reforms, most principals tried to reduce negative peer effects by spreading out the number of students with behavioral, emotional, or academic issues across classrooms. When they placed higher numbers of academically at-risk students with certain teachers, it was typically because they perceived that these students would respond better to a particular situation or that it was more efficient and effective to have an aide or special education teacher "push in" to an included classroom to help that teacher. Recent reforms appear to have resulted in more districts using organizational practices (e.g., tracking, self-contained special education classes, and inclusion) to improve performance data even when that was not ideal or beneficial for students.

John, who was consistently rated a highly effective elementary teacher in a non–Tier 1/Tier 2 suburban district, discussed how the assignment of a large number of educationally at-risk students to highly effective teachers contributes to burnout and harms students:

[Administrators are] complimenting ... [me but] it gets to be too much. ... A student ... suffered from anxiety. ... His hair would be sweaty. ... [He'd say] "I can't take it anymore. I *am on fire*." ... [I said] he could ... come up and stand next to me. ... [It] would panic the other students ... the other side ... the bipolar. ... [He'd say he] wanted to hurt someone ... screw up his face in a very scary expression. ... Another student ... [had] violent outbursts ... [would] stab with a pencil. ... [It would never pull some] to the dark side. ... [But some] are looking to misbehave. . . . [Then] that whole section in the middle . . . can go either way . . . so I am concerned about the misbehaviors . . . what it is teaching the other children in addition to how the other children are *feeling* about it. . . . [I'm] teaching a solar system lesson . . . [watching the one] prone to stabbing . . . my student with the anxiety . . . holding on to . . . my belt . . . [the school psychologist is watching a student who was inappropriately touching herself under her desk] . . . thinking, "This is like one heck of a year."

This narrative is a prime example of what I earlier described as peer effects and tipping points in the classroom. John is concerned about the negative attitudes and behaviors spreading and thereby affecting the performance and well-being of other students in the room. The chaotic environment also made it difficult to forge emotional connections with his students, which made it harder to maintain social order and create an academically stimulating learning environment.

Like John, teachers who serve large numbers of educationally at-risk students expressed that they have more academic and administrative responsibilities, including, but not limited to, increased paperwork for children with special needs under state and federal education laws. They also engage in large amounts of unpaid, *invisible work* at school and at home. For instance, John said he spent a lot of time after school on academic and administrative responsibilities because his time in the classroom was "eaten up putting out fires." The inequitable assignment of students, either to higher performing teachers or to those that administrators are trying to eliminate, co-opts teachers' backstage regions (i.e., their emotions and relationships with other students in the classroom) and offstage regions (i.e., their relationships and free time outside of the classroom) into doing unpaid, invisible work to meet state performative goals or the goals of individual administrators because, as shown, relationships in and outside of the classroom are so critical.[7] Respondents reported that these teachers have higher rates of burnout because they cannot escape the performance.

It is important to note that teachers did not necessarily object to the unequal distribution of students. Where they stood in regard to this issue depended on their views on the effects of tracking and inclusion and their beliefs about the motivations for placing students with certain teachers. Like the findings on how tracking affects students, teachers in this study had mixed views.[8] Informants agreed that teaching styles must vary depending on the needs of the class, the needs of individual students, and the attributes, experiences, and abilities of the teachers. They also agreed that "good administrators" recognize different teaching and learning styles and should somewhat try to match students with teachers. For example, one teacher may be better able to handle students with behavioral issues. Most only objected to the unequal assignment of students with educational issues if it negatively affected other students or the principal was systematically assigning the most difficult students to the same teacher(s).[9] Post-NCLB, administrative behaviors resulted in both of these outcomes, but this phenomenon was more prevalent in Tier 1 and Tier 2 schools.

Declining trust. In Chapter 5, teachers described how the use of rewards and sanctions in the classroom (social control) may reduce overall performance by creating an "us versus them" environment. Similarly, the use of rewards and sanctions to control teachers appears to have diminished school performance by escalating occupational and organizational conflict and reducing trust and social cohesion. Teachers in Tier 1 and Tier 2 schools perceived that administrators were "weeding out" those who challenged the new hierarchical/performative culture and/or using the stereotype that older teachers are "dead wood"—practice outdated teaching techniques or fail to work hard upon receiving tenure—to reduce personnel costs.[10] Shannon, a former urban elementary teacher who now supervises student teachers in a large urban district, explained:

> In the city, power has been transferred to the principals. . . . I worked with one principal closely. . . . He felt like teachers needed a kick in the butt to really shake out the wheat from the chaff. . . . [He said] schools needed to use the test scores, and the pressure, to get rid of the dead meat . . . the dead weight . . . test scores were to push teachers into leaving.

The practice of pushing more experienced (expensive) teachers to leave is misguided because, as supported in Chapter 5, high turnover reduces school effectiveness and experience typically improves performance.[11]

Declining social trust, though, also reduced school effectiveness by creating a climate of "us versus them" (reduced social cohesion) and discouraging more experienced teachers from training and socializing new ones.[12] At the heart of these divided communities was a value conflict between those who stressed (and enforced) the humanistic values of teaching and those who supported—at least on the surface—the portrayal of teaching as a clinical or technical enterprise (i.e., something that is easily standardized and measured). Those who remained loyal to the norms of teaching felt like administrators had engaged in a "divide and conquer" strategy by rewarding those who "performed" teaching but did not "feel" it. These teachers were often accused of "not liking the kids," having a "corporate, self-interested mentality," or being focused on "getting ahead" at the expense of caring for children. Debbie, a suburban elementary teacher, elaborated on this increased social conflict:

> It's almost like . . . the family side . . . [and the fake] corporate side. . . .
> [They] have all of the newest and latest things up on their walls . . . know
> the newest theory . . . [but] so busy trying to get ahead . . . that they lose
> sight of . . . the love that the children need. . . . They could talk your
> ear off about theory, and . . . probably put the theory into practice, but
> not with the heart. And that . . . is the key to teaching . . . if your heart
> is really into making a child learn . . . grow and . . . prosper, you'll find
> a way, regardless of what the theory is.

To those who did not adopt the new business mentality, the "corporate" teachers had lowered their standards or ideals to gain status, approval, better classes and duties, or to move into administration. These self-interested behaviors signaled a lack of personal and professional integrity; yet these teachers were rewarded by "a system" that valued test scores above other indicators of teacher professionalism, proficiency, and performance.

When asked to expand on those thoughts, teachers said "those teachers" did not teach spontaneously or holistically develop children as human beings; instead, they focused on those aspects of teaching that were tangible and easily measured. In short, they "taught to the test" or even engaged in cheating. Returning to Annie's narrative,

> [in] the next grade . . . children are tested at the beginning of the school
> year and . . . [the] scores are lower. . . . [The new teacher] is made to feel
> guilty . . . [yet it's obvious] they were not tested correctly at the end of the
> year . . . [given] a little more leeway, fudged . . . a little . . . certain teachers
> . . . scores are much higher than . . . the reading teacher's scores . . . for
> those same kids. . . . Certain teachers . . . have the reputation for that.

Annie's narrative shows how teachers in grades or subjects that do not have state exams could game the system by loosely grading their own "local," or school, exams. When teachers are involved in the creation of these local exams, it is easy to "teach to the test" by only covering tested material, typically in a repetitive fashion, but some reported teachers doing this for state exams as well.

Gaming the system (neglect), increased turnover (exit), and narratives of resistance (voice). Annie's statement is part of a broader story about how NCLB intended to close the achievement gap by holding schools accountable for student learning, yet (largely) resulted in dysfunctional behaviors and unintended consequences more than real improvements to public schools. Nichols and Berliner (2007, p. 49) contend that Campbell's law—the idea that quantitative social indicators distort and corrupt social processes the more they are used to regulate behaviors—explains these outcomes. Some examples documented by empirical studies include lowered state standards, a narrowed curriculum, teaching to the test, assisting students with test questions, misclassifying students as special education, employing disciplinary procedures to encourage low-performing students to be absent on test day, manipulating retention policies, providing enriched school lunch menus prior to the test, and changing answers (e.g., Figlio & Winicki, 2005; Nichols & Berliner, 2007; Ravitch, 2010). Given these findings, it is not surprising that NCLB failed to close the achievement gap. Although race-based gaps (somewhat) narrowed over the past several decades, research suggests that those gains resulted from federal antipoverty and desegregation policies versus accountability reforms.[13] In the meantime, income-based gaps have grown as a result of growing numbers of children living in poverty (Reardon, 2011).

The claim that NCLB's emphasis on tangible and testable skills resulted in dysfunctional behaviors, more than real improvements, was far more common in Tier 1 and 2 schools—where teachers described strong administrative pressure to improve test scores—but it was also more common in schools that served large numbers of underprivileged students with limited resources. Nancy, a former elementary teacher and retired elementary principal from a high need, low resource urban school, alluded to these dysfunctional behaviors:

> [NCLB led] to an emphasis on tests and some practices that might not be ideal for . . . learning . . . teaching for the tests . . . altering test scores. . . . I haven't seen that but . . . [it is possible to] skew test scores by answering questions. . . . How the assistance is given affects the answer . . . put on the test. . . . They are not physically changing it, but they are skewing it.

Teachers in these schools felt pressure to help their students compete in an environment where the deck was stacked against them; however, the resulting behaviors were, in many cases, not ideal for students.

One complaint was that the focus on data and numbers increasingly crowded out the humanistic norms of teaching, which, again, are designed to produce caring, well-adjusted, well-rounded, competent, and educated human beings. A suburban elementary teacher (Debbie) and an urban student teacher supervisor (Shannon) had this to say:

DEBBIE: Those numbers are . . . looked at and discussed . . . down to . . . 8 percent . . . in this classroom didn't answer this question correctly . . . is that going to impact your teaching this year. . . . The test . . . and the students are going to be different. Why am I looking at . . . a test . . . for a half a day? How much money was spent. . . . We're not making parts . . . we're making people . . . we're making human beings.

SHANNON: It is about the test scores. That is the ultimate measure of whether . . . [teachers and students] are considered successful. . . . The principal is . . . constantly walking into rooms or walking by rooms . . . what that translates into, is that they cannot keep their focus on student needs. . . . Science and social studies have pretty much gone by the wayside in elementary school. It is all about math and literacy. And now, with technology, it is much easier to *do* literacy . . . [and] assess the kids . . . on the computer. . . . They've spent an enormous amount of money training teachers on the technology part . . . [a study shows] test scores have not gone up on literacy, but . . . slightly in math. But if you look at the amount of money . . . I don't know how successful that is. . . . [People don't think] about what is being lost or . . . spent. They just look at the numbers. But the costs are just too high.

In these situations, it became more common for educators to turn away from communal goals and focus on individual (self-preservation) goals. Teachers called this "flying under the radar." I later refer to it as *neglect*. It includes, but is not limited to, gaming the system (e.g., teaching to the test).

Tim, a charter middle school teacher, discussed a second common narrative. The pressure to perform in ways that improved test scores resulted in increased alienation, burnout, job dissatisfaction, and health and mental health issues:

Sometimes you get depressed [*laughs*] . . . when you don't meet your goals. . . . I started antidepressants . . . it really helped me . . . that pressure can be really crushing and I needed to remove some of [it] . . . so that I could perform. I think that happens to a lot of teachers, where the pressure gets to be too much and so they have to look for something else. . . . This is definitely a product of high-stakes testing. You put a lot of pressure on yourself.

His narrative supports Hochschild's (1983) claim that alienation is the inevitable result of emotional labor *because* it commodifies the private emotional sphere for commercial purposes—meaning it turns emotions into something that can be bought and sold. Tier 1 and 2 schools were, in essence, commodifying teachers' emotions and relationships because both are critical for learning. That resulted in very high rates of burnout and turnover.

Most teachers appear to have "voluntarily" retired, left teaching, or transferred to another district; yet, prior to leaving, many had been "targeted" for increased observation and supervision, had their "support yanked" (denied resources), and/or were given classes that were "loaded" with behavioral, emotional, and academic issues. These teachers were then (inappropriately) shamed at school or grade level meetings for having lower test scores or shamed through silence as other teachers were praised. They also received poor performance reviews. Thus "voluntary exit" is a misnomer.

Just as interesting, teachers reported high rates of principal burnout and turnover. Some left or retired early due to high levels of organizational conflict and stress. Others did so to avoid engaging in morally objectionable behaviors. Continuing with Annie's narrative,

[many administrators] are leaving rather than caving. . . . . [They have to say] who are their three best and three worst teachers and then . . . [are told] to go get rid of the three worst. . . . Just because . . . [they are the] three worst teachers does not mean . . . they need to be fired. You can work with them . . . [but] administrators are being hired to come in and crack the whip. . . . [Those who left said they] could not be the kinds of administrators that *they* wanted to be. . . . [One said] "this district is a sinking ship and the only administrators left are the sharks." . . . [That administrator] was *very* well liked and couldn't stay here.

Over time, increased exit facilitated the "new culture of teaching," which was characterized by a fear of expressing opposing voices, a decline in risk taking, and mechanistic teaching styles.

Teachers in Tier 1 and 2 schools professed that they struggled to balance competing loyalties to their occupation, students, colleagues, and schools as organizations; they were especially likely to tell narratives of dissonance and resistance. The classification of these behaviors is likely to vary depending on "where you sit" (see Chapter 10).

Administrators would likely classify such behaviors as *neglect* because teachers are not carrying out district directives. Informants characterized them as a form of professional *voice* in an environment that violated professional norms but silenced opposition. The latter is apparent in a story Donna told about a district directive that was designed to contain costs and make "the numbers" look good by encouraging principals to keep referrals to special education down:

> You have to . . . feel the parent out . . . tell them . . . step by step how to get around the system of special ed in this district. . . . [I] take that risk because . . . I will never ever compromise my belief in that child . . . [by] not giving him services. . . . I've already been told . . . I was borderline on insubordination trying to help a parent get services. . . . It's not right.

Donna circumvented an administrative directive even though she risked being fired. Like the vast majority, this narrative of resistance involved protecting children, but teachers described helping colleagues and parents, even when they risked losing their jobs or being subjected to increased "surveillance," harsh language, and public shaming at faculty meetings. Together, these stories suggest that resistance was not simply a battle over what and how to teach. The performative culture compromised their personal integrity, as well as the heart and soul of their profession.

As mentioned, studies show that the personal and intrinsic value of caring draws individuals into teaching and, once there, helps them sustain their commitment to the occupation (Hargreaves, 1998; Lortie, 1975). That research is backed by other studies that find that college seniors who are "idealists"—meaning they list "service to society" as their main reason for choosing a career—are the most likely to enter teaching and then make up about 30 percent of the occupation. Unfortunately, those who strongly value service are also more likely to exit the profession (Lortie, 1975; Miech & Elder, 1996). These studies are *not* claiming that unethical people remain in teaching; they support the finding in this study that teachers' work commitments are affected by their social, economic, and political contexts, not just their personal dispositions.

My informants displayed very high levels of public service motivation, consistently working above and beyond what is formally required at work. Even so, NCLB's emphasis on tangible (i.e., testable) skills and observable work appears to have reduced teachers' commitments to things that are not specified in their contracts or measured by their evaluations. This was especially true in Tier 1 and

2 schools, where the focus on data and numbers crowded out the humanistic norms of teaching. Some tried to "fly under the radar" by staying in their classrooms. Others went along with directives that they believed violated professional norms or "voiced" through resistance rather than speaking out. Those who could not deal with what respondents described as the moral dilemmas created by a policy that focused on tangible and testable skills at the expense of other goals exited from their schools and districts; some left teaching and administration altogether. This *ethical leaving* appears to have increased across schools over time but it was still more prevalent in Tier 1 and 2 schools, where the drive for greater efficiency and accountability transformed teaching into "performing."

Social Control Under Educator Accountability (NCLB Waivers and RttT)

President Obama not only envisioned a new generation of rigorous teacher evaluation systems as the core of his efforts to build a more effective teaching workforce; he stated that RttT would diminish teaching to the test and other arguably dysfunctional behaviors by using SGMs versus raw proficiency scores (Resmovits, 2011a). Some interviews suggest that the new evaluation system did *not* change educators' priorities, practices, and behaviors. Many teachers and administrators said, for example, that APPR "would not change how they did their jobs" or that "they would continue to focus on students regardless of how they are evaluated." Other interviews identify some positives associated with the use of SGMs. Some informants claimed that principals and teachers were more motivated to focus their efforts on children who struggle academically; some principals also appear to have used SGMs to make more informed decisions about teacher tenure and this resulted in the voluntary exit of some less effective teachers. While few in number, these reports illustrate the benefits associated with SGMs and the state's new evaluation system. For the most part, though, my interviews indicate that the use of SGMs to evaluate educators resulted in dysfunctional behaviors, particularly in a high-stakes environment. This section focuses on the most commonly cited negative consequences.

Sink-or-swim mentality. Generally, teachers and principals faulted the state for implementing APPR in such a way that teachers and principals were left to sink or swim. Most teachers declared, for instance, that they had not received sufficient training to understand

SGMs or to use SGM data to improve their practice; administrators and teachers also lamented the fact that they received their data in the second month of the following school year—too late to inform student teacher assignments and make changes to instructional practices. Participants further complained that they were provided with insufficient information to improve practice owing to state administrative reforms, which were adopted to prevent cheating and teaching to the test, despite no evidence of widespread problems. On the contrary, principals and teachers alleged that President Obama's claim that RttT would diminish teaching to the test had generated policy feedback in the form of state actions to control these behaviors, such as prohibiting schools from keeping past exams and grading open-ended questions. Some maintained, though, that this "gag order" actually resulted from the state ceding authority for the testing and evaluation system to a private contractor that wanted to control the release of test questions to save money associated with generating new test questions every year.

Sam's narrative in the last chapter provides evidence of these concerns, but the gist of educators' complaints was that schools did not receive numerical data until the fall of the following year and were unable to link those data to qualitative information that could improve practice at either the school or teacher level. The comments of a current elementary teacher (Jess) and suburban elementary principal (Chris), who was also a former elementary teacher, captured these complaints:

CHRIS: As a fourth-grade teacher, I liked . . . figuring out where my students did well and where they did not . . . [to] tweak what I was doing and grow . . . do an item analysis [of the test]. . . . It improved my instruction. Now . . . we get a score . . . by teacher . . . [with] some *very* general information about what a child is struggling with . . . like word problems. . . . It does not tell you which question . . . how they answered. . . . [When] you had that test . . . [you knew and could] teach differently . . . [or] recommend extra help . . . the next year.

JESS: In the very beginning, testing was far more helpful. We could . . . go through . . . [see] who did what. . . . We get back data now . . . see a score that each kid got, but . . . don't know . . . what questions they missed. . . . We also get data saying, "In the fifth grade at your school, X percent missed question one" . . . but I don't know if they're my kids . . . or somebody else's.

As evident in the last section, some educators had used these data to "teach to the test," but informants said that most had used it to improve teaching and learning. Under APPR, educators no longer had access to sufficient information and what little they did get was too late to inform practice.

Some participants further argued that the *methodology itself* discouraged educators from using SGMs to improve practice, especially the lack of transparency and widespread perceptions that the methodology was flawed. Ben, a suburban sixth-grade teacher, offered:

> [We got our results in October which] is far too late to use them in any meaningful way to improve teaching. We would need them in the summer to reflect and figure out where to go . . . [and the] results are based on how the current group of kids . . . "grew" from the previous year. . . . [But now] the assessment . . . classroom . . . and, in our case . . . school is different because now they are in middle school. This flies in the face of everything you learn . . . factors that impact learning . . . test reliability and validity. . . . You are comparing apples and oranges. There is no basis to do this. . . . A number of universities . . . challenged . . . how the state is constructing a teacher's growth score . . . have shown it is not valid.

Again, educators acknowledged that SGMs are better than raw test scores, but the "flawed methodology" clearly reduced "buy-in"; it made many teachers less willing to use their test results to inform practice, even if they had gotten them in time to do so.

Time constraints were another factor in why many administrators and teachers were not using the data to improve practice. Educators reported being asked to implement too many new policies at once, such as APPR and the new Common Core Standards. APPR in and of itself created time constraints through additional paperwork and new responsibilities—like developing SLOs, a form of SGM—but teachers in grades and subjects that previously did not have state exams now had to create their own tests. Tom, a suburban middle school art teacher, said:

> We had to create tests for art, gym, home and careers, technology and music . . . spent *huge* amounts of time developing test questions . . . something that art teachers are not trained to do . . . on our own time. Some schools are purchasing those tests . . . [private] companies making money. . . . It is a *huge* business. Our district got almost no money . . . [but] is spending a huge amount . . . [mostly] on administrative positions. . . . [Our hours] outside of the classroom have increased . . . developing pre- and posttests, and grading and filing our paperwork for APPR. . . .

[We have] less time to prepare for . . . teaching . . . much less interacting with students.[14]

These time constraints appear to have generated a sink-or-swim mentality *in the classroom* by reducing teachers' ability to interact with and help students.

Another common complaint was that *new and struggling teachers received less help* because experienced teachers and principals had less time to mentor them. Under the previous system, tenured teachers were not typically evaluated every year. A suburban elementary teacher (Mia), high school math teacher (Brenda), and former urban psychologist/current suburban district administrator (Sally) discussed how the need to do so under APPR affected principals:

MIA: [The] number of evaluations . . . [is] outrageous. . . . An administrator . . . [said] she didn't know how she was going to competently do her job . . . [observing] everyone every year.

SALLY: We had to take a 40-hour course and two tests. . . . It was online training . . . some reading but most of it was watching, analyzing . . . and scoring videos, and then getting feedback. . . . [We] purchased the system . . . type our observations into . . . an online database where you can . . . see if the teacher has changed anything based on previous observations. . . . There was a cost and I'm sure it was high. . . . [My former urban district did not] have an assistant principal in elementary school. . . . I don't know how they're going to get it done . . . evaluations . . . discipline . . . communications with the parents . . . management of the building. And, some . . . [schools] are labeled and they're dealing with all of that.

BRENDA: [When] kids are failing or not doing well, it is looked at like it is your fault. . . . I don't think it was as much that way . . . [before RttT. It was] . . . a team effort . . . [now it is] looked at as, "Those are *your* kids . . . *your* test scores . . . *your* student that is failing. What are *you* doing wrong?" . . . They look at the numbers. . . . It is a lot of pressure on teachers.

This sink-or-swim mentality may explain some of the reported voluntary exit of teachers.

Contrived randomness and increased hierarchical controls. Participants said that socioeconomic inequality combines with market forces and state and district policies to nonrandomize test performance across schools and teachers so that some have a greater proportion of groups that struggle on standardized tests, such as ELLs, low-income students, minorities (because they are more likely to be poor), and children with learning, emotional, and behavioral issues. Brenda continued:

> People do not realize how random it really is . . . . [who you] get in your classroom. . . . One year I might do great . . . but the next year that is some other teacher. I am still working just as hard, but I have different students and those students are more needy than that other teacher's students, so now I am at the low end of the test scores. . . . That randomness is hard to handle . . . you know it is not you, but . . . [that's what] we are saying. It is all . . . the teacher.[15]

This *contrived* randomness—the nonrandom sorting of students across schools and classrooms as a result of racial and socioeconomic stratification—appears to have precipitated more hierarchical controls, as the state, school districts, principals, and teachers tried to "fix" low achievement by standardizing teaching and learning.

NCLB created the incentive for schools and districts that disproportionately serve academically at-risk students to micromanage teachers as a way of standardizing performance. RttT expanded these behaviors by shifting accountability to teachers and then attaching high-stakes consequences. School districts, for instance, used to achieve efficiency gains by clustering some special education students into a single elementary building where they could provide specialized services. Under NCLB, districts allegedly moved students back into their "feeder schools" to avoid the SINI label that was common for schools that served more needy populations. RttT then caused principals to worry about assigning more needy students to a single classroom, even though it might be in the student's best interest, because that teacher would then be in danger of a poor performance review.

Consider the narratives of a suburban special education (Nina) and sixth-grade middle school (Ben) teacher:

NINA: Districts used to . . . cluster some of the special ed kids into one or a few elementary schools for efficiency reasons, rather than hiring staff for every . . . school. But now, they have to de-cluster and send them to their home schools so that they don't get on the list.

BEN: I'm going into my nineteenth year of teaching. . . . I have a *very* good reputation within my district and school. . . . A lot of parents request me. . . . My superintendent and principal . . . [said,] "We . . . do not feel these test scores in any way show the value you bring to your students and our district. . . . You are an excellent teacher, but . . . are an ineffective teacher according to the state." . . . I had 90 percent score a 3 . . . zero score a 4 . . . zero score a 1. The remaining that *scored a 2 were all labeled* [my emphasis]. . . . Looking at kids. . . it was very close. . . . Last year, the student received a 365 and this year he received a 364 and so he showed "no growth." We don't know if they grew or did not grow. We know they dropped a point on a test. . . . The variables are enormous. Yet . . . I am being told . . . I failed.

Ben does not work in a high-need, low-resource school, yet his colleagues confirmed that he is given a disproportionate share of those who struggle academically, behaviorally, and emotionally because they excel in his class. Prior to APPR, he was consistently rated highly effective. Now, his principal needs to think about possibly placing students with a less effective teacher to prevent this highly effective one from being eliminated. Given the high stakes associated with these tests, it is not surprising that educators would reject students who struggle.

Again, some said that their districts manipulated this contrived randomness to affect school (NCLB) and teacher (RttT) performance by assigning at-risk students to highly performing teachers, encouraging or discouraging students to be present on test day (NCLB), and using student placements to retain or eliminate certain teachers (NCLB and RttT). Lorna, an urban elementary teacher, elaborated on these gaming behaviors:

[On test day, the] principal would make us go in our cars and pick up the child who was a 4. . . . She would call the parents and ask them what is wrong . . . [then say] he could take the test . . . [someone was] coming to get the child . . . the one who was not a 3 or 4, they would not be calling those parents. . . . [Others got] sent home the day of the test. . . ."You're not feeling very well." . . . [Now, they] move the good kids . . . right before the test. If they don't like a certain teacher . . . [move] their high-performing students . . . into the classrooms of other teachers . . . always give a reason . . . but it is so that they can control the test scores in ways that they can keep who they want. . . . It is a corrupt system. It is sad. Very sad.

My interviews indicate that these dysfunctional behaviors had been more common in Tier 1 and 2 schools (like Lorna's) under NCLB but spread as a result of educator accountability (RttT and NCLB waivers).

Teaching to the test. RttT and NCLB waivers also continued

NCLB's focus on ELA and mathematics at the elementary level. Informants professed that this resulted in a narrowing of what subjects were taught in elementary school. Most discussed reduced time spent teaching social studies and science, but some discussed art and music. All three policies also created the incentive to "drill and grill" tested knowledge and facts at the expense of nontested material and skills. Again, standardized tests privilege a limited amount of factual knowledge and some skills; they do not require the kinds of reasoning that are necessary for more complex forms of thinking (see National Center on Education and the Economy, 2013). As a result, recent education reforms (NCLB, NCLB waivers, and RttT) increasingly marginalized the development of critical thinking skills, problem solving skills, and noncognitive skills and behaviors (e.g., empathy, trust, tolerance of diverse opinions, perseverance, self-control, and conscientiousness). These findings are troubling because, as mentioned, research supports educators' claims that such skills and behaviors are important for individual success; they also are critical for achieving the broader mission of public schools, teaching as an occupation, and federal education policy.

One goal of public education, for instance, is to level the playing field in society. Another is to develop children's civic skills and engagement. A professed goal of federal education policy is to increase the number of students pursuing STEM. An occupational goal widely supported by teachers is to develop caring, well-adjusted, competent, and educated human beings. Participants maintained that critical thinking, problem solving, and noncognitive skills and behaviors are critical for meeting all of these goals; yet each became less salient as teachers directed their efforts toward what is measured to meet state performative goals. These behavioral changes reduced educators' ability to create a level playing field because groups that have traditionally struggled on standardized tests—special education, ELL, minority, and low-income students—were more likely to be exposed to "drill and grill" teaching as schools and educators tried to fix low achievement. This claim is evident in Veronica's narrative in Chapter 1.

Increased testing anxiety and "opting out." Research also supports educators' claims that anxiety disorders are on the rise, including severe and chronic test anxiety (McDonald, 2001; National Institutes of Health, n.d.), especially among students who struggle. By increasing the number of exams in already tested subjects (i.e., the pre- and posttest model) and expanding the testing model across subjects and to most grades, APPR disproportionately harmed these students. A high school math (Patricia), elementary (Carley), and art (Ella) teacher remarked,

PATRICIA: Students that struggle. . . . It makes them feel bad . . . harms their self-esteem over time. . . . Some of them give up. You have to really motivate them. . . . By the time they get to high school they are sick of these tests and it impacts how they feel about school.

ELLA: I had teachers in elementary school telling me their students were crying . . . because they did not do well on the pretest, or had anxiety . . . [because] they did not know the material well. . . . It was a pretest . . . [but] parents were up in arms because their child was upset. . . . No matter how hard they try to explain it, the students are upset and so the teacher feels upset. . . . Over time it leads students to dislike school, and to doubt their abilities.

CARLEY: [They gave] a field test [a week after the state exams] . . . the kids felt like they were done with testing . . . had to take this other test. . . . At the end of the year the kids want to please you and they wanted to do well. I had kids in tears. . . . They were tested out.

Like Carley, many teachers further complained that the state was using children for "data collection" by making them take a field test right after the "real" one. This created stress for children and took time away from learning. To these informants, this example illustrates that the state cares more about data and eliminating bad apples than learning and social justice issues.

Ella's narrative is important for another reason. Parental concerns about "overtesting" sometimes resulted in aggressive voice, which suppresses school performance by making it harder for educators to do their jobs (see Chapter 9).[16] State data (not seen here) and Sam's narrative in Chapter 3 support her claim that students increasingly "opted out" of state exams for similar reasons. The opt-out rate exceeded 50 percent in some counties and 70 percent in some school districts. It negatively affected public schools because there is a federal penalty for high nonparticipation rates; however, it also suppressed performance because, as supported by other research, upper-income parents were more likely to opt their children out and test scores are linked to socioeconomic background.[17] In addition, many parents (misguidedly) expressed that testing was designed to hold schools and teachers accountable, and so they refused to take the offered intervention services for their children.[18] When combined, these behaviors refute the claim of policy makers that testing would improve performance by providing parents with the information to seek available services.

Gaming the system, undermining collaboration, and cultivating an ethos of self-interest. Rather than resolving what I earlier referred to as the "two achievement gaps," participants claimed that educator accountability aggravated existing issues and created new ones. One common narrative was that high-stakes testing under NCLB discouraged students from taking more rigorous classes, such as honors and Advanced Placement (AP) courses, while the use of SGMs to evaluate teachers under RttT and NCLB waivers reduced the incentive for teachers to encourage them to do so. Ron, an urban high school AP physics teacher, described these perverse incentives:

> [The previous] teacher only wanted the "elite" students. . . . He made the class so difficult . . . to weed out students. Those kids really liked him, but he only had like 31. . . . It has increased. . . . I will have 70 . . . [because] I have a welcoming approach . . . make it challenging . . . very rigorous, but it's fun. . . . [But] the physics exam is . . . brutal. I have had excellent reviews every time I have been observed. . . . [Yet my] first year I had 66 percent pass. It blindsided me. . . . I made a lot of changes . . . redid everything so that all the homework . . . and test questions were . . . from past exams. . . . [My results] were better but only 72 percent. . . . A lot of the kids . . . would not have been in that class under the previous teacher. But I want to be inclusive . . . [not] focus on whether it's going to affect my test results. . . . You do need to teach to the test. I hate to say that, but you do have to give students a lot of opportunity to take similar exams . . . be done with the material early . . . [give] a lot of review.

Ron's desire to be inclusive is in tension with the drive to game test scores by gatekeeping courses so that students unlikely to perform well—and therefore reflect negatively on a teacher's effectiveness—are barred access. These perverse incentives are intensified in high-need, low-resource schools, like Ron's, again suggesting social justice issues.

A second common narrative was that linking job security to student test scores created the incentive to avoid children with learning, behavioral, and emotional issues. Consider the statements of two suburban elementary (Jess and Meagan) and an urban middle school English (Ronnie) teacher,

JESS: [People who] volunteer or are told . . . [to teach] a special ed population . . . along with all the paperwork . . . [must] show a year's growth. . . . Behavior problems take up a huge amount of your time and energy. . . . Teachers are . . . less willing to do . . . that.

MEAGAN: If they did that with doctors and nurses, nobody would be an oncologist or work in hospice because they serve people who are facing life-threatening circumstances; but, in teaching, people think we can have a one-size-fits-all model. . . . People are going to double-think whether they want to take more . . . needy children.

RONNIE: I am on a team that teaches special education. . . . We've been successful. . . . Will teachers be willing to take on . . . students that struggle or have attendance issues. . . . No matter what you do, that child isn't there, 50, 60 days. . . . It's going to influence your evaluation, and yet you can't physically go to their house and get them to school.

As discussed, participants believe VAMs (NCLB waivers and RttT) are an improvement over raw scores (NCLB) but still do not adequately account for these and other factors.

A third common narrative was that RttT created the incentive for teachers to game the system through SLOs—the achievement targets students must meet to show adequate growth. Under APPR, teachers set their own SLOs. The use of a pre- and posttest model allegedly encouraged some to set the bar low to show "growth." This penalized those who set high standards. Returning to the narratives of Ella and Patricia:

ELLA: The . . . implementation has been really flawed. . . . I actually heard people say . . . this is really appalling [*laughing*] . . . they tell the kids to . . . put . . . wrong answers . . . on the pretest. . . . If people want to get away with things they will find a way. It is human nature. You cannot possibly design controls to catch everything. . . . For the most part teachers work very hard and most want to do right by the kids. . . . They can make it look like they are a good teacher if . . . only . . . looking at a pre- and posttest. . . . It's sad but I'm sure it happens.

PATRICIA: I think most teachers won't manipulate the system. They are in teaching for the right reasons and have high standards because they care about the kids. . . . The teachers who do not have high standards are the ones you want to get out of teaching, but the new evaluation system won't do that. . . . Instead, it hurts the teacher who sets the bar high. . . . [With the pre- and posttest] each teacher is essentially setting their goals . . . they have to be realistic, but . . . there is room here for odd things to go on. . . . The results between teachers could be all over the place. I don't know if the process is valid.

Participants said that these realities increased the likelihood that APPR rewarded "bad apples," instead of penalizing them, while giving the teachers whom policy makers hoped to keep an "ineffective" rating.

A forth common narrative was that SGMs discouraged trust and collaboration by making teachers "compete" for good evaluations. Jess best explained why collegiality is critical and how SGMs negatively affect it:

> As an organization . . . you've got all different kinds of teachers. Some are better at handling some students. . . . We now switch kids for some subjects . . . or have students working with other teachers on certain units because they have a particular interest in the topic and have created something . . . that works well. . . . We're not going to be able to do that. . . . [They haven't figured out how] to get those scores back to individual teachers. . . . [I also] have to trust that they are going to cover the curriculum that I would have . . . that everybody is going to do what they should. . . . Before, we were more interested in how policy changes were going to impact the kids. Now . . . the talk is always about how this is going to affect me . . . it has changed the conversation . . . it is going to be less collegial. . . . It's not like the old days where the administrator could say . . . [could I change your schedule or add more students to your roster?] and you could say, "Okay, I'll take one for the team."[19]

The widespread perception that using SGMs for educator evaluations undermines collegiality and cultivates an ethos of self-interest is especially disconcerting because teachers claimed—and research shows—that collegial working environments are critical for school efficiency and effectiveness, as well as for school improvement efforts (see, e.g., Bryk & Schneider, 2002).

In short, schools need teachers to "take one for the team" by being willing to work with difficult students and perform other kinds of *invisible work*. Teachers voluntarily did so to meet the needs of students before recent education reforms. Accountability, through student test scores, silences these behaviors because their value is difficult to measure. Tom, from whom we heard earlier, declared,

> [The major problem with recent reforms] is that teaching is a profession, vocation and an art more than a job. That makes it very difficult to quantify . . . [all] the things teachers do . . . [to build] children as human beings. You can't quantify inspiration or encouragement for example, but both of them are important for helping children persevere. Most of what you do, you do in order to get the quote-on-quote "job" done, not because you're required to do it. That involves staying late, working on weekends, working during the summer and so forth. You don't see those behaviors in the classroom and you can't test them.

Under NCLB, these behaviors disintegrated in schools that micro-managed teachers and used competition to improve performance (e.g., merit pay, a strong performative discourse, better classes and duties). Causally, this related to declining trust between teachers and between teachers and administrators. Using more "individual-ized" and "objective" measures of performance (SGMs for educator evaluations) under RttT and NCLB waivers appears to have further disincentivized these behaviors; it also undermined collaboration and threatened the ethos of care by replacing it with an ethos of self-interest for some educators.

Not taking student teachers. One example of *invisible work* is serving as a supervising mentor for student teachers. Respondents claimed that growing numbers of teachers were unwilling to perform this important service. Some expressed that they had no time to do so owing to the increased paperwork and planning associated with the implementation of APPR and the new Common Core Standards; others asserted that teachers were concerned about their evalua-tions if they allowed an inexperienced student to teach their class. Shannon, a former elementary teacher and current urban student teacher supervisor, reported,

> Our school is struggling to get placements. . . . They will only take student teachers in the primary grades because there is no testing. . . . But teachers are supposed to have two experiences; one in the primary . . . and one in the upper elementary grades. For the second experience, because the teachers are under so much pressure to cover content, they don't want . . . [them]. And, if they do take them, they use them to correct papers or things that help the participating teacher. . . . It really is affecting the profession. . . . Student teachers are not getting the experiences that they need to then become proficient teachers. . . . They have to get that experience their first year on the job, which is not good. But . . . cooperating teachers . . . are under so much pressure to get good test results that they do not want to hand over their classroom to somebody who is not yet proficient. Yet, the profession depends on teachers' willingness to do just that.

These claims are troubling because student teaching influences the development and socialization of future teachers. One policy intervention could be to allow teachers to opt out of using student test scores for the year that they take a student teacher.

Increased voluntary exit and ethical leavers. NCLB and RttT also required that HQTs and effective teachers (respectively) be equitably distributed across schools. Unfortunately, this study suggests that both policies increased turnover in high-need, low-resource schools and among teachers who disproportionately serve poor and minority children and children with academic, behavioral, and emotional issues. They did so by rewarding those who teach high achievers or teach to the test. In some cases, principals used SGMs to make more informed decisions about teacher tenure, and this resulted in the voluntary exit of some less effective teachers; however, participants expressed a belief that only a small portion of those who left were less effective. Many more were *ethical leavers*. Returning to Tom's narrative:

> [APPR is changing] the way teachers feel about their jobs. I know . . . because I'm vice president of the union, grievance chair and a union negotiator. . . . We are seeing a lot of teachers . . . investigating early retirement . . . [and] a lot of younger teachers, under 5 years and . . . 10 years . . . looking to get out. . . . [They] don't like the direction teaching is going in. . . . So much of it [teaching] is building children as human beings. . . . That's what's going away and many people just want to get out. That's why they became teachers.

Reports about ethical leavers suggest that accountability policies may actually cause exit among the very types of teachers public schools need.

Summing up, Foucault (1980) argues that power is "a machinery . . . nobody owns" (p. 110) because it is (largely) exercised from within rather than imposed through violence or force; nonetheless, it "establishes inegalitarian and asymmetrical relations between individuals and groups" (p. 156). Certainly some schools imposed practices that disciplined teachers to meet state performative goals, but teachers also disciplined themselves to meet social expectations within an educational system that is unequal as a result of socioeconomic inequality, inequitable school financing, and the nonrandom sorting of students by need and ability across schools and classrooms. The words of a retired urban special education teacher and suburban district special education administrator (Valerie) capture this claim:

> [Recent reforms are based on] false ideas and statistically could never work. The notion that . . . [by] 2012 all children had to meet standards was statistically impossible because everything was still based on the bell curve. . . . So, *by definition*, some children had to fail. . . . The first . . . were special education students because, *by definition*, . . . they were

. . . having trouble learning . . . [and] ESL kids . . . struggling with the language. . . . [Then] they were recalibrating it every year to keep that normal bell curve. *By definition,* you have . . . children who are below average, or . . . not meeting standards. . . . It sets schools up to become . . . labeled. . . . Even if teachers never thought that they were going to be evaluated based on the test results . . . [they] are going to teach to that test . . . not for any personal gain, but because they care about their students. . . . [It is also] human nature to . . . [teach] what they are going to test. . . . Now, their evaluations are . . . on the line. They have a stake in teaching to the test . . . [also] an incentive to reject students that struggle because *by definition* they are going to be the ones that do not pass or grow as fast.

The end result was that accountability reforms (largely) resulted in dysfunctional behaviors and unintended consequences. Partly, this stemmed from flaws in the design of these policies, but most of these negative consequences resulted from how testing interacts with social contexts.

Discussion: The State, the Professions, and Organized Interests

Freidson (1975, p. 198) predicted that professionalism would wane owing to a widespread belief that the exclusive right to regulate a field enables members to advance their own interests at the expense of society. These concerns would make the professions vulnerable to market demands for higher profits, on one hand, and bureaucratic demands for less discretion, on the other. The data from this study support his claim but indicate that, in the field of education, the assault on professional authority started with policy makers and then trickled down. As shown, policy makers advocated using hierarchical controls (e.g., standards and testing) and market controls (e.g., competition and choice) as a way to encourage educators to serve "consumers of public services" more efficiently and effectively. They justified these reforms through rhetoric that portrayed teachers as ineffective, self-interested enemies of reform while constructing organized political and economic interests (e.g., business-economic elites, conservative think tanks, testing and publishing companies, and the charter and home school industry) as educational experts.[20] Teachers discussed five ways these changes eroded professionalism and decades of teaching reforms.

First, policy makers, the media, and organized political and economic interests pushed the idea that non-university-based programs, like Teach for America (TFA), were a way to close the achievement gap between low-income and minority children and their economically advantaged peers. Like the Peace Corps, TFA hoped to convince idealistic college graduates to work for two years in underserved areas, such as hard-to-staff (mostly urban and rural) schools. Now, the idea that it is possible to become an effective teacher with only five weeks' training has reportedly encouraged some school districts to replace more experienced (and expensive) teachers with unexperienced TFA recruits—despite empirical research showing that teachers prepared through traditional university programs more positively affect student achievement than those prepared through alternative ones like TFA.[21]

Second, since the Progressive Era, many school districts have hired district administrators with business backgrounds, but most promoted teachers to serve as principals. The misperception that former teachers are unwilling to fire ineffective ones has encouraged some districts to hire principals who have never taught, which impedes the ability of the profession to train, socialize, and police its own as a way of ensuring members remain true to core values. An urban public elementary school teacher (Lorna) described how this harms teachers and students:

> There needs to be some business structure . . . but you cannot run schools like a business . . . [or] have merit pay. . . . Teachers are not producing a product. They are working with children. . . . [Principals used to need] 10 years' experience teaching before they could apply to a principal program. . . . Now, you can . . . [attend the city's training academy] for 16 months . . . [where] they are steeped in the business model. . . . Jack Welch [GE] . . . a whole culture. . . . [You hear] the business jargon . . . [in] everything those principals say. . . . [They] look at children . . . teachers . . . in terms of money . . . get rid of a person who is making a lot because they have been there a long time . . . get rid of . . . teachers before they get tenure. . . . It is a slippery slope. . . . They stop just short of calling the children a product. . . . But underneath their language . . . they think of children as products . . . ignore the beauty . . . the diversity of the children. . . . [The] business paradigm . . . ignores their social and economic lives. . . . How can you compare a school and a teacher in an area . . . so deprived socioeconomically to . . . [those] in an affluent area . . . their scores . . . their education . . . ? It is never going to be equal.

Again, educators (largely) blamed this development on decades of antiteacher and antiunion rhetoric. They said that policy makers would never advocate staffing and governing other professions—like doctors and lawyers—with those who have no training or experience; yet the chancellor of education in this northeastern state recruited fellows that were mostly from outside the profession or with almost no teaching experience to train seasoned principals on how to evaluate teachers. Like the language used to promote TFA, these actions leave the impression that experience and training are unnecessary for mentoring, supervising, regulating, and evaluating teachers. Both also perpetuate the myth that "those who can't, teach" and that we could miraculously improve public schools *solely* by recruiting better teachers.

Third, recent education reforms weakened collaboration and reduced the time experienced teachers have to socialize new ones. Educators told me that this socialization is one of the primary ways the profession trains and polices its own. Research also supports their claims that collaborative and collegial working environments are critical for school efficiency and effectiveness, as well as for school improvement efforts, and that students perform better on state tests in schools where teachers are organizational and curricular leaders.[22] These understandings are why, as shown in Part II, one of the first things the union demanded through collective bargaining was a free period away from students so that teachers could engage in personal, organizational, and professional activities. That development led to the creation of "teacher leaders," both in terms of the curriculum and school decision-making, and encouraged individual and collective economic, political, and professional voice. Now, their "free period" has been "eaten up" by administrative demands (e.g., data), policy demands (e.g., developing SLOs and tests), and parental demands (e.g., answering phone calls and emails).

Carley, a suburban elementary teacher, articulated how these developments have affected her:

> [You can't] be a slacker. . . . These people are committed . . . professional . . . work very, very hard. . . . I am there at night working during the summer. . . . [During the year] I literally can't even get over to my desk during the day to blow my nose. . . . We cannot leave the kids unattended even to use the bathroom. . . . You are always supervising the kids . . . it weighs on you. . . . You are . . . locked in. . . . Sometimes you just really feel the intensity of that. . . . I went to my doctor . . . [for] bladder issues . . . she sees this all the time with teachers . . . no one teaches to get an easy pass. . . . [It's] a very hard job . . . physically . . . emotionally too.[23]

A recent nationally representative survey supports the claim of educators in this study that teachers in both high- and low-poverty schools do not have enough time to collaborate (W. Johnson & Berglund, 2018).

Fourth, the charter school movement has been used to restrict collective bargaining and the provision of tenure and seniority. As shown in Chapter 4, these reforms helped ameliorate the historically high turnover model that had suppressed economic, political, and professional voice and resulted in low wages and poor working conditions for teachers. By respreading that model, charter schools have put pressure on public school teachers to give in to "unsustainable" work demands. Lorna continued:

> I have a friend who was a principal in a charter school. . . . They ran those teachers into the ground . . . to the point . . . they could not teach for more than three or four years. . . . They didn't care if they burned them out because it was not like the public system where they have a need for a massive number of teachers. . . . But that now has become the philosophy of schools everywhere. . . . [You are expected to be] there until six o'clock . . . teachers give up their lunches . . . [for] staff development . . . "Chat and Chew" and "Lunch and Learn," . . . It is definitely not in the contract, but everybody is scared to death not to go.

Recent state legislative changes and court decisions have further weakened or overturned collective bargaining, tenure, and seniority.[24] When combined with the findings in Part I, these developments show how policy makers at all levels of government increasingly silenced union voice as a way to adopt their preferred reforms; yet research finds that teacher quality and student performance are better in states and charter schools that are unionized.[25]

Charter school teachers confirmed that their administrators expect to turn over all of their teachers within five years; they also agreed that the drive and potential to minimize professional discretion are magnified in charter schools because administrators view their jobs as catering to customers to make a profit and/or outperform their public school counterparts. Crystal, an urban charter school teacher, remarked,

> [We are not] giving them the rigor . . . going beyond . . . "grill-and-drill" and test preparation . . . [making them] independent readers and thinkers. . . . [We say we prepare] disadvantaged kids for college, but . . . not doing that . . . it is discouraging . . . a goal I . . . feel passionate about. . . . There are teachers whose students are not performing on tests

[as well]. . . . Now they are targeted . . . support is yanked . . . told what and how to teach . . . administrators are . . . ruthless . . . nasty to people who are on the "outs" . . . [They talk] about a model that is supposed to reform the public school . . . it is not even close. . . . It churns and burns teachers . . . turns them over and spits them out. . . . It is not creating a sustainable model. . . . [We] are creating this clash with the public school system when . . . we should be helping each other out, but the administrators view themselves as competing with the public schools.

Charter school informants further supported other participants' claims that charter schools rely more heavily on TFA recruits and that the availability of this temporary, cheap labor supply is partly why 93 percent of charters are nonunionized. In consequence, individual teachers have no protection against arbitrary treatment.

Fifth, declining economic (union) voice paved the way for transforming teaching into a technical occupation. Teaching—as a technology—emphasizes the instrumental ends of public education over its transformative and humanistic ends; the latter are difficult to measure. It also constructs children as products, like widgets, that can be shaped and molded into a standardized output. An urban special education teacher (Tracy) disclosed,

[When] I started, schools were more open to developing the person . . . making them more productive . . . with a good sense of self and what they could do and be. You gave them the foundations and perseverance to be successful, whether that was going to college or directly to work, but also to continue learning and growing. Now . . . we're just giving them curriculum . . . [not] developing children . . . the technical aspects of teaching. . . . It's more . . . harsh . . . the nurturing and the creativity . . . [is] all gone and it's very stressful . . . less humanistic. . . . It's more you have to reach this bar and sometimes you're not going to . . . [so you're] always feeling like you haven't done enough. So, I wouldn't want someone that I love . . . [getting emotional] to have a lifetime of that.

As shown, teachers began losing professional autonomy under NCLB, as school districts used scripting and other routinizing mechanisms to standardize teaching and learning and (hopefully) achieve state aims. RttT resulted in similar outcomes, but teachers voluntarily engaged in these behaviors to meet state performative goals. Either way, these policies resulted in teachers being treated as interchangeable parts in the labor process, meaning they could be switched out and replaced at any time by newer, cheaper workers.[26] These developments disincentivized individual and collective (economic, political, and professional) voice because teachers are afraid of losing their jobs; they are also less likely to benefit individually from voice or professional training in a high-turnover environment.

While some may advocate less professional discretion as a way to regulate performance, teaching as a technology also harms children. Shannon, a student teacher supervisor, explained,

> [It] has not been . . . positive for children . . . [teachers talking] about programs and scores . . . curriculum and assessment. . . . When I was teaching, the conversations were always about children. . . . You don't hear teachers talking about children . . . kids are almost like products . . . everything is focused on the kids' performance . . . outcomes and objectives . . . and what is getting lost is who they are . . . the human being . . . the human side of teaching. When you set up systems where a kid's performance reflects your success . . . then you are going to have to treat children more like products. . . . It is *really* unfortunate.

This development contributed to *ethical leaving* and, when combined with other issues—like unsustainable work demands, poor wages, and reduced status and autonomy—reduced entry into the profession. In short, it recreated the high-turnover model that unions had been redressing through economic voice (e.g., union demands for better salaries, benefits, working conditions) and political voice (e.g., policy feedback on behalf of better training, licensing requirements, smaller class sizes, a more equitable distribution of HQTs).

Certainly the economy contributed to these developments. State funding for public schools plummeted during the Great Recession and did not return to prior levels in many states.[27] Local funding also fell in 19 states. Even where it rose, local spending did not typically make up for state reductions and a decrease in inflation-adjusted federal Title I spending during the same period. The resulting revenue cuts contributed to higher class sizes and deteriorating working conditions as districts across the nation laid off teachers and support staff. Some school districts, especially those in rural areas, had to move to a four-day week.[28] Because salaries and benefits compose the majority of K–12 education spending, the Great Recession also contributed to teachers experiencing some of the worst wage stagnation of any profession. Although it varies considerably across states, average weekly wages (adjusted for inflation) actually fell by $30 a week for the nation's roughly 3.2 million full-time K–12 public school teachers between 1996 and 2015.[29] This occurred as pay for other college graduates increased by \$124 a week and resulted in teachers earning, on average, just 77 percent of the weekly wages of similarly educated graduates in 2015. This "wage penalty" has been increasing since the mid-1990s; however, teachers in many states and districts have also been asked to contribute more toward health and retirement costs—reducing the "benefit advantage" that had traditionally offset some of the wage differentials between teachers and college graduates in other fields.[30]

As with school budgets, the erosion of teacher pay cannot be blamed solely on the Great Recession. It reflects policy decisions. Most of the 25 states that were still spending less on education had enacted income and corporate tax cuts between 2008 and 2016. In fact, 8 of the 10 states with the largest reductions in education funding—Alabama, Arizona, Florida, Georgia, Idaho, Kansas, Oklahoma, and Virginia—had adopted tax cuts.[31]

Given these developments, it is not surprising that two-thirds of teachers quit before retirement or that the supply of aspiring teachers is drying up. This has resulted in a growing teacher shortage. Shortages are especially acute in those states, such as Arizona, that adopted budget cuts as a result of cutting taxes. There, districts are staffing many of the budget-related vacancies with foreigners, resulting in an increase in the J-1 visas that allow temporary employment in the United States. As in the past, though, shortages across states are especially acute in schools that primarily serve underprivileged and minority students and in mathematics, science, special education, and bilingual/English language development.[32]

According to those I interviewed, high turnover itself deprofessionalizes teaching by disincentivizing economic, political, and professional voice and the investment in professional training and development. However, recent reforms and rhetoric appear to have especially discouraged voice among younger teachers. Some feared retaliation in the form of more difficult classes, which negatively affects their test scores and provides "evidence" that justifies firing them or denying them tenure. Others feared layoffs, in a time of fiscal austerity, as voice, in the form of speaking up or protesting, could generate retaliation from their communities in the form of budget cuts during (what is perceived to be) a period of rising antiunion sentiments and perceptions that teachers are greedy.

Again, public opinion polls do not support these fears; teachers appear to be responding to public discourse and actual funding issues more than public sentiments. Nonetheless, competition for test scores and concerns about the stability of their jobs in an era of fiscal austerity pitted younger teachers against older ones because the former were more likely to be laid off. Returning to Lorna's narrative and adding the statement of a retired urban elementary teacher, who is now substitute teaching in suburban schools (Elaine),

LORNA: [When I started, teachers would] go into the rooms and shut their doors. . . . [The union got] people to collaborate . . . now . . . forcing competitiveness . . . [we're] back to . . . when teachers were isolated. . . . Why . . . give up . . . your good ideas. . . . Your scores are going to go down . . . the kids . . . become a product . . . barter with children's lives for . . . test scores.

ELAINE: I was a substitute teaching for this older teacher . . . [with] health issues . . . a very good teacher . . . [but] another teacher . . . asked me to document everything . . ."nail" this teacher . . . little things . . . like not having the "proper" documentation for . . . things I was expected to do as a substitute. . . . [They] wanted to get rid of this older teacher to preserve a job for the younger teacher . . . the first-grade team has basically shunned this teacher . . . to force her out . . . will not socialize . . . tell her anything she needs to know in order to do a good job . . . tell her, "Go ask the principal" . . . this is what is going on today . . . The collegiality is gone . . . writing off a human being. She was not as efficient and so she was expendable.[33]

Elaine's narrative is an example of how groups may use their social cohesion to (unfairly) target weaker members, but these narratives are actually describing how recent reforms combined with economic distress to reduce collegiality.

In collegial working environments, teachers work together to foster communal goals by sharing what works, mentoring new teachers, and engaging in what I referred to as *invisible work*. Many asserted that their colleagues are actually *more* important today because they help counteract the high physical and emotional demands of teaching, the effects of working in a (now) low-status occupation, and parental demands that are contrary to the interests of other children, the school, and society. Brenda, a suburban high school math teacher, professed,

[Teaching is not respected. It] is a respectable profession and I feel proud to say I'm a teacher . . . my colleagues are important for . . . [helping] me keep that in mind . . . despite what other people . . . say, teachers work very hard. . . . [Teachers in another state] doctoring test scores . . . they are being blamed for things that they have little control over . . . I

> would leave the profession before I'd do that . . . but you could see the pressure . . . their job on the line. . . . [Why] collaborate or share ideas and strategies . . . we have had great relationships . . . that is going to change. If my friend . . . has 10 fewer failures . . . I am going to look bad.

Informants perceive that competition is unhealthy for schools as organizations, teaching as an occupation, and children if not balanced by more communal norms. It perpetuates a "survival of the fittest" mentality—where some teachers hide their successes to "beat" their colleagues on the tests—and reduces teachers' willingness to engage in the invisible work that helps meet the profession's core values.

As a whole, this study supports Freidson's (2001) claim that the professions *cannot exist* without a monopoly—an exclusive right to provide services based on training and licensing requirements. The unregulated market drives down the price of services, negatively affects the profession's ability to recruit and retain members, and reduces the incentive to advance a formal body of knowledge and skills because anyone may practice. These developments negatively affect the quality of services, but something larger is at stake. Professions have a "morality"—an underlying set of values—that benefit their clients and society. Because of this, members must be *independent from those that provide them with their living* so that they will enforce the collective right and individual duty to *voice* on any developments that interfere with the "professional soul."[34] This responsibility includes judging the demands of public policies and employers and *refusing to obey* them on professional grounds.

When a profession is unable or unwilling to voice in defense of its underlying values, it has been *deprofessionalized*.[35] In terms of teaching, voice is one of the primary ways that teachers protect our most vulnerable, as well as the soul of their profession. What is at stake is the ability of teachers to meet the occupation's core moral purpose—to develop children as caring, well-adjusted, competent, *and* educated human beings. The profession is also less able to enforce and fulfill the transformative and social democratic ends of public education.

More recently, hundreds of thousands of teachers engaged in walkouts, strikes, and walk-ins at state capitols to protest the disinvestment in and the privatization of public education, as well as the deprofessionalization of teaching through a combination of low wages, reduced benefits, poor working conditions, and decreased autonomy. They also flooded the airwaves and social media with stories about working one or more part-time jobs to support their families and with images showing the increasingly inadequate learning conditions that have resulted from the long-term disinvestment in public education. The latter included tattered and outdated textbooks, broken desks and chairs, an inadequate number of desks, chairs or textbooks, and students wearing coats, hats, and gloves inside frigid classrooms because of broken or inadequate heating systems. Many further highlighted these issues by panhandling and creating GoFundMe pages to get money for their classrooms.[36]

With the public behind them, educators won victories in states across the nation, especially in those that had enacted the largest funding cuts and had the largest wage penalties for teachers.[37] These states shared three other things in common: They have RTW laws and weak unions, the state government plays an especially strong role in education policy, and they are conservative and swung heavily in favor of Donald Trump.[38] This study and news accounts suggest *the last commonality is spurious.* Certainly protests against a decade of deep cuts to public education were a threat to Republican control in some of the country's most conservative states, but some states had elected governors and legislatures from opposing parties, and union officials said that most of the protesting teachers tended to vote Republican in these "red states."[39] The voices of teachers in these states further support the claims of educators in this study that *recent protests are nonpartisan.* Teachers are voicing against what they perceive to be a decades-long war against public education and other public services. That battle justified the expansion of charter schools and other forms of school choice while asking public schools—where most Americans educate their children—to do more with less; it also squeezed teachers and many others out of the middle class while giving tax breaks to corporations and the wealthy.[40]

Some might use successful protests in what are, for the most part, weakly organized RTW states to refute the claim that unions are critical for professional, political, and economic voice. Certainly teachers led these strikes, were out ahead of their unions, and were able to directly use social media to mobilize support from parents and community members; nonetheless, they still received economic resources, including organizational support—sometimes at the expense of teachers in other, more strongly organized states. The federated structure of unions enables them to shift economic and political resources from one part of the nation to another.[41] Unions also provide more than economic resources. They are a source of social glue that helps sustain collective action through moral support and solidarity.

When unions do not have the exclusive right to represent workers, it takes longer for individuals to rise up—either because they lack the structure to unite workers or because workers fight one another rather than external threats. This allows working conditions and wages to deteriorate until workers reach a boiling point. Recent strikes in weakly organized states suggest that this is exactly what happened. Again, most of these states have an unusually strong role in education policy. Without a countervailing power to other organized economic interests (e.g., business interests), these states have historically been able to suppress union voice and so there was limited feedback against tax cuts for corporations and the wealthy, the deregulation of the private sphere, and the disinvestment in and privatization of the public sphere (Schreiber, 2018).

Ironically, the unusually strong role of these states in public education is also what made them ripe for large-scale collective action once teachers and citizens had reached a boiling point; it provided a single target to mobilize against (Schreiber, 2018). I have been referring to this as *social cohesion*. In contrast, teachers' unions in the northeastern state that is the subject of this analysis bargain for most things locally. That historically resulted in large differences in salaries and working conditions across districts, reduced professional solidarity (social cohesion), and made it more difficult to fight for teaching reforms and education policies at the state level. As shown, the state's collective bargaining law altered that situation by leading to the creation of a single state-level union that could mobilize members on behalf of state and eventually federal education reforms.

Those who seek to weaponize policy feedback by restricting union voice may wish to consider the stabilizing functions of unions and the broader benefits that unions have provided for individuals and society (see Chapters 4 and 11). The state's collective bargaining law eventually reduced the number of strikes, which was actually the goal of the policy, even though it (unintendedly) created more social cohesion among teachers. Partly it did so by imposing economic sanctions, but my interviews *strongly indicate* that unions minimize strikes in return for gaining economic security through both economic voice (collective bargaining) and political voice (policy feedback). Both forms of voice encourage incremental changes in wages and benefits and the adoption of policies that promote the health and well-being of middle- and working-class citizens over time; those incremental changes tend to prevent things from reaching a boiling point. When strikes do occur, they are more likely to be short and, in the case of education, tend to affect a single district rather than the whole state (see also Schreiber, 2018).

When combined with recent events, this study indicates that large-scale strikes and protests may become more prevalent in the post-*Janus* environment, where RTW is the law of the land for public employees. Public employees are embedded in social contexts where they often form strong social ties with clients and their communities. They are able to use the federated structure of unions, occupations, and associations (e.g., teachers' associations) to mobilize their communities on behalf of reform (policy feedback) and then aggregate that support up to the state and national levels. This political and social capital does not solely include support for strikes and protests. Retirees, for instance, described how unions encouraged pro-education parents to run for school boards and, more recently, teachers successfully used social media—not just strikes—to raise the visibility of education reform in elections. With the public behind them and the help of the two major teachers' unions, an unprecedented number of teachers *from both political parties* also successfully ran for local, state, and national office in 2018—many of them in deep red and purple states where the education cuts were the harshest as a result of tax cuts.[42]

In recent conversations with some of the educators in this study, they discussed this rising activism, especially among a younger generation of teachers who had never experienced the solidarity that was developed through mobilizing against similar conditions in the 1960s and 1970s. These conversations and the words of teachers at their convention in Pittsburgh suggest that *Janus* is reengaging teachers, rather than deterring them, as they use their social ties to convince members not to leave the union. Robert Russo, a union leader from New Jersey who served 15 days in jail in 1970 for his role in an illegal teachers strike, avowed, "We are all militant again . . . will all go to jail if we have to. . . . They are taking away rights . . . everything we have worked for . . . and people are very invigorated" (Elk, 2018).

As shown, policy feedback is not a one-way street. Policy and political reforms that stemmed from the successful mobilization of those who had been left out of the social, political, and economic gains that were produced through government policies and programs after World War II (e.g., minorities, the disabled, public sector employees) reenergized conservatives, who felt that they were being left out of the programs and policies of the Great Society. Now, the efforts of conservatives to weaponize policy feedback by defunding and defanging unions and public employees is energizing a new generation of teachers who, along with their allies, are fighting against the disinvestment in public programs (e.g., public education); the privatization of the public sector (e.g., school choice and policies that reward private-sector vendors); and the deprofessionalization of public employees (e.g., public school teachers) as a result of low wages, reduced benefits, poor working conditions, and decreased autonomy. History shows that policy makers from *any political party* could benefit from working with these newly mobilized teachers to reform and reinvest in the public services that benefit all Americans. Suppressing economic, professional, and political voice to push for policies that only benefit some may temporarily work, but it eventually results in more aggressive forms of voice, neglect, and social turbulence.

Conclusion

This study identifies some positives about the workforce policies of NCLB and RttT, such as the voluntary exit of some ineffective teachers and some improvements in practice as a result of the HQT provisions.[43] Yet both policies appear to have created additional issues—like exacerbated inequity, increased gaming, undermined collaboration, reduced professional voice, the abandonment of an ethos of care for an ethos of self-interest, an increase in ethical leaving, the desertion of HQTs from schools and students that need them the most, and a lack of development for student teachers. Participants said recent education reforms deployed a "Band-Aid" approach rather than redress the real problems that plague education. These "wicked problems" require a broader array of policy interventions to ensure children have equitable OTL. To generate positive feedback for such interventions, policy makers should encourage the expansion of groups and organizations that mobilize a broader array of citizens (e.g., unions, professions and occupations, farmers' organizations, consumer associations, and worker, consumer, and housing cooperatives). This mobilization provides a countervailing narrative to the demands of concentrated economic and political interests. At the very least, policy makers should stop creating barriers to collective voice through weaponized policies and discourse. Chapter 11 elaborates on these policy recommendations.

PART IV

Modeling Policy Feedback

Cohen (2003) shows that the Great Depression changed the way our nation thought about emergency assistance and the government. For instance, most Americans came to believe that living in a county, town, or city entitled them to a minimum level of public services. Those beliefs began to change in the 1980s, as policy makers increasingly framed the government as the problem, rather than the solution, and citizens as consumers, rather than community members, to justify deregulation, privatization, and the use of market mechanisms (e.g., choice and incentives) to regulate public services. A recent article illustrates how tying basic services to the ability to pay, rather than framing them as a right of citizenship, has transformed public services. Ordered only to respond to those who had paid a $75 municipal fee, firefighters in Tennessee doused the borders between lawns—to protect those that had paid—while allowing an unsecured mobile home to burn (Frayer, 2010). This section uses the data from this study, and the concept of public service paradigms, to develop theory about how this reconstruction of citizenship—in terms of both individual rights and communal responsibilities—influences policy feedback and democratic performance.[1] By "public service paradigm," I mean an overarching narrative about the proper role of government in society and the best way to define and achieve the public interest. These paradigms include, but are not limited to, preferred economic models, policy tools, accountability mechanisms, forms of regulation, organizational structures for public and quasi-public agencies, and managerial techniques. Chapter 8 elaborates on the concept of public service paradigms and links each paradigm to its preferred policies and forms of citizen participation (exit, voice, loyalty, and neglect). Chapters 9 and 10 use educators' narratives to explore how these paradigms influence policy feedback, the quality of public services, and democratic performance by constructing the experiences, identities, and behaviors of citizens (Chapter 9) and policy implementers (Chapter 10). Chapter 11 uses these ideas, as well as the findings from this study, to elaborate on policy recommendations that would restore democratic performance.

8

Public Service Paradigms and Policy Feedback

In theory, the public and private sectors are opposite sides of the same coin. In practice, public policies are situated within political models of governance and accompanied by economic ones to create paradigms of public service provision. These paradigms have cultural and social roots and effects. At the cultural level, they are "systems of thought and action used to regulate and organize behavior" (Stein, 2004, p. 5, discussing public policies). At the structural level, these ways of "seeing" public problems influence how society addresses them through formal and informal institutions (Gusfield, 1981). These institutions become taken for granted but structure the social, political, and economic behaviors of those who are implicitly or explicitly involved in the policy performance (e.g., policy makers, frontline workers, policy targets, interest groups, and members of society at large).[1] In this way, public service paradigms influence policy feedback and therefore future policies. This chapter explores the concept of public service paradigms. It links those paradigms to their preferred education policies and forms of citizen participation (exit, voice, loyalty, and neglect) to set up the chapters that follow, which use data from this study to examine how public service paradigms influence policy feedback, public service quality, and democratic performance by constructing the experiences, identities, and behaviors of citizens (Chapter 9) and policy implementers (Chapter 10).

Public Service Paradigms, Policy Cultures, and Education Policies

Research shows that there have been two dominant public service paradigms since World War II: traditional public administration (TPA; 1890s-1970s) and new public management (NPM; 1980s-today). These paradigms have influenced governance across Western democracies, not just in the United States. TPA is linked to Keynesian economics and NPM to neoliberalism. More recently, scholars have linked networked community governance (NCG), a less dominant model of public service provision, to theories about "public value" (Benington, 2011; Clarke & Newman, 1997). The latter includes market-based values (e.g., efficiency and individual liberty), democratic values (e.g., fairness, transparency, responsiveness, equity, justice, inclusion), and the creation of social and cultural capital. I would argue, however, that there is nothing inherent in networks that would make them better suited for producing public value. Networks may be used for social exclusion and to advance individual interests over collective ones.[2] Rather, it is more appropriate to recognize that each paradigm has a preferred way of organizing political, economic, and social relations; offers a different conceptualization of the proper role of government in society; and makes different claims about the best way for citizens to influence public policies and the quality of public services. Whether that produces public and/or private value is an empirical question. This section uses cultural theory (CT) to expand on these claims.[3]

CT relates human attitudes, beliefs, values, and behaviors to different ways of organizing social relations. These "social solidarities" vary along two dimensions: grid and group. Both are a form of social control, but *group* expresses the degree of social cohesion and *grid* describes the degree of inequality (social, political, and economic stratification).[4] From these two dimensions, CT constructs four social paradigms: egalitarianism, individualism, hierarchy, and fatalism. These cultural biases form the basis for *all* social organization, including how individuals live and work with one another; achieve and maintain social order; distribute jobs, positions, goods, and services; and control envy, greed, and malfeasance. They also foster different systems of control in the public sector, where grid denotes the extent to which public servants are controlled through rules, regulations, and standard operating procedures (SOPs) and group conveys who should provide public services—government bureaucrats and frontline workers (hierarchy), the free market (individualism), or *civil society* (egalitarianism). The latter is defined as

Fatalism
Over-/under-
governed societies
Neglect

Hierarchy
TPA/Keynesianism
ESEA
Voice

High Grid
(social control)
Asymmetrical transactions
(inequality)

Low Group
Unfettered
competition

Autonomy
(The Hermit)

High Group
(social cohesion)
Fettered
competition

Individualism
NPM/neoliberalism
NCLB/RttT
Exit

Egalitarianism
NCG/public value
professions/occupations
Loyalty

Low Grid
Symmetrical transactions

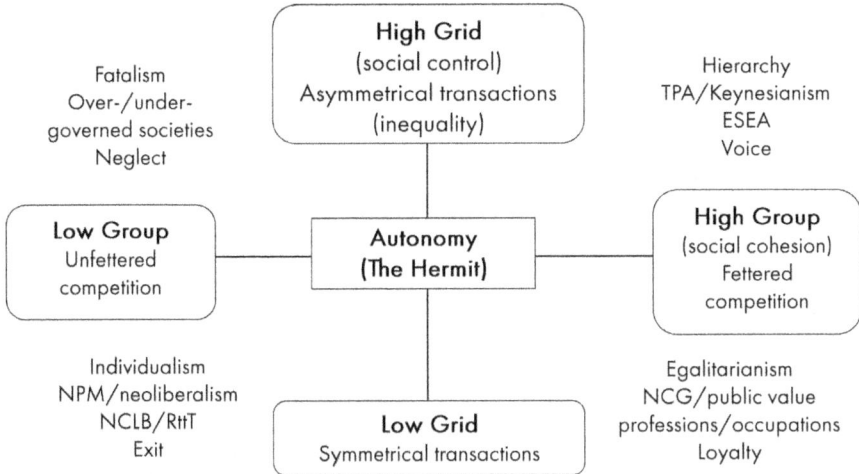

Figure 8.1. Paradigms of public service provision.

a community of citizens linked by common interests and collective activity.[5] These ideas are illustrated in Figure 8.1 and Table 8.1, which link CT to different public service paradigms.

The remainder of this section discusses each public service paradigm and links them to their preferred policies. Although the primary focus in this and later chapters is on the field of education, I provide other examples to develop and illustrate a model of how public service paradigms affect policy feedback and democratic performance that is testable through future research. The overarching claim—supported by this and other research—is that policy makers from both political parties increasingly dismantled the public sector in favor of free markets. This long-term trend had negative repercussions for civil society and democratic performance. By altering public policies (Chapter 11), policy makers could restore civil society, increase democratic participation, and improve the quality of public goods and services. The final chapter in this section shows how to do so through policy reforms.

Hierarchy: Traditional Public Administration, Keynesianism, and the ESEA

Modern public administration began during the Progressive Era (1890s–1920s) in response to urbanization, industrialization, the rise of the modern-day corporation, and unprecedented levels of

Table 8.1. Paradigms of public service provision

	Traditional public administration	New public management	Networked community governance
Conception of the public interest	Public interest is politically defined, expressed in law, and carried out by technical experts	Public interest results from the aggregation of individual interests	Public interest is the result of a dialogue about shared values
Conception of citizenship	Voters, constituents, clients, and users of public services	Customers	Coproducers of public outcomes
Role of government	Rowing: Designing and implementing policies or programs in response to politically defined objectives	Steering: Creating objectives and acting as a catalyst to unleash market forces (choice may be public, private, and/or nonprofit)	Serving: Negotiating and brokering between state, private actors, and civil society; may be steering, rowing, or staying out of the way, but the goal is to create shared values through dialogue and coproduction
Core public administration values	Efficiency	Efficiency and effectiveness	Efficiency and effectiveness, but also social democratic values and the creation of cultural, social, political, and economic capital
Governance through	Hierarchies (public sector): Administering programs through existing government agencies and/or self-regulating professions	Markets (contracts and customers): Creating mechanisms and incentive structures to achieve public objectives through the public, private and nonprofit sectors	Networks and partnerships: Building coalitions of public, nonprofit, and private organizations or interests to meet mutually agreed upon needs and goals
Preferred managerial/organizational structures	Bureaucracy: Top-down authority within public agencies; regulation of public servants and clients through rules, regulations, and procedures to ensure compliance; some discretion for professionals	Decentralized "public" organizations: Managers are responsive to elected officials and customers but have considerable discretion so long as they meet agreed upon performance objectives that control internal (agency or program objectives) or external (private or nonprofit contractors) behaviors	Collaborative governance: Managers collaborate across sectors (public, private, and nonprofit); leadership is shared internally and externally to achieve agreed upon objectives

Theory of public service motivation	Job security, pay, and benefits (e.g., health care, civil service protections)	Entrepreneurial (rewarded for effort through salary, promotion, span of control, and other forms of prestige)	Public service ethos (desire to contribute to society)
Administrative discretion	Limited	Wide latitude to meet entrepreneurial goals but controlled through incentives/performance goals	Discretion, but controlled by occupational and professional norms (mutuality)
Accountability	Hierarchical (bossism): Control by oversight and review; public servants are accountable to public managers, who are accountable to democratically elected political leaders	Contractual (choicism): Control by competition and rivalry; accumulation of self-interests results in broadly desired outcomes	Relational (groupism): Control by mutuality; attend to norms, laws, community values, and professional or occupational standards due to loyalty
	Managerialism: political, bureaucratic, and legal accountability	Consumerism: market accountability	Professionalism: professional/occupational accountability
Regulation by/policy feedback through	Voice	Exit	Loyalty
Economic theory	Public goods; Keynesianism	Public choice; neoliberalism	Networks; public value
Culture	Hierarchical	Individualist	Egalitarian/communitarian
Education policies	ESEA	NCLB, NCLB waivers, RttT, school choice policies (e.g., vouchers and charter schools)	Head Start; teaching as a profession

Note. Adapted from Benington (2011) and Clarke and Newman (1997).

immigration. The government needed to deal with the resulting social issues, and that meant grappling with economic and political ones. For instance, industrialization raised the standard of living for many, but progressive reformers charged that policy makers at all levels of government were not redressing widespread social and economic issues because they were controlled by corporate and political bosses, who used the "spoils system" to stay in power and control bureaucratic agencies. "Spoils" are what military victors take from those they conquer. In politics, the spoils system was the widespread practice of awarding government jobs to political supporters after winning elections. Both parties relied on these patronage appointments to create *loyalty*; they were used to get votes and obtain service on behalf of the party and its candidates. The resulting political corruption enriched the "haves" (e.g., politicians, wealthier Americans, the private sector) at the expense of the working classes, who struggled to meet basic needs.

Progressive Era reformers sought to make government more efficient and society less chaotic by reducing political corruption, expanding political participation (*voice*), and harnessing the power of the federal and state governments to eliminate unethical, unfair, and unsafe business practices. Some examples of political and administrative reforms include the direct election of U.S. senators (17th Amendment), suffrage for women (19th Amendment), and the adoption of civil service reforms. The latter were designed to ensure that public servants were hired and promoted based on merit; they also received due process protections to safeguard against being arbitrarily fired. Since they could not be removed simply because a new party was in town, public servants could remain politically neutral and serve Americans rather than party bosses and their political beneficiaries and benefactors. Government at all levels also increasingly intervened in the economy to protect the health and welfare of citizens. This included imposing regulations on private industry and implementing protections for workers, consumers, and the natural environment, but the Progressive Era also saw a growth in the public ownership of water, gas, and electric service. Those utilities that remained in private hands eventually came under the jurisdiction of regulatory commissions, which reviewed rates, mergers, and other business activities to prevent price gouging. All of this is what I mean by *hierarchy*.

Those who prefer *hierarchy* believe that it promotes social order and social cohesion (high group) through clearly defined roles, rules, and regulations (high grid). Informed by Keynesian economics and

TPA, this form of social organization continued to expand as the Great Depression and World War II challenged the classical view that unregulated markets would provide socially optimal solutions. According to British economist John Maynard Keynes, some goods and services would be under produced because they are *nonrivalrous* (consumption by one individual does not affect the consumption of others) and *nonexcludable* (noncontributors may still enjoy their benefits). A classic example is national defense. Everyone benefits, once provided, regardless of how little one contributes. The ability to "free-ride" off the contributions of others ensures that there will be shortages because private organizations do not reap sufficient profits.

When these goods and services provide broader societal bene-fits, as is the case with national defense, Keynes advocated shift-ing control to the public sector. He further argued that experts in government could and should use taxes and spending to manage the economy and ensure high levels of employment (fiscal policy)—even if that requires deficit spending during economic downturns and higher taxes during expansionary periods to stem inflation. These economic ideas are consistent with TPA's high trust in government and trained public managers; they expanded the size and scope of government at all levels by justifying the *decommodification* of many goods and services, meaning they were removed from the logics of the market and provided under the logics of TPA (Benington, 2011; Clarke & Newman, 1997).[6]

During the 1950s and early 1960s, these ideas were reflected in the words of economist John Kenneth Galbraith (1952, 1958) and President John F. Kennedy. The former argued that increased economic concentration (e.g., monopolies) had contributed to an affluent private sector while disinvestment had resulted in an increas-ingly impoverished public sector (e.g., public organizations, schools, roads, bridges). Rather than breaking up large corporations, he recommended that the government encourage the growth of coun-tervailing organizations—like unions, consumer and farmer associ-ations, and housing cooperatives. Such organizations could ensure the provision of safe and affordable housing, shield consumers from manipulative advertising, and protect workers from unfair and unsafe labor practices by creating the social cohesion (high group) that citizens often need to counter concentrated economic and polit-ical power; they would also spread social and economic opportunity by increasing political participation and providing citizens with the means to engage in collective political, social, and economic *voice*. Similarly, President Kennedy used the phrase "a rising tide lifts all boats" to convey how public spending on infrastructure and other goods and services distributes economic opportunity through rising income levels (Sperling, 2005).[7]

The Keynesian welfare state initially generated strong positive feedback by linking American values, attitudes, and behaviors to mass consumption. For example, government policies that supported workers' rights to organize and bargain collectively (*economic voice*) raised individual income; this increased business profits by generating increased demand for consumptive goods and reducing strikes and other clashes in the workplace (L. Cohen, 2003). Unions ensured that employees were loyal to the company, rather than a specific occupation, by negotiating wages that reflected the general cost of living and contracts that provided for health and retirement benefits. The resulting low turnover created more stable work relationships and helped transform the organization of work. Because employers were less concerned about competitors stealing their trained human capital, many began to invest in job training and promote from within. These *hierarchical work arrangements,* in turn, altered what Americans expected from their government and therefore policy feedback. The expansion of the middle class diffused access to mass-produced goods (e.g., automobiles, dishwashers, washing machines), increased homeownership, and fostered positive feedback for fiscal policy and public spending on housing (e.g., low interest federal mortgages), the construction of public colleges and universities, and social welfare programs. In contrast, there was less support for government-funded health care because growing numbers of Americans (now) received health benefits through their places of employment (Clarke & Newman, 1997; see also Chapter 11).

During the 1950s and early 1960s, this positive feedback was evident in the *bipartisan* support for the Keynesian welfare state; however, this period of relative tranquility ended as previously marginalized groups mobilized (*voice*) to seek their place within the American polity (L. Cohen, 2003). Their claim that American political, economic, and social institutions had provided unequal access to the American dream was influenced by a resurgence in left-wing scholarship after a period of demobilization during the Cold War Red Scare of the 1940s and 1950s. An example is Michael Harrington's (1962) *The Other America,* which revealed that 20 percent of the population and over 40 percent of the Black population still suffered from poverty despite overall affluence. In the field of education, this renewal is evident in books about how mass-produced, compulsory education had ignored children's emotional needs, stifled individual growth in the name of uniformity, and relegated poor and minority children to low-skilled and underpaid jobs.[8]

Within this environment, Democrats gained power at all levels of government; their electoral platform advocated policies that would reduce social tensions by extending "the blessings of American life to excluded citizens" (Matusow, 1984, p. xiv). President Lyndon Johnson's Great Society, for instance, advocated resolving the nation's social ills by bringing minorities and the poor into the economic mainstream. His War on Poverty included Title I of the ESEA. The premise behind that policy was that education could not be left to the free market or the capricious decisions of locally elected school boards; that system had helped some students while denying others the services that improved academic, economic, and other life outcomes. Rather than standardizing education, however, the ESEA set broad goals—backed by rules, regulations, and federal funding (hierarchy)—to ensure more equal OTLs; it then allowed educators to use their professional judgments to meet varying communal, familial, and student needs. Another way the Great Society sought to reduce social tensions was by expanding political engagement and *voice* in low-income and minority communities. This claim is evident in the inclusion of community action and community participation requirements (egalitarianism) in programs like Head Start.

Earlier, I argued that government programs are sites of political and social learning. Citizens are more likely to engage in public life when prior participation demonstrates the efficacy of political voice. The expansion of political and economic rewards to these marginalized groups encouraged other groups to mobilize (*voice*) and seek their place in the American polity. Some pursued various causes, such as government protection for workers, consumers, and the environment. Others supported the expansion of civil rights and liberties through federally enforced desegregation efforts and the provision of due process protections to the accused. In education, these efforts resulted in a series of federal and state court rulings that were designed to integrate public schools and extend free speech and due process protections to students, who had begun mobilizing in response to the Vietnam War. As discussed in Chapter 3, the success of these efforts is also evident in the expansion of the equity regime to ELLs, women, and the disabled.

Over time, this policy feedback mobilized other groups that felt their interests were being harmed. Some of this negative feedback (*voice*) resulted from a number of assumptions about the nature of society that were never fully accurate—and became even less so owing to rapid social and economic transformation—but had created the necessary preconditions for Keynesian welfare state expansion. For instance, the goal of full male employment rested on a gendered division of labor between the wage-earning husband and the non-wage-earning wife, who served the public realm by reproducing the private sphere of the home. This patriarchal arrangement was supposed to ensure that most citizens had their needs met through the private market (e.g., wages, pensions, health care); families with no male head of the household or an unemployed male head of the household would instead receive public assistance through the tax and insurance contributions of those who were employed. Some examples of these programs include unemployment insurance, cash assistance to families (AFDC), government-funded health care for low-income Americans (Medicaid), and food stamps. The economic and social changes of the 1970s and 1980s challenged these assumptions and preconditions through high unemployment, rising divorce rates, the spread of alternative familial arrangements (e.g., living together outside of marriage, gay or lesbian households), and the growing involvement of women in the workforce. One consequence was a decline in support for the Keynesian welfare state (Clarke & Newman, 1997).

On the left, liberals argued that the government had failed to alleviate social and economic disparities and charged that experts in government were suppressing democratic participation through paternalism disguised as professionalism (Benington, 2011; Clarke & Newman, 1997). Some also asserted that the state was actually reproducing social inequalities through racist policy designs that kept minorities, as well as poor whites, in their place. This latter claim has since been supported through empirical research.[9] Unsurprisingly, many citizens began to question the supposed neutrality of public bureaucrats and professionals under TPA and the fairness of public programs (Clarke & Newman, 1997). On the right, neoliberals and neoconservatives began mobilizing against TPA and Keynesianism, albeit for different reasons.

Like their liberal counterparts, neoliberals challenged TPA's claim that state bureaucrats and professionals are driven (and controlled) by a public service ethos; however, they argue that public servants use their "public monopoly"—the fact that only public organizations receive tax dollars to provide certain services, such as education—and their ability to hide behind professional expertise and bureaucratic rules, regulations, and red tape to build empires and evade accountability. This allegedly results in the inefficient and ineffective delivery of public services as government officials pursue their own interests at the expense of clients, citizens, and taxpayers. Neoliberals further contend that the welfare state impedes economic progress by rewarding those who "shirk"—free-ride off the labor of others—through welfare payments while penalizing those who work and invest through higher taxes. Higher taxes and expanded public programs drain investment and workers from a "wealth-creating" private sector and, by reducing business profits, inhibit entrepreneurship and impede America's ability to compete abroad (Clarke & Newman, 1997).

Neoconservatives also complain about the perverse effects of the welfare state, but they focus on how it negatively influences morality and traditional values. According to them, welfare discourages work and encourages single, female-headed households by paying benefits that exceed the minimum wage to those families with no employable male wage earner. It then leads to moral, social, and economic decline by creating a "cycle of dependency" and a permanent underclass that passes its poor work ethics and untraditional values on to children (Clarke & Newman, 1997; Murray, 1994).

Despite their differences, neoconservatives and neoliberals do not diverge in their conclusions. Both blame public servants and the welfare state for a decline in personal responsibility and America's ability to compete economically. The main difference is that neoliberals blame the public service monopoly for poor quality services; they also focus on "economic man," meaning the ways that public policies—like welfare, food stamps, SSI, Medicaid, and subsidized housing—create a disincentive to work, save, and invest. Neoconservatives contend that the professional commitment to "cultural relativism" fosters a decline in traditional values because it stresses working within the cultural mores of clients—whenever possible—to minimize the negative effects of paternalism and promote a more egalitarian and antidiscriminatory society (Clarke & Newman, 1997). Cultural relativism is part of the professional commitment to "first, do no harm."

Liberal and conservative intellectuals were not the only ones challenging TPA and Keynesianism. By the mid-1970s, a growing number of Americans were expressing skepticism about the ability of the government to foster socioeconomic equality and extend democratic participation. Americans' declining faith in government partly stemmed from a series of political and economic issues, including the resignation of president Richard Nixon, disenchantment with the Vietnam War, and the most serious economic downturn since the

Great Depression. However, as shown, concern was also mounting about the viability of capitalism and American democracy as a result of declining economic competitiveness, deindustrialization, and a series of high-profile fiscal crises in the public and private sectors. All of these weakened the nation's faith in conventional economic policy, as evident in economist Milton Friedman's claim that economic instability originated in the public, rather than the private, sector and his proposal to use the money supply, rather than fiscal policy, to create economic stability. Monetary policy shifts power away from the budget, as controlled by Congress and the president, and puts it in the hands of the Federal Reserve, which relies on economists and other fiscal experts.[10]

Monetary policy appeared to offer a nonpolitical alternative during a time when public opinion polls showed that Americans were increasingly distrustful of elected officials and of public and private institutions:

» Trust in government declined from almost 80 percent in the late 1950s to about 33 percent in 1976.
» Confidence in the private sector fell from around 70 percent in the late 1960s to about 15 percent in 1977.
» In 1959, 85 percent said that America's political institutions were "their greatest pride" in their country; in 1973, 66 percent expressed that they were "dissatisfied" with government.
» Those who believed their opinions about government did not "count much anymore" grew from 37 percent in 1966 to 61 percent in 1973. (Troy, 2005)

Americans also expressed declining faith in other forms of authority, such as the media, the military, and the professions (e.g., doctors, lawyers, priests). Moreover, for the first time in the postwar era, Americans said that they were disappointed with the present and fearful about the future (Collins, 2007).

As their faith in government declined, Americans began abandoning the public sphere and became less willing to bear collective burdens. This is evident in the phrase "not in my backyard" (NIMBY), which emerged as an increasingly distrustful America refused proposals to build landfills, prisons, factories, and even schools near their homes (Troy, 2005). Regardless of the reason, the relative affluence of the 1950s "fostered social optimism," whereas economic insecurity in the 1970s "fostered social pessimism" and "conservative denunciations of Keynesians, civil rights enthusiasts, and advocates of expansive welfare programs" (Matusow, 1984, p. 439). Social trust has continued to decline so that only one-third of Americans agree that most people can be trusted, whereas half felt that way in 1972—when the General Social Survey (GSS) first asked the question. In addition, a record high of nearly two-thirds believe that "you can't be too careful" when dealing with people (Cass, 2013).

The election of Republican president Ronald Reagan was both a sign and a consequence of growing conservatism in society. Economically, he stressed monetary policy and the use of supply-side economics to resolve economic instability. Supply-side economists argue that the best way to achieve prosperity—without increasing inflation—is to increase the supply of goods and services by providing incentives to work, save, and invest. Politically, this involved encouraging investment by providing businesses and (largely) upper-income individuals with tax incentives, deregulating the private sector, and privatizing some public services. Under New Federalism, President Reagan also proposed devolving national programs—especially those dealing with social and economic assistance—back to the states. The theory of action (Stone, 1989) was that a dynamic private market would foster economic growth; the resulting prosperity would trickle down in ways that would avert the need for social welfare programs as a rising tide lifted all boats. Although President Kennedy had used the rising tide metaphor, he was conveying that spending on public services and infrastructure would promote broader socioeconomic goals. Moreover, while he advocated tax cuts for businesses, farmers, and every income bracket, he argued that the largest proportionate reduction should go to those at the bottom of the economic ladder (Sperling, 2005). Now, that metaphor is used to suggest that those at the top will help those at the bottom by investing the resources they gained through tax cuts.

The protracted period of policy makers telling Americans that government is the *problem* (not the *solution*) and that the individual pursuit of self-interest will aggregate into a more prosperous America did not begin with President Reagan; however, he normalized this discourse. A few examples to illustrate how it spread across political parties are in order. President Johnson (D) argued on behalf of using the federal government to create a Great Society. Presidents Nixon (R), Carter (D), Reagan (R), George H. W. Bush (R), Clinton (D), George W. Bush (R), Obama (D), and Trump (R) all, in some way, told Americans that the federal government is *the* or *part of the* problem rather than the solution. It was actually President Bill Clinton, a Democrat, who boasted that "the era of big government is over" (Clinton, 1996). President Kennedy (D) said, "Ask not what your country can do for you—ask what you can do for your country" (Kennedy, 1961). Nixon told Americans that it was not selfish to want to keep their money (Nixon, 1972), and, building on the Nixon-inspired tax revolts of the 1970s, Reagan said that it was beneficial for the least well-off when America cuts taxes for the most well-off. George H. W. Bush said, "Read my lips, no new taxes" (Bush, 1988). He later reneged on that promise to reduce national budget deficits, as part of a compromise with Congress, and was not reelected. George W. Bush and Donald Trump then presided over tax cuts that, similar to those of the Reagan administration, largely benefited upper-income Americans while also ballooning federal deficits and the national debt (Dersh, 2020; Horton, 2017; Maldonado, 2019).

This discourse was not consigned to the executive branch. Discussing President Clinton's proposal to increase taxes to balance the federal budget, Representative Bob Goodlatte (R-GA) argued that "small businesses generate the bulk of this Nation's new jobs. . . . They will be the hardest hit . . . [and] when you raise taxes, you kill jobs." Representative Christopher Cox (R-CA) called the tax increase the "Dr. Kevorkian plan for our economy. It will kill jobs . . . businesses . . . kill even the higher tax revenues that these suicidal tax increasers hope to gain" (Garafolo, 2010). Former House speaker John Boehner (R-OH) claimed that raising taxes would be like "stealing from Americans" (McAuliff & Siddiqui, 2013). By co-opting taken-for-granted meanings, Republicans created new political coalitions that included "centrist" New Democrats, who moved to the right in an effort to get and keep power in a more conservative political climate. Those coalitions enabled the adoption of policies that advanced social organization through markets (individualism) while (increasingly) dismantling the public sector.

Individualism: New Public Management, Neoliberalism, and Recent Education Reforms

Individualists view the free market as the best way to efficiently and effectively meet individual wants and broader social needs. They advocate minimizing government interventions in society—including, but not limited to, bureaucratic rules, regulations, and SOPs (hierarchy)—because they view these actions as a threat to individual liberty, which they define as "freedom from" the government versus "freedom to" participate (politically, economically, and socially) as a result of public programs that promote individual and societal transformation. During the 1990s, the neoliberal wing of conservatism gained prominence within the Republican Party. As mentioned, they argued that public servants use their "public monopoly" to build empires, evade accountability, shirk their responsibilities, and pursue their own interests at the expense of citizens and taxpayers. Unlike traditional conservatives, however, they did not advocate a truncated state. Instead, they proposed using government authority to build markets and support market-like behaviors; they also advocated using market logics and mechanisms to distribute risks and rewards, evaluate government programs, hold public servants accountable, and improve the quality of public services (Apple, 2001; Benington, 2011).

Led by Newt Gingrich (R-GA), the Republican Revolution altered the political terrain in Congress even as his Contract with America altered the ideational terrain. Although education was not a part of the Contract, Republican promises to cut taxes affected resources for discretionary programs at the national level, such as education, and Republican members of Congress revived proposals to abolish the DOE and extend school choice. Gingrich and his supporters argued that the "public school monopoly" allows "Educrats" (administrators, teachers, and bureaucrats in federal and state DOEs) to promote their own interests at the expense of taxpayers, parents, and students. To rectify this issue, they advocated policies that use incentives and competition to force public schools and public school educators to reduce costs and improve service quality (e.g., merit pay and school choice in the form of charter schools and private school vouchers; Apple, 2001).[11] Economist Albert Hirschman (1970) refers to these as exit—a form of policy feedback that involves what Tiebout (1956) called "voting with your feet." Citizens may, for example, move from one school district to another or leave the public school system altogether and attend a private, religious, or charter school.

Once New Democrats, such as President Bill Clinton, moved to the right to appeal to more conservative voters, these ideas spread through NPM (policy feedback)—an approach to public administration that deploys market-oriented management techniques to improve the efficiency, effectiveness, and overall performance of public services. NPM has dominated academic and practitioner debates ever since. It includes the institutionalization of the performance in government movement through President Clinton's National Partnership for Reinventing Government

(NPR), as well as rhetoric that advocates changing the culture of a "broken" public sector by applying private-sector management techniques. Even so, President Clinton did not completely replace public management principles with the MMP. He argued that a "catalytic government" would engage in "steering rather than rowing," meaning that it would use citizen voice and choice (speaking up and competition) to monitor and enforce bureaucratic and professional responsiveness.[12]

In this way, NPM links "bottom-up" political and market accountability (voice and choice) while (theoretically) distancing "top-down" hierarchical controls through bureaucratic rules, regulations, and SOPs. As institutionalized through recent education reforms, NPM involved three assumptions: Educators need external controls to ensure that they "do right by the kids"; they would improve their work effort to obtain respectable test scores, minimize parental complaints (voice), and reduce exit from public schools; and their improved effort would significantly raise public school performance. As shown, these ideas contrast sharply with those of educators who are more closely aligned with egalitarianism.

Egalitarianism: Networked Community Governance, Head Start, and the Professions

Egalitarianism promotes social cohesion through relative social equality. Rather than adopting hierarchical interventions (social control), members of a community use networks of reciprocity to monitor and enforce compliance with group norms (social control). NCG, for instance, advocates fostering linkages between the state, markets and civil society and using citizen coproduction to promote more flexible, adaptive, and equitable responses to public problems, especially when compared to public agencies (TPA) and markets (NPM). The theory of action is that networks and interorganizational partnerships will reduce the need for more formal hierarchical controls (TPA) by enabling members to monitor one another through their social ties (Benington, 2011). When the government and private actors are able to mobilize these ties, civil society becomes an avenue to create public and private value in a similar way to how the state and markets create it under TPA and NPM. Economist Albert Hirschman (1970) refers to these ties as *loyalty*; political scientists and sociologists describe them as social capital. Either way, individuals fulfill their obligations (largely) due to feelings of trust and respect for fellow members and because they are closely aligned with the group's norms and values (social cohesion).

With respect to the professions, members adopt informal norms and formal codes of behavior—such as the Hippocratic Oath or an ethos of service—to guide day-to-day practice and introject these values—not just job skills—through formal training and on-the-job socialization. Group members then monitor and sanction those who fail to comply (Clarke & Newman, 1997; Freidson, 2001). Hood (1998) calls this form of social control and accountability "mutuality." It works through ties to colleagues and clients. Certainly, professionals are influenced by top-down managerial controls (hierarchy) and bottom-up market incentives (individualism); however, they (typically) attend to the quality of their work because they are loyal to a code of ethics and care about the subjects of their work. In these cases, the use of extrinsic incentives (the market) or hierarchical rules, regulations, and SOPs (bureaucracy) may actually crowd out the intrinsic motivations for high performance. Again, Hochschild (1983) refers to this as "care work" to denote that workers are not closely supervised, retain some autonomy over service provision, and are (typically) motivated by the personal and intrinsic value of caring to go beyond what is formally required by the job.[13]

Egalitarianism is not a dominant paradigm, but it is important to understand how this form of social regulation and accountability compares to the others. Like bureaucracy, professionalism is designed to ensure fairness through "neutrality," meaning it seeks to reduce behaviors that are based on the personal biases and prejudices of public servants. Bureaucrats and professionals also frequently deal with unwilling clients. Despite these similarities, professionalism sharply contrasts with bureaucracy. Many professions and occupations—such as teachers, physicians, nurses, and social workers—engage in *social reconstruction*. They are involved in redressing a wide array of complex social issues (e.g., homelessness, drug addiction, poverty, violence) and often (directly or indirectly) bring about change or improve society by, for example, fostering social cohesion, tolerance, and peaceful coexistence; redressing inequality; and/or developing a national identity that transcends individual, sectarian, and communal differences. Because of this, the work frequently involves sustained interactions over time and workers develop social bonds that are not typically present between bureaucrats—like those at the Department of Motor Vehicles—and citizens (Clarke & Newman, 1997). As shown in Chapter 5, these bonds are a form of social capital that improves service delivery.

Professionals also serve clients who are the coproducers of their service outcomes and typically deal with what I earlier referred to as "wicked problems," where there is widespread disagreement with respect to the definition, the cause, the appropriate solution, and the best way to measure the effectiveness of that solution (Harmon & Mayer, 1986). Teaching itself is affected by wicked problems (e.g., poverty, hunger, homelessness), but there is also no agreement on how to define and measure educator performance. Tests are one way to do so yet are only a *very* limited measure of learning.

These realities make it difficult to standardize services and hold professionals accountable through rules, regulations, and SOPs (bureaucratic hierarchies). In consequence, professionalism (largely) involves self-regulation, with some group monitoring and sanctioning of those who fail to comply with occupational norms, standards, and practices. Again, this may involve imposing social costs, such as gossip and social exclusion, but it also includes formal appeals to management. This hierarchical authority structure is bureaucratic in nature; however, managers (e.g., school administrators) are typically trained in the same profession, drawn from within the ranks, deploy collegial management styles, and decentralize decision-making with respect to service provision (Clarke & Newman, 1997). They recognize that, for the most part, those they manage do not need close monitoring from above because they are motivated to comply with group norms and practices as a result of their social ties (loyalty) to the organization, occupation, colleagues, and those they serve.

Professionalism also sharply contrasts with the market—where firms hire workers and sell products unconstrained by the state under a "buyer or worker beware" philosophy. Professions control entry through licensing and certification requirements; these regulations are enforced by the government and close off the profession to other workers. That enables the profession to regulate members through socialization and by setting standards for conduct and ongoing training. Still, it is largely one's commitment to the occupation—versus an employer, paycheck, promotion, or control by colleagues—that regulates individual behaviors. This is why those who value a paycheck or promotion and those who move up through the ranks of a vertical hierarchy (i.e., become an administrator) are often viewed as "unprofessional" or as "sell outs." They are now committed to the organization, supervisors, prestige, or a paycheck, more than the profession's norms, and are therefore less likely to view their peers as a reference point.

In short, both TPA and NPM submerged the professions within the organizational state. Yet professionalism is not compatible with bureaucracy or the market. My interviews suggest that this resulted in increased fatalism prior to educators using their social ties to fight back.

Fatalism: Contrived Randomness and Charter School Lotteries

Although *fatalism* is not a socially active culture, it is conceptually associated with under- and overgoverned societies and with excluded groups; it is characterized by neglect—withdrawal, opting out, or noncompliance—typically due to feelings of suspicion, alienation, powerlessness, dependency, and disenfranchisement.[14] CT is ambiguous about whether fatalism is a viable way to organize social relations, but fatalists stress the fickleness of the natural world and our inability to predict human behavior owing to the often unanticipated and unintended side effects of social interactions. In terms of accountability, the remedy is to build an element of chance into public administration as a way to control antisystem behaviors. This *contrived randomness* minimizes individual and collective efforts to game the system (e.g., shirking and collusion) by making the payoffs unpredictable and uncertain (Hood, 1998).

Within organizations, contrived randomness involves dividing authority so that no single individual is in control; limiting tenure and rotating staff to avoid overfamiliarity with clients; semirandomly posting employees to countries or cities where they have no social ties; engaging in unannounced or undetectable checks; and other means of reducing opportunities for shirking, collusion, and other antisystem behaviors. Examples include random tax audits, bag checks at the airport, drug and alcohol testing, the U.S. lottery system for immigrant visas, and lotteries to ensure that charter schools do not "cherry-pick" the best students in an effort to outperform their public counterparts. Behavioral responses to this kind of system vary depending on perceptions. For instance, these social controls do not necessarily need to be random. So long as they are viewed that way, they will encourage participants to self-regulate. If the system is perceived to be unfair, however, contrived randomness may actually encourage neglect and discourage cooperation and networking in their positive forms; accountability is viewed as a gaming machine where only "The House" wins (Hood, 1998). In politics, neglect includes nonvoting or nonparticipation because "You can't fight City Hall."

Discussion: Public Service Paradigms, Accountability, and Policy Feedback

CT recognizes that interests and preferences are constructed through social interactions. People use their perceptions about their natural and social worlds, and the forms of relations that are appropriate given those perceptions, to build (public and private) institutions that promote their beliefs and values. These institutions become taken for granted but influence the political, social, and economic experiences, identities, and behaviors of citizens and policy implementers.

Rival cultures may sometimes work together to achieve their objectives. TPA, for instance, combines bureaucracy with professionalism in ways that limit the market. NPM combines political and market accountability (voice and choice) in ways that theoretically distance bureaucracy and enforce professionalism. However, combining paradigms—or changing from one paradigm to the other—is likely to result in social conflict because rival cultures are largely incompatible; they stem from and foster different values. If policy makers suppress this negative feedback over long periods of time or weaponize policies to suppress voice from some while magnifying it from others, they will foster more disruptive forms of political, economic, and social action—such as riots, looting, and strikes. When viewed this way, it is evident that CT provides a lens for understanding policy disagreements, but it is also useful for improving democratic responsiveness and accountability.

Accountability is and ought to be a central theme in politics, public administration, and public policy because it is critical for democracy and effective governance. Traditionally, five forms of accountability have coexisted in public education. *Political accountability* involves oversight by elected legislatures and school boards, who defer to constituents. *Legal accountability* entails courts hearing complaints about district and legislative policies and actions. *Market accountability* occurs when parents choose to live in a community based on its schools and exit when unhappy. *Professional accountability* involves deference to occupational norms and standards of practice. *Bureaucratic accountability* is exercised when federal and state DOEs and school districts adopt rules and regulations that govern the behaviors of educators (Darling-Hammond, 1991; Gormley & Balla, 2008).

Since the Progressive Era, public schools have relied more heavily on bureaucratic and professional accountability. This was also true under the ESEA of 1965. In contrast, recent education reforms relied more heavily on a combination of political and market accountability (voice and choice). CT makes evident the flaws inherent in each form of accountability.

Bureaucratic accountability is linked to hierarchy. One downside is that public servants are held accountable for following SOPs rather than for successfully meeting the needs of citizens (Darling-Hammond, 1991). Hierarchical accountability may foster opportunism, encourage gaming behaviors, and eliminate the collective ethos that helps organizations thrive. Examples for public servants include shirking, meeting objectives in ways that are feasible but not welfare enhancing, and refusing to help colleagues or fellow citizens. These forms of *neglect* are more likely in cases where management keeps moving the goal posts once workers meet objectives (Hood, 1998). Citizens, on the other hand, may opt out of complying with policies—even those that serve the public interest (e.g., refusing to wear a mask or get vaccinated for nonmedical reasons); they may also resort to what Kagan (2003) calls *adversarial legalism*—a form of legal accountability that uses the judiciary to make public policy. These behaviors are more likely to occur when citizens are unable to get their needs met or when they distrust the government and/or fellow citizens (Hood, 1998).

Certainly, these negative outcomes may stem from bureaucratic resistance or inertia; however, they may also arise from the rhetoric and behaviors of political and economic actors (political and market accountability). The latter may manufacture a crisis in confidence or promulgate misinformation for political or economic gains, such as winning elections or earning ratings and advertising dollars in the case of the media and entertainment industry. By creating "wedge issues," these actors divide groups that would normally work together to achieve common interests. The end result is that individuals work against the common good and sometimes even their own interests (e.g., individual and collective health as a result of disinformation about masks and vaccines or voting for candidates that adopt policies to help the most well-off when not a part of that group). In these cases, citizen coproduction may contribute to issues with public service design and delivery that have little to do with the behaviors of bureaucrats. These claims are evident in recent research and public opinion polls that show political polarization and disinformation are driving a significant share of the deaths in the recent pandemic by influencing citizens' willingness to wear masks and get vaccinated (Kirzinger et al., 2021; Wood & Brumfiel, 2021).

Political-market accountability (voice and choice) is linked to individualism. Individualists extol the free market and denigrate the public sector, but the political system and the free market may *both* create social justice issues. This occurs when participation, information, and the ability to pay are systematically linked to race and class, as is the case in highly stratified societies, like the United States (see Chapter 11), where citizens have an unequal ability to engage in "voice and choice." In terms of public servants, political-market accountability may result in positive outcomes if it motivates those who would otherwise shirk or play it safe to improve their performance; however, competition may weaken trust and the collective ethos that encourages people to work together to achieve common ends (Hood, 1998). Teachers, for example, may be unwilling to share information and expertise with fellow teachers if their pay is based on how well they perform relative to others.

Professional accountability is linked to egalitarianism. One downside is that colleagues may be unwilling to police one another; they may silently accommodate unacceptable behaviors rather than training, sanctioning or expelling members from the group (Freidson, 1975). Professionals may also use their social cohesion to inappropriately reject top-down directives from managers (hierarchy), ignore bottom-up demands from clients (markets), and (unfairly) target weaker members of the group, those who are not part of a reigning group, or those who cannot be trusted to "go along." In these cases, collegiality and social cohesion impede performance, reduce trust in professional authority (and the government that enforces it), and unravel the organization through the creation of long-standing, simmering feuds (Hood, 1998).

Chapter 2 showed that policy makers tended to stress the benefits of political-market accountability while linking teachers to the flaws of bureaucracy through narratives about the "BLOB," "educrats," the "education establishment," and the "system." Certainly not everyone portrayed educators in this fashion, but narratives about the two achievement gaps implied or outright stated that educators were shirking their professional responsibilities at a cost to students and society. Such narratives include blaming the gap between low-income and minority students and their more advantaged peers on the "soft bigotry of low expectations" and between American students and their international peers on "failing" public schools.

Informants, on the other hand, discussed the benefits of professional accountability, elaborated on the negative consequences of political-market accountability, and (largely) silenced the flaws of bureaucratic accountability. According to them, the main source of accountability in education was an ethos of care, a form of professional accountability that uses social ties to encourage all members of the school community to pull their behaviors in line in ways that benefit the group. Their words suggest that TPA reinforced professional accountability through political, legal, and bureaucratic mechanisms. Teachers socialized their colleagues and policed the norms of teaching; however, state and federal DOEs and school district administrators promulgated bureaucratic rules, regulations, and SOPs to promote the consistent and nonpartial delivery of services. Principals and elected school boards also retained control over decisions about hiring and tenure, and both had the last word with respect to how the school was run. When conflicts existed, parents could pursue political, bureaucratic, and legal remedies (e.g., complaints to administrators and elected officials, ousting school board members, and taking legal action in state and federal courts). While not specifically designed for this purpose, tenure and unionization also encouraged professional voice over neglect through due process and procedural protections. As shown, professional voice tends to enforce other forms of accountability.

The paradigm of public service provision that participants were describing is a combination of TPA and NCG; their narratives suggest that NCG became more prominent as a result of the policy changes that were gained through union and professional voice (policy feedback). The idea behind NCG is that the state (hierarchy regulated by voice) and the market (individualism regulated by exit, competition, and choice) are insufficient for dealing with social and economic issues. The government must facilitate linkages between the two to redress the issues that have arisen from an increasingly complex and diverse global society. By fostering social ties (loyalty), communities and networks provide individuals with a sense of belonging, meaning, purpose, and continuity during times of social, political, and economic change or unrest. This social capital allows people to thrive amid uncertainty. Professions and occupations are especially critical for ensuring that this social capital produces public value—not just private value (e.g., individual freedom and profit)—because their *norms* encourage communitarian, egalitarian, and public-spirited behaviors; however, studies show that *public servants in general* are more likely to engage in prosocial behaviors.

This research supports all of these claims. It further indicates, however, that a public service ethos *alone* is insufficient for redressing educational inequalities owing to the ways that external factors influence educational outcomes, especially the way that market forces—often supported by government policies—have contributed to socioeconomic inequality. Under these conditions, there must be aid from higher levels of governance to provide the more equitable OTLs that increase democratic performance. I explore these claims in the next three chapters.

Conclusion

Policy scholars recognize that participation is central to the quality of many public goods and services, yet policy makers frequently ignore citizen coproduction because it is easier to influence the behaviors of public servants. Economist Albert Hirschman (1970), on the other hand, used the constructs of exit, voice, loyalty, and neglect (EVLN) to explore how citizens might influence the quality of public services in a democratic society.[15] History shows that American political culture has long been shaped by the viability of exit. Examples include policies and rhetoric that encouraged westward expansion, the movement away from rural and urban areas to the suburbs, and the use of school choice (e.g., vouchers and charter schools) as an ameliorative for inefficient and ineffective "public school monopolies." Hirschman, however, argued that the market is not necessarily the most efficient and effective way to provide goods or resolve social issues. Rather, it is some combination of EVLN that allows the identification and correction of problems in both the public and private sectors.

Exit, for instance, may weaken the propensity to voice. The provision of cheap alternatives causes a rapid degeneration of public and private organizations as the most quality conscious leave in large numbers. By encouraging individuals to voice rather than opt out (exit and neglect), loyalty may help resolve these issues; it provides institutions, organizations, and groups with the time to correct problems before they lose a critical number of dissatisfied customers, clients, or members.[16] Neglect provides a similar cushion when it denotes nonparticipation, but may also lead to a rapid degeneration in quality if it involves shirking or noncompliance. In short, voice, loyalty, and neglect provide the information and time to correct perceived and actual problems; exit may create the incentive to do so. This chapter showed how public service paradigms prefer and encourage the use of different forms of policy feedback (EVLN). The next two examine the effects of these preferences on citizen participation, policy implementation, and democratic performance.

9

Citizen Coproducers and Policy Feedback

As discussed, NPM and neoliberalism seek to reform the public sector by making it more like the private sector. The theory of action (Stone, 1989) is that citizen complaints and the competition for "customers" will stimulate public servants to alter their behaviors in ways that improve public services. In the words of Albert Hirschman (1970), both assume that the quality of public goods and services is determined by some combination of market-like consumer behaviors (e.g., exit, choice, competition) and political activity (voice). These ideas are evident in recent education reforms, which framed parental voice and choice as a way to improve public school performance and "lift all boats." This chapter uses 83 interviews with educators to explore their perceptions of how political-market accountability (voice and choice) affects citizen behaviors and public education.

Beyond Exit and Voice: Citizen Coproduction of Public Services

Chapter 2 discussed how the combination of consumer choice and public policies resulted in schools being segregated by race and socioeconomic background. Many informants disclosed that technological developments and school district organizational practices similarly resulted in segregated classrooms. Schools historically tracked students based on their "choice" to finish high school, pursue vocational training, or attend college, but those decisions were heavily influenced by a student's racial and socioeconomic background. The development of standardized and intelligence quotient testing, institutionalization of guidance counselors as an occupation, and federal funding for these kinds of administrative purposes under the National Defense Education Act of 1958 (NDEA) increasingly enabled schools to track students by "ability" (as measured by test scores), yet this, too, reportedly favored advantaged groups.[1] It was one reason why women, minorities, students with disabilities, and other marginalized groups mobilized during the 1960s and 1970s (voice); they successfully demanded a more equitable distribution of educational opportunities (policy feedback).

Educators said the resulting changes in policy triggered the mobilization of others, who felt that inclusion had harmed their interests through lowered standards. On a positive note, their concerns led to state policy changes that raised educational standards, including high school graduation requirements. Schools also began providing more rigorous programs for high-achieving students, such as gifted and talented programs and AP classes. This policy feedback created an educational "floor" (i.e., minimum standards) for most students while raising the ceiling for others (i.e., advanced college preparatory programs and other forms of accelerated instruction). Less positively, these and other developments often increased racial and socioeconomic stratification within a more inclusive system of public education.

Stratification denotes the categorization of people into groups based on indicators of (political, social, or economic) power, such as wealth, income, race, ethnicity, education, gender, ability, occupation, or social status. Participants were conveying that classrooms today are more integrated in terms of students with special needs and less overtly tracked by socioeconomic background; however, public education is still stratified in terms of the quality of experiences and opportunities afforded to low-income and minority students due to the link between test scores and socioeconomic background and the fact that students of color are disproportionately likely to be poor. Respondents portrayed accountability policies—like NCLB, NCLB waivers, and RttT—as the institutionalization of these state and local developments at the national level.

Although they did not use this language, informants were conveying that parents, in the past four decades, have increasingly viewed education as a *rivalrous good* (i.e., a competition for future wealth and status) rather than a *public good,* meaning a commodity or service that contributes to the well-being of society and is therefore provided without profit to all members. Educators were not shaming parents. They blamed this development on public discourse and policies, especially the failure of policy makers to redress changes within the larger political economy and a public discourse that focused on individual rights (freedom from the government) at the expense of collective responsibilities.

More students began attending college after World War II for three reasons: the increased outsourcing of higher paying jobs that did not require a college education to other nations, the expansion of low cost student loans, and the growth of public colleges and universities. Beginning in the 1980s, stagnating wages, the contraction of public services, rising housing costs, and other threats to the middle class intensified the competition for college placements and jobs. These developments negatively affected economic mobility and the quality of life for growing numbers of Americans (see Chapter 11). One consequence was that parents increasingly feared for their children's future. Such fears were exacerbated by a public discourse that blamed "failing" public schools for the decline in economic productivity and America's ability to compete abroad.

Within this environment, parents engaged in political and social behaviors that advanced their own children's interests but ultimately harmed the least well-off. Molly, a high school social studies teacher, explained,

[Kids] who have a lot more . . . [their] parents are very active . . . work the system . . . [demand] AP classes. . . . [It] has the effect of segregating their children . . . economically. . . . Socioeconomic background does influence testing and . . . who gets into those classes. But these parents are also connected . . . [fight to] get their children into these classes even when they might not be the top students . . . want their kids . . . with those top performers . . . get into the right college and . . . the right job. . . . There is a lot of tracking even though we got rid of . . . what you would call a non-college-based track. . . . The cafeteria, you can see them segregating themselves this way. . . . That divisiveness and competitiveness is . . . affecting schools. . . . It's not about learning. It's about . . . test results and grades . . . to get ahead.

My interviews suggest that public discourse and policies that treat parents as consumers—versus citizen coproducers—played a role in these developments. This section uses the constructs of EVLN (Hirschman, 1970) to illustrate these claims.

The Unequal Effects of Parental Exit

Hirschman (1970) argued that exit, the market form of social control, is unlikely to improve the quality of public services because it is (typically) used by the most well-off, involved, and engaged; it then leaves behind those who are the least likely to fight for reform (voice). This study supports his claim. Elaine, a retired urban elementary school teacher, best captured these complex processes:

[The community] changed over time. . . . [It had] different enclaves . . . Italian, Chinese, and so forth, but it was a neighborhood school and the parents were very engaged. . . . Maybe they did not speak English, but . . . would bring someone . . . to translate. . . . [Then] more and more parents, as they established themselves, would move . . . into the neighboring suburbs . . . it changes the whole flavor of . . . the urban district . . . each individual school . . . I saw that happen multiple times. The parents who really were strong and committed to education . . . were always the ones that would . . . [buy a home or] find an apartment in suburban districts. . . . [We used to be] much more similar to suburban schools . . . parents . . . worked for a . . . major company. . . . [Many did well but their kids] attended the city school. That really doesn't happen anymore. . . . It bothers me when people use race or nationality . . . it was across the board. The kids who stayed were having a much more difficult time in their home lives.

According to Elaine, "exit" was neither a single event nor a short-term process; it involved multiple migrations over a 20-year period. She described five negative consequences.

The school had to constantly restructure the organization of teaching and learning to accommodate population changes. These processes drained school resources. Waves of exit also continuously destroyed old social ties while making it difficult to construct new ones. Both of these trends put a lot of stress on educators, who had to deal with a community that was increasingly under social and economic duress. In her words,

You literally would not leave certain buildings in the district after dark . . . [unless] somebody was walking you. . . . It was a working community . . . [with] shops . . . stores . . . restaurants and bars . . . when I first started. . . . [Then the community was increasingly] crime-ridden . . . someone found a gun in the playground. . . . You worried about your car being broken into. . . . A teacher . . . had a parent . . . take the keys out of her pocketbook . . . [in] her desk . . . stole her car. . . . It is very difficult to go to work . . . where you do not feel safe.

That stress then encouraged some educators to leave and made it difficult to recruit new ones. In consequence, the district often had to rely on alternatively credentialed or uncredentialed teachers.

When combined, these social, economic, and organizational issues suppressed performance in Elaine's district while the transfer of more engaged parents and students enhanced the performance of the surrounding suburban schools. Exit then became the default mechanism for those who were not necessarily well-off financially yet cared deeply about education. They chose to live in an apartment in the surrounding suburban districts rather than have their children attend what they increasingly perceived to be an inferior urban public school system.

Other educators supported her claim that the normalization of suburban living among middle-class and upper-income Americans bolstered property values—and thus tax revenues—in suburban schools; exit then suppressed both in the communities they left behind. Again, state and federal aid offsets some of the resulting fiscal disparities, but per pupil spending still varies significantly across districts and unequally influences educational outcomes.

Less obviously yet still a contributor to differences in performance, suburban schools tend to be more homogenous due to policies that promoted white flight while poverty and racial discrimination locked minorities and more transient populations, such as low-income renters and newly arriving immigrants, into rural and urban areas. Educators were not blaming students. Their point was that more homogenous communities (typically) experience more social cohesion. Suburban schools may therefore invest fewer resources in organizational mechanisms that maintain social order and more in those that improve educational outcomes. The concentration of poverty in urban and rural districts when compared to suburban schools magnifies these trends. Urban and rural schools (generally) have more demands on faculty and resources owing to the link between SES and academic issues.

Exit increases educational disparities *within districts* for similar reasons. Educators provided three examples of how these *interdistrict* moves negatively affect the schools that are left behind. The first instance involved teachers who had worked in three different southern states before working in the northeastern state that is the subject of this analysis. All of them told similar narratives to Kristen,

an urban elementary teacher, about the effects of market accountability (exit) within a countywide school system:

> The southern schools use the county system. Here, everything is done
> by district. . . . It is a growing area in the South. . . . They were building
> all of these schools . . . letting all of these white families put transfer
> letters in . . . [but] all of the Hispanic and Black families would stay in
> my school. . . . My school was probably a 50–50 split [when I started], but,
> by the time I left after five years, it was 90 percent minority. . . . They
> don't use the word *segregation,* but that is what it was. . . . It is all done
> by "parental choice" [making quote signs] . . . parents write letters to go
> to these new beautiful schools. . . . Even if the minority parents wrote
> letters, which most of them didn't, it was our most motivated kids who left.

This form of exit is largely unavailable in this northeastern
state—where most children are assigned to elementary schools
based on where they live and then feed into specific middle and high
schools (if the district has more than one). Still, this narrative shows
how parental exit affects the racial and socioeconomic composition
of schools even within the same district.

The second instance was similar to what Kristen described but
involved using residential addresses as a way to opt in to specific
schools. Educators in suburban schools most often elaborated on
this phenomenon; however, educators in four urban districts told me
parents would target certain areas of the city to ensure that their children attended certain schools. In these cases, parents reportedly said
that they wanted their children to attend a specific school to make
friendship networks with people from the same or a higher socioeconomic background, yet their decisions (consciously or unconsciously)
intensified racial—not just socioeconomic—stratification between
schools. Motivations aside, parents were not choosing schools based
on the performance of the teachers. Their decisions were based on
the backgrounds of the families.

The third instance involved a combination of parental behaviors
and organizational practices that were designed to alter how students
were assigned to schools. One situation involved a large urban district
that assigned students to certain "feeder" high schools based on
where they lived but allowed students to compete for slots in "elite"
high schools. The theory of action was that this competition would
spur students to perform better in the lower grades, since placements
were based on a combination of qualifying exams and grades. The
other situation involved an urban district that had adopted a lottery

system to determine who was placed in one of its three middle schools. The school was new and the lottery system was viewed as a fair way to distribute students between the two older middle schools and the brand-new one. The district eventually eliminated the lottery system and closed one of the two older middle schools. Students were then assigned to a middle school based on where they lived. Because parental decisions were the only changing variable, these examples are a natural experiment for exploring how exit affects school performance. In both cases, it resulted in social justice issues.

Shannon, a former urban elementary teacher and urban district student teacher supervisor, described how the competition for elite high school slots put a lot of stress on students: "Everything is about test scores. . . . Students need the test scores to get into good high schools . . . need to pass the test in order to graduate." She then talked about how this system appears to be "unbiased" (i.e., based on merit) yet ignores how SES influences performance and therefore who is allowed to attend these elite high schools. This includes student performance on entrance exams, but also the fact that parents choosing where to live stratifies elementary schools by SES and therefore affects individual and collective academic performance in lower grades (e.g., peer effects; see Chapter 5). The drain of the most engaged students then negatively affects the performance of the students who are left behind in the feeder high schools. In consequence, this practice stratifies performance across schools within this urban district and reproduces socioeconomic inequality, even while promoting itself as a merit-based system.

The other example appears to be even more unbiased than Shannon's since the students were assigned by lottery. Similar to the more overt competitive mechanism used by Shannon's district, though, random assignment resulted in socioeconomic inequality because the most engaged parents opted in to the lottery. What made these narratives so compelling is that they were identical regardless of where the informant worked, which indicates that these are not self-interested responses. Two middle school English teachers, Chloe (lottery school) and Stephanie (feeder school), had the following to say:

CHLOE: [Our students] were picked by lottery . . . which is fair because anyone had a shot. . . . Nonetheless, it wasn't fair . . . who's going to follow up on that. . . . I'm not saying that the other parents did not care, but the parents who were . . . go-getters wanted their kids to be in the new school. . . . More active parents . . . tend to have children who do better

. . . have high expectations and are involved. . . . Demographically we looked very similar . . . my middle school pretended . . . we did not serve different . . . students, but we really did. . . . We are back to feeder schools . . . see a *huge* difference. . . . [Before,] we had a different clientele . . . the whole climate was different because of it . . . a lot of school pride . . . teachers felt pride, too, because our students did much better in general.

STEPHANIE: [Last] year was the first year . . . not based on a lottery. . . . [Their test scores used to be way] higher . . . the gap was crazy; but last year they were only 6 percent ahead. . . . When you level the playing field, the outcomes score-wise . . . are really similar. . . . [It looked] like we were serving the same . . . demographically . . . and the kids came from the same community, but we all knew that we weren't. . . . [The lottery students] were coming from homes where the parents were really on top of things. . . . It is not always true, but the kids who are struggling the most . . . are having trouble at home. . . . A lot of times you cannot get a working phone number. . . . Parental involvement is so important. . . . Everybody has to be involved. It really does take a village.

Just as compelling, a high school teacher told me that these unequal experiences affected the performance of children beyond middle school. Clearly this is not a case of teachers displacing blame onto parents and students to evade being held accountable. Like Shannon, their complaint was that parental sorting had long-term consequences for students.

In sum, exit negatively affects those who are left behind through the outmigration of more active parents, teacher turnover, and the increased reliance on novice, alternatively certified, or uncertified teachers. Their schools are also disproportionately likely to serve a large number of academically at-risk students (e.g., ELLs and those with academic and behavioral issues) with an inadequate level of resources. Parents care about their children yet, in exercising their right to choose, consciously or unconsciously stratify public schools by race and SES. This widens the performance gap between schools and districts by positively influencing the performance of some and negatively affecting the performance of others.

The government has not been a neutral actor in these processes (see Chapters 2 and 11). As discussed, federal, state, and local policies historically subsidized white middle-class and upper-income flight from rural and urban areas to the suburbs while isolating minorities and low-income Americans in communities with fewer economic opportunities. The organization of public schools around geographic catchment areas and the use of property taxes to fund local public services then resulted in low-income and minority children being segregated in underfunded schools. Research supports participants' claim that schools with a disproportionately large number of low-income and minority students receive less funding and that school finances influence performance.[2] Segregation negatively influences student achievement, though, even without less funding. Studies suggest that this is due to the concentration of minorities in very high poverty schools (Reardon, 2015).[3]

The Unequal Effects of Voice

Hirschman (1970) described voice as the primary way that citizens influence the quality of public services. Fennell (2001) rightly notes, however, that solely conceptualizing voice as "speaking up" minimizes how parents and students influence school quality through their everyday acts of participation. My interviews confirm her claim that speaking up and participating are *both* important; they also support Hirschman's contention that voice and exit often work together to reduce performance because those who are left behind have the least capacity to generate improvements from within. Elaine provided compelling support for this phenomenon because she retired from her urban district and is now a substitute teacher in suburban schools:

> The discipline is so much easier. . . . [The] suburban district . . . [has] three "Title I (primarily low-income) schools," but they are nothing like . . . my urban district . . . should be very similar, but . . . [even] our so-called normal kids had all kinds of issues . . . angry . . . could not focus . . . emotional issues and . . . in some cases they should be in a special needs class but . . . parents . . . just did not know how to go about doing it. . . . There are so many other issues that these children and families were dealing with. . . . Over the course of my career . . . I had to spend more and more time on discipline. And . . . paperwork . . . because of all the discipline issues.

For the most part, informants portrayed these issues as resulting from differences in resources, capacity, and experiences—not different values.

Certainly some students arrive "less ready" or lack good study habits as a result of growing up in impoverished or disordered environments, but most educators conveyed that voice—in the form of speaking up and participating—stratifies experiences because quality-enhancing behaviors are more costly for some than for others. Socioeconomic inequality especially affects the willingness and capacity of marginalized groups to participate. A suburban elementary teacher (Terry) explained,

> [It is harder for socioeconomically disadvantaged] kids for many reasons. . . . [If] everyone was relatively equal then they would not stand out . . . [but] the community is relatively affluent. . . . They are lacking in things other kids take for granted . . . suffer inside . . . know . . . other moms, dads, and kids . . . look down on them. One . . . little guy, his mom . . . had a birthday party and invited all the boys in the class. . . . I went. . . . Not one little boy from the class went. She had put so much effort into that party . . . had all the relatives there. . . . It was because the party was in a trailer park. . . . [Parents have told me they do not come to school] because of other parents. Some . . . don't have a high school education . . . don't have good teeth . . . that sounds like a weird example. They don't have the "things" that everyone else has. So they don't come.

Voice is unlikely to improve services in ways that help *all* students, as portrayed in recent education discourse, for two other reasons. It is not necessarily productive and parents may not be keeping their "eyes on the street" for everyone in the school or classroom. My interviews suggest that it is more useful to conceptualize voice as a continuum, with some forms helping individuals but having negative repercussions for other students, the classroom, and/or the school.

Participatory voice involves attempts to resolve problems in ways that are engaged yet nonthreatening. It is "democratic," because participants are willing to consider other viewpoints as well as communal concerns or needs, and tends to improve children's performance by encouraging hard work and providing outside assistance. Contrary to the "eyes on the street" narrative, though, educators said that active involvement at home is more crucial than merely being present in the school. They cited a range of behaviors, such as reading to children, helping with homework, and collaborating with teachers to develop ways to address academic, behavioral, and emotional issues—both at home and at school—so that children will thrive.

In contrast, *competitive voice* describes parental efforts to seek favorable treatment for their children through positive means; these behaviors may or may not negatively affect other children, but often undermine children's willingness to work hard by causing them to expect adults to "do it for them." *Aggressive voice* is a step beyond competitive voice. It reflects an intolerance of opposing viewpoints and entails attempts to win without regard for the effects on the community or individuals within the group. Aggressive voice negatively affects performance by reducing children's willingness to cooperate at school. It occurs when parents or students constantly challenge school or teacher actions and priorities, demand unearned or unentitled benefits, or threaten litigation to gain advantages for their own children at the expense of "other people's kids."

The most frequent examples of *aggressive voice* dealt with services for students with special needs—where parental demands were often backed by the threat of litigation if the school did not comply. It is important to note that educators acknowledged a need for strong legal protections owing to a history of discrimination against children with special needs; they also recommended that parents be strong advocates for their children. They were discussing situations where parental demands impeded their ability to maintain social order and put other students at risk of physical and/or emotional harm. One common example was when parents ignore the advice of professionals, such as doctors, counselors, social workers, or teachers. When asked to expand on this concern, informants mentioned, among other things, that parents sometimes take their children off medicine that helps control their behaviors, without the advice of physicians, or demand placement in "regular" (i.e., included) classrooms rather than self-contained classrooms for children with extreme behavioral and/or emotional issues.[4] These behaviors tend to stratify educational experiences because middle- and upper-income parents are reportedly more likely to push for services and inclusion. In these cases, it is critical for teachers to advocate for *all* children, even though it sometimes puts them at odds with (powerful) parents.

The most frequent example of *competitive voice* involved parental demands for "rigor," meaning AP classes, gifted and talented programs, and other forms of accelerated instruction. As mentioned, these demands "snowballed" as tracking was eliminated from the normalized curriculum. Participants also discussed parental requests to place their children with specific teachers. Those I interviewed did not appear to have any issues with these requests if they stemmed from parental beliefs that their children would relate better to a specific teaching style. Some of these requests, though, are due to perceptions that specific teachers are "easy graders" and will therefore help their children compete in a "race" for college placements. Others are designed to ensure that their children will be pooled with higher performing or higher SES students. All of these behaviors appear to be more prevalent in suburban schools.

Parents may or may not be aware of how these behaviors affect others in the school or classroom; however, educators—like Sarah, a suburban elementary teacher—described how these demands often create issues:

> [Teachers] make up the classrooms for . . . the following year. . . . They are supposed to make it balanced . . . highs and lows, friendships, gender, kids who should be kept away . . . or be put together. . . . It takes *days* . . . *hours* after school. . . . [A teacher in my grade] was so strict . . . teachers didn't want children . . . to be harmed so she really only got above average . . . strongly motivated . . . no behavior problems. . . . [Some parents knew and would request her so that their kids were placed] with the gifted kids. . . . [Low-income families] are not "in-the-know." . . . Upper socioeconomic neighborhoods . . . [networking and volunteering would] observe you, their child, other children . . . kids' behavior and ability . . . use this information. . . . I had a class . . . the first-grade teacher told me before I had them, "Never . . . have I had a class like this" . . . and I had to *literally* change my entire program. . . . [I felt] *horrible* . . . could not do enough . . . to make up for this class. . . . [Teachers the following year were saying] "they are *killing* me. I am going to have a nervous breakdown."

In this example, parental participation resulted in negative peer effects by pooling those with academic, behavioral, and emotional issues in the same classroom. Sarah conveys how that negatively affects the performance of these students over time, as learned behaviors transfer across grades and classrooms. She also alludes to how this creates social justice issues.

Schools with a large number of engaged parents do tend to perform better than those with mostly disengaged parents; however, voice does not necessarily "raise all boats." Middle- and upper-income parents are more likely to access the information that fosters voice and therefore the resulting benefits. There is also a fine line between aggressive, competitive, and participatory voice and sometimes parents do not realize that this line is being crossed. Sarah, who we just heard from, and Sheila, a suburban elementary speech pathologist, described these *helicopter parents*:

SHEILA: [They] hover. . . . It is *over involvement* . . . not letting their kids resolve their own problems even for minor things. . . . I am not talking about depressing or upsetting situations. . . . [It is things like] not sitting next to [a specific child]. . . . There are degrees of when a parent should get involved and those degrees seem to have been removed. . . . When you get those children in your class . . . [you have to] be on guard. . . . You do not see poorer children's parents do this. . . . [It is] going on among middle class and upper middle class . . . [with a] higher education level. . . . Their child is never the problem.

SARAH: [They] have devoted their *lives* to these kids . . . do not allow . . . any consequences . . . [saying things like] "she will be *so* upset she has to go to the workroom because she forgot to do her assignment," and you say, "We don't hang them by their toes in workroom [*laughs*]. . . . This is . . . how they learn."

The phrase often used was that some parents behave as if "Harvard is on the line . . . [*pause for effect*] in kindergarten."

When schools are aware of these issues, they may be able to mitigate them, but my interviews suggest that some teachers are uninformed. Rhonda, a suburban elementary school aide, told a particularly compelling narrative because her children attended the school where she worked and so she knew "the players":

Many of them are home and on the higher end of the socioeconomic spectrum. . . . [Some volunteer] for the right reasons . . . [but most are] only trying to help their own children . . . get the inside scoop . . . butter up the principal . . . get their child into the best classes or student council. . . . Then other kids . . . get ostracized. . . . Parents want their child to play with certain kids but not others and know who to invite over and . . . to birthday parties. . . . They are *very,* very savvy. But, the staff doesn't know . . . the "wolf in sheep's clothing" . . . [give] gifts to the teachers . . . participate in the PTA [Parent Teacher Association] . . . run the "teacher appreciation breakfasts" . . . [but are] spreading anything . . . which should be confidential. . . . The staff begins to forget that these are parents because they are always in helping. . . . It is like a network that helps advance certain kids but not others . . . tell who was in the principal's office . . . gets in trouble . . . difficulty in school . . . [families] going through a divorce . . . having financial difficulties . . . who was a good kid for their kids to play with. . . . Their kids were not choosing. . . . The parents . . . [choose children's friends] because . . . their parents were high status or . . . wanted to be friends with the kid's parents for whatever reason. . . . It is very competitive . . . trying to get their kids into the right things in elementary . . . middle . . . high school. . . . [So they] talk about who are the easy graders, even in elementary school.

Rhonda claimed teachers were stressed as a "result of all the testing" and relied on "extra hands." Some forgot that (most) parents are there to keep their "eyes on the street" for their own children or the children of parents who are in their social networks. This is one way that testing combines with a stratified participatory system to leave underprivileged children behind.

As a group, educators expressed a belief that parents are increasingly using aggressive and competitive voice to maximize their own children's consumption and compete more favorably in the race for college admissions and employment opportunities. Parents are rightfully worried about safety and concerned that their children will not exceed their own SES in today's hypercompetitive economic climate. Sheila continued:

> [It] is like an "overconcern" . . . for safety. . . . We think each generation should be [better off]. . . . Parents are worried that this will not be the case. . . . Things are tough economically. . . . Everybody wants the best for their children, but this is . . . taking it to the extreme. . . . They are not going to sit back and let him or her try to figure out things . . . through the power of suggestion or learning through experience . . . it is too risky. . . . It is more about . . . parents' maneuvering. . . . [Kids] are not allowed to be just kids. . . . Play and learn from playing . . . is a big part of development. But everything is organized for them. . . . Parents can't get them into enough activities. . . . Everybody wants that "well-rounded" child, because colleges look at that. . . . We all hope for that, but . . . children are burnt out.

Beyond the classroom examples already provided, informants discussed budgetary demands that unequally distribute services between students, such as cutting funds for some programs (e.g., sports, art, or special education) to fund others that benefit their children (e.g., AP classes) without raising taxes. They also mentioned an increased willingness to vote down school budgets because they fund programs that do not benefit their own.

Again, educators were not shaming parents. They perceive that policy makers, the media and entertainment industry, and business-economic interests contributed to the normalization of aggressive and competitive voice by politicizing education, stimulating parental fears through negative stories about public schools, failing to redress social and economic issues (e.g., school shootings, rising socioeconomic inequality), and adopting public policies that help the most well-off (see Chapters 3 and 11). This finding is important because voice—like exit—creates *spillover effects*; parents influence the behaviors of their own children, but also other parents and other people's children.

In general, informants used the language of "contagion" to show how social behaviors spread. When parents see "other people's children" gaining a competitive advantage and/or that "the squeaky wheel gets the grease," they, too, try to level the playing field. Over time, these behaviors become "normalized," meaning they are "naturalized" (extended to non-school environments), "mushroom" (become more aggressive), and "snowball" to other parents and students through peer effects.[5] Returning to Sheila's narrative,

> They get used to behaving that way. . . . It becomes how you're supposed to behave. . . . You don't even realize you're doing it because you get caught up in it . . . hanging out with people who are doing the same thing [*laughs*]. . . . So it becomes the norm . . . what "normal" people do. And things become more and more competitive, and it seems like everything is on the line even for very small matters. . . . They are doing sports and . . . other activities . . . to get into college, but it starts way back in elementary school. . . . It is *soooo* time consuming. . . . Kids are not doing their homework because they are so busy outside of school. . . . It seems counterproductive . . . I just saw on TV that parents are going to their child's jobs and complaining about their evaluation . . . job situation . . . [or] that their child did not get the job. . . . Parents call college professors and complain about . . . grades. . . . Ten years ago . . . maybe you had one. . . . [But] it mushrooms. . . . One parent does it . . . it spirals out of control because parents . . . don't want their child disadvantaged because other parents are demanding things for their children.

In extreme cases, aggressive and competitive voice impede educators' ability to create social order and may lead to a rapid degeneration in service quality.

Educators conveyed that aggressive and competitive voice erode the efficiency and effectiveness of public schools even in less extreme cases; they reduce social cohesion, necessitate more overt forms of social control, and draw educators' time and effort away from planning, teaching, and positively interacting with students. Jess, a suburban elementary teacher, elaborated on these complex social processes:

> [Parents] want to help their children, but it can be counterproductive. First, children need to learn from experience and that is not going to happen if parents are constantly "doing" things for them and not

giving them the independence to try and fail, and learn from that; to have consequences for behaviors. . . . Second, you are taking on an emotional burden that isn't yours and blowing something up perhaps out of proportion. . . . Parents have become more educated themselves, they understand . . . the importance of an AP class . . . [for] college and then getting . . . a good job . . . the pressure from the economy . . . technology. . . . They have an emotional connection to this child. . . . I respect that, but, in return, you need to respect what I'm telling you as a professional. . . . [I've learned] to just listen . . . and repeat back the emotions . . . the topics . . . [and to] back up . . . [what I say and do in the classroom, so that I can say,] "Here's what they are weak at . . . strong with . . . what you can do . . . what I'm going to do." Usually that will help. . . . [Luckily] I've always had administrators who . . . [back me up because now when] people are angry they want to go right to the top.

Similar to Jess, most teachers conveyed that they must now be able to "back up" what they say and do in the classroom because more parents today "go right to the top" when angry. Administrators then expend more effort trying to control what occurs in the classroom to reduce the "fallout" from angry parents. These are both forms of social control. In addition, as evident in Molly's and Sarah's narratives, parental demands for rigor have led to organizational practices that pool children with the most severe behavioral, emotional, and academic needs in the same classrooms, resulting in issues that require other forms of social control (e.g., detention, suspension, and expulsion). This impedes performance and creates social justice issues through the downward leveling effects of neglect.

Neglect: "Once They Get That Label, They Can't Shake It"

Hirschman (1970) does not discuss how neglect influences service quality. It was later added to his model, but the construct is implicit in his claim that *exit* is unlikely to improve performance because those who are left behind are the least likely to generate improvements. In its passive form, neglect involves withdrawal or nonparticipation, such as not voting (the political space) and not participating in class (the coproduction space). In its more active form, it involves shirking and noncompliance by disobeying laws, refusing to do homework and study for exams, or cheating on tests. Educators also described acts of sabotage, such as stealing a teacher's grade book. I would argue that these acts belong under competitive and aggressive voice. That keeps the distinction between voice—in its positive and negative forms—and neglect.

Like neglect, voice includes nonparticipation or noncompliance; however, it is action geared toward something (positive or negative) and typically involves feelings of (political or personal) efficacy and/or feelings of entitlement. Voice involves everything from active resistance to civil disobedience and conscientious objections (refusing to comply for reasons of conscience). It may even include nonvoting if a conscious intent to express opposition to a political system, government policies, or the candidates in a particular election. Neglect may sometimes be a form of protest, but it is frequently accompanied by *fatalism,* such as feeling that "You can't fight City Hall." It may also simply be a way to shirk responsibility or free ride off the contributions of others.

In the civic sphere, studies show that some citizens are less likely to vote, engage in prosocial behaviors, and mobilize on behalf of social, political, and economic causes. Research suggests that nonparticipation reflects institutional barriers more than cultural differences. For example, nonvoting is higher among young people, the poor, minorities, and those with a high school diploma or less. All of these groups have historically faced legal restrictions that suppress registration and voting (Piven & Cloward, 1988); many still do today (Boschma, 2021; Brennan Center for Justice, 2021). Similarly, my interviews suggest that nonparticipation at school is (largely) a function of structural issues rather than different values. Because of the link between poverty and academic outcomes, negative experiences at school tend to stratify participation by race and socioeconomic status.

Research supports educators' claim that parents who struggled in school often feel uncomfortable participating.[6] In addition, students often act up or opt out (noncompliance and nonparticipation) as a way of coping with limited capacity. A suburban elementary aide (Rhonda) and an urban (Kristen) elementary teacher discussed these issues:

RHONDA: The kids were usually very good at accepting the children who were low functioning or had disabilities. . . . But the students who struggle . . . felt embarrassed . . . don't want to . . . be different. . . . [Some] did not want me to help . . . would act out . . . be rude . . . So, some of the behavioral problems . . . [are] related to the learning issues. They would rather . . . I don't like using those words, but be known as the "bad kid" than the kid who had learning issues. . . . [But then it's] tough . . . for people to forget . . . you were the bad . . . [or] drug kid. . . . Once they get that label, they can't shake it.

KRISTEN: I was so nervous [my first back-to-school night]. . . . It never gets easier actually, but . . . you work hours getting your classroom set up. . . . I am there more than I am at home. It is the children's home too. . . . I make sure . . . the kids . . . respect the classroom . . . straighten things up and keep our home nice. . . . I still get giddy thinking about . . . my first classroom. . . . [We had] put out snacks for the parents to . . . feel welcome . . . I had only like five or six . . . but that was an amazing turnout. . . . [My colleague] didn't have one . . . a lot . . . did not have positive school experiences . . . to get them back into school is a big step. . . . [Now, I call home and] say, "I hope . . . you can stop in even if . . . only . . . a few minutes" . . . make it sound . . . casual so that they are not intimidated. . . . It takes a long time . . . but has helped.

These narratives show how socioeconomic inequality combines with the coproduction of educational outcomes to create challenges for educators, even when they are trying to be inclusive. They are important for another reason. Individual neglect affects collective performance through peer effects. Portes's (1998) concept of downward leveling norms is useful for explaining how this occurs.

Downward leveling norms arise from situations where group solidarity is cemented through common experiences of adversity and opposition to mainstream society. Social reproduction theorists use this concept to show how adverse experiences and/or negative perceptions about academic and employment opportunities structure low-income and minority students' optimism and conformity to the cultural standards that are imposed by schools and society. Empirical research shows that low-income and minority children are aware that the deck is stacked against them; the perception that their effort and hard work will not be rewarded in the academic and/or labor market increases the likelihood that some will opt-out (nonparticipation), self-select out of the college track in middle- and high school, develop oppositional cultures or countercultures, or refuse to display characteristics that they feel will not be rewarded in school or in life. These stances limit their compliance with school norms and standards, resulting in lower academic achievement and attainment. In this way, downward leveling norms keep some members in place while forcing more ambitious members to flee the group to succeed.[7]

When combined, this and other research suggests that schools, as communities and public institutions, are spaces where students develop "social capital" (rewards through relationships); however, loyalty to the group sometimes reinforces disengagement and other behaviors that negatively affect academic achievement and attainment. If exit becomes the default mechanism for those who are doing well, it may foster a downward academic spiral for the least advantaged by redistributing rewards (e.g., popularity or status) and punishments in ways that promote neglect, meaning growing numbers cease to generate improvements from within owing to reduced feelings of self-efficacy and a belief that voice (speaking up or participating) will not change things.

For the most part, educators blamed these social-psychological effects on living in communities that are struggling economically. The exodus of those with the most resources and capacity has replaced a vision of what is possible (hope) with what is visible (adversity). Stephanie, from whom we heard earlier, described these invisible or intangible costs:

> [It] is hard to make up for certain things. . . . [I was] a middle-of-the-road . . . [suburban] student. . . . People would say . . . "What college *are* you going to?" It was expected . . . when you have a 40 percent graduation rate, they are just trying to get kids through high school . . . be engaged enough . . . to graduate. . . . I had all my students write to colleges. . . . [They] said things like, "Why should we do that? They don't want us." I had colleges write us back that *were* really interested. . . . Kids take those kinds of things for granted in suburbia.

The proximity of adversity and remoteness of hope alters the attitudes (futility), aspirations, and behaviors (neglect) of students; they are being influenced by a belief about what they are *able* to achieve by *observing* those around them. Research supports these claims.[8] When viewed through this lens, exit does not impose costs merely through the loss of tax revenues; it does so through the ways that it affects the attitudes, beliefs, and behaviors of those who are left behind.

Students of color are more likely to be a part of what, according to educators, society views as "disposable communities"—underfunded schools, immigrant and low-income communities, living at the margin in middle- and upper-income communities—because their families are disproportionately likely to be poor, but informants portrayed socioeconomic inequality, poverty, hunger, and other "wicked problems" as having pernicious effects on children regardless of racial or ethnic background. According to them, children in these situations feel like they are "stamped" with negative social regard—irrespective of their racial or ethnic background. Kim, an urban middle school teacher, described how this affected her students:

[A girl] was tragically shot . . . in the community. The kid who acciden-
tally shot her was 15 years old . . . from a very specific neighborhood . . .
that has a lot of problems. . . . [The] school [is not violent]. . . . The kids
obey the rules. . . . [I had grieving children and they discussed how the
media made them] and everyone in the neighborhood look like they
were violent . . . bad . . . had guns. . . . The public was responding . . .
"They are all gun-toting thugs . . . welfare recipients . . . we are paying
for" . . . really brutal [comments] because they could be anonymous. . . .
The kids were expressing that it was hurtful. . . . [I started a blog and] for
once our school was in the newspaper in a positive way. . . . [Students]
saying a lot of really profound things. . . . [It was] hard for adults to smack
them down. . . . [They] had to listen. . . . The kids felt really empowered
. . . like they had a voice.

Rhonda's earlier narrative shows that children find it hard to escape
labels that result from their own behaviors, such as the "bad kid."
Kim is conveying how children encounter messages about what "society" (i.e., other children, adults, communities, and the government)
thinks about "people like them." Those messages teach them about
who matters and who does not.

Respondents agreed that parents and students care about distributive, social, and procedural justice—such as socioeconomic equality and due process—not just performance. They also care about
how "their group" is constructed by public discourse. Perceptions
of injustice or unfairness are reportedly correlated with low aspirations and negative behaviors at school, including, but not limited
to, apathy and alienation. Per Kim and others, many learn that they
are not "worthy" of societal rewards and government attention; this
influences how they *feel* about themselves, their communities, society,
and the government. She continued:

[The children talked] about the label that they were thugs. How hurtful
it was. . . . They have had other things where they were portrayed very
poorly. . . . They are not really vocal about it, but they do say things like,
"We are not all like that. Why do they say we're *all* bad?" and "Why does
that store *close* every day? I can't even get *juice* there." . . . Some of the
businesses that are near or around the school close the hour after school
lets out because they don't want *those* kids coming in. It is hurtful. . . .
They believe that a small amount of kids ruin it for everyone. And . . .
generalize that to businesses . . . schools . . . government. They often feel
like they are stamped with that . . . negative impression . . . can't escape it.

In these cases, individuals must escape the "collective"—distance themselves through exit—to avoid being part of what society has characterized as an "undeserving group." That reduces voice and social cohesion (political and social capital), making it difficult to fight for reform.

The narratives in this section convey why policy makers should not evaluate public institutions (e.g., public education and education policies), public organizations (e.g., public schools), and public servants (e.g., teachers) based on efficiency and effectiveness alone. For better or worse, public servants, institutions, organizations, and discourse convey messages about individuals and groups, including whether they are respected, deserving, undeserving, incapable, feared, hated, or pitied, and teach citizens about their rights and responsibilities in a democratic society. These messages influence citizens' willingness to participate (i.e., neglect as withdrawal) and also affect how they participate (i.e., exit, voice, and neglect as noncompliance). When parents and children perceive that they are part of a caring community, they are more likely to pull their behaviors in line in ways that promote individual and collective outcomes. Chapter 5 discussed how this improves classroom performance.

In contrast, Kassidy described how working in a racially and economically stratified suburban district, where affluent parents controlled how the school was run through aggressive and competitive voice, affected educators and students:

> You had no protection . . . the principal was as much at mercy with the parents as you. . . . It was not so much about the learning as it was about numbers and prestige . . . even in elementary school . . . to get into the best schools . . . [get] the best jobs. . . . Behavior and how they treated one another . . . [the] parents could care less about that. It was all about . . . advanced classes, and . . . a 95 or above. . . . It puts stress on the whole building. . . . They needed to get a grade . . . did not need to get it from you in a nice way, or by working for it . . . were just going to fight you for it anyway and . . . would win. . . . There was no respect for. . . your professional judgment. . . . [The school was] 90 percent [white] . . . and 10 percent Black and the Black kids cleaned the white kids' houses. . . . There was such a contrast in their lifestyles. . . . They were at such a disadvantage in every way . . . so far behind, that by third or fourth grade . . . they shut down . . . because they knew that they could not compete. . . . It was hard to work in that environment. The kids were completely segregated. They wouldn't interact with one another. Even as early as fourth grade, it was a hierarchy. They knew that these kids

were beneath them. The parents' attitudes totally affected the kids. And the kids would say things like, "You can't do this because my parent is going to x, y, z." They did not view you as an authority figure. They knew their parents were above you.

Kassidy's comment that some students "shut down" because they perceived the deck was stacked against them is a classic case of downward leveling neglect.

This narrative is an extreme case, but it shows why it is important to consider power dynamics *between* citizens, not just between public servants and citizen coproducers; it is also critical to place the behaviors of both groups within their broader political, social, and economic contexts. Many educators described the difficulties they experience when parents create situations that are unjust or unsafe for "other people's children." Anger was a prevalent emotion in these situations. In part, it reflected a total disregard for their professional expertise; however, educators also care about distributive, social, and procedural justice.

Certainly some studies find that institutional agents (e.g., administrators, teachers, coaches, guidance staff, and secretaries) are less responsive to marginal, nonconforming parents and students and act in ways that discourage them from seeking support.[9] Research also documents racial and socioeconomic biases in student–school and teacher–parent relationships and shows that public schools and public policies have historically relegated low-income and minority children to lower-tracked classes and underfunded schools.[10] Educators' narratives suggest, however, that institutional agents play a complex role in children's educational outcomes.

Administrators and teachers can and do make a difference, yet they, too, battle the pernicious effects of societal issues—like poverty, hunger, segregation, and socioeconomic inequality—on children's aspirations and behaviors. They also see children for a limited number of hours per day and days per year. Children spend far more time in their communities and with their families and peers. It is therefore not surprising that educators linked educational issues to the broader *cultural political economy*—the norms, values, mores, languages, and shared experiences that structure a nation's political, social, and economic systems, especially our nation's tolerance for (de jure and de facto) segregation, childhood poverty, and socioeconomic inequality.

If enough educators engage in *ethical leaving* (exit teaching or the district), it *may* create a teaching shortage and positively influence organizational practices or public policies, but my interviews suggest that this is unlikely. Kassidy, for instance, disclosed that her district was "never short for new hires" because it was perceived to be a good place to work owing to its relative wealth. Thus, as Hirschman (1970) predicted, exit is not a sufficient recuperative mechanism; it removes pressure for reform because the most "quality-conscious" flee. In Kassidy's case, it was teachers who could not tolerate social injustice and either left or were (overtly or covertly) pushed out because they refused to go along.

These kinds of narratives are interesting in their own right; they are especially illuminating, though, when linked to policy makers' justification for NCLB, RttT, and NCLB waivers. Policy makers argued that parental voice and choice would "raise all boats" by ensuring educators "do right by the kids." Implicitly or explicitly, they blamed the soft bigotry of low expectations for the gap between poor and minority children and their more advantaged peers. According to my interviews, this theory of action fails to acknowledge that parents have different propensities and capacities to influence educational processes, and both are highly correlated with SES. It also ignores the ways that parents—in pursing their own interests—may actually harm "other people's children." Yet this and a large body of research show that parents use their social ties and cultural capital to advance their own children at the expense of nonconnected children and families;[11] they also activate their cultural and social capital in ways that structure unequal academic, work, and life experiences for children.[12]

Differences in *cultural capital* affect the ability of low-income parents to comply with the evaluative standards of public and private institutions. This affects their children because parents transmit their engagement styles by "coaching" their children on how to interact with institutional agents to improve their educational outcomes (Lareau & Weininger, 2003). The segregation of parental social networks by SES also perpetuates inequalities. Middle- and upper-income parents tend to have more *social capital*; they also get more "bang for their buck" from their social ties. Lower SES, immigrant status, and lower levels of education tend to be associated with *less* social capital and *impede the use* of social capital as well.[13] This social disadvantage partially relates to the "architecture" of parental networks. Middle- and upper-income parents are more likely to have professionals in their networks, which provides them with the expertise, authority, and information to contest the judgments of educational gatekeepers.[14]

Within this environment, educators are often the sole barrier to the pernicious effects of socioeconomic inequality on children's educational outcomes *precisely because,* as public servants, they care about *all* children, not just their own. Yet they, too, must cope with the ways that the free market (parents choosing where to live), government policies (e.g., inequitable school financing), socioeconomic inequality, and "wicked problems" affect their jobs. When neglect stems from moral or ethical concerns and spreads to others, it may actually be salutary for institutions, organizations, and society. Those benefits will not occur, however, unless there is an open dialogue about why people are "opting out." Schools, communities, governments, and society will also fail to thrive without some level of loyalty to counter the negative effects of exit, voice, and neglect.

Loyalty: "We Take All the Blueberries"

In his book *The Blackboard and the Bottom Line,* Cuban (2004, pp. 3–5) relays a story about a successful ice cream maker telling teachers how to improve public education by running it like a business. Under cross-examination, he admitted that his success resulted from carefully selecting the finest blueberries and throwing out those that did not meet his high standards. A teacher replied, but we don't "send back our blueberries. We take them rich, poor, gifted, exceptional, abused, frightened . . . take them all! Every one! And that . . . is why it's not a business. It's a school!" It would seem more appropriate to use this story in the section on exit because it is about market behaviors; however, the words of the handful of teachers who relayed it to me suggest that it struck a chord for another reason. It conveys what gets lost when voice and choice become both the means and the ends of defining what qualifies as high-quality public services. I am referring to this as loyalty, but educators described it as a commitment to something larger than our individual selves—like the intangibles that are promoted through our common spaces, such as the common school ideal.

Their words reminded me of L. Cohen's (2003) claim that something was lost as a result of the "Consumer's Republic." The example she used was the promotion of shopping malls as the new "civic centers" of suburban towns in the 1950s. As this form of (social, economic, and political) organization drew businesses and consumers away from urban centers and small towns, people began to realize that these private spaces were not the same as the public ones that they had replaced. The owners, for instance, could restrict free speech and assembly because of their private legal status. In contrast, both are allowed—yet mostly taken for granted—in the public spaces outside of "main street" stores and businesses, like sidewalks, streets, and parks. With fewer people shopping on Main Street, though, businesses closed and there were fewer "eyes" on all "streets." Research shows that the latter provide an informal source of social control that improves public safety (J. Jacobs, 1992). Something similar occurs with teachers' presence in the hallways; however, the "eyes on the street" narrative does not hold true for parents because, in contrast to public safety, they do not necessarily share the same interests with respect to public schools. These findings are not contradictory. Rising concerns about unsafe sidewalks, streets, parks, and schools resulted in more people withdrawing into privatized spaces, like athletic clubs, private schools, and suburban enclaves; the urban and rural communities and schools that they left behind then fell into economic, political, and social decline.

Of course the suburbs have public spaces too, but the need to travel by car often isolates and disconnects citizens; they are also more likely to engage with "people like them," meaning people from similar economic, racial, and ethnic backgrounds. When people become spatially isolated by race, ethnicity, and SES, their social ties with people who are "not like them" atrophy and they increasingly become isolated by distrust of "others." These developments affect our political life for two interrelated reasons. What keeps a democratic society healthy is not solely its mechanisms for enabling citizens to participate in the political sphere or its commitment to delimiting government's "monopolization" of the private sphere. It is those "spaces" (e.g., physical places, public policies, public discourse) that sustain our *public life*, defined as the place where we engage our fellow citizens. When public life includes encounters with people who are not like us, it integrates society and improves the quality of political debate and participation by making it more likely that citizens perceive that they share things in common—despite all of their differences. This is what sociologists mean by social capital. It includes our bonding ties of close friends and family but, more critically, the linking and bridging ties that are important for our social and economic lives, as well as for democracy.

Phrased another way, the public realm binds us together as a society. Within that space, people build the social bonds that may lead to political and economic ones. Many people will never open a business or participate in politics beyond the individual act of voting. Others would never go into politics or open a business on their own, yet may do so in the company of others. The public realm conjoins our private and public lives; expands citizens' access to politics; and creates the physical spaces where individuals construct the weak (bridging and linking) ties that increase access to cultural, political, and economic capital, as well as other opportunities. All of these intangibles are what we lose when we destroy our public life. It is therefore disheartening to hear educators say that our public spaces—both real and imagined, like public schools and the public school ideal—are being destroyed by public discourse and policies that eulogize exit and competition over other public values, such as participation, equality, and justice. These developments have undermined the idea that democracy cannot work unless people *opt in for the common good*.

As shown, educators view recent education reforms as the institutionalization of these developments and perceive that these policies have implications for democracy. Those views are particularly evident in how they, versus policy makers, framed charter schools. The latter portrayed charter—especially "public" charter—schools as *David* in need of protection from *Goliath* (the public school monopoly). They deserve protection because they provide a "safety valve" for low-income and minority children who are trapped in failing public schools. Educators, in contrast, portrayed charter schools as privatized "public" spaces that do not "take all the blueberries." Chloe, an urban middle school English teacher, proclaimed,

> [Those] who follow up on the lottery are the most active and engaged parents. . . . Not always, but usually, they have the most active and engaged children. . . . They say they do not cherry-pick . . . [but charter schools] make it impossible for the kids they don't want . . . to stay . . . suspend them so much. And the parents can't keep staying home . . . have to send them back to the public schools. . . . This is above and beyond . . . [the need for safety, yet] public schools . . . have to educate them no matter what. . . . They are allowed to do all kinds of things that we are not allowed to do . . . rules requiring parents to volunteer . . . we are now supposed to "compete" . . . always being compared . . . [yet] the parent volunteer thing . . . shows you how you could cherry-pick. By creating this rule, they now have the parents who are most able or willing to volunteer . . . the most engaged . . . who have the ability to take time off from work . . . the means to get to the schools . . . available childcare.

While the population looks the same "on paper" (i.e., demographically), charter schools actually serve less needy children because the most engaged parents and those with more social and economic capital—like transportation and childcare—opt in.

Charter schools also set up contractual relationships that provide them with far more control over parents' and students' behaviors and allow them to reject "undesirable blueberries." Stephanie, who worked in a charter school before teaching in an urban middle school, described how that worked:

> [At our] morning meeting . . . [we did different] dances . . . brainwashing . . . a whole culture that is like indoctrination . . . . chant things like "knowledge is power" . . . almost corporal punishment. Students had to stand there with their hands at their side and people could call you out and yell things at you. It was really militaristic. . . . We were told that, if a kid talked back . . . we all had to gang up on the kid. . . . Places that have problems with violence, it can spiral out of control. . . . But that was not the kind of teacher I wanted to be. . . . [Some] believe that . . . strict, militaristic punishment approach works. I don't think it did.

Stephanie became an *ethical leaver*. She exited and went to work in an urban school because she objected to the teaching philosophy and the "counseling out" of needy students. In her words,

> [instead] of trying to help . . . the charter school would get rid of them . . . even the slightest problem . . . throw kids away . . . counsel them out . . . call parents for every little thing . . . bringing them in . . . tell them . . . "If you do not take your child out, we will expel them and it will be on their record forever." There were ways . . . to get these kids out without ever having to go through a formal process. . . . Charter schools say that they are not picking the cream of the crop because anyone can come in. That is true. . . . But they weed them out . . . offered me all kinds of money to stay, but . . . I went into teaching to make a difference.

These charter school behaviors were discussed by almost every urban public school educator and over half of the suburban educators in this study, but the charter school teachers I interviewed confirmed Stephanie's claims.[15]

According to these testimonies, voice and choice are misnomers when describing why some charter schools outperform public schools. Just as interesting, *all* of these stories were about "public" charter schools.[16] Thus, even in their "public" guise, charter schools are not David—in need of government support so that they may rescue other *Davids* (poor and minority children). They are a business. They have different rules than public schools. While a couple of studies have been used to claim that charter schools do not "cream skim"—take only the most motivated students—or discriminate against ELLs and students with disabilities, these findings, like much of the research on school choice, are empirically contested.[17]

Public school educators further complained that the outflow of revenues from SINI schools has harmed those who remain in the public school system, while the benefits to those who attend charter schools are minimal to nonexistent. As mentioned, students in SINI schools are allowed to transfer to public charter schools within the district. The resources follow the child so that their home districts receive less funding. Educators said that this exacerbates the already unjust way we fund public schools. First, it disproportionately harms schools where property taxes are already blighted through the exit of the most well-off. Second, charter school "cream skimming" reduces the performance of those who are left behind in the public schools through downward leveling peer effects. Third, public schools must then provide more services and invest in more expensive (and punitive) means of maintaining social order. Nancy, a retired urban school teacher and administrator, alluded to many of these issues:

> I hired teachers who had taught at charter schools . . . gained a pretty up close and personal glimpse through . . . the antidotes they shared . . . about the limitations of those schools. . . . [A lot of the issues stemmed from] being run as a business, so . . . [for example, teachers were] required to teach a certain way and to teach things at certain times. . . . [They encouraged] special needs kids and kids with behavioral issues to leave. . . . A lot of calls home and students being sent home. . . . They would be interrupted at work and so forth. . . . There are no charters in that district anymore. . . . They didn't do as good a job . . . and it was very sad because those resources follow the child . . . [and] we were left with more needy students. . . . [So, it hurt the public school, yet] for that same amount of resources, they got a much better education. . . . The parents figured it out . . . the business model did not work.

As shown in Parts II and III, more punitive forms of social control (e.g., detention or suspension) are harmful for children's development and academic outcomes, but informants said that school choice also harms us as a society by increasing segregation and exacerbating a school-to-prison pipeline that disproportionately harms students of color and students with academic, behavioral, and emotional needs.

Research supports educators' views. Charter schools perform no better, and often worse, than public schools; they have increased segregation by race, income, and language; and, they are more likely to suspend students, especially minorities and students with academic, emotional, and behavioral issues.[18] Although one study found that students in New York City public schools scored slightly higher on state math and reading tests after charter schools opened within a half mile, this finding is contested.[19]

Public school teachers further complained that charter schools are often given access to public property and sometimes share space with the public schools that they are putting out of business. They also often have more resources because they typically receive donations from the private sector. Research supports these claims.[20] This means public school students see firsthand how they are being denied equal resources. Just as problematically, when public schools close or lose space, children must leave their neighborhood schools and travel to other public schools. As shown in Chapter 6, parents expressed concerns about their children walking through unsafe spaces, exposing them to gun violence, drugs, and other dangers.

Educators in this study agreed with parents, yet also reported that school closings disrupt students' social ties and academic programs, increase behavioral issues, and decrease academic performance. Lorna, an urban elementary school teacher, explained:

> Sometimes they close the school and reopen it with a charter *in* the school or they reopen it *as* a charter school. And that is the big argument. . . . There's a charter but . . . not enough room for our children. . . . Our kids have to go elsewhere . . . because the charter recruits kids and . . . is very selective. . . . It's not right. They are using public buildings and the students are being funded by public dollars because the old school quote-on-quote failed. So, rather than give the public school more resources, we disrupt the lives of children . . . and teachers by forcing them to move to a new school. We disrupt that whole community.

Studies support that moving negatively influences children's social ties and academic achievement; a *high rate* of student mobility negatively affects overall school performance too.[21]

Educators further described how students learned different lessons about voice. Charter schools strictly regulate participatory voice yet encourage competitive voice. Tim, an urban charter school teacher, professed that one of the reasons they engage in the "group building" activities that Stephanie called "indoctrination" was to foster a sense of community and ameliorate some of the harmful effects of running schools like a business:

> It is very competitive. . . . We all try to really push each other . . . test scores dip . . . you are going to have a little bit more heat . . . to get you to step up . . . education being a business removes the joy . . . implicit rewards of learning . . . everything is tied to how well you do. . . . That creates a very individualistic and competitive environment. . . . Students are less likely to help one another . . . focused on . . . [helping] themselves get ahead. . . . It is a tightrope you are walking as a teacher . . . trying to create a communal discourse because everything is individual and numbers based . . . tied to explicit rewards. . . . If a student asks you, "Why can't I go on the field trip?" you say, "Well, let's look at the data . . . your numbers" . . . data, data, data. . . . Administrators . . . to run the school like a business . . . need to separate . . . [from us. It's] about you needing to get your . . . numbers up . . . [not] what you brought to the table. . . . [They want] you to be a little scared all the time . . . [wondering if you] would have a job . . . be replaced . . . switched out. . . . It is frustrating. . . . I've been reduced to a number.

According to Tim, this competitive environment encourages parents and students to engage in aggressive voice, but what he is actually describing is how his school needs to create social cohesion as a result of too much *competition,* which is a market-based form of social control.

Public school teachers and other charter school teachers confirmed Tim's claim that the competitive and individualistic environment at charter schools encourages aggressive voice; yet, if parents and students are too aggressive, the charter school "counsels them out." The public school must then deal with an exaggerated sense of entitlement. Returning to Chloe's narrative,

> [We] get a *huge* number of students from surrounding charter schools. . . . [Some] cannot read, and . . . all the [charter] school did was pass them on. . . . Two sisters . . . said, "You are not going to fail us! Our . . . teacher . . . [at the charter school] tried to fail us and my mother came and that teacher had to pass us." . . . They couldn't seem to understand . . . their mother didn't run the show here. . . . That's true of charter schools. . . . They want the money. . . . I have seen firsthand, but [also] . . . have heard this from many, *many* teachers. . . . The kids [from charter schools]

come in with this crazy sense of entitlement . . . of how they are going to control the teachers. . . . You are one of my 25 students . . . not the only one in this room.

Aggressive voice appears to be a negative side effect of a system that caters to parents as educational consumers while controlling parents, students, and educators through competition.

Just as importantly, public *and* charter school educators agreed that the charter school model is not sustainable for public schools. Their arguments are complicated, but the gist is that learning requires trust because it involves vulnerability.[22] While trust is important regardless of who "owns" the school (i.e., public, private, religious, or charter), different types of schools rely on different forms of trust. *Organic trust* is rooted in faith and largely unconditional. Members of social systems that are characterized by organic trust share a broad-based moral bond. In fundamentalist religious schools, for example, the actions of educators are supported—largely unquestioned—because the community shares attitudes and beliefs about the role of the school in society. This social cohesion is a form of social control that improves performance by causing people to pull their behaviors in line in ways that benefit the group. *Contractual trust* is more delimited. It is developed between parties that are involved in a transaction where the obligations and responsibilities are well specified and easily measured. Typically, a legal framework binds individuals, encourages them to carry out their obligations, and enables an aggrieved party to take action if another party fails to fulfill its part of the contract. That form of social control is evident in the contract that parents, students, and charter schools sign.

In contrast, *relational trust* is developed through sustained association over time. It is typically found in organizations and institutions that have multifaceted goals, like public schools, where the methods of achieving those goals are situation specific—versus controlled through SOPs—and obligations are diffuse in scope. It is critical for public schools (and many other public services) because learning is coproduced and it is difficult to assess if all parties are fulfilling their obligations.[23] Parents, principals, and school boards cannot be sure teachers are fulfilling their responsibilities—except through test scores that are a very limited measure of teaching and learning. Teachers cannot be certain parents are supporting the educational process at home or that principals and school boards are carrying out their responsibilities outside of the classroom. State and national policy makers cannot (easily) assess public school performance—much less determine who to reward or blame for it. These issues make it difficult to hold individuals accountable and increase the likelihood that public schools will suffer from what Olson (1965/1971) calls "collective action problems." It is in everyone's interest to promote the school's goals and objectives, yet no single actor is ultimately responsible and so no single actor may be blamed. This creates an incentive for members to free ride off the labor of others and results in public management issues.

Administrators need to create a productive work atmosphere without being certain what constitutes "good work" beyond the very limited measure of test scores. They also deal with complaints and crises without (typically) knowing if the complaint is justified and whether the crisis is symptomatic or atypical. According to J. Wilson (1991), these issues are likely to create a high degree of conflict between public managers and public servants, especially when workers deal with a clientele that is not of their choosing, such as when teachers are assigned a group of students. The inability to oust disruptive and noncontributing clients (parents and students) makes it highly likely that teachers will be driven by "situational imperatives," such as the need to keep order, while principals and school boards deal with other constraints, such as complaints from politically influential constituencies. Both groups are able to reject or deflect complaints if they are able to show that the behaviors did not occur or were justified, but this is hard to do because outcomes and outputs are difficult to observe. Administrators must therefore strike a delicate balance. Teachers will feel like they are not being "backed up" if the complaint is acted on without providing due process. Parents will feel that the school is "insensitive" if the complaint is not addressed. The resulting conflict may lead to a breakdown in trust and the withdrawal of support from the organization (i.e., reduced loyalty).

These realities are one of the reasons why teachers claimed that tenure is so critical and teaching, as a profession, stresses an *ethos of care* (Chapters 4 and 5). As shown, tenure is *not* a job guarantee; it ensures *due process,* which facilitates trust and voice. Trust is particularly critical in situations where there are asymmetric (unequal) power relations. This was the case between school boards/district administrators and teachers prior to unionization and is also the case where parents lack the specialized knowledge they need to advance the interests of their children. By helping educators foster trust and social cohesion, relationships with colleagues, parents, students, and the community reduce the need for more overt, punitive, and costly forms of social control (e.g., rules, regulations, detention, suspension, expulsions).

Relational trust is strengthened when members of a group perceive that each is willing to help the other. When teachers embody a caring commitment—beyond what is formally required by their contract—and administrators, parents, and students respond in an appreciative and supporting manner, a moral force is added to their social dynamics that becomes a source for positive action. It improves performance by helping individuals work together to achieve common ends, but it requires sustained interactions over time (i.e., loyalty).[24] Exit disrupts these dynamics.

Other research supports educators' claim that *social trust*—an environment characterized by trusting and cooperative relationships—is critical for school efficiency and effectiveness, as well as for school improvement efforts.[25] It is more critical in public schools because they remain one of the foremost places where citizens experience people who are *not* like them. On a positive note, these experiences build social, economic, and political capital; however, public schools may also become highly charged emotional spaces owing to this diversity. Carley explained,

> [I had a student who] kicked me in the stomach and tried to stab me with a pencil. . . . A lot of the kids were crying and upset. . . . Luckily I had a classroom that was open to another . . . [and my colleague helped me restrain him] until a counselor could get there. . . . The parents had taken him off his medication because he was having such a great year . . . [not] because of a doctor's note. . . . [We had] a meeting with the parents. . . . [I explained to the class that he] didn't mean to do what he did . . . [used it as a learning exercise on how to] manage anger. . . . Parents don't always know what's best . . . [don't see their child] with other children . . . in a classroom setting . . . understand the dynamics of the classroom. They're not thinking about everybody else in the classroom. . . . [Even I] as a parent . . . don't always know what's best. . . . If I expect . . . [my] child to learn and be in a school setting [then on some level I need to trust the teacher and the school]. . . . [I] wish people would trust the schools more.

Trust helps educators do their jobs by stopping issues before they occur and by delimiting aggressive and competitive voice; it is also critical for resolving problems after they occur. Carley, for instance, disclosed that this situation was remediable because her principal "backed her up," she is well respected, and she has very good relationships with her students and the surrounding community. In fact, the parents told her that they had taken their son off his medicine *precisely because* he was having such a good year with her.

Carley's narrative about trust, though, is also a commentary on the importance of loyalty. Phrased another way, exit is loyalty to one's own but disloyalty toward others. In the presence of loyalty, communities construct ties of affection and feelings of trust *over time,* including bonding ties with people like us, and the bridging and linking ties that help build relational trust and reciprocity. This *social capital* is more critical for public schools because private and charter schools often rely on organic and contractual trust to achieve social cohesion and minimize the need for social control. In fact, the importance of social trust for school (and teacher) effectiveness is part of the reason why educators stress social values—such as equality, caring, trust, participation, cooperation, and reciprocity—in addition to a commitment to procedural justice. When parents and students feel like these social and democratic values are absent, they withdraw their support and performance declines. Unfortunately, these values are "going away" as a result of recent reforms and discourse that treat parents as consumers—meaning they will improve public education through exit—rather than citizen coproducers.

One further point deserves mention. Loyalty, like voice, is generally portrayed as a positive construct, yet it, too, may have negative side effects. Downward leveling norms often arise when loyalty stems from situations where individuals cannot escape the collective. This *entrapped allegiance* harms individuals, communities, and society through withdrawal, neglect, and even criminality. Loyalty is also harmful to individuals if it is enforced through asymmetric power relations—versus allegiance—where individuals comply as a result of legal, economic, political, or social inequalities or coercion rather than free will. Research suggests that individuals in these cases may lose their capacity to know what is in their best interests (see Gaventa, 1980). As shown, this was sometimes the case with teachers prior to unionization.

Discussion: Social Capital as a Public Good

Sociologists call the accepted customs, conventions, and moral attitudes of a group or society "social mores." Like glue, social mores hold a society together by fostering social cohesion. This research

supports Tocqueville's (1994) claim that social mores improve democratic performance when they encourage participation and foster
voluntary compliance with rules, regulations, and laws. According to
him, democracy flourished in America because of the propensity to
forge strong social bonds through the creation of voluntary associations. These organizations fostered the "habits of the heart"—morals,
manners, ideals, and emotional commitments—that sustained
democracy by helping citizens counter the demands of powerful
political and economic interests, including a centralized state.

Tocqueville predicted, however, that associationism would wither
as a result of American individualism, which he viewed as both
the cause and consequence of its relative socioeconomic equality.
Once growing numbers of citizens no longer needed others to help
meet their daily needs—or they were discouraged from doing so
by American individualism—they would withdraw into the private
world of family and friends. That development would eventually
contribute to rising socioeconomic inequality by ensuring that the
least well-off lacked the social bonds (social capital) to counter the
demands of powerful political and economic actors (Goliath). The
spread of economic uncertainty would then cause growing numbers
of citizens (David) to need the government's help, yet the government
would be (largely) unresponsive owing to these citizens' inability
to collectively voice. The end result would be a spiraling decline in
socioeconomic equality *and* democracy.

While Tocqueville portrayed cultural factors as the cause of these
developments, this study suggests that the "state" has played an
active role in the decline of social capital, socioeconomic equality, and democratic performance over the past 30 years. Here, the
state includes politicians who run against the government, demean
public servants, and imply that the government steals from us when
it taxes our income to provide for the commonweal—the well-being
common to all of us. It also includes public policies and discourse
that normalize the role of parents as consumers and public schools
as a marketplace, while distancing the role of parents as citizens,
public schools as communities, and education as a public good.
The latter fostered the common school ideal, which was critical for
America's commitment to a broader vision of public education and
a willingness to tax ourselves to provide services that may or may
not benefit us individually.

According to respondents, the portrayal of public education as a
consumptive good—something that is designed to meet individual
needs and wants—rather than a collective good has encouraged

parents to engage in exit and aggressive and competitive voice over loyalty and democratic voice. It also shifted power to the most well-off parents because they are more vocal, are less likely to rely on public programs, and have the capacity to use their social and cultural capital to demand special programs for their own children—such as gifted and talented programs, more extensive special education services, and homogenously tracked classes—at the expense of "other people's children."[26] A retired suburban high school English teacher (Liam) had this to say:

> [A group] wants to start a foundation where individuals could contribute so that certain programs could continue . . . despite state aid cutbacks. They do not want to pay the taxes but they will donate money to keep certain programs. . . . The foundation will control what the money goes to. . . . It's like "only for our own," whatever "our own" is. . . . What is wrong with our system . . . [that] people . . . cannot see the benefit of a fairer distribution of wealth so that people more broadly can benefit?

When combined with fiscal austerity, the dismantling of education as a public good has reduced the nation's ability to meet the transformative and humanistic ends of a free and universal public education.

As a group, educators conveyed how public policies and discourse that treat citizens unequally, favor businesses over human beings, and eulogize the private sector while portraying the public sector as broken, inefficient, and ineffective, increase political cynicism and reduce trust in government and fellow citizens. Some examples provided by informants include the ability of businesses and the most well-off to avoid government regulation and taxes by moving their plants overseas or by hiding their assets in foreign accounts; the provision of tax breaks to the most well-off while growing numbers of citizens struggle economically; and the existence of widespread income and racial disparities in the criminal justice system. Given these issues, participants said it was not surprising that some citizens would vote down school budgets. They are one of the few areas where "consumers" of public services have direct control.

Again, research supports that a civic-oriented public discourse leverages more community support for public schools than rhetoric that focuses on children and parents as consumers and that civic engagement helps resolve collective action problems, including the willingness to tax ourselves to provide public education (Glaser et al., 2002; Goldin & Katz, 1999). In addition, studies outside of education show that the government has not been a neutral actor in the formation, maintenance, and destruction of the bonding, bridging, and linking ties that foster collective political, social, and economic action.

Bonding social capital involves networks that are inward looking and exclusive. It glues together members who are alike in background, social status, role, origin, or identity through strong ties (R. Putnam, 2000). Bridging social capital involves networks that are outward looking and inclusive; they are composed of participants from a wide range of backgrounds who are bridged by weak ties (Granovetter, 1973, 1985). Linking social capital represents the capacity of individuals or groups to leverage resources from institutions outside of a community (Woolcock, 2001). It comprises vertical connections to more powerful actors in either the public or private sector (Cote & Healy, 2001).

Historically, the American government was particularly critical for facilitating bridging and linking social ties between otherwise disconnected groups (Szreter, 2002). This is important because the state is often the only actor that has the capacity to create these ties in impoverished communities.[27] That changed as the movement to defund and privatize public services reduced government's capacity to fulfill these important functions, but public discourse about an inefficient and ineffective public sector also delegitimized and reduced public demands for policy makers to do so (policy feedback). Public discourse and policies may foster self-interested *or* civic behaviors. Framing citizens as consumers, where the focus is on the right to choose, rather than as coproducers, where the focus is on the responsibility to contribute to the commonweal—the well-being common to all of us—has fostered the former (Don't Tread On Me) and is harming those communities most in need.

Conclusion

Recent education policies and discourse largely ignore the ways that political and economic institutions interact with the social contexts of schools to inequitably structure children's educational outcomes. As shown, policy makers and business-economic interests (largely) blamed public schools and public school teachers for the two achievement gaps; they then advocated voice and choice to rectify the situation. This study, however, supports Hirschman's (1970) assertion that voice and exit—while important in their own right—have more profound effects when combined with loyalty and neglect. If growing numbers of citizens defect from supporting the commonweal, public schools will go into decline.

At stake are the "intangibles" created through those public spaces, as evident in a picture that was posted and immediately gained more than 20,000 views. It shows a Jewish man riding the subway with a younger, African American man sleeping on his shoulder.[28] A witness attached the following tagline:

> heading home on the Q train . . . young Black guy nods off on the shoulder of a Jewish man . . . doesn't move a muscle, just lets him stay . . . I asked . . . if he wanted me to wake the kid up, but he . . . responded, "He must have had a long day, let him sleep. We've all been there, right?" He was still sleeping soundly . . . 20 minutes later . . . a small gesture, but a kind one . . . wonderful reminder that every moment is a chance to do something good for another person . . . inspire . . . others . . . with our small but powerful actions.

Shocked by the popularity of the picture, the man in the photo, Isaac Theil, told a magazine,

> Maybe the photo wouldn't . . . [be] so popular if people weren't seeing a Jewish man with a yarmulke and a Black man in a hood. . . . There is only one reason that I didn't move. He was simply a human being who was exhausted. . . . [I had a] shoulder to offer him.

Someone characterized Theil's actions as "the perfect demonstration of empathy," which is the ability to "draw on past hardship to soften our hearts towards others." Theil softened his heart to a total stranger, who wasn't so strange after all.

Like the "narrative of the blueberries," this story demonstrates how our public spaces afford us the opportunity to move beyond ourselves. It also shows what gets lost when we allow our public spaces, both real and imagined—like public schools and the public school ideal—to go into decline. The market is a powerful metaphor, but educators conveyed that excessive competition is unhealthy for children, society, and democracy; it destroys our commitment to things that are larger than me, myself, and I. The next chapter builds theory about how conceptualizing public services as a marketplace has affected policy implementation and democratic performance.

10

Policy Implementation, Policy Feedback, and Democratic Performance

Until now, I have (largely) focused on how public policies and discourse affect teaching and learning; however, educators occupy the space where policy meets practice. They are critical for implementing current policies and affect future ones—both by influencing the effectiveness of government and through voting, lobbying, and other forms of political participation. This chapter uses 83 interviews with educators to explore how values, beliefs, and social contexts (e.g., school districts, local communities, occupational norms, colleagues) influence policy implementation, policy feedback, and democratic performance. It pulls together the findings from earlier chapters and is particularly useful as policy makers, researchers, and citizens consider the costs and benefits of future reforms and policies.

Public Service Paradigms and Policy Implementation

TPA and NPM represent different paradigms of public service provision, yet both allege that public servants resist implementing policies that threaten their interests (e.g., job security, chances for promotion, status in the workplace, working conditions); both also blame bureaucratic resistance for implementation failures. To resolve this issue, TPA recommends confining and channeling bureaucratic discretion through rules, regulations, and SOPs but allowing some professional discretion to personalize services; NPM advocates using competition, choice, and other market incentives to encourage bureaucrats *and* professionals to pursue state aims while also efficiently and effectively serving citizens. For the most part, these top-down (TPA) and bottom-up (NPM) solutions sideline how implementation is influenced by different social contexts. There is a similar issue in the literature on policy implementation. It recognizes that professional and occupational norms play an important role in how public servants do their jobs, yet (largely) focuses on the need to control the behaviors of what Lipsky (1980) calls "street-level bureaucrats," such as administrators and teachers. Most studies do not explore the conditions under which these norms might produce broader societal benefits rather than solely serving as a justification for policy resistance or bureaucratic and professional inertia.

In contrast, this study supports McDonnell's (1991) claim that value conflicts are at the root of many implementation issues; it also supports studies outside of the implementation field, which show that work that is primarily done to serve others or a higher purpose contributes to the development of a moral identity (see, e.g., Gardner et al., 2001). Educators, for instance, frequently characterized their issues with parents, colleagues, public policies, and organizational directives as moral conflicts; conflict was escalated when they had to negotiate competing loyalties to their schools, the norms of the occupation, and their "clients" (i.e., parents and students). The latter was especially true in the post–education reform environment, where the coproduction of educational outcomes often worked in tandem with public policies to inequitably challenge educators' ability to comply with their occupational norms and promote the broader social democratic mission of public schools.

My interviews suggest that most educators engaged in voice to resolve these issues, but moral conflicts also resulted in high rates of exit and sometimes neglect as a means of resistance. This chapter uses the concepts of EVLN to explore this claim and develop a broader theory about how public policies and discourse affect democratic performance by influencing the behaviors of public organizations, public servants, policy implementers, and citizen coproducers. The main focus is on education and educators; however, I use examples from current events to show how the analysis more broadly applies to other policy areas and public servants in general.

Again, Hirschman (1970) used EVLN to explain how *consumers* and *citizens* influence the quality of private goods and public services in democratic societies.[1] Chapter 9 focused on citizens. Here, the focus is on applying those constructs to the political and organizational behaviors of public servants and policy implementers.

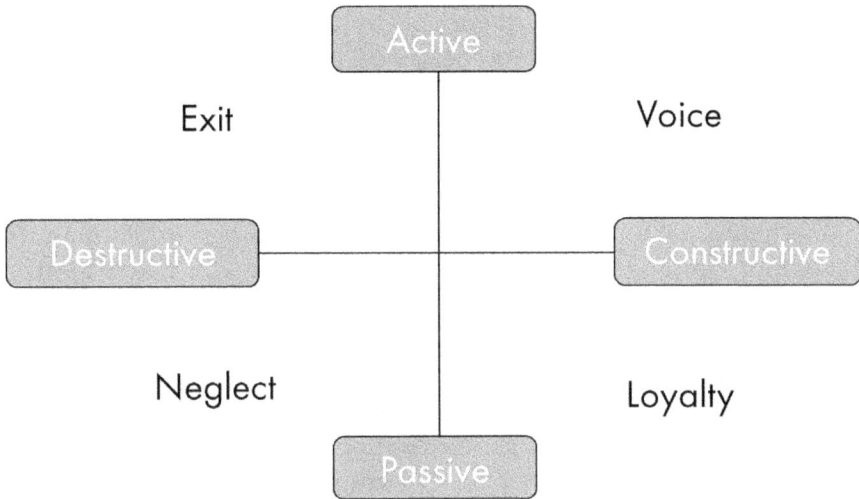

Figure 10.1. EVLN.

Theorists have already modeled EVLN for *private organizations.* That research (Farrell, 1983) advocates separating these behaviors into their constructive (voice and loyalty), destructive (exit and neglect), active (voice and exit), and passive (loyalty and neglect) forms to acknowledge their disparate effects on organizational performance (Figure 10.1). Exit, for example, often has destructive effects because the most quality-conscious clients, customers, and workers are typically the first to leave (active behavior); that removes pressure for reform (voice; active/positive behavior) and allows the organization to continue with business as usual.

This study found that EVLN similarly results in disparate effects for *public organizations, policy implementation,* and *public service provision;* however, it is more complicated to model EVLN for public servants owing to the interaction between their organizational, occupational, and citizenship roles. For instance, organizationally and occupationally, exit is still more likely for those who have the most skill, ability, and capacity—because they are more likely to have alternative employment options—but exit is tempered by occupational norms and relationships at work (loyalty). In addition, as shown in Chapter 9, public servants (educators) often need the cooperation of citizens (parents, students, and school communities) to do their jobs well and implement policies; they are also often embedded within communities where they form relationships with their clients or those they are regulating. Coercive policies are likely to have unintended consequences if policy makers do not account for these multiple roles and social contexts, especially when they create serious value conflicts.

For modeling purposes, I have separated the organizational/occupational and citizenship/political behaviors of public servants but my research suggests that these roles and behaviors often overlap. Nonetheless, public servants as citizens and policy implementers have four options when unhappy: use voice within the organization or voice through occupations, unions, interest groups, political parties, or other intermediary institutions (e.g., the news or social media); exit from the organization (district/school) or the occupation (teaching); remain but withdraw from organizational and/or political life (e.g., neglect as nonparticipation and nonvoting); or fulfill their professional and/or civic responsibilities while awaiting change (loyalty).

Loyalty in Organizational and Political Life

This section begins with loyalty because my research supports Hirschman's (1970) contention that it is an emotion that influences behavioral choices. It explains, for instance, why employees, customers, citizens, interest groups, and members of unions and political parties continue to fulfill their obligations, participate, buy products, or speak up long after exit appears to be a more rational option. They continue to vote, remain in a school district, or "buy American" even if they believe that it will not make a difference, their child might receive a better education elsewhere, or it costs more money. Loyalty, though, should not be viewed solely as a factor that causes individuals to choose voice (speaking up and participating) over exit; this research shows that it is an alternative in its own right and its effects are not always passive/positive, as previously constructed.

Moving beyond loyalty as a passive/positive construct. In its passive form, loyalty is a sentiment more than a behavior. It involves patience while awaiting change. Loyalty becomes an active/positive construct when it induces individuals to go above and beyond their obligations—without being asked, encouraged, or forced to do so—to promote civic, organizational, or occupational goals (see also Withey & Cooper, 1989). Chapter 5 provided evidence of this *loyalty with allegiance,* including *organizational citizenship behaviors* (volunteering for school committees and chaperoning school events), *occupational citizenship behaviors* (mentoring new teachers and supervising student teachers to help the occupation thrive), and *civic behaviors* in both their political form (voting, lobbying, calling elected officials) and pro-social form (donating to and volunteering for causes). In this study, those who expressed active/positive loyalty conveyed a high degree of trust in the community, administrators, colleagues, and fellow citizens; most also did so for the government. Trust was also more common among participants who demonstrated passive/positive loyalty, but loyalty appears to be closer to the construct of neglect when it reflects misinformed, incompetent, or entrapped allegiance.

Misinformed allegiance arises from ignorance or a lack of capacity. In the political space, it occurs when citizens lose sight of their interests, whether owing to an unequal distribution of political, social, or economic power or because political and economic elites have successfully used wedge issues to divide groups that would normally work together to achieve common ends. This often results in individuals working against their own interests, like voting for candidates that adopt policies to help the most well-off when they are not a part of that group. Gaventa (1980) documents these kinds of issues in Appalachia. Organizationally, it tends to arise from a lack of training, a job–skill mismatch, and/or incompetent or inadequate management. In the marketplace, misinformed allegiance occurs when customers purchase shoddy or harmful products or services based on false claims or misleading advertising.

Incompetent allegiance occurs when individuals blindly follow orders, bad policies or SOPs. They may also engage in erroneous or ritualistic behaviors owing to a lack of effort or because they are "just doing what they're told to do."

Entrapped allegiance involves compliance due to a perceived lack of free will or as a result of legal, economic, political, or social coercion. Entrapped individuals remain silent because they perceive that the costs of exit and voice are too high and/or that the likelihood of change is minimal to nonexistent. Like misinformed allegiance, it is typically—but not always—found in situations where there are asymmetric (unequal) power relations (Gaventa, 1980). Regardless of why it occurs, entrapped individuals believe that their options are to accept, adjust to, or make peace with a bad situation or leave.

Most would agree that it is harmful to provide allegiance to those who engage in behaviors that are injurious to themselves or others, but loyalty is also destructive when individuals blindly follow orders because of misinformation, incompetence, or a perceived lack of free will. In these cases, individuals (citizens, employees, public servants, and policy implementers) give up their voice. Some may withdraw while continuing to fulfill some of their (civic, occupational, or organizational) obligations; others may engage in neglect. The example I used in Chapter 9 was the spread of downward leveling norms. These behaviors harm students and are costly for schools and society, especially if they lead to criminality through a school-to-prison pipeline (neglect as a refusal to obey laws).

I elaborate on neglect among public servants later in the chapter. For now, it is important to note that, in this study, narratives about misinformed and incompetent allegiance were (typically) told about the behaviors of "others" (i.e., policy makers, colleagues, parents, or students). Entrapped allegiance was evident in educators' narratives about themselves *and* others; it was far more prominent in the words of those who worked in districts that heavily restricted professional voice. These participants conveyed feelings of resignation more than loyalty. They were also more likely to express distrust of their colleagues and fellow citizens. As such, silence should not be misconstrued as acceptance or faith in the government, the organization, their colleagues, or fellow citizens. It was passive withdrawal while carrying on with business as usual. The ability to shut their doors and teach allowed some to bide their time until they could get out (i.e., retire, leave the school or district, or leave teaching) and others to remain loyal to the occupation while withdrawing from the organization. In both cases, however, educators were less willing to engage in *invisible work* (Chapter 5) and civic behaviors.

My interviews indicate that feelings of entrapped allegiance spread over time owing to a belief that recent reforms were not designed to improve public education or the quality of the teaching workforce. Instead, policy makers blamed educators for the two achievement gaps to get schools to do more with less, avoid redressing the real issues in society, and justify privatization (e.g., charter schools, vouchers, contracts with private businesses for supplemental services and consumable learning packages). Most of those who were 40 years old or older further mentioned that recent reforms were a way to restrict or eliminate tenure and seniority as a way to fire more expensive teachers.

Chapters 3 and 6 explored these claims, but an urban middle school English teacher (Chloe) complained,

> It has become about money. There is no loyalty to . . . [those who] dedicate themselves to teaching . . . their school and . . . district. . . . [Now, they] can get rid of anyone . . . manufacture a reason. . . . The public

thinks that tenure is a guarantee. That is how it is written up in the media. . . . It guarantees jobs for bad teachers. It is never discussed . . . [that, along with seniority, it] is part of an implicit bargain. . . . Teachers get paid lower salaries in the beginning . . . [given their] high degree of education . . . work very hard during . . . and after school . . . continue . . . professional training . . . do things for the school community that are outside their jobs. In return, they make . . . [more] toward the end . . . are given due process to protect them against arbitrary treatment from administrators and . . . [the] public . . . [which has] a very strong influence on the public school system.

Entrapped allegiance is evident in the cynicism and distrust many informants expressed toward federal and state policy makers—even as they implemented testing, the Common Core, and the new evaluation system. Their words suggest that they felt like they had no recourse because their complaints about the negative effects of recent reforms had been ignored, characterized as "self-interested," or portrayed as something to be "managed," but not listened to, by policy makers.

Almost every teacher in some way expressed that society has never rewarded their hard work or level of education through their paychecks or by conferring status on the occupation. The primary way that school districts discouraged high turnover (exit)—as a result of these realities—was by protecting professional voice and rewarding loyalty and expertise through tenure and seniority; states and districts also provided health and retirement benefits to (partially) offset low wages. As shown in Chapters 3, 6 and 7, educators perceive that policy makers have reneged on this deal to save money during tough economic times or because tax cuts have reduced public revenues. These developments reduced trust (declining loyalty) in federal and state policy makers; distrust appears to have spread, for some informants, to school administrators, society, and even the union.[2]

Recent informal discussions with teachers suggest that public support for strikes in other states has restored trust in fellow citizens for many educators. However, political cynicism has grown for some respondents as a result of the Supreme Court's *Janus* decision and Mitch McConnell's argument, while serving as Senate majority leader, that the national government should provide federal aid to businesses but allow state governments to go bankrupt during the pandemic. He claimed that state governments were struggling because of mismanagement and high pension costs (as a result of giving in to unions) rather than decreased tax revenues and increased social welfare costs during a pandemic-induced recession.

As mentioned in Chapters 1 and 6, this political cynicism is not partisan. While teachers tend to have similar views on educational issues and policies, their partisan affiliations and political ideologies generally match those of citizens at large and in the communities where they live (Editorial Projects in Education, 2017). It stems from concerns about procedural and distributive justice. Many believe that recent discourse, policies, and court decisions are unfair, especially given the large bailouts for the private sector, and are designed to reduce voice among public employees and unions because these groups have the political resources to demand policies that more equitably distribute resources and opportunities to all Americans.

This research shows that loyalty is not a one-way street; people expect it to be returned. A first-year suburban art teacher (Ellen) exclaimed,

> [Money] is tight . . . people are feeling that crunch, but then it spirals out of control . . . [to] what we have now . . . [blaming education for] the country's economic situation . . . the achievement gap between different students, and . . . American students and overseas . . . human beings are not all equal in every area and societies aren't equal . . . I don't think that you can hold the teacher accountable for a gap that exists no matter how hard they work . . . hold people accountable for things that are so beyond their control . . . we don't . . . choose who and where we teach . . . We get blamed but rarely rewarded . . . when the economy is doing well . . . It makes me wonder if the government trusts us, and if they don't, then why not? My experience with teachers is that they are very hardworking . . . good citizens . . . serve the public, and provide an important role in society. So, why doesn't the government trust us? And, can we trust a government that doesn't trust us?

For better or for worse, loyalty and trust are correlated with one another in civic, political, *and* organizational life, and policy makers influence both.

This study discussed how past policies and discourse promoted white flight from urban and rural areas to the suburbs and current ones encouraged parents to flee public schools for charter and private alternatives (declining loyalty and exit). Recent education reforms and rhetoric also fostered aggressive and competitive voice among parents and taxpayers by conveying that the government does not trust public schools and public school educators. Both of these developments have contributed to declining trust and increased political cynicism among educators. Most appear to have remained loyal to their students, colleagues, and occupations while taking action (voice) to make their organizational or political environments more congruent with their norms and values; however, some exited, became more quiescent (decreased political and organizational voice), or engaged in neglect. Neglect typically resulted from conflicting loyalties and was not necessarily a negative development.

Understanding divided and conflicting loyalties. Educators provided many examples of how public policies and discourse alter the behaviors of citizens and policy implementers by constructing divided loyalties. Sometimes this is by intent—a way for policy makers to achieve political objectives by dividing groups that would normally work together to achieve common goals (divide and conquer). Yet, as evident in the words of Kristen—who worked in a high-need, low-resource, southern rural school before transferring to a high-need, low-resource, urban northern school—narratives about conflicting loyalties did not relate solely to recent reforms:

> I identify with other urban teachers. . . . they are experiencing the same thing. . . . [We have] to stick together because we . . . [are] being stigmatized. . . . [In the South] they were building new schools. . . . The "better" students were going. . . . Most of them were white. . . . Many of my friends were transferring. . . . Their test scores were always amazing and I knew that I could get a job there . . . [get] that stipend [merit pay] every year because the test scores. . . . [But I] felt that loyalty to the person who had given me . . . the chance to teach. . . . [I also feel loyal to my current administrator and district and] that loyalty is one of the things that keeps me motivated. . . . [I still feel loyal to] my school in the South . . . I just needed to be home after 9/11. . . . My dad . . . was fine, but he was up in the air that day. . . . As a teacher you always put everyone else first, but . . . I needed to put my feelings first. I've always felt guilty . . . even though I know they got a great replacement. . . . [My school and students] brought me to the bus port. . . . They were crying and I was crying. . . . An amazing paraprofessional who was my second mother . . . let me stay with them in the days after 9/11. . . . [My] classroom is a family but our school . . . too . . . your behavior is important for you . . . the group. . . . We don't have to love one another, but . . . have to live together . . . treat each other with respect. . . . Your brother can get on your nerves but he is still your brother.

Kristen describes five kinds of loyalty. She is loyal to her district, administrators, colleagues, students, and other teachers who work in high-need, low-resource environments. Teachers also mentioned being loyal to their occupation and the state. The latter claim is evident in Kristen's and Sam's earlier narratives, when they discussed being proud to work in a "gold standard state," as well as informants' stories about how the state's collective bargaining law reduced turnover (exit).

After the events of 9/11, Kristen's loyalty to her family competed with her loyalty to her school. She chose to exit (go home) but said she still feels guilty about putting her "feelings first." Although she does not say this, her statement suggests that this guilt stems from a belief that putting herself first violates the normative commitment to "do right by the kids." One way she reconciled these conflicting loyalties was by teaching in another high-need, low-resource school; this allowed her to remain loyal to what drew her to the occupation—a calling to work with underprivileged children and the educators who serve them.

As shown, loyalty to one's colleagues, school, community, and/or occupation helps educators sustain the very high levels of *work commitment* and *invisible work* that are required for good teaching; the latter directly improve the efficiency and effectiveness of public schools and indirectly do so by helping educators build trust with parents, students, and the community. The norm of competition (markets), as instituted under recent reforms, disincentivized these behaviors; it decreased the efficiency and effectiveness of public schools by reducing teachers' loyalty to the norms of the occupation (e.g., trust, collegiality, collaboration, a commitment to doing invisible work) and recreating the high turnover model of teaching (exit) that drains occupational knowledge and reduces voice.[3] Conflict between the norms of teaching (do right by the kids) and the norm of competition also appears to have increased dysfunctional behaviors—such as teaching to the test (neglect)—as teachers strive to help students succeed while also meeting policy demands in a system that rates the competition for test scores above everything else but ignores how the deck is stacked against our most vulnerable students.

Voice in Organizational and Political Life

As mentioned, Hirschman (1970) defined *voice* as the process of fighting for reform from within. Withey and Cooper (1989) argue that employees are sensitive to three things when deciding to voice: costs, efficacy, and the attractiveness of the setting. My interviews indicate that this is also true with respect to public servants, but it is the *perceived* costs, efficacy, and attractiveness that matter. Individuals make different calculations even within the same political, economic, or organizational context; they may also alter their own or others' perceptions of costs *even if* nothing changes within those settings. In addition, public servants do not solely assess the costs associated with voice. They assess *what values they will give up* by acquiescing or going along. Voice appears to be more likely when policies, directives, or parental demands conflict with the "collective conscience" (Durkheim, 1996)—a set of beliefs, ideas, morals, attitudes, and knowledge that unifies members of occupations and professions, such as an *ethos of care* (see Chapter 5).

As a whole, my interviews indicate that voice—in both its participatory and protest varieties—often involves high personal costs like time and energy, the possibility of offending superiors, colleagues, or clients, and/or the potential loss of respect from the group or influence over future issues. Exit is also costly because the individual must leave his or her work environment and possibly lose income and friends. Either way, individual actions are less likely to foster change until others join in. These realities increase the likelihood of collective action problems, where individuals find it difficult to work together to achieve common objectives (Olson, 1965/1971). It is in everyone's interest if individuals speak up, but not in the interest of any single individual to do so. Recognizing that the public sector will become increasingly less efficient and effective if growing numbers of citizens and public servants opt out (exit and neglect), TPA advocated building political, social, and economic institutions that would encourage voice and loyalty. Those institutions became more inclusive over time.

Constructing voice through political, social, and economic institutions. In terms of *citizens,* across subsequent reforms, TPA opened up the processes of government agencies to expand voice and participation. For instance, the Freedom of Information Act (1966) provides the public with access to government data, records, and other information and sunshine laws require the government to provide the public with sufficient advance notice of government meetings and to hold those meetings in places that are accessible to the public. TPA also recognized that the concentration of political, social, and economic power creates hurdles for broader democratic participation and enables powerful individuals and organized interests to use the government for private gain. To rectify the situation, it encouraged the growth of groups and organizations that foster broader collective action, such as unions, professions and occupations, farmers' organizations, consumer associations, and worker and renter cooperatives.

The community action requirements included in many Great Society programs (e.g., Head Start) are another example of government efforts to foster voice and political inclusion, especially among those who had historically suffered from low levels of participation, such as minorities, immigrants, and the poor. The Great Society further recognized that individuals are not truly free if they are hemmed in by poverty or a lack of education. It redistributed opportunity to provide marginalized groups with the knowledge and capacity to participate more fully in political, social, and economic life (e.g., Title I of the ESEA).

In terms of *public servants,* TPA separated politics from administration to ensure that bureaucrats and professionals used their expert judgment on behalf of citizens and clients—relatively free from the whims of political elites and powerful constituencies. Instead, bureaucrats and professionals are (largely) regulated by a public service ethos, but also through citizen voice in both its participatory and protest varieties. Examples of the latter include comment periods for government regulations, complaints to elected officials (political oversight), or lawsuits when something goes wrong (legal accountability). The theory of action (Stone, 1989) is that political representation would combine with bureaucratic administration and professionalism to promote the public good, including the equitable and impartial treatment of citizens.

These ideas were reflected in the Pendleton Act of 1883, which awarded federal jobs based on merit and competitive exams rather than political connections and donations. The law transformed public services so that, today, well-educated individuals and well-trained professionals seek a career in the federal government.[4] Many of these jobs are also unionized and offer tenure and seniority protections. As shown, these changes helped resolve collective action problems by encouraging loyalty and voice over exit and neglect. The federal government further promoted voice through laws like the Whistleblower Protection Enhancement Act (WPEA). That law received the vote of every member of Congress, reflecting a bipartisan consensus that the ability to safely report government waste, fraud, corruption, and wrongdoing is critical for government performance, as well as democratic governance.[5] Otherwise, public servants and public organizations may engage in waste, neglect, or even unethical behaviors, and citizens will lose trust in government.

In the state that is the subject of this analysis, these ideas are reflected in a policy that allows public servants—like teachers—to bargain collectively. One way that law encouraged economic, political, *and* professional voice over exit was by requiring nonjoiners to pay partial dues rather than free riding off the efforts of union members. This and other *resource effects* provided growing numbers of public servants, such as teachers, with a stake in collective political and economic action. As shown, collective voice improved teacher autonomy, salaries, and working conditions, which created a link in their minds between collective political participation and the ability to advance their professional interests. Such *interpretive effects* further increased political participation by altering civic predispositions and teachers' sense of political efficacy, civic duty, and group consciousness.

Just as importantly, local school districts began experimenting with tenure and seniority as a way to reduce turnover (exit) and redress teacher shortages. One unintended side effect was increased professional voice as seniority encouraged teachers to remain in the profession, thus giving them a stake in collective action, and tenure reduced the ability of districts to fire teachers for nonperformance-related issues. Prior to these administrative reforms, *effective teachers* were often removed—either because they voiced, did not curry favor with administrators, school boards, and/or powerful parents, or were too expensive as they gained more years of experience.

Participants alleged that nonperformance-based removals sometimes still occur for teachers who have not yet been offered tenure and more frequently occur in charter schools, where teachers are significantly less likely to be part of a union. To them, this demonstrates that these issues are not a historical anomaly. In fact, they said tenure and seniority are *more critical today*. The spread of market logics has fostered a broader societal disregard for professional (and other forms of) knowledge and expertise; this has contributed to the growth in aggressive and competitive voice among parents, students, and community members. These behaviors are harmful to "other people's children"—especially those who lack economic, social, and cultural capital—and require educators to use voice as a way of leveling the playing field.

Given this latter claim, it is not surprising that the two most common examples of voice in this study involved a refusal to implement (federal, state, and district) policies that harm parents and children and a willingness to counter parental demands that harm children. An urban middle school English (Stephanie) and elementary (Lorna) teacher had this to say:

LORNA: [I told my principal the] bilingual program . . . doesn't work. . . . You need to do more ESL. . . . It's making the kids feel like they are

... segregated. ... [He was Hispanic and the school] about 90 percent Hispanic. ... [It] was a very nurturing community. ... He said to me, "Will you speak to their parents. ... They want their children in separate classes . . . speaking Spanish because they do not want them to lose their culture or . . . language." I said, "They're not going to lose their culture. ... They will acquire a real feel for English and their second language will be Spanish." . . . We convinced them . . . he made me go get my ESL license. ... [We opened] an ESL class on every grade. ... Immersion . . . is the best way to learn. ... That year, all of my children in kindergarten . . . tested out of ESL. That had *never* happened . . . it continued to grow. ... The school became well known for their ESL program . . . a place where people wanted their children to go . . . [to] gain the skills they needed to do well in life. ... I had said to their parents, "You want your children to be anything . . . president of the United States . . . be bilingual, but their primary language should be English because you don't want *anything* . . . holding them back."

STEPHANIE: They are trying to have . . . us teach the same things on the same day. ... Tenured teachers can say, "No, I won't do that; it is not in the best interests of the kids."

Lorna is describing what I earlier referred to as the transformative ends of public education. These ends may make public education a site of economic, political, social, and cultural conflict because they often require *social reconstruction*. Again, by that, I mean the process of bringing about change or improving society by, for example, fostering social cohesion, tolerance, and peaceful coexistence; redressing inequality; and/or developing a national identity that transcends individual, sectarian, and communal differences. Stephanie mentions that tenure and seniority enable educators to engage in these processes by speaking out without fear of reprisal.

The professional commitment to an ethos of care helps ensure that these transformative ends do not harm individuals or marginalized groups; it also helps reduce social conflict (e.g., adversarial relationships with parents and the community) by stressing the need to be inclusive and responsive. Lorna's narrative is a classic example of these claims and shows how professional voice helps create the trust and reciprocity (social capital) that allow public schools to improve social cohesion, address important individual and societal needs, and encourage broader citizen participation.

Restrictions on voice. Up until now, I have focused on how the state may promote voice among citizens and public servants, but it is also possible to silence voice through public discourse and policies.

Historically, government actions hindered *economic voice* through actual violence (e.g., jailing and beating up strikers) and symbolic violence (e.g., portraying labor unions as communist) while restrictions on voting and registration reduced *political voice*. A growing number of states have now adopted RTW laws, which allow employees to benefit from union contracts without paying any dues. Those laws have reduced the economic *and* political power of unions by restricting their ability to use "select incentives" (Olson, 1965/1971) to encourage workers to join. The resulting decline in membership and dues (resource effects) decreased political voice (policy feedback) from organizations that represent middle- and working-class Americans. The Supreme Court's *Janus* decision has now made RTW the law of the land for all public employees and Senator Rand Paul has reintroduced a national RTW law that would do the same for private employees.[6] Meanwhile, amid rising protests and historic levels of voter turnout during the 2020 election, state lawmakers across the country have introduced or adopted legislation that will inhibit peaceful protest and restrict voting and registration, especially among minority and low-income Americans. These include more than 90 antiprotest bills introduced in at least 36 states and the adoption of nearly two dozen bills that restrict ballot access in 14 states—with more in the pipeline (Boschma, 2021; Brennan Center for Justice, 2021; Eidelman, 2021).

With respect to professional voice, state legislative changes and ongoing court decisions have greatly weakened or overturned tenure and seniority, claiming that both create opportunity gaps by making it prohibitively expensive to remove underperforming teachers.[7] At the national level, such efforts include an unsuccessful attempt by House Republicans to reinstate the Holman Rule, which enabled lawmakers to slash the pay of an individual federal worker down to a dollar or cut a specific program as part of an appropriations bill. Republican leaders said that the rule would improve accountability, efficiency, and effectiveness by enabling policy makers to more easily cut the size of the federal workforce, but many Republicans acknowledged that the rule would upend the 130-year-old civil service by making the work of the 2.1 million civil servants—now insulated from politics—vulnerable to the whims of elected officials.[8]

More successfully, President Trump restricted professional voice and threatened the impartiality of civil servants by instituting "gag orders," which blocked public servants from communicating with citizens, the media, and members of Congress. He also attacked and fired individual federal employees for alleged disloyalty without due process; involuntarily transferred senior executives; backed efforts to unmask the whistleblower who filed a complaint about his dealings with Ukraine president Volodymyr Zelensky; retweeted a post with the alleged whistleblower's name to his 68 million followers; and fired inspectors general—independent government watchdogs—when they exposed issues with waste, fraud, and abuse. Many of these actions caused even staunch Trump allies in Congress to express concern. In addition, he discursively denigrated the idea of a neutral and competent civil service through rhetoric about the need to "drain the swamp," claims that the "civil service is the problem," and language about a "deep state" of subversive bureaucrats who were thwarting the will of citizens and elected officials.[9]

This study shows that public discourse about self-interested and ineffective public servants is a form of symbolic violence that suppresses voice. It includes calling teachers "educrats," framing them as self-interested enemies of reform, and blaming the "BLOB" (big learning organization bureaucracy) for declining economic competitiveness as a way to eliminate tenure and seniority, adopt merit pay, expand charter schools (most of which are nonunionized), and promote nontraditional teacher training programs. Educators did not use the word *neoliberalism* but positioned recent reforms as part of a movement to downgrade bureaucrats, professionals, and other experts and elevate political and market actors (i.e., political and economic interests, such as private providers of supplemental services, the charter and home school industries, alternative teacher training programs, and testing and publishing companies). In the words of a suburban elementary teacher, Meagan,

> Look at the whole thing that happened in Georgia with teachers being forced to change test scores or cheat on tests. Their administrator told them . . . there would be repercussions if they did not. . . . teachers are . . . being asked to do things that go against their professional voice . . . feel compelled to do so because of fear . . . [for] their jobs. And that's what tenure was supposed to protect against. . . . We are so focused on . . . controlling for the bad apples that we are spoiling the good ones . . . putting a lot of worms in the system. I never minded the sacrifices of teaching, but now . . . I am being told I am a horrible person . . . a drain on the public. . . . It is almost like there is a scheme, for lack of a better word . . . this new evaluation system . . . focus on performance, and . . . eliminating tenure and teachers' unions . . . to get new people in who will not question things and . . . people out who will. But we are losing the consistency and the community of teaching . . . losing those learning communities.

As shown, the resulting political-market accountability has reduced educator voice by increasing hierarchical control, encouraging aggressive and competitive voice among parents, and reducing job security. New teachers appear to be most severely affected.

Moving beyond voice as a positive construct. Educators' narratives about competitive and aggressive voice among parents and students are evidence of this study's finding that voice is not always positive in its means or effects. For educators, it includes demanding the best classes or counseling out more needy students from AP classes or charter schools. My interviews suggest that aggressive and competitive voice have never been a widespread problem among public schoolteachers, but these behaviors appear to be on the rise in a system that promotes exit and competition—over voice and loyalty—as the best way to regulate educators. Recent reforms also appear to have increased voice in the form of *acts of resistance* and *sabotage.*

Acts of resistance include walkouts, strikes, sit-ins, and other acts of civil disobedience, as well as refusing to implement public policies. Acts of sabotage include creating flaws that prevent a policy from being successfully implemented or implemented as intended or voicing outside the organization without any attempt to construct reform from within. Cheating is classified as neglect because it is more typically a way to subvert the system, not change it. This claim is evident in Meagan's narrative about teachers in Georgia, as well as an earlier story about a principal that had teachers pick up higher scoring students who were absent on test day while encouraging poorly performing students to stay home.

I would argue, however, that the classification of such acts as positive or negative often depends on three things: first, the broader political, economic, and social environment; second, the means and ends of such protests; and third, who is doing the evaluating. Actions that are directed at the state yet harm citizens are more likely to be viewed negatively than those that help citizens. The perfect example is the creation of "rogue" social media accounts in response to President Trump's gag orders. The Interior Department was ordered to shut down its official Twitter account after the National Park Service (NPS) tweeted photos showing that President Trump's swearing-in had substantially smaller crowds than President Obama's in 2009. The official account was restored the next day, once the NPS deleted the tweets and apologized, but many federal agencies began restricting external communications. These actions led some public servants to create rogue accounts, such as @AltUSNatParkService, to engage in whistleblowing and cover topics that were being removed from the official sites, such as climate change.

From President Trump's perspective, these accounts are a form of subversive behavior (neglect) or an attempt to sabotage his policies (aggressive voice). Public servants, though, framed them as a way to remain loyal to the mission of their agencies and the citizens they serve; many also characterized these accounts as acts of civil disobedience in an environment where their voice, their research, and the mission of their agencies were being silenced by political appointees who appeared to be at odds with the mission of their agencies. AltUSNatParkService quickly gained 170,000 followers, almost twice as many as the official one, suggesting that many Americans viewed this as a (positive) act of resistance (voice).[10]

Many articles on *both* the right and the left advocated that public servants, during President Trump's administration, resist, engage in subversive behaviors, or exit as a way to uphold public service values and the Constitution in an environment where ample evidence suggested that voicing publicly or privately would result in personal attacks and/or being shut out, fired, or replaced with those who are less likely to speak up.[11] This study and recent events, however, suggest that it is still preferable, from a societal and governance perspective, to blow the whistle on ethical issues than to engage in exit or quiet acts of resistance. Exit typically drains the most vocal and competent public servants. Quiet acts of resistance, on the other hand, may erode trust in civil servants' ability to faithfully exercise their duties because they appear to support the claim that a "deep state" subverts the will of the electorate. Unfortunately, whistleblowing is often quite costly for individual public servants.[12] For these reasons, professional voice must be protected through legislation, such as the WPEA, and these protections must be enforced by elected officials and public agencies.

Exit in Organizational and Political Life

As mentioned, neoliberals claim that public servants use their ability to hide behind professional expertise and bureaucratic rules and red tape to pursue their own interests at the expense of citizens and taxpayers. To resolve these issues, neoliberalism advocates using market logics (i.e., exit, choice, and competition) to hold public servants accountable and improve the efficiency and effectiveness of public services. This theory of action assumes that loyalty-promoting institutions—such as tenure and seniority—increase neglect because material rewards automatically increase with service; public managers are required to exert effort to remove employees; and citizens, for the most part, cannot take their business elsewhere.[13] The ascendancy of neoliberal ideas is evident in President Trump's appointment of Betsy DeVos as secretary of education, the expansion of school choice policies (private school vouchers and charter schools), and the adoption of policies like merit pay in states and school districts across the nation.

The appointment of Betsy DeVos, for instance, is consistent with neoliberal proposals to recruit from outside of the "public service monopoly" to reform "the system." She was put in charge of the largest provider of student loans and financial aid, and the entire K–12 educational system even though she did not have a degree in education; had no expertise in pedagogy, curriculum, or school governance; did not attend or send her children to a public school; and had no direct experience with student loans, or even experience by proxy through her children. Her sole experience for the job included using her family's extraordinary wealth to lobby for neoliberal reforms, especially in Michigan, where she and her husband, Dick DeVos—an heir to the Amway fortune—have influenced every major education-related reform since the 1990s through lobbying, contributing at least $7 million in recent years to lawmakers and the state Republican Party, and serving as the chair of the Michigan Republican Party.

DeVos's efforts resulted in the state's first charter school bill. Michigan also lifted the cap on the number of charter schools, adopted a school choice voucher program, and passed tax-credit initiatives that widened the range of private and religious institutions that could receive public funds (e.g., homeschooling and virtual education). Detroit now has a greater proportion of charter schools than any city, except New Orleans, and Michigan's two-decades-long charter school initiative is one of the least regulated in the country.[14] In fact, just about anyone may open a charter school if he or she is able to raise the capital; almost 80 percent are run by for-profit organizations; and, there is almost no accountability for performance. This is especially true of for-profit charter schools because they are not required to make the same financial disclosures as nonprofit or public entities. In comparison, other states have moved to curb or ban the expansion of for-profit charters; most require a proven track record before expanding; and most subject poor performers to improvement efforts and closure if necessary.[15]

The ascendancy of neoliberal ideas is further evident in the rhetoric of former Secretary DeVos. In an op-ed piece, she urged legislators to "retire" Detroit Public Schools and "liberate all students" by allowing them to use tax dollars to attend the schools of their choice—similar to how consumers choose where to travel and shop (Zernike, 2016b). She framed school choice as

> a battle of Industrial Age versus the Digital Age . . . Model T versus the Tesla . . . old factory model versus the new internet model . . . Luddites versus the future. We must open up the education industry—and let's not kid ourselves that it isn't an industry . . . to entrepreneurs and innovators. This is how families without means will get access to a world-class education . . . start-ups, ventures, and innovation in every other area of life, but [not] education because it's a closed system, a closed industry, a closed market . . . a monopoly, a dead end. And the best and brightest innovators and risk-takers steer way clear of it. As long as education remains a closed system, we will never see the education equivalents of Google, Facebook, Amazon, PayPal, Wikipedia . . . any real innovation. (V. Strauss, 2016a)

Portraying public education as an "industry" is consistent with corporate education reformers—including those in the Bush and Obama administrations—who argue that public schools should be run like a business and regulated by competition from outside the "public school monopoly."

Like *Waiting for Superman,* the point of her speech is that, *by their very nature,* public schools are not as good as charter and private schools. The latter have allegedly uncovered the most efficient and effective ways to educate children by virtue of their business acumen. She continued to advocate that parents "judge with their feet" (exit) even after charters in Michigan repeatedly failed to deliver on their promises (Strauss, 2016a; Zernike, 2016a, 2016b). She also recommended significant cuts for public schools, as secretary of education, and advocated increased support for charter schools and private school vouchers. Again, she claimed that parents are better able to improve public education than federal bureaucrats because they "vote with their feet" for the best schools. In addition, she diverted millions of federal dollars that were primarily intended to help struggling public schools, colleges, and universities during the COVID-19 pandemic to private and religious schools. These actions and policies harmed the neediest students while helping middle- and upper-income parents and private and charter schools (C-SPAN, 2017; DeVos, 2017; Green, 2020).

As one of the nation's largest school choice laboratories, Michigan serves as a natural experiment for understanding how exit—versus hierarchy (government regulation) and professionalism—influences public service provision.

Exit and the illusion of performance. Today, Michigan ranks near the bottom for nationally representative (NAEP) fourth- and eighth-grade math and fourth-grade reading tests, but charter schools scored worse than their public school counterparts. A 2015 federal review also found that there was "an unreasonably high" percentage of charter schools on a list of the state's lowest performers; moreover, that number had doubled since 2010, after DeVos successfully lobbied to expand the number of charter schools and prohibit restrictions on the ability of failing charter schools to expand or replicate. In fact, because Michigan lacks effective mechanisms for shutting down or even improving failing charter schools, the state tolerates more low-performing charter schools than almost any other state. At the same time, the unregulated market has resulted in a glut of charter schools and a higher closure rate. More than 150 schools have opened or closed in the last seven years and it is not unusual for students and teachers to change schools annually. Even charter supporters, like the Walton Family Foundation, are concerned about the instability of the unregulated market; it withdrew its support from Detroit—where 79 percent of the state's charters are located—despite committing $1 billion over five years to expanding charters and other forms of school choice elsewhere.[16]

Again, research supports that educators' views on charter schools and other forms of school choice are not partisan; they are shared across political parties and even those educators who fervently supported President Trump expressed a high disapproval rate for DeVos and her policies (Editorial Projects in Education, 2017). Their actual concern, which is supported by accumulated national evidence—with charter schools being the most heavily researched—is that school choice does little, if anything, to boost achievement and may actually increase the achievement gap between low-income and minority students and their more affluent peers. Charter schools perform no better—and often worse—than public schools.[17] They have high attrition rates, especially for students with academic and behavioral issues;[18] and, like their Michigan counterparts, many go bankrupt and close.[19]

Similarly, research on the nation's three largest state voucher programs—located in Indiana, Louisiana, and Ohio and collectively enrolling more than one-third of the 178,000 voucher students nationwide—shows that they did not improve and may actually have reduced student learning.[20] Students in the nation's only federally funded voucher initiative, located in Washington, DC, also performed worse on standardized tests than those who did not participate.[21]

There is no question that some students benefit from charter schools and voucher programs, but empirical research does not justify the Trump administration's decision to free millions of dollars in carry-over funding to nearly triple the number of students served in DC (from about 1,100 to 3,000); divert needed coronavirus funds away from public schools; and expand charter schools and private school voucher programs across the country.

Exit and the illusion of choice. Also contrary to neoliberal rhetoric, the increasingly privatized system in Michigan did not expand choice for the least well-off—the supposed beneficiaries of these reforms. The highest performing schools are typically out of reach for low-income students; the poorest neighborhoods remain underserved despite a glut of charter schools; most charter schools do not offer transportation; and bus service in cities like Detroit is often unreliable. Mothers who do not need to work typically find it easier to navigate the system in terms of time, transportation, and other resources; however, most parents appear to find it difficult to get information because more than a dozen organizations are issuing charters and DeVos successfully lobbied to kill legislation that would have provided more transparency (Zernike, 2016b).

Indiana is another interesting natural experiment for two reasons. DeVos lobbied heavily for the establishment of Indiana's voucher program in 2011 and, as governor of the state, Vice President Mike Pence successfully fought to loosen eligibility requirements to greatly expand vouchers. He said, "There's nothing that ails our schools that can't be fixed by giving parents more choices and teachers more freedom to teach" (E. Brown & McLaren, 2016). During his tenure, Indiana eliminated the requirement that children must attend public school before receiving vouchers for other schools; raised the income cutoff, so that more middle-class families were eligible for vouchers; and lifted the cap on the number of recipients covered, so that the voucher program is now one of the nation's largest and fastest growing. Once again, the program expanded choice while not helping underprivileged students and students of color, as claimed by policy makers—like President Trump—who characterized school choice as the civil rights issue of our time. Taxpayers also have less oversight and accountability because, unlike with traditional public schools, the state has no financial reporting requirements for private schools receiving voucher funds (E. Brown & McLaren, 2016; Zernike, 2016a).[22]

Exit and the illusion of democratic choice. Like other empirical research, this study finds that school choice has not leveled the playing field in terms of providing disempowered communities with more opportunities and voice;[23] instead, it has exacerbated segregation by race, income, language, and academic and behavioral issues.[24] Charter schools, for instance, are more likely to suspend students, especially students of color and those with academic and behavioral issues. Such disciplinary actions (detention, suspensions, expulsions) raise the risk of drop out and lead to higher rates of crime and imprisonment.[25] Just as problematically, this and other research suggests that school choice weakens public school finances and thus the ability of traditional public schools to serve existing students, especially those that attend the high-need, low-resource schools that disproportionately serve minorities and our nation's most economically disadvantaged children.[26]

Given these findings, it is not surprising that school choice does little—if anything—to boost achievement and might actually increase the achievement gap; it has also contributed to Blacks and Latinx being more segregated today than at any time in the past four decades.[27] This development is unfortunate. Research shows that racial integration was the most effective federal reform for narrowing the achievement gap, but segregation is also harmful for democratic societies.[28]

At a *bare minimum,* citizens must be able to reflect on their own beliefs, values, and experiences; compare them to those of other citizens; and engage in a dialogue that acknowledges differences while finding and creating common interests. The exposure to those from different backgrounds helps children develop tolerance, compassion, and the socioemotional skills that help them engage in these activities. As shown, those skills also help individuals thrive and foster the social cohesion that improves the performance of public institutions and organizations, like public education and public schools. Thus, even if it raises achievement—and research suggests that it does not—we should question growing privatization. School choice is compromising educators' ability to produce well-rounded human beings, instill democratic character, and achieve the democratic social purposes of public schools by fostering segregation, reducing social justice, and decreasing social trust and civic engagement.

Equally troubling, for the majority of those I interviewed, is the fact that recent reforms ceded authority to nondemocratically elected actors who have a mixed record of improving achievement; they also have a stake in closing and restructuring public schools and expanding testing, supplemental services, and charter schools (e.g., testing and publishing companies; education management organizations;

the education consulting industry; private and religious providers of supplemental services; charter schools; and the DeVos, Gates, and Walton Family foundations).[29] Respondents argued that these private and quasi-private entities are not being held accountable to the taxpayers who are funding them owing to a lack of regulation.

Again, at a *bare minimum,* democratic accountability requires that those receiving public funds be held accountable to the public through democratic procedures; yet this is just the opposite of what market advocates, like DeVos, have put into place in school choice programs across the country. Instead, they have deregulated and obfuscated hiring practices, choices about the curriculum, and procedures for disciplining and expelling students. For example, it is difficult for taxpayers to hold schools accountable in Washington DC because the voucher program administrator will not provide any information on how many students attend each school, how they are performing, or how the schools spend the $15 million they receive each year; and, unlike with public schools, Congress did not require that private school recipients of public tax dollars (voucher funds) disclose this information. Similarly, of the 10 largest private school choice programs in the nation, 7 either do not require students to take standardized tests or do not require schools to make those scores public, at least 3 do not publish information about how much revenue each school receives and how many students they serve, and at least 8 have no minimum performance requirements. In consequence, parents cannot compare the performance of their children with that of their peers or their chosen school with that of other private and public schools. Taxpayers, on the other hand, cannot make decisions about whether to continue to fund an individual school or the voucher program as a whole.[30]

When asked to comment about this lack of public information, the spokeswoman for then Secretary DeVos (Liz Hill) said that parents do not need "more data sets, they need more options. . . . When a robust choice program exists and students are no longer stuck in a mandated system, the ultimate accountability . . . is whether . . . parents choose to send their children there" (E. Brown, 2017). This view is a striking departure from the government's approach since the Clinton administration, where policy makers from both parties advocated improving public schools by publishing test scores to force them to fix low achievement. Instead, Secretary DeVos argued that "liberating students" from the public school monopoly *in and of itself* is enough accountability (E. Brown, 2017). In contrast, Hirschman (1970) argued that we cannot shield children from the effects of supposedly bad schools. Because public education is so critical for democracy, the *quality of public schools affects everyone in a society*. Exit is metaphorically but not actually possible or even desirable.

Exit and public servants. Again, this and other studies find that the desire to serve and other intrinsic values are the primary reasons listed for becoming a teacher; both are also critical for job satisfaction, decisions to remain in the profession, and the willingness to engage in *invisible work*. Two sources of data suggest that this is also true for administrators. Most are former teachers and quantitative studies show that public servants in general are more active in civic affairs (Brewer, 2003) than other citizens and demonstrate more "public service motivation" (PSM)—defined as a commitment to the public interest, service to others, and self-sacrifice as measured by donations of money, time, and blood (Houston, 2005). These civic and prosocial behaviors provide society with a source of social capital.

As shown, the participants in this study displayed very high levels of PSM; they also primarily linked *job satisfaction* to intrinsic rewards and *dissatisfaction* to extrinsic rewards and external factors (e.g., work conditions, too little autonomy, the low status of educators, and the effects of public policies). Rising job dissatisfaction appears to have increased exit in the postreform environment, especially in what I earlier referred to as Tier 1/Tier 2 schools, where teachers experienced significantly increased administrative controls. Annie, a suburban speech pathologist, discussed how that resulted in high turnover:

> I've never thought of leaving my profession. I've always *loved* it, and can't imagine doing anything else. . . . [But] things . . . in our district. . . . We've had about 19 teachers retire early, quit, or leave in the last year and a half . . . the atmosphere . . . morale . . . is *extremely* low. . . . I've thought of leaving, just the district, but . . . considered [emotional pause] leaving the profession . . . losing that many friends and colleagues . . . [is] disheartening . . . lives . . . destroyed . . . financially. . . . It's affected health . . . many . . . on medication . . . the distrust in our building . . . I just can't leave. . . . This is my life. . . . I am always happy . . . with the children. . . . [But there were many] who couldn't go on . . . [felt they were losing] their health . . . dignity . . . have no say . . . just a robot . . . [that] does things one way because someone has decided . . . this is the way . . . [to] teach. . . . Many . . . who left said, "I started to lose respect for myself."

The decline in professional authority reportedly spread across national reforms, but respondents described how the characterization of educators and other public servants as inefficient, ineffective, and self-interested enemies of reform also trickled down in ways that impeded their ability to do their jobs by fostering aggressive voice and increased neglect (opting out and noncompliance) among citizen coproducers.

Studies support informants' claims that feelings of low self-efficacy contribute to burnout and high turnover;[31] however, perceptions that recent reforms were unfair and undemocratic also contributed to increased exit through *ethical leaving*, especially among those who served those most severely affected by (e.g., low-income and minority students, ELLs, and children with learning, emotional, and behavioral issues). Increased exit among federal employees during the Trump administration confirms that ethical leaving may be a broader response to concerns about fair and democratic procedures and policies that reduce professional autonomy.[32]

Given these findings, it is not surprising that a recent study shows that there is a growing teacher shortage. The problem is multipronged and complex. *Demand* for teachers increased as school districts began hiring in 2015 after years of layoffs owing to the Great Recession. Some hiring also stemmed from enrollment increases and efforts in some states and districts to reduce teacher–pupil ratios to prerecession levels and restore classes and programs that had been eliminated. Even so, *attrition* (supply side) *accounts for as much as 95 percent* of the current and predicted drought and *two-thirds of that attrition is preretirement.* Supply-side shortages are also being driven by a 35 percent decline in new entrants—from 691,000 in 2009 to 451,000 in 2014—as well as a low level of reentry among those who leave. Reentrants comprise one-third to one-half of each year's supply, but *only around one-third of those who exit ever return to teaching* (Sutcher et al., 2016).

It should be noted that teacher shortages are not uniform across states and districts. Attrition is lower where wages are higher—like the Northeast—than in more poorly compensated areas, such as the South and some parts of the West. As in the past, districts that disproportionately serve low-income and minority students have been more severely affected. Majority-minority schools, for instance, had four times as many uncertified teachers, on average, in 2013–2014 as low-minority schools. When there are not enough teachers to go around, those schools most in need of high-quality teachers are the least likely to get them (Sutcher et al., 2016; Will, 2016).

As discussed, some issues with low salaries and poor working conditions result from tax cuts and unequal school financing, but there are other factors. California, for example, issued 10,200 *intern* credentials, permits, and waivers in 2015–2016—*more than double* the 5,000 issued in 2012–2013. The state's high-poverty districts were especially likely to hire those with substandard credentials, meaning they are not fully trained, poorly trained, or teaching outside their fields, but the high cost of living played a role in this development statewide. A teacher's salary is not enough to buy a home in many areas, even with relatively higher pay compared to other states.[33] This finding is interesting because retired teachers said that their inability to afford homes in the communities where they worked was one of the contributing factors to strikes during the 1960s and 1970s. It is therefore not surprising that teachers in Los Angeles and Oakland went on strike or that most of the strikes nationwide occurred in states where public school revenues were down as a result of tax cuts (Balingit, 2018a; CBPP, 2018; D. Goldstein, 2018d).

Also of interest, the Learning Policy Institute predicts that we could *virtually eliminate teacher shortages by reducing the attrition rate.* Between 20 and 40 percent of teachers leave the profession in the first five years, a figure that rises to 50 percent in some districts, especially those that serve low-income and minority students (Blume, 2016; Sutcher et al., 2016). At 8 percent annually, the attrition rate in the United States is about twice that of countries like Finland and Singapore, which are often cited as "gold star" education systems by American reformers. Reducing this annual attrition rate in half would virtually eliminate teacher shortages (Ayers, 2016; Sutcher et al., 2016). This study suggests, however, that this is unlikely to occur in a political climate that portrays teachers' voices as "self-interested" and something to be managed, but not listened to, or restricted in an effort to adopt and implement policies that privatize public education. Certainly high turnover (exit) may signal that a school district is not performing well, but, as shown, it also occurs when policies create unsustainable working conditions and/or a socially unjust system. If these conditions persist, the government will diminish the capacity of the profession to recruit and retain teachers, which affects the pool of qualified administrators and the efficiency and effectiveness of public schools.

Neglect in Organizational and Political Life

As a behavioral construct, neglect characterizes situations where one is physically present yet not complying or opting out, such as shirking occupational responsibilities, not participating in class, and nonvoting. My interviews highlighted four types of neglect among citizens and public servants: disruptive neglect, salutary neglect, asymmetric neglect, and interpretive neglect. Most of the reported neglect in this study resulted from interpretive effects, salutary neglect, and neglect as token compliance or undue rule abidance in situations where restrictions on voice combined with power asymmetries—differences in status within an organization or between groups in a society—to negatively affect the ability to take action or cause action to be taken. There appeared to be very little disruptive neglect.

Disruptive neglect involves subverting the system for personal gain or to get even for perceived slights. Among public employees, it includes shirking and free riding off the labor of others, using absenteeism or work time for personal business, and subverting administrative directives or engaging in delay tactics to avoid implementing a policy or directive. Among students, it includes cheating and refusing to do homework or study. Citizens, on the other hand, may use offshore accounts to avoid taxes.

Salutary neglect includes cases where noncompliance or nonparticipation result from moral or ethical considerations. It may also stem from professional judgments or cases where there is a lack of necessary resources, training, or cooperation from others. In terms of the latter, public servants may delay carrying out a policy or organizational directive until further clarification or they gain the needed cooperation or resources.

Asymmetric neglect is often, but not always, a passive form of voice or resistance. It stems from a distrust of the system—either due to perceived legal, economic, political, or social coercion or because policy makers and/or public organizations (e.g., the DOE or school district administrators) are adopting unethical or harmful laws, practices, or behaviors but heavily sanctioning voice.

Citizens and public servants may also interpret policies differently. Whether these *interpretive effects* are positive or negative (largely) depends on the outcomes; however, similar to voice, people may have different views on the constructiveness of such behaviors depending on where they sit.

Neglect in organizational life. In this book, educators describe how occupational norms interact with their schools, communities, and broader cultural, political, and economic environments to influence their behaviors. These diverse, and sometimes competing, contexts create interpretive effects with respect to public policies and organizational directives *even in the same district*. The words of a suburban high school social studies teacher, Molly, illustrate this point:

[The] school notifies parents of . . . absences . . . at different intervals. . . . [If] they miss 30 . . . they're removed from the course. . . . [Some] might view that policy as a way to help parents . . . [or] protect the school or themselves. . . . A parent can't say, "I didn't know my child was going to absentee out. You can't fail him or her." It's also hard to get a student to pass a state exam when they've missed so many classes. . . . Those who view it that way . . . keep those slips on their desk . . . waiting for number 30. It bothers me. . . . There are reasons . . . [for missing] that much school and it's my job to . . . work with that student and the parents. Sometimes that means giving some leeway . . . not handing in the 30th. . . . It's important for parents to know . . . [absences, but] second chances are okay. . . . My administrator . . . cares about the kids . . . [sends them] to teachers who are willing to give that policy a little slack. Sometimes . . . [a teacher says] "so-and-so must be getting close." . . . I say, "Not yet, we have him at different times. . . . Maybe he came in late. I *really* hope that doesn't happen. He's had a tough time, but . . . trying to get his act together" . . . to shame them a little. . . . Sometimes that works. . . . My administrator . . . must know. But this is . . . how high-stakes testing distorts how teachers do their jobs. . . . [Most] are in it for the right reasons . . . but, if you make their jobs dependent on test scores, it perverts that.

Molly is making no attempt to alter the attendance policy. She clearly understands why this SOP is in place but expresses that teachers who blindly follow it—without paying attention to the individual needs and situations of their students—pervert its intent. Their *undue rule abidance* is not subversive, yet it harms students and therefore neglects the norms of teaching.

Molly is also not trying to shirk her responsibilities or make her life easier. On the contrary, she asserts that her administrator knows and supports her use of professional discretion; acknowledges that it is hard to get a student to pass state exams after missing so much school; and, keeps students in her class even after the SOP would allow her to force them to withdraw. Instead, a story she told about her most difficult student confirms that her behaviors result from a commitment (loyalty) to the norms of teaching:

I was teaching [her 11th-grade American history as a senior because she had failed under another teacher]. She was pregnant and . . . had 29 absences . . . missed a month and a half . . . has to take a state test . . . along with students who have no absences or only a few . . . [to] graduate. . . . She had no free period. . . . [We met for extra help] during lunch. When she didn't show, I would go into the cafeteria . . . walk by her table

. . . say, "Hey, you heading to the classroom?" She didn't want that. It was embarrassing, so she made sure . . . to come meet with me [*laughs*]. We would chat about the content . . . how important it was for her . . . [and her child to have] at least a high school education . . . [and] to read to her child. . . . [I gave her children's] books. . . . [In] a meeting with our administrator . . . her mother . . . other teachers . . . she told everyone . . . she couldn't stand me. . . . It was because I wouldn't give her the easy out. . . . [I'm] being shamed . . . burning up inside. . . . You're the professional . . . can't show it . . . hold that against them. . . . Sometimes, in a dark part of my mind, I'd think, "Why are you pushing so hard to keep her. . . . Your life would be easier . . . wouldn't be blamed if she fails the test" [*laughs*] . . . [but I knew it was critical that] she finish high school.

Like Lorna, Molly "walks the walk" (obeys the norms of teaching) even amid adversity to advance the transformative and humanistic ends of public education. She also engages in social reconstruction by donating children's books to a pregnant student and by discussing with her the importance of a high school education and reading to a child.

Molly further displays a high degree of personal and professional efficacy and integrity. She does not passively engage in neglect. She does so when it is salutary for her students—even when it causes her to expend more effort or risk offending administrators. Like other teachers, Molly said that testing is perverting these kinds of salutary behaviors and claimed that this is one reason why tenure is so important:

[She] loved her previous teacher. . . . He loved to tell me that she hated me . . . [Yet] she failed the course under him. . . . He basically lets the kids do what they want . . . teaches to the test and mostly it works. . . . The funny thing is, she did end up passing [with me]. . . . She came back at the end of the next year and visited me. She didn't visit him [*laughs*]. And she told me that she was sorry that she was so awful to me . . . that she read to her baby every night [*getting emotional*]. Then, she said that I was her favorite teacher because I never gave up on her [*laughs*]. . . . This is why tenure is so important. You can have a student like that who really gives a teacher a hard time and that teacher is doing the right thing, while she praises the teacher who is not doing the right thing. She got her mother involved in it, administrators, other teachers, and other students. It wasn't a problem for me because I have a really good reputation, but it could have been. Administrators can choose to listen to that if they want to get rid of a teacher, so there needs to be due process.

Tenure encourages professional voice and salutary neglect on behalf of parents and students. It also enables teachers, like Molly, to pursue the academic, humanistic, and transformative ends of public education without fear of reprisal from school boards, administrators, citizens, and uncooperative students and/or parents.

Molly does not work in a district that heavily sanctions professional voice, but, as shown, more districts began doing so in the postreform environment. In these situations, educators appear to engage mostly in token compliance rather than disruptive neglect. *Token compliance* is not the same as subverting federal, state, or district directives and policies for personal gain or to "pay back" supervisors, parents, or students for perceived slights. It was typically a passive form of professional voice in situations where differences in status between individuals and groups within an organization (power asymmetries) were used to punish unscripted or unsolicited participation. This involved following some directives, partially following others, and circumventing policies that were harmful to children or contrary to the humanistic, transformative, and academic ends of public schools and teaching as a profession.

Token compliance is evident in Chapter 7, where teachers followed the exact scripts provided when administrators popped into the room and then returned to the "real business of teaching" when they left. I also discussed the behaviors of teachers who worked in the district that pushed "the gift of time," claiming children would outgrow special needs without the benefit of services. Debbie, an elementary teacher, discussed how she subverted that directive:

> [A student was not] understanding any of the letters or sounds. . . . My administrator . . . [kept saying] "He just needs time to grow." . . . [Mom said] "I don't think so." . . . I gave her, word for word, what my administrator said . . . with a face . . . odd tone . . . said, "Did you want to talk to your doctor . . . get a letter from him?" . . . [She did and] he has a learning disability. . . . A year would not have let him grow. . . . I went against what I was told . . . without . . . saying . . . our administrator isn't going to do anything about it. . . . I would have lost my job.

From the district's perspective, Debbie engaged in subversion; from an occupational and governance perspective she engaged in passive whistleblowing against a district that was violating federal laws and harming children in order to *subvert the system* and save resources. Neglect is a rational response if districts heavily sanction those who refuse to engage in unethical behaviors but, as discussed, still not more preferable than voice from a societal and governance perspective.

Informants agreed that most of those who choose to teach do so because they care about students and most administrators are former teachers. In consequence, they both share an interest in creating a *caring* climate—one that promotes democratic and egalitarian ideals (e.g., inclusion, participation, a commitment to social and procedural justice). Educators will leave (exit) or withdraw (neglect) from organizational life in those climates that are characterized by too much competition, a lack of due process, and the absence of social justice. The words of Claire, a suburban elementary teacher, exemplify this form of neglect:

> [Some] took the abuse . . . held their tongue . . . a lot of weight gain . . . physical and mental issues . . . chest pains. . . . If there wasn't food, there were Kleenex. . . . Some people isolated themselves . . . go to your classroom, close the door . . . come out when the kids arrive . . . close the door to teach . . . stay hidden. . . . We called that "flying under the radar" . . . survival mode . . . get through the day, have another day . . . one more off the calendar.

Neglect as a withdrawal from organizational life sometimes provides public managers (e.g., public school administrators) with slack to fix problems or issues without negatively affecting the performance of public agencies (e.g., public schools). Teachers, for instance, are able to withdraw from the organization while still fulfilling their obligations in the classroom. However, widespread withdrawal will reduce the efficiency and effectiveness of public schools because teachers no longer perform necessary *invisible work.*

Claire's narrative is important for another reason. Like Debbie, it is primarily about *asymmetric* neglect—passive withdrawal due to serious issues in an organization that also heavily sanctions voice. She is not shirking her occupational responsibilities, free riding off others' contributions, or engaging in other forms of disruptive neglect. Examples of the latter included demanding the best students to improve test scores and, although no one reported such, using work time for personal business and lateness/absenteeism to disrupt school business. Stories about teachers experiencing health and mental health issues due to recent reforms suggest that absenteeism may have increased, but it appears to be a minor problem.

Neglect as a political-market response. Like other public servants, educators work in public organizations and also serve as policy implementers. Prior to recent education reforms, they were subject to five forms of accountability: bureaucratic, legal, political, market, and professional. In contrast, recent reforms primarily relied on what I referred to as political-market accountability—the ability of residents to complain, vote down school budgets, vote out school board members, or exit when unhappy to another locality with lower property taxes or better performing schools. Because educational outcomes are coproduced, neglect may be a response to these behaviors rather than public policies, organizational practices, or the behaviors of supervisors. This claim is apparent in the words of Robin, a suburban elementary teacher:

> I tell people not to go into teaching because it is not about teaching. It's about making sure children can pass a test, documenting what you do to make sure children pass, answering parental emails . . . doing anything a parent wants . . . regardless of whether . . . it's in the best interests of their child . . . [how it] might affect the classroom. . . . If it comes to a battle between our professional opinions and parents' wants, opinions, or preferences, they will win. . . . [We've had teachers] told to apologize . . . [for] a comment on a report card. . . . "We noticed a decline in their reading skills so it would be great if you could read more at home while we work on those skills in class." . . . The kids are telling you that they're not reading at home. . . . We have learned not to voice our professional opinions. . . . [Parents] insist their children need modified tests. . . . [I] give special tests that are easier . . . modified study guides. . . . We don't have a lot of professional autonomy. . . . [You] quietly do your own thing . . . pick and choose [battles] . . . stay within the lines as much as possible. . . . Parents feel like Harvard is on the line in kindergarten . . . [get upset about] a bad grade on the report card. . . . This is elementary school, where no one is going to see these grades.

Robin does not work in the same school as Claire and did not use the words "flying under the radar," but she is conveying the same behavior. As a result of administrative *and* parental behaviors, she is less willing to voice her professional opinions about what is right for children. This is an example of passive withdrawal and neglecting the norms of teaching (e.g., professional voice and a service ethic).

These behaviors have not occurred in a vacuum. Informants perceive that recent discourse and policies have negatively affected their ability to do their jobs by increasing aggressive and competitive voice and neglect among citizens. For these reasons, it was often difficult to separate narratives about neglect in response to recent education reforms and neglect in response to organizational practices and/or the behaviors of citizen coproducers. When combined with other empirical studies, though, this research supports Hood's (1998) discussion of the potential negative effects of hierarchical account-ability (e.g., bureaucratic and political) and market accountability.

According to Hood (1998), *hierarchical accountability* may foster opportunism, shirking, slowed production, and other forms of non-welfare-enhancing behaviors (neglect) if workers learn that management keeps moving the goal posts when they meet objectives. Chapter 7 provided examples of these behaviors (e.g., teaching to the test) in response to the state raising the goal posts by "renorming" the tests and the "cutoff" points when more students began to pass. An urban middle school English teacher (Stephanie) discussed how that affected educators' willingness to comply with public policies and bureaucratic and political oversight:

> [We] are under restructuring. . . . People from the state . . . popping in . . . [said in a report] we were focusing too much on the test [*laughs*]. . . . You came in days before the test. . . . That is why they have no credi-bility. . . . [Initially] I did not feel poorly about the state. . . . They were . . . trying to be helpful. . . . We improved. . . . [They] raised the bar . . . 74 percent of my students passed . . . [then] only 40. . . . I hadn't changed. . . . The ripple effect . . . [my school feels] the test means noth-ing. . . . Before, they could say . . . we are improving . . . going to continue getting better. . . . If this is something that someone can randomly move around, than they have decided to opt out . . . get back to things that are important for learning. . . . I had done everything to improve . . . yet I and my students were deemed failures, I stopped comparing them to the test . . . taught the way that I thought I should. . . . [It's] a bell curve . . . some have to fail. . . . [We] had some morale and dignity when . . . improving . . . even though . . . we would always be . . . doing worse. . . . They are . . . taking away hope . . . the improvement that we had. . . . It's very unfair. . . . People tried so hard . . . in the face of . . . violence in the city . . . [everything] these kids are up against. . . . Removing any improvement . . . was demoralizing.

Participants also mentioned how the federal government moved the "goal post" from holding schools accountable (NCLB) to holding educators accountable (RttT and NCLB waivers).

With respect to *market accountability*, this study supports Hood's (1998) contention that it may motivate those who would otherwise shirk or play it safe to improve their performance, but competition may also weaken trust and the collective ethos that encourages people to work together to achieve common ends. Participants discussed, for instance, how increased competition reduced the willingness of some teachers to engage in the *invisible work* that advances the profession and improves the efficiency and effectiveness of schools, such as taking student teachers, mentoring or helping other teachers, and volunteering to serve on committees.

Some of these dysfunctional behaviors did not harm students (e.g., providing enriched school lunch menus the week prior to testing). As a whole, though, this and other research indicates that test-based accountability created social justice issues. I already discussed how teaching to the test disproportionately affected the skills of low-income and minority students, ELLs, and students with emotional, behavioral, and academic issues. Studies further show that test-based accountability increased dropouts, suspensions, and expulsions by creating the incentive for schools to encourage low-performing students to leave. The problem was most severe for students of color and students with disabilities (Advancement Project, 2011). Although this kind of *disruptive neglect* does not appear to be the norm, this study suggests that these behaviors increased across policies (NCLB, NCLB waivers, and RttT) as educators learned that the federal and state governments would keep moving the goal posts whenever they would meet objectives.

Regardless of why these strategic and dysfunctional behaviors occurred, they have real consequences for schools as organizations, teaching as an occupation, and society. Schools as collectivities need educators to be present in the hallways and engage in other voluntary behaviors, such as chaperoning dances, supervising clubs and activities, attending sporting events, and serving on committees. The government also needs educators to voice on any developments that negatively affect parents, students, and society, including, but not limited to, exposing waste, fraud, and abuse. The refusal of some educators to voice and/or engage in *invisible work* negatively influences organizational *and* occupational performance; it also affects the implementation of public policies.

Tier 1 and 2 school informants—where educators experienced significant new administrative controls—were especially likely to describe teachers who were performing in a ritualistic manner (e.g., teaching to the test) or following administrative orders (loyalty) rather than actively or even passively voicing by neglecting unethical directives or policies; however, other participants also acknowledged that recent reforms resulted in some teachers abandoning the norms of the profession or contributing to poor performance through arguably dysfunctional behaviors. If neglect digresses into more overt acts of negligence (e.g., absenteeism, showing up late, not preparing for class), public organizations and services will quickly go into decline.

Neglect as a positive response. Molly's narrative, though, shows that neglect does not always involve shameful or subversive behaviors. It may also have positive effects. As mentioned, there is a correlation between teacher effectiveness and years of teaching. High turnover also reduces the efficiency and effectiveness of public schools by reducing social cohesion, eroding the resources invested in teacher training, and decreasing the number of available mentors for new teachers. Neglect—in the form of withdrawing while still fulfilling occupational norms and obligations in the classroom—may help school districts and society by slowing turnover while enabling teachers to alter the situation by redressing organizational, societal, or policy issues.

Another benefit of temporary withdrawal is that the emotional and physical demands of teaching are quite high and often unsustainable over long periods of time. Teaching also has a clinical side that sometimes requires (emotional) distance to diagnose and treat problem areas. In both cases, withdrawal does not reflect low job satisfaction or work motivation; rather, it is a way for teachers to fulfill their occupational obligations, while managing stress and (temporarily) conserving resources, rather than exiting. Many expressed that this was one reason why it is critical to "have the summer off." Teachers use this time for work-related activities, such as gathering knowledge, planning lessons, and engaging in professional development; it also provides a break from the intense emotion work of teaching and helps them sustain their commitment to the profession.

Neglect that stems from moral or ethical concerns is also likely to be salutary for society, public institutions (public education), and public organizations (public schools or the DOE)—especially if it is a passive way to challenge (refuse to implement) harmful policies or restore equity to the employment relationship. Like voice and exit, however, neglect is more likely to result in social, economic, or political change (policy feedback) if it spreads—so that people become concerned and start a dialogue about why so many are "opting out." As discussed, this occurred when President Obama expanded the testing regime despite polls showing that the vast majority of Americans wanted less testing. As rising numbers of parents opted their children out of state, national (NAEP), and international (PISA) exams, growing numbers of schools began receiving penalties under federal law for low test participation rates. The most recent reform—the ESSA—allowed states to decide what happens to those schools.[34] This is an example of policy feedback through a combination of voice *and* neglect; it supports Hirschman's (1970) contention that exit, voice, loyalty, and neglect are more powerful when combined.

Summing up, conceptually, it makes sense to think of EVLN as separate constructs, but this research upholds Hirschman's (1970) claim that there is considerable crossover. Loyalty is important for building and maintaining trust. It increases the likelihood that individuals will choose voice, over exit and neglect, because it typically reflects a belief that issues or problems are temporary and will (eventually) be resolved. As with neglect, though, loyalty may reflect feelings of entrapment, rather than allegiance, owing to a belief that there is little possibility of influencing decisions and/or the costs of voice and exit are too high. In this study, loyalty as entrapped allegiance reduced the likelihood that educators would engage in organizational or occupational citizenship behaviors, as well as civic and prosocial behaviors in their role as citizens. Unlike neglect, it involved acquiescence or being co-opted rather than noncompliance. Some justified giving up voice because they could remain loyal to something else, such as their school, their colleagues, or teaching as an occupation. Yet this type of loyalty is problematic if it allows public servants to remain silent in the face of serious issues. One way the government may redress this issue is by adopting policies that promote loyalty *and* voice, such as tenure and seniority.

As a whole, this study shows that occupational norms and personal views of fairness and appropriate action play a very strong role in how educators do their jobs and implement policies. When violated, most will engage in voice, but growing numbers will exit and engage in subversive or *variegated* neglect—meaning they comply in some areas, engage in token compliance in others, and/or modify or outright disobey some directives and policies—especially if voice (speaking up and engaging in protest) is restricted. For better or for worse, policy makers must take values into account. Examining education from a moral or ethical lens—versus a business-economic lens—illuminates the need to redress the broader issues that affect public school performance, such as poverty, segregation, socioeconomic inequality, and the inequitable financing of public schools. Policies that focus solely on the behaviors of educators are likely to result in unintended consequences and dysfunctional behaviors more than real improvements in public education.

Discussion: Modeling Policy Feedback

The policy implementation literature (largely) separates the democratic process of making laws from the bureaucratic process of carrying them out. Yet political scientists recognize that "policies produce politics" (Schattschneider, 1935), meaning policy makers construct the experiences, identities, and behaviors of citizens and public servants in ways that influence demands for future policies. Some policies directly influence beliefs and behaviors. Others do so through the ways they interact with social contexts. Either way, as shown in Figure 1.4 (Chapter 1), policies create "implementation feedback loops" by generating new problems or dysfunctional behaviors; negatively influencing public service quality; redistributing power and influence in ways that create new political alliances; or reconstructing the values, beliefs, interests, and preferences of citizens and policy implementers. This section uses EVLN to map these claims and develop theory about policy feedback and democratic performance. Again, this theory is useful as policy makers consider the costs and benefits of future reforms and policies (Chapter 11).

Mapping EVLN for Public Service Quality and Policy Implementation

Initial research advocated separating EVLN into constructive, destructive, active, and passive behaviors to acknowledge the disparate effects on organizational performance (Farrell, 1983). In contrast, this study found that some forms of each of these behaviors are better than others for improving the quality of public services and policy implementation. Exit with voice, for instance, is preferrable to exit without voice because it provides information for reform, indicates when citizens' choices are not a sign of quality issues, or, less benignly, exposes when exit is being used as a tool of exclusion. An example of the latter is that the organization of public schools around geographic catchment areas has created the incentive for high-wealth communities to splinter from low-wealth ones and form new school districts. This form of economic segregation has been accelerating and creates barriers to socioeconomic integration and economic opportunity (EdBuild, 2019). Voice is also more variegated than conceptualized under Hirschman's (1970) model; it has a dark side and includes everyday acts of participation. Neglect, in contrast, is portrayed as the value destroying alternative to voice, but it may actually have positive effects.

This research further indicates that perceptions about whether these behaviors are positive or negative are often a function of "where you sit." It is certainly possible to objectively categorize and evaluate these behaviors; however, there are also gray areas where the interpretation depends on who is affected, how they are affected, and who is making those judgments. It is critical to interrogate these characterizations because those in power often control the narrative, such as framing a peaceful protest (voice) as a civil disturbance or a riot (neglect) because it challenges existing (political, social, or economic) arrangements. There may also be no intent to engage in negative behaviors, yet that may be the result of certain actions, such as when delayed or token compliance (Bardach, 1977) stems from a lack of resources or when uneven compliance results from interpretive effects.

To illustrate these findings, I have graphed these behaviors according to citizen responses in the political and coproduction space (Figure 10.2), public servants' organizational behaviors (Figure 10.3), and policy implementation (Figure 10.4). All four behaviors (EVLN) are now spatially organized in the form of a circumplex, rather than clearly divided into four quadrants (active/passive and constructive/destructive behaviors). Figures 10.5–10.7 use these graphs and the data from this study to model how EVLN affects *democratic performance*. Figure 10.5 shows how citizen responses affect democratic performance and the quality of public services. Figure 10.6 portrays how the behaviors of public servants affect the performance of public agencies (e.g., the DOE and public schools). Figure 10.7 models how citizens and public servants influence policy implementation. It is important to discuss a few caveats.

First, I use the terms *constructive, benign/protective,* and *destructive* self-interest to describe differences within each of these four constructs, but I am not claiming that all behaviors are self-interested. I chose this language to convey that we do not need to agree on whether people act out of sociotropic and altruistic motivations (e.g., loyalty, compassion for others, a desire to do good in society) or solely out of self-love (i.e., individual benefits or rewards). It is enough to acknowledge that each of these constructs has positive effects in some guises and negative effects in others, that some behaviors are more self-interested than others, and that people are sometimes willing to pull their behaviors in line in ways that help the group.

Second, loyalty is at the top of the chart because, in its most positive guise, it includes the key construct of trust. Trust in the political or economic system, elected officials, other citizens, and so forth encourages the most value creating forms of EVLN. Social cohesion

Destructive voice and participation:
Blaming behaviors/no attempt to fix problems
Seeking favorable treatment at the expense of others
Attempting to "win" despite negative effects on the community
Examples include:
Not in my backyard (NIMBY)
Adversarial legalism
Intolerance of opposing views
Sabotage (e.g., terrorism, vandalizing public property, stealing a teacher's grade book)
Demands for unearned benefits, rewards, or services

ACTIVE

Active engagement:
Contact officials
Run for office
Discuss political and school issues at community forums
Letters to the editor
Actively participate in neighborhood, community and school groups

Considerate voice:
Attempt to solve problems by considering individual and community concerns
Comply when disagree but act to change situation (e.g., participate in peaceful protests)
Peacefully noncomply (e.g., conscientious objectors, civil disobedience)

Passive participation:
Vote
Contribute to campaigns
Attend school functions

Competitive voice and participation:
Getting "my fair share" without regard for the effect on the community
Comply, but what's in it for me (squeaky wheel gets the grease)?

Loyalty as active allegiance:
Speak well of the polis, schools, and community
Civic and prosocial behaviors due to faith in the "system" (e.g., the government, the school, public servants) and/or one's communal ties

Exit as active choice:
Leave/transfer with voice when unhappy

Exit as exclusion:
People "like us" (e.g., private alternatives and gated communities)

Exit as passive choice:
Leave/transfer without voice when unhappy

DESTRUCTIVE

CONSTRUCTIVE

Interpretive effects:
Interpret laws, policies, or directives differently

Disruptive neglect:
Giving the appearance of cooperating while not complying
Subverting the system (e.g., cheating on a test, using offshore accounts to avoid paying taxes)
Shirking/passing off responsibilities (e.g., not doing homework, not studying for exams, free riding off of government programs)

Asymmetric neglect:
Withdrawal, nonvoting, and nonparticipation due to restricted voice, distrust of public officials, the system, and/or fellow citizens, or feeling like "You can't fight city hall"

Salutary neglect:
Nonparticipation (e.g., nonvoting, not attending school functions) out of a belief that the country or government (e.g., economy, community, public policies, public education, public schools) are "on the right track"
Noncompliance and nonparticipation due to moral, ethical, or other considerations

Loyalty as entrapped allegiance:
Undue rule abidance due to asymmetric (unequal) power relations
Individuals comply as a result of legal, economic, political, or social coercion rather than free will

Loyalty as misinformed allegiance:
Loyalty stemming from ignorance or incapacity; citizens lose sight of their interests

Loyalty as supportive allegiance:
Patience (silent compliance while awaiting change)

PASSIVE

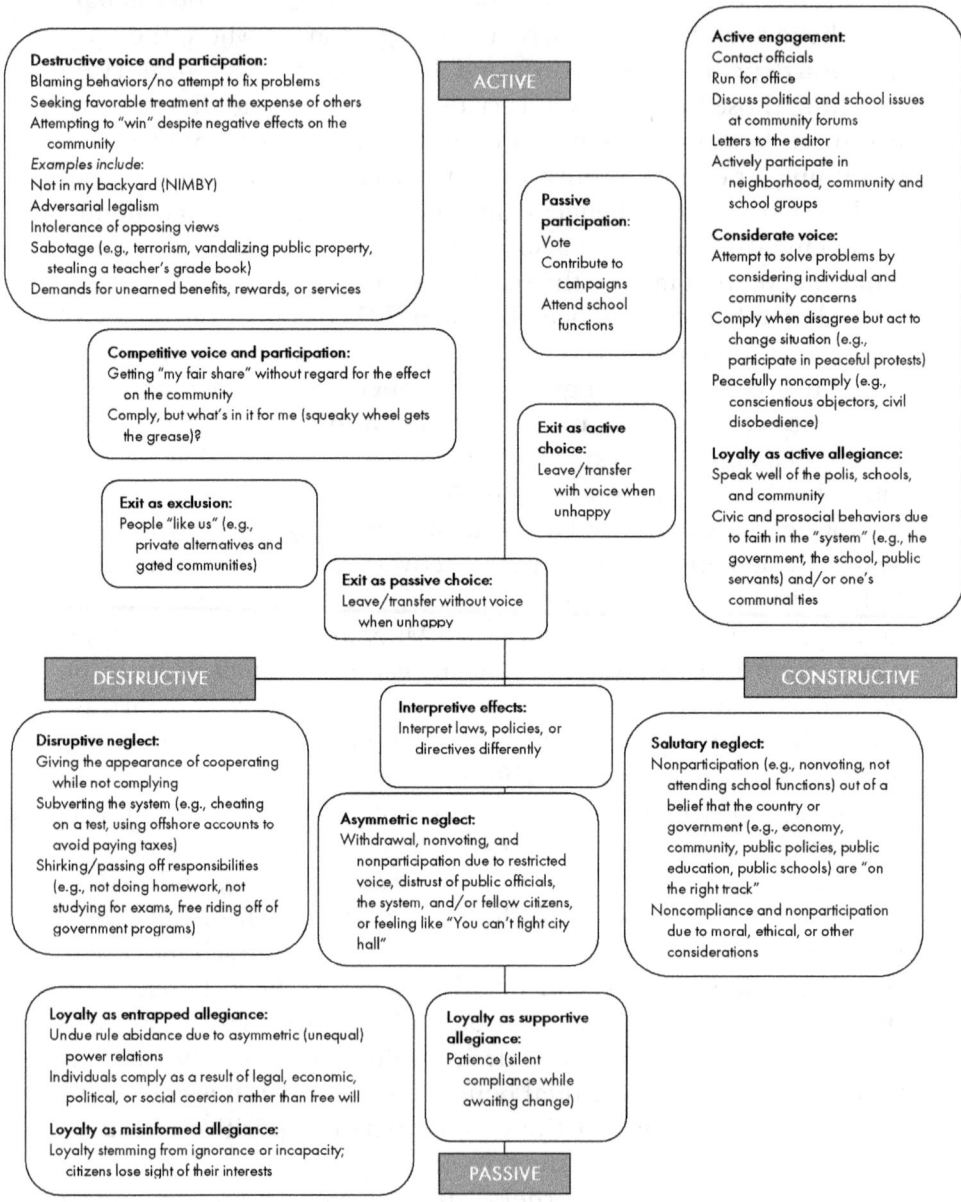

Figure 10.2. Citizen responses in the political and coproduction space.

Destructive voice and participation:
Blaming behaviors/no attempt to fix problems
Seeking favorable treatment at the expense of others
Attempting to "win" despite negative effects on the organization or others within the organization
Examples include:
Intolerance of opposing views
Demanding the best classes
Sabotage (e.g., destroying organizational property, ensuring organizational goals/policies fail)

ACTIVE

Passive voice and participation:
Engage in (private) behaviors that alter organizational goals, policies, or procedures (without voicing)
Carry out general intent of organizational goals, policies, or procedures, but adapt them to meet existing conditions (without voicing)

Considerate voice and engagement:
Comply but (overtly) act to change problem areas/get issues resolved
Attempt to solve the problem by considering individual as well as organizational concerns

Loyalty as active allegiance:
Speak well of the organization/ occupation/colleagues/government
Organizational and occupational citizenship behaviors owing to faith in the "system" (e.g., government, the organization, the occupation) and/or one's communal ties

Competitive voice and participation:
Getting "my fair share" without regard for the effect on the organization
Comply but what's in it for me (squeaky wheel gets the grease)?

Exit as active choice:
Leave/transfer with voice when unhappy

Exit as exclusion:
Covertly forced out as a result of voicing or because management/ coworkers feel "you are not one of us" or cannot be trusted to go along

Exit as passive choice:
Leave/transfer without voice when unhappy

DESTRUCTIVE

CONSTRUCTIVE

Disruptive neglect:
Giving the appearance of cooperating while not complying or conforming
Subverting the system
Shirking and free riding off the labor of others
Examples include:
Lateness/absenteeism
Using work time for personal business
Passing off responsibilities
Engaging in delay tactics until interest wanes, conditions change, or opposition builds

Interpretive effects:
Workers interpret the policy or directive differently than the organization

Salutary neglect:
Noncompliance and nonparticipation due to professional expertise or judgment and/or moral, ethical, and other considerations
Postpone carrying out a policy or directive because more clarification is needed, it is not comprehensible, there is a lack of resources, or there is a lack of necessary cooperation from others

Asymmetric neglect:
Withdrawal due to feelings of distrust in the face of serious issues, where voice is heavily restricted
Biding your time until you can get out

Loyalty as entrapped allegiance:
Undue rule abidance/following bad policies due to asymmetric (unequal) power relations
Individuals comply as a result of coercion rather than free will
Biding time until you can get out

Incompetent or misinformed allegiance:
Erroneous and ritualistic behaviors that are not done covertly, to get authority, or to construct change
Behaviors are based on old SOPs, a lack of expertise or effort, or due to "just doing as told"

Loyalty as supportive allegiance:
Patience (silent compliance while waiting for the organization to change)

PASSIVE

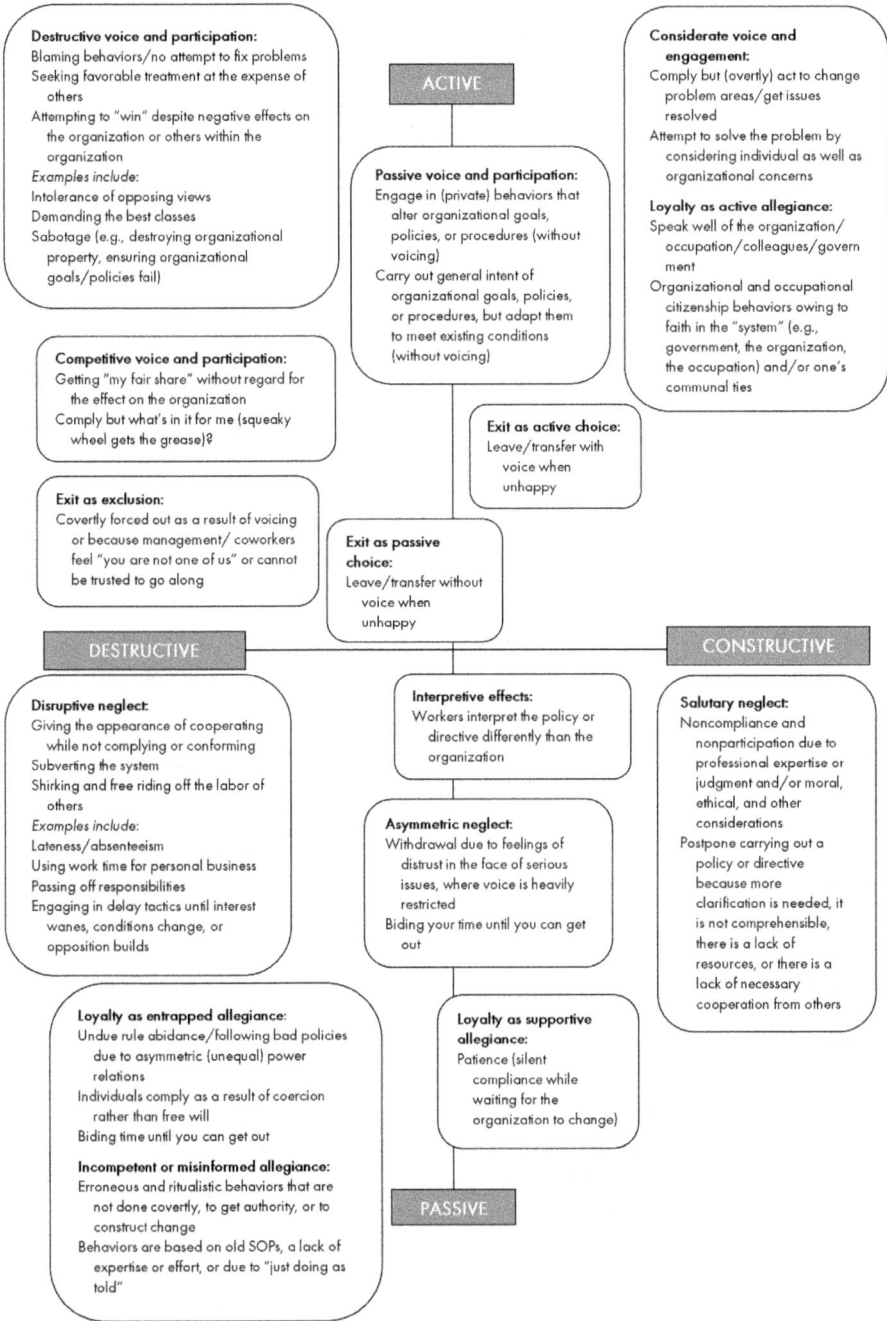

Figure 10.3. Public servants: organizational behaviors.

ACTIVE

Aggressive voice and destructive noncompliance:
Adversarial legalism
Sabotage (e.g., build flaws into policies or directives to prevent them from being implemented or implemented as intended)

Self-interested voice and destructive compliance:
Comply, but what's in it for me (squeaky wheel gets the grease)?
Blaming behaviors/no attempt to fix problems

Voice as passive resistance:
Engage in behaviors that alter the goals, practices, or procedures prescribed by a policy or directive with no attempt to change it

Voice as constructive compliance:
Implement and conform while acting to change a policy or directive

Voice as constructive non-compliance:
Engage in behaviors that alter the goals, practices, or procedures prescribed by a policy or directive while acting to change it
Examples include:
Implement a variation of a policy or directive
Carry out the general intent of a policy or directive, but adapt it to meet existing or changing conditions

Exit as exclusion:
Covertly forced out as a result of voicing or because management or coworkers feel "you are not one of us" or cannot be trusted to go along

Exit as active choice:
Leave/transfer with voice when unhappy

Exit as passive choice:
Leave/transfer without voice when unhappy

DESTRUCTIVE   **CONSTRUCTIVE**

Disruptive neglect:
Give the appearance of cooperating while not complying or conforming
Bureaucratic shirking and undue rule abidance
Delay tactics (wait for interest to wane, conditions to change, or opposition to build)
Subverting the system (e.g., encourage low performing students to stay home on test day)

Interpretive effects:
Interpret the policy or directive differently

Asymmetric neglect:
Comply but withdraw due to opposition to a policy or directive, restricted voice, feelings of distrust in the face of serious issues, and/or feeling like "You can't fight city hall"

Salutary neglect:
Noncompliance and nonparticipation due to professional expertise or judgments or moral, ethical, or other considerations
Delay until further clarification (postpone carrying out policies or directives because they are not comprehensible, there is a lack of resources, or there is a lack of necessary cooperation from others)

Entrapped allegiance:
Undue rule abidance/following bad policies or directives due to asymmetric power relations
Individuals comply as a result of coercion rather than free will
Biding time until you can get out

Incompetent or misinformed allegiance:
Blindly following bad policies or directives
Erroneous and ritualistic behaviors that are not done covertly, to get authority, or to construct change
Behaviors are based on old SOPs or due to a lack of expertise, effort, or "just doing as told"

Loyalty as supportive allegiance:
Patience (silent compliance while awaiting change)

PASSIVE

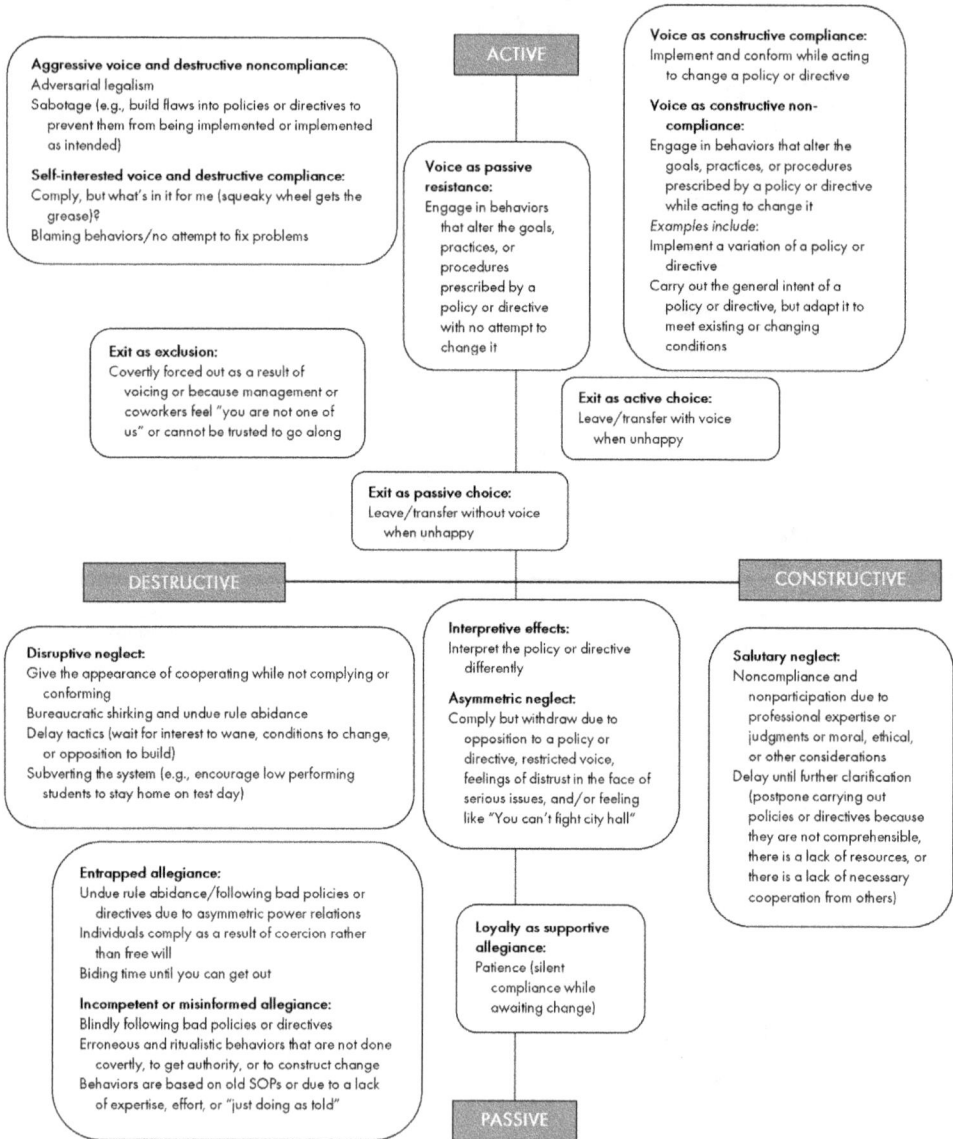

Figure 10.4. Policy implementation.

and social trust—again, defined as a belief in the honesty, integrity, and reliability of others—inspire individuals to pull their behaviors in line in ways that benefit the group. Without them, governments, organizations, and groups must exercise more social control, which is less efficient and effective than when individuals voluntarily control themselves.

Third, social cohesion *generally* improves performance but may destroy public value by serving as a tool of social exclusion and advancing private interests over collective ones.[35] Loyalty also harms society, organizations, groups, and individuals when group solidarity promotes downward leveling norms or when blind loyalty causes individuals to engage in harmful behaviors or follow bad policies or practices. An example is when loyalty to a public leader or a specific group within society encourages citizens to reject democratic norms, such as the peaceful transfer of power.

This study suggests that these issues are more likely to occur in societies with large political, social, and economic power asymmetries. Such is the case for downward leveling norms, which arise from situations where group solidarity is cemented through common experiences of adversity and opposition to mainstream society; however, as discussed in Chapter 8, it is also easier for political and economic interests to create wedge issues that promote divisive outcomes for personal and/or in-group gain. The example I used was research and public opinion polls that show political polarization and disinformation are driving a significant share of the deaths in the recent pandemic by influencing citizens' willingness to wear masks and get vaccinated (Kirzinger et al., 2021; Wood & Brumfiel, 2021). In these societies, the government must pull together the social fabric by developing socially integrating institutions (e.g., public education) and by promoting organizations that encourage voice from different groups in society (e.g., unions, occupations and professions, consumer associations, farmers' organizations, and worker, consumer, and renter cooperatives).

As shown in Figures 10.5–10.7, social cohesion, social trust, and trust in government are especially critical for democratic performance. Democratic performance improves by moving individual behaviors up and/or over to the far left corner.

Fourth, I am mapping the relationships between trust, social cohesion and control, EVLN, and democratic performance based on my interviews but have purposefully not defined *democratic performance*. Future studies need to develop that construct and then test the relationships mapped through this study. Comparisons between

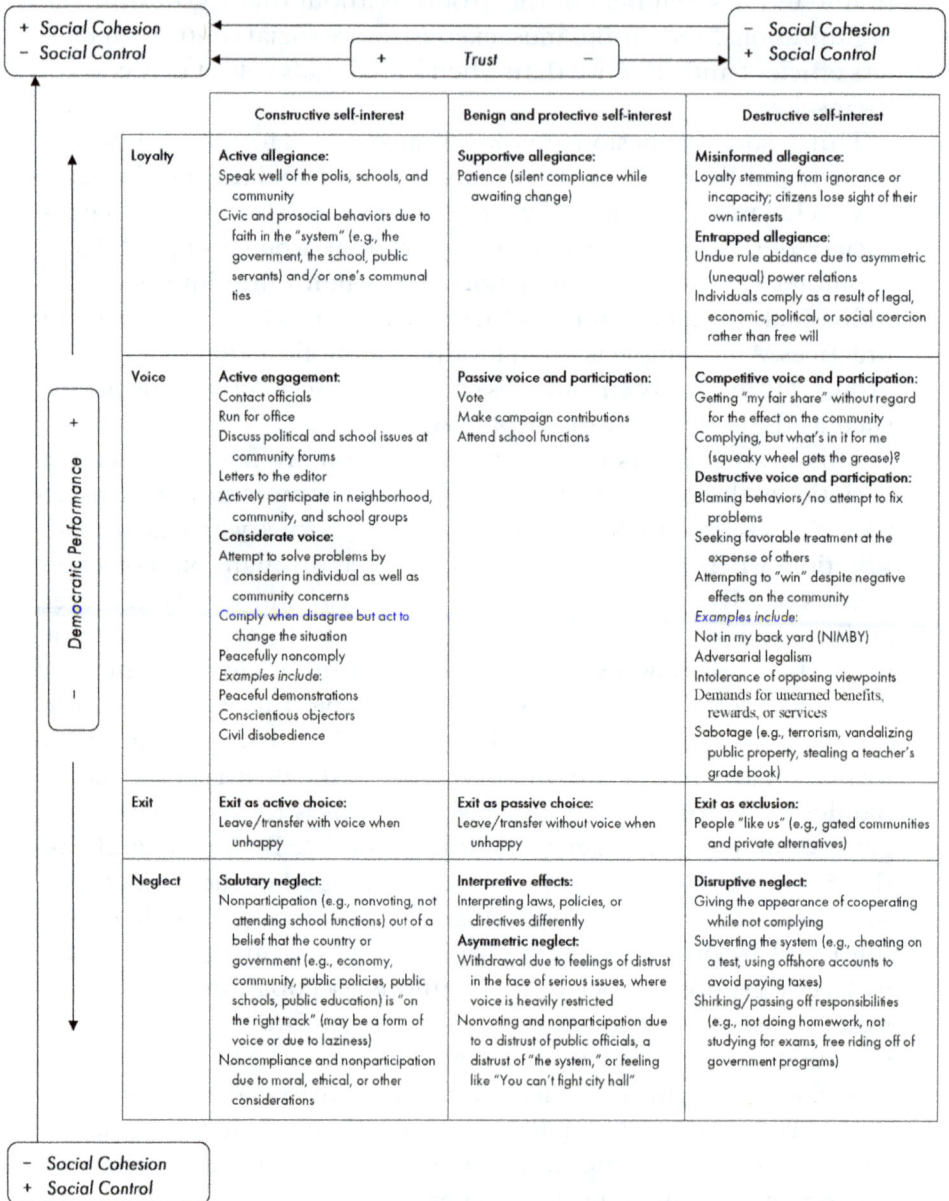

		Constructive self-interest	Benign and protective self-interest	Destructive self-interest
+ Social Cohesion / **− Social Control** ←——————————— **+ Trust −** ——————————→ **− Social Cohesion** / **+ Social Control**				
Democratic Performance (+ / −)	Loyalty	**Active allegiance:** Speak well of the polis, schools, and community. Civic and prosocial behaviors due to faith in the "system" (e.g., the government, the school, public servants) and/or one's communal ties	**Supportive allegiance:** Patience (silent compliance while awaiting change)	**Misinformed allegiance:** Loyalty stemming from ignorance or incapacity; citizens lose sight of their own interests. **Entrapped allegiance:** Undue rule abidance due to asymmetric (unequal) power relations. Individuals comply as a result of legal, economic, political, or social coercion rather than free will
	Voice	**Active engagement:** Contact officials. Run for office. Discuss political and school issues at community forums. Letters to the editor. Actively participate in neighborhood, community, and school groups. **Considerate voice:** Attempt to solve problems by considering individual as well as community concerns. Comply when disagree but act to change the situation. Peacefully noncomply. *Examples include:* Peaceful demonstrations. Conscientious objectors. Civil disobedience	**Passive voice and participation:** Vote. Make campaign contributions. Attend school functions	**Competitive voice and participation:** Getting "my fair share" without regard for the effect on the community. Complying, but what's in it for me (squeaky wheel gets the grease)? **Destructive voice and participation:** Blaming behaviors/no attempt to fix problems. Seeking favorable treatment at the expense of others. Attempting to "win" despite negative effects on the community. *Examples include:* Not in my back yard (NIMBY). Adversarial legalism. Intolerance of opposing viewpoints. Demands for unearned benefits, rewards, or services. Sabotage (e.g., terrorism, vandalizing public property, stealing a teacher's grade book)
	Exit	**Exit as active choice:** Leave/transfer with voice when unhappy	**Exit as passive choice:** Leave/transfer without voice when unhappy	**Exit as exclusion:** People "like us" (e.g., gated communities and private alternatives)
	Neglect	**Salutary neglect:** Nonparticipation (e.g., nonvoting, not attending school functions) out of a belief that the country or government (e.g., economy, community, public policies, public schools, public education) is "on the right track" (may be a form of voice or due to laziness). Noncompliance and nonparticipation due to moral, ethical, or other considerations	**Interpretive effects:** Interpreting laws, policies, or directives differently. **Asymmetric neglect:** Withdrawal due to feelings of distrust in the face of serious issues, where voice is heavily restricted. Nonvoting and nonparticipation due to a distrust of public officials, a distrust of "the system," or feeling like "You can't fight city hall"	**Disruptive neglect:** Giving the appearance of cooperating while not complying. Subverting the system (e.g., cheating on a test, using offshore accounts to avoid paying taxes). Shirking/passing off responsibilities (e.g., not doing homework, not studying for exams, free riding off of government programs)
− Social Cohesion / **+ Social Control**				

Figure 10.5. Citizen responses in the political and coproduction space.

		+ Social Cohesion − Social Control	+ Trust −	− Social Cohesion + Social Control

		Constructive self-interest	Benign and protective self-interest	Destructive self-interest
Democratic Performance (+)	Loyalty	**Active allegiance:** Speak well of the organization/occupation/colleagues/government Organizational and occupational citizenship behaviors owing to faith in the "system" (e.g., government, the organization, the occupation) and/or one's communal ties	**Supportive allegiance:** Patience (silent compliance while waiting for the organization to change)	**Entrapped allegiance:** Undue rule abidance/following bad policies due to asymmetric (unequal) power relations Individuals comply as a result of coercion rather than free will Biding time until you can get out **Incompetent or misinformed allegiance:** Erroneous and ritualistic behaviors that are not done covertly, to get authority, or to construct change Behaviors are based on old SOPs, a lack of expertise or effort, or due to "just doing as told"
	Voice	**Considerate voice and engagement:** Comply but (overtly) act to change problem areas/get issues resolved Attempt to solve problems by considering individual as well as organizational concerns	**Passive voice and participation:** Engage in (private) behaviors that alter the goals, policies, and procedures of the organization (without voicing) Carry out the general intent of organizational goals, policies or procedures, but adapt them to meet existing conditions (without voicing)	**Competitive voice and participation:** Getting "my fair share" without regard for effect on the organization Comply, but what's in it for me (squeaky wheel gets the grease)? **Destructive voice and participation:** Blaming behaviors/no attempt to fix problems Seeking favorable treatment at the expense of others Attempting to "win" despite negative effects on the organization or others within the organization Examples include: Intolerance of opposing viewpoints Demanding the best classes Sabotage (e.g., destroying organizational property, ensuring organizational goals/policies fail)
	Exit	**Exit as active choice:** Leave/transfer with voice when unhappy	**Exit as passive choice:** Leave/transfer without voice when unhappy	**Exit as exclusion:** Covertly forced out as a result of voicing or because management or coworkers feel "you are not one of us" or cannot be trusted to go along
(−)	Neglect	**Salutary neglect:** Noncompliance and nonparticipation due to professional expertise or judgments and/or moral, ethical, and other considerations Postpone carrying out a policy or directive because more clarification is needed, it is not comprehensible, there is a lack of resources, or there is a lack of necessary cooperation from others	**Interpretive effects:** Workers interpret a policy or directive differently than the organization **Asymmetric neglect:** Withdrawal due to feelings of distrust in the face of serious issues, where voice is heavily restricted Biding your time until you can get out	**Disruptive neglect:** Giving the appearance of cooperating while not complying or conforming Subverting the system Shirking and free riding off others Examples include: Lateness/absenteeism Using work time for personal business Pass off responsibilities Delay tactics (wait until interest wanes, conditions change, or opposition builds)

− Social Cohesion
+ Social Control

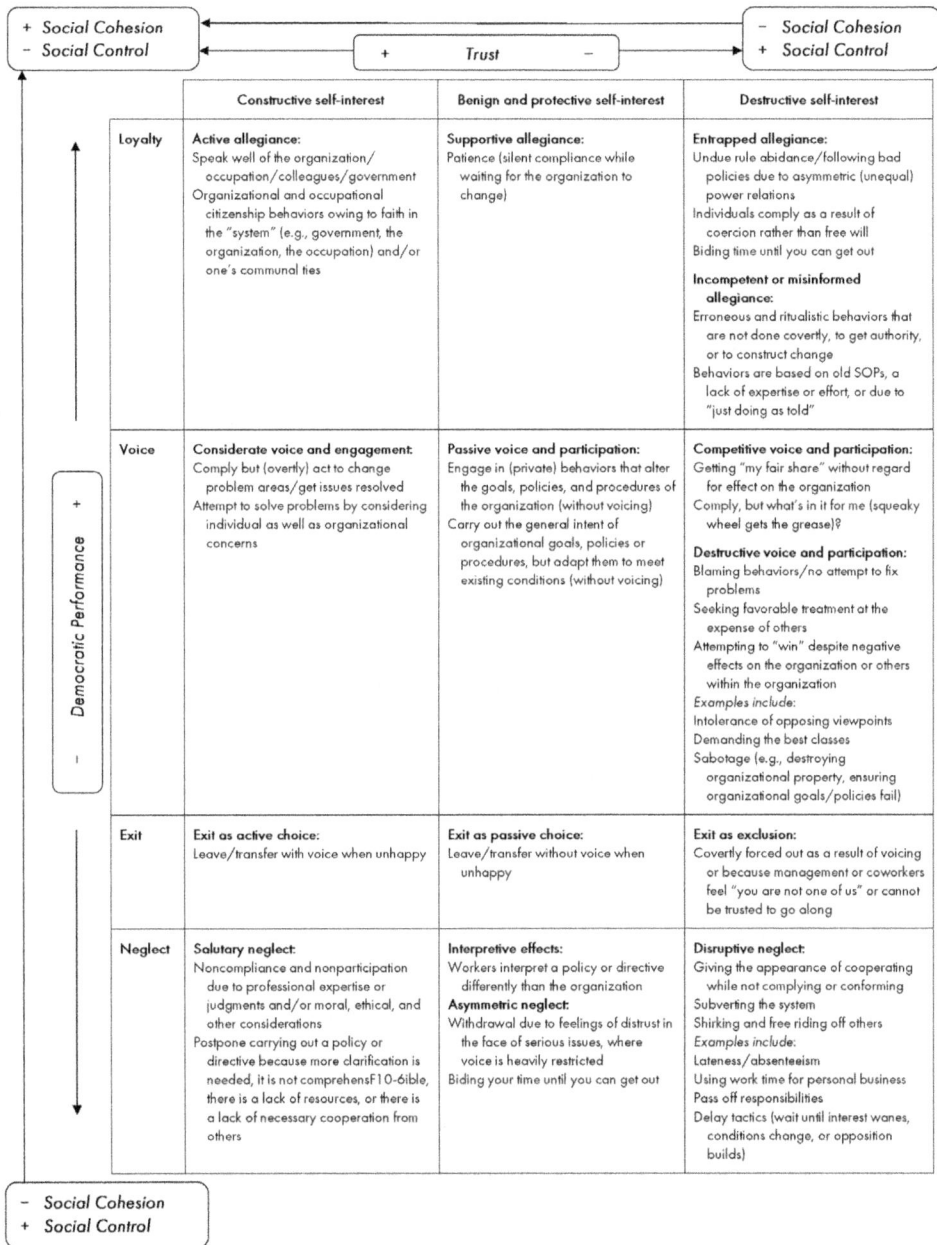

Figure 10.6. Public servants: organizational behaviors.

+ Trust −

		Constructive compliance	Constructive noncompliance	Destructive compliance	Destructive noncompliance
Democratic Performance (+ / −)	Loyalty	**Supportive allegiance:** Patience (silent compliance while awaiting change) Note: implementing a policy or directive while acting to change it (see voice) is preferable to silent compliance in terms of democratic performance; loyalty remains at the top of the chart because this study suggests it increases the likelihood of compliance with positive forms of voice		**Entrapped allegiance:** Undue rule abidance/ follows bad policies due to asymmetric power relations Individuals comply as a result of coercion rather than free will Biding time **Incompetent or misinformed allegiance:** Blindly following bad policies or directives Erroneous and ritualistic behaviors that are not done covertly, to get authority, or to construct change Behaviors are based on old SOPs, a lack of expertise, effort, or "just doing what I was told to do"	
	Voice	**Implement and temporarily conform:** Comply with a policy or directive while acting to change it	**Considerate voice:** Engage in behaviors that *alter the* goals, practices, or procedures prescribed by a policy or directive while acting to change it *Examples include:* Implement a variation of the policy or directive Carry out the general intent of a policy or directive, but adapt it to meet existing or changing conditions **Passive resistance:** Behaviors that silently alter harmful policies/directives in cases where voice is heavily restricted; judgments about whether these behaviors are positive or negative often depend on where you sit	**Self-interested voice:** Comply with a policy or directive, but what's in it for me (squeaky wheel gets the grease)? Blaming behaviors/no attempt to fix problems	**Aggressive voice:** Adversarial legalism Sabotage (e.g., build flaws into policies or directives to prevent them from being implemented or implemented as intended)
	Exit		**Exit as active choice:** Leave/transfer with voice when unhappy	**Exit as exclusion:** Covertly forced out as a result of voicing or because management or coworkers feel "you are not one of us" or cannot be trusted to go along	**Exit as passive choice:** Leave/transfer without voice when unhappy
	Neglect		**Salutary neglect:** Noncompliance and nonparticipation due to professional expertise or judgments and/or moral, ethical, and other considerations Postpone carrying out policies or directives because more clarification is needed, they are not comprehensible, there is a lack of resources, or there is a lack of necessary cooperation from others	**Interpretive effects:** Interpret the policy or directive differently **Asymmetric neglect:** Comply but withdraw due to opposition to a policy or directive, restricted voice, feelings of distrust in the face of serious issues, and/or feeling like "You can't fight city hall"	**Disruptive neglect:** Give the appearance of cooperating while not complying or conforming Bureaucratic shirking and undue rule abidance Delay tactics (delay until interest wanes, conditions change, or opposition builds) Subvert the system (e.g., encourage low performing students to stay home on test day)

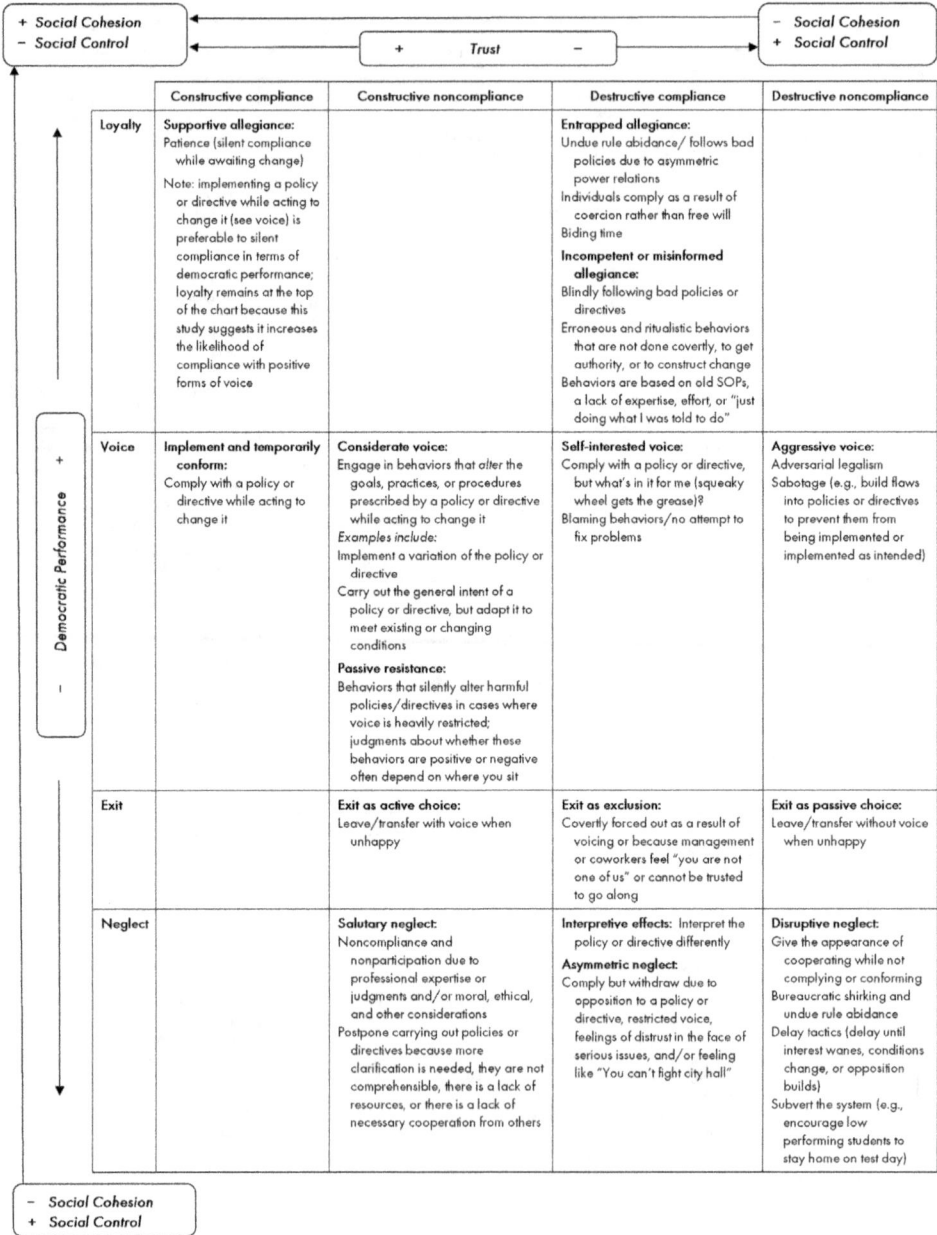

Figure 10.7. Policy implementation.

states or nations, for example, could explore the link between trust in government, social trust, and social cohesion (e.g., socioeconomic inequality and segregation) and the effectiveness of public responses to COVID-19. My interviews provide some broad parameters.

Democratic performance is broader than the efficiency and effectiveness of public services and public servants. Democratic institutions—such as public education—have broader ends. Policies that focus solely on technocratic and economic means and ends (e.g., competition, choice, performance) are likely to foster unintended consequences and dysfunctional behaviors unless tempered by more egalitarian and communitarian norms, goals, and practices.

With respect to public education, the focus on efficiency and effectiveness, as measured by test scores or consumer satisfaction, silences democratic values and other important societal goals, such as procedural justice, fairness, autonomy, and the creation of a more egalitarian, participatory, and caring society. Americans care about these ends, not just public service quality or even costs. When performance is reduced to a test score, teachers who teach to the test (neglect) are actually considered equal to those who do not, so long as the outcomes (test scores) are the same.

In the political space, the concept of democratic performance is broader than the aggregation of individual preferences and interests. By that definition, policies are democratic if they are adopted by democratically elected legislatures, regardless of how few vote or participate in government; it fails to acknowledge how the majority or powerful interests may use their political, social, and economic capital to suppress dissent and repress participation, with or without the force of law. The construct of democratic performance must also move beyond hierarchical (TPA) and market (NPM) controls that intentionally or unintentionally result in public servants blindly following policies or directives regardless of how they harm citizens, erode trust in government, and contradict their professional or occupational norms. Public institutions (e.g., public education and public policies), public organizations (e.g., the DOE and public schools), and public spaces (e.g., public schools, libraries, parks) are resources for political and social learning; each may increase civic capacity by socializing citizens and providing a place for people from different backgrounds to come together. Less positively, they may destroy public value rather than creating it.

Fifth, I have mapped organizational, citizenship, and implementation behaviors separately; however, democratic performance, including, but not limited to, the responsiveness of public servants and the quality of public services, results from the interaction between these three spheres. Public servants, for instance, are citizens as well as policy implementers; their behaviors are influenced by citizen coproducers (e.g., taxpayers, clients, parents, students), the organizations in which they work, public policies, and "wicked problems." Policies that ignore these important social contexts are likely to result in dysfunctional behaviors and unintended consequences. This is also true with respect to citizens.

The next section uses these ideas to explore the democratic performance of different *public service paradigms*—again, defined as overarching narratives about the proper role of government in society and the best way to define and achieve the public interest through, for example, democratic procedures, public policies, taxes and spending, government regulations, and the management and organization of government agencies and public programs. Public service paradigms have different effects on the behaviors of citizens and public servants; they therefore have different effects on democratic performance.

Public Service Paradigms, EVLN, and Democratic Performance

As discussed, TPA stresses voice and NPM advocates choice—a form of exit where citizens "vote with their feet" (Chubb & Moe, 1990; Tiebout, 1956)—as the best way for citizens to regulate the behaviors of elected officials and public servants. Proponents of NCG—a less dominant model of public service provision—recognize the importance of citizens for the delivery of many public goods and services; they argue that networks reduce the need for more formal hierarchical controls by enabling members to monitor one another (Benington, 2011). Teachers, for instance, use peer group accountability to ensure that colleagues adhere to occupational norms and practices; they also use their social ties to encourage parents and students to pull their behaviors in line in ways that advantage the "group" (i.e., the classroom, school, society). Either way, individuals fulfill their obligations owing to feelings of loyalty, trust, and respect for fellow members (social capital) and/or because they are closely aligned with the group's norms and values (i.e., social cohesion). In Chapter 8, I linked each paradigm to its preferred form of accountability and education policy (Table 8.1; Figure 8.1). Figure 8.1 tells a story about democratic performance, as evident in the implementation of education reforms.

The ESEA. As institutionalized under the ESEA, the Great Society recognized that neglect was a destructive alternative to exit, voice, and loyalty. Neglect is not always a sign of serious issues, such as when citizens stay home on election day or parents do not participate in school owing to disinterest or a belief that the country, government, or school are "on the right track." It becomes one if neglect is systematically tied to race, ethnicity, class, educational background, age, and gender—like in the United States, where those with a high school diploma or less, young people, minorities, and the economically disadvantaged are less likely to vote and participate in government (Piven & Cloward, 1988; U.S. Census, 2021) or at school (see Chapter 9). In addition, neglect is harmful if policy makers consistently mobilize some groups and demobilize others as a way to influence elections and weaponize policy feedback. This includes using public discourse as symbolic violence and adopting policies that discourage economic and political voice, such as laws that restrict unionization (e.g., RTW laws) and reduce citizen participation (e.g., restrictions on registration, voting, and/or protest). When the least well-off give up or are deprived of their voice, politics becomes degenerative—government policies increasingly fall into a *pattern* of allocating benefits and burdens in ways that are ineffective, inefficient, and unfair (Stone, 1997).

Those who are portrayed and treated as deserving and entitled (e.g., small businesses, scientists, the military, the middle class, homeowners) become less likely to empathize with the least advantaged because they have rarely experienced a government that neglects, burdens, or punishes them. They also are more likely to view the government as being on the wrong track when it confers benefits on poorly regarded "others" (i.e., those society views as deviants and dependents); blame the government—rather than themselves—when policies are ineffective; and advocate private alternatives—which only they routinely have the means to afford—over public services. Examples include private security, schools, health, mental health, and drug treatment services. Even when the government provides advantaged groups with resources, such as vouchers for private schools, they typically do not view themselves as claimants. The lesson that they have learned from public policies and discourse is that they are entitled to these benefits as citizens. Moreover, not viewing themselves as claimants, they are more likely to argue that others should "pull themselves up by their bootstraps" or have their needs met through their families or religious organizations. Public discourse and policies have taught them that the problems confronted by the least well-off have resulted from a failure of individual will rather than a lack of available opportunities or the inequitable treatment of citizens through political, economic, or social institutions (A. Schneider & Ingram, 2005b).

In comparison, "contenders" (e.g., Wall Street bankers, wealthy individuals, labor unions, the gun lobby) learn to get what they can through back doors because the government typically provides them with benefits through hidden side payments—such as tax breaks, government contracts, and deregulation—to avoid appearing to favor groups that are perceived to have gained their power and resources through unfair, underhanded, or self-interested actions. Despite poor social regard, contenders are rarely punished by public policies because they have political capital. That changes for those that society views as dependents and deviants (children, immigrants, the mentally ill, welfare recipients, drug addicts, criminals); both groups are less likely to perceive that they will benefit from mobilizing, lobbying, or voting because they have experienced the government as a random or unjust force in their lives. This is particularly true of those that society views as deviant. Some may escape the stigmatized group by hiding their identity; others agree with the negative stereotype but offer arguments about how they differ from the group. Soss (2005) showed, for example, that this was the case with some welfare recipients. Either way, these behaviors help some escape social stigma yet make it difficult to mobilize the "group" on behalf of change (A. Schneider & Ingram, 2005b).

Over time, these social constructions result in the so-called deserving and entitled (typically) growing stronger while the undeserving unwittingly collude with the powerful to perpetuate their own subordination. In politics, this leads to the oversubscription of policies that benefit advantaged groups and punish deviants, the undersubscription of policies that benefit dependents, and the costs of policies that benefit contenders becoming increasingly hidden so that society is unaware of them (A. Schneider & Ingram, 2005b). Within this environment, some communities and groups may function quite well, but others are only getting by and/or are struggling with exclusion or overt conflict (Woolcock & Narayan, 2000). These outcomes exist in some parts of America, where elite groups live in exclusionary enclaves while, in other communities, public infrastructure and services have either broken down or are chronically underfunded; gangs or private policing are the primary sources of law enforcement; and economic life is sustained through the informal or illegal economy because community residents suffer from isolation and a dearth of political, social, and economic resources (Fernandez-Kelly, 1995; Sullivan, 1989; Venkatesh, 2002, 2009).[36] This situation is represented in the upper left-hand quadrant of Figure 8.1 (fatalism and neglect).

The purpose of this discussion is not to make people feel guilty about what they have or their position in life or to blame individuals. It highlights *patterns* so that society may address them (Chapter 11); it also helps explain why, recognizing the dangers of fatalism and neglect, the ESEA combined hierarchy (TPA) with egalitarianism (NCG) to overcome barriers to inclusion. President Johnson argued that democratic societies cannot advance if large numbers of citizens are hemmed in by poverty or a lack of education. Professionalism would allow the government to individualize services and redress some issues, but there must be some higher level of governance—like the federal DOE—to ensure more equitable OTL. This includes federal redistributive policies to ensure that local markets—as regulated by democratically elected school boards—do not create a situation where some students get an excellent education while others receive inadequate services owing to an inequitable distribution of wealth between communities and power within communities. His argument that the government should counter the concentration of wealth and power through federal redistributive policies and by using the professions to integrate society and promote political, social, and economic transformation is consistent with theories of social capital. The federal government is creating vertical ties to other sources of wealth while strengthening local ones in communities where social, political, and economic capital are depleted and/or inequitably distributed.

Unfortunately, the ESEA never lived up to its promise to create a more egalitarian and inclusive society. As discussed in Chapter 3, the policy was never fully funded, it did not penalize states with large disparities in per pupil expenditures, and its funding formula was designed to ensure that most schools received federal support. In consequence, it was not uncommon for districts and schools with large numbers of low-income children and limited resources to be short-changed, while schools in relatively wealthy districts—with few low-income children—received benefits. Unsurprisingly, the policy did not resolve inequities between districts—either in terms of their overall level of resources or the average amount spent per pupil.[37] Just as problematically, poverty is correlated with educational achievement, regardless of race or the school a child attends (Reardon, 2011), and children of color are almost three times more likely to grow up poor as white children (Children's Defense Fund, 2020). Predictably, studies show that race-based gaps in achievement have (somewhat) narrowed due to federal antipoverty policies and desegregation efforts, but income-based gaps have continued to grow.[38]

NCLB, NCLB waivers, RttT, and the ESSA. Despite these realities, policy makers mostly blamed public schools and public school teachers for policy failure under the ESEA. Their rhetoric is consistent with neoliberal claims that public servants use their ability to hide behind professional expertise and bureaucratic rules, regulations, and red tape to build empires and evade accountability. That shirking allegedly caused the achievement gap between low-income and minority children and their more affluent peers and between American students and their international peers. To correct these deficits in performance, recent reforms advocated using parental voice and choice to enforce educators' responsiveness to citizens and taxpayers.

In theory, recent reforms distanced top-down hierarchical controls through bureaucratic rules, regulations, and SOPs.[39] In practice, these policies hierarchically managed schools and educators by tying rewards and punishments (carrots and sticks) to student test scores. As shown, they largely ignored the fact that professionalism typically involves "coproduction" and that students are nonrandomly assigned across schools and teachers, so that some are more likely to serve the least well-off. This *contrived randomness* contributed to test-based accountability being viewed as a "gaming machine" (Hood, 1998) where the deck is stacked against academically at-risk students and those who serve them. It encouraged some educators to engage in neglect (e.g., opting out of serving the neediest students, teaching to the test, encouraging academically at-risk students to stay home on test day) and others to exit.

Policy makers further failed to acknowledge that exit and voice are typically used by the most ambitious, educated, and/or economically well-off, which allows these groups to disproportionately benefit from available opportunities and services. This shifted power to those who have the most political, economic, and social capital while encouraging neglect and fatalism among the least well-off parents and students. In politics, this form of fatalism includes nonvoting and nonparticipation, which then magnifies policy feedback from the most well-off. In the coproduction space, it includes withdrawal and other forms of neglect, such as not participating in class, doing homework, or studying. Sheila, a suburban speech pathologist, characterized neglect in this way:

> You see kids shut down . . . tell me that they just put any old thing down . . . saying to you during the test "Can you please tell me what this means?"

or "Can you just read this word for me?" And of course you can't. . . . It breaks my heart . . . can you imagine having this happen over and over and over again. . . . If you are . . . reading well below grade level, there is very little you can do. So, they figure "What the heck. I'll just put anything down." And most often they are the first ones done . . . the kids who are the lowest performing. . . . And they will say to you "Oh, that was easy!" [*laughs*] . . . trying to pretend they were not struggling, and yet [you] . . . see the head down . . . the dejection . . . the tenseness and frustration and agitation. . . . [They] want to do their best but just struggle. They are biting their fingers. . . . They have testing anxiety.

The use of market incentives also discouraged cooperation and networking in their most positive forms because educators, parents, and students compete for limited rewards. When combined, neglect in the form of noncooperation and nonparticipation necessitates more costly and less egalitarian forms of social control, such as detention, suspension, and expulsions. Unsurprisingly, this research finds that recent reforms did not increase the efficiency and effectiveness of public schools or reduce the achievement gap.

Neoliberal rhetoric also advocates removing barriers to exit—such as tenure and seniority—so that public employers (e.g., schools) may quickly fire incompetent public servants (e.g., teachers), reward better performing ones (e.g., merit pay), or move employees around in ways that improve overall performance (e.g., move teachers between schools without their input). Although recent federal reforms did not specifically advocate the elimination of tenure and seniority, the expansion of the free market model across three administrations (G. W. Bush, Obama, and Trump) has provided more public funds to schools that are nonunionized and do not offer tenure and seniority (e.g., most charter schools and private schools that receive voucher funds).

This framing ignores how tenure and seniority increase loyalty among educators and citizen coproducers by incentivizing teachers to remain in the occupation, stay in high-need/low-resource schools, voice their concerns, protect the interests of children, and engage in social transformation. It also downplays the negative effects of exit on organizational performance. Some attrition is desirable, especially if it weeds out less-effective educators; however, experience improves performance, it is costly to hire and train teachers, and schools need experienced teachers to train and mentor new ones. The elimination of these loyalty-inducing institutions should be viewed as problematic for another reason. They foster an ethos of care (voice and a service ethic). This professional norm improves public school performance by developing trust and social cohesion, which in turn encourage *all* actors (e.g., educators, taxpayers, parents, students) to pull their behaviors in line in ways that advantage the group, even if that means expending extra effort.

Phrased another way, public institutions and organizations are highly dependent on feelings of loyalty because they encourage citizens and public servants to engage in *civic and other pro-social behaviors.* Loyalty with allegiance includes the key ingredient of trust. Trust is critical for democratic performance yet hard to generate in highly segregated and unequal societies because there is less social cohesion and citizens have fewer encounters with those from different backgrounds. Without that social interaction, citizens lack empathy for one another and are less willing to tax themselves to provide for the common good. Those who have been relegated to marginalized and underserved communities, on the other hand, will feel less willing to participate and comply with rules that have perpetuated an unequal and unjust society. When growing numbers of citizens opt out or engage in more harmful forms of neglect and aggressive voice, including violence, the government must engage in more overt (and expensive) forms of social control, such as school expulsions and incarceration. This further spreads distrust in government and fellow citizens across social groups. The end result is a rapid decline in democratic performance. To reverse this decay, policy makers must reduce segregation, improve socioeconomic equality, and develop institutions that build social ties (social cohesion and social trust) between disparate groups. This is what NCG is designed to do.

NCG recognizes that the state (hierarchy regulated by voice) and the market (individualism regulated by exit, competition, and choice) are insufficient for dealing with an increasingly complex and diverse global society. There is a need for linkages between the two to redress the complex issues that have arisen in modern societies, including the atrophy of social ties (Clarke & Newman, 1997). Networks of trust and reciprocity do not solely help people overcome adversity and thrive amid uncertainty. These social ties (loyalty and social cohesion) provide a sense of belonging, meaning, purpose, and continuity during times of change. By developing socially integrating institutions (e.g., public education) and promoting organizations that encourage voice from different groups in society (e.g., unions, occupations and professions, consumer associations, farmers' organizations, and worker, consumer, and renter cooperatives), the government is able to pull together the social fabric.

Durkheim (1996) argued that professions and occupations are uniquely "marked" to perform this integrative function, but my research suggests that they cannot do it alone. Certainly educators use their relationships to structure individual behaviors in ways that integrate school communities and facilitate individual *and* collective outcomes; however, their ability to do so is mediated by their social, economic and political contexts. Educators who work in high-need, low-resource schools bear an unequal cost of caring. This harms us as a society by encouraging high turnover (exit). The United States will continue to have an educational system where some do quite well but others struggle until all levels of government, especially the national government with its larger and less-regressive tax base, redress segregation, socioeconomic inequality, poverty, and the inequitable financing of public schools (see Chapter 11). Citizens are aware of these inequalities and they teach them lessons that negatively influence democratic participation and the performance of *all* public institutions.

Conclusion

Policy makers and scholars recognize that participation is central to the quality of many public goods, like education, but frequently ignore citizen coproduction because it is easier to influence the behaviors of public servants. For instance, at least since the Coleman Report (Coleman et al., 1966), scholars have known that factors outside of school account for a substantial majority of race- and income-based gaps in achievement and attainment;[40] yet, as shown, education reforms have continued to focus on within-school factors, especially the behaviors of teachers, while downplaying policies that have been shown to narrow opportunity gaps, such as offering summer learning opportunities, reducing childhood poverty, instituting low-cost housing policies, and more equitably financing public schools.[41] In fact, RttT funded states with some of the most inequitable school finance formulas (Sciarra, 2012), including the state that is the subject of this analysis. A further example is legislative changes and court decisions that greatly weakened or overturned job protections for teachers—claiming that these policies make it too expensive to remove underperforming teachers.[42] Like federal education policies, the latter blame educators for poor performance while failing to redress the underlying causes of achievement gaps between underprivileged children and their more advantaged peers, and American students and their international peers. When socio-economic inequality is accounted for, research shows that the major differences disappear in both cases.[43] No one would deny that educators are critical for both the successful implementation of education policies and the performance of public schools; however, policies that ignore the important role of parents, students, and society are unlikely to work. In this study, those policies created the very problems the government was trying to resolve. The next chapter draws lessons from these findings to develop a new educational policy agenda.

11

Educators' Voices as Policy Feedback

The United States is at a historic crossroad with respect to education reform. Teacher protests and strikes in many states had been generating support for more education funding after a decade of disinvestment owing to the Great Recession and tax cuts in many states, but the novel coronavirus and ensuing economic crisis have reduced tax revenues and raised spending for unemployment and social welfare programs.[1] Because most lower levels of government are required to balance their budgets, the resulting deficits will likely necessitate another round of cuts to education spending unless Congress provides more resources.[2] These crises occurred at a time when the need to shut down schools to "flatten the curve" and a reinvigorated BLM movement have renewed concerns about how systemic inequalities influence children's educational and life outcomes. Certainly America has a long tradition of state and local control over public education, but the federal government has a critical role to play. Education reform is therefore likely to gain more prominence in the next couple of years.[3] This chapter uses educators' voices to develop lessons from prior policies and recommendations for future ones.

Learning from Policy Feedback: Lessons from the Field

For the past three decades, policy makers have pushed a MMP that prioritizes competition, choice, and individual rights over collective responsibilities and other values, such as equity, social justice, and democratic inclusion. As shown, the MMP focuses on *freedom from* the government versus using public resources and authority to empower citizens by, for example, expanding democratic participation and access to economic opportunities (*freedom to*). In education, the movement began with *A Nation at Risk*; gained traction at the federal level under President Bill Clinton, with Goals 2000 and the IASA; and was vastly expanded under both the Bush and Obama administrations with the adoption of NCLB, NCLB waivers, and RttT. The theory of action was that parental voice and choice would raise all boats by holding educators and public schools accountable for student performance. Despite some improvements, these reforms created a wide array of new issues—such as the negative effects of overtesting (Lazarin, 2014) and a narrowed curriculum (Morton & Dalton, 2007)—while not resolving the two achievement gaps (between low-income and minority children and their academic peers and American students and their international peers).

The most recent federal reform—the ESSA—is unlikely to change these realities. It makes some genuine improvements, yet, at its core, the ESSA still promotes a punitive, test-based accountability regime that uses market-based economic tools (competition, choice, incentives, and sanctions) to improve public education.[4] Some studies support that competition forces schools to be more effective by emphasizing efforts to improve student achievement. These findings, however, are contested owing to some combination of issues with the methods, the expansiveness of the conclusions, or an inability to replicate the findings.[5] Meanwhile, this and other research finds that competition—through school choice, as currently structured, merit pay, and other reforms—puts pressure on school budgets, punishes schools and teachers that disproportionately serve low-income and other academically at-risk students, and increases segregation. What follows is a new education agenda that focuses on equity while still providing choice and ensuring opportunity for all. These broad-based policies will build the positive feedback that supports and sustains reform while also reducing achievement gaps by expanding the middle class and targeting assistance to those in need.

Lesson 1: Social and Economic Policy Is Education Policy

Research shows that the SES of parents—especially income and education—predicts academic outcomes. Poverty is associated with environmental stressors that impede educational achievement and attainment and a wide array of life outcomes, regardless of race, ethnicity, or the school a child attends.[6] These negative effects begin early; they typically persist and strengthen through high school and beyond—so that those who grow up in poverty are more likely to be poor as adults, and those chances increase sharply with time spent in poverty as a child. This is especially true for African American children (Wagmiller & Adelman, 2009), who also have the highest rate of poverty (Children's Defense Fund, 2020; 30.1%); however, America has the highest rate of childhood poverty in the developed world and children of color in general are close to three times as likely to grow up poor.[7]

Rising poverty and growing income inequality have reduced social mobility. Since 1979, the majority of gains have gone to the top 1 percent while the total share of income claimed by the bottom 90 percent has steadily declined.[8] In consequence, the percentage of adult children who earn more than their parents has been falling and the "birth lottery" (privileges associated with being born into wealth) has been growing. There is still economic mobility, yet Americans now have less than those in other economically advanced nations and the American dream—the ideal of equal opportunity and socioeconomic mobility—has become increasingly out of reach.[9] When combined, these developments have resulted in growing income-based gaps in educational achievement and attainment—especially between those at the highest end of the income distribution and all others. White affluent children score at the highest levels in the world; low-income students and students of color score similarly to those in less developed nations.[10]

To improve public school performance and reduce the two achievement gaps, the nation must redress socioeconomic inequality, decrease poverty, and address the currently unmet needs of low-income students. Otherwise, schools must redirect educational resources that could have been spent on instruction. The time is ripe for these policy interventions. Research and public opinion polls show that Americans across demographic groups, while dramatically *underestimating* the current level of wealth inequality, are very concerned about living standards for the next generation and would like to see a more equitable distribution of wealth. This finding holds even for those who are not typically associated with support for redistributive policies, such as conservatives (Leonhardt, 2013; Norton & Ariely, 2011). Research and opinion polls further support participants' claim that growing socioeconomic inequality, declining economic mobility, and perceptions of unfairness and injustice have reduced social trust and social cohesion.[11] As shown, this makes all levels of government less efficient and effective by necessitating more overt forms of social control (e.g., incarceration and student detentions, suspensions, expulsions).

For those who are interested, Bivens (2016) discusses a wide range of policies that would redistribute income, yet are either growth-neutral or would not harm overall economic growth; others have outlined policies that would redress the racial wealth gap that was largely created by government policies and is wider than the racial gap in earnings.[12] This section focuses on the income support programs that participants recommended to improve public school performance—with the exception that affordable housing and child-care are addressed under community-based supports in the next section. If done correctly, these recommendations will improve educational outcomes by promoting economic growth, broadening the middle class, redressing poverty, and more equitably spreading socioeconomic opportunity. The nation could fund these initiatives by increasing taxes at the uppermost end of the economic spectrum with little measurable effects on overall income levels or economic growth (Bivens, 2016).

Recommendation 1: Improve access to adequate nutrition. During 2020–2021, the novel coronavirus resulted in school closures and an economic crisis that reduced access to needed nutrition for millions of children and their families. Even before the COVID-19 crisis, though, 37 million people were struggling with food insecurity (U.S. Department of Agriculture [USDA], 2019). While rates vary across the nation, children are at highest risk and even relatively short periods affect their academic behaviors and educational outcomes.[13] Federal nutrition programs—such as the Supplemental Nutritional Assistance Program (SNAP; formerly the Food Stamp Program), Women, Infants, and Children (WIC), and the national school lunch program (NSLP)—help about 59 percent of food-insecure house-holds; however, a free and reduced-price breakfast and lunch are the only meals of the day for many students during the school year.

Access to adequate nutrition is even more precarious over the summer. [14] Studies show that the federal government's two main programs for feeding low-income children—the NSLP and the Summer Food Service Program (SFSP)—are very effective. Unfortunately, about one-third of eligible children live in communities that cannot participate because the current threshold—where at least 50 percent of the children in the community must be eligible for a free or reduced-price lunch—is the most restrictive in the program's history. The temporary nature of the program is another reason there are only 34 summer food sites for 100 school lunch programs. The need to reapply, recruit staff members, and dismantle the program each year is challenging for organizations that have limited budgets and resources, putting some out of business and discouraging others from applying. Even sites that serve meals after school through the Child and Adult Care Food Program (CACFP) must reapply and operate separate summer programs. Children must also eat on-site, and so weather, parental work schedules, a lack of information, and/or a lack of transportation create access issues.[15]

The lack of adequate nutrition during school vacations contributes to the "summer slide," where low-income children begin catching up during the school year and then regress over the summer months. Research attributes about 80 percent of the gap in reading between underprivileged students and their peers to this phenomenon (No Kid Hungry, 2015a). During the pandemic, Congress provided temporary, emergency benefits to relieve some of the suffering associated with the economic crisis and schools closing or operating on a reduced schedule. Recent data from the U.S. Census Bureau show that food insecurity plummeted for all households as a result of these benefits but fell the most for households with children. Unfortunately, hunger and food insecurity rose again once the aid ran out (Evich, 2021). Changes adopted during the Trump administration will further increase hunger and exacerbate income-based disparities in health and educational outcomes for a generation of young people unless reversed.[16]

A recent study that linked the school lunch program in Sweden to individual information about school children since the 1950s (e.g., how long they had access to free and nutritious lunches and their subsequent education, employment, and health outcomes) demonstrates the long-term benefits of such programs. It found that free and nutritious lunches had substantial positive effects on lifetime earnings, educational attainment, and health. The *resulting increased earnings* were significantly *higher than the cost of the meals*. Even the wealthiest students derived some value from the program; however, the gains were particularly large for the lowest income children and students that were exposed at earlier ages to the program (Alex-Peterson et al., 2017). The benefits of adopting a similar program in the United States are actually likely to be larger due to the dramatic differences in poverty and socioeconomic inequality between the two countries. The gap between the rich and poor has actually increased relative to Sweden since the 1950s, but, even then, the program was designed to improve nutrition because food shortages and hunger were uncommon there, unlike here.

Congress should expand the historically underfunded school lunch program so that free and nutritious meals are offered to all students regardless of their family's financial situation. Administratively, this reform would eliminate the costs and burdens of distributing, collecting, and certifying applications to comply with federal requirements; it would therefore provide administrators, teachers, and school food staff with more time and resources to serve the nutritious meals that improve health outcomes and success school. This recommendation would further improve health outcomes by speeding up food lines and giving children more time to eat. Research shows that students are more likely to eat less healthy foods (sweets and carbohydrates) when pressed for time. Just as importantly, it would eliminate the food stigma and lunch shaming that currently reduce participation in the program. Some students would rather go hungry than be shamed for eating inferior "welfare food." Efforts to reduce this food stigma through electronic systems that do not distinguish between those receiving a free or reduced price lunch and those paying for their meals have not eliminated the issue because low balances and unpaid lunch bills have led cash-strapped schools to publicly shame students in an effort to collect the money from parents, such as stamping children's hands with a message to their parents that they need lunch money, taking trays away from students when they reach the cashier, or giving students lower cost replacement meals (see Food Research and Action Center [FRAC], 2021).

As shown, public policies allocate more than benefits and burdens; they are sites of political and social learning. When compared with entitlement programs, means-tested and/or paternalistic policies, such as AFDC, are especially likely to discourage political participation and demand-making by conveying negative messages and differentiating between citizens in ways that foster isolation, apathy, and alienation. By providing a universal free school lunch, policy makers would eliminate food stigma and lunch shaming, improve social cohesion in schools, and increase social trust and civic engagement by treating parents and students with dignity and respect. Over the long term, this recommendation would expand economic growth by increasing demand for food, improving health and educational outcomes, and expanding economic self-sufficiency. It would also decrease gaps in achievement and reduce socioeconomic inequality because low-income students would benefit more than higher income groups—even though every student is eligible for the program. All of these outcomes would improve democratic performance.

In terms of summer food programs, Congress should lower the area eligibility threshold to 40 percent to increase the number of eligible communities and make the SFSP consistent with the 21st Century Community Learning Centers program, which is the largest federal funding source for summer and after-school programs. It should further provide start-up and technical support funding to increase site retention and expansion; allow summer meal sites to serve three meals a day; provide funding for transportation, which is particularly critical in the suburbs and rural areas; and allow sponsors to operate programs year-round by combining the CACFP and SFSP (see FRAC, 2019).

Congress should also raise the level of SNAP benefits and provide increased benefits during the summer when the 20 million children served by program are home and a family's grocery bill rises by $300 a month on average (No Kid Hungry, 2015a). In addition, Congress should make permanent the Summer Electronic Benefit Transfer for Children (Summer EBT). This USDA pilot program now operates in select states and tribal nations as a complement to summer nutrition programs; it provides $60 per summer month to purchase food—roughly the equivalent of the monthly cost per child for the school breakfast and lunch programs (FRAC, 2019). Studies show that these policies and programs are effective; a 10 percent increase in SNAP purchasing power decreases food insecurity among children by 22 percent and the Summer EBT reduces by one-third the share of children directly experiencing very low food security (Bauer, 2018).[17]

Recommendation 2: Expand access to affordable health care. The basic structure of the American health care system, where most people have private insurance through their jobs, is largely a historical accident. With so many workers diverted toward military service during World War II, employers struggled to recruit labor, especially since they could not raise pay under national wage freezes that were designed to reduce wartime inflation and stabilize the economy. Employer-provided health care served as an income support—a raise in pay—and helped some businesses compete for workers. Once the Internal Revenue Service (IRS) exempted employer-based health insurance from taxation, it became cheaper to purchase health insurance through one's job. Unions also worked to expand that model through collective bargaining. Over time, the widespread provision of health care through private employers reduced positive feedback for publicly funded health care from citizens and increased negative feedback from business-economic interests, including private insurers. Even many unions opposed public health care because they had spent a great deal of political and economic capital fighting for insurance benefits for their members (Carroll, 2017). That battle proved to be shortsighted.

The folly of tying health care access to employment became particularly evident during the COVID-19 crisis, as massive job loss wiped out the employer-based health care model; however, Americans also transfer more frequently today from job to job and even sector to sector, which puts their health insurance at risk (Chatzky, 2018). Medicaid and Medicare cover health care for some low-income and elderly Americans, respectively; nonetheless, more than 20 million children lack sufficient access to health care–even with the ACA—because they are uninsured, do not receive routine primary care, or have unmet pediatric subspecialty needs (e.g., cardiology or endocrinology).[18] Even families with coverage face hardships because health insurance is frequently inadequate, premiums and deductibles have outstripped wage growth, and only 40 percent of Americans have saved enough to cover a $1,000 emergency expense. This has contributed to rising health-related bankruptcies.[19]

Informants discussed how poor health prevents children from attending school and learning while there. Research also supports their claim that health disparities are linked to income inequality and shows that health is deteriorating for the young relative to older Americans.[20] Many income-support programs—such as SNAP and Medicaid—have a strong *investment component,* meaning they improve the prospects for a healthy and productive life, especially for children. Other progressively redistributionist policies—like Social Security, housing, and Medicare—do not reduce overall economic growth, yet have been the key driver for what little growth in income occurred for the bottom 90 percent (Bivens, 2016). Congress should reopen enrollment under the ACA, create a public option for people who cannot afford private plans, and address escalating prescription drug prices.[21]

Recommendation 3: Invest in policies and institutions that help workers earn livable wages. Since the late 1970s, we have invested in policies that have privileged a small percentage of the population under the guise that they would reinvest these gains and their investments would trickle down to other Americans through increased employment and higher wages (Bivens, 2016; B. Harrington, 2016). Contrary to the claims of policy makers, a 50-year study shows that tax cuts for the most well-off did not lift all boats by spurring investment and economic growth (Dersh, 2020); instead, research from the winners of the 2019 Nobel Prize in Economic Sciences found that this strategy intensifies economic inequality (Beniwal, 2019). The wages of most workers either remained stagnant or declined—even as worker productivity increased and business profits and the stock market boomed.[22] Declining union membership contributed to slower wage growth, rising inequality, and increased poverty; the growth in CEO and executive compensation also played a role, as upper management claimed an increased share of profits.[23] Regardless of why rising socioeconomic inequality has occurred, without livable wages, socioeconomic problems manifest in public schools. For this reason, economic policy is education policy.

Rather than continuing current (supply side) economic policies, Nobel Prize–winning research shows that a fairer way to stimulate the economy is through modest increases in taxes on the wealthiest and corporations—with the government then using those revenues to fund social welfare programs that put money into the pockets of middle- and working-class citizens; these groups then stimulate the economy through increased consumption (Beniwal, 2019). This is Keynesian economics (see Chapter 8). Policy makers should also consider raising the minimum wage, investing in American manufacturing, and adopting legislation that puts workers on a more equal footing with employers. They should further explore changing how unions are organized.

Current federal law emphasizes *enterprise-level bargaining,* where unions negotiate with a particular employer or for employees at a particular worksite. Under sectoral bargaining, unions negotiate for all workers in an entire industry (e.g., restaurant workers). Sectoral bargaining has been implemented to varying degrees and with varying degrees of success in Europe, Canada, and South America; research suggests it would increase union density, boost economic productivity, improve wages and benefits, and close racial and gender pay gaps in the United States. It may be more difficult to achieve this reform at the national level, but the successful fight for a $15 minimum wage for fast-food workers in New York State offers a way forward in terms of state level reform. While the National Labor Relations Act restricts the ability of state governments to regulate labor organizing, it allows the convening of "wage boards"—mostly defunct state institutions from the Great Depression era that have the authority to consult with unions and businesses and mandate pay and benefit scales for entire industries. This was the path used in New York and at least five other states have authorizing laws on the books (California, Colorado, Massachusetts, New Jersey, and North Dakota), with other states and cities considering them.[24]

Unionization *is* associated with lower levels of executive pay and increased wages and benefits for workers. However, union density *does not* increase unemployment or the probability of firms going out of business; it also does not harm nonunionized workers. On the contrary, unions have fought for government policies and programs that benefit a wide swath of the American public, including unemployment insurance, the 40-hour workweek, and policies that improve our quality of life (e.g., Social Security, public colleges, health care). Unionized states have a higher minimum wage and heavily unionized industries raise wages in nonunionized firms because they must compete for workers.[25] In addition, union membership is one of the strongest predictors of an area's economic mobility, with low-income children especially benefiting.[26] Research further shows that recent state minimum wage increases—some of which were quite substantial—had no measurable impact on unemployment (Bivens, 2016; Farber, 2005).

The freedom of workers to collectively negotiate with employers is a widely recognized fundamental right in democracies around the world (Bivens et al., 2017). Unions help workers gain voice in the workplace, but this research shows that they also improve democratic participation and performance by institutionalizing norms of egalitarianism, instilling a belief that individuals have rights and responsibilities (both in the workplace and as citizens), providing the capacity to act when those rights have been denied, and creating feelings of individual and collective political efficacy when those actions produce change. These norms, beliefs, and predispositions are a form of social capital; they foster future collective action because, on some level, they transfer to the children of union members and/or to others in the community, whether that is through social networks or because they see the gains made by union members.

The spread of collective bargaining after the adoption of the National Labor Relations Act in 1935 fostered decades of fairer economic growth. The decline in union membership since the 1970s corresponds with rising socioeconomic inequality, as well as the erosion of wages, benefits, and workplace protections. As shown, anti-union discourse and private sector RTW laws contributed to this decline so that union membership is far more common in the public than in the private sector—where unionization is also far lower than it is in other advanced democracies, such as France, Sweden, Denmark, Germany, and Canada.[27] Now, as a result of the

Supreme Court's *Janus* decision, RTW is the law of the land for all public employees.

Recent developments and polls support that it is time for unions to mobilize Americans.[28] About half of those I interviewed said that unions must do a better job of publicizing information about how RTW laws have weakened the labor movement, reduced wage growth, created a growing wage gap, and increased poverty; some further advocated running public service announcements similar to those that asked citizens to "look for the union label" and "buy American." In recent informal discussions, a few mentioned starting a campaign to push large companies, like Amazon, to clearly label which products are made in America to help manufacturing. To them, the inability to obtain needed medical supplies during a pandemic, due to weaknesses in the supply chain as more products are produced overseas, illustrates how the global economy has left America weaker, less equal, and more prone to health and national security issues.

Congress must support these efforts by adopting legislation—like the Protecting the Right to Organize (PRO) Act, which passed in the House. That act would redress the fundamental weaknesses in U.S. labor law that were discussed earlier in this book. It would also reverse state policies and Supreme Court decisions that have defunded and defanged unions and thereby reduced negative feedback for policies that benefit only a very small portion of Americans. In addition, states that allow the convening of wage boards and those interested in adopting such reforms could serve as laboratories of democracy for building worker power and participation and reducing economic and political inequality.

Recommendation 4: Invest in school infrastructure. A substantial body of research shows that infrastructure investments (e.g., roads, bridges, tunnels, airports, schools, hospitals, public drinking water systems) increase economic productivity (Bivens, 2012a, 2012b, 2016). For instance, improvements to school facilities—the second largest sector of public infrastructure spending after roads and highways—boost teacher retention by as much as, if not more than, salary increases. In contrast, poor-quality facilities increase absenteeism, dropouts, and suspensions and negatively affect student and educator health, task completion, and educational achievement and attainment.[29] Research shows that more than half of public schools are in need of repairs, but students in more affluent communities are far more likely to enjoy classes in bright, comfortable, and healthy buildings while those in low-wealth communities disproportionately attend classes in unhealthy, dilapidated, and obsolete facilities.[30]

Although Democrats are more likely to favor federal school infra-structure aid, these investments have historically received bipartisan support, especially during economic and other crises, and a growing number of states now legally recognize that school facilities are an important factor for creating more equal OTL. In addition, a 2015 poll found that 92 percent of Americans believe that the government should improve the quality of public school buildings.[31] The Rebuild America's Schools Act could serve as a starting point. Proposed in 2019 by House and Senate Democrats, it would have provided $70 billion for school repairs and construction, offered $30 billion in tax-credit bonds, established a national database on the condition of public school facilities, and created about 1.9 million jobs (Ujifsa, 2019b).

The Act would help redress the facilities crisis, increase teacher retention, improve educational outcomes, and raise property values—especially in low-wealth communities, many of which have not fully recovered from the Great Recession and have been dispro-portionately harmed by the practice of closing poorly performing schools under recent education reforms.[32] With 2 million acres of land, the design and operation of school facilities also significantly affects the environment. Congress should give preference to districts that preserve natural resources through, for instance, solar power and renewable energy, "green" construction, and by reducing waste through reuse and recycle policies (Filardo, 2016).

More broadly, federal infrastructure policies should be designed to create jobs and rebuild the economy in ways that especially help communities that continue to be affected by historical disparities in public policies. I discussed, for example, how federal housing policies and highway aid often divided and isolated low-income and minority communities while also encouraging white flight from urban and rural areas. By decreasing property values, these policies reduced revenues (property taxes) for public services—like parks, fire, police, and schools—in low-income communities and communities of color. These communities have also disproportionately borne the impact of environmental hazards, but race better predicts proximity to pollution and exposure to lead, unsafe drinking water, and other hazards than income alone (see, e.g., Climate Reality Project, 2021).

Socioeconomic inequality has further fostered a *digital divide*. Low-income communities and people of color have a high demand for internet access, yet often cannot afford to subscribe; race predicts disparities in broadband access even after accounting for income and other demographic factors, such as education and employment (see, e.g., Floberg, 2018). Many informants discussed how exposure to lead and other environmental hazards results in unequal educational outcomes. In recent informal conversations, they added that the inability to access the internet, and in some cases having power shutoff because of unpaid utility bills, is another way that poverty impedes academic outcomes for low-income students and students of color. This was especially true during the COVID-19 school shutdowns, but respondents said it also contributes to achievement gaps through the "summer slide."

The current economic crisis provides an opportunity to rebuild America's strength and resilience from the ground up while also promoting racial equity and reducing socioeconomic inequality. Similar to how we invest in the armed forces, intelligence gathering, and diplomacy, we must invest in people, places, research, and institutions to defend against another pandemic and escalating negative effects of global warming. In terms of the latter, participants stressed the importance of "thinking outside of the box," such as using the roofs of government buildings—like schools—for community gardens. Schools could offer summer programs where students learn, through doing, how to plant, tend, and preserve these gardens. They could keep some of the resulting harvest and donate the rest to local food pantries. Participating students would acquire life skills, socio-emotional skills, and learn about civics through action. Schools could build an environmental studies component into these programs, but they are also an environmentally friendly way to increase food production in ways that help the least well-off.

Recommendation 5: Increase access to technical, vocational, and higher education and reduce college completion gaps. Research shows that a college degree has become increasingly important for professional success and economic mobility. The fastest-growing *occupations* will not require a college diploma (health care workers, technical occupations, and service workers), but 65 percent of all newly created jobs do. Those without a high school diploma face especially limited employment options and lower earnings potential. On a positive note, educational attainment among 25- to 29-year-olds in the United States rose between 2000 and 2019 at every level (high school, associate's, bachelor's and master's degree). Less positively, racial, ethnic, and socioeconomic disparities in college attendance and completion continue to be an issue and, in some cases, have worsened.[33] The gender gap has also been getting wider since the 1980s, with American colleges and universities now enrolling roughly six women for every four males. The gender gap in college entrance and completion exists across demographic groups, but it is higher for low-income and minority males. The pandemic is likely to exacerbate these disparities.

U.S. colleges enrolled 1.5 million fewer students in 2020 than five years ago. Low-income students and students of color, particularly Native Americans, were hardest hit; however, men accounted for 70 percent of the decline and, again, enrollment decreases were especially large for low-income and minority males.[34] The pandemic's impact on college enrollment was uneven across institutions. Recessions normally increase enrollment at community colleges and other two-year institutions; instead, the pandemic and economic crisis caused a 12 percent enrollment drop. In comparison, four-year public colleges experienced declines of less than 3 percent and enrollment actually increased at some of the more selective four-year private institutions (Sparks, 2021). All of these developments have implications for the country's economic competitiveness, as well as for economic, social, and racial justice.

The willingness to invest in public colleges and universities was historically based on an egalitarian belief that merit, rather than birth or income, should determine one's ability to rise. By making college affordable for veterans, the working class, women, and people of color, this investment was one of the primary drivers of economic growth, socioeconomic mobility, and middle-class prosperity.[35] Public colleges and universities also provide other long-term social, political, and economic benefits. For instance, they help local communities thrive through increased employment, higher wages, and raised consumer spending; they also reduce crime, increase civic participation, and improve health outcomes (M. Mitchell et al., 2017). Despite these contributions, public colleges and universities are struggling as a result of long-term disinvestment.

Almost every state was still spending less on higher education in 2017 than in 2008 as a result of the Great Recession and tax cuts in many states. Most have also been shifting costs to students over the last 25 years. Certainly federal financial aid helps some students cover tuition hikes; however, it rarely covers the full cost of tuition, much less the rising costs of fees, room, and board. These developments are closing the doors of opportunity for growing numbers of citizens; there is also a concern about diminished quality as schools cut course offerings, faculty, and student services.[36] All of these issues are likely to get worse as a result of the pandemic and current economic crisis.

Reinvesting in two- and four-year public colleges and universities would help the nation keep pace with rising demand for college graduates, caregivers, skilled trades, and technical occupations (Carnevale et al., 2013). Such investments will help pull the nation out of the pandemic-related economic crisis; however, they must be done in a way that promotes racial and socio-economic justice. For example, investing more resources in community colleges, Historically Black Colleges and Universities (HBCUs), and other minority-serving institutions would disproportionately benefit students of color and low-income students. Increased funding for Pell Grants also has the potential to do so, but Congress must ensure that cash-strapped states and colleges do not use these "extra" resources to displace current investments; this has happened before and resulted in the same or higher costs for students and a smaller than predicted enrollment increase for low-income students (see Shireman, 2021).

More broadly, this research suggests that it would be better, from a governance and democratic performance perspective, to combine a variety of policy tools. Specifically, Congress and state governments should work together to expand free—or very low-cost—financial aid, halt tuition hikes at public colleges and universities, offer tuition-free community college, expand aid to HBCUs, provide partial debt forgiveness for student loans to help current graduates navigate the recession, reform the Public Service Loan Forgiveness (PSLF) program, use debt forgiveness to encourage entry into caring occupations, and destigmatize and expand vocational and technical education. This approach would focus on racial and socioeconomic justice while also increasing access, retention, and positive policy feedback for future investments in higher education.

Research shows financial aid is associated with student success. Need-based financial aid may be more equitable and less expensive than keeping tuition low, since it focuses on economically disadvantaged students; however, it is critical to keep tuition affordable because higher costs actually dissuade low-income students from enrolling—even when the net price with aid remains the same (Bowen et al., 2011; M. Mitchell et al., 2017). In addition, high debt levels decrease the probability of graduation—especially among low-income students—and impede economic growth by reducing graduate school attendance for STEM majors, rates of homeownership among young adults, and the formation of small businesses.[37]

Some informants further advocated using promised debt forgiveness to encourage entry into caring occupations (e.g., teachers, nurses, counselors, and other health and mental health care workers), especially for those who agree to work in low-resource communities, which typically experience shortages. This may be one way to integrate these occupations, many of which lack male representation and some of which lack minority representation, while also improving college completion. Many also mentioned the need to reform the PSLF program. The program is supposed to provide debt relief for public service workers, like teachers and police officers, but has been plagued by confusing requirements and other issues, since its inception in 2007; those issues have resulted in many borrowers being (inappropriately) rejected or repaying higher amounts.

Last, but not least, many skilled trades (plumbers, electricians, carpenters, etc.) are experiencing shortages despite relatively high pay. A little over half of participants advocated the destigmatization and expansion of vocational and technical education in high school and at two-year colleges to redress this issue. Congress could create a pilot project that provides funding to two-year colleges to develop partnerships with local high schools and area businesses. As part of a new vocationalism, these programs would integrate career and technical skills into educational programs during and after high school, over the summer, and/or as a one-year add-on that could be incorporated into a two- or four-year degree. Research shows that career pathway programs reduce high school dropout (Bonilla, 2018) and may reduce dropout in two-year colleges (Soares, 2010). Many also advocated increasing pathways for student transfers from community colleges to four-year public colleges and universities. Research supports their claim that four-year colleges see an increase in graduation rates when they accept more transfers from two-year colleges.[38]

When combined, these recommendations will build a strong middle class and develop the entrepreneurs and skilled workers needed to compete in a global economy. This more inclusive approach may help stem the growing gender gap, by encouraging male students to enroll and graduate, yet we should not redirect effort away from serving young women. Women remain under-represented in the nation's most highly selective colleges and universities, as well as in the highest paying fields of study (e.g., engineering and computer science). Moreover, college admissions continue to favor young, white men, owing to the emphasis on standardized testing. The point of being more inclusive, while still retaining a focus on racial and socioeconomic justice, is that younger generations (Generation X, Millennials, and Zoomers) have been particularly hard hit by two recessions and a pandemic. These developments will affect their life outcomes at a time when they will be asked to negotiate a modern global economy that requires a vast array of skills and knowledge; they will also be responsible for caring for an aging Baby Boomer generation. Being more inclusive may raise costs, but it will expand opportunity, improve social cohesion, and increase positive policy feedback through coalition building between citizens from different backgrounds (i.e., race, ethnicity, SES, age, gender).[39]

The U.S. electorate is already polarized by gender, race, ethnicity, SES, and educational attainment. Those divisions are likely to worsen if current trends continue (Thompson, 2021). Wherever possible, policy makers should adopt policies that are more inclusive to increase social cohesion. This research suggests that social cohesion, in and of itself, increases social trust; however, by treating young people with dignity and respect, these reforms will directly build social trust, increase civic engagement, and improve democratic performance over the long-term.

Lesson 2: Schools and Communities Matter

America's public schools are diverse and are becoming even more so. In the 1970s, nearly four out of five students were white, compared to just over half in 2009. By 2045, the United States will be a "majority minority" country, with non-Hispanic whites making up fewer than half the total population (Frey, 2018). Despite these demographic trends, the typical white student attends a school where three-quarters of their peers are white, while the vast majority of Latinx (80%) and African American (74%) students attend schools that are 50–100 percent minority. Many Black (15%) and Latinx (14%) students are enrolled in "apartheid schools"—those where white students make up less than 1 percent—and a large proportion (43% of Latinx and 38% of African American students) attend schools where less than 10 percent are white. Black and Hispanic students are also four times more likely to attend schools where more than 75 percent are low income, as measured by eligibility for free and reduced-price lunch. That compares to the early 1990s, when the average Black or Latinx student attended a school where approximately one-third were low income.[40] These realities are important because research shows that segregation is a large contributor to racial disparities in achievement and attainment;[41] however, concentrating low-income students in economically homogenous schools depresses those outcomes even further.[42]

Again, the negative effects of socioeconomic inequality stem from a combination of individual, school, and outside-of-school variables. School funding also plays a role. The United States is one of the few economically advanced nations where public schools that primarily serve underprivileged children receive less funding than schools that serve their more advantaged peers (Organization for Economic Co-operation and Development [OECD], 2013; Ushomirsky & Williams, 2015). This unequal funding affects every aspect of a school's ability to provide an excellent, well-rounded education, including access to HQTs, challenging courses, and better facilities.[43] Nevertheless, simply raising the level of spending is unlikely to close the two achievement gaps; public schools face complex challenges. This section focuses on strategies to improve the educational outcomes of all students while still retaining a focus on equity.

Recommendation 1: Link housing policy with education policy. Housing policy is essential for a strong system of public education for many reasons. Research shows that access to healthy, safe, and affordable housing improves educational achievement and attainment. While the effects vary by age, those who experience homelessness, housing instability, "hypermobility" (frequent moves), and substandard or unsafe housing are more likely to have learning and behavioral issues due to chronic health concerns (e.g., lead poisoning or asthma); excessive absenteeism; missed instruction; disturbances in teacher and peer relationships; and stress-induced issues with studying, retaining information, and completing assignments. Hypermobility does not affect solely those experiencing it; high rates of student mobility within a school impede the performance of other students.[44]

Housing policy is important for another reason. All else being equal, economic mobility is higher in communities where low-income individuals are more dispersed within mixed-income neighborhoods.[45] Economic mobility itself improves educational achievement, but female beneficiaries of integration have lower rates of single-parent families and children who move to better neighborhoods are more likely to stay out of trouble, graduate from high school, attend four-year colleges, be employed, earn higher pay and benefits, and live in more integrated neighborhoods with lower rates of poverty as adults. In addition, those who grow up in diverse neighborhoods and attend diverse schools are also more likely to choose diverse colleges and workplaces and send their children to integrated schools. Thus, inclusive communities promote future integration and help subsequent generations. All of these gains are larger the longer children live in socioeconomically inclusive neighborhoods.[46]

As shown, all levels of government contributed to racially and economically segregated schools by facilitating white, middle-class, and upper-income flight to the suburbs; redlining poor and minority communities; segregating public housing; and using school attendance zones and infrastructure, such as railroads, highways, difficult-to-cross avenues and boulevards, parks, rivers, and other geographic barriers, to isolate low-income and minority communities in areas that typically had few economic opportunities. Because these dividing lines were built into the physical environment, they persist in many communities to this day.[47] The removal of these and other barriers to socioeconomic inclusion would improve educational achievement and attainment; it would also foster democratic performance by increasing social trust and social cohesion. These outcomes are one reason why it is critical to adopt the broader infrastructure investments that are recommended in lesson one.

Integrated schools reduce prejudice, fear, and intolerance by allowing students to interact on equal terms with those from different backgrounds (e.g., race, ethnicity, income). Such interactions build democratic character and are critical for success in an increasingly diverse global economy. For instance, they improve socioemotional skills, by fostering an understanding of alternative perspectives, and create the social cohesion and social trust that improve democratic participation. In contrast, segregated and unequal schools reduce social trust and increase political cynicism by providing evidence of the gap between democracy in theory and democracy in action. The resulting neglect (e.g., crime and low participation) reduces the efficiency and effectiveness of public schools and other democratic institutions by necessitating more intrusive and expensive forms of social control.

More recently, the federal government and some local and state governments have begun to invest in policies that integrate communities and, therefore, schools. Research shows that these reforms may actually be more effective at closing racial and income achievement gaps than providing schools that disproportionately serve low-income and minority children with extra resources.[48] Despite these positive findings, all levels of government invest very little in these strategies.[49] Opponents argue that taxpayers and parents are not broadly supportive of such reforms because they chose to pay more for homes in communities that generally, though not always, have better-performing schools as a result of more property tax revenues (Rotherham, 2010). Proponents respond by pointing to polls where parents express that they value racially and ethnically diverse learning environments. The larger issue is that parents do not appear to know about the positive academic benefits of integration for *all* students.[50]

Another issue with these reforms are that they are not sufficient. America cannot reduce the two achievement gaps *solely* by moving high-poverty children into predominantly middle-class schools: large school districts where these strategies would be most effective are not the norm, there are often not enough good schools nearby, competition for such slots is intense, and the population of low-income students is so large that it would be difficult to achieve a sufficient mass of socioeconomic integration to ensure that enough students benefit.[51] More affluent schools are not always more effective than schools that disproportionately serve low-income children, but polls suggest that policy makers could build coalitions on behalf of integration if they better publicize its broader benefits, rather than appealing to individual self-interest, and by making housing policy more transparent and fair. It is also critical to adopt other education reforms that address the needs of low-income students within the current system. The rest of this section elaborates on these ideas.

Recommendation 2: Make housing policy transparent and fair. Compared to other economically developed nations, U.S. housing policy is poorly matched to need. The three ways federal, state, and local governments intervene in housing markets—taxes, subsidies, and regulations (e.g., zoning)—tend to benefit businesses and middle- and upper-income homeowners at the expense of low-income families and renters. Part of the issue stems from a lack of transparency. *Tax expenditures* (benefits provided through the tax code), for instance, are highly skewed toward businesses and upper-income Americans yet are mostly hidden; the costs of providing public housing and rental assistance, on the other hand, are highly visible because they are outlined in budgetary documents.[52] In addition, public discourse about so-called de facto segregation has hidden the historical contribution of housing policies to current segregation and a racial wealth gap that has made African American families more susceptible to income insecurity and less likely to own a home (Shapiro et al., 2013). In the past, these realities have made it difficult to build coalitions for housing reform, but that is changing because of the deterioration in housing affordability for a broader swath of renters and homeowners alike.

Nearly half of Americans now spend more than 30 percent of their pretax income on housing, which is above the rate advocated by researchers and policy makers. The problem is especially acute in urban areas with strong job markets—where it forces individuals either to make long commutes or give up employment opportunities. These issues impede economic performance; are contributing to global warming; and are also fostering an intergenerational wealth gap in a similar way to how earlier housing policies contributed to a racial wealth gap. In this case, rising home values have benefited older Americans—those more likely to own homes—at the expense of younger ones and minorities, who are now paying more rent because demand exceeds the supply of affordable housing.[53]

Housing reform would help promote racial and socioeconomic justice and integration; improve economic stability and growth; and redress global warming by reducing commuting. Improved transparency and fairness would also increase democratic accountability and participation by expanding the number of Americans who view the government as a source of help and opportunity. This includes new beneficiaries of housing policies and those who are currently receiving "hidden" tax benefits, many of whom are unaware of the total amount the government gives back and how those resources could be dispersed in fairer and more efficient ways if they were allocated through spending rather than returned through the tax code. The following reforms should be at the top of the list.

Recommendation 2A: Abolish or greatly reform the home mortgage interest tax deduction and redistribute the funding. Tax expenditures subsidize households and businesses by reducing the amount of taxes owed; however, they are heavily skewed toward upper-income Americans and decrease the amount of revenues that are available for other programs. Most economists agree that the home mortgage interest deduction (MID)—one of the largest tax breaks—produces few benefits, especially given its costs in terms of lost revenue and the economy. It primarily advantages the wealthiest homeowners (about 70 percent of the benefits flow to the top 20 percent) and has contributed to an affordable housing shortage; it was also a factor in the housing bubble that harmed the economy during the Great Recession.[54] The Tax Cuts and Jobs Act grandfathered in some changes, but Congress should eliminate the MID and reinvest the revenues in ways that would increase socioeconomic integration and help a broader swath of Americans. Alternatively, it could limit the MID to one home, reduce the size of a mortgage that is eligible for a tax break to $500,000, and convert the deduction to a 15 percent non-refundable tax credit. A nonrefundable tax credit provides a refund only up to the amount owed, meaning that it could reduce tax liability to zero but not below that amount. Converting the MID to a nonrefundable tax credit would allow *all* homeowners with mortgages to get a tax break, not just those with enough income to itemize their tax returns.

Recommendation 2B: Build more social housing to restore the economy and increase socioeconomic integration. Since the Nixon administration, policy makers have used negative stereotypes to justify disinvesting in public housing. Such stereotypes result from public discourse and policies that (a) linked the American dream to owning a single-family home, (b) encouraged white middle-class and upper-income flight to the suburbs, and (c) segregated public housing in areas with few jobs and resources. These developments isolated minorities and the least well-off, reduced positive feedback for public housing, and justified America's laissez-faire approach to its housing supply. Today, the U.S. Department of Housing and Urban Development (HUD) mostly uses a combination of subsidies and vouchers. The former are designed to encourage private developers to construct affordable housing; the latter help low-income Americans afford private housing. In addition, corporations and individuals receive benefits for investing in low-income housing through the Low-Income Housing Tax Credit. Because these subsidies and tax breaks are limited to 20 and 15 years, respectively, the stock of affordable housing, which has already been depleted through the tearing down or selling off of public housing, will deteriorate even further once this low-income housing gets converted to market-rate apartments.

As a result of these policy choices, public housing now constitutes less than 1 percent of the nation's housing stock and there are long waiting lists. These waiting lists are partially due to an affordability crisis, but public housing is generally more decent now because the worst developments—the high-rise projects—have mostly been torn down, leaving garden apartments, low-rise walk-ups, and single-family homes or townhomes. Nonetheless, as more Americans fight for a dwindling supply of housing that is protected from market pressures, others are pushed into private markets and rents rise. The government must then provide greater subsidies to keep rents in the private market affordable for low-income Americans at a higher cost to taxpayers, assuming Congress raises HUD's budget; otherwise, fewer get served (Dreier, 2018; Zonta, 2018).

Western Europe's positive experiences with *social housing* suggest that policy makers could change how citizens view the attractiveness of socioeconomic integration and renting versus buying a home. These programs fostered strong positive feedback for public housing by serving a mixed-income population of families and individuals, conferring benefits on renters that are more similar to those of property owners (e.g., security of tenure), and giving a broader swath of the population a stake in its expansion and upkeep. The United States also has variants of social housing, but it is far less widespread.[55] If done correctly, federal investment in social housing would integrate neighborhoods and public schools; revitalize low-income communities without triggering gentrification; reduce homelessness; and decrease housing instability by ensuring it is better matched to need. It would create jobs in mixed- and low-income communities and help local businesses (Dreier, 2018; Zonta, 2018). These investments may also be a better way to reduce commuting in areas that are experiencing rapid growth than current proposals that advocate providing a refundable tax credit for people who spend a large fraction of their income on rent.[56] They should be designed to promote green and energy-efficient development and provide broadband access to help mitigate the technological divide.

Recommendation 2C: Expand housing choice vouchers (HCVs; Section 8). HCVs are, by far, the largest housing assistance program—with families paying 30 percent of their income and HUD paying the rest up to a ceiling. Unfortunately, these subsidies help only about one-fifth of eligible families because, unlike food stamps and Medicaid, they are not an entitlement. Landlord discrimination and local resistance to the spread of low-income housing (NIMBY) have also ensured that decent apartments are mostly off-limits to voucher holders in more prosperous communities (Dreier, 2018; Zonta, 2018). The Housing Choice Voucher Mobility Demonstration project, which was previously passed by the House of Representatives, would expand the number of families receiving vouchers through the infusion of close to $30 million in federal assistance; it would also improve the ability of public housing agencies to offer the mobility support services that help families move into mixed-race, low-poverty communities.[57] It is a step in the right direction, but making Section 8 an entitlement and expanding eligibility to cover those who are slightly more prosperous could be combined with the other recommendations in this section to build a broader coalition and expand positive feedback for housing policies that integrate communities and therefore public schools.

Recommendation 2D: Update the Fair Housing Act. The federal Fair Housing Act of 1968 protects potential renters and home buyers from discrimination; however, Congress should dismantle the hidden policies and regulate the private behaviors that have contributed to both racial and socioeconomic segregation as well as an affordability crisis. It should especially bar landlord discrimination against voucher recipients and incentivize communities to reform zoning laws and other rules and regulations that specify how land may be used.[58] Many of these policies directly or indirectly hinder socio-economic (and therefore racial) integration. One example of such *exclusionary zoning laws* is the prohibition on building anything other than single-family, detached houses (e.g., townhouses, duplexes, and apartment buildings). Single-family homes increase the potential for socioeconomic segregation because they are typically the largest and most expensive form of construction. Other policies that increase costs are minimum square footage and lot size requirements. Zoning reform would expand the supply of more affordable units and help integrate schools by allowing neighborhoods and communities to build townhomes, duplexes, and apartment buildings or convert older homes into moderate and high-density housing. It is especially needed in high-opportunity areas where property values combine with zoning laws to raise building costs and therefore keep out middle- and lower-income Americans.[59]

Recent developments suggest that the affordability crisis has been changing previous beliefs that zoning is purely a local matter and that single-family homes are preferable. Minneapolis, for instance, recently discontinued single-family zoning restrictions—the first city to do so—and some communities have adopted *inclusionary zoning laws* that also require developers of market-rate apartments and condos to make some units available, either for rent or for sale, to low- and moderate-income households. The "Yes in My Backyard" (YIMBY) movement—where some urban dwellers are allying with developers to fight exclusionary zoning laws out of a desire for more affordable and inclusive housing—also directly contrasts with the NIMBY movement that, as mentioned, began to spread in the 1970s. Although state and federal policy makers have limited *direct control* over zoning, they are able to influence local behaviors and states have begun considering policies that would curtail exclusionary zoning—especially near mass transit hubs—as a way to redress the affordability crisis.[60]

At the national level, Elizabeth Warren's proposal to tackle exclusionary zoning by tying a *new pool* of local infrastructure grant money to land use reforms is a step in the right direction. It would work in a similar way as RttT, which, while unpopular, was highly successful at getting cash-strapped school districts to adopt reforms during the Great Recession in return for federal resources. Her proposal would also make it illegal for landlords to discriminate against renters with federal housing vouchers and increase the affordable stock of housing by creating a federal trust fund that finances the construction of subsidized units. This comprehensive proposal would be greatly strengthened by linking zoning reforms to a larger pool of federal funding, such as transportation and/or infrastructure aid.[61]

The post-COVID-19 economy and the current interest in federal infrastructure aid have created a historic opportunity to develop bipartisan housing reform, expand Section 8, and provide relief to a broader group of Americans. In doing so, policy makers could create positive feedback for federal housing policy while also reducing the racial and socioeconomic segregation that impedes public school performance and harms us as a society.

Recommendation 2E: Create nonrefundable tax credits for frontline workers who live in low-resource communities. As shown, educators' relationships are an informal source of social capital; they help integrate schools and communities, improve student achievement and attainment, and foster the development of a more just and egalitarian society. My interviews suggest frontline workers—such as police, EMTs, firefighters, and health, mental health, and childcare workers—are also critical for integrating and transforming society, not just for providing important services. COVID-19, 9/11, and the renewed BLM movement illustrate that, for better or worse, these public servants are especially critical during crises and disasters. Nonetheless, they are typically underpaid and overworked. In addition, many recognize the importance of the police and firefighters for healthy and safe communities, but policy makers have mostly failed to appreciate the importance of care work for our communities, society, and the economy.

Providing nonrefundable tax credits for critical health, safety, *and* care workers who live and work in low-wealth communities would increase the number of young people pursuing these careers while also reducing shortages in typically underserved low-income and minority neighborhoods. This reform could be linked with recommendation 6D in this section, which advocates expanding the number of promise neighborhoods and constructing civic empowerment zones, to build political, economic, and social capital in three ways: frontline workers would live alongside those they serve, which makes them more cognizant of local needs and concerns; they would reinvest in low-income and minority communities through their time and purchasing power, which improves local economies; and the ability to "stay local" would likely increase the overall number of minorities and low-income Americans serving in these occupations. The latter is critical for ensuring that this proposal does not trigger gentrification. It may even be a way to recruit more men into caring occupations and more women into the field of public safety.

In education, this reform would help reduce the *teacher diversity gap,* which is discussed later in this chapter.[62]

Recommendation 3: Restructure Title I and target new funding to school integration efforts. The federal government provides only about 8 percent of public school revenues and has historically underfunded its two largest policies: Title I of the ESEA and the Individuals with Disabilities Education Act (IDEA). Funding for both programs is also widely dispersed. The end result is that states with higher percentages of low-income children actually receive less funding.[63] Most state governments use some type of equalization formula (e.g., foundation aid) to bring local funding up to a floor that (theoretically) ensures students receive an adequate education; however, the combination of federal and state resources has never come close to closing the gap in per pupil expenditures created by the substantial variation in local property taxes. In consequence, public schools remain highly unequal—with the highest-poverty districts and students of color receiving less funding.[64]

As mentioned, the U.S. Supreme Court curtailed the ability of students to challenge this unequal school financing under the Fourteenth Amendment. State courts, however, have been more willing to tackle this issue, assuming there are any relative provisions in a state's constitution. Plaintiffs have won two-thirds of their cases in 45 states since 1989, but these decisions were undermined by inadequate legislative solutions and cuts in state funding during the Great Recession of 2008.[65] Since then, funding in some states—especially those that adopted tax cuts—has not returned to previous levels.[66] The economic crisis experienced during the COVID-19 pandemic is likely to result in a similar situation unless the federal government provides schools with more resources *and* structures that funding in ways that improve equity and integration.

Recommendation 3A: Increase federal funding and redistribute Title I funds. Congress should simplify the Title I funding formula and make it more progressive by phasing out the hold-harmless minimum and eliminating the small state minimum. This change would result in gains for 36 states and losses for 14 states and Washington, D.C. Most, however, would experience minimal losses (Gordon, 2016). The federal government could make this "Robin Hood" approach more palatable by raising funding levels for Title I to mitigate some or all of these losses while still ensuring that the highest-poverty schools and states receive more funding.

Recommendation 3B: Expand federal magnet school funding. The organization of public schools around geographic catchment areas has severely restricted school desegregation efforts—especially once the U.S. Supreme Court ruled out busing as a way to move students across district boundaries. Again, I am not making claims about the merits of busing. The point is that this decision was part of a movement away from federal court orders that redressed segregation. In consequence, the primary way the federal government (now) fosters integration is through funding for magnet schools. Magnet schools encourage students from surrounding suburbs to attend urban public schools through special themes (e.g., art, music, science, technology) and innovative teaching approaches and curriculum (e.g., Montessori).[67] These schools tend to cost more, owing to the need to develop the curriculum, train educators on new pedagogical approaches, provide students with transportation, and so forth; however, research shows that they promote integration and improve the educational outcomes of low-income and minority children more than charter schools.[68] They also have large waiting lists because they serve roughly equal numbers of students as charter schools yet receive far less support. Congress should increase funding for magnet schools to meet demand and stop adding riders to appropriation bills to prevent using federal funds for integration.[69] The latter have been added since the 1970s to curb protests against school busing but necessitate that magnet schools raise separate funding for transportation.

Recommendation 3C: Adopt the Strength in Diversity Act. One of the strengths of federalism is that it allows states to experiment with and tailor policies to local needs and concerns. Congress should adopt the Strength in Diversity Act, which would create a federal grant program that funds racial and economic integration in schools across the country. The Act provides funding to school districts that voluntarily develop, implement, or expand school diversity initiatives. It includes one-year or multi-year planning grants to help districts explore and collect data on different models and funding to recruit or train staff, develop community engagement plans, support specialized academic programs, and transport students (once Congress removes the ban on using federal money to pay for transportation for school desegregation efforts). The legislation is both practically and symbolically important (Belsha, 2019).

First, it gives preference to school districts that explicitly tackle racial segregation, not just economic segregation, as well as to plans that involve multiple school districts. As mentioned, the latter has been stymied since the Supreme Court's 1974 decision in *Milliken v. Bradley*. Second, it provides a roadmap for how the federal government could become more involved in helping school districts desegregate given such limitations. Third, it serves notice that the federal government values desegregation after decades of moving away from the issue. Fourth, it rewards school districts who are already engaging in desegregation efforts while incentivizing others to develop their own initiatives. The diversity of these initiatives will help create a roadmap for other districts. Fifth, the policy signals that it is possible for school districts to work together to address racial segregation by redrawing attendance zones, rather than blaming it on "de facto" housing patterns (Belsha, 2019); those are clearly important but socioeconomic and racial integration in schools will require a wide array of policy tools.

Recommendation 4: Restrict secession from school districts. The rules governing the formation of new districts are an important component of protecting economically disadvantaged students. Most states allow school districts to splinter and there are currently more than 14,000 districts across the country. As shown, the use of property taxes to fund public schools has, on its own, contributed to segregated and unequal schools, but it has also created an incentive for high-wealth communities to fence themselves off from low-wealth ones. Because most splintering involves predominately white, wealthier schools exiting from poorer, minority-dominated districts, the resulting artificial borders have become barriers to economic opportunity and integration. Unfortunately, this form of economic segregation has been accelerating.[70] Many of these communities also have a long history of racial segregation.[71]

State governments should either prohibit the formation of new districts—like Georgia and Florida have—or place restrictions on their formation. At a minimum, they should make it harder to opt out of contributing to the common good by (a) requiring that communities submit an analysis of how splintering would affect school finances and racial and socioeconomic demographics and (b) requiring the approval of both the seceding community and the district it leaves behind (EdBuild, 2017, 2019).[72] Congress should encourage states to adopt these reforms by linking them to federal education aid; an even larger incentive would be to link these reforms to infrastructure aid as part of a broader housing and infrastructure package.

Recommendation 5: Eliminate or more equitably distribute state lottery funds. State lotteries in 35 states have been presented as a way to generate funding for public education. While they make up only a small portion of education funds, they are another example of the inefficient and inequitable way America finances its schools. Lotteries raise $54 billion and only return $15 billion to schools. In addition, lottery revenues are not returned to low-income communities in proportion to their lottery contributions.[73] Eliminating lotteries is unpopular for many reasons (EdBuild, 2016a, 2016c). The federal government could encourage states to more equitably distribute these funds, though, by adjusting or withholding Title I funding.

Recommendation 6: Adopt capacity-building strategies. As discussed, informants complained that many of the so-called best practices that were promoted under recent reforms were based on the recommendations of outside actors that had a financial stake in their adoption rather than on scientific evidence or the expertise of educators. Similar to countries that outperform the United States on international measures of achievement (see Fullan, 2011), educators advocated a variety of research-based strategies that would build capacity by investing in schools as communities. I already discussed improving school infrastructure, expanding access to needed nutrition and health care, reforming housing policy, and more equitably distributing school funding; Lesson 4 provides recommendations to build capacity by improving the teaching profession. This section presents other research-based, capacity-building strategies.

Recommendation 6A: Increase access to high-quality preschool, childcare, summer learning, and extracurricular opportunities for low- and moderate-income children. Research supports informants' claim that the increased investment in outside educational opportunities by high-SES parents has contributed to unequal educational outcomes.[74] For instance, low-income children are less likely to have been exposed to preschool.[75] They also make academic gains during the school year but lose ground over the summer owing to fewer private learning opportunities (the summer slide).[76] These opportunity gaps create differences at the starting gate that are expanded over subsequent grades. Those who attend pre-K have higher test scores *and* are more likely to graduate high school, attend college, hold a job, and have higher earnings. Pre-K also reduces teenage pregnancies and the crime rate.[77] After-school and summer enrichment programs further boost achievement and engagement (Peterson, 2013). America can do better for its children while also promoting economic growth.

Research shows that the economic gains associated with expanded access to high-quality pre-K would be large enough to fully finance this societal investment over the course of decades (Bivens, 2016; Chaudry et al., 2017). One type of program that appears to be especially promising deploys a "two-generational approach" that provides parents with childcare, as well as skills to get and retain better jobs and build stronger families.[78] In recent informal discussions, educators said that the federal government should also invest significant new resources in the provision of affordable, high-quality childcare. The inability of many to return to work during the COVID-19 pandemic highlighted how critical childcare is for the economy, but it is also a fairness issue.

The lack of affordable childcare disproportionately affects women, especially women of color and those from low-income and middle-class families. Even before the pandemic, roughly half of Americans lived in so-called "child care deserts" where there is less than one licensed provider for every three children (Cohn, 2018); however, 2.3 million women dropped out of the workforce between February 2020 and 2021, as compared to 1.8 million men (Leonhardt, 2021), and women continued to leave in high numbers during August and September of 2021—even though 661,000 jobs were added. The ongoing dissolution of the child care industry was a huge contributor, but women also made up a larger proportion of dislocated public sector workers during the recession (Carrazana, 2020). Taking other long-term pandemic-related issues out of the equation, child care related unemployment alone is going to impede the income and career trajectories of (primarily) low-income and middle-class women for decades to come; in consequence, it will negatively affect the well-being and educational outcomes of their children.[79]

While some have argued that we should means test government funded child care, as discussed throughout this book, more inclusive programs improve civic engagement and democratic performance by increasing social cohesion and social trust; they are also easier to sustain in the long-run because they foster positive feedback. In comparison, the government has a long (and unsuccessful) history of means-testing programs that primarily serve women and children. Though the primary intent may have been to reduce costs, these programs create administrative hurdles that limit access for low-income Americans; they also reduce trust in the government and decrease political participation by isolating and stigmatizing recipients. The pandemic provides a historic opportunity to rectify this situation.

A recent study by the National Women's Law Center finds that a universal child-care system—one that provides affordable, reliable child care from birth to age 13—would increase workforce participation and stabilize retirement by dramatically increasing lifetime earnings and improving job security for women (and men) across the country. All of these outcomes would boost economic growth

(Leonhardt, 2021), but, again, would also boost positive feedback and trust in government by treating citizens with dignity and respect rather than isolating them through program designs and policy labels. Universal child care recognizes that women often serve as the primary, unpaid caregivers for children and parents at a cost to their careers, lifetime earnings, and retirement stability. This role has especially harmed the life outcomes of low-income women and women of color, who are also disproportionately likely to staff underpaid child care positions (Cohn, 2018; Leonhardt, 2021).

Finally, about three-fourths of those I interviewed advocated targeting enhanced funding for extended learning opportunities to the low-wealth districts that disproportionately serve low-income children and students of color. Such programs include high-quality pre-K, summer learning opportunities, extracurricular programs, advanced coursework (Advanced Placement classes and other forms of accelerated instruction), and the provision of so-called nonacademic classes (art, music, technology, and physical education). All students benefit from multiple ways of learning and knowing, but, as shown, many low-resource schools cut these programs during the Great Recession. Without increased federal assistance, they are likely to do so again in the COVID-19 fiscal environment. Even without such cuts, research shows that low-income and minority students have less access to advanced coursework due to school fiscal issues. This negatively affects their ability to compete on an even playing field for college admissions (Foundation for Excellence in Education, 2018; Martin et al., 2018).

Recommendation 6B: Provide high-need, low-resource schools with more funding to reduce class sizes. Research shows that small class sizes, especially in elementary school, increase educational achievement and attainment, improve wage earnings, and reduce poverty by enabling teachers to better tailor instruction, improve student engagement, increase time on task, and reduce time spent on classroom management. These investments also improve equity because the positive effects are typically larger for low-income and minority students.[80]

Recommendation 6C: Invest in supports that improve school safety and impede the school-to-prison pipeline. Research supports participants' claim that students are experiencing record levels of depression, anxiety, trauma (e.g., witnessing violence, experiencing abuse or the loss of loved ones), and other mental health issues. These issues have reduced academic achievement and attainment and caused the suicide rate to skyrocket.[81] Investments in school counselors, nurses, social workers, and psychologists improve attendance and academic achievement and attainment while also reducing the numbers of suspensions, expulsions, and other disciplinary incidents. These positions are critical for dealing with sick, stressed, or traumatized students yet are often the first to go as a result of fiscal distress. This makes it difficult for students to get the help and guidance they need to be successful; it also negatively affects school safety.[82]

In the aftermath of recent school shootings, governments at all levels allocated significant new resources to reduce violence and improve safety.[83] Most focused on zero-tolerance policies and visual security measures (e.g., installing metal detectors, maintaining police on-site, hiring security officers, setting up surveillance cameras, arming teachers); yet research indicates such policies do not increase school safety, are ineffective at preventing or reducing school violence, make schools feel less safe and welcoming, raise absenteeism, increase rates of student suspension and expulsion for nonthreatening behaviors (e.g., talking back or dress code violations), create an upsurge in referrals to the police, and result in increased incidences of arrest for lower-level threats (e.g., fighting, disorderly conduct, making threats without a weapon). In addition, these policies have created social justice issues by creating a school-to-prison pipeline that disproportionately affects male students, students of color, and students with disabilities. Directly, this occurs through referrals to local law enforcement for smaller infractions; indirectly these policies result in higher rates of suspension, expulsion, and absenteeism—all of which increase the risk of criminality through educational underperformance and dropout. It is one of the factors contributing to disparities in educational outcomes for these groups, including the gaps in college attendance and completion that were discussed under Lesson 1.[84] Like other recent reforms, these punitive policies also direct critical resources to private companies rather than providing public schools with resources for preventive measures.[85]

Support for redirecting resources away from zero-tolerance school policing and security policies is growing in the wake of recent BLM protests (Kamenetz, 2020). This and other research, however, indicate that it is possible to challenge the school-to-prison pipeline *without divesting in school security*.[86] My informants said that high academic achievement and attainment and positive school behaviors are more likely in school environments where students and staff feel like they are socially connected, valued, treated fairly, *and* physically and emotionally safe. They also agreed that it is critical to invest in strategies that are based on evidence; acknowledge that schools differ substantially in terms of their needs and their capacity to implement reforms; and recognize that *schools must create social order* to efficiently and effectively serve and educate students. As shown, schools, like societies, achieve social order through three mechanisms: social cohesion, social trust, and social control. This study suggests that it is far more cost effective and socially and economically just to improve social order through social cohesion and social trust, but measures for ensuring social control cannot be totally abandoned. Congress should provide the DOE with resources to improve data collection and fund research on effective approaches for improving school climate and safety, with a specific focus on preventing school violence and reducing the school-to-prison pipeline.

Strategies to create safe and supportive school climates are likely to vary depending on the district, but research shows that coercive disciplinary practices are less effective than other reforms, such as gun violence prevention, peer mediation, and restorative justice programs; school climate modifications to facilitate positive interactions between educators and students; and therapeutic and behavioral supports. These reforms promote social trust and social cohesion, restore a sense of physical and psychological safety, address mental health needs, and develop the socioemotional and other skills that improve educational behaviors and outcomes.

Congress should support these efforts by significantly increasing funding for student support services, programming, and staffing (e.g., social workers, counselors, and psychologists). Currently, 1.7 million students are in schools with no counselors, 3 million have no nurses, 6 million have no school psychologists, 10 million have no social workers, and 14 million have no counselor, nurse, psychologist, or social worker (ACLU, 2019). Congress should also allow more flexibility in the use of federal funds to develop school-based, community-based, and blended programs. In addition, the DOE should restore civil rights protections and data collection; these roles were downgraded or rescinded during President Trump's administration.[87]

Recommendation 6D: Expand the number of promise neighborhoods and construct civic empowerment zones. *Promise zones* or *promise neighborhoods* marshal the assets of the community to improve learning through "wraparound services," including pre-K, childcare, nutrition, dental, health, counseling, before- and after-school programs, summer enrichment programs, GED preparation, college preparatory classes, and second-language and child development classes for parents. Research suggests that these zones improve student attitudes and behaviors (e.g., perseverance and attendance) as well as their academic and life outcomes; they also encourage parents, students, and other community members to participate at school and in the community.[88] Earlier, I referred this as social capital. It includes bonding ties to those close to us, bridging ties to participants from a wide range of backgrounds, and linking ties that leverage resources from outside of a community, whether that is the federal government, private and nonprofit philanthropies, or business-economic interests (e.g., banks and developers). This and other research shows that school improvement efforts are more effective when they include the broader community of stakeholders.[89] Such inclusiveness is important for building social cohesion and social trust—both of which improve the willingness and capacity of citizens to participate in democratic institutions (voice) and work toward the common good.

Unfortunately, this and other research also suggests that schools do not equally prepare students for citizenship. This *civic opportunity gap* reduces voice from the least well-off, which increases the likelihood that community control over public schools will reduce educational equity.[90] To redress these issues, the federal government should fund community participation grants that foster the inclusion of historically marginalized groups in public schools and local governance, similar to the ones that were included in many Great Society programs. Community organizing would help build a political constituency that is invested in public education, committed to a more equitable distribution of resources, and has the capacity to engage in voice on behalf of policies that redress structural inequalities (policy feedback).[91]

Civic opportunity programs would vary by community, but the goal is to improve and sustain education reform by developing leadership skills; building social trust, social cohesion, and civic capacity; and creating networks that are working toward political, social, and economic justice from the ground up. At the local level, these *civic empowerment zones* would help build school capacity by engaging the community in reform, facilitating a long-run view of change, and creating the bridging and linking ties that improve access to wraparound services and social supports. Again, the latter are critical for meeting the social and economic needs of individuals and families. Such social supports ensure that children enter school ready and willing to learn and provide the resources that sustain learning over time. They may also help stem the flow of middle-class families from low-resource communities.[92] At the state and national levels, this expanded civic capacity would help counter the economic model of democracy, which, as shown, undermined the gains that were made by middle- and working-class Americans and marginalized communities under the New Deal, postwar policies, and the Great Society, as well as through unions, the civil rights movement, and the community control movement. The latter sought to give parents—especially low-income and minority parents—more voice in public schools.

Lesson 3: Political-Market Accountability Increases Educational Inequalities

Democratic theory frames education as a public good because it helps students lead independent and fulfilling lives; develops the predispositions, values, and skills needed for civic engagement and democratic participation; creates social cohesion; and fosters the inclusion of diverse constituencies in shared decision-making and local self-governance. All of these develop political, social, and economic capital (freedom to).[93] In contrast, economic models of democracy advocate using competition and choice to foster freedom from the government. The spread of these views is evident in the 47 percent increase in the number of charter schools between 2006–2007 and 2012–2013, as well as the expansion of private school vouchers across the country. Rather than building the trust, civic capacity, and social cohesion that are essential for sustaining and improving public schools, this research shows that these market-based reforms have made public education less democratic and inclusive. School choice, for instance, weakened public school capacity by disrupting social ties, increasing racial and socioeconomic segregation, and destabilizing school finances.[94] Most informants were not resistant to charter schools and a recent poll supports this study's findings that educators' views are not partisan; they are shared by teachers from different political parties and political ideologies (e.g., Editorial Projects in Education, 2017). Their broader complaint is that data have been misappropriated to justify transferring public resources to charter, private, and parochial schools and force public schools to do more with less, or go out of business.

This book shows why democracy is not synonymous with the free market and democratic accountability is not synonymous with the aggregation of private interests. Democratic participation means accepting the rights *and* responsibilities of citizenship. Educators must go beyond the technical aspects of their jobs; children must participate in class and help others; and citizens must be willing to perform their civic obligations, such as voting and paying taxes. Framing education as a good that is produced by teachers and consumed by individuals, versus a good that is produced collectively for the benefit of society, crowds out these responsibilities and reduces public education to a performance that is devoid of social value. Educators "do" teaching for good evaluations, parents "maneuver" to advance their children, and students "do" school to get ahead. Phrased another way, the focus on individual rights and wants (the market) impedes democratic performance by reducing citizens' willingness to contribute to the commonweal—the well-being common to all of us.

There is no question that some students have benefited from school choice; however, contrary to the claims of policy makers, research shows that parental choices are not an indicator of school or teacher quality.[95] Parents care about academics yet also have strong preferences for other qualities, such as a school's proximity to their homes and/or jobs, the availability of before- or after-school programs and extracurricular activities, the enrollment of high achievers, and the racial and socioeconomic backgrounds of the students.[96] The latter preferences contribute to socioeconomic and racial segregation, but that is also true of parental preferences for schools that are closer to home.[97] The lack of information, transportation, and quality schools nearby creates higher barriers to choice for underprivileged children (e.g., low SES, recent immigrants, students of color) and students with special needs.[98] In consequence, the market empowers some while "chaining others to place."[99]

Again, accumulated national evidence shows that charter schools do little, if anything, to boost achievement and increase segregation by race, income, language, and academic and behavioral issues. They are also more likely to suspend students, especially minority students and students with academic and behavioral issues.[100] These findings call into question the claim that parental choice will raise all boats. The bottom line is that charter schools could be part of an overall strategy to improve public education, but not if discourse inappropriately and inaccurately compares public schools with charter schools as a way to justify policies that defund and defang public schools and those that support them (e.g., educators and unions). This discourse alienates an important constituency that cares about children (public school educators) to justify ceding authority to nondemocratically elected actors that have a mixed record of improving achievement, as well as a financial stake in expanding accountability and school choice policies (e.g., testing and publishing companies, education management organizations, the education consulting industry, charter schools, private and religious schools, and the DeVos, Gates, and Walton Family Foundations). The latter are not being held accountable to taxpayers owing to a lack of regulation.[101]

School choice should not be expanded unless it advances equity and integration and includes mechanisms to ensure that those receiving public funds are held accountable for how those funds are spent and do not discriminate in hiring and admissions. This is particularly critical if the Supreme Court, as expected, sides with the plaintiffs in *Carson v. Makin* (2021) and requires states to fund students that attend schools that provide religious instruction versus funding tuition payments to private and parochial schools that are nonsectarian—meaning they do not provide a religious education. That decision, if rendered, will open the door to a dramatic expansion of voucher and other school choice programs, but it will also require that the federal government and state governments protect against discrimination based on race, gender, sexual orientation, and so forth. The schools involved in the lawsuit brought by parents in Carson, for instance, discriminate against LGBTQ in hiring and admissions (Carlisle & Reilly, 2021).

Recommendation 1: Use research to improve parental access to information. States and localities have made uneven investments in systems that support parental choice. Most parents fill out multiple applications because participating schools have different requirements, selection preferences, and deadlines; many also remain on waiting lists until parents with multiple offers make their decisions. This process favors those parents who have the time, knowledge, and resources to navigate the system. The adoption of universal or common enrollment systems in some cities—like Denver, Newark, New Orleans, and Washington—has streamlined and made school choice less complicated and more transparent by creating a single application for public and charter schools; yet research shows that, even under these more comprehensive systems, both high- and low-income parents need navigational assistance and more information.[102] The rapid expansion of school choice (charter school and voucher programs) has also fueled the growth of an education consulting industry, which favors those who have the economic capital to purchase these services.[103] The federal government should fund studies on how parents and students consume information, how that affects the inclusiveness of school choice programs, and what policies would alleviate informational disparities so that parents from different backgrounds are more equal in their capacity to navigate school choice.

Recommendation 2: Improve democratic accountability and make integration an explicit goal of school choice. While still few and far between, the number of public school districts and charter school networks that are using socioeconomic integration strategies has grown from 2 in 1996 to 83 public schools and 8 charter schools in 2016 (the most recent study year). The most common integration strategy is to redraw school attendance boundaries, but other strategies include developing magnet schools, adopting district-wide choice policies that explicitly consider socioeconomic diversity, and using charter school lottery processes that consider SES. Successful early adopters engaged in strong outreach, provided free transportation, and used weighted lotteries to meet diversity goals.[104] The federal and state governments should support and expand these efforts. As mentioned in the last section, the proposed Strength in Diversity Act is one way to do so but must be accompanied by proposals in this section to address other factors that have been increasing segregation by race, ethnicity, and SES—namely school choice policies.

Congress should strengthen the provision in the ESSA that advocates charter management organizations advance racial and socioeconomic integration and apply it to state governments. States should not receive federal charter school funding (or, more expansively, Title I funds) unless they make socioeconomic integration an explicit goal of their school choice (voucher and charter school) programs and target funding in ways that will increase choice fairness.[105] Before making decisions about where to grow charter schools, for example, states should be required to assess opportunities for underserved student populations (e.g., low-income students, students of color, ELLs, students with academic, emotional, and behavioral issues) and evaluate the effects of this expansion on the surrounding public schools (e.g., school closings, segregation, and budget cuts). We must also stop calling charter schools "public" if they do not serve everyone. This means federal and state DOEs must

»   conduct equity audits
»   penalize charter schools with low acceptance and high expulsion rates for educationally "at-risk" groups, meaning students from lower socioeconomic backgrounds, students of color because they are disproportionately likely to be poor, ELLs, and those with learning, behavioral, and emotional issues
»   require that charter schools comply with all federal laws and desegregation decrees

» mandate that charter schools provide detailed plans for how they will reduce current disparities in achievement, graduation, suspension, and expulsion rates for educationally at-risk groups and broaden, not replicate, existing opportunities for these groups[106]

More broadly, federal education funds should be denied to states whose educational agencies (state DOEs) do not have the authority to revoke and nonrenew charter schools that fail to meet basic standards and integrative outcomes.[107]

At a *bare minimum,* democratic accountability requires that those receiving public funds be held accountable to the public through transparent and democratic procedures. Yet market advocates, like Betsy DeVos, have deregulated school choice programs across the country in ways that obfuscate hiring and firing practices, curricular choices, procedures for disciplining and expelling students, and performance data. This makes it difficult for parents and taxpayers to hold charter schools and voucher recipient schools accountable. Yet research shows that charter schools are more likely to suffer from financial mismanagement, go bankrupt, and close.[108] A recent study also found that up to $1 billion in funding awarded by the federal Charter Schools Program (CSP) was wasted on charter schools that never opened or only opened for a brief period of time before they were shut down for poor performance, a lack of enrollment, fraud, and/or mismanagement (Burris & Bryant, 2019).

Policy makers must hold private and quasi-private actors to the same standards as public schools. The federal CSP should not be expanded until Congress provides the DOE with more resources to conduct equity audits and investigate charter school waste, fraud, and mismanagement. The DOE must also be able to hold states accountable for collecting information on any program that transfers public tax dollars to quasi-public and private entities for educational purposes (e.g., charter schools and voucher programs). This should include withholding federal education aid from states that do not publish information on how many students attend each charter school and receive vouchers, how these students are performing, and how these schools spend public tax dollars.

Private, religious, and charter schools that receive public funds should also be required to make public their procedures for grading, disciplining, and expelling students; to adopt procedures that protect educators, parents, and students against discrimination and malfeasance; and to develop processes that broaden participation in school governance. As mentioned, only 11 percent of charter schools are unionized (National Alliance for Public Charter Schools, 2018). The DOE should further prioritize offering charter school funding to schools and states that encourage teacher voice through collective bargaining and stakeholder voice through community-led models over those that cede authority to private and quasi-private entities.

Recommendation 3: Use test scores as a gauge of student performance, not to ration economic security. The publication of annual test scores provides public information to help policy makers, parents, and taxpayers evaluate schools and make decisions about funding or where to send their children. This policy tool gained widespread support based on the belief that parental voice and choice would improve public education. It presumes that parents make choices based on quality alone and that educators are stimulated to work harder for rewards (merit pay) or due to the threat of losing their jobs. These assumptions are contrary to the findings of this and other research. Instead, testing and competition have increased anxiety and mental health disorders among adolescents,[109] disproportionately penalized schools and teachers that serve students that struggle, and encouraged gaming and other dysfunctional behaviors that do not improve instruction.[110]

Participants agreed that parental participation is critical for children's educational outcomes but argued that voice and choice are not sufficient for improving public education or for leveling the playing field. The best way for parents to evaluate schools and teachers is to examine relationships in the building and the degree to which students are happy, engaged, and interact with one another through repeated visits.[111] Unfortunately, many parents do not have the time or desire to engage in these processes and so they often lack actionable information about school and teacher quality.[112] This increases the likelihood that their decisions will be tainted by personal biases, influenced by misperceptions about teaching and learning, and (inappropriately) penalize teachers and schools.[113]

In addition, the ability to access and act on information is unequally distributed in ways that harm the least well-off. As shown, middle- and upper-income parents have an informational advantage that improves their children's access to better quality schools, classes, and teachers. Some of this advantage is cultural. For example, research shows that many immigrants do not view oversight and participation as part of their parental duties because they believe "there are no bad schools"—only some "bad" students and teachers within schools.[114] Structural barriers, though, are more important. SES creates differences in the ability to access and share important online information through a technological divide (e.g., school account-ability ratings or charter school entrance requirements). Middle and upper-income parents are also more likely to have professionals in their networks. Because of this, they are better able to access and share information that is not widely available and are more likely to believe that they have the expertise and authority to contest the judgments of educational gatekeepers (see Chapter 9).[115] I have been referring to this as cultural and social capital.

The recent college admission scandal (Medina et al., 2019) and the finding that there is more grade inflation in high schools that educate wealthier students (e.g., Jaschick, 2017) support informants' claim that middle- and upper-income parents and students are more likely to obtain unearned rewards (e.g., grades, admissions to college, and acceptance into accelerated instruction and athletic programs).[116] This aggressive and competitive voice combines with institutional biases, such as legacy admissions (Larkin & Aina, 2018), to reportedly discourage hard work from those who benefit and from those who do not by providing evidence that the deck is stacked. Despite these findings, educators did not recommend restricting parental voice. Instead, as discussed in the previous section, they advocate policies that would broaden participation by fostering democratic inclusion.

Most also did not oppose using test scores as a *gauge* of student performance or to make decisions about providing more assistance to schools and students; they opposed using test scores to ration economic security for educators and students and penalize public schools.[117] Again, test scores reflect SES, more than ability or effort; segregation and inequitable resources also combine in unexpected and often unacknowledged ways to negatively affect the performance of low-income and minority students.[118] High school grades are a better predictor of college completion than college admissions exams (Bowen et al., 2011), but grade inflation in schools that educate wealthier students suggests that policy makers, colleges, and univer-sities should use caution there too.

One way to adjust for such issues would be to provide an *adversity score* that colleges may use as a factor in admissions. It would account for external factors, such as living in neighborhoods and attending schools that have high rates of poverty, segregation, and crime, as well as low rates of high school graduation, college attendance, and college completion. This reform acknowledges that the SAT and ACT are measures of accumulated advantage, rather than common yardsticks; wealthier parents are able to provide their children with experiences that increase their scores and chances of being admitted to their preferred colleges (e.g., tutoring, extracurricular activities, summer camps, courses that provide test-taking strategies); and peer effects matter. The College Board, publisher of the SAT, recently said it would add an adversity score but later withdrew the proposal (Geiser, 2015; Hartocollis, 2019). The broad based policy interventions recommended throughout this chapter are another way to more equitably distribute opportunity, including access to college.

Lesson 4: Political-Market Accountability Deprofessionalizes Teaching

Throughout this book, I have shown why the public sector is not the same as the private sector (individualism) and professionalism (egalitarianism) is not the same as bureaucracy (hierarchy). By creating a consumerocracy—where public services are evaluated based on how well they serve individual wants versus collective ends—the political imposition of market ideology has generated issues for the ethical, efficient, and effective delivery of public services. The belief that citizens need to discipline public servants to make them more responsive to individual demands has downgraded professional judgements; it may actually raise costs when combined with the philosophy that "the customer is always right" by fostering a sense of entitlement, an unwillingness to accept limits on public service provision, and aggressive voice among citizens. One example is the growth in costs associated with "adversarial legalism," or using the courts to make policy (Kagan, 2003). Parents should, of course, prioritize their children's needs, but schools and educators cannot always personalize and individualize services. School funding is constrained by democratic choices (e.g., voting on school budgets and taxes) and educators must consider the needs of all students and the community.[119]

Education is not even a true marketplace or a product in the traditional sense of the word. It is *social activity*. Parents, students, and society are involved in its production, not just its consumption—as is the case with widgets—and the success of the individual often depends on the performance of the group, as well as the ability of the group to work toward common ends. Just as importantly, it is a *public good*. The quality of a local public school affects everyone in the community, just like the quality of public education affects everyone in a society. Under these conditions, market incentives and state coercion are less likely to improve service quality, especially when they seek solely to alter the behaviors of educators. Instead, these forms of social control promote dysfunctional behaviors, such as complying with the letter of the law to improve performance without actually improving instruction (e.g., teaching to the test). The focus on efficiency and effectiveness, as measured by test scores or consumer satisfaction, also silences democratic values and other important societal goals, such as procedural justice, fairness, autonomy, equity, social justice, universal care, and the transformative and humanistic ends of public education. Americans care about these ends, not just public service quality or even costs.

Markets also do not necessarily "raise all boats," as policy makers argue they do. In fact, incentives (e.g., competition and choice) are actually designed to motivate individuals to work hard through the creation of winners and losers. Some parents now exercise more consumer rights, but their gains came at a cost for other people's children. Again, these outcomes create social justice issues because the most well-off are better able to access high quality schools, classrooms, and services for their children.

At the same time, the market generates troublesome links between public service provision and the ability to pay. One teacher told a story about a wealthy suburban district in another state that "encourages" parents to "donate" a certain amount per child every year. The newspaper then publishes how much they contributed to "recognize" (i.e., reward) those who donated above the amount and acknowledge those who contributed the suggested amount. This shames—through silence—those who do not contribute and creates a language of dependency for children whose parents cannot afford the price. As shown, such negative stigmas increase neglect among children in ways that are similar to how the stigmatization of welfare recipients and the working poor reduces political participation. Neglect in the form of reduced participation, refusing to study or do homework, or even criminality increases costs by necessitating more social control (detention, suspension, expulsion and incarceration).

That being said, research shows that highly performing teachers improve educational achievement and attainment, as well as students' lifetime earnings.[120] Conversely, high turnover increases costs and reduces performance.[121] If America wants to recruit and retain the best and the brightest to improve student achievement and attainment, it must adopt a comprehensive policy agenda that reprofessionalizes teaching—so that teachers are viewed more similarly to doctors and lawyers, like they are in other countries.

Recommendation 1: Raise teacher compensation, especially in hard-to-staff schools. Middle-class wages have been in a downward spiral for many occupations and professions. This is also true of teaching; however, American teachers earn only 60 percent of similarly educated professionals in this country—the lowest ratio of modern industrialized nations—and have experienced lower pay growth compared to those in other nations.[122] They are also about 30 percent more likely than nonteachers to work a second job. The latter is not solely attributable to summer employment, working in related positions (e.g., tutoring or coaching), or low starting salaries. About half of second positions are unrelated to teaching, teachers are more likely to work a second job all year round, and the families of many mid-career teachers qualify for benefit programs like the Children's Health Insurance Program and a free or reduced-price school breakfast and lunch. The Great Recession of 2008 and tax cuts in many states contributed to these issues, but the high cost of living consumes higher salaries in some areas—like California.[123] Most teachers also report paying out of pocket for classroom supplies and many turn to crowdfunding to make up for inadequate resources.[124]

Some policy makers have tried to portray teachers as selfish for protesting and/or going on strike (Sinclair, 2018), yet their demands included more funding for support staff, books, supplies, and capital improvements—not just higher salaries.[125] Moreover, the experiences of other highly performing countries support their claim that America would improve the recruitment and retention of high-quality teachers by making salaries more competitive with other professionals'.[126] Informants recommended combining higher starting pay with policies that would allow teachers to more quickly advance to mid-career-level salaries. These recommendations would reduce the number of teachers who need to work a second job or leave the profession. In addition, most advocated providing salary incentives to recruit teachers in hard-to-staff schools and about one-third of interviewees recommended providing salary incentives to those who teach hard-to-staff subjects (e.g., science and math). The latter recommendation is more controversial in an egalitarian occupation because it rewards teachers based on what they teach versus more equitably distributing HQTs and rewarding teachers for years of experience and education. This area needs to be studied more systematically.

Recommendation 2: Invest in polices and institutions that promote teacher voice. Teacher unions should be involved in any effort to modernize the profession. As shown, unions raise student achievement and attainment by increasing wages, raising teacher dismissal rates, and reducing turnover; they also improve funding fairness and reduce dropout rates—especially among lower-performing students.[127] To promote union voice, Congress should redress the fundamental weaknesses with U.S. labor law that educators in this study identified, such as creating penalties for school districts that refuse to negotiate in good faith. Lesson 1 discussed this and other labor reforms. Such policies are especially critical in light of the Supreme Court's *Janus* decision but also because legislative changes have weakened or eliminated teacher tenure and seniority by lengthening probation periods, linking tenure to student performance, and/or streamlining teacher dismissal processes (Joseph, 2014; Sawchuk, 2014a).

Opponents claim that unions, tenure, and seniority create opportunity gaps by making it too expensive to remove underperforming teachers; they argue that tenure and seniority are no longer necessary because the discriminatory labor practices that had historically harmed women and people of color were eliminated by the Civil Rights Act of 1964.[128] Some further contend that public school teachers do not need the same free speech protections as university professors because the latter contribute to new and sometimes controversial academic ideas (Given, 2014). This book shows that these claims are misguided and have resulted in policies that reduce teacher voice on behalf of students, colleagues, public education, and the norms of the profession.

Recent examples of why free speech and due process protections (e.g., tenure) are still needed in public schools include state and school board proposals to ban books, restrict the teaching or discussion of "culturally divisive" issues or topics (e.g., systemic inequalities or sexual orientation), place cameras in every classroom, establish reporting "tip lines," and impose fines, and in some cases, misdemeanor charges on noncomplying educators. The adopted or proposed changes are based on the unproven claims that elementary and secondary schools are teaching critical race theory (CRT), using it to rewrite history and indoctrinate students, increasing tribalism—behaviors and attitudes that stem from strong loyalty to one's own group—and harming students' self-esteem by portraying them as part of the problem based on their heritage. As a group, the educators in this study expressed strong support for parental involvement in education; however, a recent NBC analysis confirms the concerns being voiced by educators at large that a culture war is being pushed and funded by conservative think tanks, media outlets, and law firms for political reasons. At least 165 local, state, and national groups are promoting ways to control what is taught in classrooms through tactics such as disrupting school board meetings, ousting liberal school board members, and harassing parents who support teaching about equity issues—with the goal of mobilizing conservative voters in next year's midterms and beyond. Such restrictions on free speech do not appear to be supported by the majority nationwide or even where they are being proposed and adopted. This is an example, though, of how an aggressively vocal minority may harm students and society—in this case by restricting professional voice, silencing works of literature and critical parts of the nation's history, allowing parents to "spy on" other people's children, not just teachers, through cameras in the classroom, and constraining educators' ability to foster empathy, tolerance, and trust through the discussion of complex social and historical issues and the provision of help to students who are dealing with prejudice and/or issues of identity. At least one principal has been arbitrarily suspended based on the unproven accusation that he was promoting CRT (Gross, 2021; Ray & Gibbons, 2021; Shepherd, 2021).

Many of those I interviewed supported lengthening the probation period for tenure from three to five years, and most were not opposed to streamlining due process protections—so long as teachers' unions were involved in the development and implementation of these changes. As a group, though, they advocated retaining tenure and seniority while focusing on other ways to improve the profession, as discussed throughout this section.

Recommendation 3: Reward teachers for leadership roles. The current compensation system incentivizes degree attainment and years of experience over contributions to the profession and to schools. In addition, ambitious teachers must leave the classroom to gain more responsibility, even if they are talented and would prefer to teach rather than to become administrators. Recent reforms largely kept that system but linked pay and/or job tenure to performance. In doing so, these reforms rewarded those who teach high achievers, teach to the test, or teach in low-need and/or high-resource schools. Informants preferred instituting career ladders that reward teachers for an array of roles and responsibilities rather than rewarding them for student test scores. That might include training and mentoring new or struggling teachers; planning or facilitating professional development; observing teachers and giving feedback; and working with school leaders to hire teachers and make decisions about resources, instruction, and the curriculum. This recommendation is in line with professional ideology, which argues that those with training should develop new innovations and mentor and evaluate colleagues (see Chapter 5).

I discuss mentoring and evaluating colleagues in the next two recommendations, but some districts have been experimenting with rewarding teachers for leadership roles and/or accelerating the time that it takes to earn mid- to top-level salaries. Research suggests that these policies have improved instruction and school performance by retaining effective teachers (K. Miles et al., 2015). State and/or federal policy makers could facilitate these efforts by funding and disseminating studies that compare the cost and effectiveness of different district-level compensation practices. It would also be useful to have studies that compare the salaries and benefits of teachers with other professionals in each state and within different regions of the state. These studies would help school districts explore the best ways to (a) reward those that take on additional responsibilities, (b) accelerate the time that it takes to earn mid- to top-level salaries, and (c) use teacher compensation to recruit and retain teachers at a time when resources are limited.

Recommendation 4: Use principal training and peer assistance and review (PAR) to improve teacher evaluation and support continuous growth. As discussed, research shows that most teachers were deemed effective or highly effective under traditional evaluative methods (e.g., principal observation and professional development plans); poorly performing teachers were also rarely dismissed. These findings fueled demands to link teacher evaluations to student test scores.[129] Yet most teachers were still deemed effective or highly effective and were rarely dismissed under this policy reform (Sawchuk, 2013c). Informants recognized that there are issues with principal observations and professional development plans but argued that the low removal rates mostly reflect high turnover among the least effective teachers early in their careers.[130] They prefer observations and professional development plans to using student test scores because the former provide actionable and timely information for improving instruction; administrators and districts are also able to adjust these forms of evaluation to prevent teachers from being rewarded or penalized based on *whom* they serve (high achievers vs. high-need students) and *what* they teach (inclusive classrooms vs. advanced or accelerated courses). Although they argued that principal observations had been improving through the development of new instruments (e.g., Charlotte Danielson), they also said that investing in principal training would improve this form of evaluation.

Recent reforms, for the most part, ignored the role of principals in school performance; however, they are the second most important in-school variable for student achievement—after teachers—and are especially important in high-poverty schools. Effective principals improve instruction, reduce turnover, and foster school change by providing feedback through announced and unannounced classroom visits, creating positive working conditions and relationships, improving school culture, and sharing leadership responsibilities.[131] Most participants acknowledged that principals in high-poverty schools had less time to perform these important functions as a result of dealing with "wicked problems." About half said that principals *in general* need more high-quality mentoring, especially in the first three years, to help with these roles and most agreed that principals need to invest more time in conducting evaluations, offering meaningful feedback, and providing support for low-performing teachers.

State and federal financial support for ongoing principal training—especially for those who work in high-need, low-resource schools—would improve school leadership, but it needs to be restructured. That may involve funding time away from work to receive more training, in a similar way to how university professors take a sabbatical to conduct research. Research suggests that investing in partnerships with schools of education to enrich principal training and mentorship improves school leadership; it also creates a support system that ensures continuous mentorship, growth, and development by fostering relationship-building (social capital) between administrators from different districts (Center for Public Education, 2012; Mitgang, 2012).

Beyond providing more resources for principal training and mentorship, many participants suggested that the federal and/or state governments should fund and disseminate studies that examine variations in teacher dismissal rates between schools and districts. These studies should also document "best practices" with respect to teacher training and dismissal.[132] About 15 percent of the teachers I interviewed further advocated using PAR to improve teacher evaluations. PAR provides teachers with a leadership role in the development of professional standards and the evaluation of their peers. None of those I interviewed had direct experience with this form of evaluation, but consulting teachers temporarily leave the classroom (for about three to five years) so that they may provide assistance to 15–20 novice teachers and/or help experienced teachers who have been rated in need of improvement. Consulting teachers file a report after several months to a joint management–labor committee that may solely rely on their recommendation or combine it with the principal's evaluation to make decisions about reappointment or dismissal (J. Goldstein, 2008; S. Johnson & Fiarman, 2012).

PAR programs are somewhat controversial.[133] They are more expensive because schools must backfill these teaching positions. Experimental research is needed, but existing studies support that PAR improves performance through mentoring, reduced turnover, and increased collaboration, as well as through *higher dismissal rates* for ineffective teachers. Some of the increased costs are also offset through other savings, such as reduced legal costs. PAR minimizes legal challenges because review panels include administrators and teachers and are able to show that the district provided due process, as well as training and advice from experienced colleagues before dismissal.[134] These findings suggest that PAR would improve teacher professionalism (e.g., voice and training), but it also may facilitate agreement between unions, school districts, and policy makers with respect to teacher training and removal.[135]

Recommendation 5: Provide more opportunities for collaboration and professional development. Informants said that one early benefit that they gained through collective bargaining was a free period each day to grade work, develop lesson plans, engage in professional development, collaborate with colleagues, serve the school and profession, provide extra help to students, and talk with parents. All of these directly improve practice and indirectly do so by fostering relationship building. Most of this time is now reportedly devoted to meeting policy demands, such as collecting data, aligning curriculum with standards and assessments, and filing paperwork for students with special needs or behavioral issues. Unlike a generation ago, teachers are also required to get all students career and college ready—not just a small percentage of top performers. That is a positive development yet requires differentiating and adjusting instruction to meet the needs of growing numbers of ELLs (Hamm et al., 2018) and other academically at-risk students and developing the critical thinking and socioemotional skills that enable students to think outside the box, persevere amid uncertainty, and contribute to increasingly diverse workplaces. These changes necessitate additional planning time for all teachers, but especially for new teachers who are learning the ropes.

Research shows that teachers, on average, work 10 plus hours a day (Bill and Melinda Gates Foundation, 2013). Contrary to current rhetoric, those in their forties and fifties, on average, work more hours, with the exception that brand-new teachers of all ages typically work the most.[136] American teachers also work far longer hours than their OECD counterparts, who are given more time during the school day to collaborate and craft lessons (Darling-Hammond et al., 2010; OECD, 2017).

The federal government should fund a pilot project that provides school districts with resources to engage in scheduling reforms that will provide more opportunities for collaboration and professional development. Such reforms might include hiring new teachers to temporarily cover classrooms and provide participating teachers with a free period during the day or a block of time at some point during the year to collaborate with other teachers, engage in professional development, and mentor new and struggling teachers. These participating hires will gain needed skills by "learning the ropes" from those they temporarily replace while also providing the district with a pool of trained human capital if vacancies open up. Congress should also provide state DOEs with funds to study and collect data on the effectiveness of different reforms. Some states and school districts may wish to focus on providing this "free time" to teachers in their first three years or to teachers in hard-to-staff schools and subjects; others may wish to use it to meet specific needs, such as mentoring new teachers or developing and sharing curriculum and lesson plans. The main point of this reform is that teaching has undergone tremendous changes that have increased on-the-job demands, but teachers' schedules remain largely unchanged.

Informants said that school districts must also better align professional development with the needs of students and teachers. The average teacher receives fewer than 16 hours of professional development a year, far below what research suggests is needed to improve student learning, and most of that training is ineffective at changing practice—in part because it is often divorced from content and/or has too little to offer in terms of meeting student needs (Darling-Hammond et al., 2009; Hill, 2009). One lesson from this study is that professional development has become a big business—where market actors develop and sell materials to states and local school districts at a high cost with little involvement from educators.[137] This has not improved educational outcomes and is deprofessionalizing teaching. Professions advance when those who have the expertise train inductees, evaluate members, and develop innovations. The scheduling reforms discussed in this section may be a way to redress this situation.

Recommendation 6: Improve teacher induction programs. Owing to demographic changes and high turnover, beginning teachers are now the largest group in one of the largest occupations in the nation. Between 40 and 50 percent of teachers leave within the first five years, but half of all turnover occurs in about 25 percent of the nation's (predominantly high-poverty urban and rural) public schools. Research shows that teachers receive less support than those in other professions and occupations; teaching is also one of the few professions in which new employees have the exact same responsibilities as veterans (R. Ingersoll, 2012; Walker, 2019). This and other research suggest there are less traumatic ways to introduce teachers into the profession.

Studies show that teacher induction programs improve job satisfaction, teacher retention, instruction, and student achievement, but some interventions are better than others and receiving multiple types of support is better than receiving only one. Unfortunately, the most commonly provided interventions are not those that are the most successful. For instance, research supports informants' claims that having common planning time and a mentor teacher from the same subject or grade provides the strongest positive effects. Yet, by far, the most common intervention offered to new teachers is supportive communication with administrators followed by guidance and feedback from a mentor teacher. Many districts do provide common collaboration and planning time with teachers from the same grade or subject, but fewer than 20 percent reduce the teaching load or schedules for new teachers—a common way of helping beginning professors (R. Ingersoll, 2012). These realities contrast with the views of respondents in this study, who strongly advocated hiring additional teachers to reduce the teaching load for first-year teachers and some said second-year teachers as well. About half of those I interviewed mentioned that the federal government invests in medical residencies yet provides very little for teachers. It should provide more resources for teacher induction programs in general, but especially target these resources to high-need, low-resource schools, where turnover is especially high.[138]

Recommendation 7: Make teacher preparation and licensure programs more rigorous and improve clinical experiences. Average SAT scores and GPAs have gone up for teaching majors, but the highest-performing high school and college students, and students from our nation's highest-ranked universities, are still less likely to choose teaching. Raising salaries would help with recruitment; however, too many potential educators—especially teachers of color—fail state professional licensing exams and do not receive the training they need to be successful in the classroom. This reduces diversity and is unfair given the significant costs involved in becoming a licensed teacher.[139] States should publish teacher preparation program data to provide prospective candidates with indicators of effectiveness, such as the school's job placement rates, candidates' scores on state licensure exams, and student evaluations of their courses, clinical experiences, and preparation for teaching.

Given changing student demographics, the state and/or federal government should also adopt a pilot project that provides scholarships to enable prospective candidates to student teach in schools that disproportionately serve low-income students and students of color—especially those in urban and rural areas. This would help ensure that teacher candidates gain the skills and experiences they need to work with and manage diverse learners and classrooms; it would also help high-need, low-resource schools recruit effective teacher candidates postgraduation. In addition, states could improve the quality and diversity of the workforce by ensuring that licensure programs assess the skills and knowledge teachers need to be successful in the classroom and by forgoing fees for low-income candidates. Research shows that teacher licensure exams mostly rely on multiple choice questions that do not assess deep and relevant content knowledge and pedagogical skills; they are also expensive (Partelow et al., 2017; Sawchuk, 2013a, 2013b).

There is a legitimate concern that raising the selectiveness of teacher preparation programs and the quality of state licensure exams may disproportionately eliminate students of color from the teacher candidate pipeline owing to the ways that structural inequalities negatively affect educational outcomes, including test scores; however, empirical research suggests that it is possible to increase both selectivity and diversity (Lankford et al., 2014; Partelow et al., 2017).

Recommendation 8: Close the diversity gap between teachers and students. Almost 80 percent of the teaching workforce is white and 40 percent of schools have no teachers of color. The shortage of Hispanic teachers is harming the nation's fastest-growing student population—the nearly 5 million ELLs, of which roughly 75 percent are Spanish speakers. Some of this diversity gap stems from historical issues, including segregation, but teachers of color are actually losing ground among Millennials as compared to Generation X. The diversity gap is not a recruitment issue. Teachers of color enter in higher numbers today, but they also exit at much higher rates—mostly because they are far more likely to work in high-need, low-resource schools where exit is also higher among their white colleagues.[140] The male gender gap has also grown over the last 30 years.[141]

A more representative teaching workforce is important for many reasons. This and other research finds that educator diversity benefits *all* students.[142] Students of color, though, especially do better on a variety of academic outcomes if they are taught by teachers of color; they are less likely to be reported for disciplinary infractions too.[143] More research is needed, but there is also some evidence that expanding the number of male teachers, particularly in elementary school, would help reduce gender disparities in educational outcomes, especially for low-income males and minority males (Thompson, 2021). These findings are not suggesting that women cannot teach boys or that white teachers cannot teach students of color. The point is that increased diversity provides students with successful role models, which, in and of itself, may be a way to stem the school-to-prison pipeline that disproportionately harms male students and students of color because they are more likely to be disciplined, suspended, and expelled; they are therefore less likely to graduate high school.

For those who are interested, Partelow et al. (2017) provides a number of recommendations to reduce the teaching diversity gap. One program that shows promise for both recruitment and retainment is Grow Your Own Teachers.[144] The recruitment of local candidates is critical because most teachers work within 40 miles of their hometowns (Boyd et al., 2005). Colleges and universities also improve minority representation in the profession when they accommodate part-time students and offer free or reduced college tuition (B. Alvarez, 2017). Another successful approach is to provide students of color with minority mentors.[145] As already discussed, states and the federal government could join these efforts by providing more financial assistance and debt forgiveness to low-income students who pursue teaching or are currently teaching in high-need, low-resource schools. This reform would expand the middle class by making the teaching profession accessible to low-income students. While it would likely improve male representation, it would especially target minorities of both genders because, as mentioned, they are disproportionately likely to grow up poor and teach underprivileged students in underresourced schools.[146]

Discussion: Restoring the Public Sector and Reviving the Middle Class

John Dewey (1927) said that the "public does not naturally exist in society; it has to be . . . called into existence." At times in our nation's history, policy makers have done so and rallied citizens behind communal goals versus private wants. Dewey recognized, however, that those with political, economic, and social capital may distort the definition of the "public good" so that it creates "public bads" for the many on behalf of the few. Similarly, Stone (1997) notes that the state is often portrayed as a "neutral referee," yet political and economic power are intertwined in ways that often favor the most well-off. Lindblom (1982) goes one step further. He claims that there cannot be a "mutual benefit society." We do not share the same interests and so the government cannot be a "neutral referee." It must choose. Since the late 1970s, policy makers have chosen a public service paradigm that advocates dismantling the public sector while investing in policies that privilege only a small percentage of the population. The theory of action is that the most well-off will reinvest their gains in ways that will trickle down to other Americans through increased employment and higher wages.

This book argues that it is possible to disagree about the appropriate level of taxes and spending while still recognizing the importance of public goods and services. The expansion of the public sector began in the nineteenth century because the free market had produced harmful externalities that businesses either could not or would not address on their own (e.g., child labor, environmental degradation, unsafe living and working conditions). These issues went unchecked because citizens and the affected communities lacked the power to force them to do so. Advocates of TPA provided the rhetoric, policies, and legal and administrative structures to expand the regulatory state and increase political, social, and economic voice. Those changes, when combined with the economic issues in the 1970s, mobilized those who were concerned about rising taxes and government intrusion in people's lives. As constructed under neoliberalism, public choice theory provided these groups and individuals with the language to challenge the administrative structures and policies of TPA (see Chapter 8).[147]

Again, neoliberals claim that the public service monopoly allows public servants to put their own interests above the needs of citizens and society, resulting in an inefficient and ineffective public sector. The goal was to "free" people from government intrusion, but, by promoting severe cuts to the public sector, this rhetoric disproportionately harmed middle- and low-income Americans. These groups are more reliant on public services and have historically used public-sector employment as a way to enter or stay in the middle class. The same is true in many rural communities, where residents are more dependent on public services and employment because they have fewer and less diverse private employers and businesses. Neoliberalism downplays these negative side effects because it values individuals for their ability to contribute to the private economy while downgrading the (public and private) value created by committed public servants and denigrating the idea that citizens have rights to services—once authorized through democratic processes—that are funded through public tax dollars, transform and improve society, and raise the quality of their lives.

Today, state and local employees compose the smallest share of the American workforce since 1967. This sector is still larger than the 2.8 million or so who are part of a greatly shrunken federal workforce (P. Cohen & Gebeloff, 2018).[148] Part of this downsizing results from lower tax revenues during the Great Recession, but national policy makers and many state policy makers also prioritized tax cuts and therefore spending cuts to reduce the resulting deficits (P. Cohen & Gebeloff, 2018; McNichol, 2012). Neoliberals claim that smaller federal, state, and local payrolls help the economy by reducing taxes and stimulating private-sector growth; yet research shows that most of the created private-sector jobs were unstable, paid little more than minimum wage, and did not provide health insurance, paid sick days, parental leave, and other benefits. In the meantime, public servants have been financially downgraded through increased wage penalties and lower benefits. The push to privatize public services, like prisons, emergency services, and schools, has further eroded salaries and benefits.[149] All of these have contributed to a shrinking middle class (P. Cohen & Gebeloff, 2018; McNichol, 2012). When viewed through this lens, it becomes evident that the campaign to cut public services, through forced deficits and restrictions on voice (e.g., public sector collective bargaining, tenure, seniority), is an attack on the middle class; however, the resulting shortages of nurses, teachers, firefighters, paramedics, police officers, counselors, restaurant and meat inspectors, correction workers, and so forth have affected us all.

Public services are not always perfect or superior. The BLM protests, for instance, are drawing attention to how uncooperative, abusive, or alienated public servants may destroy citizens' trust in government and one another. Still, research and history show that it is possible to make working in the public sector attractive to those with an inclination to serve *all* Americans. By vocation and specialized training, these individuals may be trusted to promote the public interest over private interests or self-interests. To recruit and retain those who are committed, at the top of their class, or already accomplished professionals, the government must pay reasonable salaries, meaning not necessarily equal to those paid in the private sector but sufficient for access to the middle class; provide sufficient opportunities for professional advancement based on merit and training; and create institutions that protect voice (e.g., whistleblower protection laws). As shown, voice promotes public values and improves the efficiency and effectiveness of public services through transparency, engagement, and the exposure of waste, fraud, and abuse. It is further critical that the government be viewed as a good employer. Policy makers set standards for public *and* private employers. If the government does not "walk the walk," it will be harder to encourage private employers to voluntarily follow better practices. The government will also lose the trust of citizens who are either the victims of bad employment practices or see their tax dollars supporting those practices.

One further point deserves separate consideration. We must also change how we talk about public servants and services, not just how we regulate both. Words matter. Ridiculing and scapegoating public employees discourages dedicated and hardworking individuals from pursuing and remaining in public service, including the best and brightest teachers. *The professions*—like teaching—require enhanced control over licensing, certification, training, and service provision (see Chapter 5), but *public education* is a public good, not a monopoly—as characterized by free market advocates, like President Trump's secretary of education Betsy DeVos. All citizens have an investment in public education because it improves the quality of our society as a whole.[150] Similarly, *public schools* are not a business, an industry, a market, or a dead end; they are owned by citizens, run by locally elected school boards, and subject to democratic oversight at the state and federal levels.

As public institutions, public schools provide the space where "we the people" come together to continue and transform our democratic way of life. They do so by advancing humanistic, integrative, egalitarian, and civic ends (e.g., civic engagement and political participation)—not just economic ones (e.g., training human capital). Unlike charter, private, and religious schools, public schools may not exclude students based on race, immigration status, gender, income, special needs, and so forth. In consequence, they are one of the few places where citizens from different backgrounds work side by side—even if they are still far too segregated by race and SES.

In addition, public education is not the sum of individuals acting on their private wants; it is a commitment to something larger than ourselves—a space where citizens have obligations to one another. Public school performance is also broader than what schools "do"; it is a reflection of who "we" are. If public policies favor narrow interests or promote inequalities between individuals, groups, and communities, some schools will perform quite well. Others will struggle to educate children.

As mentioned, the United States is at a historic crossroad. Like other times in our nation's history, civil society is rising up and demanding that policy makers redress political, social, and economic inequalities. Contrary to the views of neoliberals, the private sector *and* the public sector may destroy individual liberties, socioeconomic equality, and communities; both undergoverned *and* overgoverned societies are places where individuals, groups, public institutions, and private institutions may use social, economic, and political capital for unproductive and destructive ends. The proper amount of government intervention actually depends on the society, the community, and the historical time period. The policies that were adopted during the Great Depression and the War on Poverty increased civic engagement by more equitably distributing opportunities and fostering political, economic, and social voice (freedom to). In contrast, recent discourse and policies have encouraged rising numbers of citizens to opt out. Partially this is due to the focus on individual rights (e.g., property rights, freedom from the government, Don't Tread On Me) versus communal responsibilities; however, increased economic insecurity has also reduced trust in government and fellow citizens.

Phrased another way, by shrinking the middle class and creating a growing gap between those at the top and those at the bottom, policy makers have fostered a decline in social capital *and* democracy. To regenerate both, policy makers must restore the belief that America is an opportunity society, as well as an ideal worth fighting for, by redressing inequality, expanding political participation, and promoting civility in public life. This chapter laid out a number of reforms that are consistent with NCG, egalitarianism, and communitarianism. These policy changes would temper some of the excesses of TPA and NPM. Most would redress inequality and some would promote civility in public life. Both of these are critical for improving social cohesion, social trust, civic engagement, and democratic performance.

In terms of the latter, participants did not discuss voting and other reforms that would expand democracy and so I did not include them in this chapter. However, their focus on policies that foster voice and inclusion is consistent with recent demands to (a) restore key sections of the Voting Rights Act of 1965, which were gutted by the U.S. Supreme Court's decision in *Shelby County v. Holder* (2013), and (b) reduce partisan gerrymandering by having independent commissions, rather than politicians, draw electoral districts. Partisan gerrymandering allows elected officials from both parties to pick their voters by drawing "safe districts," meaning those that favor one party over another. When combined with other decisions that have allowed almost unlimited amounts of political spending, including "dark money," the Supreme Court's refusal to redress partisan gerrymandering has reduced the incentive for policy makers from both parties to listen to voters instead of special interests.

Added to those Supreme Court decisions, Republican state legislatures have been weaponizing voting by adopting restrictions that disproportionately target Democratic constituencies. This electoral strategy is escalating as a result of historic voter turnout in November 2020, with 14 states having now enacted nearly two dozen laws and many more in the pipeline. Most restrict absentee and mail-in voting, but states are prohibiting giving food and water to voters who are waiting in line; banning extended voting hours; disallowing drive-through voting; closing polling places in minority neighborhoods; politicizing the administration and certification of elections; and allowing partisan poll watchers to challenge voter eligibility and record those who receive help filling out their ballots. The latter will increase the likelihood of voter intimidation (Boschma, 2021; Brennan Center for Justice, 2021).

What all of these decisions and policies share in common is that they reflect the view that politics is about bare-knuckled combat rather than a way to *serve* Americans. When political parties are out of power, for example, democratic norms require that they *serve* as the "loyal opposition": they peacefully transfer power; follow democratic laws and procedures; publicly (and often vehemently) debate ideas about how to govern; and use those debates to mobilize citizens and build winning coalitions from the ground up through the power of their ideas. The willingness to establish minority rule through institutions like the filibuster in the U.S. Senate, partisan gerrymandering, and voting restrictions at the state level is an assault on democracy. It has also created extreme inequality and reduced American's trust in one another and in their political, social, and economic institutions. The House of Representatives recently passed the For the People Act to redress some of these issues. As this book goes to press, it is in the hands of the Senate. Those who value American democracy will put restoring democratic norms above holding on to power by any means necessary.

Conclusion

The original ESEA recognized that public schools are a microcosm of society; it sought to foster a more democratic, inclusive, and equitable system of public education through the provision of federal resources to schools that served large numbers of economically disadvantaged children. Federal reforms since then have moved the ESEA away from that original purpose by framing resources as incentives and withholding those "rewards" if schools (NCLB) or educators (RttT and NCLB waivers) did not meet specified outcomes (i.e., test scores). These policies discounted decades of research showing that segregation, inequitable school financing, and socioeconomic status more heavily influence educational outcomes than educators. This is unfortunate because students today are more racially and ethnically diverse; schools are also highly segregated and the majority of school children now come from low-income families.

The fundamental concept behind a universal system of public education is that a person is not truly free if he or she is hemmed in by poverty and a lack of education. While the well-being of a nation's children ought to be a moral imperative, this book shows that the failure to meet children's basic needs—such as access to stable housing, adequate nutrition, and health care—also harms us as a society. Today's schoolchildren will be part of a modern global economy that requires a vast array of skills and knowledge. They will also be responsible for caring for an aging Baby Boomer generation that currently has a lot of influence over policy decisions and, in consequence, the ability to alter America's future in ways that help younger generations and therefore themselves.

Civic and economic renewal necessitates reforming the way we talk about government, public servants, and fellow citizens. It further requires public institutions and policies that more equitably distribute opportunity and the capacity to voice. Societies that turn on their weak in favor of the most well-off are unjust. They are also mistrustful. If left unattended, distrust rapidly degenerates into spaces of "us" versus "them"—creating lives that are "nasty, brutish, and short" for growing numbers of citizens. We are all connected. Supporting younger generations so that they are able *and* willing to contribute to the commonweal—the well-being common to all of us—will ensure that the United States is prepared to face the many new and grave challenges that affect us all.

Appendix A

Content Analysis of Public Discourse

The focusing questions for my interpretive analysis of public discourse were grounded in the public policy literature, especially Stone (1989, 1997), Schneider and Ingram (1990, 1993), and Ingram and Schneider (1991).

» What is the problem that is being resolved, as evidenced by the discourse? Who is being blamed? What solutions are being offered?

» What kinds of reasoning/symbolic devices are used? What kinds of causal stories are told? What is the character of the debate?

» What "public values" are being represented in the discourse (both as symbols and ideals to be maximized, and as a means of justifying policy designs and policy tools)? How are they interpreted?

» What policy tools are advocated to resolve the problem? Do the policy tools and policy design fit the problem as defined?

» How are the policy's targets socially constructed (e.g., students, parents, teachers, administrators, public schools, charter schools, private schools, state governments, the federal government)? Do the targets make sense given the definition of the problem?

» How are public versus private institutions characterized (this is coming out of the above analysis on policy targets but also in general)?

» Who are the direct/indirect beneficiaries of the policy? How are they helped by the policy? Are the beneficiaries hidden or explicit, the benefits direct, indirect, or a charade? Who is penalized by the policy? Are the penalties enforceable, explicit, or hidden?

» What does dissent/consent look like for "problem definition"? For the policy's tools or design? For the characterization of the policy's targets?

Appendix B

Interview Protocol

This interview protocol involves a series of mostly open-ended questions that are designed to explore how public policies and discourse interact with informal norms, work practices, and patterns of social relations within teaching and schools to structure educators' political and social experiences, identities, and behaviors. The questions are also designed to elicit educators' perceptions of how public policies and political discourse impact children's educational outcomes and the democratic social purposes of schools. Most administrators are former teachers. Where applicable, I asked questions about both positions.

Section 1: Questions 1–17

This section gathers data about how educators' backgrounds, teaching assignments, and school contexts influence their experiences, identities, and behaviors.

> **To be read before asking questions in this section:** *In this first part of the interview, I am going to ask you questions about your background and career, as well as questions that explore important, but less observable, influences on your identity and development as an educator.*

1. How long have you been a teacher/administrator (how long were you a teacher/administrator if you retired or left teaching/administration)? How long have you been in the current district, if different?

2. What grade(s) do/did you teach? What subject(s) or special areas (e.g., speech, reading, school psychologist, classroom aide, classroom assistant), if applicable?

3. Where did you go to school as an undergraduate? What did you study?

4. What is your highest level of education [Show Card 1]?

   CARD 1

   _____BA/BS
   _____MA/MS
   _____MA+
   _____PhD

5. I am going to show you a card, and if you are comfortable with it, I was wondering if you would pick the decade that reflects your age [Show Card 2].

   CARD 2

   _____Less than 30
   _____30 to 39
   _____40 to 49
   _____50 to 59
   _____60 or older

6. I was wondering if you would tell me why you chose to become a teacher/administrator. [Probes: What were the major attractions of the job? Do you remember any qualities about yourself that you felt would fit well with teaching/administration? What person or people or experiences influenced your decision to become a teacher/administrator? Did you consider any other occupations at the time? If yes, what and why?]

7. Did you feel well prepared to teach/be an administrator when you got your first job? [Probe: Basically, I am trying to understand what experiences you think were most influential in terms of *what* and *how* you

teach/be an administrator. For example, what classes, experiences, or jobs were best in terms of preparing you to teach/be an administrator?]

8. Was teaching/administration different from what you expected when you made the decision to enter the field? [Probe: If yes, how was it better or worse?]

9. Could you tell me a little bit about some of the rewards of your job?

10. I guess no line of work is perfect. What are the things that you like least about teaching/administration?

11. Could you tell me about a negative experience from your career as a teacher/administrator? What about a positive experience?

12. Have you ever considered leaving teaching/administration? [Probe with TLC: What was going on at the time? Why did/didn't you leave?]

13. Purely hypothetically, if you received a number of job offers at the same time, please rank the following in terms of importance to you. You may leave something blank if it is not important to you [Show Card 3].

CARD 3

_____Working with children or adolescents
_____Salary
_____Professional prestige
_____Administrative influence
_____Professional freedom and autonomy
_____Summers off
_____Job security
_____Something that interests me
_____Other—specify (you do not need to add any)

14. I wanted to talk a little bit about time. I was wondering if you could tell me how many hours on average you spend on the school premises each week (this would also include attending school functions)? On average, about how much time do you spend away from school doing schoolwork—this could include planning, grading, reading, studying, etc.? [Probe: If they talk about spending extra time at school or at home, probe for the kinds of activities they do and why. Probe whether they do other kinds of volunteer

work or volunteer for nonteaching/student-related activities or organizations.]

15. Different jobs have their own language and humor, sometimes even in the form of "sick jokes" that they use to converse with each other, build camaraderie, and relieve tension. Does teaching/administration have that? [Probes: I am trying to understand if teachers/administrators use humor to release tension and whether they share these jokes or experiences with one another?]

16. Most organizations use rules and standard operating procedures as a way of ensuring efficiency and behavioral consistency on the job. Can you explain one or two standard rules for doing things that are used by your school as an organization for teachers/administrators? [Probes: It would be nice if you could apply this to your job as a teacher/administrator. It would also help me, in terms of understanding how your school as an organization works, if you would give me at least one that you think makes your job a lot easier and one that you think imposes difficulties on your work environment.]

17. Let's talk a little bit about relationships. How important are relationships for teaching/administration, if at all? How do you view the relationships in this school between those on this card [Show Card 4]?

CARD 4
- Central administrators and building administrators
- Teachers and administrators
- Teachers and teachers
- Teachers and students
- Teachers and parents
- Administrators, teachers, and the community

Section 2: Questions 18–32

This section examines how recent education reforms impacted different groups and different aspects of teaching and schooling.

To be read before asking questions in this section: *In this part of the interview, I am going to talk with you about how recent education reforms have altered what, how, and why you teach, as well as the experiences, behaviors, and identities of different groups within your school community (if at all).*

18. Could you tell me a little bit about what you know in terms of NCLB/RttT?

19. In your opinion, what are some positive aspects of NCLB/RttT (if any)? What problems (if any) have occurred as a result of NCLB/RttT?

20. In your professional opinion, how useful are standardized tests in terms of measuring student performance? Teacher performance? School performance? How do you use standardized test results, if at all? How does your school use them? Has this changed as a result of NCLB/RttT? [Probes: How do you/teachers in your school evaluate students? What do you/teachers in your school look for in terms of learning and growth? Has this changed as a result of NCLB/RttT?]

21. Has NCLB/RttT influenced the way you do your job? [Probes: If yes, how and why? Do you view these changes as positive or negative? It would be okay if you would like to talk more generally about how NCLB/RttT has affected how teachers/other administrators do their jobs, rather than you personally.]

22. Has NCLB/RttT influenced the way you feel about your job? How you feel about your school? About your government?

23. Has NCLB/RttT influenced relationships in your school? [Probes: If yes, how and why? Do you view these changes as being positive or negative? Why?]

24. Has NCLB/RttT influenced the way teachers/administrators are evaluated, penalized, or rewarded in your school? If yes, have these changes been positive or negative? [Probes: Maybe we could start by discussing how teachers/administrators were evaluated before NCLB/RttT, and then discuss changes in how teachers/administrators are evaluated after NCLB/RttT. It might also help me if you talked about how you know if you are successful as a teacher/know teachers are

successful/know you are successful as an administrator. How do you know if you are doing the kind
of job you want to do? What do you watch for as an
indication of your effectiveness?]

25. Has NCLB/RttT influenced the way other teachers/
administrators do their jobs? How the district is being
run? Do you view these changes, if any, as positive
or negative?

26. How have students reacted to NCLB/RttT, if at all? In
your opinion, has NCLB/RttT impacted individual
students or different groups of students differently?
If yes, how so?

27. What about parents—how have they reacted to NCLB/
RttT (if at all)?

*Questions 28–32 apply only to teachers/administrators in
public schools that are being closed or restructured.*

28. Your school is labeled/under restructuring/being
closed. Could you tell me what you know about this/
how you feel about this?

29. Could you tell me a little bit about how your school
being labeled/restructured/closed has impacted you
as a teacher/administrator? [Probes: Has it influenced
how you feel about your job? About your district?
About the state? About government in general?]

30. Could you tell me a little bit about how your school
being labeled/restructured/closed has impacted
the students here? What about their parents? Other
teachers? Administrators? [Probes: Have any of these
groups talked with you personally about this issue?
Have you been present at meetings where it was
discussed by any of these groups?]

31. Did you take any action to remove the label/influence
how the school was restructured/change the decision
to close the school? If yes, how was it received? [Probe:
What about other teachers/administrators—did they
take any action that you know of? What about the
teachers' union? Students? Parents?]

32. What are your plans for when the school closes? [Probes: Will you continue teaching/being an administrator? Do you know where you will be going?]

Section 3: Questions 33–41

This section explores how forces in society at large influence public schools and teaching.

> **To be read before asking questions in this section:**
> *In this last part of the interview, the questions are somewhat broader than the personal experience questions I asked you earlier. I would particularly like to discuss other influences on public school administration and teaching, including forces within society at large.*

33. Some people think that schools should be operated like a well-run business with clear lines of authority and clearly stated responsibilities and roles. Others think that schools should be organized more loosely and that relationships among school staff should tend toward equality. Which of these two views comes closest to yours? [Probe: Do you think schools have changed over time toward one model or the other?]

34. Some people feel that we need differential policies to retain teachers. This might include, for example, creating ranks from "beginner" to "master" teacher—similar to a university system where there are lecturers, assistant professors, and so forth. It might also include a policy to retain science teachers or to encourage teachers to teach in high-need districts. It might also include merit pay (differential pay scales). How do you feel about this?

35. I was wondering if you would take a look at some recent headlines and comment on them for me. [Probes: In your opinion, what do you think is going on? What is the issue? What is at stake? Had you seen any of these stories or similar ones? Do teachers/administrators discuss stories like these with one another? Do stories like these influence how you feel

about your job? About the state? About government in general?] (Show Card 5)

CARD 5
- "School board in Rhode Island votes to fire <u>all</u> teachers in a struggling high school to improve school performance"
- "New Jersey governor urges voters to reject school budgets in districts where teachers did not accept pay freezes. Calls teachers' unions 'greedy'"
- "For kids' sake, power to fire teachers crucial!"
- "Washington D.C. public schools fire 226 'ineffective teachers'"
- "Wisconsin Governor Scott Walker signs law restricting union bargaining rights"
- "Idaho Governor Butch Otter signs law phasing out tenure for new teachers, restricting collective bargaining, and instituting merit pay"

36. I have heard teaching referred to as an art, a job, an occupation, a profession, and a vocation. Which comes closest to describing your views about teaching? Have your views changed over time?
37. Would you describe teaching/administration as an "emotional job"? This could be because you have to manage your own emotions to do the job well, or manage other people's emotions, or the job itself brings out emotions.
38. Do you think the "job" of teaching/administration has changed over time? [Probes: What about the "job" of public schools? It would help me if you would explain what you think the "job" of public schools is, and then explain whether you think that "job" has changed over time.]
39. What about people's attitudes about teachers, administrators, and public schools? Do you think they have changed over time? [Probes: I mean here the general public, government officials, students, parents, etc. It would be okay if you would like to choose a specific group or if you prefer to address this question in general.]

40. Do you think society has changed in ways that have impacted public schools and/or your job as a teacher/administrator?

41. If you were allowed to go back and "do it all over again," would you become a teacher/administrator? If not, what might you choose to do? If someone close to you said they wanted to become a teacher/administrator, how would you respond?

Appendix C

Interview Data for Administrators and Teachers

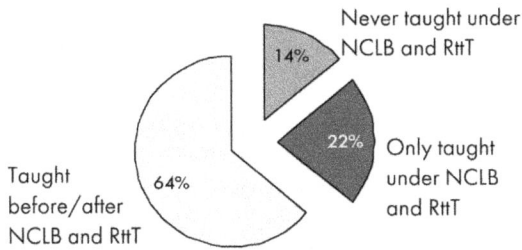

Figure C.1. Interviews by NCLB and RttT status. $N = 83$ interviews with teachers and administrators.

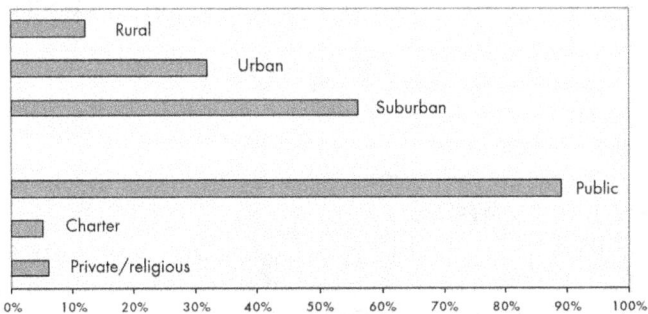

Figure C.2. Interviews by school type and context. $N = 39$ school districts. Statewide, about 44% of students attend urban schools, 43%

suburban/town, and 13% percent rural. Some teachers taught in more than one school. Each of these schools was counted in cases where teachers (a) taught in more than one school *and* (b) compared and contrasted those schools in the interview. For the most part, this involved new teachers who moved as a result of layoffs or to find a permanent position, although it also included experienced teachers who had moved between schools.

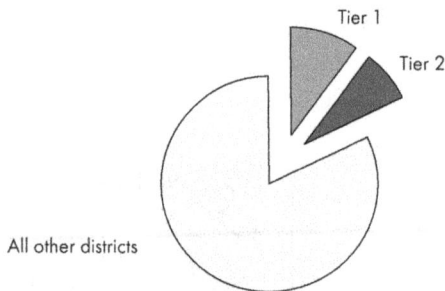

Figure C.3. Interviews by district managerial controls. $N = 39$ school districts. Some teachers taught in more than one school. Each of these schools was counted in cases where teachers (a) taught in more than one school *and* (b) compared and contrasted those schools in the interview. For the most part, this involved new teachers who moved as a result of layoffs or to find a permanent position, although it also included experienced teachers who had moved between schools.

The sample of Tier 1 and 2 districts included two high-need, low-resource urban school districts, both of which had schools that were labeled under NCLB; two urban charter schools; and three suburban districts, none of which was in danger of being labeled under NCLB. Two of the suburban districts served average-need students with an average level of resources. The other district served low-need students with a high level of resources.

» Tier 1 = 4 districts (1 urban, 2 charter, and 1 suburban): Public managers standardized and routinized teaching to ensure job consistency and (theoretically) improve educational outcomes. Standardization was achieved through top-down hierarchical controls but was often backed by explicit rewards and incentives.

» Tier 2 = 3 districts (1 urban and 2 suburban): Public managers adopted a very strong "performative" discourse that was often backed by explicit rewards.

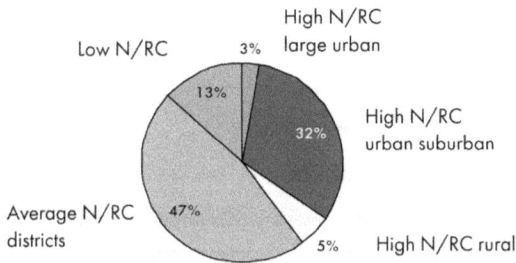

Figure C.4. Interviews by school district need and resource capacity. $N = 39$ school districts. Some teachers taught in more than one school. Each of these schools was counted in cases where teachers (a) taught in more than one school *and* (b) compared and contrasted those schools in the interview. For the most part, this involved new teachers who moved as a result of layoffs or to find a permanent position, although it also included experienced teachers who had moved between schools. The DOE for the northeastern state that is the subject of this analysis classifies school districts according to the needs of the school population (e.g., rates of student poverty and limited English proficiency) and their resource capacity (e.g., the income and property wealth of the district's residents). This graph shows the interviews according to these classifications. Low-N/RC districts would have a proportionately higher ability to meet the needs of their students than high-N/RC districts owing to some combination of student needs/district resources. The ability of average-N/RC districts to meet the needs of their students would be somewhere in between.

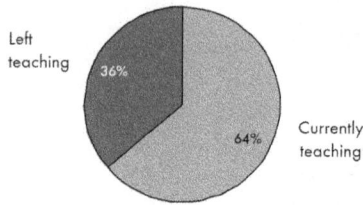

Figure C.5. Interviews by teaching status. $N = 83$ interviews with teachers and administrators.

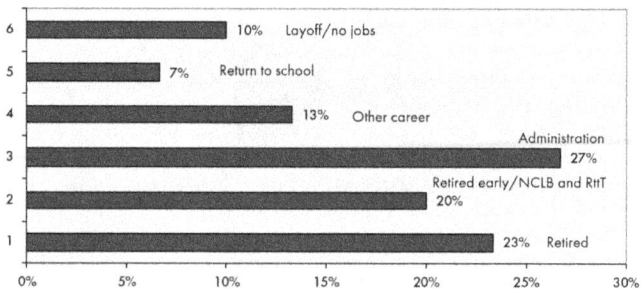

Figure C.6. Reasons for leaving teaching. $N = 83$ interviews with teachers and administrators.

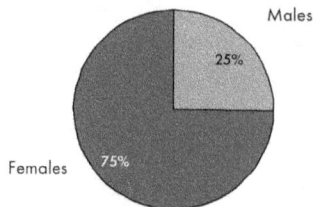

Figure C.7. Interviews by gender. $N = 83$ interviews with teachers and administrators.

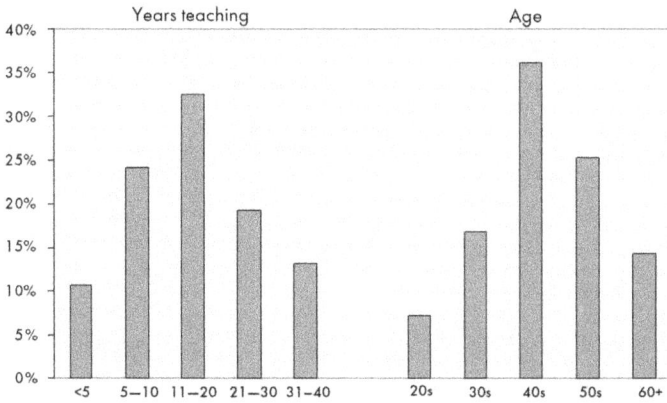

Figure C.8. Interviews by age and years teaching. $N = 83$ interviews with teachers and administrators. Average years teaching = 17. Average age = 43 years. Statewide, nearly 50% of teachers are 33–48 years old.

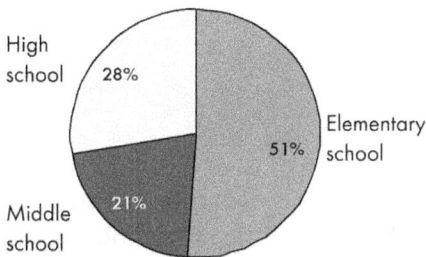

Figure C.9. Interviews by level taught. $N = 83$ interviews with teachers and administrators. Statewide, about 45% of students attend elementary, 23% grades 6–8, and 32% grades 9–12.

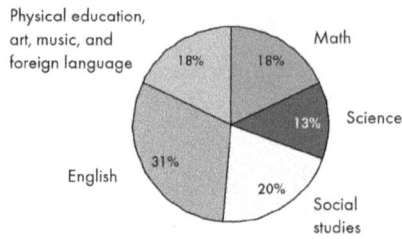

Figure C.10. Interviews by subject area. $N = 34$ interviews with teachers and administrators. Five teachers taught in more than one subject. These numbers do not include elementary teachers who teach multiple subjects. They only include secondary subject area teachers (math, science, English, social studies, foreign language, art, music, and physical education) and teachers in K–12 who teach art, music, and physical education.

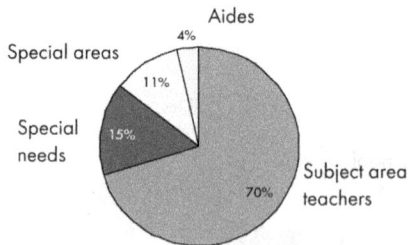

Figure C.11. Interviews by job title. $N = 83$ interviews with teachers and administrators. Special needs = speech, school psychologist, special education, reading, ESL, and AIS. Special areas = art, gym, library, foreign language, and music. Subject area = elementary teachers and secondary math, science, English, and social studies teachers.

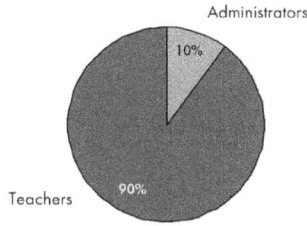

Figure C.12. Administrators versus teachers. $N = 83$ interviews with teachers and administrators.

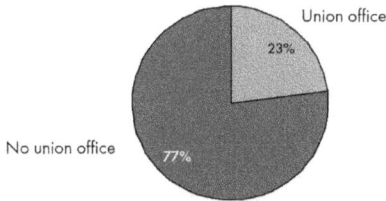

Figure C.13. Interviews by whether the teacher at one time held union office. $N = 83$ interviews with teachers and administrators.

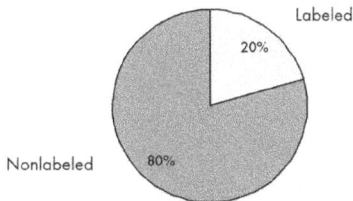

Figure C.14. Interviews by whether the teacher at one time worked in a labeled school. $N = 83$ interviews with teachers and administrators.

References

Aaronson, D., Barrow, L., & Sander, W. (2007). Teachers and student achievement in the Chicago public high school. *Journal of Labor Economics, 25*(1), 95–135.

Abdulkadiroglu, A., Pathak, P., Schellenberg, J., & Walters, C. (2017). *Do parents value school effectiveness?* (Working Paper No. 23912). NBER. https://www.nber.org/papers/w23912

Abrams, L., & Gibbs, J. (2002). Disrupting the logic of home–school relations: Parent involvement strategies and practices of inclusion and exclusion. *Urban Education, 17*(3), 384–407.

ACLU. (2019, March 4). *Cops and no counselors: How the lack of school mental health staff is harming us.* https://www.aclu.org/issues/juvenile-justice/school-prison-pipeline/cops-and-no-counselors

ACLU. (n.d.). *Felony disenfranchisement laws* [Map]. https://www.aclu.org/issues/voting-rights/

Adler, M. (2013). Findings vs. interpretation in "The long-term impacts of teachers" by Chetty et al. *Education Policy Analysis Archives, 21*(10), 1–11.

Advancement Project. (2011, March). *Federal policy, ESEA reauthorization, and the school-to-prison pipeline.*

http://www.advancementproject.org/resources/entry/ federal-policy-esea-reauthorization-and-the-school-to-prison-pipeline

AFT. (2015, November 30). *Why we support the Every Student Succeeds Act.* American Federation of Teachers. http://www.aft.org/node/10807

Ahmad, F., & Boser, U. (2014, May 4). *America's leaky pipeline for teachers of color.* Center for American Progress. https://www.americanprogress.org/issues/race/reports/2014/05/04/88960/americas-leaky-pipeline-for-teachers-of-color/

Ahmed-Ullah, N. (2011, December 19). Uproar continues over plans for south side schools. *Chicago Tribune.* http://www.chicagotribune.com/news/ct-xpm-20111-21-9-ct-met-closing-protest-20111220-story.html

Ahmed-Ullah, N. (2012, February 21). Protestors gather at Emanuel's house to protest CPS plans. *Chicago Tribune.* http://www.chicagotribune.com/politics/ct-rahm-emanuel-protests-12302-0151229-story.html

Aikens, N. L., & Barbarin, O. (2008). Socioeconomic differences in reading trajectories: The contribution of family, neighborhood, and school contexts. *Journal of Educational Psychology, 100*(2), 235.

Alexander, D., & Lewis, L. (2014). *Condition of America's public school facilities: 2012–13.* National Center for Education Statistics. https://nces.ed.gov/ pubs2014/2014022. pdf

Alexander, K., Entwisle, D., & Olson, L. (2007). Lasting consequences of the summer learning gap. *American Sociological Review, 72,* 167–180.

Alex-Peterson, J., Lundborg, P., & Rooth, D. (2017, December). *Long-term effects of childhood nutrition: Evidence from a school lunch reform.* IZA Institute of Labor Economics. https://ftp.iza.org/dp11234

Algozzine, R., Daunic, A., & Smith, S. (Eds.). (2010). *Preventing problem behaviors: Schoolwide programs and classroom practices.* Corwin Press.

Allegretto, S. (2018, April 4). *Teachers across the country have finally had enough of the teacher pay penalty.* Economic Policy Institute. https://www.epi.org/publication/ teachers-across-the-country-have-finally-had-enough-of-the-teacher-pay-penalty/

Allegretto, S., & Mishel, L. (2016, August 9). *The teacher pay gap wider than ever.* Economic Policy Institute. https://www.epi.org/publication/the-teacher-pay-gap-is-wider-than-ever-teachers-pay-continues-to-fall-further-behind-pay-of-comparable-workers/

Allensworth, E., Ponisciak, S., & Mazzeo, C. (2009). *The schools teachers leave: Teacher mobility in Chicago public schools.* Consortium on Chicago School Research.

Alvarez, B. (2017). *A growing recruitment strategy for a diverse teacher workforce.* NEA. http://neatoday.org/2017/05/24/grow-your-own-teacher-diversity/

Alvarez, L. (2011, March 16). Florida House approves ending tenure for new teachers. *New York Times.* https://www.nytimes.com/2011;03/17/us/17florida.html

Alvarez, L. (2013, December 2). Seeing the toll, schools revise zero tolerance. *New York Times.* https://www.nytimes.com/2013/12/03/education/seeing-the-toll-schools-revisit-zero-tolerance.html

Alyani, N., Mariana, Y., Osman, M., & Bachok, S. (2014). Factors influencing parents' decision in choosing private schools. *Procedia, 153,* 242–253.

American Association of Colleges for Teacher Education. (2018). *Colleges of education: A national portrait.* https://aacte.org/resources/research-reports-and-briefs/ colleges-of-education-a-national-portrait/

American Educational Research Association, American Psychological Association, & National Council of Measurement in Education. (1999). *Standards for educational and psychological testing.* AERA.

American Psychological Association. (n.d.). *Education and socio-economic status.* https:// www.apa.org/pi/ses/resources/publications/factsheet-education.pdf

American Statistical Association. (2014). *ASA statement on using value added models for educational assessment.* https://www.amstat.org/asa/files/pdfs/POL-ASAVAM-Statement.pdf

Amlung, S. (2010, March 19). *Back from the brink: How the UFT saved New York from bankruptcy.* New York Teacher.

Anagnostopoulos, D. (2003). The new accountability, student failure, and teachers' work in urban high schools. *Educational Policy, 17*(3), 291–316.

Anagnostopoulos, D., & Rutledge, S. (2007). Making sense of school sanctioning policies in urban high schools. *Teachers College Record, 109*(5), 1261–1302.

Andrias, K., Madland, D., & Wall, M. (2019, December 11). *A how-to guide for state and local workers' boards.* Center for American Progress. https://www.americanprogress.org/article/guide-state-local-workers-boards/

Annie E. Casey Foundation. (2012). *The first two years of Atlanta's Dunbar learning complex: Climbing the ladder of reading proficiency.* http://www.aecf.org/m/resourcedoc/AECF-ClimbingTheLadderOfReadingProficiency-2012-Full.pdf

Annie E. Casey Foundation. (2014). *Creating opportunity for families: A two generational approach.* http://www.aecf.org/m/resourcedoc/aecf-CreatingOpportunityforFamilies-2014.pdf

Apple, M. (2001). *Educating the "right" way.* Routledge.

Arcacia, E. (2006). Achievement and enrollment status of suspended students: Outcomes in a large, multicultural school district. *Education and Urban Society, 38*(3), 359–369.

Armentrout, M. (2018, July 20). Mark Janus quits state job for conservative think tank gig after landmark ruling. *Chicago Sun Times.* https://chicago.suntimes.com/2018/7/20/18409126/mark-janus-quits-state-job-for-conservative-think-tank-gig-after-landmark-ruling

Associated Press. (2018a, April 5). Kentucky legislators send tax cuts for wealthy, tax hikes for the other 95 percent to governor's desk. *Washington Post.* https://www.washingtonpost. Com/news/wonk/wp/2018/04/05/kentucky-lawmakers-pass-tax-cuts-for-wealthy-tax-hikes-for-other-95-percent/

Associated Press. (2018b, May 3). Striking Arizona teachers win 19% raise, end walkout. *LA Times.* http://www.latimes.com/nation/nationnow/la-na-arizona-teachers-20180503-story.html

Auguste, B., Hancock, B., & Laboissière, M. (2009). *The economic cost of the U.S. education gap.* McKinsey.

Ayers, R. (2016, November 22). The feds, and the New York Times, double down on strategies that fail our students. *Huffington Post.* http://www.huffingtonpost.com/rick-ayers-/the-feds-and-the-new-york_b_12522954.html

Ayscue, J., Frankenberg, E., & Seigel-Hawley, G. (2017, March). *The complementary benefits of racial and socioeconomic diversity in schools.* National Coalition on School Diversity. https://school-diversity.org/pdf/DiversityResearchBriefNo10.pdf

Bachtell, J. (2013, March 13). A fog of lies surrounding Chicago school closings. *Peoples' World.* http://peoplesworld.org/a-fog-of-lies-surrounding-chicago-school-closings/

Badger, E., & Cameron, D. (2015, July 16). How railroads, highways and other man-made lines racially divide America's cities. *Washington Post.* https://www. washingtonpost.com/news/wonk/wp/2015/07/16/how-railroads-highways-and-other-man-made-lines-racially-divide-americas-cities/

Bakeman, J. (2018, January 10). The rise and fade of education's "opt out" movement. *The Medium.* https://medium.com/s/new-school/the-rise-and-fade-of-educations-opt-out-movement-13250787e7f4

Baker, A. (2014, July 3). Lawsuit challenges New York's teacher tenure laws. *New York Times.* https://www.nytimes.com/2014/07/04/nyregion/lawsuit-contests-new-yorks-teacher-tenure-laws.html

Baker, B. (2014, August 15). Are teachers' unions really the scourge of the nation? *Washington Post.* https://www.washingtonpost.com/news/answer-sheet/wp/2014/08/15/are-teachers-unions-really-the-scourge-of-the-nation/

Baker, B., Farrie, D., & Sciarra, D. (2018, February). *Is school funding fair? A national report card.* Rutgers Education Law Center. https://drive.google.com/file/d/1BTAjZuqOs8pEGWW6oUBotb6omVwlhUJI/view

Baker, B., & Ferris, R. (2011). *Adding up the spending: Fiscal disparities and philanthropy among New York City charter schools.* National Education Policy Center. http://nepc.colorado.edu/

Baker, B., & Miron, G. (2015). *The business of charter schooling: Understanding policies that charter operators use for financial benefit.* National Education Policy Center. https://nepc.colorado.edu/publication/charter-revenue

Baker, P., Haberman, M., Hakim, D., & Schmidt, M. (2020, February 14). Trump fires impeachment witnesses Gordon Sondland and Alexander Vindman in post-acquittal purge. *New York Times.* https://www.nytimes.com/2020/02/07/us/politics/alexander-vindman-gordon-sondland-fired.html

Bakija, J., Cole, A., & Heim, B. (2012). Job and income growth of top earners and the causes of changing income inequality: Evidence from U.S. tax return data. https://web.williams.edu/Economics/wp/BakijaColeHeimJobsIncomeGrowthTopEarners.pdf

Baldi, S., Jin, Y., Skemer, M., Green, P. J., & Herget, D. (2007). *Highlights from PISA 2006 performance of U.S. 15-year-old students in science and mathematics literacy in an international context.* National Center for Education Statistics.

Balfanz, R., & Legters, N. (2004). Locating the dropout crisis: Which high schools produce the nation's dropouts. In G. Orfield (Ed.), *Dropouts in America: Confronting the graduation crisis* (pp. 57–84). Harvard Educational Press.

Balingit, M. (2018a, April 2). Fed up with school spending cuts, Oklahoma teachers walk out. *Washington Post.* https://www.washingtonpost.com/news/education/wp/2018/04/02/fed-up-with-school-spending-cuts-oklahoma-teachers-prepare-to-walk-out/

Balingit, M. (2018b, June 2). From the classroom to the campaign trail: Emboldened teachers run for office. *Washington Post.* https://www.washingtonpost.com/local/

education/see-teacher-run-educators-move-from-the-classroom-to-the-campaign-trail

Bandura, A. (1977). *Social learning theory*. Prentice Hall.

Banfield, E. (1958). *The moral basis of a backward society*. Free Press.

Bardach, E. (1977). *The implementation game: What happens after a bill becomes a law*. MIT Press.

Barnett, W. (2008). *Preschool education and its lasting effects: Research and policy implications*. Education and Public Interest Center & Education Policy Research Unit. https://nieer.org/wp-content/uploads/2016/08/PreschoolLastingEffects.pdf

Barnett, W., & Nores, M. (2013). *Equitable access to quality preschool*. Center for Early Learning Outcomes. http://ceelo.org/wp-content/uploads/2013;10/SLIDES_EquitableAcesstoQualityPrek.pdf

Baron, E. (2017). *The effect of teachers' unions on student achievement: Evidence from Wisconsin's Act 10*. https://ssrn.com/abstract=3001417

Baroody, K. (2011). *Turning around the nation's lowest-performing school: Five steps districts can take to improve their chances of success*. Center for American Progress. http://www.americanprogress.org/issues/2011;02;pdf/five_steps.pdf

Bauer, L. (2018, July 25). *Reducing food insecurity among households with children is still a challenge for the United States*. Brookings Institution. https://www.brookings.edu/blog/up-front/2018/07/25/reducing-food-insecurity-among-households-with-children-is-still-a-challenge-for-the-united-states/

Begley, S. (2017, January 25). There's now an unofficial National Parks account tweeting against President Trump. *Time*. http://time.com/4648607/nps-national-park-service-twitter-donald-trump/

Beland, D. (2005). Ideas and social policy: An institutionalist perspective. *Social Policy and Administration, 39*(1), 1–18.

Bell, A. (2019, February 15). *HUD funding bill will launch housing voucher mobility demonstration*. Center on Budget and Policy Priorities. https://www.cbpp.org/blog/hud-funding-bill-will-launch-housing-voucher-mobility-demonstration

Bell, T. (1988). *The thirteenth man*. New York: Free Press.

Belsha, K. (2019, July 11). What it means when Democratic frontrunners say they support Strength in Diversity Act. *Chalkbeat*. https://www.chalkbeat.org/2019/7/11/21121013/what-it-means-when-democratic-frontrunners-say-they-support-the-strenth-in-diversity-act

Bemelmans-Videc, M. L., Rist, R., & Vedung, E. (Eds.). (2007). *Carrots, sticks and sermons: Policy instruments and their evaluation*. Transaction.

Benington, J. (2011). From private choice to public value? In J. Benington & M. Moore (Eds.), *Public value: Theory and practice* (pp. 31–51). Palgrave Macmillan.

Beniwal, V. (2019, October 21). Taxing the rich to fund welfare is the Nobel winner's growth mantra. *Bloomberg News*. https://www.bloomberg.com/news/

articles/2019-10-21/taxing-the-rich-to-fund-welfare-is-nobel-winner-s-growth-mantra

Bensonsmith, D. (2005). Jezebels, matriarchs, and welfare queens: The Moynihan Report of 1965 and the social construction of African-American women in welfare policy. In A. Schneider & H. Ingram (Eds.), *Deserving and entitled: Social constructions and public policy* (pp. 105–110). State University of New York Press.

Berchick, E., Barnett, J., & Upton, R. (2019). *Health insurance coverage in the United States: 2018.* U.S. Census Bureau. https://www.census.gov/library/publications/2019/demo/p602-67.html

Berlin, J., & Bentle, K. (2018, June 29). What Wisconsin says about what could happen to Illinois unions after *Janus. Chicago Tribune.* https://www.chicagotribune.com/news/data/ct-union-membership-after-janus-htmlstory.html

Berliner, D., & Biddle, B. (1996). *The manufactured crisis: Myths, fraud, and the attack on America's public schools. Basic Books.*

Bettinger, E. (2005). The effect of charter schools on charter students and public schools. *Economics of Education Review, 24*(2), 133–147.

Bidgood, J. (2019, March 6). West Virginia raises teachers' pay to end statewide strike. *New York Times.* https://www.nytimes.com/2018/03/06/us/west-virginia-teachers-strike-deal.html

Bidgood, J., & Robertson, C. (2018, March 8). West Virginia walkouts a lesson in the power of a crowd-sourced strike. *New York Times.* https://www.nytimes.com/2018/03/08/us/west-virginia-teachers-strike.html

Bifulco, R., Cobb, C., & Bell, C. (2009). Can interdistrict choice boost student achievement? The case of Connecticut's interdistrict 61 magnet program. *Education Evaluation and Policy Analysis, 31*(4), 323–345.

Bifulco, R., & Ladd, H. (2006). The impacts of charter schools on student achievement: Evidence from North Carolina. *Education Finance and Policy, 1*(1), 50–90.

Bill and Melinda Gates Foundation. (2013). *Primary sources: America's teachers on teaching in an era of change.* http://www.scholastic.com/primarysources/PrimarySources3rdEditionWithAppendix.pdf

Bivens, J. (2012a). *Why the bipartisan commitment to public investment should go beyond rhetoric.* Economic Policy Institute. https://www.epi.org/publication/ib362-bipartisan-commitment-to-public-investment/

Bivens, J. (2012b). *More extraordinary returns: Public investments outside of "core" infrastructure.* Economic Policy Institute. https://www.epi.org/ publication/bp348-public-investments-outside-core-infrastructure/

Bivens, J. (2016). *Progressive redistribution without the guilt.* Economic Policy Institute. https://files.epi.org/pdf/107762.pdf

Bivens, J., Engdahl, L., Gould, E., Kroeger, T., McNicholas, C., Mishel, L., Mokhiber, Z., Shierholz, H., von Wilpert, M., Wilson, V., & Zipperer, B. (2017). *How today's*

unions help working people. Economic Policy Institute. https://files.epi.org/
pdf/133275.pdf

Bivens, J., Gould, E., Mishel, L., & Shierholz, H. (2014). *Raising America's pay: Why it's
our central economic policy challenge.* Economic Policy Institute. https://www.epi.org/
publication/raising-americas-pay/

Bivens, J., & Mishel, L. (2013). *The pay of corporate executive and financial professionals as
evidence of rents in top 1 percent incomes.* Economic Policy Institute. https://www.epi.
org/publication/pay-corporate-executives-financial-professionals/

Bivens, J., & Shierholz, H. (2018, December 12). *What labor market changes have
generated inequality and wage suppression?:* Economic Policy Institute. https://files.
epi.org/pdf/148880.pdf

Blair, J. (2002, November 6). Unions' position unheeded on ESEA. *Education Week.*
https://www.edweek.org/ew/articles/2002/11/06/10esea.h22.html

Blankley, B. (2019, February 21). Boosted by *Janus* ruling, Senator Rand Paul
introduces Right to Work Act for 4th time. *Watchdog.* https://www.watchdog.org/
national/boosted-by-janus-ruling-sen-rand-paul-introduces-right-to/article_
a827f7ec-35171-1e99-7537-75d1af6cf57.html

Blume, H. (2016, November 29). California faces a looming teacher shortage, and the
problem is getting worse. *LA Times.* http://www.latimes.com/local/education/la-
me-edu-california-teacher-shortage-20161129-story.html

Blumenthal, R. (2002, December 5). Recalling New York at the brink of bankruptcy.
New York Times, B3.

Bonilla, S. (2019). *Connecting high school, college and the labor market: Evidence on the
scale-up of career pathways in California.* Stanford Center for Education Policy
Analysis. https://cepa.stanford.edu/sites/default/files/wp190-3-v201905.pdf

Borman, G., & Dowling, M. (2008). Teacher attrition and retention: A meta-analytic
and narrative review of the research. *Review of Educational Research, 78*(3), 367–409.

Boschma, J. (2021, May 28). *Fourteen states have enacted 22 laws making it harder to vote.*
CNN. https://www.msn.com/en-us/news/politics/fourteen-states-have-enacted-
22-new-laws-making-it-harder-to-vote/ar-AAKuDr5

Boser, U., & Straus, C. (2014, July 23). *Mid- and late-career teachers struggle with paltry
incomes.* Center for American Progress. https://cdn.americanprogress.org/wp-
content/uploads/2014/07/teachersalaries-brief.pdf

Bosetti, L., & Pyryt, M. (2007). Parental motivation in school choice. *Journal of School
Choice, 1*(4), 89–108.

Bosk, C. (2003). *Forgive and remember: Managing medical failure.* University of Chicago
Press.

Bottari, M. (2018, February 22). Behind *Janus*: Documents reveal decade-long plot
to kill public sector unions. *In These Times.* Retrieved from https://inthesetimes.
com/features/janus_supreme_court_unons_investigation.html

Bourdieu, P. (1986). The forms of capital. In J. Richardson (Ed.), *Handbook of theory
and research for the sociology of education* (pp. 241–258). Greenwood Press.

Bourdieu, P. (1999). *The weight of the world*. Polity Press.

Bourdieu, P. (2000). Cultural reproduction in social reproduction. In R. Arum & I. Beattie (Eds.), *The structure of schooling* (pp. 56–68). McGraw-Hill Higher Education.

Bowen, W., Chingos, M., & McPherson, M. (2011). *Crossing the finish line: Completing college at America's public universities*. Princeton University Press.

Bowles, S., & Gintis, H. (1976). *Schooling in capitalist America*. Basic Books.

Bowles, S., & Gintis, H. (2000). Beyond the educational frontier: The great American dream freeze. In R. Arum & I. Beattie (Eds.), *The structure of schooling* (pp. 112–120). McGraw-Hill Higher Education.

Boyd, D., Grossman, P., Lankford, H., Loeb, S., & Wyckoff, J. (2006). How changes in entry requirements alter the teacher workforce and affect student achievement. *Education Finance and Policy, 1*, 176–216.

Boyd, D., Lankford, H., Loeb, S., Rockoff, J., & Wyckoff, J. (2008). The narrowing gap in New York City teacher qualifications. *Journal of Policy Analysis and Management, 27*(4), 793–818.

Boyd, D., Lankford, H., Loeb, S., & Wyckoff, J. (2005). Explaining the short careers of high-achieving teachers in schools with low-performing students. *American Economic Review, 95*(2), 166–171.

Bracey, G. (2000). *Bail me out: Handling difficult data and tough questions about public schools*. Corwin Press.

Bracey, G. (2008, November 13). The U.S. produces the lion's share of top scoring students. *Huffington Post*. http://www.huffingtonpost.com/gerald-bracey/the-u-s-produces-the-lion_b_143740.html

Brady, D., Baker, R., & Finnigan, R. (2013). When unionization disappears: State-level unionization and working poverty in the United States. *American Sociological Review, 78*(5), 872–896.

Braun, H., Jenkins, F., & Grigg, W. (2006). *A closer look at charter schools using hierarchical linear modeling*. National Center for Education Statistics.

Brenan, M. (2021, September 2). *Approval of labor unions at highest point since 1965*. Gallup. https://news.gallup.com/poll/354455/aproval-labor-unions-highest-point-1965.aspx

Brenan, M. (2017). *Nurses keep healthy lead as most honest, ethical profession*. Gallup. https://news.gallup.com/poll/224639/nurses-keep-healthy-lead-honest-ethical-profession.aspx

Brennan, M. (2011, May). The impacts of affordable housing on education: A research summary. *Insights*. https://nchh.org/ resource-library/cfhp_insights_impacts-of-affordable-housing-on-education.pdf

Brennan Center for Justice. (2021, April 1). *Voting laws roundup: March 2021*. https://www.brennancenter.org/our-work/research-reports/voting-laws-roundup-march-2021

Brewer, G. (2003). Building social capital: Civic attitudes and behavior of public servants. *Journal of Public Administration Research and Theory, 13*(1), 5–26.

Briney, A. (1958). Should teachers be politically active? *Journal of Teacher Education, 9*(7), 7–11.

Briscoe, F., & Khalifa, M. (2013). "That racism thing": A critical race discourse analysis of conflict over the proposed closure of a Black high school. *Race, Ethnicity, and Education, 18*(6), 739–763.

Brookhart, S., & Freeman, D. (1992). Characteristics of entering teacher candidates. *Review of Educational Research, 62*(1), 37–60.

Brookings Institution. (2017). *The current state of scientific knowledge on pre-kindergarten effects*. https://www.brookings.edu/wp-content/uploads/2017/04/duke_prekstudy_final_4–41–7_hires.pdf

Broussard, M. (2014, July 15). Why poor schools can't win at standardized testing. *Atlantic*. https://www.theatlantic.com/education/archive/2014/07/why-poor-schools-cant-win-at-standardized-testing/374287

Brouwers, A., & Tomic, W. (2000). A longitudinal study of teacher burnout and perceived self-efficacy in classroom management. *Teaching and Teacher Education, 16*, 239–253.

Brown, E. (2016a, August 26). A southern city wants to secede from its school district, raising concerns about segregation. *Washington Post*. https://www.washingtonpost.com/local/education/a-southern-city-wants-to-secede-from-its-school-district-raising-concerns-about-segregation/2016/08/25/13ce53986–94f-11e69–9bf-f0cf3a6449a6_story.html

Brown, E. (2016b, April 14). California appeals court upholds teacher tenure, a major victory for unions. *Washington Post*. https://www.washingtonpost.com/ local/education/california-appeals-court-upholds-teacher-tenure-a-major-victory-for-unions/2016/04/14/8dde2d940–2971–1e69–d363–3d198ea26c5_story.html

Brown, E. (2017, July 15). Trump wants to spend millions more on school vouchers. But what's happened to the millions already spent? *Washington Post*. https://www.washingtonpost.com/local/education/trump-wants-to-spend-millions-more-on-school-vouchers-but-whats-happened-to-the-millions-already-spent/2017/07/15/ab6002a86–2671–1e78–4a1-a26b75ad39fe_story.html

Brown, E., & McLaren, M. (2012, November 17). Quality controls lacking for D.C. schools accepting federal vouchers. *Washington Post*. https://www.washingtonpost.com/local/education/quality-controls-lacking-for-dc-schools-accepting-federal-vouchers/2012/11/17/062bf97a-1e0d-11e2-b647-bb1668e64058_story.html

Brown, E., & McLaren, M. (2016, December 26). How Indiana's school voucher program soared and what it says about education in the Trump era. *Washington Post*. https://www.google.com/amp/s/www.washingtonpost.com/amphtml/local/education/how-indianas-school-voucher-program-soared-and-what-it-says-about-education-in-the-trump-era/2016/12/26/13d1d3ec-bc971–1e69–1ee-1adddfe36cbe_story.html

Brown, E., & McLaren, M. (2017, April 27). Nation's only federally funded voucher program has negative effect on student achievement, study finds. *Washington Post.* https://www.washingtonpost.com/local/education/federal-study-of-dc-voucher-program-finds-negative-impact-on-student-achievement/2017/04/27/e545ef282–5361–1e7-bb9d-8cd6118e1409_story.html

Brown, F. (2020, May 1). Can Dr. Birx and Dr. Fauci serve President Trump in good conscience? *Washington Post.* https://www.washingtonpost.com/outlook/can-birx-and-fauci-serve-the-president-in-good-conscience/2020/ 05/01/837347308–b0b-11ea-ac8a-fe9b8088e101_story.html

Bruegel, I., & Warren, S. (2003). Family resources and community social capital as routes to valued employment in the UK? *Social Policy and Society, 2*(4), 319–328.

Brummet, Q. (2014). The effect of school closings on student achievement. *Journal of Public Economics, 119,* 108–124.

Bryk, A., & Schneider, B. (2002). *Trust in schools: A core resource for improvement.* Russell Sage Foundation.

Bryk, A., Schneider, B., & Kochanik, J. (1996). *Social trust: A moral resource for school improvement.* Department of Education, Office of Educational Research and Improvement.

Buckley, J., & Schneider, M. (2007). *Charter schools: Hope or hype?* Princeton University Press.

Buckley, J., Schneider, M., & Shang, Y. (2004, February). *The effects of school facility quality on teacher retention in urban school districts.* National Clearinghouse for Educational Facilities. http://www.ncef.org/pubs/teacherretention.pdf

Buckley, J., Schneider, M., & Shang, Y. (2005). Fix it and they might stay: School facility quality and teacher retention in Washington, D.C. *Teachers College Record, 107,* 1107–1123.

Buerger, C., & Bifulco, R. (2019). The effect of charter schools on districts' student composition, costs, and efficiency: The case of New York state. *Economics of Education Review, 69,* 61–72.

Bumiller, E. (2002, January 9). Focusing on home front, Bush signs education bill. *New York Times.* http://www.nytimes.com/2002/01/09/us/focusing-on- home-front-bush-signs-education-bill.html

Burch, P. (2008). *Hidden markets.* Routledge.

Burchinal, M., McCartney, K., Steinberg, L., Crosnoe, R., Friedman, S., McLoyd, V., Pianta, R., & NICHD Early Child Care Research Network. (2011). Examining the Black–White achievement gap among low-income children using the NICHD Study of Early Child Care and Youth Development. *Child Development, 82*(5), 1404–1420.

Burgess, S., Greaves, E., Vignoles, A., & Wilson, D. (2014). What parents want: School preferences and school choice. *Economic Journal, 12,* 1262–1289. https://doi.org/10.1111/econj.12153

Burian-Fitzgerald, M. (2005). *Average teachers' salaries and returns to experience in charter schools.* Michigan State University. http://www.tc.columbia.edu/ncspe/working-papers/OP101.pdf

Burris, C., & Bryant, J. (2019). *Asleep at the wheel: How the federal charter schools program recklessly takes taxpayers and students for a ride.* Network for Public Education. https://www.networkforpubliceducation.org/

Burris, C., & Strauss, V. (2017, August 28). Do traditional public schools benefit from charter competition? *Washington Post.* https://www.washingtonpost.com /news/answer-sheet/wp/2017/08/28/do-traditional-public-schools-benefit-from-charter-competition/

Burt, A. (1982). *Toward a structural theory of action.* Academic Press.

Burtless, G. (1996). *Does money matter? The effect of school resources on student achievement and adult success.* Brookings Institution Press.

Bush, G. H. W. (1988, August 18). *RNC acceptance speech.* American Presidency Project. http://www.presidency.ucsb.edu/ws/?pid=25955

Bush, G. W. (2001, January 20). *Inaugural address.* The American Presidency Project. http://www.presidency.ucsb.edu/ws/?pid=25853

Bush, G. W. (2006). *Address to the NAACP annual convention.* http://georgewbush-whitehouse.archives.gov/news/releases/2006/07/20060720.html

Bushaw, W., & Lopez, S. (2010). The 42nd annual Phi Delta Kappa/Gallup Poll of the public's attitudes toward the public schools. *Phi Delta Kappan, 92*(1), 8–26.

Bushaw, W., & McNee, J. (2009). The 41st annual Phi Delta Kappa/Gallup Poll of the public's attitudes towards the public schools. *Phi Delta Kappan, 91*(1), 8–23.

Butler, E., & Beeghley, L. (1974). The consequences of intelligence testing in the public schools before and after segregation. *Social Problems, 21*(5), 740–754.

Caldwell, P. (2018, November/December). How pissed-off parents and teachers could expel Scott Walker from office. *Mother Jones.* https://www.motherjones.com/politics/2018/10/tony-evers-profile-scott-walker-wisconsin-education-teachers/

Calkins, A., Guenther, W., Belfiore, G., & Lash, D. (2007). *The turnaround challenge: Why America's best opportunity to dramatically improve student achievement lies in our worst-performing schools.* Mass Insight Education & Research Institute. http://www.massinsight.org/

Cama, T. (2017, January 26). House Dems: Trump's federal "gag orders" likely illegal. *The Hill.* http://thehill.com/policy/energy-environment/316347-house-dems-trumps-federal-gag-orders-likely-illegal

Cambor, K. (1999). Bad apples. *The American Prospect.* http://prospect.org/article/bad-apples

Camera, L. (2015, December 3). Proposed new education law shrinks federal footprint. *U.S. News & World Report.* http://www.usnews.com/news/articles/2015/12/03/proposed-new-education-law-shrinks-federal-footprint

Camera, L. (2018a, October 11). Teachers crowdfund millions for classroom supplies. *U.S. News & World Report*. https://www.usnews.com/news/education-news/articles/20181–01–1/teachers-crowdfund-millions-for-classroom-supplies

Camera, L. (2018b, January 31). Will Trump help rebuild America's schools? *U.S. News & World Report*. https://www.usnews.com/news/the-report/articles/20180–13–1/infrastructure-spending-for-schools-if-history-repeats-itself-no

Camera, L., & Cook, L. (2016, June 1). Title I: Rich school districts get millions meant for poor kids. *U.S. News & World Report*. https://www.usnews.com/news/articles/20160–60–1/title-i-rich-school-districts-get-millions-in-federal-money-meant-for-poor-kids

Camilli, G., Vargas, S., Ryan, S., & Barnett, W. (2010). Meta-analysis of the effects of early education interventions on cognitive and social development. *Teachers College Record, 111*(3), 579–620.

Campanile, C. (2015, April 13). Affluent parents are against Common Core: Study. *New York Post*. https://nypost.com/2015/04/13/affluent-parents-are-against-common-core-study/

Campbell, A. (2003). *How policies make citizens: Senior political activism and the American welfare state*. Princeton University Press.

Carey, K. (2006). *Hot air: How states inflate their educational progress under NCLB*. https://eric.ed.gov/?id=ED502115

Carey, K. (2016, May 17). Why GOP and teachers are uniting to stop Obama effort to help poor schools. *New York Times*. https://www.nytimes.com/2016/05/18/upshot/why-poor-districts-receive-less-government-school-funding-than-rich-ones.html

Carey, K. (2017, February 23). Dismal voucher results surprise researchers as DeVos era begins. *New York Times*. https://mobile.nytimes.com/2017/02/23/upshot/dismal-results-from-vouchers-surprise-researchers-as-devos-era-begins.html

Carini, R. (2002). *Teacher unions and student achievement*. National Education Policy Center. https://nepc.colorado.edu/sites/default/files/chapter10-Carini-Final.pdf

Carini, R., Powell, B., & Steelman, L. (2000). Do teacher unions hinder educational performance? Lessons learned from state SAT and ACT scores. *Harvard Educational Review, 70*. http://hepg.org/her-home/issues/harvard-educational-review-volume-70-issue-4/herarticle/lessons-learned-from-state-sat-and-act-scores_130

Carlisle, M., & Reilly, K. (2021, December 6). This Supreme Court case could take a "wrecking ball" to separation of church and state. *Time*. https://time.com/6125676/maine-religion-schools-supreme-court-carson-makin/

Carneiro, P., Crawford, C., & Goodman, A. (2007). *The impact of early cognitive and non-cognitive skills on later outcomes*. Centre for the Economics of Education. https://discovery.ucl.ac.uk/16164.pdf

Carnevale, A., Smith, N., & Strohl, J. (2013, June). *Recovery: Job growth and education requirements through 2020*. Georgetown University Center on Education and the Workforce. https://georgetown.app.box.com/s/tll0zkxt0puz45hu2lg6

Carnoy, M., Garcia, E., & Khavenson, T. (2015, October 30). *Bringing it back home. Why state comparisons are more useful than international comparisons for improving U.S. education policy.* Economic Policy Institute. http://www.epi.org/publication/bringing-it-back-home

Carnoy, M., & Rothstein, R. (2013). *What do international tests really show about U.S. student performance?* Economic Policy Institute. http://www.epi.org/publication / us-student-performance-testing/

Carr, S. (2012, December 13). In southern towns, "segregation academies" are still going strong. *Atlantic.* https://www.theatlantic.com/national/archive/2012/12/in-southern-towns-segregation-academies-are-still-going-strong/266207/

Carrazana, Ch. (2020, October 2). 865,000 women left the workforce in September. *19th News.* https://19thnews.org/2020/10/women-job-losses-2020-recession/

Carroll, A. (2017, September 5). The real reason the U.S. has employer-sponsored health insurance. *New York Times.* https://www.nytimes.com/2017/09/05/upshot/the-real-reason-the-us-has-employer-sponsored-health-insurance.html

Case, A., & Katz, L. (May 1991). *The company you keep: The effects of family and neighborhood on disadvantaged youths* (Working Paper No. 3705). NBER.

Cass, C. (2013, November 30). Americans don't trust each other anymore. *Business Insider.* https://www.businessinsider.com/americans-dont-trust-each-other-anymore-20131–1

Cassella, M., & Mueller, E. (2020, June 25). A lack of child care is keeping women on unemployment rolls. *Politico.* https://www.politico.com/news /2020/06/25/child-care-women-unemployment-339012

Casselman, B. (2014, April 30). Race gap narrows in college enrollment, but not in graduation. *FiveThirtyEight.* https://fivethirtyeight.com/features/race-gap-narrows-in-college-enrollment-but-not-in-graduation

Casselman, B. (2015, April 3). The tax deductions economists hate. *Five Thirty-Eight.* https://fivethirtyeight.com/features/the-tax-deductions-economists-hate/

Castrechini, S., & London, R. (2012). *Positive student outcomes in community schools.* Center for American Progress. https://cdn.americanprogress.org/wp-content/uploads/issues/2012/02/pdf/positive_student_outcomes.pdf

CBS News. (2018, March 7). *A closer look at Oklahoma's 4-day school week.* https://www.cbsnews.com/news/a-closer-look-at-oklahomas-four-day-school-week/

Center for Public Education. (2012). *The principal perspective.* http://www.centerforpubliceducation.org/principal-perspective

Center for Research on Education Outcomes. (2013). *National charter school study 2013.* Stanford University. http://credo.stanford.edu/documents/ NCSS%202013%20Final%20Draft.pdf

Center on Budget and Policy Priorities. (2018, March 26). *State tax cuts: A key factor in AZ, OK teacher pay crises.* Https://www.cbpp.org/blog/state-tax-cuts-a-key-factor-in-az-ok-teacher-pay-crises

Center on Budget and Policy Priorities. (2019, September 12). *Policy basics: Federal tax expenditures.* https://www.cbpp.org/research/federal-tax/policy-basicsfederal-tax-expenditures

Center on Education Policy. (2006). *From the capital to the classroom: Year 4 of the No Child Left Behind Act: Summary and recommendations.* http://www.cep-dc.org/displayDocument.cfm?DocumentID=301

Center on Education Policy. (2008). *A call to restructure restructuring: Lessons from the No Child Left Behind Act in five states.* Author.

Center on Education Policy. (2012). *Schools with federal improvement grants face challenges in replacing principals and teachers.* Author.

Center on Great Teachers and Leaders. (2014). *Timeline of relevant educator effectiveness research and policy.* American Institute for Research. http://www.gtlcenter.org /sites/default/files/143–355_Tchr_Effctvness_Tmln-508_Final_100114.pdf

Center on Reinventing Public Education. (2014, February). *Coordinating enrollment systems across school sectors: An overview of common enrollment systems.* https://www.crpe.org/sites/default/files/Pub_EnrollmentSpotlight_Feb2014_0.pdf

Charter discipline: The impact on students. (2013, February 19). *Education Week.* http://www.edweek.org/ew/section/infographics/charter-discipline-infographic.html

Chatzky, J. (2018, April 24). Job hopping is on the rise. *NBC News.* https://www.Nbcnews.com/better/business/job-hopping-rise-should-you-consider-switching-roles-make-more-ncna868641

Chaudry, A., Morrissey, T., Weiland, C., & Yoshikawa, H. (2017). *Cradle to kindergarten: A new plan to combat inequality.* Russell Sage Foundation.

Chen, M. (2014, April 7). Why are students and teachers opting out of standardized testing? *Nation.* http://www.thenation.com/blog/179214/teachers-and-students-opt-out-defy-testing-machine#

Chetty, R., Friedman, J., Hilger, N., Saez, E., Schanzenbach, D., & Yagan, D. (2011). How does your kindergarten classroom affect your earnings? Evidence from Project STAR. *Quarterly Journal of Economics, 126*(4), 1593–1660.

Chetty, R., Friedman, J., & Rockoff, J. (2011). *The long-term impacts of teachers: Teacher value-added and student outcomes in adulthood* (Working Paper No. 17699). National Bureau of Economic Research.

Chetty, R., Friedman, J., & Rockoff, J. (2014). Measuring the impacts of teachers II: Teacher value-added and student outcomes in adulthood. *American Economic Review, 104*(9), 2633–2679.

Chetty, R., Grusky, D., Hell, M., Hendren, N., Manduca, R., & Narang, J. (2016). *The fading American dream: Trends in absolute income mobility since 1940* (Working Paper No. 22910). NBER.

Chetty, R., Hendren, N., & Katz, L. (2016). *The effects of exposure to better neighborhoods on children: New evidence from the Moving to Opportunity Project.* https://scholar.

harvard.edu/hendren/publications/effects-exposure-better-neighborhoods-children-new-evidence-moving-opportunity

Chetty, R., Hendren, N., Kline, P., & Saez, E. (2014). *Where is the land of opportunity: The geography of intergenerational mobility in the United States* (Working Paper No. 19843). NBER.

Chetty, R., Hendren, N., Kline, P., Saez, E., & Turner, N. (2014). *Is the United States still a land of opportunity? Recent trends in intergenerational mobility* (Working Paper No. 19844). NBER.

Children's Defense Fund. (1975). *School suspensions: Are they helping children?* Washington Research Project.

Children's Defense Fund. (2020). *The state of America's children, 2020.* https://www.childrensdefense.org/wp-content/uploads/2020/02/The-State-Of-Americas-Children-2020.pdf

Children's Health Fund. (2016, November). *Unfinished business: More than 20 million children in U.S. still lack sufficient access to essential health care.* Physicians for a National Health Plan. https://pnhp.org/news/20-million-children-lack-sufficient-access-to-health-care/

Chiles, N. (2017, March 31). *Everyone pays a hefty price for segregation, study says.* NPR. https://www.npr.org/sections/codeswitch/2017/03/31/ 522098019/everyone-pays-a-hefty-price-for-segregation-study-says

Chin, T., & Phillips, M. (2004). Social reproduction and child-rearing practices: Social class, children's agency, and the summer activity gap. *Sociology of Education, 77,* 185–210.

Chivas, D. (2010). A school fails in Brooklyn (Parts 1–4). *AOL News.* http://www.aolnews.com/brooklyn-school/article/metropolitan-corporate-academy-did-failing-brooklyn-school-get-failed-by-the-system/19522399

Chokshi, N. (2018, March 30). How to get $29 million for classroom projects? Just ask. *New York Times.* https://www.nytimes.com/2018/03/30/us/donors-choose-donation-ripple.html

Chubb, J., & Moe, T. (1990). *Politics, markets, and America's schools.* Brookings Institution Press.

Ciechalski, S. (2020, May 6). Connecticut teacher cares for student's baby brother as family recovers from coronavirus. *NBC News.* https://www.nbcnews.com/news/us-news/connecticut-teacher-cares-student-s-baby-brother-family-recovers-coronavirus-n1201601

Clarke, J., & Newman, J. (1997). *The managerial state.* Sage.

Climate Reality Project. (2021, April 6). *Environmental racism: What it is and how you can fight it.* https://www.climaterealityproject.org/blog/environmental-racism-what-it-and-how-you-can-fight-it

Clinton, W. J. (1993, January 23). *1996 state of the union address.* Clinton White House Archives. https://clintonwhitehouse4.archives.gov/WH/New/other/sotu.html

Clotfelter, C., Ladd, H., & Vigdor, J. (2005). Who teaches whom? Race and the distribution of novice teachers. *Economics of Education Review, 24,* 377–92.

Cody, A. (2012, March 30). NEA's Priority Schools focus on teacher expertise, parent, and community involvement. *Education Week.* http://blogs.edweek.org/ teachers/ living-in-dialogue/2012/03;teachers_get_a_very_mixed.html

Cohen, D., & Moffitt, S. (2009). *The ordeal of equality: Did federal regulation fix the schools?* Harvard University Press.

Cohen, L. (2003). *A consumers' republic: The politics of mass consumption in America.* Vintage Books.

Cohen, P., & Gebeloff, R. (2018, April 22). Public servants are losing their foothold in the middle class. *New York Times.* https://www.nytimes.com/2018/04/22/business/ economy/public-employees.html

Cohen, R. (2016, August 2). California's Ed Reform wars. *American Prospect.* http:// prospect.org/article/california%E2%80%99s-ed-reform-wars

Cohen, R. (2018a, September 28). Elizabeth Warren introduces plan to expand affordable housing and dismantle racist zoning practices. *Intercept.* https:// theintercept.com/2018/09/28/elizabeth-warren-affordable-housing-bill

Cohen, R. (2018b, January 8). Public school buildings are falling apart, and students are suffering for it. *Washington Post.* https://www.washingtonpost.com/news/ posteverything/wp/2018/01/08/public-school-buildings-are-falling-apart-and-students-are-suffering-for-it/

Cohen, R. (2019, January 29). Coming off LA strike victory, a new wave of teacher protests takes hold. *Intercept.* https://theintercept.com/2019/01/29/la-teachers-strike-virginia-colorado-california/

Cohn, J. (2018, December 6). Finding decent child care is a huge struggle for some families, new report shows. *Huffington Post.* https://www.huffpost.com/entry/ finding-licensed-child-care-report_n_5c089013e4b069028dc66697

Cohn, S. (2015, May 29). An American workplace war that's reached a tipping point. *CNBC.* https://www.cnbc.com/2015/05/29/the-right-to-work-battle-has-reached-a-tipping-point.html

Coleman, J., Campbell, E., Hobson, C., McPartland, J., Mood, A., Weinfeld, F., & York, R. (1966). *Equality of educational opportunity.* National Center for Educational Statistics. http://library.sc.edu/digital/collections/eeoci.pdf

Collins, R. (2007). *Transforming America: Politics and culture during the Reagan years.* Columbia University Press.

Communities in schools. (2010). *CIS national evaluation: Five year summary report.* http://www.comunitiesinschools.org/media/uploads/attachments/Communities_ In_Schools_National_Evaluation_Five_Year_Summary_Report.pdf

Communities in schools. (2017, August). *Phi Delta Kappan.* https://www. communitiesinschools.org/press-room/resource/2017-national-pdk-poll/

Conner, J., & Zaino, K. (2014). Orchestrating effective change: How youth organizing influences education policy. *American Journal of Education, 120*(2), 173–203.

Cooper, H., Nye, B., Charlton, K., Lindsay, J., & Greathouse, S. (1996). The effects of summer vacation on achievement test scores: A narrative and meta-analytic review. *Review of Educational Research, 66*(3), 227–268.

Corbin, J., & Strauss, A. (2008). *Basics of qualitative research: Techniques and procedures for developing grounded theory.* Sage.

Corcoran, S. (2010). *Can teachers be evaluated by their students' test scores? Should they be? The use of value-added measures of teacher effectiveness in policy and practice.* Annenberg Institute. http://www.annenberginstitute.org/products/Corcoran.php

Cordes, S. (2017). *New York charter schools outperform traditional public schools: More evidence that cream-skimming is not driving charters' success.* National Education Policy Center. http://nepc.colorado.edu/thinktank/review-nyc-charters

Cordes, S. (2018). In pursuit of the common good: The spillover effects of charter schools on public school students in New York City. *Education Finance and Policy, 13*(4), 484–512.

Cordova-Cobo, D., Fox, L., & Wells, A. (2016, February 9). *How racially diverse schools and classrooms can benefit all students.* The Century Foundation. https://tcf.org/content/report/how-racially-diverseschools-and-classrooms-can- benefit-all-students/

Corley, C. (2013, March 22). *Chicago teachers, parents riled by plan to close 54 public schools.* Northeast Public Radio. http://www.npr.org/2013/03/22/175014378/chicago-to-close-54-public-schools

Cote, S., & Healy, T. (2001). *The well-being of nations: The role of human and social capital.* Organization for Economic Co-operation and Development.

Council for American Private Education. (2013). *Survey identifies why parents choose private schools.* CAPE Outlook. https://www.capenet.org/pdf/Outlook390.pdf

Cross, C. (2004). *Political education: National policy comes of age.* Teachers College Press.

C-SPAN. (2017, May 24). *Fiscal year 2018 education budget.* https://www.c-span.org/video/?4287141-/education-secretary-betsy-devos-pressed-accountability-charter-schools&live

Cuban, L. (2004). *The blackboard and the bottom line.* Harvard University Press.

Cuban, L. (2010). *As good as it gets: What school reform brought to Austin.* Harvard University Press.

Cuellar, M. (2013). *For each and every child—a strategy for education equity and excellence.* Equity and Excellence Commission. http://www2.ed.gov/about/bdscomm/list/eec/equity-excellence-commission-report.pdf

Dark, T. (1999). *The unions and the Democrats: An enduring alliance.* ILR Press.

Darling-Hammond, L. (1991). Accountability mechanisms in big city school systems. *ERICDigest,* no. 71.

Darling-Hammond, L. (1996). What matters most: A competent teacher for every child. *Phi Delta Kappan, 78*(3), 193–200.

Darling-Hammond, L. (2013). *Getting teacher evaluation right: What really matters for effectiveness and improvement.* Teachers College Press.

Darling-Hammond, L., Amrein-Beardsley, A., Haertel, E., & Rothstein, J. (2012). Evaluating teacher evaluation. *Phi Delta Kappan, 93*(6), 8–15.

Darling-Hammond, L., Holtzman, D., Gatlin, S. J., & Heilig, J. (2005). Does teacher preparation matter? Evidence about teacher certification, Teach for America, and teacher effectiveness. *Education Policy Analysis Archives, 13*(42). http://epaa.asu.edu/epaa/v13n42/v13n42.pdf

Darling-Hammond, L., Wei, R., & Andree, A. (2010). *How high-achieving countries develop great teachers.* Stanford Center for Opportunity Policy in Education. http://edpolicy.stanford.edu/sites/default/files/publications/ how-high-achieving-countries-develop-great-teachers.pdf

Darling-Hammond, L., Wei, R., Andree, A., & Richardson, N. (2009). *Professional learning in the learning profession.* National Staff Development Council. http://www.researchgate.net/publication/237327162_Professional_Learning_in_the_Learning_Profession_A_Status_Report_on_Teacher_Development_in_the_United_States_and_Abroad

Darrah, J., & DeLuca, S. (2014). "Living here has changed my whole perspective": How escaping inner-city poverty shapes neighborhood and housing choice. *Journal of Policy Analysis and Management, 33*(2), 350–384.

David, R., & Hesla, K. (2018, March). *Estimated public charter school enrollment, 2017–2018.* https://www.publiccharters.org/sites/default/files/documents/201803/FINAL%20Estimated%20Public%20Charter%20School%20Enrollment%2C%20 20171–8.pdf

Davidson, J. (2018, September 9). Top civil servants leaving Trump administration at a quick clip. *Washington Post.* https://www.washingtonpost.com/politics /2018/09/10/top-civil-servants-leaving-trump-administration-quick-clip/

Davies, G. (2007). *See government grow: Education politics from Johnson to Reagan.* University Press of Kansas.

Davis, G. (2015, December 11). President Obama signs into law a rewrite of No Child Left Behind. *New York Times.* https://www.nytimes.com/2015/12/11/us/politics/president-obama-signs-into-law-a-rewrite-of-no-child-left-behind.html

Day, C., & Leitch, R. (2001). Teachers' and teacher educators' lives: The role of emotion. *Teaching and Teacher Education, 17,* 403–415.

DeArmond, M., Jochim, A., & Lake, R. (2014, July). *Making school choice work.* Center on Reinventing Public Education. https://www.crpe.org/publications/making-school-choice-work

DeBray, E. (2006). *Politics, ideology, and education: Federal policy during the Clinton and Bush administrations.* Teachers College Press.

DeBray-Pelot, E. (2007). Dismantling education's iron triangle. In C. Kaestle & A. Lodewick (Eds.), *To educate a nation: Federal and national strategies of school reform* (pp. 64–89). University Press of Kansas.

Dee, T. (2012). *School turnarounds: Evidence from the 2009 stimulus* (Working Paper No. 120–4). Program on Education Policy and Governance.

Dee, T., & West, M. (2011). The non-cognitive returns to class size. *Educational Evaluation and Policy Analysis, 33*(1), 23–46.

DeFilippis, J. (2001). The myth of social capital in community development. *Housing Policy Debate, 12*(4), 781–806.

De la Torre, M., Allensworth, E., Jagesic, S., Sebastian, J., Salmonowicz, M., Meyers, C., & Gerdeman, R. (2012). *Turning around low-performing schools in Chicago.* Consortium on Chicago School Research.

De la Torre, M., & Gwynne, J. (2009, October). *When schools close: Effects on displaced students in Chicago public schools.* Consortium on Chicago School Research. http://ccsr.uchicago.edu/sites/default/files/publications /CCSRSchoolClosings-Final.pdf

DeLuca, S., & Rosenblatt, P. (2011). Increasing access to high performing schools in an assisted housing voucher program. In P. Tegeler (Ed.), *Finding common ground: Coordinating housing and education policy to promote integration* (pp. 35–37). Poverty and Race Research Action Council. https://www.prrac.org/pdf/HousingEducationReport-October2011.pdf

Denice, P., & Rosenfeld, J. (2018, August 15). Unions and nonunion pay in the United States, 1977–2015. *Sociological Science.* https://www.sociologicalscience.com/articles-v52–35–41/

Dersh, I. (2020, December 27). 50-year study of tax cuts on wealthy shows they always fail to "trickle down." *Salon.* http://www.salon.com/2020/12/27/50-year-study-of-tax-cuts-on-wealthy-shows-they-always-fail-to-trickle-down/

Derthick, M. (1972). *New towns in-town: Why a federal program failed.* Urban Institute Press.

Designs for Change. (2012). *Chicago's democratically led elementary schools far out-perform Chicago's "turnaround schools": Yet turnaround schools receive lavish extra resources.* Designs for Change.

DeVos, B. (2017, May 22). *Prepared remarks by U.S. Secretary of Education Betsy DeVos to the American Federation for Children's National Policy Summit.* https://www.ed.gov/news/speeches/prepared-remarks-us-secretary-education-betsy-devos-american-federation-childrens-national-policy-summit

Dewey, J. (1927). *The public and its problems.* Wallow.

Diamond, J., & Spillane, J. (2004). High-stakes accountability in urban elementary schools: Challenging or reproducing inequality? *Teachers College Record, 106*(6), 1145–1176.

Dickson, E. (2020, July 3). Coronavirus is killing the working mother. *Rolling Stone.* https://www.rollingstone.com/culture/culture-features/working-motherhood-covid-19-coronavirus-1023609/

Dillon, S. (2011, November 5). Merger of Memphis and county school districts revives race and class challenges. *New York Times.* https://www.nytimes.com/2011/11/06/

education/merger-of-memphis-and-county-school-districts-revives-challenges.
html

Dinham, S., & Scott, C. (1998), A three domain model of teacher and school
executive satisfaction. *Journal of Educational Administration, 36*(4), 362–378.

Dinham, S., & Scott, C. (2000). Moving into the third, outer domain of teacher
satisfaction. *Journal of Educational Administration, 38*(4), 379–396.

Dobbie, W., & Fryer, R. (2011). Are high-quality schools enough to increase
achievement among the poor? Evidence from the Harlem children's zone.
American Economic Journal: Applied Economics, 3(3), 158–187.

Dodenhoff, D. (2007). *Fixing the Milwaukee public schools: The limits of parent-driven
reform.* Wisconsin Policy Research Institute. http://www.wpri.org/BI-Files/Special-
Reports/Reports-Documents/vol20no8.pdf

Domonoske, C. (2016, October 19). *Interactive redlining map zooms in on America's
history of discrimination.* NPR. https://www.npr.org/sections/thetwo-
way/2016/10/19/498536077/interactive-redlining-map-zooms-in-on-americas-
history-of-discrimination

Dowdall, E. (2011, October). *Closing public schools in Philadelphia: Lessons from six
urban districts.* The Pew Charitable Trust: Philadelphia Research Initiative. http://
www.pewtrusts.org/uploadedFiles/wwwpewtrustsorg/Reports/Philadelphia_
Research_Initiative/Closing-Public-Schools-Philadelphia.pdf

Dowdall, E. (2013, February 11). *Shuttered public schools: The struggle to bring old buildings
to new life.* The Pew Charitable Trust: Philadelphia Research Initiative. http://www.
pewtrusts.org/~/media/assets/2013/02/11/philadelphia_school_closings_report.
pdf

Dreier, P. (2018, April 16). Why America needs more social housing. *American Prospect.*
https://prospect.org/infrastructure/america-needs-social-housing/

Dryfoos, J. (2002). Full-service community schools: Creating new institutions. *Phi
Delta Kappan, 83*(5), 393–399.

Duncan, A. (2009, June 8). *States open to charters start fast in "Race to
Top"* [Press release]. The White House. http://www2.ed.gov/news/
pressreleases/2009/06/06082009a.html

Duncan, G., & Magnuson, K. (2011). The nature and impact of early achievement
skills, attention skills, and behavior problems. In G. Duncan & R. Murnane (Eds.),
Whither opportunity? Rising inequality, schools, and children's life chances (pp. 47–69).
Russell Sage Foundation.

Duncan, G., Morris, P., & Rodrigues, C. (2011). Does money really matter? Estimating
impacts of family income on young children's achievement with data from
random-assignment experiments. *Developmental Psychology, 47*(5), 1263–1279.

Dunn, C., Kenney, E., Fleischhacker, S., & Bleich, S. (2020). Feeding low-income
children during the COVID-19 pandemic. *New England Journal of Medicine.* https://
doi.org/10.1056/NEJMp2005638

Durkheim, E. (1996). *The division of labor in society.* Free Press.

Dynarski, S., Hyman, J., & Schnzenbach, D. (2013). Experimental evidence on the effect of childhood investments on postsecondary attainment and degree completion. *Journal of Policy Analysis and Management, 32*(4), 692–717.

Dynarski, M., & Kainz, K. (2015). *Why federal spending on disadvantaged students (Title I) doesn't work.* Brookings Institution. https://www.brookings.edu/ research/why-federal-spending-on-disadvantaged-students-title-i-doesnt-work/

EdBuild. (2016a, March 3). *Betting big on school funding.* https://edbuild.org/content/betting-big-on-school-funding

EdBuild. (2016b). *Dividing lines: Gated school districts.* http://viz.edbuild.org/ maps/2016/dividing-lines-2014/

EdBuild. (2016c). *Lotteries as school funding: The game is rigged.* http://viz.edbuild.org/ maps/2016/lottery/

EdBuild. (2016d, February 11). *Playing the game and missing the point: The wrong education funding conversation.* https://edbuild.org/content/playing-the-game-and-missing-the-point-the-wrong-education-funding-conversation

EdBuild. (2017, June). *Fractured: The breakdown of America's school districts.* https:// edbuild.org/content/fractured/fractured-full-report.pdf

EdBuild. (2019). *Fractured: The accelerating breakdown of America's school districts, 2019 update.* https://edbuild.org/content/fractured

EdBuild. (n.d.). *Non-White school districts get $23 billion less than White districts despite serving the same number of students.* https://edbuild.org/content/23-billion

Edelman, M. (1988). *Constructing the political spectacle.* University of Chicago Press.

Editorial Projects in Education. (2017, December 12). Educator political perceptions: A national survey. *Education Week.* https://epe.brightspotcdn.com/ be/2b/1bc98850470e9fecf8f8085a3284/educator-political-perceptions-education-week-12-12-2017.pdf

Edsource. (2017, February 8). *Worsening teacher shortage puts more underprepared teachers in classrooms, report says.* https://edsource.org/2017/worsening-teacher-shortage-puts-more-underprepared-teachers-in-classrooms-report-says/576770

Egalite, A., & Kisida, B. (2016, August 19). *The many ways teacher diversity may benefit students.* Brookings Institution. https://www.brookings.edu/blog/brown-center-chalkboard/2016/08/19/the-many-ways-teacher-diversity-may-benefit-students/

Eidelman, V. (2021, April 27). *States are passing laws targeting peaceful protesters.* CNN. https://www.cnn.com/2021/04/26/opinions/laws-target-peaceful-protesters-eidelman/index.html

Eight questions for Chester Finn. (2010, April 1). *Economist.* http://www.economist. com/blogs/lexington/2010/04/education_reform

Eisenbrey, R., & Kroeger, T. (2017, May 18). *A tale of two states (and what it tells us about so-called "right-to-work" laws).* Economic Policy Institute. http://www.epi. Org/blog/a-tale-of-two-states-and-what-it-tells-us-about-so-called-right-to-work-laws/

Elementary and Secondary Education Act, P.L. 891–0 (1965).

Elesser, K. (2019, December 11). Lawsuit claims SAT and ACT are biased—here's what research says. *Forbes.* https://www.forbes.com/sites/kimelsesser/2019/12/11/lawsuit-claims-sat-and-act-are-biased-heres-what-research-says/

Elesser, K. (2016, July 1). Is the College Board making the SAT more difficult for women? *Forbes.* https://www.forbes.com/sites/kimelesser/2016/07/01/is-the-college-board-making-the-sat-more-difficult-for-women/

Elk, M. (2018, May 16). North Carolina teachers join wave of strikes with one-day walk-out. *Guardian.* https://www.theguardian.com/us-news/2018/may/16/north-carolina-teachers-strikes-walkout-unions

Elmore, R. (1987). Instruments and strategy in public policy. *Review of Policy Research, 7*(1), 174–186.

Emma, C., Wermund, B., & Hefling, K. (2016, December 9). DeVos' Michigan schools experiment gets poor grades. *Politico.* http://www.politico.com/story/2016/12/betsy-devos-michigan-school-experiment-232399

Engberg, J., Gill, B., Zamarro, G., & Zimmer, R. (2012). Closing schools in a shrinking district: Do student outcomes depend on which schools are closed? *Journal of Urban Economics, 71*(2), 189–203.

Epstein, D. (2011). *Measuring inequity in school funding.* Center for American Progress. http://www.Americanprogress.org/wp-content/uploads/issues/2011/08/pdf/funding_equity.pdf

Erickson, H. (2017). How do parents choose schools, and what schools do they choose? A literature review of private school choice programs in the United States. *Journal of School Choice, 11*(4), 491–506.

Etzioni, A. (1988). *The moral dimension: Toward a new economics.* Free Press.

Etzioni, A. (1969). *Semi-professions and their organization: Teachers, nurses, social workers.* Free Press.

Evertson, C., & Randolph, C. (1989). Teaching practices and class size: A new look at an old issue. *Peabody Journal of Education, 67*(1), 85–105.

Evich, H. (2021, May 7). Hunger rates plummet after two rounds of stimulus. *Politico.* https://www.politico.com/news/2021/05/07/hunger-rates-plummet-after-stimulus-485604

Evich, H. (2019, August 5). It feels like something out of a bad sci-fi movie. *Politico.* https://www.politico.com/story/2019/08/05/ziska-usda-climate-agriculture-trump-1445271

Fagan, J. G., & Holland, C. R. (2002). Equal opportunity and racial differences in IQ. *Intelligence, 30*, 361–387.

Fairclough, N. (1989). *Language and power.* Longman.

Farber, H. (2005). Nonunion wage rates and the threat of unionization. *ILR Review, 58*(3), 335–352.

Farrell, D. (1983). Exit, voice, loyalty, and neglect as responses to job dissatisfaction: A multidimensional scaling study. *Academy of Management Journal, 26*(4), 596–607.

Feintzeig, R. (2014, June 10). U.S. struggles to draw young, savvy staff. *Wall Street Journal.* https://www.wsj.com/articles/u-s-government-struggles-to-attract-young-savvy-staff-members-1402445198

Feldman, M., Skoldberg, K., Brown, R., & Horner, D. (2004). Making sense of stories: A rhetorical approach to narrative analysis. *Journal of Public Administration Research and Theory, 14*(2), 147–170.

Fennell, L. (2001). Beyond exit and voice: User participation in the production of local public goods. *Texas Law Review, 80*(1), 1–88.

Fernandez-Kelly, M. (1995). Social and cultural capital in the urban ghetto: Implications for the economic sociology of immigration. In A. Portes (Ed.), *The economic sociology of immigration: Essays on networks, ethnicity, and entrepreneurship* (pp. 213–247). Russell Sage.

Fiarman, S. E. (2009). *Teachers leading teachers: The experiences of Peer Assistance and Review consulting teachers* (Unpublished doctoral dissertation). Harvard University.

Fiddiman, B., Jeffrey, A., & Sargrad, S. (2018, December 19). *Smart investments for safer schools.* Center for American Progress. https://www.americanprogress.org/issues/education-k-12/reports/2018/12/19/464445/smart-investments-safer-schools/

Figlio, D. (2007). Boys named sue: Disruptive children and their peers. *Education Finance and Policy, 2,* 376–394.

Figlio, D., & Karbownik, K. (2016). *Evaluation of Ohio's EdChoice scholarship program: Selection, competition, and performance effects.* Thomas Fordham Institute. https://files.eric.ed.gov/fulltext/ED575666.pdf

Figlio, D., & Page, M. (2002). School choice and the distributional effects of ability tracking: Does separation increase inequality? *Journal of Urban Economics, 51,* 497–514.

Figlio, D., & Winicki, J. (2005). Food for thought? The effects of school accountability plans on school nutrition. *Journal of Public Economics, 89*(2/3), 381–394.

Filardo, M. (2016). *State of our schools: America's K–12 facilities 2016.* 21st Century School Fund. https://eric.ed.gov/?id=ED581630

Fine, M. (1991). *Framing dropouts: Notes on the politics of an urban public high school.* State University of New York Press.

Fineman, S. (2000). Emotional arenas revisited. In S. Fineman (Ed.), *Emotion in organizations* (2nd ed., pp. 1–24). Sage.

Fingerhut, H. (2018, June 5). *More Americans view long-term decline in union membership negatively than positively.* Pew Research. https://www.pewresearch.org/fact-tank/2018/06/05/more-americans-view-long-term-declinie-in-union-membership-negatively-than-positively/

Finn, J., Gerber, S., & Boyd-Zaharias, J. (2005). Small classes in the early grades, academic achievement, and graduating from high school. *Journal of Educational Psychology, 97*(2), 214–223.

Finn, J., Pannozzo, G., & Achilles, C. (2003). The "whys" of class size: Student behavior in small classes. *Review of Educational Research, 73*(3), 321–368.

Finnigan, K., & Gross, B. (2007). Do accountability policy sanctions influence teacher motivation? Lessons from Chicago's low-performing schools. *American Educational Research Journal, 44*(3), 594–629.

Finnigan, K., & Lavner, M. (2012). A political analysis of community influence over school closure. *Urban Review, 44*(1), 133–151.

Firestone, W., & Corbett, H. (1988). Planned educational change. In N. Boyan (Ed.), *Handbook of research on educational administration* (pp. 321–340). Longman.

Fischer, F., & Forester, J. (1993). *The argumentative turn in policy analysis and planning.* Duke University Press.

Fischer, W., & Sard, B. (2017, March 8). *Federal housing spending is poorly matched to need.* Center on Budget and Policy Priorities. https://www.cbpp.org/research/ housing/ chart-book-federal-housing-spending-is-poorly-matched-to-need

Flavin, P., & Griffin, J. (2009). Policy, preferences, and participation: Government's impact on democratic citizenship. *Journal of Politics, 71*(2), 544–559.

Floberg, D. (2018, December 13). The racial digital divide persists. *Free Press.* https:// www.freepress.net/our-response/expert-analysis/insights-opinions/racial-digital-divide-persists

Food Research and Action Center (2021, April). *Top 10 reasons to support free health school meals for all.* https://frac.org/blog/top-10-reasons-to-support-free-health-school-meals-for-all

Food Research and Action Center (2019, July). *Hunger doesn't take a vacation: Summer nutrition status report 2019.* https://frac.org/wp-content/uploads/frac-summer-nutrition-report-2019.pdf

Ford, D. (2005). *Intelligence testing and cultural diversity: Pitfalls and promises.* National Research Center on the Gifted and Talented. https://nrcgt.uconn.edu/ newsletters/winter052/

Fordham, S., & Ogbu, J. (2000). Black students' school success: Coping with the "burden of acting white." In R. Arum & I. Beattie (Eds.), *The structure of schooling* (pp. 303–309). McGraw-Hill Higher Education.

Fossey, R. (1994). Open enrollment in Massachusetts: Why families choose. *Educational Evaluation and Policy Analysis, 16*(3), 320–334.

Foucault, M. (1980). *Power/knowledge: Selected interviews and other writings* (C. Gordon, Ed.). Pantheon.

Foucault, M. (1995). *Discipline and punish: The birth of the prison* (2nd ed.). Vintage Books.

Foundation for Excellence in Education. (2018). *College and career pathways: Equity and access.* https://www.excelined.org/wpcontent/uploads/2018/10/ExcelinEd.Report. CollegeCareerPathways.CRDCAnalysis.2018.pdf

Frankenberg, E. (2010). *Choice without equity: Charter school segregation and the need for civil rights standards.* Civil Rights Project. http://civilrightsproject.ucla.edu/ research/k-12-education/integration-and-diversity/choice-without-equity-2009-report/frankenberg-choices-without-equity-2010.pdf

Frankenberg, E., Lee, C., & Orfield, G. (2003). *A multiracial society with segregated schools: Are we losing the dream?* Civil Rights Project at Harvard.

Frankenberg, E., Siegel-Hawley, G., & Wang, J. (2011). Choice without equity: Charter school segregation. *Educational Policy Analysis Archives, 19*(1). http://epaa.asu.edu/ojs/article/view/779

Fraser, N. (1989). Talking about needs: Interpretive contests as political conflicts in welfare-state societies. *Ethics, 99,* 291–313.

Frayer, L. (2010). Because of unpaid fee, firefighters let home burn. *AOL News.* http://www.aolnews.com/nation/article/firefighters-let-home-burn-after-finding-owner-didnt-pay-annual fee/19662595

Freeman, R. (1986). Unionism comes to the public sector. *Journal of Economic Literature, 24*(1), 41–86.

Freeman, R., Han, E., Madland, D., & Duke, B. (2015). *Bargaining for the American dream: What unions do for mobility.* Center for American Progress. https://www.americanprogress.org/issues/economy/reports/2015/09/09/120558/bargaining-for-the-american-dream/

Freidson, E. (1975). *Doctoring together: A study of professional social control.* University of Chicago Press.

Freidson, E. (2001). *Professionalism: The third logic.* University of Chicago Press.

Frey, W. (2014, December 12). *New projections point to a majority minority nation in 2044.* Brookings Institution. https://www.brookings.edu/blog/the-avenue/2014/12/12/new-projections-point-to-a-majority-minority-nation-in-2044/

Friedman, D. (2020, April 7). Trump declares war on watchdogs. *Mother Jones.* https://www.motherjones.com/politics/2020/04/trump-declares-war-on-watchdogs/

Fullan, M. (2011). *Choosing the wrong drivers for whole system reform. Centre for Strategic Education.* http://michaelfullan.ca/wp-content/uploads/2016/06/13396088160.pdf

Fuschillo, A. (2018, August 14). The troubling student-to-counsel ration that doesn't add up. *Education Week.* https://www.edweek.org/ew/articles/2018/08/14/the-troubling-student-to-counselor-ratio-that-doesnt-add.html

Galbraith, J. (1952). *American capitalism: The concept of countervailing power.* Houghton Mifflin.

Galbraith, J. (1958). *The affluent society.* Hamish Hamilton.

Galletta, A., & Ayala, J. (2008). Erasure and survival: Creating a future and managing a past in a restructuring high school. *Teachers College Record, 110*(9), 1959–1985.

Gamoran, A. (1986). Instructional and institutional effects of ability grouping. *Sociology of Education, 59,* 185–198.

Gamoran, A. (1992). The variable effects of high school tracking. *American Sociological Review, 57,* 812–828.

Garafolo, P. (2010, August 10). Flashback: In 1993, GOP warned that "Clinton 's tax plan would 'kill jobs,' 'kill the current recovery.'" *Think Progress.* http://thinkprogress.org/economy/2010/08/10/173450/1993-quotes/

Garcia, D. (2008). The impact of school choice on racial segregation in charter schools. *Educational Policy, 22*(6), 805–829.

Gardner, H., Csikszentmihalyi, M., & Damon, W. (2001). *Good work: When excellence and ethics meet.* Basic Books.

Gaventa, J. (1980). *Power and powerlessness: Quiescence and rebellion in an Appalachian valley.* University of Illinois Press.

Geiger, K., Garcia, M., & Pearson, R. (2018, June 27). U.S. Supreme Court gives Rauner major victory over labor, in ruling that could undercut public worker unions nationwide. *Chicago Tribune.* https://www.chicagotribune.com/politics/ct-met-bruce-rauner-janus-afscme-20180604-story.html

Geiser, S. (2015, October). *The growing correlation between race and SAT scores: New findings from California.* Center for Studies in Higher Education. https://www.rops.cshe_.10.15.geiser.racesat.10.26.2015.pdf

Gershenson, S., Hart, C., Lindsay, C., & Papgeorge, N. (2017, March). *The long-run impacts of same-race teachers.* Iza Institute of Labor Economics. http://ftp.iza.org/dp10630.pdf

Gewertz, C. (2018, April 3). ESSA offers testing flexibility. So why aren't states using it? *Education Week.* https://www.edweek.org/policy-politics/essa-offers-testing-flexibility-so-why-arent-states-using-it/2018/04

Ginsburg, A., & Smith, M. (2018a, September 12). Revisiting SIG: Why critics were wrong to write off the federal School Improvement Grant Program. *FutureEd.* https://www.future-ed.org/wp_content/uploads/2018/09/FutureEdSIGReport.pdf

Ginsburg, A., & Smith, M. (2018b, September 12). Why it's wrong to write off the SIG Program. *FutureEd.* https://www.future-ed.org/why-its-wrong-to-write-off-the-federal-sig-program/

Glaser, M., Denhardt, J., & Hamilton, L. (2002). Community v. self-interest: Citizen perceptions of schools as civic investment. *Journal of Public Administration Research and Theory, 12*(1), 103–127.

Glazerman, S., & Dotter, D. (2017). Market signals: Evidence on the determinants of school choice from a citywide lottery. *Education Evaluation and Policy Analysis, 39*(4), 593–619.

Goffman, E. (1959). *The presentation of self in everyday life.* Anchor.

Gold, E., Simon, E., Mundell, L., & Brown, C. (2004). Bringing community organizing into the school reform picture. *Nonprofit and Voluntary Sector Quarterly, 33*(3), 54–76.

Goldhaber, D., Theobald, R., & Tien, C. (2015). *The theoretical and empirical arguments for diversifying the teacher workforce: A review of the Evidence.* Center for Education Data and Research. http://m.cedr.us/papers/working/CEDR%20WP%2020159–.pdf

Goldin, C., & Katz, L. (1999). Human capital and social capital: The rise of secondary schooling in America, 1910–1940. *Journal of Interdisciplinary History, 29*(4), 683–723.

Goldring, E., & Hausman, C. (1999). Reasons for parental choice of urban schools. *Journal of Education Policy, 14*(5), 469–490.

Goldstein, D. (2018a, August 21). How do you get better schools? Take the state to court, more advocates say. *New York Times.* https://www.nytimes.com/2018/08/21/us/school-segregation-funding-lawsuits.html

Goldstein, D. (2018b, December 4). Nation's first teachers' strike at Charter Network begins in Chicago. *New York Times.* https://www.nytimes.com/2018/12/04/us/chicago-charter-strike.html

Goldstein, D. (2018c, May 2). Teacher pay is so low in some U.S. school districts that they've recruited overseas. *New York Times.* https://www.nytimes.com/2018/05/02/us/arizona-teachers-phillippines.html

Goldstein, D. (2018d, April 2). Teachers in Oklahoma and Kentucky walk out: "It really is a wildfire." *New York Times.* https://www.nytimes.com/2018/04/02/us/teacher-strikes-oklahoma-kentucky.html

Goldstein, D., & Burns, A. (2018, April 12). Teacher walkouts threaten Republican grip on conservative states. *New York Times.* https://www.nytimes.com/2018/04/12/us/teacher-walkouts-threaten-republican-grip-on-conservative-states.html

Goldstein, D., & Dias, E. (2018, April 12). Oklahoma teachers' strike. *New York Times.* https://www.nytimes.com/2018/04/12/us/oklahoma-teachers-strike.html

Goldstein, J. (2008, Fall). Taking the lead with Peer Assistance and Review, the teaching profession can be in teachers' hands. *American Educator.* https://www.aft.org/sites/default/files/periodicals/goldstein.pdf

Goldstein, J. (2010). *Peer review and teacher leadership: Linking professionalism and accountability.* Teachers College Press.

Goldstein, L. (1999). The relational zone: The role of caring relationships in the co-construction of the mind. *American Educational Research Journal, 36*(3), 647–673.

Goldstein, L. (2002). *Reclaiming caring in teaching and teacher education.* Peter Lang.

Gomez, I., & Benson, L. (2018, April 11). *Oklahoma teachers are swarming to run for office.* CNN. https://www.cnn.com/2018/04/11/health/oklahoma-teachers-registering-for-office-trnd/index.html

Gonzales, R. (2018, April 20). *Arizona teachers vote to strike, sparking statewide walkout.* NPR. https://www.npr.org/sections/thetwo-way/2018/04/20/604185559/arizona-teachers-vote-to-strike-sparking-first-ever-statewide-walkout

Goodman, P. (1962). *Growing up absurd: Problems of youth in the organized system.* Vintage.

Gordon, N. (2016, March 28). *Increasing targeting, flexibility, and transparency in Title I of the Elementary and Secondary Education Act to help disadvantaged students.* Brookings Institution. https://www.brookings.edu/research/increasing-targeting-flexibility-and-transparency-in-title-i-of-the-elementary-and-secondary-education-act-to-help-disadvantaged-students/

Gormley, W., & Balla, S. (2008). *Bureaucracy and democracy: Accountability and performance* (2nd ed.). CQ Press.

Gottlieb, B. (1975). The contribution of natural support systems to primary prevention among four social subgroups of adolescent males. *Adolescence, 10*(38), 207–220.

Gould, E. (2015). *2014 continues a 35-year trend of broad-based wage stagnation.* Economic Policy Institute. https://www.epi.org/publication/stagnant-wages-in-2014/

Gould, E., & Kimball, W. (2015). *"Right-to-work" states still have lower wages.* Economic Policy Institute. http://www.epi.org/publication/right-to-work-states-have-lower-wages/

Government Accountability Office. (1995, February). *School facilities: Condition of America's schools.* https://www.gao.gov/assets/230/220864.pdf

Government Accountability Office. (2010). *Many challenges arise in education students who change school frequently.* https://www.gao.gov/products/GAO-114-0

Government Accountability Office. (2011). *School Improvement Grants: Early implementation under way but reforms affected by short time frames.* https://www.gao.gov/products/GAO-117-41

Government Accountability Office. (2012, June). *Additional federal attention needed to help protect access for students with disabilities.* https://www.gao.gov/assets/600/591435.pdf

Government Accountability Office. (2014, January). *Recent trends in federal civilian employment and compensation.* https://www.gao.gov/products/GAO-142-15

Grabar, H. (2018a, December 7). Minneapolis confronts its history of housing segregation. *Slate.* https://slate.com/business/2018/12/minneapolis-single-family-zoning-housing-racism.html

Grabar, H. (2018b, November 8). Scott Walker's war on the public sector came back to bite him. *Slate.* https://slate.com/business/2018/11/scott-walker-lost-wisconsin-education-unions.html

Graham, K. (2013, March 4). *A look at a scary walk by students.* http://articles.philly.com/20130-30-4/news/37412867_1_peirce-src-member-sylvia-simms

Granovetter, M. (1973). The strength of weak ties. *American Journal of Sociology, 78,* 1360–1380.

Granovetter, M. (1985). Economic action and social structure: The problem of embeddedness. *American Journal of Sociology, 91*(3), 481–510.

Greenberg, J., McKee, A., & Walsh, K. (2013). *Teacher prep review: A review of the nation's teacher preparation programs.* NCTQ. https://www.nctq.org/dmsView/Teacher_Prep_Review_2013_Report

Greene, J., & Kahlenberg, R. (2012). Unions and the public interest: Is collective bargaining for teachers good for students? *Education Next.* https://www.educationnext. Org/unions-and-the-public-interest/

Greenhouse, S. (2015, August 19). How to get low-wage workers into the middle class. *Atlantic*. https://www.theatlantic.com/business/archive/2015/08/fifteen-dollars-minimum-wage/401540/

Greenstone, D. (1969). *Labor in American politics*. Knopf.

Grissmer, D., Flanagan, A., & Williamson, S. (1998). Why did the Black–white score gap narrow in the 1970s and 1980? In C. Jencks & M. Phillips (Eds.), *The Black–white test score gap* (pp. 182–226). Brookings Institution Press.

Gross, T. (2021, June 24). *Uncovering who is driving the fight against critical race theory in schools*. NPR. https://www.npr.org/2021/06/24/1009839021/uncoveringwho-is-driving-the-fight-against-critical-race-theory-inschools

Gross, B., & Gross, R. (Eds.). (1985). *The great school debate: Which way for American education?* Simon and Schuster.

Gross, N., Gaicquinta, J., & Bernstein, M. (1971). *Implementing organizational innovations: A sociological analysis of planned educational change*. Basic Books.

Gunn, D. (2018, April 24). What caused the decline of unions in America? *Pacific Standard*. https://psmag.com/economics/what-caused-the-decline-of-unions-in-america

Guryan, J. (2001). *Desegregation and Black dropout rates* (Working Paper No. 8345). National Bureau of Economic Research. https://www.nber.org/papers/w8345

Gusfield, J. (1981). *The culture of public problems: Drinking-driving and the symbolic order*. University of Chicago Press.

Gusfield, J. (1986). *Symbolic crusade: Status politics and the American temperance movement*. University of Illinois Press.

Gutmann, A. (1999). *Democratic education*. Princeton University Press.

Hacker, J. (2006). *The great risk shift: The new economic insecurity and the decline of the American dream*. Oxford University Press.

Hall, P. (1993). Policy paradigms, social learning, and the state: The case of economic policymaking in Britain. *Comparative Politics, 25*(3), 275–296.

Hall, A., & Yoder, J. (2019, March 26). *Does homeownership influence political behavior? Evidence from administrative data*. http://www.andrewbenjaminhall.com/homeowner.pdf

Hamilton, M., Heilig, J., & Pazey, B. (2014). A nostrum of school reform? Turning around reconstituted urban Texas high schools. *Urban Education, 49*(2), 182–215.

Hamm, K., Schochet, L., & Novoa, C. (2018). *The Trump plan to cut benefit programs threatens children*. Center for American Progress. https://www.americanprogress.org/issues/early-childhood/reports/2018/04/10/449262/trump-plan-cut-benefit-programs-threatens-children/

Han, E. (2016). *The myth of union's overprotection of bad teachers: Evidence from the district–teacher matched panel data on teacher turnover*. Wellesley College. http://haveyouheardblog.com/wp-content/uploads/2016/07/Han_Teacher_dismissal_Feb_16.pdf

Hanks, A., Solomon, D., & Weller, C. (2018, February 21). *Systemic inequality: How America's structural racism helped create the Black–White wealth gap.* Center for American Progress. https://www.americanprogress.org/issues/race/reports/2018/02/21/447051/systematic-inequality/

Hansen, M., & Quintero, D. (2017, September 29). *Teacher diversity gaps and their evolution under Trump.* Brookings Institution. https://www.brookings.edu/blog/brown-center-chalkboard/2017/09/29/teacher-diversity-gaps-and-their-evolution-under-trump/

Hanson, A. (2021, September 20). *Education attainment statistics.* Educationdata.org. https://educationdata.org/education-attainment-statistics

Hanushek, E. (1989). The impact of differential expenditures on school performance. *Educational Researcher, 18*(4), 45–51.

Hanushek, E. (2002). Publicly provided education. In A. Auerback & M. Feldstein (Eds.), *Handbook of public economics* (Vol. 4, pp. 2045–2141). North-Holland.

Hanushek, E. (2009). Teacher deselection. In D. Goldhaber & J. Hannaway (Eds.), *Creating a new teaching profession* (pp. 165–180). Urban Institute Press.

Hanushek, E., Kain, J., & Rivkin, S. (2004). Why public schools lose teachers. *Journal of Human Resources, 39*(2), 326–354.

Hanushek, E., Kain, J., Rivkin, S., & Branch, G. (2005). *Charter school quality and parental decision making with school choice.* National Bureau of Economic Research.

Hargreaves, A. (1998). The emotional practice of teaching. *Teaching and Teacher Education, 14*(8), 835–854.

Hargreaves, A. (2000). Mixed emotions: Teachers' perceptions of their interactions with students. *Teaching and Teacher Education, 16,* 811–826.

Hargreaves, A. (2001, March 10–14). *The emotional geographies of teachers' relations with colleagues.* Paper presented at the Spencer Foundation Invitational Conference on Social Geographies of Educational Change: Context, Networks, and Generalizability, Barcelona, Spain.

Harmon, M., & Mayer, R. (1986). *Organizational theory for public administration.* Little, Brown.

Harrington, B. (2016). *Capital without borders: Wealth managers and the one percent.* Harvard University Press.

Harrington, M. (1962). *The other America: Poverty in the United States.* Penguin Books.

Harris, D. (2007). *The promises and pitfalls of alternative teacher compensation approaches.* Great Lakes Center for Education Research and Practice. http://greatlakes-center.org/docs/policy_Briefs/Harris_Merit%20Pay.pdf

Harris, D. (2011). *Value-added measures in education.* Harvard University Press.

Harris, D., & Larsent, M. (2015). *What schools do families want and why?* Education Research Alliance of New Orleans. https://educationresearchalliancenola.org/files/publications/ERA1402-Policy-Brief-What-Schools-Do-Families-Want_170804_163150.pdf

Harris, E. (2015, February 11). Report faults charter school rules on discipline of students. *New York Times*. https://www.nytimes.com/2015/02/12/nyregion/report-faults-charter-school-rules-on-discipline-of-tudents.html

Harris, M., & Hoover, J. (2003). Overcoming adversity through community schools. *Reclaiming Children & Youth, 11*, 206–210.

Hartocollis, A. (2019, August 27). SAT "adversity score" is abandoned in wake of criticism. *New York Times*. https://www.nytimes.com/2019/08/27/us/sat-adversity-score-college-board.html

Hassel, E., & Hassel, B. (2009). The big U-turn: How to bring schools from the brink of doom to stellar success. *Education Next, 9*(1). https://www.educationnext.org/the-big-uturn/

Hastings, J., Kane, T., & Staiger, D. (2005). *Parental preferences and school competition: Evidence from a public school choice program*. National Bureau of Economic Research.

Hawkins, B. (2017, August 1). *When charter schools open neighboring schools get better a new study finds 7 reasons why*. The 74 Million. https://www.the74million.org/article/when-charter-schools-open-neighboring-schools-get-better-a-new-study-finds-7-reasons-why/

Heckman, J., & Kautz, T. (2012). Hard evidence on soft skills. *Labour Economics, 19*, 451–464.

Helm, J. (2016, December 8). Finland's schools were once the envy of the world. Now, they're slipping. *Washington Post*. https://www.washingtonpost.com/local/education/finlands-schools-were-once-the-envy-of-the-world-now-theyre-slipping/2016/12/08/dcfd0f56-bd601-1e69-lee-1adddfe36cbe_story.html

Henderson, A., & Mapp, K. L. (2002). *A new wave of evidence: The impact of school, family, and community connections on student achievement*. Southwest Educational Development Laboratory.

Herndon, J. (1969). *The way it spozed to be: A report on the classroom war behind the crisis in our schools*. Bantam Books.

Hertel-Fernandez, A. (2018). Policy feedback as political weapon: Conservative advocacy and the demobilization of the public sector labor movement. *Perspectives on Politics, 16*(2), 364–379.

Hess, A. (2017, July 14). *The 5 highest and lowest paying states for teachers in the US*. CNBC. https://www.cnbc.com/2017/07/14/the-5-highest-and-lowest-paying-states-for-teachers-in-the-us.html

Hess, F., & Leal, D. (2005). School house politics: Expenditures, interests, and competition in school board elections. In W. Howell (Ed.), *Besieged: School boards and the future of education politics* (pp. 228–253). Brookings Institution Press.

Hess, F., & McGuinn, P. (2002). Seeking the mantle of "opportunity": Presidential politics and the educational metaphor, 1964–2000. *Educational Policy, 16*(1), 72–95.

Hess, F., & Petrilli, M. (2009). *No Child Left Behind*. Peter Lang.

Hess, G. (2003). Reconstitution—three years later: Monitoring the effect of sanctions on Chicago high schools. *Education and Urban Society, 35*(3), 300–327.

Hickrod, A., Hines, E., Anthony, G., Dively, J., & Proyned, G. (1992). The effect of constitutional litigation on education finance: A preliminary analysis. *Journal of Education Finance, 18*(2), 207–208.

Hill, H. (2009). Fixing teacher professional development. *Phi Delta Kappan, 90*(7), 470–477.

Hirschman, A. (1970). *Exit, voice and loyalty: Responses to decline in firms, organizations and states.* Harvard University Press.

Hirst, E., & Doyle, B. (2013, March 28). Mayor says negotiations over, but protesters march on. *Chicago Tribune.* http://www.chicagotribune.com/news/ct-xpm-20130–32–8-chi-rally-march-in-loop-today-against-cps-closings-20130327-story.html

Hochschild, A. (1983). *The managed heart: Commercialization of human feeling.* University of California Press.

Hofferth, S., Boisjoly, J., & Duncan, G. (1998). Parents' extrafamilial resources and children's school attainment. *Sociology of Education, 71*, 246–268.

Hohle, R. (2012). The color of neoliberalism: The "modern southern businessman" and postwar Alabama's challenge to racial desegregation. *Sociological Forum, 27*(1), 142–146.

Holland, G. (2014). Child poverty in U.S. at its highest point in 20 years. *Los Angeles Times.* http://www.latimes.com/science/sciencenow/la-sci-sn-child-poverty-20141021-story.html

Honig, M. (2006). Complexity and policy implementation: Challenges and opportunities for the field. In M. Honig (Ed.), *New directions in education policy implementation* (pp. 1–24). State University of New York Press.

Hood, C. (1998). *The art of state: Culture, rhetoric, and public management.* Clarendon Press.

Hood, C. (1991). A public management for all seasons. *Public Administration, 69*(1), 3–19.

Horsley, S., & Totenberg, N. (2018, June 27). *Supreme Court deals blow to government unions.* NPR. https://www.npr.org/2018/06/27/606208436/supreme-court-deals-blow-to-government-unions

Horton, E. (2017, October 23). *The legacy of the 2001 and 2003 Bush tax cuts.* Center on Budget and Policy Priorities. http://cbpp.org/research/federal-tax/the-legacy-of-the-2001-and-2003-bush-tax-cuts

Horvat, E., Weininger, E., & Lareau, A. (2003). From social ties to social capital: Class differences in the relations between schools and parent networks. *American Educational Research Journal, 40*(2), 319–351.

Houston, D. (2005). "Walking the walk" of public service motivation: Public employees and charitable gifts of time, blood, and money. *Journal of Public Administration Research and Theory, 16*(1), 67–86.

Hout, M., & Elliott, S. (2011). *Incentives and test-based accountability in education.* National Academies Press.

Howell, W., West, M., & Peterson, P. E. (2008). The 2008 Education Next–PEPG survey of public opinion. *Education Next, 8*(4). http://educationnext.org/the-2008-education-nextpepg-survey-of-public-opinion/

Hoxby, C. (1994). *Does competition among public schools benefit students and taxpayers?* (Working Paper No. 4979). National Bureau of Economic Research. https://www.nber.org/papers/w4979

Hoxby, C. (2004a). *Achievement in charter schools and regular public schools in the United States: Understanding the differences.* Harvard University. http://post.economics.harvard.edu/faculty/hoxby/papers/hoxbycharter_dec.pdf

Hoxby, C. (2004b). *A straightforward comparison of charter schools and regular public schools in the United States.* Harvard University. http://post.economics.harvard.edu/faculty/hoxby/papers/charters_040909.pdf

Hoxby, C., & Muraka, S. (2007). *New York City's charter schools overall report.* New York City Charter Schools Evaluation Project.

Hoxby, C., & Rockoff, J. (2004). *The impact of charter schools on student achievement: A study of students who attend schools chartered by the Chicago charter school foundation.* Department of Economics, Harvard University.

Hrebenar, R., & Thomas, C. (2004). Interest groups in the states. In V. Gray & R. Hanson (Eds.), *Politics in the American states* (pp. 100–128). Congressional Quarterly Press.

Humphrey, D., Koppich, J., Bland, J., & Bosetti, K. (2011). *Peer review: Getting serious about teachers' support and evaluation.* SRI International.

Hunt, D. (2006). Social capital, teacher perceptions of control and implications for the school work environment. *Journal of Research in Education, 16*, 4–20.

Hurlburt, S., LeFlock, K., Therriault, S., & Cole, S. (2011). *Baseline analyses of SIG applications and SIG-eligible and SIGG-awarded schools.* Institute of Education Sciences, U.S. Department of Education. https://ies.ed.gov/ncee/pubs/20114019/pdf/20114019.pdf

I am part of the resistance inside the Trump administration. (2018, September 5). *New York Times.* https://www.nytimes.com/2018/09/05/opinion/trump-white-house-anonymous-resistance.html

Ingersoll, D. (2003). *Who controls teachers' work? Power and accountability in America's schools.* Harvard University Press.

Ingersoll, R. (2001). Teacher turnover and teacher shortages: An organizational analysis. *American Educational Research Journal, 38*(3), 499–534.

Ingersoll, R. (2012, May 16). Beginning teacher induction: What the data tell us. *Education Week.* https://www.edweek.org/ew/articles/2012/05/16/kappan_ingersoll.h31.html

Ingersoll, R., Merrill, L., & Stuckey, D. (2014, April). *Seven trends: The transformation of the teaching force.* CPRE. http://www.cpre.org/sites/default/files/workingpapers/1506_7trendsapril2014.pdf

Ingraham, C. (2014, October 29). Child poverty in the U.S. is among the worst in the developed world. *Washington Post.* http://www.washingtonpost.com/blogs/wonkblog/wp/2014/10/29child-poverty-in-the-us-is-among-the-worst-in-the-developed-world/

Ingram, H., & Schneider, A. (1991). The choice of target populations. *Administration and Society, 23*(3), 333–356.

Ingram, H., & Schneider, A. (1993). Constructing citizenship: The subtle messages of policy design. In H. Ingram & S. Smith (Eds.), *Public policy for democracy* (pp. 68–97). Brookings Institution Press.

Ingram, H., & Schneider, H. (2005). Constructions by moral entrepreneurs and policy analysts. In A. Schneider & H. Ingram (Eds.), *Deserving and entitled: Social constructions and public policy* (pp. 219–221). State University of New York Press.

Ingram, H., & Smith, S. (Eds.). (1993). *Public policy for democracy.* Brookings Institution Press.

Ingram, M. (2017, January 25). Trump administration puts gag order on several government agencies. *Fortune Magazine.* http://fortune.com/2017/01/24/trump-gag-order/

Isaacs, J., & Magnuson, K. (2011). *Income and education as predictors of children's school readiness.* Brookings Institution. https://www.brookings.edu/research/ income-and-education-as-predictors-of-childrens-school-readiness/

Jack, J., Gold, E., & Levin, S. (2012) *Description of 8 Philadelphia schools slated for closure or phase-out.* Research for Action. http://www.otlcampaign.org/blog/2013/04/05/color-school-closures

Jackman, R., & Miller, R. (2005). *Before norms: Institutions and civic culture.* University of Michigan Press.

Jackson, C. (2009). Student demographics, teacher sorting and teaching quality: Evidence from the end of school desegregation. *Journal of Labor Economics, 27*(2), 213–256.

Jackson, C., Johnson, R., & Persico, C. (2015). *The effects of school spending on educational and economic outcomes: Evidence from school finance reforms* (Working Paper No. 20847). National Bureau of Economic Research. http://www.nber.org/papers/w20847

Jackson, K. (1987). *Crabgrass frontier: The suburbanization of the United States.* Oxford University Press.

Jackson, K., Wigger, C., & Xiong, H. (2018, January). *Do school spending cuts matter? Evidence from the Great Recession* (Working Paper No. 24203). National Bureau of Economic Research. http://www.nber.org/papers/w24203

Jacob, B. (2002). Where the boys aren't: Non-cognitive skills, returns to school and the gender gap in higher education. *Economics of Education Review, 21*(6), 589–598.

Jacobs, J. (1992). *The death and life of great American cities.* Vintage.

Jacobs, L., & Mettler, S. (2018). When and how new policy creates new politics: Examining the feedback effects of the Affordable Care Act on public opinion. *Perspectives on Politics, 16*(2), 345–363.

Jencks, C., & Phillips, M. (1998). *The Black–white test score gap.* Brookings Institution Press.

Jennings, J. (1990). Economic competitiveness the Sputnik of the eighties. In L. Marcus & B. Stickney (Eds.), *Politics and policy in the age of education* (pp. 4–16). Charles C. Thomas.

Jochim, A., DeArmond, M., Gross, B., & Lake, R. (2014, July). *How parents experience public school choice.* Center on Reinventing Public Education. https://www.crpe. org/sites/default/files/crpe_how-parents-experience-public-school-choice.pdf

John, T. (2016, May 17). Girls outperform boys on technology and engineering test. *Time.* https://time.com/4338723/girls-outperform-boys-test-technology-engineering-skills/

Johnson, R. (2011). *Long-run impacts of school desegregation and school quality on adult attainments* (Working Paper No. 16664). National Bureau of Economic Research. https://www.nber.org/papers/w16664

Johnson, S., & Birkeland, S. (2003). Pursuing a "sense of success": New teachers explain their career decisions. *American Educational Research Journal, 40*(3), 581–617.

Johnson, S., & Fiarman, S. (2012). Teacher evaluation: What's fair? What's effective? *Educational Leadership, 70*(3), 20–25. http://www.ascd.org/publications/educational-leadership/nov12/vol70/num03/The-Potential-of-Peer-Review.aspx

Johnson, S., Kardos, S., Kauffman, D., Lieu, E., & Donaldson, M. (2004). The support gap: New teachers' early experiences in high-income and low-income schools. *Education Policy Analysis Archives, 12*(61), 1–25.

Johnson, S., Kraft, M., & Papay, J. (2011). *How contexts matter in high-need schools: The effects of teacher working conditions on their professional satisfaction and their students' achievement.* http://scholar.harvard.edu/files/mkraft/files/johnson_kraft_papay_teacher_working_conditions_final.pdf

Johnson, S., Papay, J., Fiarman, S., Munger, M., & Qazilbash, E. (2010). *Realizing the potential of peer assistance and review.* Center for American Progress. https://www.americanprogress.org/issues/education-k-12/reports/2010/05/11/7791/teacher-to-teacher/

Johnson, W., & Berglund, T. (2018). *The prevalence of collaboration among American teachers.* RAND Corporation. https://www.rand.org/pubs/research_reports/RR2217.html

Joint Center for Housing Studies. (2018). *The state of the nation's housing.* Harvard University. https://www.jchs.harvard.edu/state-nations-housing-2018

Jones, J. (2014, August 28). *Americans approve of unions but support "Right to Work."* Gallup. https://news.gallup.com/poll/175556/americans-approve-unions-support-right-work.aspx

Jones, J. (2016, August 31). *In U.S., slim majority again sees unions as helping economy.* Gallup. https://news.gallup.com/poll/195245/slim-majority-again-sees-unions-helping-economy.aspx

Jones, M., & McBeth, M. (2010). A narrative policy framework: Clear enough to be wrong? *Policy Studies Journal, 38*(2), 329–353.

Joseph, N. (2014, August). *The NCTQ teacher trendline: July 2014.* National Council on Teacher Quality. https://www.nctq.org/blog/July-2014:-Teacher-Tenure

Journey for Justice Alliance. (2014, May). *Death by one thousand cuts: Racism, school closures, and public school sabotage.* http://www.j4jalliance.com/wp-content/uploads/2014/02/J4JReport-final_05_12_14.pdf

Kaestle, C., & Lodewick, A. (2007). Introduction. In C. Kaestle & A. Lodewick (Eds.), *To educate a nation: Federal and national strategies of school reform* (pp. 1–11). University Press of Kansas.

Kagan, R. (2003). *Adversarial legalism: The American way of law.* Harvard University Press.

Kahlenberg, R. (2012–2013, Winter). From all walks of life: New hope for school integration. *American Educator.* https://www.aft.org/ae/winter20122–013/kahlenberg

Kahlenberg, R. (2018a, April 11). Reviving the Fair Housing Act at 50. *American Prospect.* https://prospect.org/civil-rights/reviving-fair-housing-act-50/

Kahlenberg, R. (2018b, August 2). Taking on class and racial discrimination in housing: Cory Booker's big idea to rein in exclusionary zoning. *American Prospect.* https://prospect.org/civil-rights/taking-class-racial-discrimination-housing/

Kahlenberg, R. (2018c, April 9). *Updating the Fair Housing Act to make housing more affordable.* Century Foundation. https://tcf.org/content/report/updating-fair-housing-act-make-housing-affordable/

Kahne, J., & Middaugh, E. (2008). *Democracy for some: The civic opportunity gap in high school.* Center for Information and Research in Civic Learning.

Kamenetz, A. (2020, June 23). *Why there's a push to get police out of school.* NPR. https://www.npr.org/2020/06/23/881608999/why-theres-a-push-to-get-police-out-of-schools

Kamenetz, A., & Lombardo, C. (2018, April 2). *Teachers are marching ahead of their unions, in Oklahoma and Arizona.* NPR. https://www.npr.org/sections/ed/2018/04/02/597358137/teachers-are-marching-ahead-of-their-unions-from-oklahoma-to-arizona

Kane, M. (2002). Validating high-stakes testing programs. *Educational Measurement: Issues and Practice, 21*(1), 31–41.

Kane, M. (2006). Validation. In R. Brennan (Ed.), *Educational measurement* (4th ed., pp. 17–64). Praeger.

Kane, T., & Staiger, D. (2002). The promise and pitfalls of using imprecise school accountability measures. *Journal of Economic Perspectives, 16*(4), 91–114.

Kantor, H., & Lowe, R. (2006). From New Deal to no deal: No child left behind and the devolution of responsibility for equal opportunity. *Harvard Educational Review, 76*(4), 474–502.

Katz, L., & Krueger, A. (2016). *The rise and nature of alternative work arrangements in the United States* (Working Paper No. 22667). National Bureau of Economic Research. https://www.nber.org/papers/w22667

Katz, M. (1990). *The undeserving poor.* Pantheon.

Katznelson, I. (2005). *When affirmative action was white: An untold story of racial inequality in twentieth-century America.* W. W. Norton.

Katznelson, I., & Weingast, B. (Eds.). (2005). *Preferences and situations: Points of intersection between historical and rational choice institutionalism.* Russell Sage Foundation.

Kaushal, N., Magnuson, K., & Waldfogel, J. (2011). How is family income related to investments in children's learning? In G. Duncan & R. Murnane (Eds.), *Whither opportunity? Rising inequality, schools, and children's life chances* (pp. 187–205). Russell Sage Foundation.

Keller, B. (2005, April 20). NEA files "No Child Left Behind" lawsuit. *Education Week.* https://www.edweek.org/ew/articles/2005/04/20/33suit_web.h24.html

Kemple, J. (2015). *High school closures in New York City: Impacts on students' academic outcomes, attendance, and mobility.* Research Alliance for New York City Schools. https://research.steinhardt.nyu.edu/research_alliance/publications/hs_closures_in_nyc

Kennedy, J. F. (1961, January 20). *Inaugural address.* John F. Kennedy Presidential Library. www.jfklibrary.org/archives/other-resources/john-f-kennedy-speeches/inaugural-address-19610120

Kerbow, D. (1996). *Patterns of urban student mobility and local school reform.* Center for Research on the Education of Students Placed at Risk.

Kerr, J. (2015, December 2). No Child Left Behind rewrite passes House easily. *Huffington Post.* http://www.huffingtonpost.com/entry/no-child-left-behind-vote_565fb881e4b08e945fee181c

Kettl, D. (2002). *The transformation of governance: Public administration for twenty-first century America.* Johns Hopkins University Press.

Kettl, D., & DiIulio, J. (1995). *Inside the reinvention machine: Appraising government reform.* Brookings Institution Press.

Kidder, W., & Rosner, J. (2002). How the SAT creates "built-in-headwinds": An educational and legal analyses of disparate impact. *Santa Clara Law Review, 43,* 131–212.

Kilgore, E. (2018, April 2). Teachers go on strike in two more red states. *New York Magazine.* http://nymag.com/daily/intelligencer/2018/04/teachers-go-on-strike-in-two-more-red-states.html

Kingdon, J. (1984). *Agendas, alternatives, and public policies.* Little, Brown.

Kirp, D. (2012, May 19). Making schools work. *New York Times.* http://www.nytimes. com/2012/05/20/opinion/sunday/integration-worked-why-have-we-rejected-it. html

Kirshner, B., Gaertner, M., & Pozzoboni, K. (2010). Tracing transitions: The effect of high school closure on displaced students. *Educational Evaluation and Policy Analysis, 32*(3), 407–429.

Kirzinger, A., Kearney, A., Hamel, L., & Brodie, M. (2021, November 16). *The increasing importance of partisanship in predicting COVID-19 vaccination status.* Kaiser Family Foundation COVID-19 vaccine monitor. https://www.kff.org/coronavirus-covid-19/poll-finding/kff-covid-19-vaccine-monitor-media-and-misinformation/

Klein, A. (2010, June 15). NEA eyes Congress as high court refuses NCLB case. *Education Week.* https://www.edweek.org/ew/articles/2010/06/09/35nea.h29.html

Klein, A. (2015, November 30). ESEA reauthorization: The Every Student Succeeds Act explained. *Education Week.* http://blogs.edweek.org/edweek/ campaign-k-12/2015/11/esea_reauthorization_the_every.html

Klein, A. (2018a, July 23). Anti-test movement slows to a crawl. *Education Week.* http:// www.edweek.org/ew/articles/2018/07/23/anti-test-movement-slows-to-a-crawl. html

Klein, A. (2018b, May 24). Approved ESSA plans: Explainer and key takeaways from each state. *Education Week.* https://www.edweek.org/ew/section/multimedia /key-takeaways-state-essa-plans.html

Klein, M. (2018, July 14). Charter school CEOs get massive paychecks thanks to private doners. *New York Post.* https://nypost.com/2018/07/14/charter-school-ceos-get-massive-paychecks-thanks-to-private-donors/

Klein, R. (2015a, December 9). "No Child Left Behind": Overhaul Passes Senate in Milestone Vote. *Huffington Post.* http://www.huffingtonpost.com/entry/no-child-left-behind-overhaul_566704e4e4b079b281901766

Klein, R. (2015b, June 3). This is what it takes to get a teacher fired around the country. *Huffington Post.* https://www.huffingtonpost.com/entry/teacher-tenure-map_n_7502770

Kochan, T., Kimball, W., Yang, D., & Kelly, E. (2018, January 17). *Worker voice in America: A current assessment and exploration of options.* http://iwer.mit.edu/wp-content/uploads/2018/01/worker-voice-paper-1_16_18_tablesintext12pt.pdf

Kohl, H. (1967). *36 Children.* New American Library.

Konish, L. (2019, February 11). *This is the real reason most Americans file for bankruptcy.* CNBC. https://www.cnbc.com/2019/02/11/this-is-the-real-reason-most-americans-file-for-bankruptcy.html

Koretz, D. (2002). Limitations in the use of achievement tests as measures of educators' productivity. *Journal of Human Resources, 37*(4), 752–777.

Koretz, D. (2008). *Measuring up: What educational testing really tells us.* Harvard University Press.

Kozol, J. (1968). *Death at an early age.* Bantam.

Kraft, M., & Papay, J. (2014). Can professional environments in schools promote teacher development? Explaining heterogeneity in returns to teaching experience. *Educational Evaluation and Policy Analysis, 36*(4), 476–500.

Krants-Kent, R. (2008). Teachers work patterns: When, where, and how much do U.S. teachers work? *Monthly Labor Review*, pp. 52–59. https://www.bls.gov/opub/mlr/2008/03/art4full.pdf

Krezmien, M., Leone, P., & Achilles, G. (2006). Suspension, race, and disability: Analysis of statewide practices and reporting. *Journal of Emotional and Behavioral Disorders, 14*(4), 217–226.

Krueger, A., & Whitmore, D. (2001). The effect of attending a small class in the early grades on college test taking and middle school test results: Evidence from Project STAR. *Economic Journal, 111*(468), 1–28.

Krueger, A., & Whitmore, D. (2002). Would smaller classes help close the Black–white achievement gap? In J. Chubb & T. Loveless (Eds.), *Bridging the achievement gap* (pp. 11–46). Brookings Institution Press.

Kunichoff, Y. (2014, June 5). One year after closings, how are Chicago's public schools now? *In These Times*. http://inthesetimes.com/working/entry/16804/CTU_report_CPS_chicago_closing

Kyriacou, C. (2001). Teacher stress: Directions for future research. *Educational Review, 53*(1), 27–35.

Lacireno-Paquet, N., & Brantley, C. (2012). Who chooses schools, and why? The characteristics and motivations of families who actively choose schools. In G. Miron, K. Welner, P. Hinchey, & W. Mathis (Eds.), *Exploring the school choice universe: Evidence and recommendations* (pp. 65–88). Information Age.

Laczko-Kerr, I., & Berliner, D. (2002). The effectiveness of "Teach for America" and other under-certified teachers on student academic achievement: A case of harmful public policy. *Education Policy Analysis Archives, 10*(37). http://epaa.asu.edu/epaa/v10n37/

Ladd, H. (2012). Education and poverty: Confronting the evidence. *Journal of Policy Analysis and Management, 31*(2), 203–227.

Ladd, H., & Sorensen, L. (2014). *Returns to teacher experience: Student achievement and motivation in middle school* (Working Paper No. 112). CALDER.

Ladd, H., & Zelli, A. (2002). School-based accountability in North Carolina: The responses of school principals. *Educational Administration Quarterly, 38*(4), 494–529.

Lafer, G. (2011, September 15). *Right to work: The wrong answer for Michigan's economy.* Economic Policy Institute. https://www.epi.org/publication/right-to-work-michigan-economy/

Lafer, G. (2012a, February 7). *Right to work: A failed policy.* Economic Policy Institute. https://www.epi.org/publication/ib326right-to-work-new-hampshire-update/

Lafer, G. (2012b, January 11). What "right to work" means for Indiana's workers: A pay cut. *Nation*. https://www.thenation.com/article/what-right-work-means-indianas-workers-pay-cut/

Lafortune, J., Rothstein, J., & Schanzenback, D. (2016, February). *School finance reform and the distribution of student achievement* (Working Paper No. 22011). National Bureau of Economic Research. https://www.nber.org/papers/w22011.pdf

Lahm, S. (2017, December 7). Opting out of standardized testing? Get ready to be labeled "not proficient." *Progressive.* https://progressive.org/public-school-shakedown/opting-out-of-standardized-testing-get-ready-to-be-labeled/

Lam, W. (1996). Institutional design of public agencies and coproduction: A study of irrigation associations in Taiwan. *World Development, 24*(6), 1039–1054.

Lamont, M., & Lareau, A. (1988). Cultural capital: Allusions, gaps and glissandos in recent theoretical developments. *Sociological Theory, 6,* 153–168.

Landy, M. (1993). Public policy and citizenship. In H. Ingram & S. Smith (Eds.), *Public policy for democracy* (pp. 19–44). Brookings Institution.

Lankford, H., Loeb, S., McEachin, A., Miller, L., & Wyckoff, J. (2014). Who enters teaching? Encouraging evidence that the status of teaching is improving. *Educational Researcher, 43*(9), 444–453.

Lankford, H., Loeb, S., & Wyckoff, J. (2002). Teacher sorting and the plight of urban schools: A descriptive analysis. *Educational Evaluation and Policy Analysis, 24*(1), 37–62.

Lareau, A. (2000). *Home advantage: Social class and parental intervention in elementary school.* Rowman and Littlefield.

Lareau, A. (2003). *Unequal childhoods: Class, race, and family life.* University of California Press.

Lareau, A., & Horvat, E. (1999). Moments of social inclusion and exclusion: Race, class, and cultural capital in family–school relationships. *Sociology of Education, 72,* 37–53.

Lareau, A., & Weininger, E. (2003). Cultural capital in educational research: A critical assessment. *Theory and Society, 32*(5/6), 567–606.

Larkin, M., & Aina, M. (2018, November 4). *Legacy admissions offer an advantage—and not just at schools like Harvard.* NPR. https://www.npr.org/2018/11/04/663629750/legacy-admissions-offer-an-advantage-and-not-just-at-schools-like-harvard

Lasky, S. (2000). The cultural and emotional politics of teacher–parent interactions. *Teaching and Teacher Education, 16*(8), 843–860.

Lassiter, M. (2006). *The silent majority: Suburban politics in the sunbelt south.* Princeton University Press.

Lawless, J., & Fox, R. (2001). Political participation of the urban poor. *Social Problems, 48*(3), 362–385.

Layton, L. (2015a, June 7). How Bill Gates pulled off the swift Common Core revolution. *Washington Post.* https://www.washingtonpost.com/politics/how-bill-gates-pulled-off-the-swift-common-core-revolution/2014/06/07/a830e32e-ec341-1e39-f5c-9075d5508f0a_story.html

Layton, L. (2015b, December 10). Obama signs new K–12 education law that ends No Child Left Behind. *Washington Post.* https://www.washingtonpost.com/

local/education/obama-signs-new-k-12-education-law-that-ends-no-child-left-behind/2015/12/10/c9e58d7c-9f511-1e5-a3c5-c77f2cc5a43c_story.html

Lazarin, M. (2014, October 16). *Testing overload in America's schools.* Center for American Progress. https://www.americanprogress.org/issues/education-k-12/reports/2014/10/16/99073/testing-overload-in-americas-schools/

Leachman, M. (2017, November 29). *K–12 funding in some states still far below pre-recession levels.* Center on Budget and Policy Priorities. https://www.Cbpp.org/blog/k-12-funding-in-some-states-still-far-below-pre-recession-levels

Leachman, M., & Figueroa, E. (2019, March 6). *K–12 school funding up in most 2018 teacher-protest states, but still well below decade ago.* Center on Budget and Policy Priorities. https://www.cbpp.org/research/state-budget-and-tax/k-12-school-funding-up-in-most-2018-teacher-protest-states-but-still

Leachman, M., Masterson, K., & Figueroa, E. (2017, November 29). *A punishing decade for school funding.* Center on Budget and Policy Priorities. https://www.cbpp.org/research/state-budget-and-tax/a-punishing-decade-for-school-funding

Lee, A. (2020, March 31). *Math teacher shows up at student's front porch to give her a one-on-one lesson while social distancing.* CNN. https://www.cnn.com/2020/03/31/us/coronavirus-math-lesson-teacher-trnd/index.html

Lee, J. (2006). *Tracking achievement gaps and assessing the impact of NCLB on the gaps: An in-depth look into national and state reading and math outcome trends.* Civil Rights Project. https://www.civilrightsproject.ucla.edu/

Lee, J., & Reeves, T. (2012). Revisiting the impact of NCLB high-stakes school, accountability, capacity and resources: State NAEP 1990–2009 reading and math achievement gaps and trends. *Education Evaluation and Policy Analysis, 34*(2), 209–231.

Leetaru, K. (2017, January 25). What the "rogue" EPA, NPS, and NASA twitter accounts teach us. *Forbes.* http://www.forbes.com/sites/kalevleetaru/2017/01/25/what-the-rogue-epa-nps-and-nasa-twitter-accounts-teach-us-about-the-future-of-social/

LeFloch, K., Birman, B., O'Day, J., Hurlburt, S., Mercado-Garcia, D., Goff, R., Manship, K., Brown, S., Therriault, S., Rosenberg, L., Angus, M., & Julsey, L. (2014). *Case studies of schools receiving school improvement grants: Findings after the first year of implementation.* National Center for Education Evaluation and Regional Assistance, Institute of Education Sciences, U.S. Department of Education.

Leithwood, K., Harris, A., & Strauss, T. (2010). *Leading school turnaround: How successful leaders transform low-performing schools.* Jossey-Bass.

Lemann, N. (1999). *The big test: The secret history of the American meritocracy.* Farrar, Straus, and Giroux.

Leonhardt, D. (2013, July 22). In climbing income ladder, location matters. *New York Times.* https://www.nytimes.com/2013/07/22/business/in-climbing-income-ladder-location-matters.html

Leonhardt, M. (2021, April 12). *Universal child care could boost women's lifetime earnings by $130 billion—and ensure more stable retirement options.* CNBC. https://www.cnbc.com/2021/04/12/universal-child-care-could-boost-womens-earnings-by-130-billion-dollars.html

Levenson, E., & Jorgenssen, S. (2018, March 6). *West Virginia governor signs bill to give striking teachers pay raise.* CNN. https://www.cnn.com/2018/03/06/us/west-virginia-teachers-strike/index.html

Levin, E., & Meni, D. (2016, June 30). The biggest beneficiaries of housing subsidies? The wealthy. *Talk Poverty.* https://talkpoverty.org/2016/06/30/biggest-beneficiaries-housing-subsidies-wealthy/

Levine, M. (2016, February). *Deunionization in Wisconsin and metro Milwaukee: A statistical overview.* Center for Economic Development. https://uwm.edu/ced/wp-content/uploads/sites/431/2018/11/deunionization-of-wisconsin.pdf

Levinson, M. (2007). *The civic achievement gap.* Center for Information and Research in Civic Learning.

Lewin, S. (1996). Economics and psychology: Lessons for our own day from the early twentieth century. *Journal of Economic Literature, 34*(3), 1293–1323.

Lewin, T. (2010, July 23). Once a leader, U.S. lags in college degrees. *New York Times.* https://www.nytimes.com/2010/07/23/education/23college.html

Lewis, R. (2013, November 9). *Detroit gun violence claims 17 lives in past 10 days.* http://america.aljazeera.com/articles/2013/11/9/detroit-violenceskyrockets amidbankruptcyrestructuring.html

Libassi, C. (2018). *The neglected college race gap: Racial disparities among college completers.* Center for American Progress. https://cdn.americanprogress.org/content/uploads/2018/05/22135501/CollegeCompletions-Brief1.pdf

Lieberman, R. (2001). *Shifting the color line: Race and the American welfare state.* Harvard University Press.

Lieberman, M. (2021, October 12). How bad are school staffing shortages? What we learned by asking administrators. *Education Week.* https://www.edweak.org/leadership/how-bad-are-school-staffing-shortages-what-we-learned-by-asking-administrators/2021/10

Lindblom, C. (1982). Another state of mind. *American Political Science Review, 76*(1), 9–21.

Lindsay, C., Lee, V., & Lloyd, T. (2018, June 21). *The prevalence of police officers in US schools.* Urban Institute. https://www.urban.org/urban-wire/prevalence-police-officers-us-schools

Lipman, P., & Haines, N. (2007). From accountability to privatization and African American exclusion: Chicago's "Renaissance 2010." *Educational Policy, 21*(3), 471–502.

Lipsky, M. (1980). *Street-level bureaucracy: Dilemmas of the individual in public services.* Russell Sage Foundation.

Loeb, S., Darling-Hammond, L., & Luczak, J. (2005). How teaching conditions predict teacher turnover in California schools. *Peabody Journal of Education, 80*(3), 44–70.

Loeb, S., & Miller, L. C. (2006). *A review of state teacher policies: What are they, what are their effects, and what are their implications for school finance?* Institute for Research on Education Policy and Practice, School of Education, Stanford University.

Loeske, D. (2007). The study of identity as cultural, institutional, organizational, and personal narratives: Theoretical and empirical integrations. *Sociological Quarterly, 48*, 661–688.

Logue, J. (2016, April 15). Messages that aren't easily erased. *Inside Higher Ed.* https://www.insidehighered.com/news/2016/04/15/pro-trump-chalkings-inflame-many-campuses

Longo-Schmid, J. (2016). Teachers' voices: Where policy meets practice. In K. Hewitt & A. Amrein-Beardsley (Eds.), *Student growth measures: Where policy meets practice* (pp. 49–71). Palgrave.

Lortie, D. (1975). *Schoolteacher: A sociological study.* University of Chicago Press.

Losen, D., Hodson, C., Keith, M., Morrison, K., & Belway, S. (2015, February 23). *Are we closing the gap on school discipline?* Center for Civil Rights Remedies. https://civilrightsproject.ucla.edu/resources/projects/center-for-civil-rights-remedies/school-to-prison-folder/federal-reports/are-we-closing-the-school-discipline-gap

Loveless, T. (2006, August). *The peculiar politics of No Child Left Behind.* Brookings Institution. https://www.brookings.edu/research/the-peculiar-politics-of-no-child-left-behind/

Lovett, I. (2010). Teacher's death exposes tensions in Los Angeles. *New York Times.* http://www.nytimes.com/2010/11/10/education/10teacher.html

Lubienski, C., Scott, J., & DeBray, E. (2011, July 22). The rise of intermediary organizations in knowledge production, advocacy, and educational policy. *Teachers College Record.* http://www.tcrecord.org/Content.asp?ContentId=16487

Lucas, S., & Berends, M. (2002). Sociodemographic diversity, correlated achievement, and defacto tracking. *Sociology of Education, 75*, 328–348.

MacLeod, J. (2000). Teenagers in Clarendon Heights: The hallway hangers and the brothers. In R. Arum & I. Beattie (Eds.), *The structure of schooling* (pp. 276–287). McGraw-Hill Higher Education.

Madland, D., & Rowell, A. (2017). *Attacks on public-sector unions harm states: How Act 10 has affected education in Wisconsin.* Center for American Progress Action Fund. https://cdn.americanprogressaction.org/content/uploads/sites/2/2017/11/15074954/ImpactofWisconsinAct10-brief.pdf

Madland, D., & Wall, M. (2020, March 2). *What is sectoral bargaining?* Center for American Progress Action Fund. https://www.americanprogressaction.org/issues/economy/news/2020/03/02/176857/what-is-sectoral-bargaining/

Magnet Schools of America. (2012). *A review of research on magnet schools.* https://magnet.edu/research-category/magnet-school-research

Magnet Schools of America. (n.d.). *A snapshot of magnet schools*. https://magnet.edu/getinvolved/research-studies/snapshot-of-magnet-schools-report

Malanga, S. (2018, Spring). Life after *Janus*. *City Journal*. https://www.city-journal.org/html/life-after-janus-15841.html

Malen, B., & Rice, J. (2004). A framework for assessing the impact of education reforms on school capacity: Insights from studies of high-stakes accountability initiatives. *Education Policy, 18*(5), 631–660.

Maldonado, C. (2019, October 10). Trump tax cuts helped billionaires pay less taxes than the working class in 2018. *Forbes*. http://www.forbes.com/sites/camilomaldonado/2019/10/10/trump-tax-cuts-helped-billionaires-pay-less-taxes-than-the-working-class-in-2018/?sh=5154353128f0

Manna, P. (2006). *School's In: Federalism and the national education agenda*. Georgetown University Press.

Mansbridge, J. (1980). *Beyond adversarial democracy*. University of Chicago Press.

Mansbridge, J. (1990a). *Beyond self-interest*. University of Chicago Press.

Mansbridge, J. (1990b). Self-interest in political life. *Political Theory, 18*(1), 132–153.

Manzo, F. (2017, May 10). Union membership declined in "right-to-work" states and increased in collective bargaining states last year. *Illinois Update*. https://illinoisupdate.com/2017/05/10/union-membership-declined-in-right-to-work-states-and-increased-in-collective-bargaining-states-last-year/

Marinell, W., & Coca, V. (2013). *Who leaves and who stays? Findings from a three-part study of teacher turnover in NYC middle schools*. Research Alliance for New York City Schools. http://media.rancy.org/2011/002

Martin, C., Boser, U., Benner, M., & Baffour, P. (2018). *A quality approach to school funding: Lessons learned from school finance litigation*. Center for American Progress. https://www.americanprogress.org/issues/education-k-12/reports/2018/11/13/460397/quality-approach-school-funding/

Martinez, T., Chandler, A., & Latham, N. (2013). *Case study: School discipline reform in California*. California Endowment. https://www.issuelab.org/resource/case-study-school-discipline-reform-in-california.html

Mathematica Policy Research. (2010). *The evaluation of charter school impacts*. Institute of Education Sciences. http://ies.ed.gov/ncee/pubs/20104029/pdf/20104029.pdf

Mathis, W. (2009). *NCLB's ultimate restructuring alternatives: Do they improve the quality of education?* Education and the Public Interest Center and Education Policy Research Unit. http://epicpolicy.org/publication/nclb-ultimate-restructuring

Mathis, W. (2011, August 25). No Child Left Behind on steroids. *Washington Post*. https://www.washingtonpost.com/blogs/answer-sheet/post/no-child-left-behind-on-steroids/2011/08/25/gIQA92bzdJ_blog.html

Mathis, W., & Cordes, S. (2017). *Report's use of data and analysis is inadequate to address the question of cream-skimming*. National Education Policy Center. http://nepc.colorado.edu/newsletter/2017/05/examination-new-york

Matsudaira, J., & Patterson, R. (2017). Teachers' unions and school performance: Evidence from California charter schools. *Economics of Education Review, 61*, 35–50.

Matusow, A. (1984). *The unraveling of America: A history of liberalism in the 1960s.* Harper Torch Books.

Maul, A., & McClelland, A. (2013). *Review of national charter school study 2013.* National Education Policy Center. http://nepc.colorado.edu/thinktank/review-credo-2013

Maxwell, L. (2014, August 19). U.S. school enrollment hits majority minority milestone. *Education Week.* http://www.edweek.org/ew/articles/2014/08/20/01demographics.h34.html

Maxwell, L. (2016). School building condition, social climate, student attendance and academic achievement: A mediation model. *Journal of Environmental Psychology, 46*, 206–216.

Maynard-Moody, S., & Musheno, M. (2003). *Cops, teachers, counselors: Stories from the front lines of public service.* University of Michigan Press.

McAuliff, M., & Siddiqui, S. (2013, February 28). John Boehner compares tax proposals of White House to stealing. *Huffington Post.* http://www.huffingtonpost.com/2013/02/28/john-boehner-taxes-stealing_n_2782608.html

McBeth, M., Shanahan, E., Arnell, R., & Hathaway, P. (2007). The intersection of narrative policy analysis and policy change theory. *Policy Studies Journal, 35*(1), 87–108.

McCaffrey, D., Koretz, D., Lockwood, J., & Hamilton, L. (2004). *The promise and peril of using value-added modeling to measure teacher effectiveness. RAND Corporation.*

McCaffrey, D., Sass, T., Lockwood, J., & Mihaly, K. (2009). The inter-temporal variability of teacher effect estimates (Working Paper No. 20090–3). National Center on Performance Incentives. https://my.vanderbilt.edu/performanceincentives/files/2012/10/Annotated_Bibliography__ValueAdded_Studies.pdf

McCarl, R. (2010). *The myth of the "highly qualified" teacher.* Mackinac Center for Public Policy. https://www.mackinac.org/13909

McCarthy, J., & Hoge, D. (1987). Social construction of school punishment. *Social Forces, 65*(4), 1101–1120.

McDonnell, L. (1991). Ideas and values in implementation analysis: The case of teacher policy. In A. Odden (Ed.), *Education policy implementation* (pp. 241–258). State University of New York Press.

McDonnell, L., & Elmore, R. (1987). Getting the job done: Alternative policy instruments. *Educational Evaluation and Policy Analysis, 9*(2), 133–152.

McDonough, P. (1997). *Choosing college: How social class and schools structure opportunity.* State University of New York Press.

McElwee, S. (2014, October 23). Why the voting gap matters. *Demos.* https://www.demos.org/research/why-voting-gap-matters

McGirr, L. (2002). *Suburban warriors: The origins of the new American right.* Princeton University Press.

McGuinn, P. (2006). *No Child Left Behind and the transformation of federal education policy, 1965–2005.* University Press of Kansas.

McLaughlin, M. (1993). What matters most in teachers' workplace context? In J. Little & M. McLaughlin (Eds.), *Teachers' work: Individuals, colleagues, and contexts* (pp. 79–103). Teachers College Press.

McNeal, M. (2011, July 6). More states defiant on NCLB compliance. *Education Week.* http://www.edweek.org/ew/articles/2011/07/06/36nclb.h30.html

McNeal, R. (1999). Parental involvement as social capital: Differential effectiveness on science achievement, truancy, and dropping-out. *Social Forces, 78*(1), 117–144.

McNichol, E. (2012, June 15). *Some basic facts on state and local government workers.* Center on Budget and Policy Priorities. https://www.cbpp.org/research/some-basic-facts-on-state-and-local-government-workers

McNicholas, S., Mokhiber, Z., & von Wilpert, M. (2018, February 21). *Janus and fair share fees: The organizations financing the attack on unions' ability to represent workers.* Economic Policy Institute. https://files.epi.org/pdf/142063.pdf

MDRC. (2014, October). *New findings show New York City's small high schools boost college enrollment rates among disadvantaged students.* https://www.mdrc.org/news/press-release/new-findings-show-new-york-city-s-small-high-schools-boost-college-enrollment.

Mead, J. (2013). *Why the gap? Special education and New York City charter schools.* National Education Policy Center. http://nepc.colorado.edu/thinktank/review-why-the-gap

Mead, J., & Preston, G. (2012). *Chartering equity: Using charter school legislation and policy to advance equal educational opportunity.* National Education Policy Center. http://nepc.colorado.edu/

Mead, J., & Weber, M. (2016). *Special education and English language learner students in Boston charter schools.* National Education Policy Center. http://nepc.colorado.edu/

Mead, S. (2010, October 29). The limits of socioeconomic integration. *Education Week.* https://blogs.edweek.org/edweek/sarameads_policy_notebook/2010/10/the_limits_of_socioeconomic_integration.html

Medina, J. (2014, June 10). Judge rejects teacher tenure in California. *New York Times,* p. A1.

Mediratta, K., Shah, S., & McAlister, S. (2009). *Community organizing for stronger schools: Strategies and successes.* Harvard Education Press.

Merriam, S. (1998). *Qualitative research and case study applications in education.* Jossey-Bass.

Merry, R. (1980, August 13). Teacher group's clout on Carter's behalf is new brand of special-interest politics. *Wall Street Journal,* p. 2.

Mesecar, D. (2015, January 15). *The rise and fall of supplemental services: Policy implication for government markets.* American Enterprise Institute. https://files.eric.ed.gov/fulltext/ED555546.pdf

Methvin, E., & Herndon, T. (1979). Annotating a Reader's Digest article: "The NEA: A Washington lobby run rampant." *Phi Delta Kappan, 60*(6), 420–423.

Mettler, S. (2002). Bringing the state back in to civic engagement: Policy feedback effects of the G.I. Bill for World War II veterans. *American Political Science Review, 96*(2), 351–365.

Mettler, S., & Soss, J. (2004). The consequences of public policy for democratic citizenship: Bridging policy studies and mass politics. *Perspectives on Politics, 2,* 55–73.

Meyer, J., & Rowan, B. (1977). Institutionalized organizations: Formal structure as myth and ceremony. *American Journal of Sociology, 83*(2), 340–363.

Michelman, B. (2016). Title I: The engine of equity and accountability. *Policy Priorities, 22*(4), 1–7.

Mickelson, R. (2011a, October). *The reciprocal relationship between housing and school integration.* National Coalition on School Diversity. https://school-diversity.org/pdf/DiversityResearchBriefNo7.pdf

Miech, R. A., & Elder, G. H., Jr. (1996). The service ethic and teaching. *Sociology of Education, 69*(3), 237–253.

Milanowski, A., Heneman, H., & Finster, M. (n.d.). *Peer evaluation of teachers in Maricopa County's teacher incentive fund program.* Teacher Incentive Fund. https://files.eric.ed.gov/fulltext/ED560211.pdf

Miles, K., Pennington K., & Bloom, D. (2015). *Do more, add more, earn more: Teacher salary redesign lessons from 10 first-mover districts.* Center for American Progress. https://www.americanprogress.org/issues/education-k-12/reports/2015/02/17/106584/do-more-add-more-earn-more/

Miles, M., & Huberman, A. (1984). *Qualitative data analysis: A sourcebook of new methods.* Sage.

Mills, J., Egalite, A., & Wolf, P. (2016). *How has the Louisiana scholarship program affected students?* Education Research Alliance for New Orleans. https://educationresearchalliancenola.org/

Mills, J., & Wolf, P. (2017, June). *The effects of the Louisiana Scholarship Program on student achievement after three years.* Education Research Alliance for New Orleans. https://educationresearchalliancenola.org/files/publications/Mills-Wolf-Effects-of-LSP-on-Student-Achievement-After-Three-Years.pdf

Min, S. (2019, January 16). *Most Americans couldn't cover a $1,000 expense.* CBS News. https://www.cbsnews.com/news/most-americans-couldnt-cover-a-1000-expense/

Mintrop, H. (2004). *Schools on probation: How accountability works (and doesn't work).* Teachers College Press.

Mintrop, H., & Trujillo, T. (2005). Corrective action in low performing schools: Lessons for NCLB implementation from first-generation accountability systems. *Education Policy Analysis Archives, 13*(48), 1–27.

Miron, G. (2011). *Review of "Charter schools: A report on rethinking the federal role in education."* National Education Policy Center. http://nepc.colorado.edu/

Miron, G., Evergreen, S., & Urschel, J. (2008). *The impact of school choice reforms on student achievement.* National Education Policy Center. http://epsl.asu.edu/epru/documents/EPSL-08030262-EPRU.pdf

Miron, G., Mathis, W., & Welner, K. (2015, February). *Review of separating fact from fiction.* National Education Policy Center. http://nepc.colorado.edu/

Miron, G., & Nelson, C. (2001). *Student academic achievement in charter schools: What we know and why we know so little.* National Center for the Study of Privatization in Education, Teachers College, Columbia University. http://ncspe.org/keepout/papers/00041/590_OP41.pdf

Miron, G., & Urschel, J. (2010). *Equal or fair? A study of revenues and expenditure in American charter schools.* Education and the Public Interest Center and Education Policy Research Unit. http://epicpolicy.org/

Miron, G., & Urschel, J. (2012). The impact of school choice reforms on student achievement. In G. Miron, K. Welner, P. Hinchey, & W. Mathis (Eds.), *Exploring the school choice universe: Evidence and recommendations* (pp. 65–88). Information Age.

Miron, G., Urschel, J., Mathis, W., & Tornquist, E. (2010). *Schools without diversity: Education management organizations, charter schools, and the demographic stratification of the American school system.* National Education Policy Center. http://nepc.colorado.edu/publication/schools-without-diversity

Miron, G., Urschel, J., & Saxton, N. (2011). *What makes KIPP work? A study of student characteristics, attrition, and school finance.* National Center for the Study of Privatization in Education, Teachers College, Columbia University. http://www.ncspe.org/

Miron, G., & Welner, K. G. (2012). Introduction. In G. Miron, K. Welner, P. Hinchey, & W. Mathis (Eds.), *Exploring the school choice universe: Evidence and recommendations* (pp. 1–16). Information Age.

Mishel, L. (2012, August 29). *Unions, inequality, and faltering middle-class wages.* Economic Policy Institute. https://www.epi.org/publication/ib342-unions-inequality-faltering-middle-class/

Mishel, L. (2015). *The opportunity dodge.* American Prospect. https://prospect.org/power/opportunity-dodge/

Mishel, L., & Davis, A. (2015, June 21). *Top CEOs make 300 times more than typical workers.* Economic Policy Institute. https://files.epi.org/2015/top-ceos-make-300-times-more-than-typical-workers.pdf

Mishler, W., & Rose, R. (2001). What are the origins of political trust? Testing institutional and cultural theories in post-communist societies. *Comparative Political Studies, 34,* 30–62.

Mitchell, C. (2016, August 8). As nation's students become more diverse, teaching corps hasn't kept pace. *Education Week.* http://blogs.edweek.org/edweek/learning-the-language/2016/08/students_are_more_diverse_teachers_aren't.html

Mitchell, M., Leachman, M., & Masterson, K. (2017, August 23). *A lost decade in higher education funding.* Center on Budget and Policy Priorities. https://www.cbpp.org/research/state-budget-and-tax/a-lost-decade-in-higher-education-funding

Mitgang, L. (2012). *The making of the principal: Five lessons in leadership training.* Wallace Foundation. https://www.wallacefoundation.org/knowledge-center/Documents/The-Making-of-the-Principal-Five-Lessons-in-Leadership-Training.pdf

Moe, T. (2006). Political control and the power of agent. *Journal of Law, Economics, and Organization, 22*(1), 1–29.

Moe, T. (2011). *Special interest: Teachers unions and America's public schools.* Brookings Institution Press.

Monaghan, A. (2014, November 13). U.S. wealth inequality—top 0.1% worth as much as the bottom 90%. *Guardian.* https://www.theguardian.com/business/2014 / nov/13/us-wealth-inequality-top-01-worth-as-much-as-the-bottom-90

Moore, S., Donaldson, M., Sick-Munger, M., Qazilbash, E., & Papay, J. (2007). *Leading the local: Teacher union presidents speak on change, challenges.* Educator Sector.

Morgan, S., & Poppe, E. (2012). The consequences of international comparisons for public support of K–12 education: Evidence from a national survey experiment. *Educational Researcher, 41*(7), 262–268.

Morton, B., & Dalton, B. (2007). *Changes in instructional hours in four subjects by public school teachers of grades 1 through 4.* National Center for Education Statistics. https://eric.ed.gov/?id=ED497041

Moser, M., Brown, H., Frank, R., Reynolds, T., Landberg, E., Alston, A., & Rosaldo, S. (2003). *The demand for information for educational decision making in the District of Columbia: A public discourse.* District of Columbia State Education Office.

Murnane, R., Willett, J., Kemple, J., Olsen, R., & Singer, J. (1991). *Who will teach: Policies that matter.* Harvard University Press.

Murphy, J. (1991). Title I of ESEA: The politics of implementing federal education reform. In A. R. Odden (Ed.), *Education policy implementation* (pp. 65–80). State University of New York Press.

Murphy, J., & Meyers, C. (2007). *Turning around failing schools: Leadership lessons from organizational sciences.* Corwin Press.

Murray, C. (1994). *Losing ground: American social policy, 1950–1980.* Basic Books.

Nakamura, R., & Smallwood, F. (1980). *The politics of policy implementation.* St. Martin's Press.

Naring, G., Briet, M., & Brouwers, A. (2006). Beyond demand-control: Emotional labour and symptoms of burnout in teachers. *Work and Stress, 20*(4), 303–315.

Nathanson, L., Corcoran, S., & Baker-Smith, C. (2013). *High school choice in NYC.* Research Alliance. https://steinhardt.nyu.edu/research_alliance/publications/hs_choice_low_achieving_students

National Alliance for Public Charter Schools. (2018). *Unionized charter schools, 2016–17.* https://www.publiccharters.org/sites/default/files/documents/20180–2/Unionized%20Charter%20Schools%2020161–7_0.pdf

National Association of Elementary School Principals. (n.d.). *A framework for safe and successful schools.* https://www.naesp.org/sites/default/files/Framework%20for%20 Safe%20and%20Successful%20School%20Environments_FINAL_0.pdf

National Center for Education Evaluation and Regional Assistance. (2017, January). *School Improvement Grants: Implementation and effectiveness.* Institute of Education Sciences. https://ies.ed.gov/ncee/pubs/20174013/pdf/20174013.pdf

National Center for Education Statistics. (2010a). *Percentage of public school 4th-graders in low-poverty and high-poverty schools, by race/ethnicity: 2009.* https://nces.ed.gov/ pubs2010/2010015/figures/figure_7_5b.asp

National Center for Education Statistics. (2010b). *PISA 2009 results.* http://nces. ed.gov/surveys/pisa/pisa 2009highlights.asp

National Center for Education Statistics. (n.d.-a). *Charter schools: Fast facts.* https:// nces.ed.gov/fastfacts/display.asp?id=30

National Center for Education Statistics. (n.d.-b). *Number and percentage distribution of public elementary and secondary school students, by percentage of students racial/ethnic group enrolled in the school and student's racial/ethnic group: Selected years, fall 1995 through fall 2015.* https://nces.ed.gov/programs/digest/d17/tables/dt17_216.55.asp

National Center for Education Statistics. (n.d.-c). *Number and percentage distribution of public elementary and secondary school students, by percentage of minority enrollment in the school and student's racial/ethnic group: Selected years, fall 1995 through fall 2014.* https://nces.ed.gov/programs/digest/d16/tables/dt16_216.50.asp

National Center on Education and the Economy. (2013). *What does it really mean to be college and work ready?* Author.

National Commission on Educational Excellence. (1983). *A nation at risk: The imperative for educational reform.* http://www.ed.gov/pubs/NatAtRisk/risk.html

National Commission on Teaching and America's Future. (2007). *The high cost of teacher turnover.* https://eric.ed.gov/?ie=ED498001

National Commission on Teaching and America's Future. (2010). *Who will teach: Experience matters.* http://nctaf.org/wp-content/uploads/2012/01/NCTAF-Who-Will-Teach-Experience-Matters-2010-Report.pdf

National Commission on Teaching and America's Future. (2011). *State of the states: Trends and early lessons on teacher evaluation and effectiveness policies.* http://www.nctq. org/p/publications/docs/nctq_stateOfTheStates.pdf

National Committee for Responsive Philanthropy. (1999). *One billion dollars for ideas: Conservative think tanks in the 1990s.* Author.

National Conference of State Legislatures. (n.d.). *Chart on right to work states.* http:// www.ncsl.org/research/labor-and-employment/right-to-work-laws-and-bills.aspx

National Council on Disability. (2018). *Broken promises: The underfunding of IDEA.* https://www.ncd.gov/sites/default/files/NCD_BrokenPromises_508.pdf

National Council on Teacher Quality. (2014). *National summary: Are new teachers being prepared for college and career readiness standards?* https://www.nctq.org/

dmsView/2014_State_Teacher_Policy_Yearbook_National_Summary_NCTQ_ Report

National Education Association. (2015, December 2). *NEA welcomes historic step to usher in new era in public education.* http://www.nea.org/home/64735.htm

National Institutes of Health. (n.d.). *Any anxiety disorder.* https://www.nimh.nih.gov/ health/statistics/any-anxiety-disorder.shtml

National Opportunity to Learn Campaign. (2013, April 23). *The color of school closures.* http://www.otlcampaign.org/blog/2013/04/05/color-school-closures

National Right to Work Committee. (2016). *Right to work states timeline.* https://nrtwc. org/facts/state-right-to-work-timeline-2016/

Naylor, B. (2019, November 18). *Impeachment hearings illustrate longstanding conflict throughout Trump's presidency.* NPR. https://www.npr.org/2019/11/18/780563096/ impeachment-hearings-illustrate-longstanding-conflict-throughout-trumps-presiden

Ness, A. (2017, August 2). Teachers spend hundreds of dollars a year on school supplies. That's a problem. *Education Week.* https://www.edweek.org/tm/ articles/2017/08/02/teachers-spend-hundreds-of-dollars-a-year.html

Newfield, C. (2011). *Unmaking the public university.* Harvard University Press.

Newlin Carney, E. (1994, June 18). Still trying to reinvent government. *National Journal,* pp. 1442–1444.

Newton, X., Darling-Hammond, L., Haertel, E., & Thomas, E. (2010). Value-added modeling of teacher effectiveness: An exploration of stability across models and contexts. *Education Policy and Analysis Archives, 18*(23). http://epaa.asu.edu/ojs/ article/view/810/858

New York City Working Group on School Transformation. (2012, April). *The way forward: From sanctions to supports.* Annenberg Institute for School Reform. http:// annenberginstitute.org/pdf/SchoolTransformationReport.pdf

New York University. (2016, October 5). *Students of all races prefer teachers of color, finds NYU Steinhardt study.* https://www.nyu.edu/about/news-publications/news/2016/ october/students-of-all-races-preferteachers-of-color—finds-nyu-steinh.html

Ng, J., & Peter, L. (2010). Should I stay or should I go? Examining the career choices of alternatively licensed teachers in urban schools. *Urban Review, 42,* 123–142.

Nias, J. (1996). Thinking about feeling: The emotions in teaching. *Cambridge Journal of Education, 26*(3), 293–306.

Nichols, S., & Berliner, D. C. (2007). *Collateral damage: How high-stakes testing corrupts America's schools.* Harvard Education Press.

Nichols, S., Glass, G., & Berliner, D. (2006). High-stakes testing and student achievement: Does accountability pressure increase student learning? *Education Policy Analysis Archives, 14*(1). http://epaa.asu.edu/epaa/v14n1/

Nixon, R. M. (1972, October 21). Radio address on the philosophy of government. In *Public papers of the president of the United States* (pp. 997–1000). Washington, DC: Office of the Federal Register, National Archives and Records Service.

No Child Left Behind, P.L. 1071–10 (2001).

Noddings, N. (1992). *The challenge to care in schools.* Teachers College Press.

Noddings, N. (1995). *The challenge to care in schools: An alternative approach to education.* Teachers College Press.

No Kid Hungry. (2015a, June 30). *Summer hunger is too expensive to ignore.* https://www.nokidhungry.org/sites/default/files/NKH_MicroReport_SummerHunger.pdf

No Kid Hungry. (2015b). *Summer nutrition program social impact analysis.* http://bestpractices.nokidhungry.org/resource/summer-nutrition-program-social-impact-analysis

No Kid Hungry. (2020, April 8). *Facts about child hunger in America.* https://www.nokidhungry.org/who-we-are/hunger-facts

Norton, M., & Ariely, D. (2011). Building a better America—one wealth quintile at a time. *Perspectives on Psychological Science, 6*(1), 9–12.

Nownes, A., Thomas, C., & Hrebenar, R. (2007). Interest groups in the states. In V. Gray & R. Hanson (Eds.), *Politics in the American states: A comparative analysis* (9th ed., pp. 98–126). CQ Press.

Oakes, J. (1985). *Keeping track: How schools structure inequality.* Yale University Press.

Oakes, J., & Rogers, J. (2005). *Learning power: Organizing for education and justice.* Teachers College Press.

Obama, B. (2010, July 29). *Obama education status quo morally inexcusable.* http://www.whitehouse.gov/blog/2010/07/29/president-obama-education-status-quo-morally-inexcusable

O'Brien, E., & Dervarics, C. (2013). *Which way up? What research says about school turnaround strategies.* Center for Public Education, National School Boards Association.

O'Brien, M. (2014, October 22). The bottom 90 percent are poorer today than they were in 1987. *Washington Post.* http://www.washingtonpost.com/blogs/wonkblog/wp/2014/10/22/the-bottom-90-percent-are-poorer-today-than-they-were-in-1987/

O'Day, H. (2002). Complexity, accountability, and school improvement. *Harvard Educational Review, 72*(3), 1–31.

Odden, A. (1991). The evolution of education policy implementation. In A. Odden (Ed.), *Education policy implementation* (pp. 1–12). State University of New York Press.

Olson, M. (1971). *The logic of collective action: Public goods and the theory of groups.* Harvard University Press. (Original work published 1965)

Opfer, C., & Han, J. (2017, August 15). Labor organizing in right-to-work states is numbers game. *Bloomberg BNA.* https://www.bna.com/labor-organizing-righttowork-n73014463154/

Orfield, G. (2009). *Reviving the goal of an integrated society: A 21st century challenge.* Civil Rights Project. http://civilrightsproject.ucla.edu/

Orfield, G., & Frankenberg, E. (2014). *Brown at 60: Great progress, a long retreat and an uncertain future.* Civil Rights Project. http://civilrightsproject.ucla.edu/

Orfield, G., Kucsera, J., & Siegel-Hawley, G. (2012). *E pluribus . . . separation: Deepening double segregation for more students.* Civil Rights Project. http://civilrightsproject. ucla.edu/

Orfield, G., & Lee, C. (2005). *Why segregation matters: Poverty and educational inequality.* Civil Rights Project at Harvard University. http://civilrightsproject.ucla.edu/ research/k-12-education/integration-and-diversity/why-segregation-matters- poverty-and-educational-inequality/orfield-why-segregation-matters-2005.pdf

Orfield, G., & Lee, C. (2006). *Racial transformation and the changing nature of segregation.* Civil Rights Project at Harvard University. http://civilrightsproject.ucla.edu/

Orfield, M. (2015). Milliken, Meredith, and metropolitan segregation. *UCLA Law Review, 62*(2), 364–462.

Organization for Economic Co-operation and Development. (2011). *Building a high- quality teaching profession: Lessons from around the world.* http://www2.ed.gov/about/ inits/ed/internationaled/background.pdf

Organization for Economic Co-operation and Development. (2013). *Education at a glance 2013: OECD indicators.* http://www.oecd.org/education/eag2013%20(eng)— FINAL%2020%20June %202013.pdf

Organization for Economic Co-operation and Development. (2017). *Education at a glance 2017: OECD indicators.* https://www.oecd-ilibrary.org/education/education- at-a-glance-2017_eag-2017-en

Orr, M., & Rogers, J. (2010). *Public engagement for public education: Joining forces to revitalize democracy and equalize schools.* Stanford University Press.

Osborne, D., & Gaebler, T. (1992). *Reinventing government: How the entrepreneurial spirit is transforming the public sector.* Plume.

Ospina, S., & Dodge, J. (2005). It's about time: Catching method up to meaning— the usefulness of narrative inquiry in public administration research. *Public Administration Review, 65*(2), 143–157.

Ossei-Owusu, S. (2013, July 16). Turn off the lights: Public school closings, minority youth and bleak futures. *Huffington Post.* http://www.huffingtonpost.com/shaun- osseiowusu/turn-off-the-lights-publi_b_3592473.html

Ostrom, E. (1996). Crossing the great divide: Coproduction, synergy and development. *World Development, 24*(6), 1073–1087.

Otterman, S. (2010, October 12). Lauded Harlem schools have their own problems. *New York Times.* https://www.nytimes.com/2010/10/13/education/13harlem.html

Paige, R. (2003a, March 12). *Paige blasts "soft bigotry of low expectations": Says every school must teach every student to high level with high standards.* National Right to Read Foundation. http://www.nrrf.org/paige31–20–3.htm

Paige, R. (2003b, March 12). *Remarks before the Commonwealth Club of California.* http:// www.nje3.org/index.php/remarks-of-the-honorable-rod-paige

Paige, R. (2004, February 23). *Secretary Paige issues apology for comment about NEA.* http://www2.ed.gov/news/pressreleases/2004/02/02232004.html

Paige, R. (2007). *The war against hope: How teachers' unions hurt children, hinder teachers, and endanger public education.* Thomas Nelson.

Palumbo, A., & Scott, A. (2005). Classical social theory I: Marx and Durkheim. In A. Harrington (Ed.), *Modern social theory* (pp. 40–62). Oxford University Press.

Papay, J. (2011). Different tests, different answers: The stability of teacher value-added estimates across outcome measures. *American Educational Research Journal, 48*(1), 163–193.

Papay, J., & Johnson, S. (2012). Is PAR a good investment? Understanding the costs and benefits of teacher peer assistance and review programs. *Educational Policy, 26*(5), 696–729.

Partelow, L., Spong, A., Brown, C., & Johnson, S. (2017). *America needs more teachers of color and a more selective teaching profession.* Center for American Progress. https://cdn.americanprogress.org/content/uploads/2017 /09/15120738/ TeacherDiversity-report1.pdf

Patashnik, E. (2008). *Reforms at risk: What happens after major policy changes are enacted?* Princeton University Press.

Payne, C. (2010). *So much reform, so little change.* Harvard Education Press.

PDK. (1998–2018). Gallup poll of the public's attitudes toward the public schools. *Phi Delta Kappan.* https://pdkpoll.org/

PDK. (2001, August 23). Public schools get highest ratings in 30 years. *Phi Delta Kappan.* https://news.gallup.com/poll/4819/public-schools-get-highest-ratings-years.aspx

PDK. (2015, December). Testing doesn't measure up for Americans. *Phi Delta Kappan.* https://www.region10.org/r10website/assets/File/pdkpoll47_2015.pdf

PDK. (2017, September). *Academic achievement isn't the only mission: Americans overwhelmingly support investments in career preparation, personal skills.* https:// pdkpoll.org/wp-content/uploads/2020/05/pdkpoll49_2017.pdf

PDK. (2018, September). Teaching: Respect but dwindling appeal. *Phi Delta Kappan.* https://kappanonline.org/magazine-issue/the-50th-annual-pdk-poll-of-the-publics-attitudes-toward-the-public-schools/

Pear, R. (2004, February 24). Education chief calls union "terrorist," then recants. *New York Times,* p. A20.

Peltier, M. (2011, March 24). *Florida law backs merit pay, ends tenure for new teachers.* Reuters. https://www.reuters.com/article/us-florida-teachers-idUSTRE72N7K320110324

Peske, H., Liu, E., Johnson, S., Kauffman, D., & Kardos, S. (2001). The next generation of teachers: Changing conceptions of careers in teaching. *Phi Delta Kappan, 4*(83), 304–311.

Peterson, T. K. (2013, February 5). *Expanding minds and opportunities: Leveraging the power of afterschool and summer learning for student success.* 50 State After School Network. http://www.statewideafterschoolnetworks.net/content/expanding-minds

Pew Research Center. (2014). *The rising cost of not going to college*. https://www.
pewsocialtrends.org/2014/02/11/the-rising-cost-of-not-going-to-college/

Pew Research Center. (2019, January 24). *Public's 2019 priorities: Economy, health care,
education and security all near top of list*. https://www.people-press.org/2019/01/24/
publics-2019-priorities-economy-health-care-education-and-security-all-near-top-
of-list/

Phillips, M. (2011). Parenting, time use, and disparities in academic outcomes. In G.
Duncan & R. Murnane (Eds.), *Whither opportunity? Rising inequality, schools, and
children's life chances* (pp. 207–228). Russell Sage Foundation.

Pierson, P. (1993, June 13). When effect becomes cause: Policy feedback and political
change. *World Politics*, pp. 595–628.

Pierson, P. (1996). The new politics of the welfare state. *World Politics, 48*(2), 143–179.

Pilkington, E. (2017, August 30). Rightwing alliance plots assault to "defund
and defang" America's unions. *Guardian*. https://www.theguardian.com/us-
news/2017/aug/30/rightwing-alliance-unions-defund-defang

Pincus, F. (1985). From equity to excellence: The rebirth of educational conservatism.
In B. Gross & R. Gross (Eds.), *The great school debate: Which way for American
education?* (pp. 329–344). Simon and Schuster.

Pinsker, J. (2015, July 23). America is even less socially mobile than most economists
thought. *Atlantic*. https://www.theatlantic.com/business/archive/20/15/07/
america-social-mobility-parents-income/399311/

PISA. (2001). *Knowledge and skills for life: First results from PISA 2000*. OECD Publishing.

Piven, F., & Cloward, R. (1989). *Why Americans don't vote*. Pantheon Books.

Pizmony-Levy, O., & Saraisky, N. (2016, August). *Who opts out and why: Results from
a national survey on opting out of standardized tests*. Teachers College, Columbia
University. https://www.tc.columbia.edu/media/news/docs/Opt_ Out_National-
Survey——FINAL-FULL-REPORT.pdf

Pollak, S., & Luby, J. (2015, July). Poverty's most insidious damage: The developing
brain. *JAMA Pediatrics, 169*(9), 822–829.

Portes, A. (1998). Social capital: Its origins and applications in modern sociology.
Annual Review of Sociology, 24, 1–24.

Portes, A. (2000). The two meanings of social capital. *Sociological Forum, 15*(1), 1–12.

Portnoy, J., & Rein, L. (2017, January 4). House Republicans revive obscure rule that
allows them to slash the pay of individual federal workers to $1. *Washington Post*.
https://www.washingtonpost.com/local/virginia-politics/house-republicans-
revive-obscure-rule-that-could-allow-them-to-slash-the-pay-of-individual-federal-
workers-to-1/2017/01/04/4e80c990-d2b21-1e69–45a-76f69a399dd5_story.html

Potter, H., Quick, K., & Davies, E. (2016). *A new wave of school integration: Districts
and charters pursuing socioeconomic diversity*. Century Foundation. https://tcf.org/
content/report/a-new-wave-of-school-integration/

Pressman, J., & Wldavsky, A. (1984). *Implementation* (3rd ed.). University of California
Press.

Prothero, A. (2015, February 3). Consultants steer parents through maze of school choice. *Education Week*. http://www.edweek.org/ew/articles/2015/02/04/consultants-steer-parents-through-maze-of-school.html

Putnam, H., & Walsh, K. (2019). *A fair chance: Simple steps to strengthen and diversify the teacher workforce*. National Council on Teacher Quality. https://www.nctq.org/publications/A-Fair-Chance

Putnam, R (1995). Bowling alone: America's declining social capital. *Journal of Democracy, 6*(1), 65–78.

Putnam, R. (2000). *Bowling alone: The collapse and revival of American community*. Simon and Schuster.

Putnam, R., Leonardi, R., & Nanetti, R. (1994). *Making democracy work: Civic traditions in modern Italy*. Princeton University Press.

Radin, B. (2006). *Challenging the performance movement: Accountability, complexity, and democratic values*. Georgetown University Press.

Rainie, L., Keeter, S., & Perrin, A. (2019, July 22). *Trust and distrust in America*. Pew Research. https://www.pewresearch.org/politics/2019/07/22/trust-and-distrust-in-america/

Ravitch, D. (1985). *The troubled crusade: American education: 1945–1980*. Basic Books.

Ravitch, D. (2010). *The death and life of the great American school system: How testing and choice are undermining education*. Basic Books.

Ray, R., & Gibbons, A. (2021, November). *Why are states banning critical race theory?* Brookings Institution. https://www.brookings.edu/blog/fixgov/2021/07/02/why-are-states-banning-critical-race-theory/

Raymond, M. E. (2009). *Multiple choice: Charter school performance in 16 states*. Stanford University Press.

Reardon, S. (2009). *Review of "How New York City's charter schools affect achievement."* National Education Policy Center. http://nepc.colorado.edu/ thinktank/review-how-New-York-City-Charter

Reardon, S. (2011). The widening academic achievement gap between the rich and the poor: New evidence and possible explanations. In R. Murnane & G. Duncan (Eds.), *Whither opportunity? Rising inequality and the uncertain life chances of low-income children* (pp. 91–115). Russell Sage Foundation Press.

Reardon, S. (2015). *School segregation and racial academic achievement gaps*. Center for Education Policy Analysis. https://cepa.stanford.edu/sites/default/ files/wp151–2v201510.pdf

Reardon, S., Grewal, E., Kalogrides, D., & Greenberg, E. (2012). Brown fades: The end of court-ordered school desegregation and the resegregation of American public schools. *Journal of Policy Analysis and Management, 31*(4), 876–904.

Reardon, S., Kalogrides, D., Fahle, E., Podolsky, A., & Zarate, R. (2018). The relationship between test item format and gender achievement gaps on math and ELA tests in fourth and eighth grades. Educational Researcher, 284-294. https://journals.sagepub.com/doi/pdf/10.3102/0013189X18762106

Reardon, S., & Yun, J. (2002). *Private school racial enrollments and segregation.* Civil Rights Project, Harvard University.

Reay, D. (1998). *Class work: Mothers' involvement in their children's primary schooling.* University College London.

Reay, D. (2004a). Exclusivity, exclusion, and social class in urban education markets in the United Kingdom. *Urban Education, 39*(5), 537–560.

Reay, D. (2004b). Mostly "roughs and toughs": Social class, race and representation in innercity schooling. *Sociology, 38,* 1005–1023.

Reay, D., & Lucey, H. (2003). The limits of "choice": Children and inner city schooling. *Sociology, 37,* 121.

Rebarger, T., & Zgainer, A. (2014). *Survey of America's charter schools.* Center for Education Reform. https://www.edreform.com/wp-content/uploads/2014/02/2014CharterSchoolSurveyFINAL.pdf

Rebell, M. (2007). *Ensuring successful remedies in education adequacy litigations: A comparative institutional perspective.* Campaign for Educational Equity, Teachers College, Columbia University. http://www.centerforeducationalequity.org/events-page/equity-symposia/2007-equal-educational-opportunity-what-now/papers/Ensuring-Successful-Remedies-110–40–7.pdf

Reckdahl, K. (2015, December 15). Training more Black men to become teachers. *Atlantic.* https://www.theatlantic.com/education/archive/2015/12/programs-teachers-african-american-men/420306/

Reich, R. (1988). *The power of public ideas.* Harvard University Press.

Reiley, L. (2019, December 4). Trump administration tightens work requirements for SNAP, which could cut hundreds of thousands from food stamps. *Washington Post.* https://www.washingtonpost.com/business/2019/12/04/trump-administration-tightens-work-requirements-snap-which-could-cut-hundreds-thousands-food-stamps/

Reininger, M. (2011). *Hometown disadvantage? It depends on where you're from.* Educational Evaluation and Policy Analysis. http://eepa.aera.net/

Research for Action. (2013a, March). *School closings policy.* PACER: Issue Brief. http://www.researchforaction.org/wp-content/uploads/2013/03/RFA-PACER-School-Closing-Policy-Brief-March-2013.pdf

Research for Action. (2013b, February). *School District of Philadelphia school closings: An analysis of student achievement.* http://www.researchforaction.org/wp-content/uploads/2013/02/RFA-School-Closure-AYP-Analysis-Feb-2013-Revised_Closing-and-Consolidations.pdf

Resmovits, J. (2011a, September 23). No Child Left Behind reform: Will Obama's waiver plan really diminish "teaching to the test"? *Huffington Post.* http://www.huffingtonpost.com/2011/09/23/no-child-left-behind-reform- obama_n_978450.html

Resmovits, J. (2011b, July 26). With No Child Left Behind overhaul stalled, more schools "failing." *Huffington Post.* http://www.huffingtonpost.com/2011/07/26/no-child-left-behind-failing-schools_n_910067.html

Resmovits, J. (2015, December 10). Obama signs Every Student Succeeds Act, marking the end of an era. *L.A. Times.* http://www.latimes.com/local/education/standardized-testing/la-me-edu-essa-obama-signs-end-no-child-left-behind-20151210-story.html

Restuccia, A. (2018, March 30). Federal workers spill on life in Trump's Washington. *Politico.* https://www.politico.com/story/2018/03/30/trump-washington-civil-servants-492347

Restuccia, A., Guillen, A., & Cook, N. (2017, January 24). Information lockdown hits Trump's federal agencies. *Politico.* http://www.politico.com/story/2017/01/federal-agencies-trump-information-lockdown-234122

Rhodes, J. (2014). *An education in politics: The origins and evolution of No Child Left Behind.* Cornell University Press.

Rice, D. (2019, August 26). *Strengthening housing vouchers should be priority in 2020 funding bills.* Center on Budget and Policy Priorities. https://www.cbpp.org/research/housing/strengthening-housing-vouchers-should-be-priority-in-2020-funding-bills

Rice, D., Schmit, S., & Matthews, H. (2019, April 26). *Child care and housing: Big expenses with too little help available.* Center on Budget and Policy Priorities. https://www.cbpp.org/research/housing/child-care-and-housing-big-expenses-with-too-little-help-available

Rice, J., & Croninger, R. (2005). Resource generation, reallocation, or depletion: An analysis of the impact of reconstitution on school capacity. *Leadership and Policy in Schools, 4*(2), 73–104.

Rice, J., & Malen, B. (2003). The human costs of education reform: The case of school reconstitution. *Educational Administration Quarterly, 39*(5), 635–666.

Rich, M. (2016a, March 16). Charter schools suspend Black and disabled students more, study says. *New York Times.* https://www.nytimes.com/2016/03/17/us/charter-schools-suspend-black-and-disabled-students-more-study-says.html

Rich, M. (2016b, April 13). Teacher tenure is challenged again in a Minnesota lawsuit. *New York Times.* https://www.nytimes.com/2016/04/14/us/teacher-tenure-is-challenged-again-in-a-minnesota-lawsuit.html

Rich, M., & Hurdle, J. (2013, March). Rational decisions and heartbreak on school closings. *New York Times.* http://www.nytimes.com/2013/03/09/education/rational-decisions-and-heartbreak-on-school-closings.html

Ripley, A. (2014, June 17). Higher calling: To improve our schools, we need to make it harder to become a teacher. *Slate.* https://slate.com/human-interest/2014/06/american-schools-need-better-teachers-so-lets-make-it-harder-to-become-one.html

Rivkin, S., Hanushek, E., & Kain, J. (2005). Teachers, schools and academic achievement. *Econometrics, 73*(2), 417–458.

Roberts, S. (2006a, December 28). Infamous "drop dead" was never said by Ford. *New York Times*, p. A30.

Roberts, S. (2006b, December 31). When the city's bankruptcy was just a few words away. *New York Times*, p. A24.

Rockoff, J. (2004). The impact of individual teachers on student achievement: Evidence from panel data. *American Economic Review, 94*(2), 247–252.

Roe, E. (1994). *Narrative policy analysis*. Duke University Press.

Romo, V. (2018, April 12). *Arizona governor agrees to 20 percent raise for protesting teachers*. NPR. https://www.npr.org/sections/thetwo-way/2018/04/12/602023664/arizona-governor-agrees-to-20-percent-raise-for-protesting-teachers

Ronfeldt, M., Loeb, S., & Wyckoff, J. (2013). How teacher turnover harms student achievement. *American Educational Research Journal, 50*(1), 4–36.

Roscigno, V., & Ainsworth-Darnell, J. (1999). Race, cultural capital, and educational resources: Persistent inequalities and achievement returns. *Sociology of Education, 72*(3), 158–178.

Rosenbaum, J., & DeLuca, S. (2008). What kinds of neighborhoods change lives? The Chicago Gautreaux Housing Program and recent mobility programs. *Indiana Law Review, 41*, 653–662.

Rosenbaum, J., & DeLuca, S. (2014). Does changing neighborhoods change lives? The Chicago Gautreaux Housing Program. In D. Grusky (Ed.), *Social stratification: Race, class and gender in sociological perspective* (pp. 393–399). Westview Press.

Rosenberger, L., & Schulman, L. (2017, April 14). How President Trump's State Department is sabotaging America's future leadership. *Washington Post*. https://www.washingtonpost.com/news/posteverything/wp/2017/08/14/how-president-trumps-state-department-is-sabotaging-americas-future-leadership/

Rosenfeld, J. (2018, August 13). *The meaning of labor's win in Missouri*. American Prospect. https://prospect.org/article/meaning-labors-win-missouri

Rosenfeld, J., Denice, P., & Laird, J. (2016, August 30). *Union decline lowers wages of nonunion workers*. Economic Policy Institute. https://files.epi.org/pdf/112811.pdf

Rosenholtz, S. (1991). *Teachers' workplace: The social organization of schools*. Teachers College Press.

Rosenthal, A. (1966). Pedagogues and power: A descriptive survey. *Urban Affairs Review, 2*(1), 83–102.

Rosner, J. (2001). Disparate outcomes by design: University admissions tests. *Berkeley La Raza Law Journal, 12*(2), 377–386.

Rossman, S. (2018, March 30). Teachers are striking all over. What is going on? *USA Today*. https://www.usatoday.com/story/news/nation-now/2018/03/30/teachers-striking-oklahoma-west-virginia-arizona-kentucky/472742002/

Rotherham, A. (2010, October 28). Does income-based school integration work? *Time*. http://content.time.com/time/ nation/article/0,8599,2027858,00.html

Rothstein, J. (2000). Does competition among public schools benefit students and taxpayers? A comment on Hoxby. *American Economic Review, 97*(5), 2026–2037.

Rothstein, J. (2009). Student sorting and bias in value-added estimation: Selection on observables and unobservables. *Education Finance and Policy, 4*(4), 537–571.

Rothwell, J., & Massey, D. (2010). Density zoning and class segregation in U.S. metropolitan areas. *Social Science Quarterly, 91*(5), 1123–1143.

Roy, J., & Mishel, L. (2005). *Advantage none: Re-examining Hoxby's finding of charter school benefits* (Briefing Paper No. 158). Economic Policy Institute.

Rueben, K., & Randall, M. (2017, November 27). *Balanced budget requirements: How states limit deficit spending.* Urban Institute. https://www.urban.org/research/publication/balanced-budget-requirements

Rumberger, R., & Larson, K. (1998). Student mobility and school functioning in the early grades. *Journal of Educational Research, 89*(6), 365–369.

Rusk, D. (2011). "Housing policy is school policy": A commentary. In P. Tegeler (Ed.), *Finding common ground: Coordinating housing and education policy to promote integration* (pp. 21–30). Poverty and Race Research Action Council. https://www.prrac.org/pdf/HousingEducationReport-October2011.pdf

Sack, J. (2001, December 5). ESEA negotiators near accords, but snags remain. *Education Week,* pp. 21, 28, 31.

Sahlberg, P. (2011). *Finnish lessons: What can the world learn from educational change in Finland.* Teachers College Press.

Salamon, L. (Ed.). (2002). *The tools of government: A guide to the new governance.* Oxford University Press.

Saltzman, G. (1985). Bargaining laws as a cause and consequence of the growth of teacher unionism. *Industrial and Labor Relations Review, 38*(3), 335–351.

Saltzman, G. (1988). Public-sector bargaining laws really matter: Evidence from Ohio and Illinois. In R. Freeman & C. Ichniowski (Eds.), *When public sector workers unionize* (pp. 41–78). University of Chicago Press.

Samberg, L., & Sheeran, M. (2000). *Community school models.* Coalition for Community Schools. http://eric.edu.gov/?id=ED466996

Sampson, R., Sharkey, P., & Raudenbush, S. (2008). Durable effects of concentrated disadvantage on verbal ability among African-American children. *Proceedings of the National Academy of Sciences of the United States of America, 105*(3), 845–852.

Santelices, M., & Wilson, M. (2010). Unfair treatment? The case of Freedle, the SAT, and the standardization approach to differential item functioning. *Harvard Education Review, 80*(1), 106–133. https://bearcenter.berkeley.edu/sites/default/files/Wilson%20%2322.pdf

Sartain, L., Stoelings, S., & Krone, E. (2010). *Rethinking teacher evaluation: Findings from the first year of the Excellence in Teaching Project in Chicago public schools.* Consortium on Chicago School Research. https://consortium.uchicago.edu/sites/default/files/publications/Teacher%20Eval%20Final.pdf

Sattin-Bajaj, C. (2014). *Unaccompanied minors: Immigrant youth, school choice, and the pursuit of equity. Harvard Education Press.*

Sawchuk, S. (2013a, October 14). Groups honing real-time teacher-performance exam. *Education Week.* https://www.edweek.org/ew/articles/2014/10/15/08performance. h34.html

Sawchuk, S. (2013b, May 14). States' teacher-exam bar set low, federal data show. *Education Week.* http://www.edweek.org/ew/articles/2013/05/15/31tests.h32.html

Sawchuk, S. (2013c, February 5). Teachers' ratings still high despite new measures. *Education Week.* http://www.edweek.org/ew/articles/2013/02/06/20evaluate_ ep.h32.html

Sawchuk, S. (2014a, September 23). Due process laws vary for teachers by state. *Education Week.* https://www.edweek.org/ew/articles/2014/09/24/05tenure.h34. html

Sawchuk, S. (2014b, December 3). Higher academic standing seen among recent New York teacher hires. *Teacher Beat.* http://blogs.edweek.org/edweek/ teacherbeat/2014/12/higher_academic_standing_seen_in_recent_new_york_ teacher_hires.html

Scafidi, B., Sjoquist, D., & Stinebrickner, T. (2008). Race, poverty, and teacher mobility. *Economics of Education Review, 26,* 145–159.

Schanzenback, D., Boddy, D., Mumford, M., & Nantz, G. (2016, March). *Fourteen economic facts on education and opportunity.* The Hamilton Project. http://www. hamiltonproject.org/assets/files/education_facts.pdf

Schattschneider, E. (1960). *The Semisovereign people: A realist's view of democracy in America.* Holt, Rinehart, and Winston.

Schmidt, V. (2008). Discursive institutionalism: The explanatory power of ideas and discourse. *Annual Review of Political Science, 11,* 303–326.

Schmitt, J. (2018, January 25). *Biggest gains in union membership in 2017 were for younger workers.* Economic Policy Institute. https://www.epi.org/publication/biggest- gains-in-union-membership-in-2017-were-for-younger-workers

Schneider, A., & Ingram, H. (1990). Behavioral assumptions of policy tools. *Journal of Politics, 52*(2), 510–529.

Schneider, A., & Ingram, H. (1993). Social construction of target populations: Implications for politics and policy. *American Political Science Review, 87*(2), 334–347.

Schneider, A., & Ingram, H. (1997). *Policy design for democracy.* University Press of Kansas.

Schneider, A., & Ingram, H. (2005a). A response to Peter deLeon. *Public Administration Review, 65*(5), 638–640.

Schneider, A., & Ingram, H. (Eds.). (2005b). *Deserving and entitled: Constructions and public policy.* State University of New York Press.

Schneider, M. (2002, November). *Do school facilities affect academic outcomes?* National Clearinghouse for Educational Facilities. http://www.ncef.org/pubs/outcomes.pdf

Schneider, M., & Buckley, J. (2002). What do parents want from schools? Evidence from the internet. *Educational Evaluation and Policy Analysis, 24*(2), 133–144.

Schneider, M., Marschall, M., Teske, P., & Roch, C. (1998). School choice and culture wars in the classroom: What different parents seek from education. *Social Science Quarterly, 79*(3), 489–502.

Schofield, J. (2005). Review of research on school desegregation's impact on elementary and secondary school students. In J. Banks & C. M. Banks (Eds.), *Handbook of research on multicultural education* (pp. 597–616). Macmillan.

Schott Foundation. (2013). *The color of school closures.* http://www.otlcampaign.org/sites/default/files/school-closings.jpg

Schreiber, N. (2018, June 27). Labor unions will be smaller after Supreme Court decision but maybe not weaker. *New York Times.* https://www.nytimes.com/2018/06/27/business/economy/supreme-court-unions-future.html

Schuetz, J. (2018, July 10). *Under US housing policies, homeowners mostly win, while renters mostly lose.* Brookings Institution. https://www.brookings.edu/research/ under-us-housing-policies-homeowners-mostly-win-while-renters-mostly-lose/

Schuetz, J. (2020, January 7). *To improve housing affordability, we need better alignment of zoning, taxes, and subsidies.* Brookings Institution. https://www.brookings.edu/policy2020/bigideas/to-improve-housing-affordability-we-need-better-alignment-of-zoning-taxes-and-subsidies/

Schulman, L. (2018, September 7). Civil servants can't stop Trump. Stop asking them to. *Washington Post.* https://www.washingtonpost.com/outlook/civil-servants-cant-stop-trump-stop-asking-them-to/2018/09/06/6dd7ccbc-a6eb-11e8-a6569–43eefab5daf_story.html

Schutz, P., & Pekrun, R. (2007). *Emotion in education.* Academic Press.

Schutz, P., & Zembylas, M. (Eds.). (2009). *Advances in teacher emotion research: The impact on teachers' lives.* Springer.

Schwartz, H. (2010). *Housing policy is school policy: Economically integrative housing promotes academic success in Montgomery County, Maryland.* Century Foundation. https://tcf.org/assets/downloads/tcf-Schwartz.pdf

Schwarz, A., Stiefel, L., & Chalico, L. (2007). *The multiple dimensions of student mobility and implications for academic performance: Evidence from New York City elementary and middle school students.* Education Finance Research Consortium.

Schweinhart, L., Barnett, S., & Belfield, C. (2005). *Lifetime effects: The High/Scope Perry Preschool Study through age 40.* High/Scope Foundation. https://highscope.org/perry-preschool-project/

Sciarra, D. (2012, December 18). Latest Race to the Top grants go to states at bottom of school funding equity. *Huffington Post.* http://www.huffingtonpost.com/david-sciarra/race-to-the-top-funding_b_2317281.html

Scott, J. (2009). The politics of venture philanthropy in charter school policy and advocacy. *Educational Policy, 23*(1), 106–136.

Semuels, A. (2017, July 5). From "not in my backyard" to "yes in my backyard." *Atlantic.* https://www.theatlantic.com/business/archive/2017/07/yimby-groups-pro-development/532437/

Senior, J. (2010). The junior meritocracy. *New York Magazine.* http://nymag.com/news/features/63427/

Shanahan, E., Jones, M., & McBeth, M. (2011). Policy narratives and policy processes. *Policy Studies Journal, 39*(3), 535–561.

Shapiro, T., Meschede, T., & Osoro, S. (2013, February). *The roots of the widening racial wealth gap: Explaining the Black–White economic divide.* https://heller.brandeis.edu/iasp/pdfs/racial-wealth-equity/racial-wealth-gap/roots-widening-racial-wealth-gap.pdf

Shear, M., & Anderson, N. (2009, July 23). President Obama discusses new "Race to the Top" program. *Washington Post.* http://www.washingtonpost.com/wp-dyn/content/article/2009/07/23/AR200907230293

Shen, A. (2013, May 6). *Chicago school officials admit shuttering schools won't save as much money as they thought.* Think Progress. http://thinkprogress.org/education/2013/05/06/1962561/chicago-schools-save-money/

Shepard, L. (1987). The case for bias in tests of achievement and scholastic aptitude. In S. Modgil & C. Modgil (Eds.), *Arthur Jensen: Consensus and controversy* (pp. 177–190). Falmer Press.

Shepherd, K. (2021, September 1). Texas parents accused a Black principal of promoting critical race theory. The district has now suspended him. *Washington Post.* http://www.washingtonpost.com/nation/2021/09/01/texas-principal-critical-race-theory/

Shireman, R. (2021, September 15). *The campaign to double the Pell Grant is well-intentioned, but must lead to improved affordability and diversity.* Century Foundation. https://tcf.org/content/commentary/campaign-double-pell-grant-well-intentioned-must-lead-improved-affordability-diversity/

Shores, K., & Steinberg, M. (2017, August). *The impact of the Great Recession on student achievement: Evidence from population data.* Center for Education Policy Analysis. https://cepa.stanford.edu/content/impact-great-recession-student-achievement-evidence-population-data

Simms, M., Eversberg, D., Dupuy, C., & Hipp, L. (2018). Organizing young workers under precarious conditions: What hinders or facilitates union success. *Work and Occupations, 45*(4), 420–450.

Simon, E. (2013, March 4). Are school closings the new urban renewal? *Notebook.* http://thenotebook.org/blog/13596/school-closings-new-urban-renewal

Simon, S. (2013, November 18). Duncan: I'm sorry for "moms" remark. *Politico.* https://www.politico.com/story/2013/11/secretary-education-arne-duncan-clumsy-phrasing-white-moms-remark-100017

Simpson, G., & Fowler, M. (1994). Geographic mobility and children's emotional/behavioral adjustment and school functioning. *Pediatrics, 93*(2), 303–309.

Sinclair, H. (2018, April 4). Oklahoma governor Mary Fallin: Teachers on strike are like "teenagers who want a better car." *Newsweek.* http://www.newsweek.com/oklahoma-governor-mary-fallin-teachers-strike-are-teenagers-who-want-better-871423

Skiba, R., Michael, R., Nardo, A., & Peterson, R. (2002). The color of discipline: Sources of racial and gender disproportionality in school punishment. *Urban Review, 34*(4), 317–342.

Snyder, M. (2012, October 7). *Police: Enter Detroit at your own risk.* http://theeconomiccollapseblog.com/archives/police-enter-detroit-at-your-own-risk

Soares, L. (2010). *The power of education–industry partnerships.* Center for American Progress. https://www.americanprogress.org/issues/economy/reports/2010/10/04/8518/the-power-of-the-education-industry-partnership/

Somin, I. (2017, November 6). Mortgage interest deduction mostly benefits the rich—end it. *Hill.* https://thehill.com/opinion/finance/358922-mortgage-interest-deduction-mostly-benefits-the-rich-end-it

Soss, J. (1999). Lessons of welfare: Policy design, political learning, and political action. *American Political Science Review, 93*(2), 363–380.

Soss, J. (2005). Making clients and citizens: Welfare policy as a source of status, belief and action. In A. Schneider & H. Ingram (Eds.), *Deserving and entitled: Social constructions and public policy* (pp. 291–328). State University of New York Press.

Southern Education Foundation. (2015, January). *Low income students now a majority in the nation's public schools.* https://www.southerneducation.org/wp-content/uploads/2019/02/New-Majority-Update-Bulletin.pdf

Sparks, S. (2021, June 4). College enrollment dip hits students of color the hardest. *Education Week.* https://www.edweek.org/teaching-learning/college-enrollment-dip-hits-students-of-color-the-harest/2021/06

Sparks, S., & Klein, A. (2018, April 24). Discipline disparities grow for students of color, new federal data show. *Education Week.* https://www.edweek.org/leadership/discipline-disparities-grow-for-students-of-color-new-federal-data-show/2018/04

Sperling, G. (2005, December 18). How to refloat these boats. *Washington Post,* p. B3.

Spiegelman, M. (2018). *Public school teacher spending on classroom supplies.* National Center for Education Statistics. https://files.eric.ed.gov/fulltext/ED583062.pdf

Spillane, J., Diamond, J., Burch, P., Hallet, T., Jita, L., & Zolterns, J. (2002). Managing the middle: School leaders and the enactment of accountability policy. *Educational Policy, 16*(5), 731–762.

Spradley, J. (1979). *The ethnographic interview.* Holt, Rinehart, and Winston.

Starkman, D. (2014). The $236,500 hole in the American dream. *New Republic.* https://newrepublic.com/article/118425/closing-racial-wealth-gap

Starz, D. (2018, March 23). *Why are teachers more likely than others to work a second job?* Brookings Institution. https://www.brookings.edu/blog/brown-center-chalkboard/2018/03/23/why-are-teachers-more-likely-than-others-to-work-second-jobs/

Stein, S. (2004). *The culture of education policy.* Teachers College Press.

Steiner, L. (2009). *Tough decisions: Closing persistently low-performing schools.* Retrieved from http://www.centerii.org/survey/downloads/Tough_Decisions.pdf

Stone, D. (1989). Causal stories and the formation of policy agendas. *Political Science Quarterly, 104*(2), 281–300.

Stone, D. (1993). Clinical authority in the construction of citizenship. In H. Ingram & S. Smith (Eds.), *Public policy for democracy* (pp. 45–67). Brookings Institution.

Stone, D. (1997). *Policy paradox: The art of political decision making.* W. W. Norton.

Stone, D. (2005). Foreword. In A. Schneider & H. Ingram (Eds.), *Deserving and entitled: Social constructions and public policy* (pp. ix–xiii). State University of New York Press.

Stotko, E. M., Ingram, R., & Beaty-O'Ferrall, M. E. (2007). Promising strategies for attracting and retaining successful urban teachers. *Urban Education, 42,* 30–51.

Strauss, R. (2013). *Remedial education: Federal education policy.* Council on Foreign Relations, Renewing America Progress Report and Scorecard. http://www.cfr.org/united-states/remedial-education-federal-education-policy/p30141

Strauss, V. (2013, June 1). Philadelphia passes "doomsday" school budget. *Huffington Post.* https://www.washingtonpost.com/blogs/answer-sheet/wp/2013/06/01/philadelphia-passes-doomsday-school-budget/

Strauss, V. (2015, March 26). No, Finland isn't ditching traditional school subjects. Here's what's really happening. *Washington Post.* https://www.washingtonpost.com/news/answer-sheet/wp/2015/03/26/no-finlands-schools-arent-giving-up-traditional-subjects-heres-what-the-reforms-will-really-do/

Strauss, V. (2016a, December 8). A sobering look at what DeVos did to education in Michigan and what she might do as secretary of education. *Washington Post.* https://www.washingtonpost.com/news/answer-sheet/wp/2016/12/08/a-sobering-look-at-what-betsy-devos-did-to-education-in-michigan-and-what-she-might-do-as-secretary-of-education/

Strauss, V. (2016b, December 21). To Trump's education pick, the U.S. public school system is a "dead end." *Washington Post.* https://www.washingtonpost.com/news/answer-sheet/wp/2016/12/21/to-trumps-education-pick-the-u-s-public-school-system-is-a-dead-end/

Stringfield, S., & Yakimowski-Srebnik, M. (2005). Promise, progress, problems and paradoxes of three phases of accountability: A longitudinal case study of the Baltimore City Public Schools. *American Educational Research Journal, 42*(1), 43–75.

Strunk, K., & Grissom, J. (2010). Do strong unions shape district policies? Collective bargaining, teacher contract restrictiveness and the political power of teachers' unions. *Educational Evaluation and Policy Analysis, 32*(3), 389–406.

Sullivan, M. (1989). *Getting paid: Youth crime and work in the inner city.* Cornell University Press.

Sunderman, G. (2001). Accountability mandates and the implementation of Title I schoolwide programs: A comparison of three urban districts. *Educational Administration Quarterly, 37*(4), 503–532.

Sunderman, G. L., & Payne, A. (2009). *Does closing schools cause educational harm? A review of the research.* Mid-Atlantic Equity Center Information Brief. http://maec.ceee.gwu.edu/sites/default/files/Does Closing Schools Cause Educational Harm_1.14.2010.pdf

Sutcher, L., Darling-Hammond, L., & Carver-Thomas, D. (2016). *A coming crisis in teaching? Teacher supply, demand, and shortages in the U.S.* Learning Policy Institute.

Sutherland, I., & Lee, M. (1989). Teachers' social capital: Giving of oneself. *Early Child Development and Care, 53*, 29–35.

Sutherland, I., Lee, M., & Trapp-Dukes, R. (1993). Teachers' reported use of social capital. *Journal of Early Childhood Teacher, 14*(1), 4–10.

Sutton, R. (2007). Teachers' anger, frustration, and self-regulation. In P. Schutz & R. Pekrun (Eds.), *Emotion in education* (pp. 259–274). Academic Press.

Sutton, R., & Wheatley, K. (2003). Teachers' emotions and teaching: A review of the literature and directions for future research. *Educational Psychology Review, 15*(4), 327–357.

Swanson, C., & Schneider, B. (1999). Students on the move: Residential and educational mobility in America's schools. *Sociology of Education, 72*(1), 54–67.

Swift, A. (2017, August 30). *Labor union approval best since 2003, at 61%.* Gallup. https://news.gallup.com/poll/217331/labor-union-approval-best-2003.aspx

Szreter, S. (2002). The state of social capital: Bringing back in power, politics, and history. *Theory and Society, 31*(5), 573–621.

Taylor, A. (2018, November 7). Florida's move to allow ex-felons to vote brings U.S. closer to international norms. *Washington Post.* https://www.washingtonpost.com/world/2018/11/07/floridas-move-allow-ex-felons-vote-brings-us-closer-international-election-norms/

Taylor, K. (2015a, October 29). At a Success Academy Charter School, singling out pupils who have "got to go." *New York Times.* https:/www.nytimes.com/2015/10/30/nyregion/at-a-success-academy-charter-school-singling-out-pupils-who-have-got-to-go.html

Taylor, K. (2015b, April 6). At Success Academy Charter Schools, high scores and polarizing tactics. *New York Times.* https://www.nytime.com/2015/04/07/nyregion/at-success-academy-charter-schools-polarizing-methods-and-superior-results.html

Teachman, J., Paasch, K., & Carver, K. (1996). Social capital and dropping out of school. *Journal of Marriage and the Family, 58*(3), 773–783.

Teske, P., Fitzpatrick, J., & Kaplan, G. (2006). The information gap? *Review of Policy Research, 23*(5), 969–981.

Teske, P., Fitzpatrick, J., & Kaplan, G. (2007). *Opening doors: How low-income parents search for the right school.* Daniel J. Evans.

Thompson, D. (2021, September 14). Colleges have a guy problem. *The Atlantic.* https://www.theatlantic.com/ideas/archive/2021/09/young-men-college-decline-gender-gap-higher-education/620066/

Thompson, M., Ellis, R., & Wildavsky, A. (1990). *Cultural theory.* Westview Press.

Tiebout, C. (1956). A pure theory of local expenditures. *Journal of Political Economy, 64*(5), 416–424.

Toch, T. (1991). *In the name of excellence: The struggle to reform the nation's schools, why it's failing, and what should be done.* Oxford University Press.

Tocqueville, A. (1994). *Democracy in America.* Everyman's Library.

Toosi, N. (2017, April 21). State Dept. official reassigned amid conservative media attacks. *Politico.* https://www.politico.com/story/2017/04/21/sahar-nowrouzzadeh-reassigned-state-department-237466

Torpey, I. (2018, April). *Measuring the value of education.* U.S. Bureau of Labor Statistics. https://www.bls.gov/careeroutlook/2018/data-on-display/education-pays.htm

Tough, P. (2009). *Whatever it takes.* Mariner Books.

Touryalai, H. (2014, February 21). $1 trillion student loan problem keeps getting worse. *Forbes.* http://www.forbes.com/sites/halahtouryalai/2014/02/21/1-1-trillion-student-loan-problem-keeps-getting-worse/

Troy, G. (2005). *Morning in America: How Ronald Reagan invented the 1980s.* Princeton University Press.

Tschannen-Moran, M. (2004). *Trust matters: Leadership for successful schools.* Jossey-Bass.

Tucker, R. (Ed.). (1978). *The Marx–Engels reader.* W. W. Norton.

Tyack, D. (1974). *The one best system: A history of American urban education.* Harvard University Press.

Tyack, D., & Cuban, L. (1995). *Tinkering toward Utopia.* Harvard University Press.

Tyler, L. (2011). *Toward increasing teacher diversity: Targeting support and intervention for teacher licensure candidates.* Educational Testing Service and National Education Association. http://www.nea.org/home/42951.htm

Ujifsa, A. (2016, January 14). Opt-out activists aim to build on momentum in states. *Education Week.* https://www.edweek.org/ew/articles/2016/01/14/opt-out-activists-aim-to-build-on-momentum.html

Ujifsa, A. (2019a, March 26). DeVos says Trump budget means "freedom" in education; Democrats call it "cruel." *Education Week.* http://blogs.edweek.org/edweek/campaign-k-12/2019/03/betsy-devos-trump-education-budget-house-democrats-hearing.html

Ujifsa, A. (2019b, January 2). Schools would get $100 billion for repairs, rebuilding in Democrats' bill. *Education Week.* http://blogs.edweek.org/edweek/campaign-k-12/2019/01/schools-repair-rebuild-100-billion-democrats-infrastructure.html

Umhoefer, D. (2016, November 27). For unions in Wisconsin, a fast and hard fall since Act 10. *Milwaukee Journal Sentinel.* https://projects.jsonline.com/news/2016 /11/27/ for-unions-in-wisconsin-fast-and-hard-fall-since-act-10.html

Underwood, J. (2018, March 26). The state of teacher tenure. *Phi Delta Kappan, 99*(7), 76–77.

Urschel, J. L., Yat Aguilar, M. A., & Dailey, B. (2012). *Profiles of for-profit and nonprofit Education Management Organizations.* National Education Policy Center. http:// nepc.colorado.edu/publication/EMO-profiles-101–1

U.S. Bureau of Labor Statistics. (2015, December). *Occupational employment projections to 2024.* https://www.bls.gov/opub/mlr/2015/article/occupational-employment-projections-to-2024.htm

U.S. Bureau of Labor Statistics. (2019, January 18). *Union members summary.* https:// www.bls.gov/news.release/union2.nr0.htm

U.S. Census. (2021, April 29). *2020 Census redistricting data.* https://www.census. gov/newsroom/press-releases/2021/2020-presidential-election-voting-and-registration-tables-now-available.html

U.S. Department of Agriculture. (2019, September 4). *Household food insecurity in the United States.* https://www.ers.usda.gov/topics/food-nutrition-assistance/food-security-in-the-us/key-statistics-graphics.aspx

U.S. Department of Education. (2002). *No Child Left Behind: A desktop reference.* Retrieved http://www2.ed.gov/admins/lead/account/nclbreference/reference. pdf

U.S. Department of Education. (2006). *Title I accountability and school improvement from 2001 to 2004.* https://eric.ed.gov/?id=ED491292

U.S. Department of Education. (2009). *Race to the Top program: Executive summary.* http://www2.ed.gov/programs/racetothetop/executive-summary.pdf

U.S. Department of Education. (2011). *An overview of school turnaround.* http://ww2. ed.gov/programs/sif/sigoverviewppt.pdf

U.S. Department of Education. (2012). *Summary of considerations to strengthen state requests for ESEA flexibility.* http://www.ed.gov/sites/default/files/considerations-strengthen.pdf

U.S. Department of Education. (2014). *Guiding principle: A resource guide for improving school climate and discipline.* https://www2.ed.gov/policy/gen/guid/school-discipline/guiding-principles.pdf

U.S. Department of Education. (2016). *The state of racial diversity in the educator workforce.* https://www2.ed.gov/rschstat/eval/highered/racial-diversity/state-racial-diversity-workforce.pdf

Ushomirsky, N., & Williams, D. (2015, March). *Funding gaps: Too many states still spend less on educating students who need the most.* Education Trust. https://edtrust.org/ resource/funding-gaps-2015/

U.S. House of Representatives. (2001a). *Leave no child behind*. Hearing before the Committee on Education and the Workforce. 107th Cong., 1st sess. (Serial No. 1075–).

U.S. House of Representatives. (2001b). *No Child Left Behind*. Hearing on H.R.1. Committee on Education and the Workforce. 107th Cong., 1st sess. (Serial No. 1079–).

U.S. House of Representatives. (2001c). *No Child Left Behind, communication from the president*. Committee on Education and the Workforce. 107th Cong., 1st sess. (H. Doc 1073–4).

U.S. House of Representatives. (2001d). *Transforming the federal role in education for the 21st century*. Hearing on H.R.1, H.R. 340, Committee on Education and the Workforce. 107th Cong., 1st sess. (Serial No. 1071–0).

Uslaner, E. (2002). *The moral foundations of trust*. Cambridge University Press.

Uslaner, E. (2010). *Corruption, inequality, and the rule of law: The bulging pocket makes the easy life*. Cambridge University Press.

Uslaner, E. (2012). *Segregation and mistrust: Diversity, isolation, and social cohesion*. Cambridge University Press.

U.S. Senate. 2001. *President Bush's educational proposals*. Hearing of the Committee on Health, Education, Labor, and Pensions. 107th Cong., 1st sess. (S.Hrg. 1078–).

Valencia, R. R., & Suzuki, L. A. (2000). *Intelligence testing and minority students: Foundations, performance factors, and assessment issues*. Sage.

VanderStaay, S. (1994). Stories of (social) distress: Applied narrative analysis and public policy for the homeless. *Journal of Social Distress and the Homeless, 3*(4), 299–319.

VanHeuvelen, T. (2018). Moral economies or hidden talents? A longitudinal analysis of union decline and wage inequality, 1973–2015. *Social Forces, 97*(2), 495–530.

Van Sciver, J. (1990). Teacher dismissals. *Phi Delta Kappan, 72*(4), 318–319.

Vedung, E., & van der Doelen, F. (2007). The sermon: Information programs in the public policy process, choice, effects, and evaluation. In M. Bemelmans-Videc, R. Rist, & E. Vedung (Eds.), *Carrots, sticks and sermons: Policy instruments and their evaluation* (pp. 103–128). Transaction.

Venkatesh, S. (2002). *American project: The rise and fall of a modern ghetto*. Harvard University Press.

Venkatesh, S. (2009). *Off the books: The underground economy of the urban poor*. Harvard University Press.

Vevea, R. (2012, February 17). Questioning the fairness of a detention fee. *New York Times*. http://www.nytimes.com/2012/02/17/education/at-noble-street-schools-in-chicago-detention-costs-5.html

Vinovskis, M. (2009). *From a Nation at Risk to No Child Left Behind*. Teachers College Press.

Vinzant, J., & Crothers, L. (1998). *Street-level leadership: Discretion and legitimacy in front-line public service*. Georgetown University Press.

Vivea, B. (2013, January 15). 40 percent of closed schools now privately run. *Catalyst Chicago*. http://www.catalyst-chicago.org/news/2013/01/15/2074/map-40-percent-closed-schools-now-privately-run

Voght, K. (2020, June 12). America's child care system is in a crisis. Joe Biden will soon release a plan to fix it. *Mother Jones*. https://www.motherjones.com/politics/2020/06/biden-warren-child-care-coronavirus/

Waddington, R., & Berends, M. (2017). *Impact of Indiana choice scholarship program: Achievement effects for students in upper elementary and middle school*. CREO. http://creo.nd.edu/images/people/Waddington__Berends_Indiana_Voucher_Impacts_06.24.17.pdf

Wagmiller, R., & Adelman, R. (2009). *Childhood and intergenerational poverty: The long-term consequences of growing up poor*. National Center for Children in Poverty. http://www.nccp.org/publications/pub_909.html

Walker, T. (2019, March 13). *5 key trends in the teacher workforce*. NEA. http://neatoday.org/2019/03/13/5-trends-in-the-teaching-profession/

Wallace, J., Goodkind, S., Wallace, C., & Bachman, J. (2008). Racial, ethnic, and gender differences in school discipline among U.S. high school students: 1991–2005. *Negro Educational Review, 59*(1–2), 47–62.

Warren, E. (2019, March 16). My housing plan for America. *Medium*. https://medium.com/@teamwarren/my-housing-plan-for-america-20038e19dc26

Weaver, K. (2010). Paths and forks or chutes and ladders? Negative feedbacks and policy regime change. *Journal of Public Policy, 30*(2), 137–162.

Weaver, V., & Lerman, A. (2010). Political consequences of the carceral state. *American Political Science Review, 104*(4), 817–833.

Weidner, V. (2005). Information and information use for school choice under a statewide voucher program. *Politics of Education Association Bulletin, 29*(2), 1–5.

Weiner, D., Lutz, B., & Ludwig, J. (2009). *The effects of school desegregation on crime* (Working Paper No. 15380). National Bureau of Economic Research. http://www.nber.org/

Weiner, L. (2012). *The future of our schools: Teachers unions and social justice*. Haymarket Books.

Weisman, J., & Paley, A. (2007, March 15). Dozens in GOP turn against Bush's prized "No Child" act. *Washington Post*. http://www.washingtonpost.com/wp-dyn/content/article/2007/03/14/AR2007031402741.html

Weiss, J. (1993). Policy design for democracy: A look at public information campaigns. In A. Schneider & H. Ingram (Eds.), *Policy design for democracy* (pp. 99–118). Lawrence University Press of Kansas.

Weiss, J. (2007). Public information. In L. Salamon (Ed.), *The tools of government: A guide to the new governance* (pp. 217–254). Oxford University Press.

Weiss, J., & Tschirhart, M. (1994). Using public information campaigns as policy instruments. *Journal of Policy Analysis and Management, 3*(1), 82–110.

Wells, A. (2015). *Diverse housing, diverse schooling: How policy can stabilize racial demographic change in cities and suburbs.* National Education Policy Center. https://nepc.colorado.edu/publication/housing-school-nexus

Wells, A., & Crain, R. (1992). Do parents choose school quality or school status? A sociological theory of free market education. In P. W. Cookson (Ed.), *The choice controversy* (pp. 65–82). Corwin Press.

Welner, K. (2001). *Legal rights, local wrongs: When community control collides with educational equity.* State University of New York Press.

Welner, K. (2013, September 24). The bottom line on charter school studies. *Washington Post.* http://www.washingtonpost.com/blogs/answer-sheet/wp/2013/09/24/the-bottom-line-on-charter-school-studies/

Welner, K., & Weitzman, D. (2005). The soft bigotry of low expenditures. *Equity and Excellence in Education, 38,* 242–248.

West, A. (1980). *The National Education Association: The power base for education.* Free Press.

Western, B., & Rosenfeld, J. (2011). Unions, norms, and the rise in U.S. wage inequality. *American Sociological Review, 76*(4), 513–537.

Whitman, D. (2015, September). *The surprising roots of the Common Core: How conservatives gave rise to "Obamacore."* Brookings Institution. https://www.brookings.edu/wp-content/uploads/2016/06/Surprising-Conservative-Roots-of-the-Common-Core_FINAL.pdf

Whortman, P., & Bryant, F. (1985). School desegregation and Black achievement. *Sociological Methods and Research, 3*(13), 289–324.

Wildavsky, A. (1987). Choosing preferences by constructing institutions: A cultural theory of preference formation. *American Political Science Review, 81*(1), 3–21.

Wilhelm, K., Dewhurst-Savellis, J., & Parker, G. (2000). Teacher stress? An analysis of why teachers leave and why they stay. *Teachers and Teaching: Theory and Practice, 6*(3), 291–304.

Will, M. (2016, August 22). Help wanted: Teacher-shortage hot spots. *Education Week.* http://www.edweek.org/ew/articles/2016/08/24/help-wanted-teacher-shortage-hot-spots.html

Will, M. (2018a, February 13). Are teachers' unions on the brink of demise? *Education Week.* https://www.edweek.org/ew/articles/2018/02/14/are-teachers-unions-on-the-brink-of.html

Will, M. (2018b, August 9). Enrollment is down at teacher colleges. So they're trying to change. *Education Week.* https://www.edweek.org/ew/articles/ 2018/08/09/enrollment-is-down-at-teacher-colleges-so.html

Will, M. (2018c, May 22). Will the largest teachers' union lose 10 percent of its members? *Education Week.* http://blogs.edweek.org/edweek/teacherbeat/2018/05/nea_budget_membership_loss.html

Will, M. (2019, December 3). Enrollment in teacher-preparation programs is declining fast. Here's what the data show. *Education Week.* https://www.eduweak.

org/teaching-learning/enrollment-in-teacher-preparation-programs-is-declining-fast-heres-what-the-data-show/2019/2

Williams, J. (2015, September 17). *Parents' hunger strike reveals flaws in Chicago's education reforms.* http://news.yahoo.com/parents-hunger-strike-reveals-flaws-chicagos-education-reforms-220126550.html

Willingham, D. (2010, April 5). What NAEP reading scores really show. *Washington Post.*

http://voices.washingtonpost.com/answer-sheet/daniel-willingham/willingham-misunderstanding-na.html

Willis, P. (2000). Elements of culture. In R. Arum & I. Beattie (Eds.), *The structure of schooling* (pp. 260–275). McGraw-Hill Higher Education.

Wilson, D., Olaghere, A., & Kimbrell, C. (2017). *Effectiveness of restorative justice principles in juvenile justice: A meta-analysis.* https://www.ncjrs.gov/pdffiles1/ojjdp/grants/250872.pdf

Wilson, J. (1980). *The politics of regulation.* Basic Books.

Wilson, J. (1991). *Bureaucracies: What government agencies do and why they do it.* Basic Books.

Winkler, A., Scull, J., & Zeehandelaar, D. (2012, October). *How strong are teacher unions? A state-by-state comparison.* Thomas Fordham Institute.

Winters, N. (2017). Labor unions as activist organizations: A union power approach to estimating union wage effects. *Social Forces, 95*(4), 1451–1478.

Withey, M., & Cooper, W. (1989). Predicting exit, voice, loyalty, and neglect. *Administrative Science Quarterly, 34*(4), 521–539.

Wolf, R., & Korte, G. (2018, June 27). Supreme Court deals major financial blow to nation's public employee unions. *USA Today.* https://www.usatoday.com/story/news/politics/2018/06/27/supreme-court-deals-blow-public-employee-labor-unions/590440002/

Wood, D., & Brumfiel, G. (2021, December 5). Pro-Trump counties now have far higher COVID death rates. Misinformation to blame. *NPR.* https://www.npr.org/sections/health-shots/2021/12/05/1059828993/data-vaccine-misinformation-trump-counties-covid-death-rate

Wood, D., Halfon, N., Scarlata, D., Newacheck, P., & Nessim, S. (1993). Impact of family relocation on children's growth, development, school function, and behavior. *Journal of the American Medical Association, 270*(11), 1334–1338.

Woolcock, M. (2001). The place of social capital in understanding social and economic outcomes. *Canadian Journal of Policy Research, 2*(1), 11–17. http://www.oecd.org/dataoecd/5/13/1824913.pdf

Woolcock, M., & Narayan, D. (2000). Social capital: Implications for development theory, research and policy. *World Bank Research Observer, 15*(2), 225–249.

Wright, S., Horn, S., & Sanders, W. (1997). Teacher and classroom context effects on student achievement: Implications for teacher evaluation. *Journal of Personnel Evaluation in Education, 11*, 57–67.

Yan, H., & Smith, T. (2018, April 9). *Oklahoma teachers' walkout gains momentum in its 2nd week*. CNN. https://www.cnn.com/2018/04/09/us/oklahoma-teachers-walkout/index.html

Yettick, H., Wexler, E., & Anderson, S. (2008). Parental decision-making and educational opportunity. In K. Welner & W. Chi (Ed.), *Current issues in education policy and the law* (pp. 99–120). Information Age.

Yglesias, M. (2019, July 30). America's dual housing crisis and what Democrats plan to do about it, explained. *Vox*. https://www.vox.com/2019/7/30/20681101/housing-crisis-democrats-2020-warren-harris-booker-castro

Yin, J., & Sargrad, S. (2018, November 9). *Education in the 2018 Midterms*. Center for American Progress. https://www.americanprogress.org/issues/education-k-12/news/2018/11/09/460742/education-2018-midterms/

Zeigler, H. (1967). *The political life of American teachers*. Prentice Hall.

Zernike, K. (2015, October 24). Obama administration calls for limits on testing in schools. *New York Times*. https://www.nytimes.com/2015/10/25/us/obama-administration-calls-for-limits-on-testing-in-schools.html

Zernike, K. (2016a, November 23). Betsy DeVos, Trump's education pick, has steered money from public schools. *New York Times*. https://www.nytimes.com/2016/11/23/us/politics/betsy-devos-trumps-education-pick-has-steered-money-from-public-schools.html

Zernike, K. (2016b, December 12). How Trump's education nominee bent Detroit to her will on charter schools. *New York Times*. https://www.nytimes.com/2016/12/12/us/politics/betsy-devos-how-trumps-education-nominee-bent-detroit-to-her-will-on-charter-schools.html

Zimmer, R., Gill, B., Booker, K., Lavertu, S., Sass, T., & Witte, J. (2009). *Charter schools in eight states: Effects on achievement, attainment, integration, and competition*. RAND Corporation.

Zimmerman, A. (2017, August 18). Why charter schools are good neighbors. *Atlantic*. https://www.theatlantic.com/education/archive/2017/08/why-charter-schools-are-good-neighbors/535638/

Zonta, M. (2018, July 24). *Homes for all*. Center for American Progress. https://www.americanprogress.org/issues/economy/reports/2018/07/24/452645/homes-for-all/

Zubrzycki, J. (2012, October 16). School shutdowns trigger growing backlash. *Education Week*. http://www.edweek.org/ew/articles/2012/10/17/08closings_ep.h32.html

Notes

Chapter 1

1. See, e.g., Carneiro et al. (2007), Heckman and Kautz (2012), and Jacob (2002).

2. In a recent opinion poll, the majority of Americans rated six professions "high" or "very high" on honesty and ethics. In order, they are nurses, military officers, teachers, medical doctors, police officers, and pharmacists. Only members of Congress and lobbyists received majority negative ratings. The remaining 14 occupations were rated "average." Views sometimes change. Nurses have been ranked first every year except one, when Gallup included firefighters after the 9/11 terrorist attacks; the rating of pharmacists, although high, dropped five points, possibly reflecting the opioid crisis; and the ratings of the clergy, while still positive, have fallen. Republicans are much more likely to rate police officers, military officers, the clergy, pharmacists, and judges "very high" or "high." Democrats offer more positive ratings for news reporters (Brenan, 2017).

3. See Balingit (2018a, 2018b), Center on Budget and Policy Priorities (CBPP; 2018), R. Cohen (2019), D. Goldstein and Burns (2018), Kilgore (2018), Gomez and Benson (2018), Leachman (2017), Leachman and Figueroa (2019), Leachman et al. (2017), and Rossman (2018).

4. Like other policy issues, education has become more polarized, but there is widespread agreement with respect to testing. A majority agreed that there was too much emphasis on testing (64%) and opposed the Common Core State Standards (54%)—the K–12 academic benchmarks adopted by 43 states and the District of Columbia. A majority also advocated using multiple measures, such as student work, observations, and grades, to evaluate students; agreed that the best way to measure the success of a school is by whether students are engaged and feel hopeful about the future rather than by tests; and opposed using student test scores to evaluate teachers. The ability of parents to rate and rank schools was one of the key reasons policy makers pushed recent reforms (see Chapter 2); however, fewer than one in five public school parents said knowing how standardized test scores in their community compared with scores from other districts, states, or countries was important. Moreover, while those polled expressed support for charter schools, 57 percent opposed vouchers, which Betsy DeVos, secretary of education in the Trump administration, pushed to expand. The political divide was most stark in this area. Republicans were equally divided (46% in favor and 46% opposed), while Democrats strongly opposed vouchers (71% against and 16% in favor). Finally, a majority agreed that the federal government should play no role in holding schools accountable (PDK, 2015). These views repudiate the policies of the G. W. Bush, Obama, and Trump administrations.

5. In this poll, 73 percent said that they would support teachers in their community if they went on strike for more pay, including close to 9 in 10 Democrats and about 6 in 10 Republicans—with independents falling in between. That figure rises to 78 percent for public school parents—those most directly affected by a strike. There are regional differences. Southerners (78%) are more likely than northeasterners (67%) or midwesterners (69%) to support a teacher strike for higher pay; westerners fall in between (74%). Four in 10 southerners and westerners say they would "strongly" support a strike, compared with the Northeast (28%) and Midwest (23%).

6. NCLB and the ESSA both amended the ESEA of 1965. NCLB waivers and RttT are examples of executive policy making rather than legislation adopted by Congress (see Chapter 2).

7. The policy feedback literature sometimes includes public ideas and discourse in the definition of "political institutions" (Beland, 2005; Reich, 1988; Schmidt, 2008). This research uses the term *institution* to convey the branches of government, and the formal and informal rules of the game, including public policies. Bifurcating institutions from ideas and discourse allows for the analysis of changes in both.

8. Social Security increased political participation by providing recipients with a stake in national politics, especially those from low- or moderate-income levels who were more dependent on their benefits (Campbell, 2003). The community participation requirements included in many Great Society programs, like Head Start, increased political participation by providing previously marginalized groups with the knowledge and capacity to participate more fully in political life. It also increased political participation in other programs, which suggests that there is a connection between resource and interpretive effects (Soss, 1999).

9. See, e.g., H. Ingram and Smith (1993), Lawless and Fox (2001), A. Schneider and Ingram (1997, 2005b), and Soss (1999, 2005).

10. For example, many states do not allow former felons (and those who served sentences for misdemeanors in some states) to vote, and policy makers have historically restricted the political participation of the poor, the young, minorities, and the mentally disabled through restrictions on voting and registration and by clustering minorities—such as African Americans, Hispanics, and Native Americans—into minority majority legislative districts. This gerrymandering affects their representation in state legislatures and Congress and weakens support for welfare state expansion and carceral reform (ACLU, n.d.; Piven & Cloward, 1988; A. Schneider & Ingram, 1993; V. Weaver & Lerman, 2010). Some states are turning back laws that restrict voting for former prisoners (A. Taylor, 2018).

11. President Kennedy issued Executive Order 10988 allowing federal employees to bargain collectively; those rights were codified in the Civil Reform Act of 1978. By the late 2000s, 32 states required local school boards to bargain collectively with teachers, while 14 permitted collective bargaining, and 5—Georgia, North Carolina, South Carolina, Texas, and Virginia—prohibited it altogether (Winkler et al., 2012).

12. Southern and western states make up most of the lowest tier of unionized workers (U.S. Bureau of Labor Statistics [BLS], 2019). Act 10 was passed within months of Scott Walker and Republicans gaining control of the governor's office and the state legislature in 2010. Republicans also cut health insurance, pensions, and education funding, which resulted in an 8–10 percent reduction in take-home pay for teachers. Two side effects of fewer public-employee union members were the reduction in the number of Democratic lawmakers in the state senate and assembly and the adoption of a "right-to-work" law in 2015 that reduced private-sector union membership. Scott Walker won three elections before being defeated in 2018 by Tony Evers, who, ironically, is a former teacher and state superintendent of education (Caldwell, 2018; Grabar, 2018b; Levine, 2016; Umhoefer, 2016).

13. See Armentrout (2018), Geiger et al. (2018), Horsley and Totenberg (2018), Malanga (2018), and Wolf and Korte (2018). Efforts to overturn *Abood* fell short in 2012, 2014, and 2016. In the 2016 case, the Supreme Court deadlocked 4–4 with respect to a Southern California teacher's argument that her free speech was violated by being forced to pay about $650 a year in agency fees. The Obama administration sided with the union. After Senate Majority Leader Mitch McConnell denied a confirmation hearing for Judge Merrick Garland (President Barack Obama's pick for the court), President Trump appointed conservative Justice Neil Gorsuch, resulting in a 5–4 vote for *Janus*. Pilkington (2017) and Bottari (2018) document how right-wing activists and a network of conservative think tanks with outposts in all 50 states launched a nationwide campaign to deprive Democrats of a major source of support and funding by "defunding and defanging" public-sector unions. The alliance of 66 state-based think tanks is spearheaded by the State Policy Network (SPN) and has an annual budget of $80 million. Mark Janus, who worked as a $71,000 per year child support specialist in the Illinois Department of Healthcare and Family Services, has since announced he quit his job to work as a senior fellow for the Illinois Policy Institute, the conservative think tank that helped bankroll his case.

14. See Berlin and Bentle (2018), Cohn (2015), Gunn (2018), Manzo (2017), National Right to Work Committee (2016), and Opfer and Han (2017). Less than 11 percent of the workforce is now unionized, a drop from 35 percent during World War II. That decline stems from the private sector, especially since the 1980s, with membership plummeting from about 17 percent in 1983 to 6 percent. In comparison, more than one in three public workers belong to a union, a percentage that has held relatively steady for decades (Pilkington, 2017; Wolf & Korte, 2018).

15. At the time of the *Janus* decision, workers in 28 states had RTW laws (National Conference of State Legislatures, n.d.), meaning employees could not be required to pay fair share agency fees. RTW laws varied from state to state, but covered most private employees (other than railroad and airline workers) while most federal employees were exempt. After *Janus,* all federal, state, and local public employees are covered (Wolf & Korte, 2018).

16. See, e.g., Will (2018a, 2018c). Predicting the *Janus* decision, the conservative nonprofit Freedom Foundation began acquiring lists of public employees, as well as hiring and training canvassers to convince union members to leave once they no longer had to pay agency fees. Along with going door to door, they developed plans to visit government buildings; assemble opt-out materials for human resource departments; create a toll-free call center; flood social media, mail, and email; and fund cable television ads to spread the news about employees' opportunity to cease paying union fees by opting out. The Freedom Foundation is funded by wealthy conservative groups and individuals, such as the Sarah Scaife Foundation, which is backed by the estate of right-wing billionaire Richard Mellon Scaife; the Donors Trust, which—like Americans for Prosperity—is a conservative advocacy group that is part of the SPN and has received millions from conservative billionaire brothers Charles and David Koch; the Richard and Helen DeVos Foundation, backed by the family of U.S. secretary of education Betsy DeVos; and the SPN, which is chaired by a vice president of the Lynde and Harry Bradley Foundation. Another SPN member, the Mackinac Center for Public Policy—a Michigan-based nonprofit that is tied to the Koch-backed Americans for Prosperity—launched the "My Pay, My Say" website to inform public employees of their rights under *Janus*. The website offers an automated system for workers to generate letters to their unions opting out of dues (Bottari, 2018; McNicholas et al., 2018; Pilkington, 2018).

17. Approval for unions has increased among almost every major demographic subgroup since 2016. One exception is labor union members; their aggregate approval rate has been no lower than 75 percent since 2001, hit 93 percent in 2019, and is currently at 86 percent. Approval is relatively high among young adults ages 18-34 (77%) and those with annual household incomes under $40,000 (72%). Although approval rates vary sharply by partisan affiliation, with 90 percent of Democrats, 47 percent of Republicans, and 66 percent of independents viewing unions favorably, current approval rates *for every partisan group* are more than 20 points higher than their lowest rates between 2001 and 2020 (Brenan, 2021).

18. See, e.g., Etzioni (1988), Mansbridge (1980, 1990a, 1990b), and Stone (1997).

19. Implementation emerged as a formal field of inquiry in the 1960s. Odden (1991) and Honig (2006) distinguish different stages of research by the variables and units of analysis studied. Both became more complex over time.

20. See Bardach (1977), Derthick (1972), Firestone and Corbett (1988), N. Gross et al. (1971), Murphy (1991), and Pressman and Wildavsky (1984).

21. Honig (2006) suggests that many of these biases were influenced by the individualistic assumptions prevalent in political science and economics, where most of the implementation research was located at the time.

22. Certainly some policy scholars have explored how policies, people, and places matter in terms of policy implementation. Lipsky (1980), for example, found that the practices, routines, and behaviors of frontline implementers sometimes diverged from policy goals but showed how this often reflected the need for "street-level bureaucrats" to juggle multiple tasks and worldviews to meet the needs of clients. His study encouraged researchers to examine how hierarchical controls might alienate street-level bureaucrats from the very ideals that had drawn them to public service (see also Maynard-Moody & Musheno, 2003; Vinzant & Crothers, 1998). In the field of education, some scholars have expanded their research to account for schools as organizations, school culture, and teacher networks (e.g., Honig, 2006; Odden, 1991). These studies indicate that people's actions cannot be divorced from their social settings or the larger political and economic institutions that structure their social interactions; however, many deal with schoolwide reforms more than implementation per se, and none deal with policy feedback.

23. E.g., Bandura (1977), Burt (1982), Etzioni (1988), Katznelson and Weingast (2005), S. Lewin (1996), Mansbridge (1990), and Wildavsky (1987).

24. F. Fischer and Forester (1993), Roe (1994), Stein (2004), and Stone (1997) offer a critique of traditional approaches.

25. NPA is increasingly being used in political science, public policy, and public administration to understand how beliefs and issues of identity influence behavior, explain policy change, find solutions to recalcitrant policy problems, resolve conflicts in groups and organizations, and connect policy makers with researchers and practitioners (e.g., Feldman et al., 2004; F. Fischer & Forester, 1993; Loeske, 2007; Longo-Schmid, 2016; Ospina & Dodge, 2005; Roe, 1994; Stone, 1997; VanderStaay, 1994).

26. As a method, ethnographic interviewing recognizes that language is the most important medium through which people transmit culture. It allows researchers to get inside informants' heads by facilitating a discussion about their social worlds (Spradley, 1979).

27. I was able to ensure a diverse data sample due to a unique "data set"—available through the state DOE website—that groups schools according to the needs of their students (e.g., rates of student poverty and limited English proficiency) and district capacity (e.g., the income and the property wealth of the district's residents). It also describes other important features of schools and school districts, including, but not limited to, whether they are located in urban, suburban, or rural communities.

28. Some informants are reported as working in more than one school district. This included administrators who taught in different districts than their current one and teachers who changed districts *and* spoke about both districts. In all cases, I have changed the names of the participants; however, in three cases, I used two different names for a participant to reflect their different work experiences because their work situations—when combined with their narratives—were unique enough to make them possibly identifiable.

29. Although I am discussing the components of my analysis as if they were separate, I "memoed" throughout to keep an ongoing record of my analysis, ideas, questions, and so forth and moved back and forth between theory, memos, and coding to construct relationship(s) between analytic themes, categories, and concepts (Corbin & Strauss, 2008).

Part I

1. See H. Ingram and Schneider (1991), A. Schneider and Ingram (1993, 2005b), and Stone (2005).

2. The theory of target groups acknowledges that "real" differences exist, but argues that perceptions that a group is "positive" or "negative" are socially constructed and that policy makers magnify or reduce differences to achieve political ends.

3. See A. Schneider and Ingram (1993, 2005b), as well as Gusfield (1981), for the cultural construction of drunk driving as a policy problem, and Nelson (1984) for the construction of child abuse as a social and political issue.

4. See Fraser (1989), Stein (2004), H. Ingram and Smith (1993), and A. Schneider and Ingram (1993, 1997, 2005b).

Chapter 2

1. Upon assuming office, President Reagan advocated four strategies in education: consolidating federal programs into a block grant and reducing spending; abolishing the DOE; providing federal tax credits to parents who paid tuition at private schools; and providing poor children with vouchers that they could redeem at the private or public school of their choice. He justified these reforms by excoriating public education for promoting "uniform mediocrity" (Toch, 1991, p. 23). In contrast, his first secretary of education, Terrell Bell, was a centrist Republican who, as a former district administrator, believed that public education was in desperate shape and that the federal government had an important role to play to redress the issue. In his memoirs, he describes how he decided to "stage an event that would jar the people into action" (T. Bell, 1988, p. 115) on behalf of the nation's public schools, colleges, and universities, similar to how the Soviet Union's launch of Sputnik—the world's first earth satellite—had seized the attention of Americans and resulted in the adoption of the National Defense Education Act of 1958. He created the task force for these purposes. The subsequent report is an example of policy makers purposefully generating negative feedback to overturn the status quo.

2. Concerns about public school quality had been building among education scholars, conservative intellectuals, and business groups and were reflected in a number of studies at that time. However, *A Nation at Risk* conferred political legitimacy on these ideas because it was sponsored by the DOE. It also escalated the publication of reports and books excoriating public education even though the report's findings were contested (Cross, 2004; Davies, 2007; B. Gross & Gross, 1985; Manna, 2006; Ravitch, 1985; Toch, 1991; Vinovskis, 2009). For a discussion of how educational data were misused to create a crisis of confidence in America's public schools at that time, see Berliner and Biddle (1996) and Bracey (2000).

3. By spring 2000, 40 states were using standardized test scores to rate school performance. Most published the information in school report cards that ranked schools on a variety of indicators (Kane & Staiger, 2002).

4. President Clinton was not the first to push accountability. The 1988 reauthorization of the ESEA required districts to assess the effectiveness of then labelled Chapter 1 (Title I) programs and develop improvement plans for underperforming schools, but Congress failed to adopt President George H. W. Bush's "America 2000," which called for the development of voluntary national standards and exams, school report cards, merit pay for teachers, school choice demonstration projects, and alternative certification for principals and teachers (McGuinn, 2006).

5. The Great Society actually included health care (Medicare and Medicaid), food stamps, job training, and public service employment; however, it favored providing services that would help economically marginalized citizens help themselves (e.g., education and job training) rather than direct interventions in the labor market through large-scale job creation or income redistribution like the New Deal (Kantor & Lowe, 2006).

6. Research shows that *Brown v. the Board of Education* reduced the high school dropout rates of African Americans, while integration had no effect on the graduation rates of white students. *Brown* also improved the occupational attainments and earnings, and adult health status, of African Americans; decreased their rates of incarceration, homicide, and homicide victimization; and reduced police spending (see Balfanz & Legters, 2004; Guryan, 2004; R. Johnson, 2011; G. Orfield & Lee, 2005; D. Weiner et al., 2009). For more on this topic, see Chapter 9, note 3.

7. D. Cohen and Moffitt (2009), Cross (2004), Kantor and Lowe (2006), and Stein (2004) discuss issues with the ESEA.

8. In *Swann v. Charlotte-Mecklenburg Board of Education* (1971), the Supreme Court unanimously upheld busing as a constitutional remedy to address de facto segregation—the prevailing pattern of segregation in the North and West—and achieve racial balance in schools. However, in *Milliken v. Bradley* (1974), the Court overturned a Detroit plan to transfer students outside school district boundaries to address de facto segregation, holding that school districts were not obligated to desegregate unless it was proven that district lines had been purposely drawn with racist intent (M. Orfield, 2015). *Milliken* was decided amid rising grassroots suburban populism, including violence in the streets, antibusing crusades, taxpayer revolts, and other movements designed, for some, to preserve race- and class-based spatial patterns and, for others, to reduce property taxes, which fund half the costs of schooling. These events took place as growing numbers of citizens were suffering from economic insecurity due to *stagflation* (inflation combined with a recession). Others were concerned about rapid changes in their children's schooling as a result of school busing and integration. These newly engaged "suburban warriors" (McGirr, 2002) built up the parapolitical sphere on behalf of change. This included funding conservative think tanks, electing "anti-tax-and-spend" school boards, and lobbying for tax limitation measures, such as Proposition 13 in California and 2 ½ in Massachusetts (McGirr, 2002; Toch, 1991). This discussion is not making claims about the merits or pitfalls of school busing to remedy segregation. The point is that, since *Milliken,* the federal courts have moved away from redressing segregation, as evident in the Supreme Court's decision in *Parents Involved v. Seattle School District* (2007) and the release of more than 200 medium- and large-sized districts from desegregation orders between 1991 and 2009. The latter decisions gradually increased segregation in these districts relative to those that remained under court order (Reardon et al., 2012).

9. Because homeownership is a key source of economic security and wealth, the government also contributed to a racial wealth gap that continues to this day and is larger than the wage gap. For more on these policies, see Badger and Cameron (2015), L. Cohen (2003), Domonoske (2016), Hanks et al. (2018), K. Jackson (1987), Katznelson (2005), Lassiter (2006), Shapiro et al. (2013), and Starkman (2014).

10. Private employers and unions exacerbated these issues by excluding African Americans from higher paying blue-collar (manual labor) and white-collar (e.g., office and management) jobs. This impeded their ability to compete with working-class and upper-income whites for homes in neighborhoods with better-funded schools (Katznelson, 2005). Two other examples are the expansion of private and religious academies and adoption of policies that offered school choice within countywide school districts; research shows that both of these were used to resegregate the South (Carr, 2012; Hohle, 2012; and Reardon & Yun, 2002).

11. In terms of research at that time, Hanushek (1989) argued that resources (inputs) would not (consistently) improve outcomes because some schools use funds effectively, while others do not; Burtless (1996) provided a counterargument.

12. For how these tactics construct policy change, see M. Jones and McBeth (2010), McBeth et al. (2007), A. Schneider and Ingram (2005b), Shanahan et al. (2011), and Stone (1997, 1989).

13. J. Wilson (1980) argued that public policies create four different types of politics (client, interest group, majoritarian, and entrepreneurial) depending on how they diffuse or concentrate costs and benefits. He focused on *tangible* costs and benefits, yet acknowledged the existence of *psychological* ones (e.g., people being more attuned to losses than gains). Unlike Stone (1989, 1997), he did not discuss how policy makers strategically manipulate *perceptions* about costs and benefits to effect political change.

14. One example of the emerging conservative presence was the EXPECT Coalition. It was founded in 1998 to organize family and education groups that felt they had been excluded in policy debates (DeBray-Pelot, 2007).

15. Chester Finn described the BLOB as a "synonym for [the] 'education establishment'—the myriad adult interest groups and institutional forces that . . . control American public education and live off it . . . [like] teacher unions . . . administrator groups, textbook publishers, software vendors, colleges of education, state and district bureaucracies, and so on. Like a 'blob' they're without any clear shape or mission other than self-preservation. And . . . uncommonly difficult to move out of the way on behalf of the needs and interests of children" ("Eight Questions for Chester Finn," 2010).

16. Tax breaks, for example, mobilize beneficiaries but the general public remains quiescent because the costs are largely hidden in the form of less revenue for other programs that improve the general welfare. Budget deficits are less likely to generate negative feedback than cutting programs because they levy taxes on future generations to provide present benefits.

17. This supports J. Wilson's (1980) claim that people are more sensitive to losses than gains; however, in some policy areas, the government directly provides services for some while subsidizing the market for others. Housing, for instance, is largely distributed according to individual taste, need, and the ability to pay, but the government subsidizes homeownership through tax deductions (tax expenditures) while funding public housing through budget expenditures. Political conflict is minimal for the former (tax expenditures) because they are hidden in the tax code.

In contrast, public housing typically engenders heated political debate because the government is overtly providing benefits to a concentrated group (e.g., low-income families); opponents are also able to use moral reasoning to stigmatize the beneficiaries. This includes using the rhetoric of "welfare queens" to convey that poor single mothers cheat the system and are unworthy of government largesse (Schneider & H. Ingram, 2005). My qualitative analysis suggests that proponents struggled to gain widespread support for the *Robin Hood approach* for similar reasons. Public schools are (largely) funded through property taxes. The property tax system has resulted in more revenues for school districts with thriving local economies and more expensive homes. Those households are also subsidized through federal and state tax breaks. To offset the resulting revenue differences, Congress must justify why some communities or children deserve preferential treatment (i.e., concentrated benefits) through a highly visible adjustment to the budget. One problem is that educational performance has typically been portrayed as "merit based"—related to effort—rather than resulting from structural factors like socioeconomic inequality, segregation, or unequal school financing. This bias implicitly or explicitly blames poor and minority children (and the schools that serve them) for underachievement. Meanwhile, homeowners have been portrayed as being entitled to tax breaks. The early ESEA justified federal intervention in education by constructing poor children as "culturally deprived." Policy makers claimed federal spending would benefit the nation (diffuse benefits) by enabling poor children to become contributing members of society. Research shows that this framing and the resulting policy design stigmatized poor children—many of whom were minorities due to a high poverty rate—in ways that impeded their educational progress (Stein, 2004).

18. New (centrist/conservative) Democrats first proposed these reforms at the end of President Clinton's second term in office under the Public Education Reinvestment, Reinvention, and Responsibility Act. Known as the 3Rs, it included proposals that had been advanced across many decades. It received only 11 votes in the Senate, all from New Democrats.

19. Also like New Democrats, Bush tried to provide a "third way." He acknowledged that some, in "reaction to these disappointing results . . . have decided . . . there should be no federal involvement. . . . Others suggest we merely add new programs. . . . There must be another way . . . to a more effective federal role" (U.S. House of Representatives, 2001c, pp. 1–2).

20. Policies involving *entrepreneurial politics* are unlikely to be adopted unless they have someone to mobilize apathetic and unconnected individuals because they concentrate costs on one group while diffusing benefits onto a larger population that is not organized. In the case of public smoking bans, entrepreneurial politics involved convincing citizens to fight smokers and the entertainment industry (e.g., restaurants, bars). The latter had a strong incentive to mobilize and protect their interests; the former did not see themselves as a group.

21. Senator Jeffords (I-VT) said, "There is no question that we need to improve our Nation's schools. . . . [Performance] declines relative to . . . other nations as students move through the grades. . . . Almost half of all adults have either dropped out of high school or . . . not pursued . . . post-secondary. . . . [We had to] raise the cap on the number of H-1B visas because this Nation is lacking . . . skilled employees" (*Congressional Record*, December 18, 2001, S1336667).

22. The best example of this framing is Senator Kennedy's remarks during the debates on the Conference Report (*Congressional Record*, December 17, 2001, S13322), but the narrative diffused across parties, as evident in Congressman Boehner's (R-OH) statement: "Robert Kennedy . . . called the achievement gap between disadvantaged students and their peers . . . 'a stain on our national honor.' We cannot let this tragedy continue unchecked" (U.S. House of Representatives, 2001a).

23. There were some partisan differences. Liberals were still more interested in the level of resources; conservatives continued to favor localism over federal control. However, the language of "money *alone* is not the answer, reforms are also needed" (New Democrats and Republicans), "money is not the *sole* solution, but accountability will not improve public education unless the federal government better targets Title I funds" (liberals), and "the federal government needs to provide state and local governments with more flexibility through block grants while holding public schools accountable through school choice" (conservatives) provided common ground. The language of *tinkering* also enabled members to advocate more resources by pushing specific federal programs, such as reading or teacher training, without overtly stating that "money is the answer."

24. This narrative emerged in response to growing criticism from both the left and the right once reports began to circulate about how the AYP provision would result in large numbers of schools being identified as failing. Even G. W. Bush began to back away from more rigorous accountability (Bumiller, 2002; Sack, 2001).

25. When opinion polls asked whether students should be required to pass a standardized test to be promoted to the next grade, yes votes (77%) exceeded those that said no (20%) or expressed no opinion (3%); however, Americans did not support the claim that testing is the only—or even the best—way to improve the quality of education. Most preferred paying teachers more, with providing schools with more resources and using standardized tests to hold schools accountable basically tied for second. At the same time, Americans were divided over whether there is too much (30%), not enough (23%), or about the right amount (43%) of testing, and a wide margin believed examples of a student's work (68%) were better than standardized tests (26%) for measuring academic achievement (PDK, 2001).

26. I am not claiming that no one discussed issues with testing. These concerns were evident early in the debates when Democrats were more likely to discuss the pathologies of testing and conservatives were more likely to discuss the pathologies of federal control through testing. Still, many of these pathologies were actually negative tales about the behaviors of public school educators, including concerns about cheating, "teaching to the test," or narrowing the curriculum by teaching only tested content and subject areas (math and ELA). These concerns about testing were largely silenced during the Conference Report debates. Moreover, those who discussed issues still largely argued in favor of NCLB.

27. Senator Carper (D-DE) mentioned that Senator Kennedy (D-MA) had been left out of initial discussions but became a leader in the development and adoption of NCLB (*Congressional Record,* December 17, 2001, S13335–S13336). Owing to the contested presidential election between Gore/Lieberman (D) and Bush/Cheney (R), Joe Lieberman, a New Democrat, was also not invited to the initial meeting yet he too was part of the working alliance that translated Bush's blueprint into NCLB.

28. See Blair (2002) and DeBray-Pelot (2007). Teachers blocked vouchers and the Straight A's block grant.

29. Not everyone framed non–public school others as victims of the self-interested education establishment. Congressman Payne (D-NJ), an African American, engaged in a soliloquy with Dr. Foster in response to her claim that "public officials" did not support "allowing low-income parents to escape poor-performing schools . . . fighting and funding the fight against school choice." He said "there is nobody fighting it . . . no ads . . . you have got the airways all by yourself . . . no organized effort . . . practically all of these Congressmen . . . [pushing] vouchers . . . don't talk about vouchers in their community, because people in their community don't want vouchers . . . have good public schools. . . . Why can't we do in our inner cities what you have . . . [by improving] the public school system" (U.S. House of Representatives, 2001d).

30. See, e.g., the testimonies of Congresswoman Slaughter (D-OH) and Congressman Etheridge (D-NC) (*Congressional Record*, December 13, 2001, H10083, H10099).

31. Congressman Ballenger (R-NC) stated, "I know . . . [the elimination of] private school choice is . . . a sticking point. . . . I ask that we look at the reforms this bill does provide and not what it does not. Do not throw the baby out with the bathwater. . . . [It] allows public school choice . . . children in failing schools to obtain tutoring by private or religiously-affiliated educators" (*Congressional Record*, May 22, 2001, H2398). Senator Mikulski (D-MD) said she was voting for NCLB because, as "a pragmatist," she did not want the legislation to "be an example of the perfect is the enemy of the good" (*Congressional Record*, December 18, 2001, S13370).

32. When rising in opposition, Congresswoman Rivers (D-MI) said, "Less bad is not good. It is not legitimate to argue for passage of a flawed proposal on the basis that it could be worse" (*Congressional Record*, May 22, 2001, H2404).

33. An example of members using their relationships to pressure one another to vote for NCLB is the soliloquy between Congressmen Souder (R-IN) and Ballenger (R-NC). Souder stated, "I remember as a kid, I heard . . . Nixon say we are all Keynesians now . . . [well] we are all liberals now in education. . . . Not . . . many conservatives . . . are going to stand up under the pressures that we are under, and against the polls, and oppose this bill" (*Congressional Record*, May 22, 2001, H2410). Ballenger (R-NC) tried to put conservatives at ease by saying "just a few minutes ago, the Assistant Secretary told me that my conservative friends should remember that the management of the Department has changed, and their ideas will have some influence there" (*Congressional Record*, May 22, 2001, H2398). Souder then responded that the "next president will not be George W. Bush," and we may "have someone who is going to ram this stuff down our throat . . . and rue the day . . . we pass a bill with less flexibility, more money, more bureaucracy, and now national testing" (*Congressional Record*, May 22, 2001, H9008). Just as interesting, liberals—like Senator Paul Wellstone (D-MN)—then tried to shame conservatives into respecting ideological boundaries to prevent the adoption of NCLB (*Congressional Record*, December 18, 2001, S13368).

34. See, e.g., the testimonies of Senators Ted Kennedy (D-MA) and John McCain (R-NM) (*Congressional Record*, December 17, 2001, S13324, and December 18, 2001, S13385).

35. When political interests link policy problems to heated events or controversies in the larger political culture, they are using a policy surrogate to expand the conflict and gain a competitive advantage (Shanahan et al., 2011).

36. The language of state and local entitlement was not uniform and was used to both support and oppose NCLB. Some—mostly conservative opponents of NCLB—argued that state and local governments were entitled by the U.S. Constitution, "know more about their children than Washington bureaucrats," serve as "laboratories of democracy" (encourage the participation of different groups at the local level and therefore develop many different policy solutions that may be tested and copied by other states if successful), and were more efficient and effective because they are "closest to the people." Most members combined these arguments with statements about the need for freedom and flexibility, but the definition of *freedom* varied by partisan affiliation. Republicans focused on giving state and local governments more *freedom from* the federal government (i.e., block grants) and parents more *freedom from* the public school monopoly (i.e., choice). Democrats stressed *freedom to* perform better through the infusion of more and better targeted federal resources. In addition, Republicans often portrayed state and local governments in positive ways, but then separated public schools from local governments to convey that public services were inferior to private ones, while still conveying that "local" is superior to "national."

37. Despite these similarities, members were far more likely to *overtly* frame at-risk schools (SINI and schools that served large numbers of economically disadvantaged students) in *both* positive and negative ways. Typically, this was done to support providing or withholding resources or to justify penalizing poorly performing schools through labeling, restructuring, school closures, and/or competition. Even when these narratives blamed insufficient resources, the valance was typically negative; members conveyed that these schools and teachers were inferior.

38. Senator Lieberman, a New Democrat, claimed that public schools were in need of reinvigoration (*Congressional Record*, December 18, 2001, S13398); Senator Sessions (R-AL) complained, "We have too many schools where children are locked into a failing system. . . . Nobody even knows or cares that they are falling behind. They can't go to any other school. They are required by law to attend this dysfunctional school" (*Congressional Record*, December 18, 2001, S13394).

39. Some Democrats used similar language. Senator Bayh (D-IN), a New Democrat, said NCLB contains "a robust commitment to parental choice and the inclusion of market forces within our public education system, while still retaining the genius of a public education, which is the implicit guarantee of a good education for everyone, not just those who would do well in a purely market-based system. . . . We have public school choice . . . [and] supplemental services . . . a choice for afterschool, summer school, and weekend tutorials . . . a meaningful, determined commitment to charter schools, making them an integral part of the public education system, to give more vitality . . . innovation . . . accountability to public schools through charter schools" (*Congressional Record*, December 17, 2001, S13331–S13332).

40. Senator Gregg (D-NH) stated, "One of those images that stands out . . . [is governor] Faubus, from Arkansas . . . [and the] National Guard . . . standing in the school door . . . [not letting African American children] in the school. . . . Today what we have are people standing in that school door not letting kids out, locking them in those schools which are not teaching . . . because the bureaucracy and the labor unions fear the option of giving parents a choice. . . . This is not about education. This is about the power of political groups to influence the process. When you have lost generation after generation of kids to schools that are failing . . . and you know that every child who goes through that school is not going to have a chance to participate in the American dream . . . a civil right is . . . being denied. . . . We have an obligation . . . to first give that child an option to get a decent education and, second, to put real pressure on that public school system to improve . . . [but choice] affronts the power politics of Washington, DC, which are structured around bureaucracies and labor unions that will at all costs defend their turf" (*Congressional Record*, June 12, 2001, S6064).

41. The rhetoric about poor and minority children often conveyed or implied that it would take courage or heroism to "take a gamble" on their behalf. Congressman Boehner (R-OH) said, "[It reflects] a willingness . . . to take a gamble on behalf of our poorest students . . . the courage . . . to challenge conventional thinking and party orthodoxy . . . our President . . . his courage in proposing these reforms and his courage in continuing to press for them. . . . During his campaign . . . [he] took a courageous stand. . . . It was a bold and courageous move . . . without a sound, basic education, the chance at the American dream does not exist" (*Congressional Record,* December 13, 2001, H10092 and H10103–H10104).

42. The statement of Senator McCain (R-AZ) is a good example of both ways of framing parents. He stated that NCLB ensures "parents are better informed . . . by providing pertinent information regarding their child's school. . . . Parents are our first teachers. Our first classroom is the home, where we learn the value of hard work, respect, and the difference between right and wrong. . . . The home is the most important Department of Education. Parental involvement is the best guarantee that a child will succeed in school. I am genuinely excited . . . [about] reforms taking place across the country—namely school vouchers and charter schools—that are wisely built on this premise: Let parents decide where their children's educational needs will best be met. . . . School choice stimulates improvement and creates expanded opportunities for our children to get a quality education" (*Congressional Record,* 2001, December 18, S13385).

43. Congressman George Miller (D-CA) claimed, "[NCLB] is built upon a deep and uncompromising belief . . . that all of America's children can learn . . . an impoverished child does not mean a child that cannot learn. . . . [It redirects] resources to dramatically enhance the opportunities for success. . . . We cannot guarantee the success, but we can provide the opportunity" (*Congressional Record,* December 13, 2001, H10102–H10103).

44. For instance, Congressman Isakson (R-GA) stated, "Robert Browning was once asked . . . what his definition of education was and what it meant to a human being. His answer was very simple: education makes a people easy to lead, difficult to drive; easy to govern and impossible to enslave. . . . The poor and most disadvantaged children in America's public schools are in fact enslaved today by ignorance" (*Congressional Record,* July 18, 2001, H4124).

45. A panel of the U.S. Court of Appeals for the Sixth Circuit ruled 2–1 in 2008 that states and districts were not required to spend their own funds to comply with NCLB due to a clause that said "Nothing in this act shall be construed to . . . mandate a state or any subdivision . . . spend any funds or incur any costs not paid for under this act." That language had first been added to several federal education statutes in 1994. The full U.S. Court of Appeals for the Sixth Circuit deadlocked 8–8, and the Supreme Court refused to hear the case (Keller, 2005; A. Klein, 2010).

46. See Loveless (2006) and PDK (2015) for an analysis of changing public attitudes on NCLB.

47. SIG was expanded in 2009 under the American Recovery and Reinvestment Act (ARRA). The goal was to turn around 5,000 of the nation's lowest performing schools by providing temporary grants in exchange for implementing one or more of four interventions: (a) transformation (replacing the principal, restructuring the school, and evaluating teachers and principals using student test scores); (b) turnaround (fire the school's principal and teachers and allow the new principal to rehire no more than 50% of the faculty); (c) restart (convert the school to a charter school); and (d) closure (close the school and transfer students to another school). Transformation was the most common model, followed by turnarounds (Hurlburt et al., 2011).

48. Education commissioner Arne Duncan's claim that the opt-out movement was limited to parents' concerns about their children's test scores was not accurate. Compared to the general public, opt-out activists were more opposed to using test scores to judge teacher performance, but were also more concerned about the underfunding of public schools, the CCSS, and the corporatization/privatization of education. For example, while the general public ranked increased school funding as fourth of five important ideas for improving schools, opt-out activists rated it second (Pizmony-Levy & Saraisky, 2016).

49. The 1,000-plus-page ESSA legislation was approved by a vote of 359–64 in the House and 85–12 in the Senate. Senator Lamar Alexander (R-TN and chairman of the Senate HELP Committee) and Senator Patty Murray (D-WA and ranking HELP chair) worked with their House counterparts—Representatives John Kline (R-MN) and Robert Scott (D-VA)—to bring both sides together (Kerr, 2015; R. Klein, 2015a; Layton, 2015b).

50. Representative John Kline (R-MN), for instance, claimed Washington had been micromanaging the nation's classrooms for too long and said the ESSA would "turn the page on the failed status quo" by restoring local control (Kerr, 2015). White House press secretary Josh Earnest, on the other hand, praised the bill because it would "reduce over-testing and one-size-fits-all federal mandates" (Kerr, 2015). In terms of interest groups, NEA president Lily Eskelsen García stated that the ESSA "took a historic step to usher in a new era in public education that will ensure every child has equal opportunity to a high quality education regardless of ZIP Code." She gave praise that it would for "the first time since . . . [NCLB empower] educators as trusted professionals to make school and classroom decisions while keeping the focus on students most in need" (National Education Association [NEA], 2015). Eric Heins, president of the California Teachers Association, said he was excited to "help usher in a new era of local control and reform . . . that recognizes the potential of all children" (Resmovits, 2015).

51. President Obama claimed that he supported the ESSA "because it's good for the students . . . communities . . . [and] our economy. . . . It really goes to the essence of what we are about. . . . There is nothing more essential to living up to the ideals of this nation than to make sure every child is able to live up to their God given potential" (Layton, 2015b).

52. For more statements from policy makers and interest groups about pragmatism, unleashing excellence by restoring power to local communities, linking education reform to an improved economy, and providing students a chance to succeed versus an equal OTL, see AFT (2015), Kerr (2015), R. Klein (2015a), Layton (2015b), and NEA (2015).

53. Most states did not take advantage of the offered flexibility. For instance, the ESSA invited up to seven states or groups of states to participate in a pilot that would use performance tasks and other types of student work instead of state tests. Only Louisiana, New Hampshire, and Puerto Rico submitted applications by the April 2 deadline. States could also allow districts to use nationally recognized high school tests, like the SAT or ACT, instead of the state's high school exams. Some states were already using the former under their NCLB waivers. Only three took advantage of the change under the ESSA. States further did not take advantage of the provision that allowed them to administer interim tests during the year and combine the results into a summative score—instead of a single end-of-the year test. This change would have redressed teachers' concerns that end-of-year tests do not provide timely and actionable information for parents, students, and teachers to make adjustments during the year. It would have also reduced the need to cram too much material into the early part of the year to meet the testing window, but then having "slack" at the end (A. Klein, 2018b). All of these changes presented technical challenges for already-burdened state DOEs. Psychometricians, for example, warned against combining assessments into one summative score, stating it might produce invalid results; there were also concerns that college entrance exams did not align with state curriculum and therefore might produce invalid results (Gewertz, 2018; A. Klein, 2018b).

Chapter 3

1. Federal and state court decisions protected affirmative action, special education, and busing to integrate public schools; the courts also provided free speech and due process protections to students, who had begun mobilizing as a result of the Vietnam War. In terms of curricular and organizational changes, most were designed to increase graduation rates and thereby extend higher educational opportunities to a wider margin of students. Many high schools, for instance, began offering electives in business, the arts, and the humanities and/or teaching vocational classes, such as auto mechanics and beautician training. They also created social studies as a discipline by expanding the history curriculum to include political science, economics, sociology, and psychology in addition to American and world history. Other reforms provided "life adjustment skills" and improved students' mental health and self-esteem. The latter is evident in the institutionalization of health education programs, which taught nutrition, sex education, and the dangers of drug and alcohol abuse. In addition, schools tried to reduce discipline problems and the dropout rate by expanding extracurricular activities to include a wider variety of after-school sports and clubs; by easing the transitions between elementary, junior, and high school; and by making all levels of education more student-friendly. Many districts, for example, substituted "middle schools" for junior high to provide more services for children within smaller learning environments. Others allowed high school students to leave during free periods or spend free time in student lounges— contingent on good behavior. Districts also began abandoning corporal punishment, removing dress codes for students and teachers, and including students in decision-making processes (Hayes, 2004; Toch, 1991).

2. Unemployment reached 9 percent in spring 1975—its highest level since 1941—and skyrocketing energy costs pushed inflation into the double digits. This "stagflation" undermined economic security (Collins, 2007).

3. For a discussion of how economic concerns led to growing conservatism, see Collins (2007), Jennings (1990), Matusow (1984), and Troy (2005). The use of flexible labor practices has continued, and there has been a huge increase in subcontracted, temporary, and irregular work since 2005 (Katz & Krueger, 2016). Many of these practices reflect the importance of consumerism in a capitalist economy, especially its emphasis on rapid changes in demand as a way to increase consumption and business profits. Within this environment, it makes less sense to train and promote from within since the needed skills and knowledge constantly shift with changing demand.

4. As discussed in Chapter 1, total union membership has suffered a 70-year decline; union members now make up less than 11 percent of the workforce, a drop from 35 percent during World War II (Wolf & Korte, 2018). Private-sector unions have especially declined since the 1980s, with membership plummeting from about 17 percent of the workforce in 1983 to 6 percent today (Pilkington, 2017). Government policies and actions contributed to this decline, including the growth in states adopting RTW laws. In comparison, more than one in three public workers belong to a union, a percentage that has remained relatively steady for decades (Berlin & Bentle, 2018; Cohn, 2015; Gunn, 2018; Manzo, 2017; National Right to Work Committee, 2016; Opfer & Han, 2017). This is likely to change because RTW is now the law of the land for public employees as a result of the Supreme Court's *Janus* decision.

5. By the 1920s, three large companies dominated American auto manufacturing: General Motors, Ford, and Chrysler. American companies in the 1970s struggled with increased competition from foreign auto manufacturers and rising oil prices. Chrysler was bailed out by a $1.5 billion federal loan in 1979 (Troy, 2005).

6. See Amlung (2010), Blumenthal (2002), and Roberts (2006a, 2006b). Ford never explicitly said "drop dead." He was actually a moderate but adopted a tough love approach over the objections of his then vice president, Nelson Rockefeller, who had been the governor of New York.

7. NAEP was established in 1968 by Congress to sample the nation's students and measure annual progress.

8. For support of these claims, see B. Gross and Gross (1985), Pincus (1985), National Committee for Responsive Philanthropy (1999), Toch (1991), and Vinovskis (2009).

9. See, e.g., Cuban (2004), Tyack and Cuban (1995), Layton (2015a), Pincus (1985), Toch (1991), Tyack (1974), and Whitman (2015). Governors focused on developing human capital as a way to attract business investment and bolster their state economies. This included giving business-economic interests a prominent place in education reform efforts. Toch (1991, p. 18) writes, "No fewer than thirty-six states campaigned for . . . a $3.5 billion assembly plant for the Saturn automobile." GM later said they chose Tennessee due to its "school-reform package." Governor Lamar Alexander (TN) would eventually chair the National Governors Association (NGA) and then become a U.S. Senator. The NGA has since played a prominent role in all national education debates.

10. The statement of Jim, a rural high school math teacher, exemplifies the views of others: "[In] the . . . 1990s, the economy was doing very well. Private businesses were making a lot of money. The stock market was booming. Everybody was happy. . . . [They didn't] care that teachers were not participating in the boom, but they were not questioning teacher salaries . . . neither did they . . . say, 'Wow, we must be doing a good job educating everyone because the economy is booming.' But, when things are not going well . . . the economy is doing poorly . . . must be those teachers slacking off. And when people in the private sector . . . lose their jobs . . . [they] question why public servants are . . . making a salary . . . want us to give up our salaries and benefits. . . . They forget . . . teaching is end-loaded. . . . A teacher is making $80,000 a year but . . . started out at $9,000. . . . Paid into the retirement system our entire careers. The people before us . . . did not . . . [but made] even less money when they started. . . . This is their only benefit for decades of public service."

11. For studies at the time, see Berliner and Biddle (1996) and Bracey (2000). Lubienski et al. (2011) discuss the rise of intermediary organizations in knowledge production, advocacy, and education reform.

12. In public opinion polls at the time, Americans rated the lack of financial support either first (PDK, 2000) or second (PDK, 2001) among the problems faced by public schools; claimed the amount of money spent on public schools differed from district to district a great deal (29%) or quite a lot (29%; PDK, 2001); said the amount spent affected the quality of education a great deal (38%) or quite a lot (30%; PDK, 2001); and listed finances as the main obstacle to improving public schools in their communities (PDK, 1999). Most also thought federal taxes (37%) were the best way to finance public schools, followed by state (33%) and local property taxes (21%; PDK, 1998).

13. Ted, a retired rural high school English teacher and former district union president, had this to say about concerns that businesses would move to other states or overseas if not provided with tax exemptions: "[The union] fought to have schools funded through general tax revenues, but the business lobby wanted to keep taxes down. . . . And, the state needs the tax revenues . . . so they want to create incentives for businesses to come here and stay here. They don't want them moving down south where unions are not as strong or overseas. . . . Business leaders . . . look at profit. . . . By keeping schools tied to property taxes, they are better able to restrict tax increases because it impacts parents and that creates an alliance there."

14. Paul, from whom we heard earlier, told this narrative about politicians framing taxes in general as the problem: "[Taxes] became *the* big issue . . . [in] political campaigns. . . . 'It's your money . . . government is not using your money wisely. . . . Government is the problem, not the solution. . . . I will put more money back in your pocket." . . . [By] appealing to people on that level . . . [they] created a national discourse that valued those kinds of appeals . . . [with] long-term consequences . . . a growing debt and a nastier public life. . . . [They did it to win] elections, but it appealed to people's baser selves. . . . [Implied their money] was not being spent wisely or going to 'others' . . . that they would be better off if the government didn't get the money."

15. There was more than one type of narrative about how symbolic violence spreads. Many discussed, for example, how older teachers are now framed as "dinosaurs" to empower citizens to question their higher salaries, encourage them to retire early, and thereby reduce taxes. Sherry, a rural elementary teacher, said, "[During] the budget vote, I got a question as the union rep . . . [about] why one teacher was making X . . . I realized it was me . . . and they knew they were talking about me. . . . I said, 'Yes, well I started here making $8,600 a year' [*laughs*]. . . . 'I have been here for 34 years.' . . . Someone said . . . I should retire so that someone else could have a job . . . make less money . . . [and] someone else would not be laid off. . . . I would do it if I thought it would make a difference but . . . that person will be gone next year . . . when they have to lay off another person. . . . Older teachers are . . . portrayed as 'dinosaurs.' . . . When I started, the older teachers were my mentors. Expertise is not the equivalent of being stale or prehistoric. . . . I am constantly changing what I am doing. . . . This is public rhetoric or public language. You see it in the newspapers . . . experienced teachers are being treated as dinosaurs . . . resistant to change. . . . [I'm not ready] to leave my classroom . . . my children."

16. Educators said the spread of market policies accelerated after *A Nation at Risk,* when state governments gave legitimacy to groups that had been marginalized in education debates during the 1960s and 1970s (e.g., conservative intellectuals and business-economic groups). It is important to note, however, that the proposals promoted by the latter groups were not uniform or uniformly supported across conservative interests and policy makers. Labeled "centrist conservatives," Republicans *and* (New) Democrats at the state and national levels supported standards and testing to hold schools accountable. Neoliberals, on the other hand, focused on reforming schools through choice (B. Gross & Gross, 1985; Kaestle & Lodewick, 2007). Nonetheless, all of these are consistent with the MMP.

17. For studies during this period that elaborated on how data were misused in ways that created a crisis of confidence in public schools and justified state accountability reforms, see Berliner and Biddle (1996) and Bracey (2000).

18. For studies at the time, see, e.g., Berliner and Biddle (1996) and Bracey (2000). See B. Baker et al. (2018), Epstein (2011), EdBuild ($23 billion), and Ushomirsky and Williams (2015) for evidence of funding gaps and how they disproportionately affect low-income and minority students.

19. See Baldi et al. (2007), Bracey (2008), Carnoy et al. (2015), Carnoy and Rothstein (2013), and NCES (2010b). Other cultural differences mentioned by educators include the inequitable financing of public schools in the United States and the low pay/poor status of the teaching profession.

20. Shanker conceptualized charter schools as an alternative to the elite public high schools that compete for highly performing students in many U.S. cities.

21. For studies that show teachers are the most important in-school variable, see Aaronson et al. (2007), Chetty, Friedman, and Rockoff (2011), Chetty, Friedman et al. (2014), Hanushek (2009), Rivkin et al. (2005), and Wright et al. (1997). Adler (2013) demonstrates that these studies influenced public discourse and education reform despite being criticized. For example, after the publication of the study by Chetty, Friedman, and Rockoff (2011), the *New York Times* claimed we could "raise a single classroom's lifetime earnings by about $266,000" if we replaced a poor teacher with an average one; President Obama used this datum in his State of the Union address. In addition, NCLB mandated students be taught by highly qualified teachers (HQTs) and that HQTs be equitably distributed across schools. To obtain HQT status, teachers had to hold a bachelor's degree, obtain a state teaching certificate/license, and demonstrate content-area knowledge. RttT and NCLB waivers further shifted the focus to outputs through teacher accountability: An effective teacher is one who can grow a student's achievement over time as measured by student test scores. RttT awardees were also required to ensure the equitable distribution of HQTs across schools (Center on Great Teachers and Leaders, 2014; McCarl, 2010; U.S. DOE, 2009).

22. See Boyd et al. (2005), Clotfelter et al. (2005), Hanushek et al. (2004), Lankford et al. (2002), Scafidi et al., (2008), and Sutcher et al. (2016).

23. See Butler and Beeghley (1974), Fagan and Holland (2002), Ford (2005), Geiser (2015), Jencks and Phillips (1998), Kidder and Rosner (2002), Lemann (1999), Santelices and Wilson (2010), Shepard (1987), and Valencia and Suzuki (2000).

24. Continuing with Liam's narrative, "there have been cases where unions have used poor judgment . . . should have delayed a raise or taken a freeze. . . . [But school districts] have the power in collective bargaining, which many districts like mine have used to actually keep salaries down and get concessions. . . . You would have to be an idiot in this poor economic environment to go in and make excessive demands. . . . That is a sure way to make the community angry with you. So, collective bargaining does put constraints on the actors involved."

25. See Eisenbrey and Kroeger (2017), Gould and Kimball (2015), and Lafer (2011, 2012a, 2012b).

26. Meagan works as an elementary teacher in a suburban school, but this narrative did not vary across social groups. A retired urban administrator and former urban elementary teacher, Nancy, said, "[Tenure is] about due process . . . with a profession where . . . people could come in and make all kinds of false accusations . . . a teacher needs something to back them up. . . . There was a teacher I would have liked to have kept . . . they were in the first year . . . definitely deserved the second year . . . [but] butted heads with someone in the building . . . [whose husband] served on the Board. . . . [She] created a false read on this person's abilities . . . there's a lot of politics that come into play at times."

27. Research shows that service, altruism, and intrinsic motivations are the primary reasons for becoming a teacher and are critical for job satisfaction and the decision to remain in teaching (Brookhart & Freeman, 1992; Lortie, 1975; Miech & Elder 1996; Ng & Peter, 2010; Stotko et al., 2007).

28. Administrators made similar arguments. Returning to Nancy's narrative, "[you] mainly have teachers who are there to really do the job, but there are people that . . . [shouldn't be there] . . . just came in, did their job, and left. I didn't . . . want to be working with a person . . . [who] reflected poorly on the profession. . . . [We] want to get rid of ineffective teachers . . . sometimes you could talk to a teacher . . . let them understand that it's just not their calling and they would be smart enough to leave. . . . Nobody wants a weakling. . . . Teachers don't want it any more than administrators. . . . The parents are not going to be happy. . . . [It drains] the strength of that building."

29. Again, administrators made similar arguments. Nancy continued, "[Sometimes, it was a] shuffle game. . . . Teachers would apply to . . . other buildings. . . . [With seniority] the person who has more experience . . . [moves] over a new person. That was actually tested a few times in our district and we . . . didn't have to take the person just because they had more experience. . . . [Before] you would start to play all kinds of games to . . . [not get] that candidate. . . . Like when you would actually post your openings . . . [or] get the word out and make it less attractive for a person you would not want . . . to hire. . . . There are known quantities in all districts . . . you would try to . . . not get them. . . . [What] occurred, while I was an administrator, was that we did not move people into tenure as readily."

30. See Chapter 9, notes 19 and 20. Liam, a retired high school English teacher and former district union president, offered this narrative about how the media and entertainment industry portrays teachers as self-interested in ways that make accountability reforms appear to be commonsense: "[A review about how a film] was sympathetic to teachers and showed why they were worried about what was going on . . . [said] something like 'It was nice to hear teachers talking about the welfare of students rather than about salaries and contracts.' How condescending and misleading. This is the liberal *New York Times* and is written by an intellectual . . . implying teachers only care about themselves. . . . Even if that was the case, and it isn't, why would teachers not be concerned about salaries? Everyone wants to earn a decent living. You can be concerned about that and still care for children . . . those of us who have been around . . . know how hard we had to work to get teachers . . . more humane working conditions and a living wage. . . . [We] play an important role in society and work hard. . . . Now, we are back to people claiming we are self-interested if we want some control over the conditions of our work. That we should give back what we have fought for so that they can reduce taxes, but then we say the teacher is the most important thing for learning and education is critical for America to compete in the world. It is totally paradoxical."

31. Four of the children were Black or Hispanic and lived in troubled neighborhoods. The one white student lived in the suburbs of Silicon Valley. Unlike the other children, her high school had excellent facilities, test scores, and graduation rates; however, her family was worried she would slip through the cracks due to poor test scores.

32. Guggenheim interviews charter school leaders, such as Geoffrey Canada, who—according to the film—escaped a "failure factory" in Harlem, graduated from Harvard, and then created the Harlem Children's Zone to "change the system." He also interviews Bill Gates, whose philanthropy foundation has invested millions of dollars in expanding charter schools in addition to funding education research. The other "educational leaders" are Michelle Rhee, the former chancellor of public schools in Washington, D.C., who gained a national reputation for closing schools and firing educators, and Howard Fuller, the former superintendent of Milwaukee Public Schools who is a nationally recognized advocate of charter schools and private school vouchers.

33. Lorna, an urban elementary teacher, described how she and a parent reacted to the movie's portrayal of teachers: "I never unclenched my hands. I walked out and there was an African American woman with her kids. . . . I said to the children, 'Do

you like your teacher at school?' And they said, 'We loooooooooovvvvve our teacher!'
... [The mother] said, 'I came to see this because I love what goes on in my children's
lives and I wanted to see what they were saying about teachers. It was such a vile
portrayal of teachers.'"

34. My interviews suggest that these claims are not self-serving since retirees, like
Liam, made the same arguments: "[It] overlooks the fact that charter schools take
the cream of the crop.... [Jeffrey Canada] imposes discipline rules ... demands
certain commitments from the parents ... students wear uniforms. He interferes with
individual freedoms ... restricts student voice. We would not get away with this in
public schools ... he has the autonomy to create and enforce an environment where
there is no fighting or bad behavior and, more importantly, the parents commit to
support that.... They also have funding ... for smaller class sizes and materials....
I would argue that, if we ... gave the right kind of support to all public schools and
gave teachers more autonomy, you could run a successful public school system."

35. Studies support educators' claims about how Finland differs from the United
States in ways that improve performance (see, e.g., Sahlberg, 2011). While Finland
recently began retooling its educational system in response to declining test scores,
it is not making its system similar to ours—recognizing instead that their scores
are being driven by global, technological, and socioeconomic factors (Helm, 2016;
Strauss, 2015). For a critique of how the media and policy makers misinterpret data
with respect to Finland and the United States, see Ayers (2016).

36. Paul, a retired middle school English teacher and former union president, said,
"[Societal] norms have changed.... A large part of it is the consumer culture [my
italics].... We own an awful lot ... glamorize ownership and downplay nurturing
or caring for the group.... If I would be cutting the lawn, a neighbor would come
over and stop and chat ... it was normal to pitch in and help neighbors.... That
doesn't happen anymore. People are so busy making a living, and part of this is
making enough to have a certain level of living, which is far beyond what anybody
ever expected to have in my generation, that they don't have time for one another ...
they are working longer hours to have 'more' individually, and ... having less time
with their children, family, friends, and neighbors ... people also feel, because they
work so hard and yet don't seem to get ahead, possessive about their income and less
inclined to help others. It is a vicious circle ... fear ... that their children will not
be better off unless they do all of these kinds of activities.... All of this fuels the
competition ... people do more and more for their children, so they have to do more
and more for their children ... [and] a selfish way of looking at things that was not
prevalent a generation ago."

37. Teachers often described this reduced status in terms of society but still placed
the blame on business-economic and political elites, including the media. Molly, a
suburban high school social studies teacher, explained, "When I was growing up,
the teacher was always right. I am not saying that's the right attitude, but if a teacher
called home ... I was in a lot of trouble. Today, parents don't back up the school or
teacher.... Some do, but many don't. You always hear negative things about teachers
in the media. And a lot of movies portray teachers ... and public schools in negative
ways. I think people, as a result, are less trustful about public schools and teachers....
[That] impacts teaching ... there is more hostility and divisiveness."

38. See American Association of Colleges for Teacher Education (2018), Ayers (2016),
Cass (2013), PDK (2018), Sutcher et al. (2016), and Will (2018b).

39. See Holland (2014), Hout and Elliot (2011), Kirp (2012), Ladd (2012), J. Lee
(2006), J. Lee and Reeves (2012), Monaghan (2014), M. O'Brien (2014), Reardon
(2011), Schofield (2005), and Whortman and Bryant (1985). See also Chapter 9, note 3.

40. Chapter 2 supports the views expressed by almost all of those I interviewed that policy makers from both parties have increasingly framed public schools, public school educators, and unions in negative ways to justify market-based reforms. Retirees, as well as teachers in their forties and older, were more likely to specifically discuss the negative framing of unions. Paul continued, "it's like this, you can . . . look at government as this group that is a 'them,' as opposed to 'us.' Or, you can look at government like it's 'we the people.' Similarly, you can look at a teachers' union like it belongs to 'the teachers' and an individual teacher like he or she is a union member. But, we are just people. It could be the teacher . . . [helping] their community or . . . the unionist. . . . It is very difficult to distinguish that someone is doing something as a person or as a union member. But teachers *very frequently* took out of their own pocket . . . for students. They bought individual items for students who could not afford them, but they also bought stuff for classrooms and for families in our community. If there was a fire or something going on, teachers raised money through their union. . . . The union would collect money for students who had gotten in a bad way . . . an illness or an accident. . . . [We also] collected money for other teachers for the same reason."

Chapter 4

1. See F. Hess and Leal (2005), Hrebenar and Thomas (2004), Moe (2011), Nownes et al. (2007), and Strunk and Grissom (2010).

2. For commentaries on the costs and benefits of collective bargaining, tenure, and seniority, see B. Baker (2014), Cambor (1999), Greene and Kahlenberg (2012), and Moe (2011). There are ongoing lawsuits in different states, but legislative changes have already greatly weakened or overturned tenure and seniority. Opponents claim these policies create opportunity gaps by making it expensive to remove underperforming teachers (see B. Baker, 2014; E. Brown, 2016; R. Klein, 2015b; Medina, 2014).

3. Paul, a retired middle school English teacher and former union president, stated, "PERB wasn't bad, but it still is an unlevel playing field. The people who run PERB are mostly former administrators and lawyers. They have a hierarchical mind-set . . . [treat] law students and new lawyers . . . [as] a glorified slave. . . . That's different from a professional mind-set [where you are equal once credentialed and socialized]. . . . PERB serves as a forum for the resolution of disputes, but all of the powers are still with the administrative side. . . . PERB has things they can do to unions and their members that are nasty financially and otherwise . . . [but] none of those tools to bear on the other side. . . . The main benefit . . . was for press releases. If PERB ruled in favor of us, we could use that as a headline [to legitimize our claims]. . . . But it's always risky going to PERB because they have teeth for us but not for them. In the years I was president of the union, I think we were the only district that got a positive [ruling] out of PERB [*laughs*]."

4. A former rural high school English teacher and district union president (Ted) described as follows the differences between the NEA and AFT at the time the state adopted a collective bargaining law: "[The leader of the AFT led] the largest local . . . out on strike in 1962. . . . [The NEA] did not see themselves as a union . . . did not wish to be militant . . . [and] were treated with a kind of paternalistic bent. If they were given a raise, there was no rhyme or reason why one person got $100 and another got $50, other than maybe the administrator liked you better or you had that administrator's daughter in class [*laughs*]. Then, you had the . . . [AFT] bargaining collectively and making really fast gains in . . . salaries and benefits. . . . That bill . . . narrowed the gap between the two. . . . It took a while . . . was *really* difficult to get the members to accept . . . in their hearts . . . they were equal to administrators. . . . A lot of teachers . . . did not want to unionize. . . . The image of the union was that it was militant . . . the teamsters . . . "the thugs" [*laughs*].

5. Liam, a retired high school English teacher and district union president, described how hard he had to work to reunite teachers after the strike: "I was really surprised by . . . the bitterness and anger . . . [against those who] crossed the picket line. . . . The 'scabs,' as they were called, were isolated. People would not dine with them . . . leave the room when they came in. . . . People felt they had been stabbed in the back. . . . I ended up having to mediate a lot of conflict as the head of the union. . . . It was not good for the union to have this bitterness. . . . [These] teachers were my teachers too. . . . There were many reasons why people crossed. . . . [Some] were the sole income for the family, some were just afraid to voice. . . . [One woman] was very religious and . . . a pacifist. She actually turned the money over that she made . . . to the union to help pay the fines . . . people who were really hurting economically. . . . Teachers are human beings, like everyone else, and . . . felt betrayed by the principals . . . the board . . . the superintendent and the community. . . . Our salaries were the lowest in the area and our class sizes the highest, and the community had benefited for a long time from low taxes. It was time to give back."

6. Paul's discussion of why teachers in his suburban district went on strike and what occurred in the aftermath shows why the uneven playing field, even after the adoption of the collective bargaining law, necessitated social cohesion: "The district was not negotiating in good faith . . . demanding that the union accept a half hour added to the teachers' workday before their team would negotiate other areas . . . attempting to provoke a strike. . . . [It] did not think the union was strong enough to do it . . . that was indeed the prediction given to the board. . . . [And the] superintendent was quoted in the evening newspaper . . . saying about teachers, 'It's like with children. You've got to explain . . . what the rules are so there won't be any misunderstanding.' . . . [Our] members were enraged by his comparison to children. . . . [We voted 87% in a secret ballot to strike and, after the strike, we plead] our case. . . . PERB stated . . . [our school board] had indeed provoked the strike by demanding the half hour concession as a prerequisite. . . . The fines and penalties were still imposed. However, the amount of time that dues deduction was refused the union was cut by half. . . . Between the end of the strike and . . . [the following year, we filed] ten grievances . . . mostly due to the district not complying [with the contract. For example, the district required] . . . a reason for 'emergency leave' . . . [and lost. It also denied] my request for the [20 days'] release time that previous [union] presidents had been granted. . . . PERB reversed that position. The district then took offense at an article in the union newspaper, in which a board member was . . . misquoted. . . . [We apologized but] the superintendent placed a reprimand in my personnel file. . . . It was grieved and won. . . . The district may not put a letter of reprimand . . . for union . . . activities not pertaining to . . . job performance."

7. In Illinois, for instance, AFSCME bargains on behalf of more than 75,000 public employees, and more than 90 percent are members. Nonmember (fair share agency) fees are set by hundreds of Illinois locals and usually amount to about 80 percent of members' dues (Geiger et al., 2018). In terms of teachers, West (1980) shows how the NEA successfully lobbied to end teachers' ability to associate with their local NEA without paying dues to the state and national NEA. In the state that is the subject of this analysis, public employees, like public school teachers, could not be compelled to join the union but, prior to *Janus*, were required to pay partial fees to the union that represents them at the bargaining table. That state policy has now been nullified by *Janus*.

8. Interestingly, two teachers said mandatory agency fees were initially unpopular with many rank-and-file members, even though the union lobbied for it. Continuing with Paul's narrative: "[The union had a legal right] to speak for all teachers, even those who were not members. Eventually, the state also required nonmembers to pay dues. . . . [It] was not designed to help unions. . . . [My district] voted against it. . . . This was . . . after we had gone on strike and those teachers were scabs. . . . There was still a lot of bitterness . . . it was like 98 percent that went on strike so that 2 percent was not going to make a difference for us but . . . [the state union] wanted the dues . . . [since] we have to represent these teachers [in contract negotiations] and . . . provide legal services for *all* of the teachers in any district that had a union by law . . . and so *all* teachers should have to pay dues. This was an economic argument, not a political one. . . . [The state] could have . . . taken those nonmembers out of the . . . [union's] responsibility. . . . Instead, they chose to make nonmembers pay [partial] dues but said that the dues of nonmembers could not be used for political purposes."

9. When collective bargaining is removed from the analysis, scores drop in *all states.* See Carini (2002), Carini et al. (2000), and Nelson et al. (1996).

10. B. Baker (2014) finds a correlation between states with strong teacher unions and more adequate overall funding levels. There is an even stronger correlation between states with weak unions (ranked 45th to 50th) and funding levels that are particularly low. These states also had less funding fairness, meaning high-poverty districts are systematically more likely to have fewer resources per pupil. The relationship is also robust for more competitive wages for teachers in states with stronger unions. While adjusted NAEP scores are somewhat—though not systematically—lower in states with weaker unions, they are *not* systematically lower in states with stronger ones. This latter finding challenges the position that unions suppress academic performance by reducing work effort and protecting "bad teachers." In addition, there was little relationship between union strength and the achievement gap between low-income and minority children and their peers. Although states with the largest growth in NAEP scores tended to have weaker unions, that was linked to the fact that they also had the lowest performance levels and therefore had further to grow. He concludes that there is a relationship between unionization and funding fairness, which studies show affects achievement and attainment; unionization also affects the relative competitiveness of teachers' wages, which studies show influence school districts' ability to recruit and retain HQTs. Recent studies of Act 10 more directly support these conclusions. As mentioned, it was adopted by Wisconsin in 2011 and significantly limited union power by restricting fund-raising and limiting the scope of collective bargaining. Act 10 reduced average test scores and did so largely at the lower half of the student achievement distribution. Declining achievement stemmed from a large reduction in teachers' salaries, a significant increase in turnover, and a decrease in teacher experience (Baron, 2017; Madland & Roxwell, 2017).

11. Other studies support that mandatory collective bargaining laws increased union membership (Freeman, 1986; Saltzman, 1985, 1988) and suggest that these laws may have increased political participation among teachers by creating a link between political engagement and teachers' occupational interests (Briney, 1958; Rosenthal, 1966; Zeigler, 1967).

Chapter 5

1. At McDonald's, workers are coached to smile and say "Welcome to McDonald's, may I take your order please?"

2. Jobs involving emotional labor meet three criteria: "They require face-to-face or voice-to-voice contact with the public . . . require the worker . . . produce an emotional state in another person—gratitude or fear for example . . . [and the employer is able to exercise] through training and supervision . . . a degree of control over the emotional activities of employees" (Hochschild, 1983, p. 147).

3. See, e.g., Day and Leitch (2001), Hargreaves (1998, 2000, 2001), Lasky (2000), Lortie (1975), Nias (1996), Schutz and Pekrun (2007), Schutz and Zembylas (2009), and Sutton (2007).

4. Some focused on using humor in the classroom, others discussed energy or enthusiasm, and many admitted there is a place for felt or feigned anger or disappointment, so long as these emotions are regulated.

5. See Case and Katz (1991) and Figlio (2007). Peer effects may be one reason why empirical research shows inputs—such as teachers' salaries, student–teacher ratios, and so forth—are not *consistently* linked with improved student achievement and attainment.

6. Teachers also model how to show emotions. Brian, a retired urban elementary teacher, offered this story: "I was never afraid to show my emotions. . . . [While reading a story, I would have to] stop and compose myself if it was sad. . . . The kids would say, "Look, he's crying!" [*speaking in a whisper*] I was not afraid to show anger if it was deserved . . . get them to understand. . . . You are a human being. You feel emotions. I feel emotions too."

7. See, e.g., Carneiro et al. (2007), Heckman and Kautz (2012), and Jacob (2002).

8. Some examples of these verbal and nonverbal cues include joking and laughing when discussing the need to motivate students, displaying tense posture, and using formal speech, meaning they stopped using contractions.

9. Paul, a retired suburban middle school English teacher, explained, "My parents used to say 'Do right by the kids.' And it's a good expression. Teachers should approach their profession that way: 'Do right by the kids.' They might get in trouble with the administrators. They might get in trouble with the parents . . . [but they] should be doing what they feel is the right thing for the kids."

10. As evident in the words of a suburban speech pathologist (Annie) and elementary teacher (Kelly), informants also discussed "comforting parents" and providing actual assistance—often at a cost to their own well-being:

KELLY: [I had a child with] emotional issues, and I probably spent the entire year with this child and . . . his mother and father . . . getting them as much help and services as I possibly could . . . working with the social worker . . . bringing them clothing, food . . . one-on-one time with the little boy . . . after school . . . before school . . . through first grade and second grade . . . the mom still taking . . . the domestic violence. . . . It just feels like . . . [getting emotional] no matter what I did or . . . anybody did. . . . Nothing seemed to work.

ANNIE: The psychologist and I had to meet with [a mother] . . . and . . . inform . . . her [that her] child was mentally retarded. And she burst into tears and put her head down on the table . . . sobbed for 20 minutes. . . . We could not console her . . . get her to even lift her head up off the table. . . . She herself was limited so . . . it just devastated her [*said very emotionally*] that her child . . . inherited her genes . . . is how she said it. . . . I'll never forget that experience as long as I live [*getting quieter*]. . . . It's still with me . . . a horrible memory for me.

11. Male and female teachers told similar narratives, as did educators from different backgrounds. For instance, a retired rural high school social studies teacher (Joe) said, "[A student] got arrested for breaking into a shoe store . . . the son of tenant farmers . . . lived in a dirt floor cabin, and . . . liked to wear women's shoes. . . . I was newly married . . . went to the sheriff . . . [said he] was a good kid . . . a senior . . . I would love to have him graduate. . . . I got the court and the sheriff to let . . . [him live] with us the last three or four months. . . . He graduated and I gave him a suit . . . [and he] walked across the stage. The folks came over . . . didn't even say thank you to my wife, but I feel very good about it. . . . If you are worth anything as a teacher, you're going to get involved personally with your students . . . help . . . with their problems beyond the classroom. . . . The academic relationship . . . develops into other things."

12. Educators from all backgrounds conveyed these ideas. Sharon, an urban high school art teacher, explained, "I invest an enormous amount of time in my job . . . am there more than I am home. . . . When I come home I'm completely exhausted. . . . I don't think . . . my children and my husband . . . suffer, but it is a hard job. . . . You invest yourself. . . . If you don't, then you . . . teach, but you are not a teacher. It is a lifestyle. . . . You live it. . . . [It] is what you talk about . . . think about before . . . [bed and] in the morning when you're eating your cereal and on the way into work. . . . It just consumes you. It is everything you think about."

13. Other studies support no significant gender differences (Hargreaves, 1998) or variations between elementary, middle, and high school teachers (Sutton, 2007) in terms of emotion management. Even so, secondary teachers in this study more frequently expressed using humor or engaging students in conversations about their outside interests rather than the more overt verbal or physical displays of caring used by elementary teachers, such as "side hugs" (i.e., standing side by side and putting an arm around a child's shoulder). Consistent with Hargreaves (1998), this study suggests that elementary teachers also display and suppress more intense emotions than secondary teachers. They spend more time with students and may therefore develop stronger affective ties, but occupational norms more strongly encourage expressing strong positive emotions and discourage expressing strong negative emotions in the primary grades owing to how both influence children's development.

14. Teachers' narratives suggest there are limits to this feeling rule. For instance, some teachers discussed the need to negotiate between developing caring relationships and maintaining some professional distance to meet the clinical side of teaching. Teachers also sometimes need to create distance to manage their emotions and perform their jobs, especially with recalcitrant students and parents.

15. Principals like Loretta, who is also a former urban elementary school teacher, made similar remarks: "[Teaching is] very emotional. . . . The kids . . . become your own. You take ownership. . . . If you don't . . . [you are not] doing your job well. . . . If somebody . . . [misbehaves] on a trip . . . [it's like my own child] misbehaved."

16. Educators were not opposed to appropriate uses of anger in the classroom. Brenda, a suburban high school math teacher, elaborated on appropriate and inappropriate ways to deal with anger: "[Once] or twice a year I . . . get mad. . . . They are like, "whoa" [*laughs*]. But I think they need to know that. . . . Emotions are part of life. . . . Mostly, I find that being respectful of my students means they are going to respect me back. I really don't have any discipline problems. . . . You cannot shout at your kids . . . [or] talk down to them. They don't respond to that. . . . But you can use your own emotions to motivate them. As long as you are not out of control with your temper, it is fine to let them know when they push too far or to yell to get their attention and wake them up a little bit [*laughing*], especially first thing in the morning. I am not yelling at them, I am just being loud [*laughs*]. And they laugh at me and that's good too. It's also good for them to see your excitement. . . . They know when you love what you teach . . . they respond to that."

17. For example, teachers in one school covered the classes of a fellow teacher who had lost her husband and was struggling to meet the demands of the job and care for two small children. The teacher was relatively new and had not accumulated leave. Colleagues each gave up a free period to teach one of her classes so that she would not have to return before she was emotionally prepared to do the job. These caring behaviors also helped students because they were taught by an experienced teacher, who was known by the students and their families, rather than by a long-term substitute or a succession of substitutes. Stories like this were not uncommon but mostly involved short-term commitments or helping colleagues in ways that were not specifically related to teaching classes.

18. Brian, a retired urban elementary teacher, discussed the importance of relationships at work as follows: "[The] better I get to know you, the more I am willing to do for you. . . . You have to do that for students, but . . . [also] for the school to run well. . . . A happy workplace is an effective workplace. I've worked in schools that were not happy, and it is cold. . . . You walk by and do not speak in the halls . . . the kids know it . . . can sense it. I didn't have that problem . . . because I . . . would always take the time to make someone laugh. . . . It made it easier to do the job and help others do the job. . . . The kids are better off."

19. See Brookhart and Freeman (1992), Lortie (1975), Miech and Elder (1996), Ng and Peter (2010), and Stotko et al. (2007).

20. A large body of research shows that teachers' work experiences influence their emotions and well-being (see, e.g., Day & Leitch 2001; Hargreaves, 1998, 2000, 2001; Noddings, 1992; Nias, 1996; Schutz & Pekrun, 2007; Schutz & Zembylas, 2009).

21. In Durkheim's (1996, pp. liv–lv) words, "a society made up of an extremely large mass of unorganized individuals which an overgrown state attempts to limit and restrain, constitutes a veritable sociological monstrosity. For collective activity is always too complex to be capable of finding expression in the single organ of the state. . . . The State is too remote from individuals, its connections with them too superficial and irregular to . . . penetrate the depths of their consciousness and socialize them from within. . . . A nation cannot be maintained unless between the state and individuals, a whole range of secondary groups are interposed. These must be close enough to the individual to attract him strongly to their activities and . . . absorb him into the mainstream of social life."

22. These findings are consistent with quantitative studies outside of education, which find that public servants are more active in civic affairs than other citizens and may be a source of social capital in society. Brewer (2003), for example, shows that public employment predicts civic participation; Houston (2005) finds that government employees demonstrate more "public service motivation"—defined as "a commitment to the public interest, service to others, and self-sacrifice" and measured through donations of money, time, and blood.

23. See Brouwers and Tomic (2000), Lortie (1975), D. Ingersoll (2003), R. Ingersoll (2001), Kyriacou (2001), Naring et al. (2006), and Wilhelm et al. (2000).

24. See Boyd et al. (2005), Hanushek et al. (2004), S. Johnson and Birkeland (2003), and Marinell and Coca (2013).

25. See Boyd et al. (2005), Clotfelter et al. (2005), Hanushek et al. (2004), R. Ingersoll (2001), Lankford et al. (2002), and Scafidi et al. (2008).

26. See Allensworth et al. (2009), Buckley et al. (2005), R. Ingersoll (2001), S. Johnson and Birkeland (2003), S. Johnson et al. (2004), Lobe et al. (2005), McLaughlin (1993), and Peske et al. (2001). Studies find that teacher satisfaction is influenced by teaching as an occupation, schools as organizations (i.e., work conditions), and outside factors (i.e., society at large); teachers are also motivated by intrinsic rewards (see Dinham & Scott, 1998, 2000; R. Ingersoll, 2001; S. Johnson & Birkeland, 2003; Lobe et al., 2005; Lortie, 1975; Rosenholtz, 1991).

27. See Rockoff (2004). Some studies suggest that teachers plateau early in their careers (Rivkin et al., 2005), but more recent research challenges these findings (Ladd & Sorensen, 2014).

28. See Allensworth et al. (2009), Borman and Dowling (2008), and Ronfeldt et al. (2013).

29. See Allensworth et al. (2009), Bryk and Schneider (2002), and S. Johnson and Birkeland (2003).

30. See, e.g., Kraft and Papay (2014) and S. Johnson et al. (2011).

31. See L. Goldstein (2002), Hargreaves (1998), Hunt (2006), Nias (1996), Noddings (1995), Sutherland et al. (1993), Sutherland and Lee (1989), and Sutton and Wheatley (2003).

32. See Goldstein (1999), Jennings and Greenberg (2008), Noddings (1992), Sutherland and Lee (1989), Sutherland et al. (1993), and Sutton and Wheatley (2003).

Part III

1. Congress funded RttT through an economic stimulus package—the American Recovery Reinvestment Act (ARRA) of 2009—which set some funding aside for education. Most of the money was used to mitigate teacher layoffs, but $5 billion was set aside for competitive grants of which most was used for RttT.

2. As part of the 2015–2016 budget, lawmakers in this northeastern state approved a change in the APPR system. Teachers and principals continued to earn one of four ratings: highly effective, effective, developing, or ineffective (HEDI); however, the new APPR framework replaced the three-component system (20 percent for student growth, 20 percent for student achievement, and 60 percent for observations) with a system where student performance and observation scores were weighted and combined into a matrix to determine a final overall rating. The overhaul reflected the governor's view that too many teachers were receiving high ratings. The state then reversed course, approving emergency regulations that put the system on hold for four years (until the 2019–2020 school year). APPR ratings were still calculated for advisory purposes, but not used to make decisions regarding tenure, improvement plans, or other employment issues for teachers. Principals were no longer evaluated based on student growth scores. The temporary moratorium—pending review on the use of test scores in teacher and principal evaluations—was recommended by a task force appointed by the governor. My interviews took place under the original system, but I continued to have informal conversations with some of the educators in this study through October 2020.

Chapter 6

1. See Bemelmans-Videc et al. (2007), Elmore (1987), McDonnell and Elmore (1987), Salamon (2002), and A. Schneider and Ingram (1990).

2. See Bemelmans-Videc et al. (2007), Rist (2007), A. Schneider and Ingram (1997), Weiss (1993), and Weiss and Tschirhart (1994).

3. PICs typically bypass public and private institutions and communicate directly with individuals in an effort to change how they think and act (Weiss, 1993); however, recent education reforms used public information to mobilize schools as communities and teaching as an occupation. NCLB did so by naming and shaming schools. NCLB waivers and RttT focused more clearly on naming and shaming educators—requiring, for instance, that states develop teacher and principal evaluation and support systems that are partly based on student progress over time. School districts used those systems to provide feedback to parents and educators and to make personnel decisions. In addition, all three policies required states to implement aggressive interventions in the lowest performing schools (U.S. DOE, 2002, 2009, 2012). As such, social contexts are quite important.

4. Vedung and van der Doelen (2007) acknowledge that PICs are often paternalistic yet argue that they are less coercive than other regulatory tools. Weiss (1993, 2007), however, finds that PICs often distort democratic processes, disempower citizens, and induce passivity; the effects are cumulative and long term. PICs are not necessarily biased against low-status groups, but they send out strong moral messages, and moral reasoning is frequently deployed in ways that justify and maintain status differences (see, e.g., Gusfield, 1986).

5. See Chapter 3, note 23 for studies on how testing institutionalizes the effects of class, race, ethnicity, and gender on the performance of children. Reardon et al. (2018) found that boys outperform girls on state tests that rely more heavily on multiple-choice questions—a common way to assess math knowledge—while girls outperform boys on tests when a larger proportion of the total score is determined by constructed response questions, where students write their own answers in a sentence or an essay. These differences explained about 25 percent of the variation in gender achievement gaps between states. Another example is that standardized tests, textbooks, and supporting teaching materials come from about three companies. Because standardized test questions are based on specific knowledge that is contained in the textbooks and supporting materials, the inability for low-resource schools to purchase them disadvantages their students (for support of this claim, see Broussard, 2014).

6. Ginny, who worked as an aide in an urban school prior to becoming a social studies teacher, explained how students' personal characteristics, backgrounds, and experiences affect test performance as follows: "The student has to want to pass that test and our kids come from such crazy backgrounds. I've . . . seen students . . . refusing to work or finish [the test] . . . that's not the teacher's fault . . . the teacher only has that student for six hours a day. There are a lot of other things going on at home and in their communities that affect their performance and . . . motivation . . . [In my school, so many students] have gone through life with inadequate health care and nutrition. They live in dysfunctional homes. . . . They're trying to deal with really chaotic environments . . . they tell you . . . [but] I've seen kids go home over the holidays and come back having dropped a lot of weight because there's no food. . . . They feel angry. . . . Many of them drop out."

7. See Chapter 2, note 6 and Chapter 9, note 3 for research that supports that segregation negatively influences academic achievement and attainment. See Chapter 9, note 2 for research that finds that inequitable financing negatively affects academic achievement and attainment. Like other education research, the latter studies show that resources matter.

8. See American Statistical Association (2014), Corcoran (2010), D. Harris (2007, 2011), McCaffrey et al. (2004), McCaffrey et al. (2009), Newton et al. (2010), Papay (2011), and Rothstein (2009).

9. Mary is an elementary teacher, but this narrative did not change across social groups. An art teacher (Gloria) told me, [The] fourth graders coming into art class after they took the math test . . . were actually saying, "I'm freaking out" . . . [because] how hard the test was. They were upset. . . . [As a student] I hated testing. I could remember the information but . . . I would blank. I had total testing anxiety. Or, I . . . knew the information but would not read the question right and get the answer wrong. . . . Kids were talking about those kinds of issues . . . felt a lot of pressure and . . . panicked. . . . That affects them over the long term, feeling like they are not good

test takers and . . . being ranked below their peers no matter how hard they work. . . .
Some . . . give up.

10. Soss (2005), for instance, found that some AFDC recipients stress how they
possess "normal" or "mainstream" values to differentiate themselves from other
"undeserving" recipients and avoid the social stigma attached to welfare. Reay (2004b)
found that 10- and 11-year-olds from poor and working-class backgrounds who
attended "demonized schools" in England—where no one wanted to go because they
were stigmatized—would describe "people like them" who went "there" but were
successful because they had not succumbed to drugs, gang membership, and bullying.
See also Reay and Lucey (2003) and A. Schneider and Ingram (2005b).

11. Anger against the stigmatization of teachers is evident in the narrative of a
suburban elementary teacher (Diane): "I really don't think parents know how much
of our own time and money we spend on our classroom. It is like a dirty little secret of
teaching. . . . [You have to] invest a lot of your income in your students and children
. . . to do the job well. . . . It is part of the rage I feel when I hear teachers being called
greedy. Let's see politicians invest their own time and money into their jobs instead
of asking for handouts from voters. I do it willingly because I love the kids and it is a
source of pride for me that my classroom is a warm and inviting place where children
feel safe to learn, but it hurts when I am labeled greedy. . . . I know that it is not me
personally . . . it is teachers . . . being labeled, but . . . you feel like, 'Why do I work so
hard and . . . care so much when I am . . . disrespected by the very people I serve?' I
mean, if government is labeling me greedy, how can we expect parents and students
to respect me? It feels really harsh and unfair. I am not the one who is bankrupting
this country . . . [or] who is in the paper for all sorts of unethical behaviors."

12. This narrative did not vary by occupational position or work status. A retired
urban elementary teacher (Elaine) and suburban administrator and former urban
psychologist (Sally) exclaimed,

ELAINE: [Suburban teachers have no idea] what it is like to work in urban schools . . .
take all of the support for granted. . . . This is a little mean-spirited, but . . . they
are overprivileged . . . don't get what it is like to work in an urban school, and yet
you feel like they are somewhat judgmental . . . about the kids and the teachers . . .
like they buy in to the idea that, because our test results are not on par with theirs,
that we must not work as hard. . . . The teachers I knew worked very hard under
very difficult working conditions.

SALLY: I worked in two very . . . different schools. . . . [Teachers in the] urban district
. . . are paid less . . . [than the suburban school] I am now in . . . yet they were
better. . . . They have to be because of what they deal with. They could go to a
suburban school but the suburban teachers in my current district could not go
there.

13. The Obama administration vastly expanded SIG under the ARRA by offering
temporary RttT grants (Hurlburt et al., 2011; U.S. DOE, 2011).

14. For empirical studies that support informants' claim that *the threat of reconstitution*
does not improve performance, see Anagnostopoulos (2003), Anagnostopoulos and
Rutledge (2007), Diamond and Spillane (2004), Finnigan and Gross (2007), Ladd
and Zelli (2002), Leithwood et al. (2010), Malen and Rice (2004), Mintrop (2004),
O'Day (2002), Spillane et al. (2002), Stringfield and Yakimowski-Srebnik (2005), and
Sunderman (2001).

15. For empirical studies on schools that have *actually been reconstituted*, see Dee
(2012), de la Torre et al. (2012), Designs for Change (2012), Mathis (2009), Mintrop
and Trujillo (2005), and E. O'Brien and Dervarics (2013). The federal DOE recently
published a study of the SIG program by two nonpartisan research organizations—

Mathematica and the American Institute for Research. Test scores, graduation rates, and college enrollment were no different in schools that received SIG grants (National Center for Education Evaluation and Regional Assistance, 2017). President Trump's secretary of education, Betsy DeVos, used these findings to argue that there is no point in offering more federal resources to struggling schools; however, a recent report by FutureEd, a nonpartisan think tank at Georgetown, disputed this claim and pointed to flaws in the study (Ginsburg & Smith, 2018a, 2018b). Other studies also show that resources matter (see, e.g., Chapter 9, note 2).

16. See Center on Education Policy (2008, 2012), de la Torre et al. (2012), Hamilton et al. (2014), G. Hess (2003), Le Floch et al. (2014), Mathis (2009), E. O'Brien and Dervarics (2013), J. Rice and Croninger (2005), and J. Rice and Malen (2003).

17. See Baroody (2011), Calkins et al. (2007), Murphy and Meyers (2007), and Hassel and Hassel (2009).

18. See L. Cohen (2003), K. Jackson (1987), Katznelson (2005), and Lassiter (2006).

19. See Bachtell (2013), de la Torre and Gwynne (2009), Dowdall (2011), Research for Action (2013a), E. Simon (2013), Steiner (2009), and Sunderman and Payne (2009).

20. A recent study by the Pew Charitable Trusts estimates that more than 300 public school buildings stand vacant in a dozen cities—costing taxpayers millions in maintenance costs, not to mention the costs of depreciation and the blighting effects that empty buildings have on their surrounding neighborhoods (Dowdall, 2013).

21. See Corley (2013), Dowdall (2013), and Shen (2013). A similar situation occurred in Philadelphia, where 3,700 employees were slated to lose their jobs as a result of closing 23 schools to address a $304 million deficit. Parents voiced concerns about students walking through unsafe environments; studies found that the school closures had not improved student achievement (Graham, 2013; Research for Action, 2013b; V. Strauss, 2013).

22. For support of these claims, see Briscoe and Khalifia (2013), Brummet (2014), de la Torre and Gwynne (2009), Engberg et al. (2012), Galletta and Ayala (2008), Kirshner et al. (2010), Research for Action (2013a, 2013b), and Steiner (2009).

23. For studies that support how school closures negatively affect student performance, see de la Torre and Gwynne (2009), Kirshner et al. (2010), and Lipman and Haines (2007). See Chapter 9 for informants' discussion of how moving negatively influences children's social ties and achievement and Chapter 9, note 21 for studies that support this claim.

24. See Kirshner et al. (2010) and Research for Action (2013b). A recent study (Kemple, 2015) concluded that the 29 high school closures in New York City did not harm students because some made positive gains. On closer inspection, these gains were similar to those made in other low-performing high schools at that time. In addition, students *still* did not fare well, with just 56 percent graduating within four years, which suggests that school closures are not a sufficient intervention. The study also did not examine how these students benefited from another policy intervention that had been implemented at the time—the transition to smaller schools in New York City. This is important because prior studies show that smaller schools have a positive effect on students (see MDRC, 2014). Just as problematically, the study only measured the effects of school closures on high school students who would have been transitioning anyway and are less likely to need community schools than younger students.

25. See, e.g., Jack et al. (2012), Journey for Justice Alliance (2014), National Opportunity to Learn Campaign (2013), New York City Working Group on School Transformation (2012), Ossei-Owusu (2013), Rich and Hurdle (2013), and Sunderman and Payne (2009). A map created by the Schott Foundation (2013) shows the correlation between school closures and the percentage of African American and Latino students in Chicago, New York, and Philadelphia. In Chicago, where approximately 100 schools have been closed since 2001, 88 percent of students affected were African Americans (Journey for Justice Alliance, 2014; Shen, 2013). African American students were the majority population in 90 percent of the 49 elementary schools closed in Chicago, and nearly 60 percent of those schools had a high concentration of special needs students (Kunichoff, 2014).

26. The decision to close schools sparked numerous rallies and hearings, where thousands waited in line for hours to speak, including students. The rhetoric of policy makers contrasted sharply with those affected. Educators and citizens offered rational, normative, *and* emotional responses, such as arguing that these schools were the hearts of their communities. Policy makers, like President Obama's secretary of education, Arne Duncan, focused on rational responses. He claimed, for instance, that closing low-performing schools requires "the courage to do the right thing by kids. . . . When a school continues to perform in the bottom 5 percent . . . and isn't showing signs of growth or has graduation rates below 60 percent, something dramatic needs to be done." Those affected, however, blamed school failures on society and the government, claiming that the schools had suffered from a dearth of economic and social resources. They also argued that New York City was ignoring the effects of school closings on the community and creating a "shell game" where "bad" schools were closed and then children were sent to other "bad schools." In the process, the city exacerbated an already segregated system because, as more schools were closed and replaced by charter schools, there were fewer public options for low-income and minority students, homeless children, refugees, and children with special needs. Others noted that the decision unfairly stigmatized those teachers who worked with underprivileged children (Chivas, 2010).

27. See Rich and Hurdle (2013), Williams (2015), and Zubrzycki (2012).

28. See, e.g., Ahmed-Ullah (2011, 2012), Hirst and Doyle (2013), and New York City Working Group on School Transformation (2012).

29. For these reasons, a coalition of parents, students, practitioners, school reformers, policy makers, and other stakeholders in New York City advocate other reforms, such as creating a network of struggling schools and using this zone to build capacity by engaging the community in reform and providing wraparound social supports (New York City Working Group on School Transformation, 2012). These programs would vary by community but focus on social justice and teacher professionalism rather than punitive sanctions based on test scores (Cody, 2012).

30. These narratives were remarkably consistent across those I interviewed. Compare the narrative of Jack (elementary principal) in the following quote with the words of Chris (elementary principal) in this book chapter: "I think they're trying to make it more objective by . . . [converting it to a number] so that you can compare teachers to one another. . . . There were problems with teachers' evaluations being subjective, but . . . we have come a long way. . . . Danielson has been a positive development. . . . [And] quantifying something does not make it objective. . . . [It's also] hard to quantify good teaching. There is a technical side . . . [and] a professional side. . . . You have to have certain skills, like being able to craft a lesson plan and understand child . . . and adolescent development . . . have specific content knowledge. . . . [It] is a profession because you need to constantly develop those skills and content knowledge. But it's definitely an art too. As a principal, I shouldn't walk into every room in, say, third grade and see them teaching the exact same lesson even if they're teaching the exact same thing. . . . You have to reach students. The kids are different and so the lesson should be different, but the teachers are different too. They've got different interests and passions and so the lesson should reflect those because that's how teachers get kids excited about things, by bringing their own personalities and interests to what they're teaching. . . . People who have never taught have a hard time grasping that and so they think you can quantify teaching, like Teacher A gets a 99 and Teacher B gets a 95, as if that means anything. It might and it might not. They may have been equally good, but by putting numbers onto each individual category, they ended up four points different [*laughs*]. Once you realize that, it really calls into question the fact that we're attaching stakes to these numbers."

31. Some also claimed that the state was trying to make the tests less predictable to curtail "teaching to the test." A suburban elementary teacher (Jess) said, "[This] year . . . they purposely tried to make these tests less predictable. . . . There was a concern about teaching to the test. So, they've become extremely more challenging. . . . I heard the word 'evil' used . . . the third-grade test used passages that were really more for fifth graders . . . [and students] had to be good readers to take the math test. . . . Last year, they randomly raised the bar for math. . . . It feels like . . . [the] cutoff points are a political decision rather than based on knowledge about what it means to be educated. Yet our evaluations are now going to be based on test score data as if it shows whether we educated the child or not."

32. Chloe, an urban eighth-grade English teacher, had this to say about RttT: "Half the money went straight to the state . . . [DOE. Now] the governor is completely changing the deal, which was already a deal with the devil . . . to get federal dollars. . . . He wants to have 40 percent of our evaluations based on our student test scores . . . 20 percent state tests and 20 percent local tests . . . then the state decided only certain tests were good enough. . . . [Districts] have to buy those tests or use the state tests."

33. A suburban high school English teacher (Liam) complained, "[The] federal government is not being held accountable in terms of resources. . . . Congress has failed to fully fund P.L. 94-142 . . . children with disabilities. . . . Now, we are saying that all children must pass the same tests. . . . Our union has put in many resolutions to get full funding . . . politicians . . . say it is unrealistic . . . given this fiscal . . . [and] antitax environment. . . . And I say, 'Is it unrealistic and idealistic to expect politicians to help children with special needs by fully funding existing programs?'"

34. Don, a suburban high school social studies teacher, explained how recent reforms let parents off the hook: "Parents have a *maaaaaajorrrrrr* role. . . . I see that child for 45 minutes a day. . . . Unless it is reinforced at home, it is basically a pillar without a foundation. You cannot build on something without a foundation. . . . There needs to be accountability at home. . . . In high school they care because graduation is on the line. . . . In middle school, nothing is on the line. . . . [Some will not] put in real effort. . . . The problem is the disconnect with the concept of human nature. . . . You also have to be realistic . . . a special ed kid . . . at the third-grade level . . . taking a test with seventh and eighth graders. That is not a realistic test. You have to be accountable for something that is reasonable."

35. Meagan focused on teachers, but most educators also described how labeling is undemocratic and unfair for students. Heidi, a suburban high school math teacher, said: "[It's not fair because] we all have different gifts. Some kids aren't cut out for math or not good test takers, but that doesn't mean they're failures. . . . [Some] teachers . . . have mostly high-needs students . . . request those students because they care about them and . . . they're good with those students and they want to make a difference. It's not fair to compare those teachers to . . . [those with] no or few high-needs students."

36. Kathy, a suburban elementary teacher, discussed how these developments relate to economic insecurity: "[People] are afraid . . . the economy is doing poorly and they feel like America is not keeping up globally. . . . They are looking for someone to blame . . . a scapegoat. . . . Unfortunately teachers and public schools are it. . . . There is also less money because the economy is not doing well . . . property taxes are lower because of everything with housing . . . [they're also] cutting funding for education . . . schools are really getting hit from all ends. . . . [Now they talk] about firing all teachers because they are ineffective. I'd like to know how you are deciding they are ineffective; by what standards are you judging them . . . you do not see these kinds of things for other occupations or professions . . . including our elected officials—many of whom only work six months out of the year—and no one is calling them 'greedy.' . . . They make a whole lot more . . . telling teachers and schools that they need to do more with a whole lot less. Who is holding them accountable?"

37. Retirees made similar comments. Two retired suburban elementary teachers stated the following:

JOHANNA: If we were using this kind of language to talk about the government, you would have parents complaining . . . have something put into your file. Yet politicians talk this way about teachers. Then . . . they talk about how important education is. How do you expect children to respect their teachers and respect public education, when all they hear are negative things about both? Why would they value either?

SOPHIA: [Unions] are being scapegoated because it is something concrete that we can latch on to. People are struggling economically . . . want someone to blame. But that is the very reason we need unions. If the teachers were not protected, they would be fired left and right during tough times because they make an easy target. . . . This is getting worse because of the media and politicians. You rarely hear anything good about teachers. It's always negative stories and they are using these stories to hold teachers accountable while letting everyone else off the hook. People are scared about the future and politicians are blaming public schools and teachers and teachers' unions. As if holding them accountable will resolve all our social . . . and economic problems.

38. I intentionally did not ask educators about their political affiliations. Instead, I asked if recent education reforms had affected their political experiences, identities, and behaviors and allowed informants to choose which—if any—to elaborate on. Because of this, it is difficult to provide an accurate count of those who may have switched political parties as a result of recent reforms and discourse. Most did not volunteer their political affiliations. When they did, it was typically done as a way to express that they were Republicans but were unhappy with recent reforms and discourse like other teachers (i.e., they were expressing that the unhappiness with recent reforms was not partisan). This is evident in Don's narrative in Chapter 3, but a suburban elementary teacher (Fred) remarked, "I am a Republican and I'm a teacher. There are a few of us out there [*laughs*]. . . . We need to stop worrying about politics and worry about children. . . . [They] are going to be running the world and taking care of us. . . . How about we give them the tools they need to do that. . . . People are frustrated, they're angry, and . . . looking to hold someone accountable. . . . It's pass the buck . . . . point to your left and right . . . so nothing gets done."

39. A suburban (Liam) and urban (Barb) district union president described these issues as follows:

BARB: I hated the way it was done. . . . We were called and told that we had to vote that day . . . so that the state would get the money. . . . We didn't really know exactly what it [RttT] was. . . . [Then] APPR all came out of that. . . . They want teachers held accountable like they would in the business world, but in the business world . . . you get to select who you are hiring. I don't get to pick . . . the 25 bodies that are going to sit in front of me so that I achieve really high. I get what I'm given and then I have to work from there.

LIAM: The union agreed to one thing and then . . . [the state] adopted another. . . . For whatever reason, the union did not want any discussion of the effects of . . . APPR . . . refused to make it an issue in the hearings or anywhere else. They sent a letter to the commissioner and nowhere did it mention the new evaluation system, only Common Core. And teachers are totally up in arms about it. It is a flawed system. . . . They actually had someone at these hearings . . . to "defuse" the situation . . . and get teachers to just focus on Common Core. It turns out that they had made this deal with the governor . . . took the position that . . . [at least] it would be implemented at the local level . . . [where the union could bargain with the district about] which tool they used to evaluate teachers.

So, teachers had this perception that the union was pushing this, not just the governor. . . . There was a whole Facebook revolution . . . in a large urban city against the mayor, and yet everyone is tiptoeing around the governor. . . . I have heard that the governor said, "Stop whining, this is here to stay. You've got this . . . law . . . protecting collective bargaining . . . leave this alone. It could be worse." And, the union is . . . under threat . . . [but many young teachers feel] alienated . . . master's degrees from good universities . . . [yet] being micromanaged . . . like there is no purpose to the union. . . . As a union, you are always fighting American individualism . . . now they feel . . . the union was part of this straightjacket.

Chapter 7

1. Some examples of creative activities included writing and enacting plays, creating a class newspaper, debating government policies and critical issues, and conducting "book talks."

2. This narrative did not vary across social groups, including tested and nontested subjects, occupations, and work status. Consider the words of a suburban high school art (Ellen) and elementary (Veronica) teacher:

ELLEN: [Students] bring enough stress on their own. . . . It's hard to see a student that has issues at home and . . . [all] you can do is to make their day the best it can be at school. . . . [Now] teachers feel so much stress about data and deadlines . . . records and reports . . . you just have to wonder . . . [is] that data worth all of this stress. . . . It's very time-consuming . . . [takes time away from] preparing the students for life or college, or even just working with . . . students. It takes your energy.

VERONICA: Some of them have just accepted that they don't do well. . . . They're not good test takers and repeatedly giving them a test is not going to change that. . . . They're all different kinds of learners . . . tactile . . . kinesthetic . . . musical . . . visual . . . social learners. . . . All of these . . . are being penalized by a system that only focuses on test-taking skills.

3. Hobbes, Tocqueville, and Durkheim focused on the negative effects of an excessive pursuit of self-interest and individual rights, including, but not limited to, the loss of social ties. For example, Durkheim argued that healthy individuals are more likely to live in communities that impose a sense of duty, obligation, or commitment to a higher social purpose. According to him, anomie—a condition in which norms and values disintegrate or disappear—results from social structures where individuals pursue their own goals and interests, unfettered by social controls, as well as in communities where social regulations have broken down. He linked both conditions to rapid economic change under modern capitalism. Marx, on the other hand, expressed concern about how social control damages the individual and leads to alienation and powerlessness. He argued that the "commodification" of social life—the act of turning something into an item that can be bought or sold—would spread under capitalism and increasingly force individuals to direct their labor toward the goals of those who own the means of production. In the process, they would become estranged from the product of their labor, lose a sense of selfhood, and become alienated from their natural and social worlds. In spite of their differences, Marx and Durkheim were both concerned about the emergence of modern capitalism, especially how the division of labor and spread of market relations would reduce social solidarity and the ability of society to regulate and reproduce itself (Durkheim, 1996; Palumbo & Scott, 2005; Tucker, 1978).

4. Crystal, an urban elementary charter school teacher, charged, "There is a lot of ego involved. . . . It is a just a . . . launching pad . . . administrators view themselves as competing with the public schools. . . . It is a résumé builder."

5. These narratives were remarkably similar across Tier 1 and 2 schools. Lorna, an urban elementary teacher, said, "[When] children . . . are learning . . . you don't want to interrupt it and move on . . . because you have to stick to a schedule. . . . [But administrators] were being trained to do the gotcha thing. . . . 'It is 8:29 and you're supposed to be here but you're actually there.' . . . [They] would stand outside the classroom and play gotcha. . . . I would say to them, 'You are . . . taking spontaneity out of the classroom . . . impeding learning . . . [and] their ability to relate to their students. There are reasons for being off schedule . . . you are making people paranoid and they can't teach.' This is especially true of the new teachers . . . not experienced enough . . . to adjust their schedules the second they would see them. . . . [The principals were] being trained . . . in a certain way because people were saying that nobody was being fired . . . bad teachers were just being moved through the system. . . . [Now] a certain percentage . . . has to get . . . an unsatisfactory. . . . What if you have a wonderful school? What if you have a terrible school where 50 percent should be getting an unsatisfactory rating?"

6. Kelly is a classroom teacher, but these narratives were similar even among "neutral observers," meaning educators who were not affected by these kinds of administrative controls. For example, a speech pathologist (Annie) who worked in the same school as Kelly told me, "There are a lot of walk-throughs . . . when administrators . . . just walk into classrooms. . . . They're told to ask . . . the students what they're learning and why they're learning it. And, if you hear your child say 'I don't know!' . . . you get very upset. It's very scary. . . . In the pre-K through 2 building, you can't always get that from children. So there's a lot of nervousness. . . . What are they going to ask the students? What are the students going to say? What are they going to think of the lesson I'm doing?"

7. Sociologist Erving Goffman (1959) portrayed social interaction as a form of theatrical performance where people present themselves in ways that will make an impression and earn "acceptance from the audience." To do so, they adapt their appearance and their spoken and body language to their social contexts. Social contexts include the particular time and place, as well as their "audience." He divides these interactions into front, back, and offstage regions. *Front stage actions* include situations where we interact with others in a public or professional setting. These behaviors are visible to the audience. *Backstage performances* are what we do when no one is watching. They include our inner feelings, as well as those situations where we can be at home and "step out of character." *Off-stage regions* are outside of the performance. For example, a waitress may smile at an unhappy customer (front stage) while feeling angry inside (backstage), and then go to the kitchen and have a laugh at the customer's expense with her coworkers (offstage). Backstage and offstage regions are often coopted into the performance. In our waitress example, she is playing the role of a loyal insider and giving her colleagues "a laugh," while her colleagues are helping her decompress from the strain of performing "people work." Thus she hides her true (backstage) emotions even while coopting her (offstage) colleagues into the performance. Goffman argues that the boundaries between these regions are important because they help performers manage when, how, and who has access to the performance. By co-opting teachers' back and offstage regions, recent reforms removed their ability to manage who has access to the performance, when, and how.

8. See Figlio (2007), Figlio and Page (2002), Gamoran (1986, 1992), Lucas and Berends (2002), and Oakes (1985).

9. Teachers also objected to student placements when they felt that the needs of one child were being put above the safety of other children, certain parents were consistently using their connections or access to information to advantage their children, or placements were based on who the principal favored or disfavored.

10. On average, schools spend approximately 80 percent of the budget on salaries and fringe benefits.

11. A retired suburban elementary teacher (Sophia) discussed and refuted negative stereotypes about older teachers and described what gets lost when schools push them out: "[I was substitute teaching in a southern state and they] kept asking me if I wanted to teach [*laughing*]. . . . I was just doing it because I loved the kids . . . [but the younger teachers would go] on and on to me about how amazing I was . . . all of the things I had the kids do . . . if you are a teacher, you have that mentality. You don't go in to just get a wage for subbing and then leave. . . . Teachers are hardworking people. It does not matter if you are at the beginning of your career or if you are retired, like me. . . . They are selling this myth that new teachers are 'fresh' and 'better' because they want to get rid of teachers at the end of the career because we make more . . . [and] to justify getting rid of tenure. But you don't suddenly stop working because you have tenure. . . . There is a lot to be said for being new and . . . up on all the new stuff, but there is also a lot to be said for experience. . . . They don't look at what's lost. It always comes back to money. It is sad . . . because the older teachers were the ones who socialized the new teachers in terms of what's expected . . . how they should behave in the classroom or with parents. . . . People need that . . . advice at the beginning of their career. Student teaching is not enough. It was not the principal doing that. It was other teachers."

12. Kassidy, a suburban elementary teacher, described the effects of this reduced social cohesion as follows: "[Everyone] was a little bit more out for themselves . . . like, 'Hey, I have my own issues . . . need to do what I need to do to keep my own standing' . . . like that mentality. . . . In the city, where it is every man for himself [*laughs*] . . . no one can stop and help the blind person cross the street [*laughing*]. It was very competitive. It was not a community in any sense of the word. I don't know what kept people there. . . . It wasn't for me."

13. See Hout and Elliot (2011), Kirp (2012), Ladd (2012), J. Lee (2006), Schofield (2005), and Whortman and Bryant (1985).

14. Tom had to develop his own tests, but those who did not also discussed additional paperwork, new responsibilities, and time constraints associated with APPR and the Common Core. A suburban elementary teacher (Jess) said, "[With RttT] . . . we're collecting data all the time. I can remember one time last year saying to the kids, 'You've got to stay busy for a minute, I've got to get these scores in,' and thinking this is what it's come to . . . not working with kids because I'm . . . plugging in numbers . . . they needed by the end of the morning. . . . It started out as a way of . . . testing kids to be sure they were learning . . . that was a good basic idea . . . get everybody to a certain level . . . break down test scores by socioeconomic groups, racial groups and so on. . . . Then there were penalties . . . if you didn't meet certain standards."

15. This narrative was consistent even across those who were not affected, suggesting these concerns are not self-interested. For instance, a retired suburban elementary teacher (Sophia) told me, "[Before, we used state tests] to give us a general idea of how the child was doing and how we were doing. . . . Now, they're talking about merit pay and people being fired. . . . It is so insane. . . . Teachers from the grade before would try to make the classes relatively even in terms of behavioral or learning issues, but some years it would work out that your class was much more difficult than the other classes of the grade. Now, you had a class that, through no fault of the children . . . struggled with tests or with learning. But it is also through no fault of the teacher. . . . You need to do the best you can for every child . . . get every child the help they need, but children are not born equally in terms of abilities and aptitudes and . . . circumstances . . . their home lives . . . these things affect the test scores. How can you hold one individual accountable?"

16. A high school suburban math teacher (Patricia) added the following to Ella's narrative: "[The] pressure in high-needs schools is due to low performance because they are worried about state sanctions but . . . [high-resource/low-needs schools] have it too because the parents are very worried about getting their kids into not just college, but quote-on-quote good colleges . . . because then they will get good jobs and do well in life and it is very competitive. . . . Sometimes they don't have a realistic grasp on their child's ability and level of motivation and are looking outside their child to understand why he or she is not performing to where they believe he or she should be. . . . It gets emotional because there are high stakes."

17. See, e.g., Campanile (2015), Pizmony-Levy and Saraisky (2016), and Reardon (2011). A national survey found the typical opt-out *activist* is a highly educated, white, married, liberal, middle- and upper-income parent of a child in a public school. The movement, however, brings together Democrats (46.1 percent), Republicans (15.1 percent), independents (33.3 percent), and supporters of other parties (5.5 percent). Opt-out activists were not solely opposed to high-stakes testing. Compared to the general public, they were more critical of using testing to judge student and teacher performance but also disapprove of the Common Core and the corporatization/privatization of education. Moreover, while the general public ranked increased school funding as fourth of five important ideas for improving schools, opt-out activists rated it second (Pizmony-Levy & Saraisky, 2016).

18. Jess, a suburban elementary teacher, explained, "I've had many parents say, when I try to explain test scores from fourth grade at that first fifth-grade parent conference, 'Oh, I don't care about that, that's for you people.' . . . I do not think parents and students are held accountable. No one is being . . . retained anymore. Parents can opt kids out of extra help. . . . They just write a letter saying, 'I understand he or she qualified, but no thanks.' Not many do, but there are some . . . especially in the summertime . . . [opt out of] summer school classes . . . [or] after-school tutoring."

19. Again, this narrative did not vary across social groups. An experienced suburban elementary (Kathy) and high school social studies (Don), two experienced urban special education (Nina and Tracy), and a new suburban art (Gloria) teacher stated the following:

KATHY: [APPR is creating] a lot of tension and dissension in the work
environment. . . . [It's a] problem not just for teachers but for students. . . . People
think that teachers go into their classroom and close their door and teach, but
that is simply not the case. We need to work together to educate children, whether
that is because we have different special area teachers, like art, music, or gym . . .
or because we have other professionals who help specific children, like speech
and reading teachers. . . . We also have to work together to make building-level
decisions that affect all children. We don't have to love one another, but we do
have to work together or else children will not get the education they deserve.

DON: I have a colleague who is a very good teacher and we are constantly sharing ideas
and lesson plans with one another. . . . [If] it is about money, I think teachers are
not going to be willing to do that.

NINA: It is . . . a collaborative effort in schools. It is going to create a problem. I think
people aren't going to be willing to share their ideas and lessons or help their
colleagues.

TRACY: As a special education teacher, I . . . share my students with other teachers. . . .
In a co-teaching model, the success of that program is 90 percent how you get
along. . . . [If it] becomes more of a power struggle between the two professionals
. . . the program is not as effective, and you are really not able to have the freedom
of modifying the curriculum and implementing new strategies.

GLORIA: [You need] to have teachers be willing to help one another. . . . Younger
teachers are up on . . . changes, like with technology . . . because they . . . [have]
grown up with it . . . can help older teachers with that, but then there are things
that older teachers can help . . . with because it takes years of experience to
develop strategies, like with discipline. . . . If you create a lot of competition
between teachers for test scores, then that collaboration is going to go away.
When teachers work together as a team, I think the kids really benefit.

20. Although not a prominent narrative, Mr. Connor from the Family Research
Council testified during the House hearings that homeschooling demonstrates the
value of uncertified teachers. As discussed, certification regulates entry into an
occupation and is one of the ways the state promotes professionalism. Not everyone
agreed with his claim. Congressmen Owens and Payne (D-NJ) challenged him,
resulting in the following exchange (U.S. House of Representatives, 2001d):

MR. CONNOR: What I said . . . was that I was not aware of any studies that showed that
students excelled simply because their teachers were certified.

MR. PAYNE: I didn't hear "simply." . . . I don't think home-schooled children are a
good example. People that teach their children at home are not just a typical
person . . . off the street. . . . I am glad you clarified it, because I fly a lot, I like to
have experienced pilots. . . . I may have to be operated on, and . . . I was going
to get nervous that this didn't grow and grow . . . that we simply do not need
experience.

21. See, e.g., Boyd et al. (2006), Darling-Hammond et al. (2005), and Laczko-Kerr
and Berliner (2002).

22. See Bryk and Schneider (2002), Bryk et al. (1996), W. Johnson and Berglund
(2018), and Tschannen-Moran (2004).

23. Administrators, retirees, and those from different occupations supported the
narratives of current teachers. A retired suburban special education supervisor
and former special education teacher (Valerie) had this to say: "Calling teachers
greedy, and . . . highly paid professionals who work part-time is ludicrous. When you
actually compare teachers with other professionals with the same level of education
. . . teachers do not make a lot of money . . . work a lot over the summer, reflecting

on what they taught . . . reading . . . developing new lessons, revamping old lessons, and engaging in professional development. Teachers come in early to set up the classrooms. They don't have time during the school year to do these things. . . . I don't know any other professionals or nonprofessionals who can . . . literally be on . . . all day with almost no breaks. . . . You may have the planning period, but it is taken up with parent phone calls, meeting with other teachers, working with students. . . . This is just an aside . . . I have a kidney stone . . . my doctor . . . said, 'You probably don't drink enough water. . . . You were either a nurse or a teacher.' . . . You have an audience *every minute of the day.*"

24. At the national level, this includes the Supreme Court's *Janus* decision. Florida is an excellent example of state legislation (L. Alvarez, 2011; Peltier, 2011). Lawsuits are ongoing in many states, but some have been unsuccessful (see, e.g., A. Baker, 2014; E. Brown, 2016; Medina, 2014; Underwood, 2018).

25. For research that shows teacher quality and student performance are better in states that are unionized, see Nelson et al. (1996), Carini et al., (2000), and Carini (2002); Matsudaira and Patterson (2017) show performance is better in charter schools that are unionized.

26. In the words of Meagan, a suburban elementary teacher, "[it] isn't fair that teachers are being made to feel like they are dinosaurs or . . . should leave because they have been teaching for a long time. . . . [It] takes . . . their entire career to get . . . [an income] commensurate with their level of education and training. . . . Their salaries are end-loaded. . . . I don't trust the government any longer. . . . they are targeting the best of the best. We cost them money . . . so we have to go. . . . It also involves the teachers' retirement system. If you don't get to retirement age, that saves them a huge amount of money. . . . And, if they don't need good grounds to get rid of you? Great. They can get rid of whoever is the most expensive. It is all numbers. They are trying to run schools like a business. . . . It is all about the bottom line."

27. Leachman et al. (2017) show that 19 states were still spending less per student in 2016, adjusted for inflation, than before the Great Recession, and 12 states— Oklahoma, Texas, Kentucky, Alabama, Arizona, West Virginia, Mississippi, Utah, Kansas, Michigan, North Carolina, and Idaho—actually cut funding for schools in the 2017–2018 school year by at least 7 percent from 2008 levels. Leachman and Figueroa (2019) show that 2018 K–12 school funding was up in most teacher protest states yet still well below a decade ago.

28. See CBS News (2018), CBPP (2018), Leachman (2017), and Leachman et al. (2017). The number of public K–12 teachers and other school workers has fallen by 135,000 since 2008, while the number of students has risen by about 1.4 million (Leachman, 2017).

29. The five lowest paying states for high school teachers are Oklahoma, with an annual mean wage of $42,460, and then Mississippi ($43,950), South Dakota ($44,210), North Carolina, ($45,220), and West Virginia ($45,240) (A. Hess, 2017). The five highest paying states are Alaska ($82,020), followed by New York ($81,410), Connecticut ($76,260), New Jersey ($75,250), and California ($74, 940) (A. Hess, 2017).

30. There are gender differences. In 1960, teaching was a lucrative profession for women, who earned 14.7 percent more than comparable female workers. Teachers are still predominantly female (about 77%), but female teachers now have a 15.6 percent wage penalty. That penalty is higher for male teachers (26.8 %) (Allegretto, 2018; Allegretto & Mishel, 2019). Also, compared to 10 years ago, teachers are contributing—on average and adjusted for inflation—nearly $1,500 more per year toward health premiums. Most of this correlates with broader increases in health care costs; however, states and districts have also increased teacher contributions. Ten years ago, teachers contributed about 35 percent toward the premium cost for a family plan; now it's about 38 percent. States have also been changing teacher pension plans as a result of a $1.1 trillion pension shortfall. Many have not fully recouped investment losses from the last recession, but some have not made the contributions required to keep the plans fully funded. Owing to these issues, 48 states have adopted some kind of pension reform since the market crash in 2008. In most cases, teachers are offered a hybrid plan that combines elements of a traditional pension with a 401(k)-style account. This shifts more investment risk to workers (Chang, 2018). Most states further reduced the payouts for new hires and increased the amount current workers contribute for retirees (Loboskco, 2018). As a result, only about $3 of every $10 states and districts contribute to teacher pension plans goes toward the benefits of current teachers. The rest pays past pension debt, meaning current teachers are paying the pensions of an older generation (Chang, 2018).

31. See Allegretto and Mishel (2019), Leachman (2017), and Leachman et al. (2017). For example, Kentucky slashed taxes for corporations and wealthy individuals while raising them on 95 percent of state residents (Associated Press, 2018a). Arizona and Oklahoma cut taxes sharply in the years before the Great Recession of 2007–2009, and then continued to cut taxes afterward (CBPP, 2018). Because of this, General Fund dollars (as a share of personal income) are down 30 percent in Arizona and 35 percent in Oklahoma since 2006, and there is less revenue for public schools and other public programs. Both states also have supermajority requirements to raise revenue, which tends to lock in tax cuts once enacted and makes it difficult to redress funding shortages in education. Since salaries and compensation for teachers and other employees make up the majority of K–12 education spending, these funding cuts have resulted in low pay and teacher shortages in both states. In Arizona, over 60 percent of teacher positions are either vacant or filled by people who do not meet standard teaching requirements (CBPP, 2018).

32. See CBPP (2018), D. Goldstein (2018c), and Sutcher et al. (2016).

33. Many teachers discussed how policy-related time constraints harmed relationships with students. A brand-new suburban art teacher (Gloria) told me, "I think that one of the bad things with testing and the new evaluation system is that teachers . . . have less time to form those connections with students . . . that is a hard thing for teachers right now."

34. Durkheim (1996) refers to this as the "collective conscience," meaning a set of shared ideas, beliefs, morals, attitudes, and knowledge that unifies a social group or a society by providing members with a sense of belonging and identity and by controlling their individual behaviors.

35. Freidson (2001) writes, "Professional ethics must claim an independence from patron, state, and public that is analogous to what is claimed by religious congregation. . . . It is professionals who are 'crusaders' seeking Justice, Health, Truth, and Salvation. . . . Transcendent values add moral substance to the technical content of disciplines. Professionals claim the moral as well as the technical right to control the uses of their discipline, so they must resist economic and political restrictions. . . . They are obliged to be their moral custodians" (pp. 220–222).

36. See R. Cohen (2018b), Kamenetz and Lombardo (2018), Levenson et al. (2018), Park (2018), Reilly (2017), and Sedgwick (2018).

37. In West Virginia, the Republican-controlled government gave teachers and state employees a 5 percent raise; the Republican legislature in Kentucky overrode the governor's veto and increased funding for public schools; and the backlash against severe service reductions spurred Republican-held legislatures to enact tax increases in Oklahoma and Kansas. Teachers in Arizona secured a 30 percent raise over three years despite Governor Doug Ducey, a first-term Republican, championing tax cuts and private alternatives to public schools (Allegretto, 2018; Allegretto & Mishel, 2019; Associated Press, 2018a, 2018b; Bidgood, 2019; CBPP, 2018; D. Goldstein, 2018d; D. Goldstein & Dias, 2018; Gomez & Benson, 2018; Gonzales, 2018; Levenson & Jorgenssen, 2018; Romo, 2018; Yan & Smith, 2018).

38. See D. Goldstein (2018d), D. Goldstein and Burns (2018), National Conference of State Legislatures (n.d.), and Schreiber (2018).

39. See, e.g., Balingit (2018a), CBPP (2018), D. Goldstein and Burns (2018), and Kilgore (2018).

40. Like the teacher strikes during the 1970s in this northeastern state, some evidence suggests paternalism played a role in rising teacher anger. For instance, Oklahoma governor Mary Fallin (R) portrayed teachers as being childish for demanding increased education funding and compared teachers going on strike for salary increases to "a teenager wanting a better car." She also falsely claimed that the antifascist group Antifa was one of the "outside groups" involved in the teachers' protests (Sinclair, 2018). This is a classic case of symbolic violence.

41. See also R. Cohen (2019), Kamenetz and Lombardo (2018), and Schreiber (2018).

42. For stories about increased political participation, see Balingit (2018b), CBPP (2018), D. Goldstein and Burns (2018), Gomez and Benson (2018), Levenson and Jorgenssen (2018), and Yan and Smith (2018). The country's largest teachers' union (the NEA) gave 70 teachers mentoring and support to run for office last year through its "See Educators Run" seminar and had 170 more apply by mid-2018 (Balingit, 2018b).

43. See also Boyd et al. (2008) and Loeb and Miller (2006).

Part IV

1. Hall (1993) defines policy paradigms as a "framework of ideas and standards that specifies not only the goals of policy," but also the kinds of "instruments that can be used to attain" those goals; paradigms define the "very nature of the problems" that government programs and policies "are meant to address" (p. 279).

Chapter 8

1. The idea of a policy "performance" comes from Edelman (1988).

2. See Bourdieu (1986, 2000), DeFilippis (2001), and Portes (1998, 2000). R. Putnam (2000) calls this the "dark side of social capital."

3. CT was developed in anthropology by Mary Douglas (1970, 1986) and introduced to political science and public administration by Wildavsky (1987) and Hood (1998), respectively.

4. When *group* affiliations are strong, people spend large amounts of time interacting with other members of their social unit and the group structures their individual thoughts and actions. When they are weak, individuals negotiate their social environments and are free to compete for social, political, and economic rewards relatively unconstrained by their duties to others. Conversely, people's behaviors in high-*grid* environments are circumscribed by rules, regulations, and social conventions, such as their station, position in a social or organizational hierarchy, or ascribed characteristics (e.g., gender, class, race, ethnicity). In low-*grid* environments, individuals freely compete based on aptitude or ability (Thompson et al., 1990; Wildavsky, 1987).

5. See Thompson et al. (1990), Wildavsky (1987), and Hood (1998).

6. TPA advanced social reform by bringing professions and occupations under its organizational umbrella. Clarke and Newman (1997) call this the "organizational settlement."

7. President Kennedy initially used the "rising tide lifts all boats" metaphor to counter political criticism that a federal dam project was "pork barrel spending," a pejorative term that denotes that public tax dollars are being used to secure votes (Sperling, 2005).

8. See, e.g., Goodman (1962), Herndon (1969), Kohl (1967), and Kozol (1968).

9. Research shows that the South used its power within the U.S. Congress and the Democratic Party to ensure that federal programs (largely) denied opportunities to African Americans. Typically, this was achieved through two mechanisms. When programs were more inclusive in terms of eligibility, southern congressmen ensured that the policy's design would provide greater discretion. Local officials—such as governors, legislators, mayors, and state and local bureaucrats—could then set up and administer federal programs in ways that were congruent with local mores rather than policy intent. An example is the federal Aid to Families with Dependent Children (AFDC) program, where state legislatures established very low stipend levels and unsympathetic state and local bureaucrats discouraged qualified Blacks from applying. Conversely, programs that were federally administered were fashioned in ways that kept African Americans out. For instance, farm workers and domestic help were excluded from old age insurance, which effectively barred the vast majority of African American workers in the South from receiving benefits. One side effect was that these policy designs also kept poor whites in their place (Katznelson, 2005; Lieberman, 2001).

10. See Jennings (1990), Matusow (1984), Schulman (2007), and Toch (1991).

11. Republicans would eventually relent in terms of their efforts to eliminate the DOE, but only after President Clinton's (D) crushing defeat of Robert Dole (R) in the 1996 election. By then, education had become a major political issue, and many attributed Dole's loss to the party's antigovernment stance, especially proposals to abolish the DOE and establish private school vouchers. Both were highly unpopular with voters. From that point on, Republicans (largely) supported increased education spending; however, proposals to privatize education (e.g., vouchers and other forms of school choice) and devolve decision-making to state and local governments remained salient with conservatives (DeBray, 2006; F. Hess & McGuinn, 2002; McGuinn, 2006).

12. See Hood (1991), Kettl (2002), Kettl and DiIulio (1995), Newlin Carney (1994), Osbourne and Gaebler (1992), and Radin (2006).

13. Hochschild (1983) contrasts care work with emotional labor, where emotions are prescribed and monitored by management as part of the capitalist labor process. Many service workers, for example, are provided with work scripts to sell an experience along with a work product. In these jobs, emotions have "exchange value," meaning they are sold for a wage.

14. See Hood (1998), Thompson et al. (1990), and Wildavsky (1987).

15. Theorists have added the fourth construct—neglect—to Hirschman's (1970) model, but he hinted at the construct with his claim that firms need a "cushion" of less alert customers to ensure they have sufficient time and resources (slack) to make needed changes after more alert customers have complained or exited.

16. Hirschman (1970) used the example of the inefficient and ineffective train system in Nigeria. It appeared to be a public monopoly but was actually harmed by the most quality-conscious customers exiting via the trucking system.

Chapter 9

1. Under the "hidden curriculum," schools tracked students based on their "choice" to finish high school or attend college; low-income and minority students were not encouraged to attend college and so they were tracked into classes with poorer quality teachers and curriculum. After World War II, schools began tracking students based on "merit," but low-income and minority students were still disproportionately grouped into lower tracked classes owing to the link between testing and SES and because minorities are disproportionately likely to be poor. Their point is that high school completion and college attendance were normalized after World War II and therefore became more critical for economic security. This resulted in groups competing for educational resources to ensure college acceptance and completion. Educational historians support informants' claim, but high school completion grew before World War II—even though it was not normalized until after the war. The GI Bill of 1944 then dramatically increased college enrollment by providing assistance to help servicemen transition to civilian life (Ravitch, 1985).

2. A number of recent studies took advantage of the spending cuts during the Great Recession to examine how school funding influences performance. The Great Recession reduced student achievement through lower funding; the recessionary effect was more concentrated for low-income and minority children and students who were exposed to the recession at an older age (K. Jackson et al., 2015; Shores & Steinberg, 2017). In contrast, higher funding as a result of successful challenges to state finance formulas (funding inadequacy lawsuits) improved student performance, decreased achievement gaps between low- and high-income districts, increased student retention and adult earnings, and reduced adult poverty (K. Jackson et al., 2015; LaFortune et al., 2016; Martin et al., 2018; Rebell, 2007). Despite successful challenges in state courts, the highest poverty school districts and students of color still receive less funding owing to inadequate legislative solutions (B. Baker et al., 2018; Epstein, 2011; Ushomirsky & Williams, 2015).

3. Research confirms that the movement away from efforts to integrate schools since the 1970s has widened the achievement gap between low-income and minority students and their peers. Segregation is a large contributor to disparities in educational achievement and attainment (G. Orfield & Lee, 2005; Reardon, 2015), with the 1980s being both the high-water mark for integration and the period when the "achievement gap" between white and Black students was reduced to its narrowest (Grissmer et al., 1998; Jencks & Phillips, 1998). As mentioned, integration as a result of the 1954 Supreme Court's *Brown* decision reduced the high school dropout rates of African Americans while having no effect on the graduation rates of white students; it also increased African Americans' occupational attainments and earnings, improved adult health status, and decreased rates of incarceration, homicide victimization, and homicide arrests (see Chapter 2, note 6). The focus on integrating public schools began to recede in the 1980s amid public backlash over forced busing. New rulings by a more conservative U.S. Supreme Court limited remedies to redress segregation that appeared to be based on market decisions (de facto segregation as a result of people choosing where to live and work)—the prevailing pattern in the North and West—even though housing and zoning policies had contributed to this supposed "de facto" segregation (see Chapter 2, note 8). The Reagan administration's reductions in aid for education and social welfare programs also took place during this period. Not surprisingly, the achievement gap began to widen again (Grissmer et al., 1998). Research shows that segregation also gradually increased in districts that were released from desegregation orders by federal courts between 1991 and 2009 relative to those that remained under court order (Reardon et al., 2012). Today, Black and Hispanic students are four times more likely than white students to be isolated in high-poverty schools, where more than 75 percent are eligible for free and reduced-price lunch (NCES, 2010b, n.d.-b, n.d.-c). The increased isolation of these groups mostly reflects neighborhood segregation (G. Orfield & Frankenberg, 2014; G. Orfield et al., 2012; G. Orfield & Lee, 2006). While per pupil spending in high-poverty schools in some cases meets or exceeds that of low-poverty schools, poverty and segregation suppress student performance; concentrating low-income students in racially and economically homogenous schools depresses it even further. These outcomes result from a combination of school-level variables and variables associated with growing up in low-SES families and living in high-poverty neighborhoods. For example, high-poverty schools struggle to recruit and retain HQTs; children are also surrounded by conditions that negatively affect learning, such as high crime, violence, and other indicators of economic and social distress. Segregation results in other issues too. For instance, children who are removed from mainstream society are less likely to be exposed to mainstream English—a necessity for future success (Sampson et al., 2008). Integrated housing positively affects children and schools by breaking up these patterns of segregation and concentrated poverty (Schwartz, 2010; Wells, 2015). Along with zoning reforms, funding to integrate housing is one of the key policy reforms advocated in Chapter 11. Research shows that school-based interventions matter (e.g., smaller classes, access to highly qualified teachers, professional development, full-day kindergarten, and extra services for children with special needs); however, housing policies that focus on economic integration are actually more effective. These studies confirm that resources are critical (school-based interventions), but school and neighborhood SES are more critical for academic achievement and attainment (see Chapter 11, note 47). Because minorities are disproportionately likely to be poor, these policies will also reduce segregation. Given the tremendous need for affordable housing—especially among younger generations—and growing support for housing and zoning reforms (see Chapter 11), these policies are a better way to integrate schools than busing, which created tremendous backlash (reduced social cohesion) that placed a heavy burden on minority children. Adopting the Strength in Diversity Act is also critical (see Chapter 11).

4. One teacher, for example, told a story about a student whose parents constantly threatened legal action unless the school provided services above and beyond those required for their child to be successful. By the time the student got to high school, the teachers were legally obligated by the child's individualized education plan (IEP) to meet and provide the parents with their lesson plans and class materials at the beginning of each week. They also had to provide test dates and a detailed outline and study guide weeks in advance. The parents had successfully demanded the inclusion of those concessions in their child's IEP and were aggressive about preventing teachers from changing their lesson plans and test dates—even if they needed to do so based on how other students were reacting to the material.

5. See Chapter 5, note 5.

6. Lareau and Horvat (1999), for instance, found that past experiences of discrimination and unfair treatment affect the participation of African American parents.

7. E.g., Bourdieu (2000), Bowles and Gintis (1976, 2000), Fordham and Ogbu (2000), Lareau and Horvat (1999), MacLeod (2000), and Willis (2000).

8. For example, Sullivan (1989) and Fernandez-Kelly (1995) found that teenagers in African American communities often lacked information about available jobs and employer expectations owing to high rates of unemployment in their communities; this limited their ability to obtain legitimate work and encouraged informal or illegal forms of employment.

9. See, e.g., Fine (1991) and Gottlieb (1975).

10. E.g., Lareau and Horvat (1999), Oakes (1985), and Roscigno and Ainsworth-Darnell (1999).

11. Senior (2010) describes how upper-income parents in New York City begin grooming their children as young as age four for Ivy League colleges. This involves using their networks (i.e., social capital) to get their children into elite pre-K and other programs and providing tutors and test preparation to ensure that they possess the cultural capital to perform well on preschool entrance exams. Similarly, Reay (2004a) found that school choice policies and gifted and talented programs in England have exacerbated inequality, increased segregation, and created polarization within and between schools because middle-class families engage in practices that aid the advancement of their children at the expense of the less privileged. Owing to these kinds of cases, Bruegel and Warren (2003) argue that studies need to distinguish between competitive social capital, which is used by parents (or students) to improve individual outcomes, and collective social capital, which is used on behalf of all children in a class or school.

12. Many studies find that class, race, ethnicity, and gender affect parents' ability to intervene on behalf of children (e.g., Abrams & Gibbs, 2002; Fernandez-Kelly, 1995; Hofferth et al., 1998; Horvat et al., 2003; Lareau, 2000, 2003; Lareau & Horvat, 1999; Lareau & Weininger, 2003; McDonough, 1997; R. McNeal, 1999; Sullivan, 1989). Other studies suggest that parental differences reflect unequal resources more than capacity (Chin & Phillips, 2004; Reay, 1998).

13. Hofferth et al. (1998) found that parents giving, but not receiving, assistance is negatively related to their children's school performance in low-SES families. Their study suggests that the nature and quality of parents' social ties matter. Low-SES families may have access to "low-resource" ties that help them "get by" but not "get ahead." This possibility is also suggested by R. McNeal (1999), who found that—even at comparable levels of investment—single-parent, low-SES, and minority families get less "bang for their buck." The findings of Horvat et al. (2003) may partially explain these findings. Working-class and low-income parents were "rich" in kinship networks, yet these social ties did not improve their children's schooling because they intervened individually rather than collectively; middle-class parents organized collective efforts to change school policies in ways that benefited their own children.

14. See, e.g., Horvat et al. (2003) and Lareau (2000, 2003).

15. A suburban high school social studies teacher (Don) exclaimed, "This is all coming from the business model . . . [the idea that] we can do things one way and be really efficient. But the business model also says . . . when you get a bad product, you send it back. My products are human beings. I don't send them back. . . . If we were a charter school, we could."

16. This claim is evident in Crystal's statement about why her urban elementary charter school outperformed the nearby urban public school: "Parents and students have to sign a contract . . . saying the kids will be in school, be there on time, be engaged, etc. . . . People say that we take the best of the community. . . . I do think that is true. The parents are very involved and very appreciative of the opportunity for their children, and they support us. . . . You can say, 'This is what I expect. . . . You have to sign their homework notebook every day.' And they have to do it to be a part of our community. We set the rules. We don't expel kids, but we can actively talk to parents and encourage them to go elsewhere and let them know that we cannot provide what their child needs because we are a small school. And they do leave after being 'encouraged' [*using finger quotes*] to do so."

17. See Cordes (2017), Mathis and Cordes (2017), J. Mead (2013), and J. Mead and Weber (2016).

18. Charter schools have a mixed record. In some areas, like Boston, charter schools appear to be doing relatively well, but this is not the case in other areas, such as Nevada (Center for Research on Education Outcomes, 2013; Hoxby & Muraka, 2007; Hoxby & Rockoff, 2004; see also Welner, 2013). The design and quality of current empirical research varies, but cumulative research suggests that charters perform no better—and often worse—than traditional public schools and even the most promising findings do not support policy makers' claims that charter schools will close the achievement gap (Bettinger, 2005; Bifulco & Ladd, 2006; Braun et al., 2006; Center for Research on Education Outcomes, 2013; Hanushek et al., 2005; Mathematica Policy Research, 2010; Maul & McClelland, 2013; Miron, 2011; Miron et al., 2008; Miron & Nelson, 2001; Miron & Urschel, 2012; Raymond, 2009; Reardon, 2009; Roy & Mishel, 2005; Zimmer et al., 2009). Charter schools also have high attrition rates, especially for students with academic and behavioral issues (Buckley & Schneider, 2007; GAO, 2012; Miron et al., 2011; Vevea, 2012), and are more likely to suspend students—especially minorities and students with academic, emotional, and behavioral issues (*"Charter Discipline,"* 2013; Frankenberg, 2010; GAO, 2012; E. Harris, 2015; Rich, 2016a; K. Taylor, 2015a, 2015b; Vevea, 2012). Suspensions raise the risk of drop out and lead to higher rates of crime and imprisonment (Rich, 2016a). There is also substantial evidence that charter schools exacerbate segregation by race, income, language, and academic and behavioral issues (B. Baker & Ferris, 2011; Frankenberg, 2010; Frankenberg et al., 2003; Frankenberg et al., 2011; Garcia, 2008; Miron et al., 2015; Miron et al., 2010; Miron et al., 2011; Rich, 2016a). These findings are troubling given that the expressed purpose for expanding charter schools is to advance equity by closing the achievement gap. Moreover, charter schools are more likely to suffer from financial mismanagement and less likely to have transparent accountability mechanisms (B. Baker & Miron, 2015). As mentioned, educators in this study claimed that the media either expand the findings of current studies beyond what the research suggests or inappropriately characterize the findings in ways that appear to support more public funding for charter schools. Research supports this perception; it also supports their claim that many of the studies with favorable findings have been carried out by partisan researchers, conservative think tanks, and advocacy groups that use the research to justify expanding school choice (Miron, 2011; Miron et al., 2008; Miron et al., 2015; Miron & Nelson, 2001; Miron & Urschel, 2012). For example, one of the most prominent studies (Center for Research on Education Outcomes, 2013) that charter advocacy groups use to justify expansion actually found only very slight gains in reading and none in math; those gains were almost all explainable by charter school enrollment. Similarly, a recent study suggested that New York City public schools performed slightly higher in math and reading when located within a half mile of a charter school or in co-located schools—public schools that are housed in the same building as a charter school (Cordes, 2018). News commentaries were quick to cite this study as evidence supporting policy makers' views that competition from charter schools would improve public school efficiency and effectiveness; however, a further analysis supports teachers' views in this study. The bottom line is that these charter schools had little to no effect on student achievement in the traditional public schools and were less effective at improving student achievement than other interventions, such as increased resources for public schools (Burris & Strauss, 2017). Other studies that appear to support that competition forces public schools to be more effective (e.g., Hoxby, 1994, 2004a, 2004b) are contested by scholars because of problems with the methods and/or an inability to replicate the findings (Rothstein, 2000; Roy & Mishel, 2005). Two further examples include scholarly challenges to the finding of recent studies that charter schools in Boston and New York City do not "cream skim" or discriminate against ELLs and students with disabilities (Cordes, 2017; Mathis & Cordes, 2017; J. Mead, 2013; J. Mead & Weber, 2016). See also Chapter 9, note 19.

19. This and other studies suggest that school choice weakens the finances of public schools and impedes their ability to serve existing students (see Arsen & Ni, 2011; Emma et al., 2016). One recent study found that students in New York City public schools performed 0.02 standard deviations higher in math and reading on annual statewide tests after charters opened within a half mile; students in co-located schools—public schools where a charter school is housed in the same building— performed 0.06 and 0.08 standard deviations higher on reading and math tests, respectively; and, there were no positive or negative effects on students in public schools that were located between one-half mile and three miles away. When charter schools opened nearby, parents and teachers reported slightly more positive perceptions of parental engagement, school safety, and academic expectations (Cordes, 2018). These findings were widely reported by the news media as showing that charter schools improve public schools despite being contested (see, e.g., Hawkins, 2017; Zimmerman, 2017). Hawkins works for *The 74,* which was funded in part by the charter-friendly foundations of Education Secretary Betsy DeVos and Bill Gates, but the story was widely reported in news media sources across the spectrum. Even ignoring the issues with the study, other research shows that it would be more effective to reduce class size or introduce a whole host of other reforms in public schools than to introduce charter schools as a way of improving public school performance. In fact, the major finding for why surrounding public schools improved was that they increased instructional expenditures and spending on other staff (Burris & Strauss, 2017). This supports informants' arguments that resources matter. Another recent study (Buerger & Bifulco, 2019) found that charter schools in New York State negatively impact the finances and operations of school districts in the short term, owing to economies of scale, but may lead to improved efficiency in districts in the long term. The authors rightfully note, however, that they cannot assess the reason for efficiency gains; they may have nothing to do with charter schools. More research is needed; however, once again, the bottom line is that charter schools have little to no effect on student achievement and are less effective than other interventions, especially increased resources. For these reasons, respondents argued that any study that pushes charter schools is widely praised by the media and think tanks because it benefits the private sector, while any findings that help public schools, which serve everyone, are downplayed.

20. Charter schools appear to have less revenue per pupil ($9,883) than public schools ($12,863), but this is misleading due to their unique funding formulas and because charter schools receive private revenues that are absent from national data (Miron & Urschel, 2010). They also expend resources in very different ways than public schools. While more research is needed on charter school finances, an in-depth examination of KIPP shows that they spend more than their host districts as a result of private funds. The higher level of resources combines with selective entry (i.e., the relative absence of students with disabilities and ELLs) and higher attrition rates for low-performing students to help KIPP improve its aggregate results (Miron et al., 2011). Moreover, an in-depth study of New York City charter schools shows that spending varies widely due to private donors; however, the most well-endowed charters receive an additional $10,000 per pupil. These charter schools serve, on average, far fewer students who are classified as ELL or very low income. In consequence, they are able to devote more of their budgeted resources toward teaching students; this means they are more resource intensive even when spending less. While the outcomes of these charter schools vary widely, on average, they *do not* outperform public schools in New York City (B. Baker & Ferris, 2011). Miron and Urschel (2010) further support the claims of both traditional and charter school educators in this study that charter schools expend less on teacher salaries and more on administrative personnel. For a list of some of the salaries of charter school CEOs and how they are boosted by private donors, see M. Klein (2018). In terms of support for respondents' claim that closing public schools has benefitted the private sector in the form of cheap, public buildings, one study found that, of the 75 Chicago Public Schools (CPS) that were closed, consolidated, or phased out over 12 years, 40 percent (30 schools) were then run by private operators under CPS contract, 40 percent by the district, and 15 were vacant, demolished, housing private schools or being used as district administrative offices (Vivea, 2013). A recent Pew study supports that 42 percent of vacated school buildings are sold to charter schools. Another 12 percent are used for other educational purposes, such as private schools or universities (Dowdall, 2011).

21. See Brennan (2011), GAO (2010), Kerbow (1996), Rumberger and Larson (1998), Schwarz et al. (2007), Simpson and Fowler (1994), Swanson and Schneider (1999), Teachman et al. (1996), and Wood et al. (1993). Schwarz et al. (2007) found that most move to schools with lower test scores than their previous schools.

22. Ronnie, an urban middle school English teacher, described how trust affects learning. "[Trust is important because] you're asking them to take risks. . . . Try things they haven't done, put themselves out there with their writing or their ideas. . . . If they don't trust you . . . think you're going to shut them down or be sarcastic or make fun of them, you don't have them. They have to trust that they can make a mistake or throw something crazy out there. . . . Every class makes a social contract as to what is accepted and what's not and they all sign it and I sign it. . . . No sarcasm, no put-downs, all those kinds of things are first on the list when they develop their rules. And they really do follow it."

23. Public schools are a prime example of what J. Wilson (1991) calls "coping organizations." Unlike craft, production, and procedural organizations, neither outputs nor outcomes are (easily) observed.

24. R. Putnam (1995) writes that generalized reciprocity involves an ongoing relationship of exchange that may be imbalanced at any given time but involves an expectation that the imbalance will be rectified at a future date.

25. E.g., Bryk and Schneider (2002), Bryk et al. (1996), and Tschannen-Moran (2004).

26. Valerie, a retired urban special education teacher and suburban district special education administrator, remarked on differences in parental demands between a low-resource urban district and a wealthy suburban district. She also discussed how parental demands may be harmful to "other people's children." She said: "In the small city district, parents hardly ever came to meetings, even the legal IEP. . . . The wealthy suburban district, it was rare that a parent did not come . . . [and] parents will bend over backwards and pay attorneys a great deal of money . . . get doctors to say all sorts of things to get their child identified, because then their child might get an aide . . . (or) different modifications . . . don't have to do the same homework . . . or get extended time for tests, homework and projects. . . . If a student with a disability breaks the code of conduct . . . they cannot be suspended for more than 10 days within the school year, without the committee on special education meeting to determine if that behavior was related to their disability. . . . [There was also] a group called 'Parents for Excellence' . . . dedicated to the students who excelled in school. . . . They pushed for more AP courses and more electives. But nobody was pushing for the kids . . . in the middle . . . [so] sometimes the needs of those kids did not get the attention they deserved. . . . You had to hope that there were people in the building who were making decisions that maybe were not popular with the most vocal . . . but were in the interest of the whole community . . . make sure that the needs of the many are being met and not being sacrificed because a group of parents are pushing for courses for their specific group of children and the dollars are following the squeaky wheel."

27. Jackman and Miller (2005) show that institutions—more than cultural heritage—shaped attitudes and behaviors in ways that unequally structured political and economic performance in Italy and increased citizens' distrust of government. Overpopulation, deforestation, and a shortage of arable land caused extreme "economic precariousness" and resulted in poor health, "little work, irregular work, little money, high prices, hunger and other economic . . . difficulties." In the 1950s, conditions improved in southern Italy due to the massive out-migration of residents from that region. The reduced labor supply led to a labor shortage and increased wages. Political parties also developed a new interest in the region because its instability made it ripe for the formation of new political coalitions. Over time, the development of new political and economic institutions resulted in positive changes in attitudes and behaviors. In short, trust was hindered or generated through the performance of political and economic institutions, rather than cultural patterns. Their findings challenge the work of Banfield (1958) and R. Putnam et al. (1994), which claimed cultural factors explained the poor political and economic performance of southern Italy. Similarly, Mishler and Rose (2001) found that social trust in eastern and central Europe was a function of government performance and conduct, not cultural factors. See also Lam (1996) and Ostrom (1996).

28. See http://www.huffingtonpost.com/2013/11/06/sleeping-stranger-subway-picture_n4228826.html

Chapter 10

1. Again, theorists have added the fourth construct—neglect—to Hirschman's model, but he hinted at the construct with his claim that firms need a "cushion" of less alert customers to ensure they have sufficient time and resources (slack) to make needed changes after more alert customers have complained or exited.

2. A suburban elementary teacher, Diane, exclaimed: "[The] things that are happening now are based on money. They want to change tenure now so they can get rid of the higher-paid teachers. . . . They didn't care about tenure when things weren't so bad fiscally. But, if you keep the younger teacher you are saving thousands of dollars. . . . I don't trust the government any longer."

3. Like her more experienced counterparts in Chapter 8, a brand-new teacher, Ellen, discussed why competition—as a means of controlling teachers' work—creates issues in education: "[Most] go into . . . and stay in teaching and work hard . . . because they love it and they might not need an incentive. . . . [Pay isn't] the main motivation. . . . Job security is more important. . . . [Competition] will create a little animosity. . . . People feel like they are less of a community. . . . It pits individuals against one another instead of encouraging them to work together. . . . You . . . lose that collaboration."

4. President George Washington made most of his appointments based on merit, but subsequent presidents increasingly appointed political friends and supporters; this

so-called spoils system dominated federal appointments during the administration of Andrew Jackson. President Chester Arthur signed the Pendleton Act after the assassination of President James Garfield by a disgruntled job seeker.

5. The WPEA enhanced the Whistleblower Protection Act of 1989 and made federal whistleblower rights stronger than at any time in history (Cama, 2017; Government Accountability Project, n.d., see https://whistleblower.org/whistleblower-protection-enhancement-act-wpea/)

6. This is the fourth time Senator Rand Paul introduced the National Right to Work Act. It removes language under the 1945 Taft–Harley National Labor Relations Act and Railway Labor Act, which authorized union officials to require dues from nonunion workers as a condition of their employment (Blankley, 2019).

7. Like RTW laws, Wall Street and Silicone Valley philanthropists are sponsoring this movement, including lawsuits and legislation (A. Baker, 2014; R. Cohen, 2016; Medina, 2014; Rich, 2016b).

8. The bill is named after the Indiana congressman who devised it in 1876 (Portnoy & Rein, 2017).

9. Senator Rand Paul also exposed the alleged whistleblower. President Trump began issuing gag orders less than a week after his inauguration, when he blocked public servants in several government agencies—such as the Environmental Protection Agency (EPA); the Departments of Agriculture, the Interior, and Health and Human Services (HHS); and the National Aeronautics and Space Administration (NASA)—from communicating with the public and the media. The EPA, for example, was ordered to freeze all grants, contracts, and other agreements until further notice and was prohibited from discussing these changes with reporters or on social media. The restriction on public information sparked fear among many because—in most cases—President Trump had also appointed cabinet secretaries who appeared to be at odds with the missions of their agencies. Democrats especially took issue with the restrictions on communicating with Congress, arguing that these gag orders violated laws designed to protect whistleblowing and other forms of voice, such as the WPEA. See AP News (2019), P. Baker et al. (2020), Begley (2017), Bella (2020), Cama (2017), Cheney and Everett (2020), Davidson (2018), Desidario (2020), Friedman (2020), Ingram (2017), Leetaru (2017), McGraw and Toosi (2020), Miller and Rose (2020), Naylor (2019), and Toosi (2017).

10. See Begley (2017), Leetaru (2017), and Restuccia et al. (2017).

11. See P. Baker et al. (2020), Bassin (2018), Bella (2020), F. Brown (2020), Cassidy (2016), Cheney and Everett (2020), R. Cohen (2016), Friedman (2020), Henneberger (2016), McEldowney (2018), McGraw and Toosi (2020), Miller and Rose (2020), Schulman (2018), Toosi (2017), and J. Wilson (2017). For actual acts of resistance, see "I Am Part" (2018) and Woodward (2018).

12. Certainly not all federal employees had issues with the Trump administration (see, e.g., Restuccia, 2018), but a "mass exodus" of Senior Executive Service (SES) members and other career civil servants occurred as a result of President Trump's rhetoric and actions. For example, he attacked and fired individual federal employees for alleged disloyalty, proposed cuts to compensation and benefits, involuntarily transferred senior executives, froze new hiring, eliminated public management fellows, denigrated civil servants, and gagged or attempted to gag those who expressed dissent. His poor record of filling political appointees also contributed to senior executive exit by creating a more challenging environment for those who (normally) dealt directly with appointed leaders. Not all of this accelerated exit was related to issues within the Trump White House. It was partially due to baby boomer retirements and declining interest in working for the federal government.

The decline in interest from young people, however, relates to negative discourse about government and public servants and supports the findings of this study (see F. Brown, 2020; Davidson, 2018; Feintzeig, 2014; GAO, 2014; Naylor, 2019; Rosenberger & Schulman, 2017; Schulman, 2018; Toosi, 2017).

13. For these claims in education, see Chubb and Moe (1990) and Moe (2006, 2011).

14. DeVos's resistance, for example, killed a bill that would have stopped failing charter school operators from creating new schools. She also successfully lobbied against the establishment of a Detroit Education Commission, which would have developed a grading system for *all* schools, evaluated which neighborhoods in the city most needed schools, prevented those that earned below an A or B from expanding without the commission's sign-off, and closed schools that earned an F for three years in a row. DeVos argued that this kind of oversight would create too much bureaucracy and limit choice. The legislation passed in the state's Senate but failed in its House of Representatives after the Republican caucus reminded its members how the DeVoses withheld financial support when they had opposed a bill to lift the cap on charter schools and then flooded Republicans with $1.45 million in donations in seven weeks once they agreed to the bill (Strauss, 2016a; Zernike, 2016a, 2016b).

15. See Emma et al. (2016), Strauss (2016a, 2016b), and Zernike (2016a, 2016b).

16. See Emma et al. (2016), Strauss (2016a, 2016b), and Zernike (2016a, 2016b).

17. See Center for Research on Education Outcomes (2013), Mathematica Policy Research (2010), Miron (2011), Miron et al. (2008), Miron and Nelson (2001), and Miron and Urschel (2012). See also Chapter 9, note 18.

18. See Buckley and Schneider (2007), *GAO (2012), Miron et al. (2011), and Vevea (2012)*. See also Chapter 9, note 18.

19. See Buckley and Schneider (2007), Burch (2008), and Center for Research on Education Outcomes (2013).

20. See E. Brown and McLaren (2016), Carey (2017), Figlio and Karbownik (2016), Mills et al. (2016), Mills and Wolf (2017), and Waddington and Berends (2017). Voucher proponents are using the most recent studies to argue that those who participate in these programs improve over time. These recent studies might suggest the results are in some cases less negative, but they are still either negative or statistically insignificant (Mills & Wolf, 2017; Waddington & Berends, 2017). Again, these findings support the complaints of those in this study that any nonnegative finding is used to support privatization while downplaying a large body of research showing that investing more money in public schools would achieve better results.

21. Congress created the DC Opportunity Scholarship Program in 2004. It serves about 1,100, mostly African American and Latinx, students a year. Students are given up to $8,452 to attend a private elementary or middle school and up to $12,679 for high school. It is funded through additional revenues—about $15 million a year—rather than by taking funds away from public schools. The analysis reviewed data for more than 1,700 students who participated in these lotteries from 2012 to 2014 (E. Brown, 2017; E. Brown & McLaren, 2017).

22. Recent data suggest that taxpayers now help thousands of middle-class families pay for choices that they had already made rather than expanding choice for the least well-off. For instance, a growing proportion of those receiving vouchers (31%) do not qualify for free or reduced-price lunch, more than half of voucher recipients (52%) have never been in the state's public school system (i.e., they were already enrolled in a private school when they began receiving public funds), and private school enrollment grew by only 12,000, while the number of voucher recipients grew by 29,000 (E. Brown & McLaren, 2016).

23. As shown, the least well-off have fewer choices because there are often no better alternatives nearby; they frequently lack the necessary resources, such as transportation; and the most well-off are better able to use their social and cultural capital to obtain needed information and/or access to better-quality schools. For instance, recent studies found that the three top barriers to choice are understanding eligibility requirements (33%), arranging transportation (26%), and getting information about the schools (25%). Parents with less than a high school diploma were *far more likely* to list transportation (72%) and informational barriers (58%) than their more educated peers. The same was true, to a lesser extent, of parents with children who had special needs. They were more likely to list finding adequate information (36%), equally likely to list understanding eligibility requirements (33%), and less likely to list transportation (18%) as barriers to choice. In some cities, like Detroit, the problem was a lack of good schools versus a lack of choice (DeArmond et al., 2014; Jochim et al., 2014).

24. See B. Baker and Ferris (2011), Frankenberg (2010), Frankenberg et al. (2003), Frankenberg et al. (2011), Garcia (2008), Miron et al. (2015), Miron et al. (2010), Miron et al. (2011), and Rich (2016a). See also Chapter 9, note 18.

25. See "Charter Discipline" (2013), Frankenberg (2010), GAO (2012), E. Harris (2015), Rich (2016a), K. Taylor (2015a, 2015b), and Vevea (2012). See also Chapter 9, note 18.

26. This and other research suggests that school choice weakens the finances of public schools and impedes their ability to serve existing students (see, e.g., Emma et al., 2016). One study found that students in New York City public schools performed *slightly* higher on math and reading tests after charters opened within a half mile (Cordes, 2018); however, this finding is contested (Burris & Strauss, 2017). As discussed in Chapter 9, note 19, the finding was widely reported in ways that magnified its benefits while ignoring the issues with the study. This supports participants' complaint that the media and think tanks push any study that supports charter schools, which serve a small percentage of students, while downplaying those that support more funding for public schools, which serve everyone. See also Chapter 9, note 18.

27. See G. Orfield (2009) and G. Orfield et al. (2012).

28. See, e.g., Kirp (2012), J. Lee (2006), Schofield (2005), and Whortman and Bryant (1985).

29. For support of these claims, see Prothero (2015), Urschel et al. (2012), and Ravitch (2010).

30. See E. Brown (2017) and E. Brown and McLaren (2012).

31. For studies that support these findings, see Dinham and Scott (1998, 2000), R. Ingersoll (2001), S. Johnson and Birkeland (2003), Lobe et al. (2005), and Rosenholtz (1991).

32. See this chapter, note 11. Exit as a result of a perceived assault on professional autonomy is evident in a story about the Agriculture Department's leading climate change scientist quitting because his and other research was gagged by the Trump administration (Evich, 2019).

33. A recent survey of 211 school districts in California found that three-quarters were facing difficulties filling positions; however, 83 percent of the districts with the largest concentrations of low-income students reported having teacher shortages compared with 55 percent of the districts with the fewest. Almost 30 percent of districts reported that the high cost of living—relative to teacher salaries—has played a role. The number of underprepared teachers more than doubled in the past three years as districts filled vacant positions with those who are either not fully trained or teaching outside their fields of specialty. High-poverty districts were especially likely to report filling vacancies with substitutes (29%) or teachers who have substandard credentials (71%) as compared to low-poverty districts (13% and 30%, respectively). As with the nation, math, science, and special education were especially likely to be backfilled with teachers who had not yet completed, or in some cases even started, teacher preparation programs (Blume, 2016; Edsource, 2017).

34. While teachers were more likely to disapprove of NCLB than the general public, 69 percent of Americans polled by *Education Next* in 2008 said that they wanted the testing provisions of NCLB substantially altered (Howell et al., 2008). For a discussion of the opt-out movement and a description of the ESSA, see Chen (2014) and A. Klein (2015).

35. See Bourdieu (1986, 2000), DeFilippis (2001), and Portes (1998, 2000).

36. Detroit, for example, filed for Chapter 9 bankruptcy in July 2013. It has an unemployment rate of over 18 percent and is one of the most violent cities in the nation. The Detroit Police Officer Association actually passed out flyers at a rally that said "Enter Detroit at your own risk" and citizens formed the Detroit 300 to fight crime. Among other things, the Detroit 300 make citizens' arrests (Lewis 2013; Snyder 2012).

37. See D. Cohen and Moffitt (2009), Cross (2004), Kantor and Lowe (2006), and Stein (2004). The ESEA's policy rhetoric and design further contributed to differences in performance through the downward leveling effects of neglect. While accountability was not entirely absent, as some critics would later claim, regulatory compliance largely involved showing that federal funds had reached eligible students (Kantor & Lowe, 2006). In terms of Title I, for instance, schools were "rewarded" money based on the qualifying combination of high poverty and low-test scores. The sole requirement was that they demonstrate services had been provided to low-income students. This distributive formula had three unintended side effects. First, it resulted in the removal of Title I students from "regular" (included) classrooms for large portions of the day. These "pull-out programs" were the easiest way to demonstrate regulatory compliance since schools hired practitioners and paraprofessionals to provide Title I students with instruction in separate classrooms. Second, schools had no incentive to mainstream children back into "regular" (included) classrooms because it would result in the loss of Title I funds and jobs, as well as larger class sizes—especially in schools that were already struggling with depleted resources. Third, the policy labeled low-income children "culturally deprived" and offered "compensatory education" as a way to justify federal involvement in education and contain costs by targeting aid to select groups. This "language of deficits" negatively affected children's self-esteem and feelings of self-efficacy. The slower pace of learning in self-contained classrooms then combined with behavioral changes (neglect) to magnify achievement gaps between Title I children and their peers (Kantor & Lowe, 2006; Stein, 2004).

38. See Hout and Elliot (2011), Kirp (2012), Ladd (2012), J. Lee (2006), J. Lee and Reeves (2012), Reardon (2011), Schofield (2005), and Whortman and Bryant (1985).

39. Some neoliberals do not support standards and testing, but others view the information as being useful for parents who want to choose schools and teachers.

40. See Cuellar (2013), Hout and Elliot (2011), Ladd (2012), and Reardon (2011).

41. For a discussion of this issue and policies that have been shown to narrow opportunity gaps, see Ladd (2012).

42. See A. Baker (2014), R. Cohen (2016), Medina (2014), and Rich (2016b).

43. See Bracey (2008), Carnoy and Rothstein (2013), Ladd (2012), National Center for Education Statistics (2010b), R. Strauss (2013), and Willingham (2010).

Chapter 11

1. Education ranked second among the topics that were discussed in 2018 gubernatorial campaign ads and third among voters' priorities in 2019 (Pew Research Center, 2019; Yin & Sargrad, 2018).

2. States combine rules differently, but the governor must propose a balanced budget in 44 states; legislatures must pass a balanced budget in 41 states and the District of Columbia; and, the governor must sign a balanced budget in 40 states (Rueben & Randall, 2017).

3. NCLB passed in 2001 and should have been reauthorized every five years versus four years under the ESSA. Congress failed to reauthorize NCLB in 2007; it continued to be the law of the land (as modified by NCLB waivers and RttT) until the adoption of the ESSA in 2015. It is unclear what Congress and the Biden administration will do in terms of the ESSA.

4. One such improvement under the ESSA is that states may no longer rely solely on test scores for decisions about rewarding and sanctioning schools. They must also incorporate other factors that affect a student's OTL, such as student and teacher engagement, English-language proficiency, school climate, graduation rates, and access to and success in advanced coursework (e.g., accelerated instruction and advanced placement classes).

5. See Chapter 9, notes 18 and 19.

6. See American Psychological Association (n.d.), G. Duncan et al. (2011), Isaacs and Magnuson (2011), Schanzenbach et al. (2016), and Wagmiller and Adelman (2009). Examples of environmental stressors associated with poverty include living in unsafe neighborhoods, attending schools that lack resources, an increased exposure to lead, limited access to healthy and adequate nutrition, moving and changing schools frequently, and impeded parenting due to the stress of struggling to meet daily needs. These issues alter academic preparedness and influence a wide array of outcomes (e.g., physical and psychological health and well-being, longevity, cognitive development, socioemotional processing, academic achievement and attainment, dropout rates, gainful employment, and level of income). One recent study found that poverty itself affects children's brain development in ways that impede educational and life outcomes (Pollak & Luby, 2015).

7. Children have the highest rate of poverty of any age group in America. The current child poverty rate (16%) is nearly 1.5 times higher than the rate among those aged 18–64 years (11%) and 2 times higher than among those aged 65 years and older (10%). Children are considered poor if the annual income for a family of four is below the federal poverty line of $25,701 (Children's Defense Fund, 2020). Poverty has a geographic component. For instance, it is especially acute in the South and West. *Low-income students*—those who qualify for a free or reduced-price lunch—increased from less than 32 percent in 1988 to 51 percent in 2013 (during the time the national government was adopting education reforms). See Children's Defense Fund (2020), Ingraham (2014), and Southern Education Foundation (2015).

8. See Bivens (2016), Bivens and Mishel (2013), Monaghan (2014), and M. O'Brien (2014).

9. See Chetty, Grusky et al. (2016), Mishel (2015), and Pinsker (2015).

10. As discussed in Chapter 3, federal antipoverty and desegregation policies (somewhat) narrowed race-based gaps in achievement; however, the growth in socioeconomic inequality and child poverty increased income-based gaps (for citations, see Chapter 3, note 39).

11. Uslaner (2010) shows that trust rises with wealth; it has declined as the gap between the nation's rich and poor has grown. He contends that this negatively affected our public life because more Americans felt shut out and thus lost their sense of a shared fate. Public opinion polls support this conclusion. African Americans have historically expressed less faith in "most people" than white Americans, with nearly 8 in 10 saying "you can't be too careful" in 2012. They are also less likely to participate in public life as a result of segregation and other inequalities (Cass, 2013; Piven & Cloward, 1989; Uslaner, 2002, 2012). Yet African American trust has mostly remained stable across the 25 General Social Surveys (GSS) since 1972 (Cass, 2013). Declining trust is being driven by changing attitudes among white Americans and dropped off in the 1980s (Cass, 2013), which was also a time of growing socioeconomic inequality.

12. See, e.g., Hanks et al. (2018), Shapiro et al. (2013), and Starkman (2014).

13. Food insecurity is defined as not enough food for every family member to lead a healthy life, owing to smaller portions than needed, skipping meals, and not being able to afford nutritious food. It does not necessarily mean there is nothing to eat. Students suffering from food insecurity are twice as likely to repeat a grade—due to stress, an inability to pay attention, malnutrition, and poor physical and mental health—and are more likely to experience social and behavioral issues. The USDA (2019) reports that 13.9 percent of households with children experience food insecurity compared to the national average of 11.1 percent. This figure increases for households with children under six years of age (14.3%) and for those headed by a single woman (27.8%) or single man (15.9%). Of the counties with the highest rates of food insecurity, 87 percent are in the South and 78 percent are in rural areas. Other demographics that are disproportionately affected by food insecurity are large urban centers and Black and Hispanic households. It should be noted that children who are somewhat above the official food insecure threshold also experience worse health and developmental outcomes (No Kid Hungry, 2020).

14. Fewer than 4 million children access the summer meals program, compared to about 22 million receiving a free or reduced-price lunch during school. SNAP provides low-income families with money to purchase food, but benefits do not increase over the summer, when children are at home. Women, Infants, and Children (WIC) primarily helps children under the age of five and pregnant or breast-feeding women (Bauer, 2018; FRAC, 2019; No Kid Hungry, 2015a, 2015b, 2020).

15. See FRAC (2019) and No Kid Hungry (2015a, 2015b, 2020).

16. See No Kid Hungry (2015a) for a discussion of the summer slide as it relates to hunger and this chapter, note 76 for more on the summer slide. Congress provided increased funding for SNAP and child nutrition programs under the Families First Coronavirus Response Act (FFCRA) and Coronavirus Aid, Relief, and Economic Security (CARES) Act. These benefits were temporary. It also provided historic levels of aid to families and businesses in the form of a cash stimulus. Food insecurity plummeted as a result of this funding, especially among households with children, but has been increasing since the aid ran out (Evich, 2021). Changes during the Trump administration will increase hunger over the long term unless reversed. He tightened work requirements for SNAP and denied a path to citizenship for those who receive public benefits (the public charge rule). These changes disallowed or discouraged the most vulnerable from applying for SNAP, resulting in increased hunger among adults and children (Dunn et al., 2020; Reiley, 2019).

17. Researchers should use the FFCRA as a natural experiment for understanding the effectiveness of different approaches to hunger. It allows states to request waivers to provide temporary, emergency benefits to households that are already enrolled in SNAP for children who would normally receive free or reduced-price meals but are not in school. Pilot tests—though preliminary and small scale—suggest that this approach works. Because Congress scaled up the program to deal with school closings and the economic crisis associated with COVID-19, researchers have an opportunity to study different state and local approaches (Dunn et al., 2020).

18. See Children's Health Fund (2016). In 2018, 27.5 million people (8.5%) did not have health insurance at any point during the year. This is a 7.9 percent increase from the 25.6 million in 2017 (Berchick et al., 2019).

19. See Min (2019) and Konish (2019). Medical issues contributed to two-thirds (66.5%) of bankruptcies—either due to the high costs of care or time out of work. Other contributors were unaffordable mortgages or foreclosures (45%); spending or living beyond one's means (44.4%); providing help to friends or relatives (28.4%); student loans (25.4%); and divorce or separation (24.4%). The ACA did not change the proportion of medical-related bankruptcies despite gains in coverage and access (Konish, 2019).

20. Declines in health are larger for middle- and low-income Americans; health is deteriorating for the young relative to the old (Schanzenbach et al., 2016).

21. While running for president in 2020, Senator Warren offered a plan that was a transition between current policies and the Medicare for All plan provided by Senator Sanders. In recent informal discussions, some informants discussed her plan. By creating a public option, lowering prescription drug prices, addressing corruption in the health care industry, and strengthening Medicare and Medicaid, her plan would have improved public health while putting more income into the hands of those who need it the most. It should be noted, though, that my original interviews took place before recent proposals by Senators Warren and Sanders. It is therefore unclear where educators would stand on these two options.

22. See Bivens et al. (2014), Gould (2015), and Mishel and Davis (2015).

23. See Bakija et al. (2012), Bivens (2016), Bivens and Mishel (2013), Bivens and Shierholz (2018), Brady et al. (2013), Denice and Rosenfeld (2018), Farber (2005), Mishel (2012), Mishel and Davis (2015), Rosenfeld et al. (2016), VanHeuvelen (2018), and Western and Rosenfeld (2011). From 1978 to 2014, top management compensation increased by close to 1,000 percent. While CEOs earned 20 times more than their line workers in 1965, the ratio is now 271 to 1 (Mishel & Davis, 2015). Deunionization explains about one-third and one-fifth of increased wage inequality among men and women, respectively (Mishel, 2012).

24. For a good summary of sectoral bargaining and how to promote it through state and local workers' boards, see Andrias et al. (2019) and Madland and Wall (2020). The PRO Act was adopted by the House in 2019 by a vote of 224–194. It would weaken RTW laws in 27 states and increase the number of workers covered by collective bargaining agreements. It creates penalties for companies that violate labor law (e.g., retaliating against workers who are trying to unionize), gives workers more power during disputes (e.g., permitting them to participate in collective or class action lawsuits, allowing injunctions against employers that engage in unfair labor practices), and expands the definition of unfair labor practices (e.g., replacing or discriminating against workers who participate in strikes, requiring or coercing workers to attend employer meetings that discourage union membership). See https://www.govtrack.us/congress/votes/116-2020/h50

25. See Denice and Rosenfeld (2018), Freeman et al. (2015), Greenhouse (2015), Mishel (2012), and Winters (2017).

26. Chetty, Hendren, Kline, and Saez (2014) show that the rate of single motherhood is most strongly correlated with mobility; however, income inequality, the high school dropout rate, residential segregation, and the amount of social capital—measured by voter turnout and participation in community organizations—are also critical for explaining why some communities are closer to other economically advanced nations. Freeman et al. (2015) used the same methodological approach and added the relationship between socioeconomic mobility and union membership, a variable not considered in the original study. Union membership was one of the strongest predictors of an area's mobility; low-income children especially benefited.

27. According to the BLS (2019), more than one-third of government employees (37%) belong to a union versus 6 percent of all private-sector employees. Less than 11 percent of the overall workforce is unionized, a drop from 35 percent during World War II. That decline stems from the private sector, especially since the 1980s when President Reagan broke the airline controller's strike. Membership plummeted from about 17 percent in 1983 to 6 percent today. Public-employee union membership has held relatively steady for decades (Pilkington, 2017; Wolf & Korte, 2018).

28. Polls show that support for RTW laws rose since 1957, but this and other research suggests that "branding" played a role (Blankley, 2019). These laws do not create a right to work. They allow workers to benefit from the gains made by their dues-paying colleagues. This may be changing. A movement that had been getting older and smaller is growing stronger and younger. For instance, voters in Missouri killed a RTW initiative (Rosenfeld, 2018); 53 percent of Americans (53%) now approve of labor unions; a little over 50 percent believe declining membership has been bad for workers (Fingerhut, 2018; J. Jones, 2014; Swift, 2017); and, a recent survey of nonunion, nonmanagerial workers found that half would support a unionization drive in their workplaces (Kochan et al., 2018). Although union approval is on the upswing, it is still on the low end of Gallup's nearly 80-year trend (it was as high as 75% in the 1950s). Still, the huge increase in subcontracted, temporary, and irregular work since 2005 (Katz & Krueger, 2016) would normally reduce union membership; yet unstable pay, the rise in precarious work, and other economic and social issues (e.g., a lack of affordable housing) are actually increasing support from younger workers (Bivens et al., 2017; BLS, 2019; Simms et al., 2018).

29. See Buckley et al. (2004, 2005), Camera (2018b), Filardo (2016), Maxwell (2016), and M. Schneider (2002).

30. School infrastructure has been on the policy agenda since 1996, when a GAO (1995) report said that 28 million students attended schools with significant structural problems, including 15,000 schools that were circulating air that was unsafe to breathe. The American Society of Civil Engineers recently gave public schools a D+ after finding that more than 53 percent would need repairs, renovations, and modernizations (Camera, 2018b). The school infrastructure crisis is especially acute in older industrial cities where buildings, on average, are 60–70 years old, compared to the 45-year average for the United States as a whole (Alexander & Lewis, 2014; R. Cohen, 2018b). A study of more than 146,559 school improvement projects from 1995 to 2004 found that high-wealth zip codes had more than three times the capital investment of the lowest-wealth zip codes (Filardo, 2016) where school infrastructure competes with other essential aspects of school district operations (e.g., salaries and instructional equipment) due to inequitable school financing. Local governments fund about 82 percent of capital costs, on average, with states funding most of the remainder; however, the amount varies and 12 states provide no school capital funding. The federal government contributes almost nothing to capital construction (about 0.02%); most of what it does contribute is through the Federal Emergency Management Agency (FEMA) and is for natural disasters. The funding distribution for *capital expenditures* compares to the 45 percent state and 10 percent federal contribution to *operating costs*. Because low-wealth districts find it harder to borrow and obtain capital investment, they often find it difficult to make needed repairs. This creates short- and long-term costs because proper maintenance increases operational efficiency and extends the life-span of facilities. Low-wealth districts also frequently use their funds for basic repairs, such as new roofs, while wealthier ones invest in upgrades, such as new science labs (Camera, 2018b; Filardo, 2016).

31. See Camera (2018b), Filardo (2016), and Ujifsa (2019b). The poll was commissioned by the U.S. Green Building Council (Filardo, 2016). President Franklin Roosevelt provided more than $1 billion for school construction and repairs as part of the New Deal; President Dwight Eisenhower provided funding for school construction projects through the National Interstate and Defense Highways Act and the National Defense Education Act; and, President Bill Clinton provided $1.2 billion for school renovations. President Barack Obama proposed $20 billion for school modernization in the American Recovery and Reinvestment Act, which was designed to bring the nation out of the Great Recession; however, Congress rejected this part of his proposal. President Donald Trump advocated bolstering K–12 schools as part of a broader infrastructure plan throughout his first years in office; he included a $1.5 trillion infrastructure package in his 2018 State of the Union but did not mention schools in that proposal.

32. The legislation has since been reintroduced as the Reopen and Rebuild America's Schools Act and two other pieces of legislation have been added: the Save Education Jobs Act and the Learning Recovery Act. A recent report by the 21st Century School Fund estimates that the nation needs to invest about $145 billion per year to provide healthy and safe twenty-first-century learning environments and new construction that would accommodate growing enrollments over the coming decades. According to Filardo (2016), schools spend about $50 billion annually on maintenance and operations and another $49 billion on new school construction and capital development.

33. See Auguste et al. (2009), BLS (2015), Bowen et al. (2011), Carnevale et al. (2013), Casselman (2014),), Hanson (2021), T. Lewin (2010), Libassi (2018), Pew Research Center (2014), and Torpey (2018). Those without a high school diploma can expect to earn $27,040 a year, compared to $60,996 for college graduates.

34. See Sparks (2021) and Thompson (2021). In the summer of 2020, the National Clearinghouse Research center launched a new monthly report called "Stay Informed" to provide policy makers and college leaders with updates on college enrollment during the pandemic. Those reports are available at https://nscresearchcenter.org/stay-informed. The College Board produced a report based on data from the National Clearinghouse Research center. It is available at https://research.collegeboard.org/pdf/enrollment-retention-covid2020.pdf

35. America's investment in higher education after World War II resulted in the highest college attendance rates in the world and contributed to the nation's global economic leadership. Progress has slowed since the mid-1970s; the current completion rate of 56 percent puts the United States near the bottom of economically developed countries (Bowen et al., 2011; Casselman, 2014;).

36. States and, to a lesser extent, local governments provide about 53 percent of revenues for public colleges and universities. Of 49 states analyzed (all except Wisconsin), 44 spent less per pupil in 2017 than in 2008. Only Indiana, Montana, Nebraska, North Dakota, and Wyoming were spending more on higher education in 2017 than in 2008 (M. Mitchell et al., 2017).

37. See Bowen et al. (2011), M. Mitchell et al. (2017), and Touryalai (2014).

38. Students who begin at two-year colleges are less likely to graduate than those who begin at four-year colleges, but they are more likely to graduate if they transfer to a four-year college than students who started at the four-year institution as freshmen (Soares, 2010).

39. For more on the gender gap in SATs and ACTs, see Elesser (2016, 2019). As mentioned, research shows that boys tend to do better on standardized math tests while girls do better in reading. A recent study suggests that the test format is partly to blame. Boys outperform girls on state tests that rely more heavily on multiple-choice questions—a common way to assess math knowledge—while girls outperform boys on tests where a larger proportion of the total score is determined by constructed response questions, where students write their own answers in a sentence or an essay. These differences explained about 25 percent of the variation in gender achievement gaps between states (Reardon et al., 2018). Female students actually outperform male students in terms of average math grades, but score lower on the SATs and ACTs. The gender gap in engineering and computer science majors may dissipate over time. In 2014, for example, eighth grade girls outperformed boys in technology and engineering skills on the first national test administered by the federal government—the Technology & Engineering Literacy (TEL) test (John, 2016).

40. See NCES (2010a, n.d.-b, n.d.-c), G. Orfield and Frankenberg (2014), G. Orfield and Lee (2006, 2005), and G. Orfield et al. (2012). Segregation has increased despite the dramatic suburbanization of nonwhite families and growth in white migration to urban centers. Eight of the 20 states reporting the highest number of students in apartheid schools are located in the South or states bordering the South, but the nation's largest metropolitan areas also report severe racial isolation.

41. See Chapter 9, note 4.

42. Research consistently shows that the SES of a child and his or her classmates (primarily measured by family income and parental education) predicts academic success. Low-income children learn best when surrounded by middle-class peers (Aikens & Barbarin, 2008; Coleman et al., 1966; Jencks & Phillips, 1998; Rusk, 2011; Schwarz, 2010).

43. See Chapter 9, note 3.

44. See Brennan (2011), GAO (2010), Kerbow (1996), Rumberger and Larson (1998), Simpson and Fowler (1994), Swanson and Schneider (1999), Teachman et al. (1996), and Wood et al. (1993). The effects of moving on individual outcomes vary by age, but highly mobile students are disproportionately likely to be poor and Black, and most move to schools with lower test scores than their previous ones (Schwarz et al., 2007).

45. Children who move at a younger age from a low- to a high-mobility area are almost as mobile as those who spend their entire childhoods in a higher-mobility area (Chetty, Hendren et al., 2016). A recent study of segregation shows that, if segregation in Chicago—the fifth highest segregated area—were reduced to the median of the 100 largest metropolitan areas, it would increase gross domestic product, raise income levels and lifetime earnings, lower the homicide rate, and reduce police and corrections costs in Chicago and its surrounding environs (Chiles, 2017).

46. See Brennan (2011), Chetty, Hendren et al. (2016), Darrah and DeLuca (2014), DeLuca and Rosenblatt (2011), Grissmer et al. (1998), Guryan (2001, 2004), R. Johnson (2011), Kahlenberg (2012–2013), G. Orfield and Lee (2005), Mickelson (2011), Rosenbaum and DeLuca (2008, 2019), Schwartz (2010), D. Weiner et al. (2009), and Wells (2015).

47. See Domonoske (2016) and Badger and Cameron (2015).

48. See, e.g., Schwarz (2010).

49. Some socioeconomic integration policies have been more successful than others. For instance, federally funded housing choice vouchers (HCVs, formerly called Section 8) have the potential to improve children's educational and life outcomes; however, it is critical to provide active counseling and location assistance to encourage moves that reduce racial isolation and provide access to better neighborhoods, schools, and labor markets. At the local level, inclusionary zoning laws—like the one in Montgomery County, Maryland—have improved children's educational outcomes by requiring real estate developers to set aside a certain portion of the housing stock for rent or purchase at below-market prices. This enables low-income families to buy or rent housing in higher-income school districts. About 80 districts are taking steps to integrate schools by SES and more than 100 municipalities employ inclusionary zoning policies (Kahlenberg, 2012–2013). Montgomery County is particularly interesting because it provides a natural experiment for understanding the effects of school-based interventions (e.g., smaller classes, access to highly qualified teachers, professional development, full-day kindergarten, and extra services for children with special needs) as compared to housing policies that focus on economic integration. Schwartz (2010) found that low-income students who were randomly assigned to low-poverty schools performed better on math and reading exams than their peers in high-poverty schools despite the provision of extra resources; by the end of elementary school, the initial, large achievement gaps between these highly economically disadvantaged children and their more advantaged peers in the district were cut by half for math and one-third for reading. Roughly two-thirds of the benefits came from school and one-third from neighborhood integration. Her study is not suggesting that resources do not matter; it confirms that school and neighborhood SES are more critical.

50. A recent poll shows that 70 percent prefer that their children attend racially diverse schools, but only about 50 percent agree that diversity is important for learning (PDK, 2017).

51. Only about 20 percent of students would be able to choose a better-performing school if various school-zoning boundaries were not an issue (S. Mead, 2010; Rotherham, 2010).

52. Federal policies (e.g., tax expenditures and program spending) disproportionately favor upper-income households and homeownership over renting. About 60 percent benefit households with incomes above $100,000 and those with incomes of $200,000 and above receive, on average, four times more than those with incomes below $20,000. Less than 30 percent of federal housing spending in 2015 went to renters—even though they accounted for 36 percent of the nation's households and 60 percent of those with severe housing cost burdens. Lower-income renters are far more likely to devote a very high share of their income to housing; they are also more likely to experience homelessness, housing instability, and overcrowding. The latter burdens are concentrated on the lowest-income families. Federal programs are highly effective at helping the most vulnerable (e.g., elderly people, people with disabilities, homeless veterans, low-income families with children) avoid homelessness, housing instability, and overcrowding; they also free up income for other needs, such as food, medical care, and childcare. Unfortunately, these programs are deeply underfunded (W. Fischer & Sard, 2017; Levin & Meni, 2016; D. Rice, 2019; D. Rice et al., 2019; Zonta, 2018). The mortgage interest deduction (MID) is by far the largest U.S. housing subsidy. It costs around $60 billion, and most of the benefits go to wealthy families. In comparison, HUD spent $35 billion on HCVs and public housing. The Low Income Housing Tax Credit (LIHTC)—the primary program that encourages new development of below-market apartments—costs the federal government around $8 billion a year (Schuetz, 2018, 2020).

53. See Dreier (2018), Joint Center for Housing Studies (2018), and Shapiro et al. (2013). Millions of homeowners have also not recovered from the mortgage meltdown. Homeownership is much lower for millennials than it is for older generations when they were in their twenties and thirties. Increased demand for apartments and a focus on building high-end luxury units has resulted in shortages of affordable housing and rising rents.

54. The cost of all federal income tax expenditures is higher than Social Security, the combined cost of Medicare and Medicaid, or the combined cost of defense and nondefense discretionary spending (CBPP, 2019). Studies refute that the MID promotes the American dream of homeownership. About 70 percent of the benefits flow to the top 20 percent, who would own homes without it. Low-income and middle-class Americans receive almost no benefits—either because they do not own their homes, do not itemize their mortgage deduction (about two-thirds of Americans), or both. By creating an incentive to borrow and buy more expensive homes, it has encouraged the development of large, single-family homes at the expense of multifamily rental units for low-income and middle-class Americans (Casselman, 2015; CBPP, 2019; Somin, 2017). For more on this topic, see this chapter notes 50 and 51.

55. Direct government subsidies cover less than 4 percent of America's housing stock, as compared to 15–40 percent in Western Europe. Examples of where housing is viewed as a social provision, more than a commodity, in the United States include cities with rent control laws, which provide tenants with additional rights to housing security and affordability, and mutual housing associations, community land trusts, and limited-equity cooperatives. Under the latter, residents gain security and affordability in return for limiting the extent to which they may profit from the sale of their homes or units. Many local governments also provide low-income families with subsidies to purchase homes but require them to resell to other low-income households and limit price increases through "deed restrictions" (Dreier, 2018).

56. As proposed by Senator Cory Booker and then-Senator Kamala Harris, this tax credit would help people in economic opportunity zones where wages are higher yet not high enough to cover the high cost of living for many. Their proposal would likely increase economic output and reduce greenhouse gasses by reducing commuting; however, it would set up a system where poorer areas are subsidizing wealthier ones. Government-funded demand would also likely result in landlords raising rents, thereby dissipating the offered assistance. The real issue in these areas is a lack of supply of lower-cost housing (Yglesias, 2019). Nonetheless, their proposal could be part of a coalition-building strategy.

57. The Housing Choice Voucher Mobility Demonstration project also funds research to determine the most cost-effective programs. Some of the services that help ensure program success include landlord outreach, financial coaching, housing search assistance, and postmove support (A. Bell, 2019).

58. These laws, rules, and regulations were historically adopted to limit the negative effects of housing and commercial development on neighborhoods and communities (e.g., protect homeowners from toxic dumps or prevent tall buildings from blocking sunlight) but were used for racial and socioeconomic exclusion. The U.S. Supreme Court struck down racial zoning in *Buchanan v. Warley* (1917). It upheld exclusionary zoning laws in *Euclid v. Ambler* (1926).

59. See Kahlenberg (2018a, 2018c), Rothwell and Massey (2010), and Schuetz (2018).

60. See Dreier (2018), Kahlenberg (2018a, 2018c), Semuels (2017), and Grabar (2018a).

61. See R. Cohen (2018a), Schuetz (2018), Warren (2019), and Yglesias (2019).
Democratic presidential candidates Julian Castro and Corey Booker both advocated
linking zoning reforms to larger federal funding streams (Kahlenberg, 2018b).

62. Research shows teachers prefer to work close to where they grew up (Reininger,
2011). This is likely true for other frontline workers.

63. See Camera and Cook (2016), Dynarski and Kainz (2016), Michelman (2016),
National Council on Disability (2018), and Schanzenback et al. (2016).

64. See Chapter 3, note 18. School districts where more than 75 percent of students
are nonwhite receive $23 billion less than districts where more than 75 percent of
students are white (EdBuild, n.d.).

65. See Martin et al. (2018) and Rebell (2007).

66. See Chapter 7, note 27.

67. See Chapter 2, note 8 for a discussion of how federal courts have moved away
from desegregation orders.

68. See Bifulco et al. (2009), David and Hesla (2018), and Magnet Schools of America
(2012, n.d.).

69. New York State used federal school-improvement funding to improve integration
and educational outcomes by expanding magnet schools. This integration approach
may work for other states.

70. See EdBuild (2016b, 2017, 2019). Since 2000, 71 communities have attempted
to secede—47 were successful, and 9 are still in the process of pursuing secession.
EdBuild (2016b) shows that secession has often created "island school districts"—a
wealthy district encircled by a low-income one.

71. A good example of this is Memphis, Tennessee. White students fled in the 1970s
rather than attend classes with Blacks under a desegregation plan. The city fought
a decades-long battle with the surrounding suburbs of Shelby County. Two districts
continued to share revenues from a countywide property tax until 2010, when the
urban school district was dissolved and placed under the control of the Shelby
County School Board. A few years later, the Tennessee state legislature overturned
the state's ban on the formation of new school districts and adopted one of the most
permissive approaches to secession among the 30 states that allow it. Six Shelby
County communities promptly seceded and formed their own school districts—with
an average student poverty rate of 11 percent as compared to the 33 percent in the
remaining district. Secession also resulted in the district's budget being cut by 20
percent, the closing of seven Memphis schools in the 2014–2015 school year, and
the layoff 500 teachers in 2015 and 2016 (Dillon, 2011). E. Brown (2016a) provides a
similar narrative about Birmingham, Alabama.

72. Nine states have the authority to require that school districts merge. Thirty
states allow local school systems to splinter. Of the latter, 20 require the approval
of a state agency, but only 6 are required to consider how it would affect racial and
socioeconomic demographics, 9 to provide a financial impact study, and only a few to
gain voter approval from both communities (EdBuild, 2017).

73. California has one of the largest data sets on state lotteries and public schools.
The vast majority of neighborhoods pay more into the lottery than they get back in
education funding, but the losses are not equitably distributed. Each district gets
about $164 per student; however, low-income communities contribute four times
more than upper-income ones. This means they get, on average, $51 less per student
than they would receive if allocations were commensurate with lottery spending;
the wealthiest districts get $101 more. Phrased another way, the highest-income
areas invest $1.80 for every dollar they receive through the lottery. The poorest
communities pay $6.00 for every dollar they receive (EdBuild, 2016a, 2016c, 2016d).

74. Investment in outside educational opportunities among parents in the top-fifth income brackets nearly tripled between the 1970s and the 2000s; spending by parents in the bottom fifth increased only slightly. Another investment—time spent reading and helping children learn—also contributes to unequal school readiness and educational outcomes (Kaushal, Magnuson, & Waldfogel, 2011; Phillips, 2011).

75. See Barnett (2008), Barnett and Nores (2013), Brookings Institution (2017), Burchinal et al. (2011), Camilli et al. (2014), and R. Strauss (2013).

76. See Alexander et al. (2007), Chin and Phillips (2004), Cooper et al. (1996), and Lareau (2003).

77. See Carolina Abecedarian Project (n.d.), Chaudry et al. (2017), G. Duncan and Magnuson (2011), and Schweinhart et al. (2005).

78. Early research suggests that this two-generational approach greatly increases those reading at or above grade level in kindergarten (Anne E. Casey Foundation, 2012, 2014).

79. See Cassella and Mueller (2020), Dickson (2020), and Voght (2020).

80. See Chetty, Friedman, Hilger et al. (2011), Dee and West (2011), Dynarski et al. (2013), Evertson and Randolph (1989), Finn et al. (2005), Finn et al. (2003), C. Jackson et al. (2015), and Krueger and Whitmore (2001, 2002).

81. See ACLU (2019), National Institutes of Health (n.d.), and McLeod et al. (2012). The suicide rate for children between the ages of 10 and 17 went up by 70 percent between 2006 and 2016 (ACLU, 2019).

82. The average student-to-counselor ratio is 482 to 1, nearly double the recommended level (Fuschillo, 2018). The majority of states do not meet recommended student-to-nurse ratios and 47 states and Washington, D.C. do not meet the recommended student-to-counselor ratio (ACLU, 2019).

83. The majority of public schools (55%) reported no serious incidents in 2015–2016. Among those that did, most (99%) involved fights, robberies, or threats with no weapon. Sex-based bullying accounted for the largest portion of reported incidents (41%). Black, Native American, and multiracial students are more likely to face harassment based on race, sex, and disability (Sparks & Klein, 2018).

84. See ACLU (2019), Arcacia (2006), Balfanz and Legters (2004), Fiddiman et al. (2018), Lindsay et al. (2018), Losen et al. (2015), Nance (2016), Skiba et al. (2002), Sparks and Klein (2018), Thompson (2021), and Wallace et al. (2008).

85. There are disagreements on how to redress these issues, such as stronger gun control laws, arming educators, expelling students, using disciplinary strategies that encourage students to make better decisions without expelling them, investing in visual security measures, investing in support staff, and fostering a school climate that improves students' socioemotional well-being. Recent reforms favor hiring police officers over other support staff (e.g., counselors, nurses, and psychologists) and have contributed to a growing private security industry (ACLU, 2019; Lindsay et al., 2018). For instance, 1.7 million students are in schools with police but no counselors; 3 million with police but no nurses; 6 million with police but no school psychologists; 10 million with police but no social workers; and 14 million with police but no counselor, nurse, psychologist, or social worker (ACLU, 2019).

86. Teachers' unions had already been working with community groups, such as the Alliance to Reclaim Our Schools, to find ways to reverse the school-to-prison pipeline. Reform in states like California and the 2014 adoption of U.S. DOE guidelines that limited the use of expulsions, suspensions, and police referrals to keep students in school are two examples of successful policy feedback. See L. Alvarez (2013), U.S. DOE (2014), Martinez et al. (2013), and the Alliance to Reclaim Our Schools website at http://reclaimpublicednow.org/

87. The DOE downgraded and/or rescinded the enforcement of civil rights protections, including, but not limited to, guidelines for transgender restrooms and the collection of civil rights data during the Trump administration. The ESSA should somewhat ameliorate these rollbacks by requiring that states and districts report on a variety of civil rights indicators for racial and other subgroups (e.g., information about absenteeism, suspensions, expulsions, and referrals to the police); however, these federal administrative changes should be reversed. See ACLU (2019), D. Wilson et al. (2017), Fiddiman et al. (2018), and National Association of Elementary School Principals (n.d.).

88. See, e.g., Algozzine et al. (2010), Castrechini and London (2012), "Communities in Schools" (2010), Dobbie and Fryer (2011), Otterman (2010), and Tough (2008).

89. See, e.g., Dryfoos (2002), M. Harris and Hoover (2003), and Samberg and Sheeran (2000).

90. See, e.g., Kahne and Middaugh (2008), Levinson (2007), and Welner (2001).

91. See Bryk and Schneider (2002), Bryk et al. (1996), Conner and Zaino (2014), Gold et al. (2004), Mediratta et al. (2009), Oakes and Rogers (2005), and Orr and Rogers (2010).

92. See Cody (2012) and New York City Working Group on School Transformation (2012).

93. See, e.g., Gutman (1999), Oakes and Rogers (2005), and Orr and Rogers (2011).

94. Research supports these conclusions (see Chapter 9, notes 18 and 19). Two recent studies found that charter schools have a negative effect on the finances and operations of traditional public schools in the short term but may improve efficiency and effectiveness in the long term; however, these findings are contested (see Chapter 9, note 19).

95. Parents' satisfaction with their children's school does not predict whether they transfer to another public or private school. The academic performance of the receiving school is also relatively far down the list in terms of parental preferences; parents often enroll their children in lower-performing schools (Alyani et al., 2014; Bifulco & Ladd, 2006; Council for American Private Education, 2013; Miron & Welner, 2012; Miron & Urschel, 2012).

96. See Abdulkadiroglu et al. (2017), Bosetti and Pyryt (2007), Burgess et al. (2014), Erickson (2017), Fossey (1994), Goldring and Hausman (1999), D. Harris and Larsent (2015), Hastings et al. (2007), Nathanson et al. (2013), M. Schneider and Buckley (2002), M. Schneider et al. (1998), and Wells and Crain (1992).

97. See Chapters 9 and 10. Johanna, a retired suburban elementary teacher, had this to say about how parental choice often reflects students' SES and therefore segregates schools by socioeconomic background: "When I started . . . [the school] had the wealthiest neighborhoods. . . . They were building new homes. . . . [A friend was] visiting one of the homes when a petitioner came around . . . wanted the homes not to go below $350,000 so they could keep the 'rif-raf' out. . . . This was 20 years ago. That was a very expensive home. . . . [The] school changed drastically over time . . . [due to redistricting and] is now a Title I [low-income] school. . . . [Many moved away to another] district which was an 'up-and-comer' . . . 'better' area [*using finger quotes*]."

98. See Burgess et al. (2014), Center on Reinventing Public Education (2014), DeArmond et al. (2014), Jochim et al. (2014), and Nathanson et al. (2013). Many studies confirm that parents prefer schools that are closer to home (Burgess et al., 2014; Erickson, 2017; Goldring & Hausman, 1999; D. Harris & Larsent, 2015; Nathanson et al., 2013).

99. Bourdieu (1999) describes this as geographic and social positioning. He argues that those "who are deprived of capital are . . . physically or symbolically held at a distance from goods that are the rarest socially; they are forced to stick with the most undesirable and the least rare persons or goods. The lack of capital . . . chains one to a place" (p. 127).

100. See Chapter 9 for evidence from my interviews and Chapter 9, note 18 for other studies.

101. For support of these claims, see Chapters 3, 9, and 10 of this book and Prothero (2015), Urschel et al. (2012), and Ravitch (2010).

102. Under common enrollment systems, families submit one application that ranks their preferences; they receive a match based on those preferences and the admission standards of the schools. Most systems do not provide parents with sufficient information about school performance, the curriculum, and enrollment processes, but even parents in cities with the most comprehensive information systems reported information (Center on Reinventing Public Education, 2014; DeArmond et al., 2014; Jochim et al., 2014).

103. See Center on Reinventing Public Education (2014) and Prothero (2015).

104. These districts and charter networks are located in 32 states, but most are in California, Florida, Iowa, New York, Minnesota, and North Carolina (Ayscue et al., 2017; Potter et al., 2016).

105. There should be some flexibility because strategies are likely to vary across states and districts (e.g., redressing shortages in low-income areas, reducing slots in middle- and upper-income areas, providing transportation to low-income students, addressing information asymmetries).

106. These plans might include evidence in the form of a school's philosophy, methodological approach, recruitment plans, and student outcomes.

107. See J. Mead and Preston (2012) for more ideas on charter school reforms that advance equity and opportunity.

108. See B. Baker and Miron (2015), Buckley and Schneider (2007), Burch (2008), Burris and Bryant (2019), and Center for Research on Education Outcomes (2013).

109. See this chapter's notes 95 and 96 for studies that show that parental choices are not an indicator of school or teacher quality. Anxiety disorders among adolescents have grown in tandem with standardized testing. Two-thirds of high school students report experiencing uncomfortable levels of test anxiety and one in four has, at some point, experienced severe and chronic test anxiety (National Institutes of Health, n.d.).

110. See Chapter 7. Sophia, a retired suburban elementary teacher, illustrated these gaming behaviors as follows: "[My colleague] had the parents fooled. . . . Parents would . . . request . . . her, not realizing that she was not meeting the needs of the children. . . . I am trying to put it politely. . . . She used to fix the scores [laughing]. I would get children who scored exceptionally well on the tests with her, and . . . couldn't read or write . . . or there would be more serious problems where I would want to refer the child for testing for a disability but . . . it would be questioned. . . . The reading teacher . . . [and] psychologist . . . knew . . . so I . . . did not have to delay getting help. . . . Parents all thought she was a good teacher because their children would get good test results."

111. The importance of observing schools in action may explain why parents give their local public schools higher grades than public schools in general (Bushaw & Lopez, 2010; Bushaw & McNee, 2009). They see these relationships firsthand while public discourse focuses on "failing public schools."

112. See Dodenhoff (2007), Lacireno-Paquet and Brantley (2012), Moser et al. (2003), M. Schneider and Buckley (2006), Teske et al. (2006, 2007), Weidner (2005), and Yettick et al. (2008).

113. Returning to Johanna's narrative: "[A parent asked] who I thought were the 'best' teachers so that she could get her child in the 'right' placement. . . . [I said every] child is different . . . a teacher who is great with two children in one family and then have a third child in the same family not mesh. . . . Learning is complex. There are personalities involved. . . . [She'd heard a male teacher was not good and] did not want her daughter in that class . . . [because of] his private sex life. . . . He was an amazing . . . very effective teacher. . . . The kids really loved him."

114. See Glazerman and Dotter (2017) and Sattin-Bajaj (2014).

115. See Chapter 9 for how SES affects parental participation and advantages the most well-off children, but continuing with Johanna's and Sophia's narratives:

JOHANNA: [The] wealthiest neighborhoods . . . ran the school. . . . The PTA . . . were the room mothers . . . had a lot of access . . . [used] that power to help their own children and the children of the moms in their own clique.

SOPHIA: [There] is an idea that teachers need someone on the outside to, I don't want to use the word *police*, but . . . serve as watchdogs. . . . The state is starting to open up that door, and it scares me because . . . they may be there to "help out," but they are often there to check out what is going on, not just with the teacher but with other children too. Then, they take that home and gossip or pass it on to other parents, and that can be very harmful to the children. . . . They do not care about other people's children, just their own.

116. The scandal involved cheating on the SATs and ACTs and bribing college admissions and athletic coaches to get children into elite schools like Georgetown, Stanford, the University of Southern California, and Yale.

117. This study indicates that student test scores will only positively influence practice if they provide timely, transparent, clear, and reliable information that is perceived to be accurate and fair. Otherwise, schools may engage in misguided disciplinary actions, fail to remove ineffective educators, and be unable to offer the appropriate assistance to educators who are in need of growth or professional development. Teachers, on the other hand, will lack the information they need to improve practice and provide help to students who struggle. These issues demoralize educators and encourage *withdrawal behaviors* (e.g., attrition and isolation), gaming, and other unintended consequences (e.g., teaching to the test, switching to better-performing schools, or rejecting students who struggle). They also increase neglect among parents and students. As discussed, many of these issues could have been avoided if policy makers had listened to educators rather than using discourse and institutions to weaponize policy feedback in ways that silenced their voices.

118. See Chapter 3, note 23 for studies on how testing institutionalizes the effects of class, race, ethnicity, and gender on performance. For instance, standardized tests, textbooks, and supporting teaching materials come from about three companies. Because standardized test questions are based on specific knowledge that is contained in the textbooks and supporting materials, the inability for low-resource schools to purchase them disadvantages their students (for support of this claim, see Broussard, 2014).

119. Diane, a suburban elementary teacher, explained, "[Treating] parents as consumers . . . is like the customer is always right but what if they are not . . . [and there are] cases where helping one person is bad for other people . . . may lead to bad things for the whole. . . . Parents are mostly only looking out for the interests of their individual child. You have to have people who are thinking about the whole. Teachers need to do this and it is not always popular. . . . [They're] always talking about taxpayer rights like those are the only people who matter."

120. See Chetty, Friedman, Hilger et al. (2011) and Chapter 3, note 21, esp. Chetty, Friedman, & Rockoff (2011) and Chetty, Friedman et al. (2014).

121. See the discussion section of Chapter 5.

122. See Allegretto and Mishel (2019) and OECD (2011, 2017).

123. See Boser and Straus (2014) and Startz (2018).

124. Ninety-four percent of teachers report paying out of pocket for school supplies (Chokshi, 2018). Spiegelman (2018) found that the average public school teacher spent $479 in the 2014–2015 school year, but this and other studies suggest the figure is between $600 and $1,000 a year (Ness, 2017). There are no official estimates of total crowdfunding; however, the total from the three most popular vehicles—DonorsChoose.org, GoFundMe, and PledgeCents—was $200 million in 2017. Some examples of what these donations purchased include paper, pencils, pens, iPads, furniture, and field trips. This figure is close to the $210 million it costs the federal government to give teachers a $250 tax deduction (Camera, 2018a).

125. There are many examples of altruism and teachers going beyond the confines of their jobs during recent strikes, as well as the recent COVID-19 school shutdowns. These include making lunches for their students during a strike because they worried some would not eat if not in school and tutoring their students by sitting outside their front doors during the shutdowns. One teacher even cared for the baby brother of her student as the family recovered from the coronavirus (Bacon, 2018; Ciechalski, 2020; A. Lee, 2020).

126. See OECD (2011, 2017). Starting U.S. teachers earn more than the OECD average (about $42,500 in elementary school compared to the OECD average of $31,000) but earn, on average, only up to 60 percent of professionals with similar education levels—the lowest relative earnings across all OECD countries.

127. See the discussion sections in Chapters 4 and 7. Recent studies found that Act 10, which was adopted by Wisconsin in 2011 to significantly limit the scope of collective bargaining and restrict fund-raising, reduced average test scores; losses occurred largely at the lower half of the student achievement distribution. Studies suggest that declines in achievement resulted from a large reduction in teacher salaries, significant increases in teacher turnover, and the hiring of less-experienced teachers (Baron, 2017; Madland & Roxwell, 2017).

128. See B. Baker (2014), E. Brown (2016b), R. Klein (2015b), and Medina (2014). The Civil Rights Act of 1964 bars discrimination on the basis of race, color, religion, sex, or national origin.

129. See, e.g., Darling-Hammond (1996), Sartain et al. (2010), and Van Sciver (1990).

130. For example, research supports respondents' claim that principals are not consistent in their evaluations of the same teacher and that some principals inflate their ratings compared to other observers (Sartain et al., 2010). However, educators said that recent improvements, such as the Danielson Framework, are helping to redress some of these issues with principal observations.

131. See Center for Public Education (2012) and S. Johnson et al. (2011). Highly effective principals have three or more years of experience overall and at least three years of experience in a particular school.

132. Public colleges and universities are a critical resource for principal training and research but also help administrators create networks that share what does and does not work across school district boundaries (social capital).

133. PAR programs are controversial because they are more expensive since districts must pay those who replace peer evaluators in the classroom. Some also argue that they hinder the principal's ability to run the school, reduce social cohesion by violating norms of collegiality among teachers, and decrease dismissal rates because teachers are unwilling to sanction their own (S. Johnson & Fiarman, 2012; Milanowski et al., n.d.).

134. See J. Goldstein (2008, 2010), Humphrey et al. (2011), S. Johnson et al. (2010), S. Johnson and Fiarman (2012), and Papay and Johnson (2012). There is a need for experimental studies that compare and contrast PAR with other methods of evaluating teachers and providing professional development. Federal and/or state policy makers could support these efforts through a pilot project that funds the additional costs of using PAR in a handful of districts. Researchers could then compare similar schools in the district (i.e., two elementary, middle, and high schools with similar student populations); the only difference would be that some schools used PAR and others used observations or professional development plans to evaluate teachers and make personnel decisions.

135. The AFT and NEA both support peer review (J. Goldstein, 2008; Rosales, 2015). Research suggests that the best way to improve PAR effectiveness and to ensure buy-in is to choose teachers through a rigorous, competitive process; ensure PAR is cosponsored by the teachers' union; and return consulting teachers to the classroom after three to five years so that they will continue to be viewed as peers (Fiarman, 2009; J. Goldstein, 2008; S. Johnson & Fiarman, 2012; S. Johnson et al., 2010; Milanowski et al., n.d.).

136. An analysis of the American Time Use Survey (ATUS) supports the finding in this study that older teachers work longer hours. Teachers aged 50 and older worked more hours per week overall and significantly more hours than teachers in their thirties (6.7 hours more per week) and twenties (5.1 hours more per week). Teachers in their forties also worked more than those in their thirties. All teachers, however, work long hours. Teachers also work at home during the week and on Sundays more than other professionals (Krants-Kent, 2008).

137. Participants complained that most "professional development" has been developed by "market actors" (testing and publishing companies) with little input from teachers and without rigorous field studies. Hill (2009) supports this claim and provides an excellent analysis of how to improve professional development.

138. Research supports respondents' claim that the combination of a year-long, high-quality clinical experience and early career mentoring improves teacher retention and performance. See https://nctresidencies.org/about/residency-model-teacher-mentor-programs/

139. See Greenberg et al. (2013), National Center on Teacher Quality (2014), Murnane et al. (1991), Partelow et al. (2017), H. Putnam and Walsh (2019), Ripley (2014), and Sawchuk (2014b).

140. African American teachers have especially high rates of exit. There are many reasons for diversity gaps at all levels of the teacher pipeline. Students of color have significantly lower college enrollment rates overall, not just in teacher education programs; they also score lower on licensure exams that serve as a barrier to entry. However, research suggests that the diversity gap mainly stems from retention issues among teachers of color (Ahmad & Boser, 2014; R. Ingersoll et al., 2014; U.S. DOE; Walker, 2019).

141. The teacher workforce is 76 percent female—up from 67 percent in 1987. The number of minority public school teachers increased from 305,200 in 1987–1988 to 760,000, but this has not closed the teacher–student racial gap. The uptick is primarily due to rising numbers of Hispanic teachers, which is a positive development for the nation's growing number of ELLs (Hansen & Quintero, 2017; Maxwell, 2014; C. Mitchell, 2016; Partelow et al., 2017; Walker, 2019).

142. See Ahmad and Boser (2014), Cordova-Cobo et al. (2016), Egalite and Kisida (2016), New York University (2016), Partelow et al. (2017), and U.S. DOE (2016).

143. See Ahmad and Boser (2014), Gershenson et al. (2017), Goldhaber et al. (2015), and Partelow et al. (2017).

144. The program works with local colleges and universities and community organizations to recruit local community members as a way to diversify the teacher workforce. It also helps prospective candidates get certified and ensures that they are provided with mentoring during the first two years. The vast majority of participants (85%) are teachers of color (B. Alvarez, 2017; Reckdahl, 2015). See also this chapter, note 144.

145. See Ahmed and Boser (2014), Partelow et al. (2017), and Tyler (2011).

146. Male educational aspirations have been falling for decades. This is true even for middle-class males; however, males without college degrees have been especially hard hit since the 1970s due to the deindustrialization of America. Job loss, disintegrating nuclear families, the rise in incarceration rates, especially for men, and rising deaths of despair are affecting all children but may especially affect school and career success for male children due to a lack of stable role models. This is one reason why it is important to increase the number of male teachers. Boys also tend to focus on short-term gains more than girls. Economically, this involves working right away rather than taking out loans to attend college and then achieve better jobs. Thompson (2021) provides a great discussion of some of these issues. "Grow Your Own Teacher" programs when combined with financial assistance or debt forgiveness may be one way to address both of these issues because it provides mentors in the community to help future teachers achieve school and career success and discuss available financial assistance and the long-term gains of putting off entrance into the workforce.

147. Public choice theory uses economic tools and logics (e.g., self-interest) to understand, frame, and resolve issues of political science. It is used, for example, to understand how individuals, such as voters, elected officials, and bureaucrats, might behave in various political and institutional settings (e.g., elections, Congress, government agencies).

148. Most state and local government functions involve the provision of services (e.g., police, firefighters, teachers). In consequence, wages and salaries make up about one-third of state and local spending. That rises to about 44 percent after adding benefits, such as health insurance and retirement. The nearly 7 million teachers, aides, and support staff working in K–12 education make up the largest share of state and local government employees by far, but protective service workers (police officers, firefighters, correction officers), workers in the field of higher education, health care workers (public hospitals and clinics), and transportation workers (road maintenance workers and bus drivers) are also prominent (McNichol, 2012).

149. State and local employees are twice as likely to have a college or advanced degree but earn about 4–11 percent less than private-sector workers with similar job characteristics and levels of education. Although benefits are typically more generous, the wage penalty is not offset by pensions, health insurance, and other benefits. It is also not spread out evenly. Low-wage state and local workers earn a small amount more than private-sector workers with similar job characteristics and levels of education; high- and middle-wage public-sector workers earn less than their counterparts in the private sector (McNichol, 2012). As shown, public school teacher earnings have fallen even further behind those of comparable workers since the mid-1990s. Teacher pay is actually up in states like New York and California—where teachers have strong collective bargaining rights—but significantly down in others, especially in right-leaning states that have restricted collective bargaining rights and adopted tax cuts. Teachers are also being asked to pay a rising share of health and retirement benefits (P. Cohen & Gebeloff, 2018).

150. Public education is both a consumption good and a public good. Consumption goods are exogenously produced and then individually consumed. The classic case is a widget where a decline in quality is unrelated to consumer behaviors or actions. Public goods are non-rivalrous and non-excludable. Consumption by one individual does not affect the consumption of others and, once provided, non-contributors may also receive benefits. This is the case with national defense where everyone in a nation benefits regardless of whether they have contributed to its provision. Typically, public goods and services are provided by the state because they are viewed as producing broader societal benefits but are under-produced because people may "free-ride" (benefit without contributing to the costs of production). The end result is that private organizations do not reap sufficient rewards from their production. From the viewpoint of individual consumers (i.e., parents) and producers (i.e., public schools), education does not meet the defining characteristics of a public good. Individual parents can and do shop around for good schools and, as shown, their individual consumption affects others. Alternatively, schools can and do lock individual students out. Even so, public education generates benefits for society at large from which no one may be excluded, regardless of how little they contribute (e.g., the political, social and economic benefits of an educated populace). Because of these larger benefits, people care about public education beyond the utility it provides to them as individual "consumers." This means that full exit is not possible but free riding (by some) is inevitable. Within this environment, parents play dual roles. As consumers of public education, they want their children to have a competitive advantage post-graduation. As citizens, they care about whether children as a whole are getting a good education. This may be for altruistic or patriotic reasons, but it may also be because local public school performance influences property values. When these two roles conflict, parents will likely weight their role as a consumers (exit) over their role as citizens (loyalty). This is also true with respect to voicing on behalf of their children. Parents may sometimes ignore self-interest in favor of the public good, yet concern for the community is likely to pale when it affects the future well-being of their children. Either way, their decisions have societal consequences.

Index